verbs have 4 conjugation

1st — stem ending $\bar{a}$
2nd — " " $\bar{e}$
3rd " " $\check{e}$
4th " " $\bar{i}$

D1248607

Latin Fundamentals

Early Manuscript of Vergil (about A.D. 400) in the Vatican Library. The portion here shown contains the Aeneid, Book XII, lines 576 to 598.—*From the Palaeographical Society "Facsimiles of Manuscripts."* (For transliteration and translation, see Appendix, pp. 409–10.)

Latin Fundamentals

by ERNEST L. HETTICH, Ph.D.

Professor of Classics · Washington Square College · Director of the Libraries
New York University

and A. G. C. MAITLAND, M.A. (Oxon.)

Associate Professor of Classics · Washington Square College
New York University

Third Edition

COMPLETELY REVISED BY
A. G. C. MAITLAND

New York   PRENTICE-HALL, INC.

PRENTICE-HALL CLASSICS SERIES

Caspar J. Kraemer, Jr., Ph.D., Editor

Qui studet optatam cursu contingere metam
Multa tulit fecitque puer; sudavit et alsit.

Preface

SINCE THE CHIEF PURPOSE of *Latin Fundamentals* has remained constant throughout its five modifications during the past twenty years, the following extracts from the original preface are still representative of that purpose:

This book is primarily intended for students beginning Latin in college. It is hoped that it will also prove useful as a review book for the upper classes of secondary schools.

The aim has been concise exposition and adequate illustration of syntax from the Latin-English standpoint.

Synthetic Latin has been avoided as early as possible and wherever possible in order to familiarize the student with the rugged idiom of Latin and its essential differences from English.

Forms have been rapidly developed, and introduced only when ready to use in sentences. Full paradigms are given in connection with the lessons. Type-forms have been recapitulated in the appendix. Wherever practicable the words used for this purpose are different from those inflected in the lessons.

The vocabulary is of wide range and is compiled from the sentences, not *vice versa*. Since this condition will confront the student when he begins reading an author, it has been thought wise to accustom him to it as soon as possible.

English-Latin exercises have been purposely confined to a small compass, since the primary aim of the book is to train the student to read and not to write Latin. A teacher who feels the need of further English-Latin material will readily adapt some of the numerous Latin-English examples. He will, for instance, in the teaching of indirect discourse, put controlling verbs in front of suitable Latin sentences chosen from earlier lessons.

In many exercises two sets of Latin-English sentences have been provided. Those in the "A" set are simpler, shorter, and narrowly illustrate the principles in the lesson; the "B" set may be used in connection with a second or review study of the lesson.

The authors heartily concur with the "secondary" objective of the study of Latin, viz., the induction of the student into an understanding of the ancient civilizations. They believe that the reading

of the actual thoughts and sayings of the ancients is an adequate
means to the attainment of that objective.   The primary objective
. . . is the acquisition of the ability to read Latin.

E.L.H.

A.G.C.M.

This third edition, like the second, endeavors even further to sim-
plify and classify according to difficulty the examples selected for
practice in translation.   Substitutes have been found for many examples that a wide range of classroom experience has revealed as
unsuitable by reason of their compression or difficulty.   In response,
too, to the suggestions of college teachers from many parts of the
country, footnotes have been added to clarify many points previously
left obscure, and full meanings have been included in all lesson
vocabularies and not left to the general vocabulary as before.

To provide additional material for connected reading, there have
been included several stories from Medieval Latin, which it is hoped
will appeal not only to regular students but to other adults whose
work in fields such as English may require practice in reading Latin
of this style.

What seems to be at first sight a marked increase in the total
number of lessons is to be explained by the redivision of old lessons
into more assimilable units and the inclusion of several review lessons,
whose omission will not in the least affect the continuity of the general development.   There are five completely new lessons.   Every
exercise has been recast; many paragraphs have been rewritten.

The treatment of the dative with verbs may seem unduly postponed.   Its present position is attributable more to convenience in
rearranging paragraph numbers than to any other consideration.
Both lessons XLIV and XLV may therefore be lifted from their
present position and taken earlier at the discretion of the instructor.

Docendo discimus.   Throughout the second revision an attempt
has been made to incorporate wherever possible what little metal
has been smelted from the ore of many a dusty year of teaching
experience—years that have served to bring home ever more clearly
the unyielding integrity of this great language and its demands for
constant flexibility and imaginative adjustment on the part of those
who teach and learn it.

My sincerest thanks are due for the many helpful and stimulating
criticisms and suggestions of friends and colleagues.   Especially do

I wish to express my appreciation to the co-author of all previous incarnations of this book, Professor Ernest L. Hettich, Director of the Libraries at New York University, to whom all proof has been submitted and whose tolerant consent to many modifications and additions was rendered invaluable by the frequent inclusion of a timely improvement; to Professor Casper J. Kraemer, Jr. the general editor of this series, at whose wise if surgical insistence much necessary amputation was carried out; and to Professor J. F. C. Richards, of Columbia University, for a generous list of emendations and improvements in detail, many of which I have gratefully adopted. Thanks are due also to my former colleague, Mr. Kenneth Lucas, of the Poly Prep Country Day School, for some help on the vocabularies.

Quare, thanks to such thorough and generous criticism, and if the great Roman teacher will forgive the impertinence, *in his quoque libris erunt eadem aliqua, multa mutata, plurima adiecta, omnia vero compositiora et quantum nos poterimus elaborata.*

A.G.C.M.

Contents

xi

Latin Fundamentals

Grammatical Survey

1. Language is made up of words. These words may be classified for the sake of convenience according to the part, rôle, or function they perform in communicating thought. It has been found that the following classes comprehend the various rôles or **parts of speech**:

Noun	Verb	Conjunction
Pronoun	Adverb	Interjection
Adjective	Preposition	

2. The noun.—A noun is the name by which persons or things are designated. (The word "things" is here used in the widest sense to include not only material objects and places but also abstract ideas and conceptions of the mind.)

	ENGLISH		LATIN
(a)	*Caesar*	(proper)	Caesar
(b)	*Rome*		Rōma
(c)	*woman*		mulier
(d)	*wine*	(common)	vīnum
(e)	*song*		carmen
(f)	*joy*	(abstract)	gaudium
(g)	*crowd*	(collective)	turba

3. A **proper noun** (**nōmen proprium**) is the name belonging to a particular person or place, as (a) and (b) above.

4. A **common noun** (**nōmen appellātīvum**) is the name common to a whole class of persons or things and may be used to designate any individual of the class, as (c), (d), and (e) above.

5. An **abstract noun** is the name of a quality, idea, state, or action

I

as distinct from a concrete object or material "thing" (in the narrower sense of the word), as (f) above.

6. A **collective noun** is the name of a number of individuals (whether persons, animals, or things) considered as a unit, as (g) above.

7. The noun function of a word is frequently designated by the term **substantive.**

8. The pronoun.—A pronoun is a word used as a substitute for the actual name of a person or thing. It saves us the trouble or the monotony of repeating a noun already used.

The noun for which a pronoun is substituted is called the **antecedent** of the pronoun.

ENGLISH		LATIN
(a) *we* (instead of *Messrs. Hettich and Maitland*)	(personal)	nōs
(b) *it* (instead of *the book*)		is
(c) *those*	(demonstrative)	illī
(d) *who?*	(interrogative)	quis?
(e) *himself* (e.g., "He taught *himself*")	(reflexive)	sē
(f) *-self* (e.g., "He *himself* will lead you")	(intensive)	ipse
(g) *anyone*	(indefinite)	aliquis
(h) *who* (e.g., "The man *who* was talking is my brother")	(relative)	quī

9. A **personal pronoun** is a pronoun which indicates grammatical person. **Person**, in grammar, is that attribute of a noun or pronoun which indicates whether the noun or pronoun used designates the speaker or writer (**first person**), the person or thing addressed (**second person**), or the person or thing about which something is said or written (**third person**).

10. A **relative pronoun** performs the double action of a pronoun and a conjunction (**18**). See also subordinate clauses (**68b**).

11. The adjective.—An adjective is *an added word*, i.e., a word added to a noun in order to *describe, limit, qualify*, or *modify* its meaning.

ENGLISH	LATIN
white	**albus**

Note that, when the adjective *white* is added to the noun *horse*, the concept of *horse* is altered, *qualified*, or *modified*, and that the resulting phrase *white horse* is much more limited in its application than the simple word *horse*.

12. An adjective like **albus**, *white*, is called a **descriptive** adjective. The meaning of the noun *horse* may be limited in other ways, e.g., *that horse*. Here we mean one particular horse and, though no descriptive particulars are given, all other horses are ruled out of consideration. Such an adjective is called a **demonstrative** adjective (**dēmōnstrō**, *point out*).

13. The so-called *articles* of English (indefinite, *a, an*; and the definite, *the*) do not appear in Latin. However, the demonstrative adjective-pronoun **is, ea, id** often closely approximates the English definite article *the* in meaning.

14. The verb.—A verb is a word which makes a **predication**, i.e., a word which, in relation to a noun or pronoun called its **subject**, makes an assertion, asks a question, or issues a command or request.

ENGLISH	LATIN
The horse is white.	**Equus** *est* **albus.**
Where is the horse?	**Ubi** *est* **equus?**
Give us this day our daily bread.	**Pānem nostrum cotīdiānum** *dā* **nōbīs hodiē.**

The **subject** in the first two examples is **equus**, *horse*; in the third example it is **tū**, *thou* (i.e., *God*), understood though not expressed.

15. The adverb.—An adverb is a word added to a verb to *limit, qualify*, or *modify* the range of its meaning. The adverb is related to the verb in the same way as the adjective is related to the noun.

ENGLISH	LATIN
The ambassador was addressed arrogantly.	**Lēgātus** *superbē* **appellātus est.**

The adverb **superbē**, *arrogantly*, limits or modifies the idea of the verb **appellātus est**, *was addressed*, by specifying the manner in which the ambassador was addressed and, incidentally, ruling out of consideration other possible ways in which he might have been addressed.

An adverb may also limit or modify the meaning of an adjective or of another adverb.

ENGLISH	LATIN
especially suitable	*maximē* idōneus
long *enough*	*satis* diū

16. The following sub-classification of adverbs is useful:

Adverbs of **manner**	e.g.,	*quickly*	celeriter
of **time**	"	*formerly*	quondam
of **place**	"	*there*	ibi
of **degree**	"	*sufficiently*	satis

Adverbs of these four classes answer respectively the questions: *How?* (i.e., *In what way?*), *When?*, *Where?*, and *How much?* or *To what extent?*

17. The preposition.—A preposition is a word used with a noun or pronoun called its **object** to show a relation existing between that object and some other word or words. A preposition (**praepositum**) is so named because it is almost invariably placed (**positum**) in front of (**prae**) its object.

ENGLISH	LATIN
Returning **to** *the city*	**Rediēns** *ad* **oppidum**

Many relations which in English are expressed by prepositions are expressed in Latin by *case* (**49**) formations.

18. The conjunction.—A conjunction is a word which joins together (**coniungō**) and shows the relation between ideas rather than words. A closer consideration of the nature of conjunctions must be postponed until the discussion of sentences and clauses (**67**).

ENGLISH	LATIN
You **and** *he are citizens.*	**Tū** *et* **ille cīvēs estis.**
i.e., *You are a citizen* **and** *he is a citizen.*	

19. The interjection.—An interjection is a word that is "thrown in among" (**interiectum**) the other words of a communication and has no grammatical connection with them; its purpose is to emphasize or give emotional expression to the speaker's thought.

ENGLISH	LATIN
Good!	**Euge!**

Inflection

20. If you were to look in an English dictionary for the noun *books* and the participle *leading,* you would not find them separately listed as such, but would have to look under the forms *book* and *lead.*   Similarly, *whom* and *his* would be treated under *who* and *he.* This illustrates the fact that, in the English language, nouns, verbs, and pronouns undergo changes in form to indicate slight changes in meaning.   Such changes in the forms of words are known as *inflections.*

21. The Latin language inflects not only verbs, nouns, and pronouns, but also adjectives.   Latin is, in fact, a *highly inflected* language.   A close parallel among the modern languages of Western Europe is German.   All fully developed languages, in fact, need approximately the same number of permutations of the basic idea contained in a given word, and the devices employed to achieve these effects vary greatly.   Latin achieves them largely by means of *inflections,* whereas English makes wider use of separate auxiliary words—pronouns, prepositions, and such assisting verbs as *shall, have, may,* etc.

22. Conjugation.—The inflection of a verb is called *conjugation.* An obvious need in rendering the meaning of the verb *lead* more specific is to evolve forms that tell whether the subject of the verb is *speaking, spoken to,* or *spoken of.*   In other words, the verb must be inflected for **person** (**9**).   Latin has a separate verb form for each person:

1st	**dūcō**	*I lead*
2nd	**dūcis**	*you lead*
3rd	**dūcit**	*he leads*

Notice that English indicates the *person* by *pronouns,* which are not necessary in Latin because the Latin ending is of itself sufficient to make the distinction. Notice also that in one form (*he leads*) English employs both devices, inflectional ending and pronoun.

23. Since the subject of the verb may be one or more than one, a second distinction is necessary. Here again Latin has a separate set of forms for the three persons. In other words, the verb must be inflected to show **number**. The forms in (**22**) are all *singular*; the following are *plural*:

1st	dūcimus	*we lead*
2nd	dūcitis	*you lead*
3rd	dūcunt	*they lead*

Note that English again depends wholly upon pronouns.

24. Another important question that arises is whether the subject of the verb is the *agent* or the *victim* of the action—whether it is *leading* or *being led*. This question is answered by inflecting the verb for **voice**. The **active voice** indicates that the subject of the verb is the agent or doer of an act; the **passive voice** that it is the victim or receiver.

ACTIVE	PASSIVE
dūcit, *he is leading*	**dūcitur**, *he is being led*

Again the distinction is made in Latin by an inflectional ending; English uses both the auxiliary verb *is being* and the inflectional form *led* (from *lead*). In some tenses (**25**) Latin also uses auxiliary verbs to form the passive voice.

25. Still another question that arises with regard to the act stated by our verb is *When?* This question is answered by inflecting the verb for *tense* (Old French *tens*, from Latin **tempus**, *time*). The simplest divisions of tense or time are *present*, *past*, and *future*. But since questions of the completeness of the given act are involved, our verb is inflected to meet not only these three obvious requirements but also other refinements of them. The Latin language has *six* tenses in the indicative mood (**37**).

26. The present tense.—This usually indicates either (a) an activity that is going on *now* (at the time of writing or speaking):

      dūcit   *he is leading*

or (b) an activity that is habitual or general:

      dūcit   *he leads*, i.e., *he is a leader* (as a general thing)

27. The imperfect tense.—This usually indicates (a) an activity that *was* going on or *continued* to go on in the past:

dūcēbat   *he was leading* (the commonest meaning)
            or
            he kept on leading (less frequent)

or (b) an activity that *was* customary or habitual:

dūcēbat   *he used to lead,* i.e., *he was a leader*
            (as a usual thing)

28. The future tense.—This indicates an activity which has not yet occurred but is expected or promised for a time later than the present:

dūcet   *he will lead*

29. The perfect tense.—The perfect tense has two aspects, the **aorist perfect** and the **true perfect.**

30. The **aorist perfect** indicates an activity as completed and done with at some time before the present.

Eō diē cōpiās Rōmam *dūxit.*
*On that day he **led** his troops to Rome.*

31. The true perfect, usually called in English grammars the **present perfect**, indicates two aspects of an activity: first, that it started in the past, and second, that it is either completed or operative (or both) in the present:

Cōpiās Tarentum *dūxit* ut hanc sēditiōnem opprimat.
*He **has led** his troops to Tarentum to suppress the revolt* (which is now taking place there).

32. The pluperfect tense (**plūs quam perfectum**, *more than perfect*) indicates an activity as having occurred previous to some point of time in the past, i.e., as past with respect to a past:

Mutinam vēnit.   Prīdiē cōpiās Placentiā *dūxerat.*
*He came to Mutina.   On the previous day he **had led** his troops from Placentia.*

33. The future perfect tense indicates an activity that will be completed in the future and before some definite point of time in the future:

> **Cum hoc caput perficiētur cōpiās ad omnēs Italiae urbēs dūxerit.**
>
> *When this section is finished, he **will have led** his troops to all the cities of Italy!*

34. Tenses that refer to present or future time are called **primary** tenses; those that refer to past time are called **secondary** (or **historical**) tenses.

The **primary** tenses of Latin are the **present**, the **future**, the **true perfect**, and the **future perfect**.

The **secondary** tenses of Latin are the **imperfect**, the **aorist perfect**, and the **pluperfect**.

Observation.—It should be noted that the foregoing discussion of tenses is applicable in its entirety only to the *indicative mood* (**37**). The meaning of the tenses of the *subjunctive* mood will be treated in sec. **212**.

35. There are, of course, in any fully developed language, a large number of shades of difference in the time and kind of activity expressed by the verb. The six varieties of tense inflection which Latin offers are helped to meet these many requirements by adverbial modifiers. No two languages are exactly parallel in the devices they employ to express tense distinctions; the student of a new language must here, as in every other part of the language, absorb new idioms as he meets them and must constantly bear in mind that he is translating not *words* merely but *ideas*. Take, for example, the so-called "progressive" form of the English present-perfect tense —*he has been leading*, which means that he *was* and *still is leading*. Latin has no direct parallel to this form, but this does not mean that Latin cannot express the idea. It can do so by means of the adverb **iamdiū**, *for a long time now*, and the present tense of the verb, i.e., **dūcit**. This illustration of the difference in the idiom of the two languages is interesting because so many foreigners who have learned English persist in using the Latin mode of expression. They say

I am living in this apartment for two years now.

instead of

I have been living in this apartment for two years.

36. Another question that arises about a verb is *What is the attitude of the speaker or writer toward the communication he is making?* Is he making a bare statement of fact or asking a question about facts? Is he issuing an order or making a request? Is he stating something as possible or probable? Is he giving utterance to a wish or request? Light on these and other similar questions is shed, in Latin, by the form of inflection in which the verb appears. These various *manners* or *aspects* in which the verb may appear are known as **moods** or **modes** (**modī**, *manners*). In the words of the grammarian Priscian (fl. A.D. 512), **modī sunt dīversae inclīnātiōnēs animī** (*attitudes, shifts, variations, swayings, alterations, changes of the human mind*) **quas varia consequitur dēclīnātiō** (*which are expressed by changes in conjugation*).

The Latin verb has three *moods*, the **indicative**, the **imperative**, and the **subjunctive**. But see sec. **41** *obs.*

37. The indicative mood in general is used in making statements or in asking questions directly.

He is leading the troops.	**Cōpiās** *dūcit.*
Where is he leading the troops?	**Quō cōpiās** *dūcit?*

38. The imperative mood is used to issue a command or make a request.

Lead the troops to Naples. **Dūc cōpiās Neāpolim.**

39. The subjunctive mood has a wide range of meaning which it would be impracticable to explain at this point. Its use in Latin is highly important; no proper understanding of the language is possible until the student has acquired a strong sense of the implications of the subjunctive mood. Its specific uses will be explained at appropriate places in the ensuing text.

> *If he should lead his troops to Brindisi, it would be a good thing.*
> **Sī cōpiās Brundisium** *dūcat,* **bene** *sit.*

Notice the English auxiliaries *should* and *would*. The subjunctive as a distinct form of the verb has, in English, almost disappeared; but the indispensable subjunctive idea is often expressed by these and other such auxiliary verbs.

40. The verb forms discussed up to this point have all been limited by a *subject* in respect to *person* and *number*. They are therefore called **finite** forms (**fīnis**, *limit*). All verbs in the indicative, imperative, and subjunctive moods are **finite** verbs. There are, however, forms in which the action of a verb may be expressed so generally as to be free from the limitations imposed by a *subject*. These are the **infinitive**, the **gerund**, the **supine**, and the **participle**.

41. The infinitive states the action of a verb in an abstract manner, usually (though not always in Latin) without *predicating* the notion of the verb about a subject, e.g.:

Active	Passive
to lead, **dūcere**	*to be led*, **dūcī**
to have led, **dūxisse**	*to have been led*, **ductus esse**

Observe that the *infinitive* appears in both voices, that it shows distinctions of tense, but that it is infinite ("unlimited") as to person and number.

In actual use the infinitive fulfills the function of a noun, e.g.:

To lead the troops to Capua will be dangerous.
Capuam cōpiās *dūcere* perīculōsum erit.

In addition to being inflected for voice and tense, the infinitive retains in syntax (**55**) other characteristics of its verbal origin (**185**).

Observation.—In view of the fact that the infinitive in certain of its functions in Latin, notably in indirect statement (**196**), takes a subject, it is sometimes spoken of as a fourth *mood* of the verb.

42. The gerund is a verbal noun of the active voice, and is therefore a general abstract name of the activity or state expressed by the verb. In English the gerund has the ending *-ing*, e.g., *leading*. Used as the subject of a verb, it is almost the equivalent in meaning of the present infinitive active:

Leading⎱
To lead⎰ *is difficult.*

Latin uses the infinitive in this relation:

Dūcere est difficile.

But in relations other than that of subject, e.g., as object of a preposition or in various other case (**49**) relations, the gerund is freely employed in Latin.

fit for leading⎱ aptus ad *dūcendum*
fit to lead   ⎰

Like the infinitive, the gerund retains in syntax various characteristics of its verbal origin (**238**).

Unlike the infinitive, the gerund is not inflected for voice and tense, but is always present and active in meaning.

Being essentially a noun in function, the gerund is inflected for case (**49**).

43. The supine is another form of verbal noun. It is found in Latin but does not exist in English. It is restricted to two idiomatic uses which will be explained and illustrated at the appropriate place in the ensuing lessons (**241**). It will be the practice in this book in all word-lists to give the supine of verbs (where the form exists) as being the most convenient form to commit to memory for the derivation of other necessary forms. (See definition of *principal parts* of verbs, **45**.)

44. The participle (pars, *part* + capiō, *take*) partakes of the meaning and function of the verb and shows the verb in adjective form, e.g.:

   *a soldier **leading** a horse*   mīles equum *dūcēns*

Observe that the participle *leading* (dūcēns) limits, qualifies, and generally serves to identify the noun *soldier* in exactly the same manner as the adjective *brave* in the phrase, *a brave soldier*.

Many participles become by usage adjectives, and practically lose all verbal significance. For example, we may speak in English of a *leading* citizen, whereby some part of the literal meaning of the verb *lead* is sacrificed. There are many similar instances in Latin, e.g., **potēns**, which strictly means *being able* but comes to mean *powerful*, also.

The participle shows variations of voice and tense:

leading   **dūcēns** (present active)
(having been) led   **ductus** (perfect passive)

Latin has four participles, as follows:

present active   ——
future active   future passive (gerundive, a verbal adjec-
                    tive of the passive voice)
——   perfect passive

Being essentially an adjective, the participle is inflected for gender, number, and case (**47–49, 51**).

Though it is an adjective, the participle, like the infinitive and the gerund, has not lost all the characteristics of its verbal origin: it may govern a case (**235**).

The participle both in English and in Latin is used in building up certain conjugational forms of the verb:

He has been **led**.   **Ductus** est.

45. Principal parts.—Since a normal verb has six tenses, three persons, two numbers, and two voices, it is obvious that it can take seventy-two (6 × 3 × 2 × 2) different shapes in the indicative mood alone, to say nothing of the subjunctive mood with forty-eight forms (four tenses only), the imperative, infinitives, etc.   If we were under the necessity of learning as a separate act of memory each one of these numerous forms for each and every verb in the language, we should be in sad case indeed.   As a matter of fact, one verb is very like another in its inflections and, once we have mastered the principles of conjugation, we need only remember a bare minimum of forms for each verb.   We can speak in English, for example, of the act of *singing* in relation to any person, number, tense, and voice if we hold fast to the three forms:

sing   sang   sung

The necessity of knowing these parts may easily be illustrated by considering the verb *bring*. From present tense *I sing*, past tense *I sang*, and present tense *I bring*, it would be a mistake to deduce past tense *I brang*. Language does not operate in quite so simple a manner. In order to speak correctly of *bringing* in all its possible relations, we must know the forms:

    bring   *brought*   *brought*

(a) The key forms of the verb from which all other forms may be derived are called the **principal parts** of the verb. In English these parts are the *present tense*, the *past tense*, and the *past participle*.

(b) In Latin, the principal parts are as follows:

First person singular present indicative active—**dūcō**, *I lead*
Present infinitive active   —**dūcere**, *to lead*
First person singular perfect indicative active—**dūxī**, *I led*
Supine   —**ductum**, (*to lead*)

The Latin verb is relatively regular in its inflections, and practically all the verbs in the language can be divided into four groups or **conjugations** called **first conjugation**, **second conjugation**, etc.

A few verbs in every language are so anomalous that a mere knowledge of the principal parts is not a sufficient guide to the complete conjugation. For example, the parts of the English verb *be* according to the conventional scheme would be

    be   *was*   *been*

These forms obviously offer no clue to such irregularities as *am*, *is*, *are*, and *were*.

46. Declension is the name given to the inflection of nouns, pronouns, and adjectives to indicate **gender**, **number**, and **case**, and these parts of speech are said to be **declined**. This word is derived from **dē** + **clīnō**, *bend down*, i.e., the derived forms are "bent away" from the nominative (**64a**) case (**cāsus rēctus**, *the straight case*) to make the **oblique** or crooked cases (a term which applies to all but the nominative).[1]

47. Gender is properly the classification of objects according to sex. All nouns are of **masculine, feminine,** or **neuter** gender.

---

[1] There are five declensions in Latin. It was Quintus Remmius Palaemon (fl. A.D. 35–70) of Vicentia, teacher of Quintilian, who first distinguished four of them.

The **masculine** (mās, *male*) gender marks objects of the male sex.

The **feminine** (fēmina, *woman*) gender marks objects of the female sex.

The **neuter** (neuter, *neither*) gender marks objects as sexless.

But in Latin, as in many other languages, there exists the phenomenon of **grammatical** gender, whereby the names (particularly of sexless objects) may be of any of the three genders, e.g.:

> **nummus**, *a coin*, is masculine
> **mēnsa**, *a table*, is feminine
> **dōnum**, *a gift*, is neuter

Nouns denoting male and female beings, however, are respectively masculine and feminine:

> **nauta**, *a sailor*, is masculine
> **fīlia**, *a daughter*, is feminine

In accordance with this principle, some nouns such as **cīvis**, *a citizen*, **incola**, *an inhabitant*, may be of either gender according as the words in any particular context mean a man or woman. Such nouns are said to be of *common* gender.

Observation.—Inasmuch as the gender of each noun is fixed from the outset, only adjectives and pronouns are, properly speaking, inflected for gender.

48. Whereas every noun has its own fixed gender, it is **declined** to indicate number, the **singular** forms indicating one object of the class designated by the noun, the **plural** forms more than one:

> *sailor*   **nauta**
> *sailors*   **nautae**

Just as in English, there is considerable variety in the manner of forming the plural. English in most words forms the plural by adding the inflectional ending -*s*, but a variety of changes accompany the addition of the ending to certain classes of nouns. Furthermore, English possesses many anomalous plural forms, some survivals of Anglo-Saxon declensions, some borrowed from other modern languages, a large number taken bodily from Latin and Greek, e.g., *basis*, pl. *bases*; *phenomenon*, pl. *phenomena*. In Latin, nouns may be divided into *five* convenient groups according to the type of endings employed. These groups are called arbitrarily the **first declension,** **second declension,** etc.

49. Case.—Consider the following English sentences:

> *The **professor** is not at his desk.*
> *The **professor's** brother is here.*
> *You may see the **professor** later.*

Let us now for the noun *professor* substitute the masculine personal pronoun:

> **He** *is not at his desk.*
> **His** *brother is here.*
> *You may see **him** later.*

It is obvious from the foregoing that nouns and pronouns have varying forms according to the sense relations in which they are employed. These declensional forms constitute the concept of **case.** In English, nouns have a distinctive form only in the so-called **possessive case,** indicated usually in the singular by the ending -*'s* and in the plural by -*s'*; only the personal pronouns *I, thou, he, she, we, they,* and the relative and interrogative *who* and *who?* have three case forms.

Consider also the following sentences:

> *I like **him**.*   ***Eum** amō.*
> *I gave **him** the book.*   ***Eī** librum dedī.*

Though the word *him* is used in both sentences in English, the precise relation of the pronoun to the rest of the words is not quite the same, as can be seen by re-wording the second sentence to read

> *I gave the book to **him**.*

The substitution of *to him* for *him* in the former sentence would be utterly meaningless.

Observe that Latin distinguishes the two uses by the separate case forms **eum** and **eī.** Latin is much richer in case forms than English, and herein lies one of the cardinal differences between the idioms of the two languages: whereas English depends upon a fixed order of words or upon prepositions to indicate the precise relations of nouns and pronouns, Latin makes much freer use of case forms.

50. English grammar ordinarily recognizes only three cases:

The **nominative**—used as subject of a verb.
The **possessive.**
The **objective**—used as object of verbs and of prepositions.

Only in certain pronouns are there distinct forms for nominative and objective, e.g., *I* and *me*; *she* and *her*; *who* and *whom*.

51. Latin has *five* important cases: the **nominative**, the **genitive**, the **dative**, the **accusative**, and the **ablative.**[2] The general meaning of these terms will be discussed below under syntax (**64**). Since each case has a singular and a plural form, it is obvious that every Latin noun appears in ten shapes. Often, however, the same form does duty for more than one case, e.g., **rēgibus** may be either dative or ablative plural of the noun **rēx**, *king*, just as in English the pronoun *her* is sometimes *possessive* and sometimes *objective*.

Pronouns and adjectives (including participles) are declined to show gender, number, and case. Such words will therefore theoretically appear in thirty different forms; but here again there is considerable duplication, e.g., **bonīs** (dative and ablative plural) is used in six of the thirty possible relations of the adjective **bonus**, *good*.

52. Derivation and word-building.—The words *like, unlike, dislike, likely*, and *likelihood* all possess a common element, the base or stem *like*. The last four are not, however, inflectional forms of the first but are entirely new words derived or built up from the simple word by prefixes and suffixes. Latin builds up more complex words from simple roots in the same manner. It will become increasingly evident to the discerning student as he proceeds that many of the prefixes and suffixes of Latin have been taken over into English with but slight change. Another method of building new words is the joining of two or more simple words to make a compound, e.g., *shoe* and *maker* may be joined to form the word *shoemaker*.

53. Comparison of adjectives and adverbs.—One form of word-building that closely resembles an inflection, and is sometimes so called, is the **comparison** of adjectives and adverbs to show the amount or **degree** of their applicability to the words they modify.

---

[2] The less important sixth and seventh cases, the vocative and locative, will be discussed later.

Thus, if a road measures thirty feet across, we should say it possessed the quality of *wideness* and would designate it by the attribute *wide* (via *lāta*). This is the **positive degree** of the adjective. If a second road is forty feet across, we say that in comparison with the first it possesses the quality of wideness in a greater degree and call it a **wider** *road* (via *lātior*). This is the **comparative degree.** If a third road is ninety feet across, it would be, of the three, the **widest** *road* (via *lātissima*). This is the **superlative** degree. For other refinements of the meaning of the comparative and superlative degrees in Latin, see sec. **158.**

Adverbs also are capable of comparison:

Positive:	*fast*	**celeriter**
Comparative:	*faster*	**celerius**
Superlative:	*fastest*	**celerrimē**

54. Vocabulary forms of nouns, pronouns, and adjectives.—Just as all forms of the verb can be deduced from four principal parts, so can all forms of nouns, pronouns, and adjectives be derived (when once the principles of declension have been mastered) from certain key forms.

The **vocabulary forms** of the noun requisite for this purpose are the **nominative** and **genitive** cases **singular**; in addition, it is necessary to learn the **gender** of each noun.

For adjectives we must memorize the **three** different **gender** forms of the **nominative singular**; for adjectives of one small class it is needful to know also the **genitive singular.**

Pronouns are declined very much like adjectives, but present certain irregularities which must be dealt with when they are encountered.

SYNTAX

55. For the most part, we have treated words thus far as if they existed as separate entities. In actual speech, of course, words are arranged in groups to communicate thought. The most fundamental of these groupings is the **sentence.**

A **sentence** is a complete communication from one mind to another and is either (1) an assertion (**declarative** sentence), (2) a question (**interrogative** sentence), (3) a command, request, or entreaty (**imperative** sentence), or (4) an emotional outburst in the form of a statement or question (**exclamatory** sentence).

Syntax (Greek **syn**, *together* + **tattō**, *arrange*) or **construction** (Latin **con-**, *together* + **struō**, *arrange*) is the process of arranging words correctly in sentences; it is also the name given to the collective body of grammatical principles governing such arrangement. For the proper apprehension of a sentence, it is not enough to know the meanings of words as separate symbols: we must understand also how to construe the words in relation to one another.

56. A sentence consists in its simplest form of a (noun) subject and a (verb) predicate (**14**):

SUBJECT|PREDICATE
Soldiers|*fight.*

For the subject-noun, a pronoun may be employed:

They|*fight.*

Since in Latin the verb itself shows both person and number, the pronoun is often dispensed with, and there can be a complete sentence consisting of a single word that includes both subject and predicate; or perhaps it is better to say that the unexpressed subject is understood or inferred from the inflectional ending of the verb:

Pugnant = (*They*) *fight.*

Few sentences, however, are as simple as this. Both subject and verb usually possess **modifiers** or **adjuncts** to amplify and explain their meaning:

> *The eager volunteer* **soldiers** *of a free people engaged in the defense of their homes and their liberties* | *always* **fight** *bravely and enthusiastically because they feel that they have more at stake than mere mercenary hirelings of tyrannous potentates.*

In the foregoing ambitious sentence all the words before the vertical line constitute the complete subject, the words after the line the complete predicate. The simple subject and the simple predicate are the two words in bold-face type. The simple subject *soldiers* is modified by the adjectives *the*, *eager*, and *volunteer*, and by the adjective-equivalent *of a free people*, etc. The simple predicate *fight* is modified by the adverbs *always*, which tells when, and *bravely* and *enthusiastically*, which tell how the soldiers fight; and by the adverb-equivalent, *because they feel*, etc., which tells why they fight.

57. Types of verbs: objects and complements.—In a sentence such as

>   *Horses run.*

we have the expression of a thought that is simple, to be sure, but that is also complete and satisfying. But if we say

>   *He killed.*

you are not satisfied, although the words constitute a subject and a predicate and therefore, by definition, a formally complete sentence. You at once ask *Whom?* or *What did he kill?* and your mind is not at rest until you receive some such answer as

>   *He killed a fly*, or
>   *He killed my love for him.*

In such sentences as the last two, the action of the verb is said to pass or go across (**trāns + eō**) from the subject to an object. A verb like *kill* that requires such an object to complete its meaning is accordingly called a **transitive** verb. A verb like *run* that requires no such complement is said to be **intransitive**.

58. A transitive verb, however, does not always require an object; or, at least, the object need not be expressly stated.

>   1. *He **leads me** to the city-hall.*
>   2. *This street **leads** to the city-hall.*

In (1) the verb *leads* has the object *me*. In (2) the verb is used in a completely satisfying statement without an object, though possibly an indefinite object *anyone* is understood. A transitive verb used in this way is called a **verb absolute.**

59. Some verbs merely serve to connect the subject with a descriptive adjective or to state an identity, partial or complete, between the subject and another noun. Such verbs are called **copulative** (**cōpula**, *link*).

1. *The house is white.*
2. *A man's home is his castle.*
3. *He is considered clever.*
4. *He was elected alderman.*

In (1) and (3) the adjectives *white* and *clever* are called **predicate adjectives** in contradistinction to **attributive adjectives**, which modify their nouns directly, e.g., "the *white* house." In (2) and (4) the nouns *castle* and *alderman* are called **predicate nouns**.

60. Direct object.—A direct object indicates the person or thing (1) affected or (2) effected or produced by the action of the verb.

1. *He read the **book*** (which was already in existence).
2. *He wrote a **book*** (which had no existence until he wrote it).

61. Indirect object.—An indirect object designates the person or thing *to whom* something is *given, said,* or *done.* In Latin the indirect object is in the **dative** (**datus**, from **dō**, *give*) case.

*I gave **him** the money.*
*I told **her** my opinion.*
*I did **them** a favor.*

Him, her, and *them* are **indirect** objects in the preceding sentences; *money, opinion,* and *favor* are **direct** objects. A rough and ready test of the indirect object is that it answers the question *to* or *for whom* or *what?* = Latin **cui?** (dative case) rather than the questions *whom?* or *what?* = Latin **quem?** or **quid?** (accusative case).

62. Double direct object.—The nature of the meaning of certain verbs both in Latin and in English permits of two direct objects to complete the meaning.

Thus:

Whom *did you ask?* Ans. **Him.**
What *did you ask?* Ans. *A simple **question.***
*I asked **him** a simple **question.***

Applying our test, you will notice that the substitution of *to him* for *him* in the foregoing sentence would be incorrect English. The use of the dative instead of the accusative would be equally incorrect in Latin.

63. Phrases.—A phrase is a group of words used as the equivalent of a part of speech and not containing a subject or predicate. A phrase normally consists, in its simplest form, of a preposition and its object.

*They fought **with vigor**.*

The phrase *with vigor* performs the same grammatical function as the adverb of manner *vigorously* in the sentence

*They fought **vigorously**,*

and is accordingly an adverbial phrase of manner.

*She treated him with the care **of a mother**.*

The adjective phrase *of a mother* performs the same grammatical function as the adjective *motherly* in the sentence

*She treated him with **motherly** care.*

Note that approximately the same idea can be expressed by the use of the possessive case:

*She treated him with a **mother's** care.*

Thus the possessive case of a noun in English, since it limits the meaning of another noun, is also an adjective-equivalent.

Observation.—Latin, like English, employs prepositional phrases both adjectival and adverbial, but it also makes free use of the oblique cases of nouns without a preposition to do the work of adjectives and adverbs.

64. General meaning of the Latin cases.—

(a) The **nominative** case is used as the subject of a *finite* verb.

(b) The **genitive** case is used as the equivalent of the English *possessive*. It also expresses approximately the range of ideas covered by the English preposition *of*. The genitive case of a noun is, syntactically considered, almost invariably an **adjective-equivalent**.

(c) The **dative** case is used for the *indirect* object of a verb and also takes in most of the relations expressed by the English prepositions *to* and *for*.

(d) The **accusative** case is used for the *direct* object of a verb, for the subject of *infinitive* verbs, and for the object of the *great* *majority of prepositions*. Prepositional phrases in Latin are almost invariably **adverb-equivalents**. The accusative is also used without prepositions in certain adverbial expressions.

(**e**) The **ablative** case expresses in general the range of ideas covered in English by the prepositions *in, on, at, by, from, with*, etc. A few commonly used prepositions in Latin govern the ablative. The ablative, both when used with and when used without a preposition, is almost invariably an **adverb-equivalent**.

(**f**) One small class of Latin nouns has a distinct form of the **vocative** case to denote the person or thing addressed. In all other nouns the vocative function is taken care of by the nominative form.

(**g**) Names of towns and a few other nouns have a special **locative** form to indicate the place *where* or *in which* a person or thing is or acts.

Observation.—It should be kept in mind that in English, as well as in Latin, a given preposition does not always have precisely the same meaning. For this reason, it would be a mistake to regard the statement above concerning the use of the Latin cases as useful in anything more than a very general sense. Consider, for example, the English preposition *of*. In the expression *the house **of** my father*, the preposition denotes *possession*, and the corresponding idea in Latin would be rendered by means of the genitive case of the word for *father*. But, in the expression *deprived **of** his money*, the same preposition denotes not possession but *separation*. The latter idea in Latin would be expressed by the ablative case of the word for *money*. Again, in the sentence *He is walking **with** his brother*, the preposition *with* means *in the company of*. When we say, however, *He is walking **with** crutches*, we certainly do not mean in the company of crutches but *by means of* crutches. And in the sentence *He is walking **with** difficulty* we are dealing with still a different meaning of the preposition. Since Latin makes distinctions between these various ideas, it is obvious that no simple rule of thumb will guide the student as to the use of the Latin cases in detail, but he will have to master each separate function as it is encountered. *The student is particularly to be warned against word-for-word translations. Not words are to be translated, but ideas.*

65. Clauses.—A clause is a group of words forming part of a larger sentence but containing within itself a subject and a predicate.   Clauses may be either **independent** (main) or **subordinate** (dependent).

An **independent** clause is one that, taken by itself, constitutes a complete sentence:

Dogs are generally liked because they are friendly.

A **subordinate** clause is one that is used as a part of speech:

*Dogs are generally liked **because they are friendly**.*

The words in bold-face type do not make an independent sentence. They constitute an adverb-equivalent limiting the verb *are liked* by answering, with respect to that verb, the question *why?*

66. Sentences classified according to clausal structure.—A sentence containing a single clause is called a **simple** sentence.

A sentence containing two or more independent clauses is called a **compound** sentence.

He lives in New York|but his sister lives in Florida.

Here we have in reality two simple sentences made into one by the device of connecting them with a conjunction.

A sentence that contains one independent and one or more subordinate clauses is called a **complex** sentence.

She lives in Florida|because she prefers the warmer climate.
    (INDEPENDENT)   (SUBORDINATE)

A sentence containing two or more independent and at least one dependent clause is called a **compound-complex** sentence.

He lives in New York,|but his sister lives in Florida|because
    (INDEPENDENT)   (INDEPENDENT)
she prefers the warmer climate.
    (SUBORDINATE)

67. Classification of conjunctions.—Conjunctions that connect independent clauses are called **coördinating** conjunctions.   They apparently connect also similar parts of speech or their equivalents, e.g., two or more adjectives, or an adjective and an adjective-equivalent.

Sentences in which coördinating conjunctions are so used are in reality elliptical.   (See the example given in sec. **18**.)

Subordinating conjunctions are those that introduce subordinate clauses and connect them with the main or independent clause.

68. Subordinate clauses are classified according to the parts of speech for which they stand as equivalent into

(a) **Substantive** (noun) clauses:

> *I know **that he is here**.*

The subordinate clause is the object of the verb *know* and therefore a **noun-equivalent**.

(b) **Adjectival** clauses:

> *The man **whom you met last night** is my brother.*

The subordinate clause modifies the noun *man* and is therefore an **adjective-equivalent**.   Adjectival clauses are introduced by *relative pronouns* rather than by conjunctions.

(c) **Adverbial** clauses:

> *Call me **when you are ready**.*

The subordinate clause modifies the verb *call* and is therefore an **adverb-equivalent**.

69. Adverbial clauses and subordinating conjunctions classified according to sense.—

Clause		*Conjunction*
(a) **Temporal**	introduced by	*when, after, until,* etc.
(b) **Conditional**	"	" *if, unless,* etc.
(c) **Causal**	"	" *since, because,* etc.
(d) **Concessive**	"	" *although, though,* etc.
(e) **Final** (or **Purpose**)	"	" *that, in order that*
(f) **Consecutive** (or **Result**)	"	" *that, so that*
(g) **Proviso**	"	" *provided that, if only*

Boys should start by learning to decline nouns and conjugate verbs; otherwise they cannot arrive at an understanding of what follows. Even to offer this advice would be superfluous were it not for the fact that most teachers, over-eager to show rapid progress, begin with topics that should be treated later, and, preferring to show off their pupils' ability in more flashy performances, later have to lose time because of their attempt to save it.

—QUINTILIAN, *The Training of the Orator*, I, 4, 22

Your Introduction—How to Pronounce and Spell Latin

70. Vowels.—

LONG	SHORT
ā as in *father*	a as in *adrift*
ē as in *they*	e as in *eh?* (clipped short) or as *é* in French *été*
ī as in *machine*	i as *y* in *merry*
ō as in *note*	o as in *renovate*
ū as in *rude*	u as *oo* in *look*

Note.—y was introduced at a comparatively late period to represent the sound of *v* (upsilon) in words borrowed from the Greek, and has a pronunciation intermediate between that of u and i (Latin), like the French *u* or the German *ü*.

71. Consonants.—These are like their English counterparts, except the following:

b before **s** and **t** is pronounced like **p.** **Urbs** is therefore pronounced **urps, obtineō** as **optineō.**

c[1] has always the English hard *c* (*k*) sound (as in *can*), never the English soft *c* (*s*) sound (as in *cider*).

g has always the English hard *g* sound (as in *gun*), never the English soft *g* (*j*) sound (as in *gem*).

---

[1] In the abbreviations **C.** and **Cn.** the letter retains its original value of **G.** Hence *Gaius* Iūlius **Caesar** and *Gnaeus* **Pompeius.**

i is used in Latin not only as a vowel but also as a consonant. When used as a consonant, **i** has the sound of the English consonantal *y* (as in *yolk* and *yes*). In some texts this sound of **i** is represented by the symbol **j**, which did not exist as a symbol in Latin. Most modern editions of Latin writers have given up the use of **j**, and use **i** for both the vowel and consonant sounds, e.g., **Iānuārius**.

k is rarely encountered. It occurs only in the two words **Kalendae** and **Karthāgō**, and of these, the latter is more often spelled with **C**.

s is always pronounced with the sharp hissing sound (as in *sun*), never with the *z* sound (as in *ties*).

t always has the sound of *t* in *ten*, never of *t* in *nation*.

u See **v**.

v The sound of the English *v* (as in *victory*) did not exist in Latin. The symbol **v** was used to represent **u**, which, like **i**, may be either a vowel or a consonant. **V** is retained in most modern texts to represent the consonantal sound of **u**,[2] which is equivalent to the English *w*, e.g., **via**, pronounced *wĭ-a*. In our texts, **u** stands for the vowel sound.

x is a combination of the English hard *c* and *s*, e.g., **vix**, pronounced *wicks*.

z The sound of **z** did not originally exist in Latin. It was introduced at the same time as **y** to represent the sound of ζ (zeta) in words borrowed from the Greek. It is usual to pronounce it as a combination of *d* and *s*, though it was more probably pronounced like *s* and *d*.

ph, th, ch were probably pronounced like **p, t, k**, respectively, followed by an aspirate, or "breathing," *h*. For convenience, we may pronounce **ph** like **f**, **th** like **t**, and **ch** like the German *ch*, or like *k* plus *h*. The nearest we can approach to this last in English is in words like *blockhouse*.

---

[2] Except after **s** and **q**, e.g., **suāvis**, **suādeō**, **quī**. Here **u** is, strictly speaking, a semi-vowel; but inasmuch as it does not make a separate syllable, it is best considered as a consonant and pronounced like the English **w**. **Quī** should really be spelled **qvī**, for the **u** is consonantal, usually represented by the symbol **v**, and pronounced like **w**. But in **cui** and **huic**, **ui** is a diphthong. Cf. **quum** = **qvum**, pronounced *kwum*, which was contracted later to **cum**. If the initial **u** in **quum** had been a vowel, the resulting contraction would have been **cūm**.

72. Classification of consonants.—Classes of consonants are frequently given names, chiefly in accordance with the organs which produce the sounds of those consonants.   For our purposes the most important classes are:

    (a) *Mutes*: **b, c, d, g, p, t**
    (b) *Liquids*: **l, r**
    (c) *Nasals*: **m, n**

For certain of our purposes, it is convenient to subdivide the mutes into three groups:

(1) Those formed with the lips (*labials*, **b, p, ph**).
(2) Those formed with the tongue and teeth (*linguals* or *dentals*, **d, t, th**).
(3) Those formed with the palate and throat (*palatals* or *gutturals*, **g, c, ch**).

73. Diphthongs.—The Greek word means "double vowels."   The diphthongs of classical Latin (**ae, au, ei, eu, oe, ui**) are true combinations of the two vowels that compose them.

ae is pronounced as the *ie* in *pie*.
au as *ou* in *house* (cf. German *haus*).
ei as in *eight*.
eu as *e* (short) plus *oo*, pronounced in rapid succession.
oe as *oi* in *oil*.
ui as in *quit* (French *huit*).   In English *suit*, the *u* predominates.   In French *suite*, *i* predominates.   In Latin, each vowel of the diphthong retains its full value, *oo + ee* being pronounced rapidly.   This diphthong occurs only in **cui** and **huic**.

74. Syllabification.
    (a) A Latin word has as many syllables as it has vowels or diphthongs.
    (b) In the division of words into syllables, a single consonant between two vowels is pronounced with the following vowel, e.g., **mā-ter, me-li-ō-ri-bus.**
    (c) Where two or three consonants occur together, the first is pronounced with the preceding vowel, the other one or two with the following vowel, e.g., **mit-tō, tem-pes-tā-ti-bus, il-lus-tris.**

Observation 1.—In pronunciation, **x** is two consonants, but it is obviously impossible to divide it in writing. In this book, words like **dīxit** are divided **dīx-it** rather than **dī-xit**. The actual pronunciation is *deek-sit*.

Observation 2.—When the combination of a mute and a liquid occurs, as in **patris**, the division may be either **pat-ris** or **pa-tris**. The latter is the more usual.

Observation 3.—Compound words are divided according to derivation into their original parts, e.g., **abest** is divided **ab-est** (prep. + verb); **movēnsque** is divided **mo-vēns-que**.

75. Quantity.—Quantity is the term used to denote the time taken in pronouncing a vowel or syllable.

(a) Vowels and syllables are regarded as either long or short.

(b) Vowels are either long or short by *nature*. (See sec. **70.**)

(c) A syllable containing a long vowel or a diphthong is long by nature, e.g., **Rō-mā-nī, pau-cae.**

(d) A syllable may also be long by *position*. A syllable is long by position when its vowel is followed by two or more consonants, or by one of the double consonants **x** and **z**.

Observation 1.—Occasional exceptions to this rule are words like **patris** (cf. **74c**, Obs. 2). Normally divided **pa-tris**, in which case the syllable **pa-** is short, it may for purposes of poetry be divided **pat-ris** to make the first syllable long. This observation applies only to the combination of a mute and a liquid, e.g., **tr.**

Observation 2.—Although the quantity of most vowels will have to be learned as a matter of observation as each new word is encountered, the following rules will be found helpful:

(1) A vowel before another vowel or **h** is short.
(2) A vowel before final **m**, **r**, or **t** is short.
(3) A vowel before **nt** and **nd** is short.
(4) A vowel before **nf** or **ns** is long.

(e) All syllables not covered by the rules in (c) and (d) are short, e.g., **mo-nu-e-rat.**

76. Accent.—

(a) Words of two syllables are accented on the first syllable.

(b) Words of more than two syllables are accented on the **penult** (last syllable but one) if that syllable is long, e.g., **scrī-bē'-bam, in-cau'-tus, con-vo-can'-tur**; on the **antepenult** (last syllable but two) if the penult is short, e.g., **ex-er'-ci-tus**, **sen-ten'-ti-a**, **con'-vo-cat**, **nō-bi-lis'-si-mus**.

(c) When enclitics such as **-que** and **-ne** are joined to another word, the accent of the resulting combination falls on the syllable immediately preceding the enclitic. An enclitic is a word which, having no accent of its own, is always suffixed to another word. Thus we get the accent **fīlia'-que**.

EXERCISE

Divide into syllables, mark the accent, and pronounce:

Caesar	vēnit	vī	conderet
hortōrum	Iūnō[3]	submergere	trabs
honōrēs	iūdicium[3]	dēsertor	persevērandō
haud	īnstaurātī	praecipuē	obstipuēre
maximīs	gāza	caelō	maestissimus
adytum	diēbus	moenia	heu
foedera	nūllō	Teucrī	cui
diēī	glaciē	poēta	exercituī

---

[3] The initial *i* is consonantal and is pronounced like the *y* in *year*.

The Latin language is modelled under the influence of that great instrument of thought, the verb.

—GEORGE GRANVILLE BRADLEY

LESSON I

Indicative of the Verb *Sum*

77. In the conjugation of the Latin verb, distinctions of the person and number are indicated by adding to the various tense stems the **personal endings.** The essential difference between Latin and English is that Latin expresses by means of these variable endings what English expresses by means of pronouns, prepositions, and auxiliary verbs. It is therefore essential in the understanding of Latin to study carefully the *endings* of words.

For the indicative active the personal *endings* are as follows:

SINGULAR	PLURAL
1. -ō, or -m	-mus
2. -s	-tis
3. -t	-nt

78. Conjugation in the indicative mood of *sum, I am.*—

SINGULAR	PLURAL
PRESENT	
1. sum, *I am*	sumus, *we are*
2. es, *you are (thou art)*	estis, *you are*
3. est, *he, she, it is*	sunt, *they are*
IMPERFECT	
1. eram, *I was, used to be*	erāmus
2. erās	erātis
3. erat	erant

30

SINGULAR   PLURAL

FUTURE

SINGULAR	PLURAL
1. erō, *I shall be*	erimus
2. eris	eritis
3. erit	erunt

(a) The verb *to be* is highly irregular in all Indo-European languages. It would, therefore, be more confusing than helpful to analyze for the beginner its various stems and the way in which these are combined with the personal endings. The student must simply commit the paradigm to memory. More will be said of stem analysis in connection with the regular conjugations.

Note that a substantive or adjective used to complete the meaning of **sum** stands in the nominative case (a predicate nominative), e.g., *Rōmānus* sum. Cf. sec. **101**.

VOCABULARY

crās, *adv.,* tomorrow
cŭr, *interrog. adv.,* why?
et, *conj.,* and
Eurōpa, *n.,* Europe
heri, *adv.,* yesterday
hodiē, *adv.,* today

in, *prep.,* in (*followed by nouns ending in* -ā; *see* **87** *for explanation*)
-ne, *enclitic,*[1] indicates a question
nōn, *adv.,* not (*precedes verb*)
quia, *conj.,* because
Scōtia, *n.,* Scotland
sum, esse, *verb,* I am, to be

Guess the English equivalents of geographical names not given. The long mark over the final -ā in Latin nouns will be explained later.

EXERCISE A

1. Sum in Americā; sumus in Virginiā.
2. Nōn sumus in Āfricā.
3. Crās erimus in Novā Scōtiā.
4. Hodiē estis in Californiā.
5. Heri erātis in Flōridā. Flōrida et California sunt in Americā.
6. Cūr nōn erās in Scōtiā?

---

[1] Literally, *enclitic* means a word that leans backward or leans for support on the preceding word. It cannot stand alone. Compare the *-n't* in English *isn't*. **-Ne** (like **-que**) should be suffixed to the first word in the sentence, which should be an important word, preferably a verb.

7. Nōn eram in Scōtiā quia Scōtia nōn est in Americā.

8. Rōma erat in Italiā; Rōma est in Italiā; Rōma erit in Italiā.

9. Crās erunt in Americā; hodiē sunt in Britanniā.

10. Cūr nōn erātis heri in Californiā?

11. Nōn erāmus heri in Californiā quia in Britanniā erāmus, et California nōn est in Britanniā.

12. Crās eritis in Germāniā; hodiē estis in Italiā et Italia est in Europā.

EXERCISE B *THURS. ORAL*

1. You (*sing.*) were in Germany.

2. We are not in Britain today; we are in California.

3. Why were you (*pl.*) in Italy yesterday?

4. We were in Italy because Rome is in Italy.

5. You (*pl.*) will be in Virginia tomorrow; today you are in Florida.

6. California and Florida are in America.

7. Germany and Italy are in Europe.

8. Tomorrow they will be in California.

9. I am in America; she is in Africa.

10. Why are you (*sing.*) not in Nova Scotia?

11. I am not in Nova Scotia because I am in Italy and Italy is in Europe. (It) is not in America.

Let us remember that we do not learn Latin for the pleasure of declining **rosa,** *the rose, or to conjugate irregular verbs and shine in examinations, but to penetrate by means of this language, which is not dead but deathless, into a magnificent realm which remains unknown to the majority of mankind, I mean the realm of human thought.*

—From the French of RENÉ BOYLESVE

LESSON II

First Conjugation, Indicative Active— Tenses from the Present Stem

79. First conjugation: *amāre, to love.*—

PRINCIPAL PARTS

amō, first person singular, present indicative,[1] active
amāre, present infinitive, active
amāvī,[2] first person singular, perfect indicative, active
amātum, supine (**43, 241**)

INDICATIVE

SINGULAR	PLURAL
PRESENT	
1. amō (*contracted from* amā-ō)	amā-**mus**
2. amā-**s**	amā-**tis**
3. ama-**t**	ama-**nt**
IMPERFECT	
1. amā-**ba-m**	amā-**bā-mus**
2. amā-**bā-s**	amā-**bā-tis**
3. amā-**ba-t**	amā-**ba-nt**

---

[1] Note that Latin has only one form for *I love, I do love, I am loving,* etc.
[2] *I loved* or *have loved.* This form will be discussed in Lesson III.

33

SINGULAR	PLURAL
FUTURE	
1. amā-b-ō	amā-bi-mus
2. amā-bi-s	amā-bi-tis
3. amā-bi-t	amā-bu-nt

The verbs of the first conjugation are known as ā-verbs, because the long ā characterizes their stem.

(a) The present stem is **amā-**. The present tense is formed by adding the personal endings directly to this stem. In the first person singular, **amā-ō** quite naturally becomes **amō**. Before -t and -nt of the third person singular and plural, -ā- becomes -a-. See sec. **75**, Obs. 2.

(b) The tense sign of the imperfect is -bā-, and the imperfect tense is formed by the present stem **amā-** plus the sign of the imperfect -bā- plus the personal endings -m, -s, -t, etc. In which forms is the -ā- of the tense sign short? Cf. (a).

(c) The sign of the future in this conjugation is -bi-. The present stem **amā-** plus -bi- gives **amābi-**. Add the personal endings -ō, -s, -t, etc., noticing that the -i- of the tense stem disappears in the first person singular and changes to -u- in the third person plural.

Note on the use of vocabularies.—The student should accustom himself as early as possible to using the general vocabulary at the end of the book. To encourage this practice, there have been incorporated in the review exercises a number of words which do not appear in the special vocabularies or in footnotes. Sometimes a variety of meanings for a particular word will be found, for English has a far richer store of words than Latin. The student should learn to exercise his judgment in selecting the meaning appropriate to the context of the sentence with which he is dealing. Those whose tongue was Latin used their language to express their thoughts. In a translation we should not strive to replace the Latin words by English words, or *vice versa*; we should rather proceed from the form given in one of the two languages to the thought expressed, and then find in the language into which the passage is to be translated the form which best corresponds to this thought.

VOCABULARY

amō, amāre, amāvī, amātum,[3] love
aut . . . aut, either . . . or
exspectō, -āre, -āvī, -ātum,[3] wait, wait for
hūc, *adv.*, here, hither
ibi, *adv.*, there, in that place
illūc, *adv.*, there, thither
labōrō, -āre, *etc.*, work; strive
mox, *adv.*, soon
ōrō, *I*,[4] pray, ask
parō, *I*, prepare, make ready

portō, *I*, carry
probō, *I*, approve
properō, *I*, hasten, hurry
pugnō, *I*, fight
quō, *interr. adv.*, where? to what place?
sed, *conj.*, but
superō, *I*, overcome
ubi, *adv.*, where, in what place?
vocō, *I*, call

EXERCISE A   *THURS.*

1. Portant, pugnās, amātisne? ōrābitis, labōrābō.
2. Vocābāmus, ōrābam, parābis, portābās, properābitisne?
3. Es, probābō, portātis, nōn pugnābimus.
4. Crās in Italiā eritis et labōrāre parābitis.
5. Nōn exspectābimus sed properābimus.
6. Cūr pugnātis? Pugnāmus quia nōn probāmus.
7. Quō properātis? Cūr nōn exspectātis?
8. In Āfricā nōn eram; in Germāniā labōrābam.
9. Cūr ōrās? Cūr nōn labōrāre parās?
10. Ubi sunt? Ibi sunt. Hūc nōn properant.
11. Quō properābunt? Hūc properābunt et superābunt.
12. Ubi estis? Hīc sumus. Quō properat? Illūc properat.
13. Labōrāre est ōrāre.

EXERCISE B

(1) They are carrying; we shall carry; you (*sing.*) were carrying.
(2) She will call; he was hurrying; I was preparing. (3) They make ready; they will be; we were. (4) Why are you (*pl.*) working? Where were they hurrying? (5) Why do you (*sing.*) approve? (6) Soon we shall be fighting. Soon you (*pl.*) will pray. (7) Were they waiting (or) were they working? (8) We are getting-ready to fight. (9) Work is prayer. (*To work is to pray.*)

---

[3] This fourth principal part and its uses will be explained later.
[4] Since the principal parts of most first conjugation verbs follow a regular pattern, we shall hereafter mark such verbs in vocabularies with the Roman numeral *I*. In the few instances where a first conjugation verb *is* irregular, the principal parts will be given in full.

LESSON III

First Conjugation, Indicative Active—Perfect, Pluperfect, and Future Perfect Tenses

80. The perfect stem of *amō*—

(**a**) The third principal part of **amō** is **amāvī**, a form composed of the stem[1] **amāv-**, to which is added the special personal ending -ī for the first person singular and other special personal endings as noted below. These endings for the perfect active tense are different from any other personal endings in Latin, but once you have learned them you can add them to the perfect active stem to form the perfect active tense of every verb in Latin, thus:

amāv-*ī*	amāvī, *I have loved, or I loved*
" -*istī*	amāvistī, *you have loved, you loved*
" -*it*	amāvit, *he has loved, he loved*
" -*imus*	amāvimus, *we have loved, we loved*
" -*istis*	amāvistis, *you have loved, you loved*
" -*ērunt*	amāvērunt, *they have loved, they loved*

(**b**) Although **sum**, being irregular, changes in its third principal part to the stem **fu-**, the same set of personal endings is added to form its perfect tense, thus:

| fu-*ī* | fuī, *I have been, I was* |
| fu-*istī* | fuistī, *you have been, you were,* etc. |

(**c**) Pluperfect and future perfect tenses are formed as follows. To the perfect stem, **amāv-** (in the case of **amō**) and **fu-** (in the case of **sum**), we simply add the complete imperfect of **sum** to form the pluperfect tense, thus:

| amāv-*eram* | amāveram, *I had loved* |
| amāv-*erās* | amāverās, *you had loved,* etc. |

---

[1] In the perfect tense, stem and base are identical; in the present tense they differ slightly, e.g., present *base* of **amō** is **am-**; present *stem* is **amā-**.

36

fu-*eram*   fueram, *I had been*
fu-*erās*   fuerās, *you had been*, etc.

Similarly, to form the *future* perfect we add to this same perfect
stem the complete *future* of **sum**, except for the last form, the *third
person plural*, where **-erint** is used instead of **erunt**, thus:

amāv-*erō*   amāverō, *I shall have loved*
amāv-*eris*   amāveris, *you will have loved*
amāv-*erit*   amāverit, *he will have loved*
amāv-*erimus*   amāverimus, *we shall have loved*
amāv-*eritis*   amāveritis, *you will have loved*
amāv-*erint*   amāverint, *they will have loved*

So, too, by adding its own future to the perfect stem of **sum**:

fu-*erō*   fuerō, etc., *I shall have been*, etc.

but

fu-*erint*   fuerint, *they will have been*

(**d**) Perfect infinitives are likewise formed by adding **-isse** to this
same perfect stem, thus:

amāv-*isse*   amāvisse, *to have loved*
fu-*isse*   fuisse, *to have been*

EXERCISE A

1. Ubi fuistis heri? In Americā fuimus.
2. Cūr hūc properāvistī? Hūc properāvī quia labōrāre parābam.
3. Fuerātis in Italiā et pugnāverātis.
4. In Āfricā labōrābāmus et superāvimus.
5. Quō properāvistī? Cūr nōn exspectāvistī?
6. Portāveris, vocāveram, superāverint, fuerātis, probābātis.
7. Nōn laudāvit quia nōn probāvit. Probābisne?
8. Ubi fuērunt? Hūc properāvērunt.
9. Fueritis, sumus, erunt, erās, estis, erimus.
10. Vocāvī, exspectāverāmus, labōrāveris, ōrāverat.

EXERCISE B

(1) We shall have been.   (2) I used to be.   (3) They will be.
(4) You (*sing.*) had worked; we have called; he will have overcome.
(5) They have prepared to fight.   (6) Why have you (*pl.*) hurried
here?   (7) We have hurried here because we are preparing to fight.[2]
(8) I had carried; he did not approve; they will have called.   (9) To
be[2] or not to be; to fight or not to fight.   (10) Are you (*pl.*) working?   (11) We are not working today; we shall prepare to work[2]
tomorrow.

---

[2] Use the present active infinitive, the second "principal part."

Amat victōria cūram.

Victory favors those who take pains.

Lesson IV

Nouns of the First Declension—
Simple Uses of the Five Cases

81. First declension nouns: *stella*, *star*.—

	SINGULAR	PLURAL
Nom.	stell-a	stell-ae
Gen.	stell-ae	stell-ārum
Dat.	stell-ae	stell-īs
Acc.	stell-am	stell-ās
Abl.	stell-ā	stell-īs

(a) There is also a *vocative* case, or case of direct address, which, in this declension, is identical in form with the nominative: e.g., ō stella, *O star!*

82. Gender of first declension nouns.—Nouns of the first declension are feminine, with the exception that those denoting male beings are masculine, e.g., **agricola**, *farmer*.

83. Case of the subject; agreement of subject and verb.—The subject of a finite Latin verb is in the *nominative* case, and the verb agrees with the subject in person and number.

Agricola labōrat.	*The farmer is working.*
Agricolae labōrant.	*The farmers are working.*
Ubi est agricola?	*Where is the farmer?*

84. Direct object.—The direct object of a verb is put into the *accusative* case.

Silvās amō.   *I love the forests.*

39

85. Genitive of the possessor.—Ownership is denoted by the *genitive* case of the noun indicating the possessor.

Aurīga *rēgīnae* equās verberat.
*The charioteer lashes the **queen's** mares.*

86. Indirect object.—The indirect object of a verb is put into the *dative* case.

Hastam *nautae* dedimus.   *We gave the **sailor** a spear.*
Viam *rēgīnae* mōnstrō.   *I show the **queen** the way.*

87. Local ablative.—A noun in the *ablative* case governed by the preposition **in** forms, with the preposition, an adverbial phrase of place. So used, **in** may therefore be translated *within, in, on, at,* or *among,* as the context demands.

in Italiā   *in Italy*
in īnsulīs   *among the islands*
in viā   *on the road*

88. Word order.—A regular uninflected language like English does its grammatical work almost entirely through its word order. It makes a vast difference whether we say, *The man kills the tiger* or *The tiger kills the man.*

In Latin, the inflections of words largely remove the necessity for a rigid word order. Here a change in word order marks a change in emphasis, while the fundamental idea in the statement made remains unchanged. **Aurīga equam verberat** means *The charioteer lashes the mare.* **Equam aurīga verberat** does not mean *The mare lashes the charioteer,* because **equam** has the accusative inflection and **aurīga** the nominative. The words in this order mean *It is the mare that the charioteer is lashing.* **Verberat aurīga equam** means *It is a lashing that the charioteer is giving the mare.*

Unless special effects like those of the last two examples are desired, adopt as your normal word order **Aurīga equam verberat**— subject, object, verb. Direct objects usually precede indirect; genitives usually precede the words on which they depend; adverbial modifiers usually precede the verbs they modify.

VOCABULARY

aedificō, *I,* build
agricola, -ae, *m.,* farmer[1]
cōpiae *(pl.), f.,* troops
diū, *adv.,* long, for a long time
dō, dare, dedī, datum *(irreg.),* give.
(*For short* **a** *of stem and other irregularities, see* Appendix **47.**)
errō, *I,* wander, roam
fīlia, -ae, *f.,* daughter *(dat. & abl. pl.,* **fīliābus**)
hasta, -ae, *f.,* spear
incitō, *I,* arouse, stir up
īnsula, -ae, *f.,* island
Italia, -ae, *f.,* Italy

mōnstrō, *I,* show, point out
nauta, -ae, *m.,* sailor
prōvincia, -ae, *f.,* province
puella, -ae, *f.,* girl
rēgīna, -ae, *f.,* queen
Rōma, -ae, *f.,* Rome
semper, *adv.,* always
sīc, *adv.,* thus, so
silva, -ae, *f.,* wood, forest
spectō, *I,* look at
via, -ae, *f.,* road, way
vīta, -ae, *f.,* life; way of living
vīlla, -ae, *f.,* country house
volō, *I,* fly

EXERCISE A

Identify these forms: agricolīs (2), puellae (3), silvam, īnsulārum, porta, prōvinciā, fīliābus (2), rēgīnās.

EXERCISE B

1. Dare, mōnstrāre, nāvigāverint, incitāverātis, dederō.
2. Cōpiās incitābimus.
3. Hasta volat.
4. Ubi est Rōma? Rōma in Italiā est.
5. Stellās nautārum fīliābus mōnstrāvit.
6. Dedistīne hastās nautīs?
7. Est[2] via in īnsulā.
8. Nautae puellās in viā exspectābant.
9. Poēta esse labōrās.
10. Sīc vīta erat.
11. Vīllamne in Italiā aedificāre parās?
12. Semper agricolae stellās spectant.
13. Puella et rēgīna diū in īnsulā errābant.
14. Vīllās in prōvinciā aedificāvimus.

---

[1] Nouns will always be given in this form. The meaning: *Nom.,* **agricola;** *Gen.,* **agricolae;** *Gender, masculine.*
[2] Translate *there is.*

EXERCISE C

(1) (There)[3] are girls on the island.   (2) Where did the sailors wander?   (3) I have stirred up the provinces.   (4) We shall over-come the troops.   (5) In Italy (there)[3] were roads and city-gates. (6) For-a-long-time we fought and roamed in the forests of Italy. (7) We were farmers always.   (8) He gives; they had given; we were giving; you (*sing.*) gave.   (9) We showed the farmer the road.

[3] Words in parentheses are not essential in the Latin and are not to be trans-lated.

Ab ōvō ūsque ad māla.

From A to Z. From soup to nuts.[1]

—HORACE, *Satires* I, 3, 6

LESSON V

Nouns of the Second Declension— Instrumental Ablative

89. Second declension nouns: *hortus* (m.), *garden; dōnum* (n.), *gift.*

SINGULAR

NOM.	hortus	dōnum
GEN.	hortī	dōnī
DAT.	hortō	dōnō
ACC.	hortum	dōnum
ABL.	hortō	dōnō

PLURAL

NOM.	hortī	dōna
GEN.	hortōrum	dōnōrum
DAT.	hortīs	dōnīs
ACC.	hortōs	dōna
ABL.	hortīs	dōnīs

(a) Nouns in **-us** have a special form for the vocative singular in **-e**, e.g., **ō amīce!** *O friend!* Nouns in **-ius** have the vocative in a single **-ī** (like the genitive singular), e.g., nom., **Vergilius**, voc., **ō Vergilī**. The accent of the nominative is retained—**Vergi'lī**, although the penult is short.

(b) In neuter nouns the accusative case is always the same as the

---

[1] Literally *from the egg to the apples*, typical respectively of the first and last courses of a Roman banquet.

nominative. The plural nominative and accusative end in -a. These rules apply with very few exceptions to all neuters in all declensions.

90. Gender in the second declension.—Nouns of the second declension ending in -um in the nominative singular are neuter. All others, with few exceptions (see sec. **96b**), are masculine.

91. Instrumental ablative.—A noun denoting the means or instrument by which an action is performed is put into the ablative case.

Virgā equum verberat.   *He lashes the horse with a switch.*

VOCABULARY

ad, *prep. w. acc.*, to, toward
amīcus, -ī, *m.*, friend[2]
aqua, -ae, *f.*, water
bellum, -ī, *n.*, war
Britannia, -ae, *f.*, Britain
carrus, -ī, *m.*, wagon
cibus, -ī, *m.*, food
collocō, *I*, place; place in position
dē, *prep. w. abl.*, about, concerning
equus, -ī, *m.*, horse
et . . . et, both . . . and
ferrum, -ī, *n.*, iron
forum, -ī, *n.*, forum, market-place

Gallus, -ī, *m.*, a Gaul
in, *prep. w. acc.*, into
nātūra, -ae, *f.*, nature
oppidum, -ī, *n.*, town
pecūnia, -ae, *f.*, money
poēta, -ae, *m.*, poet
-que, *enclitic*, and
saxum, -ī, *n.*, stone
servus, -ī, *m.*, slave, servant
Sicilia, -ae, *f.*, Sicily
taurus, -ī, *m.*, bull
templum, -ī, *n.*, temple

EXERCISE A

Identify these forms: equōs, templa, Gallīs, poētae, oppida, equīs, servō, ferrī, amīce.

EXERCISE B

1. Servī cibum et aquam carrīs in[3] oppidum portābant.
2. Et dōna et pecūniam servīs agricolae dabunt.
3. Ad[3] forum properābō.
4. Quō errāvit taurus? Taurus in hortum errāvit. Ubi nunc taurus est? In hortō est.
5. Vergilī[4] servī saxa portābant.
6. Puellae ad[3] templum properāvērunt.

---

[2] *Nom.*, amīcus; *Gen.* amīcī; *Gender, masculine.*
[3] See sec. **94**.
[4] Contracted genitive, see sec. **92b**.

7. Estne templum in forō Trāiānī?

8. Silvae dōna nātūrae sunt.

9. Quō portās saxa?   In hortum portō.

10. Dōna in templīs collocāveram.

11. Vīllās ferrō et saxīs aedificāmus.

12. Ubi fuistis?   Fuimus in Britanniā, Rōmānōrum prōvinciā.[5]

13. Rōmānī in Italiā habitant, Gallī in Galliā habitant, Graecī in Graeciā habitant.

14. Ēborācum (*York*) in Britanniā, Novum Ēborācum in Americā est.

EXERCISE C

1. Where have I been?   I have been in Sicily, a province[5] of the Romans.

2. The horses are carrying food into[3] the market-place.

3. There is iron in the province (of) Britain.[5]

4. The slaves will place the gifts of the Gauls in the temples of Trajan.

5. Shall you give gifts and money to the poet's slaves?

---

[5] See sec. **95** on apposition.

IN -abl
INTO -acc.

LESSON VI

Nouns of the Second Declension (Concluded)—
Dative of the Possessor—*In* and *Ad* with
the Accusative—Apposition

92. Other second declension nouns: *ager* (m.), *field;* *puer* (m.),
boy; *vir* (m.), *man;* *gladius* (m.), *sword;* *praemium* (n.), *reward.*—

SINGULAR

NOM.	ager	puer	vir	gladius	praemium
GEN.	agrī	puerī	virī	gladī	praemī
DAT.	agrō	puerō	virō	gladiō	praemiō
ACC.	agrum	puerum	virum	gladium	praemium
ABL.	agrō	puerō	virō	gladiō	praemiō

PLURAL

NOM.	agrī	puerī	virī	gladiī	praemia
GEN.	agrōrum	puerōrum	virōrum	gladiōrum	praemiōrum
DAT.	agrīs	puerīs	virīs	gladiīs	praemiīs
ACC.	agrōs	puerōs	virōs	gladiōs	praemia
ABL.	agrīs	puerīs	virīs	gladiīs	praemiīs

(a) Notice that most of the nouns in **-er** drop **-e-** in inflection;
a few retain it. Which these few are must be learned by observation,
but English will be of some help. Observe that *agri-culture*, derived
from **ager, agrī**, loses **-e-**, whereas *puer-ile*, derived from **puer, puerī**,
retains it.

(b) In the genitive of nouns in **-ius** and **-ium**, **-iī** contracts to a
single **-ī**. The accent of the nominative is retained. Thus the
accent of the genitive of **cōnsilium**, *plan*, is **cōnsi′lī**.

(c) Treat **vir** as if it had simply lost the **-us** of the nominative
singular.

46

93. Dative of the possessor.—The *dative* case may be used with the verb **sum** to denote a possessor.

>*Agricolīs sunt* **agrī.**
>*The farmers have* (literally, *to the farmers are*) *fields.*

94. Place to which.—In and **ad** followed by the *accusative* case express the place to which, into which, or against which a person or thing moves. With names of towns and cities[1] the preposition is omitted.

In oppidum **properat.**	*He hurries to town* (*into town*).
Ad Italiam **properat.**	*He hurries toward Italy.*
In Gallōs **properat.**	*He hurries against the Gauls.*
Rōmam **properat.**	*He hurries to Rome.*

95. Apposition.—When to a noun *A*, a second noun *B* is added, and *B* is merely another name for *A*, or gives additional information about it, *B* is called an *appositive*, and the two nouns are said to be in *apposition*. An appositive always stands in the *same case* as its noun.

>**Mārcus,** Iūlī *amīcus,* in oppidō est.
>**Marcus, the friend** of *Julius, is in the town.*

Amīcus is here nominative, being in apposition to the subject of the sentence, **Mārcus.**

>**Gallus** *puerō Mārcō* **gladium mōnstrat.**
>*The Gaul shows **the boy Marcus** (his) sword.*

Mārcō is dative because it agrees with the indirect object **puerō.**

>**In** *īnsulā Siciliā* **habitant.**
>*They live in **the island** (of) **Sicily.***

Explain the case of **Siciliā.** Notice that the Latin says "the island Sicily," where the English says "the island *of* Sicily."

---

[1] And **domus,** *home* (sec. **151**); **rūs,** *country* (as opposed to town).

VOCABULARY

ager, agrī, *m.*, field
caper, caprī, *m.*, goat
fīlius, fīlī, *m.*, son
gladius, gladī, *m.*, sword
liber, librī, *m.*, book

puer, puerī, *m.*, boy
studium, studī, *n.*, zeal, enthusiasm
taurus, taurī, *m.*, bull
vir, virī, *m.*, man
praemium, praemī, *n.*, reward

EXERCISE A

Identify these forms: gladiōs, caprīs, fīlī (2), studiīs, fīliī, caprōrum, virīs, librum, pecūniae, cibō, bella, praemia, Sicilia.

EXERCISE B

1. Agricolīs et taurī et caprī sunt.
2. In agrōs Gallōrum errābāmus.   In hortō rēgīnae errābās.
3. Puerī puellaeque in templum Minervae properābunt.
4. Dominō sunt servī quī (*who*) in vīllā cibum parant.
5. Trāiānus Fortūnae fīlius erat.
6. Dedistī-ne argentum Mārcō, agricolae fīliō?
7. Librōs, studī praemium, puerō dedī.
8. Fuistī-ne in Galliā, patriā Gallōrum?
9. Virī gladiīs et hastīs in oppidō pugnāvērunt.

EXERCISE C

(1) You (*sing.*) will give the horses food and water.   (2) I shall show the road to Brutus, Cassius' friend.   (3) Will the men be in Italy long?   Will they hasten into the provinces?   (4) We were waiting in the market-place for Marcus, the friend of the farmers. (5) The Gauls fought long and bravely with swords and stones. (6) The master has a country house, a garden, and slaves on the island of[2] Sicily.   (7) You will hasten (*sing.*) to your friends in the city.[3]   (8) To have praised; to be; to wander; they will overcome; did you (*sing.*) give? we are praising.   (9) The charioteer's horses are wandering into the farmer's field.   (10) I was-looking-at the stars.

---

[2] See sec. **95**, example 3.
[3] Say *into the city to* (*your*) *friends* (**in** + acc. + **ad** + acc.).

Servā mē, servābō tē.

Scratch my back and I'll scratch yours.

—PETRONIUS

LESSON VII

Gender—Adjectives of the First and Second Declensions—Agreement of Adjective— Predicate Noun and Predicate Adjective —Modal Ablative

96. Gender.—Review sec. **47.** The following general rules will be found useful:

(a) Names of months, mountains, rivers, peoples, and winds are masculine, e.g., **Iānuārius**, *January*; **Iūra**, *the Jura mountains*; **Rhēnus**, *Rhine*; **Gallī**, *Gauls*; **Zephyrus**, *west wind*.

(b) Names of countries, islands, cities, and trees are feminine, e.g., **Britannia**, *Britain*; **Sicilia**, *Sicily*; **Ephesus**, *Ephesus*; **ulmus**, *elm*.

Review secs. **82** and **90.** Rules for gender in the third, fourth, and fifth declensions will be given in due course. Notice, as you proceed, that certain nominative singular endings are associated with certain genders; e.g., **-us** (in the second declension) is masculine, and **-a** is feminine.

97. Adjectives of the first-second declension.—

	M.	F.	N.
		SINGULAR	
Nom.	bonus	bona	bonum
Gen.	bonī	bonae	bonī
Dat.	bonō	bonae	bonō
Acc.	bonum	bonam	bonum
Abl.	bonō	bonā	bonō

49

PLURAL

Nom.	bonī	bonae	bona
Gen.	bonōrum	bonārum	bonōrum
Dat.	bonīs	bonīs	bonīs
Acc.	bonōs	bonās	bona
Abl.	bonīs	bonīs	bonīs

(a) The vocative singular masculine is **bone**.

(b) Compare this paradigm with the paradigms of the nouns **hortus** (m.), **stella** (f.), and **dōnum** (n.).

(c) The genitive singular masculine of adjectives in **-ius** ends in **-iī**; vocative in **-ie**.

Some adjectives omit the ending of the nominative singular masculine, e.g., **līber**, *free*; cf. **vir** among nouns.

M.   F.   N.

SINGULAR

Nom.	līber	lībera	līberum
Gen.	līberī	līberae	līberī
Dat.	līberō	līberae	līberō
Acc.	līberum	līberam	līberum
Abl.	līberō	līberā	līberō

PLURAL

Nom.	līberī	līberae	lībera
Gen.	līberōrum	līberārum	līberōrum
Dat.	līberīs	līberīs	līberīs
Acc.	līberōs	līberās	lībera
Abl.	līberīs	līberīs	līberīs

(d) Compare this paradigm with the paradigm of **puer**. Note also English *liberal*.

98. Adjectives[1] in which the nominative singular masculine would be otherwise unpronounceable insert an e before the r (*Hilfsvokal* or "helping vowel"), e.g., **pulcher**, *beautiful*.

---

[1] And comparable nouns like **ager**.

	M.	F.	N.

SINGULAR

	M.	F.	N.
Nom.	pulcher	pulchra	pulchrum
Gen.	pulchrī	pulchrae	pulchrī
Dat.	pulchrō	pulchrae	pulchrō
Acc.	pulchrum	pulchram	pulchrum
Abl.	pulchrō	pulchrā	pulchrō

PLURAL

	M.	F.	N.
Nom.	pulchrī	pulchrae	pulchra
Gen.	pulchrōrum	pulchrārum	pulchrōrum
Dat.	pulchrīs	pulchrīs	pulchrīs
Acc.	pulchrōs	pulchrās	pulchra
Abl.	pulchrīs	pulchrīs	pulchrīs

(a) Compare this paradigm with the paradigm of **ager**. Note also the English *pulchritude*. This type of paradigm is far commoner than that of **līber**.

99. Agreement of adjective and noun.—An adjective agrees with the noun it modifies in gender, number, and case. For this reason, in the English-to-Latin exercises, always write the noun first; and then select the appropriate form of the adjective, e.g., **gladius ferreus**, *iron sword*; **agricolae bonō**, *to the good farmer* (dative); **bella longa**, *long wars*; **rēgīnārum pulchrārum**, *of beautiful queens* (gen.).

100. Declension of a noun with an adjective.—

	SINGULAR	SINGULAR
Nom.	dōnum pulchrum	nauta validus
Gen.	dōnī pulchrī	nautae validī
Dat.	dōnō pulchrō	nautae validō
Acc.	dōnum pulchrum	nautam validum
Abl.	dōnō pulchrō	nautā validō

	PLURAL	PLURAL
Nom.	dōna pulchra	nautae validī
Gen.	dōnōrum pulchrōrum	nautārum validōrum
Dat.	dōnīs pulchrīs	nautīs validīs
Acc.	dōna pulchra	nautās validōs
Abl.	dōnīs pulchrīs	nautīs validīs

101. Predicate noun and predicate adjective.—In Latin, as in English, nouns and adjectives referring to or modifying the subject may stand in the predicate after a copulative verb (**59**).

Mārcus est *agricola.*	*Marcus is a farmer.*
Hortī sunt *pulchrī.*	*The gardens are beautiful.*
Caelum *serēnum* est et *siccum.*	*The sky is clear and bright.*

Note that the predicate noun agrees with the subject in *case.* The predicate adjective really modifies the subject, and, therefore, like any other adjective, agrees with it in *gender, number,* and *case.*

102. Modal ablative.—The manner of an action is expressed by a noun in the ablative case preceded by the preposition **cum.** If the noun is modified by an adjective, **cum** may be omitted.

Cum studiō labōrant.
They work with zeal (or, *zealously*).

Gallī *magnā audāciā* pugnāvērunt.
The Gauls fought with great daring.

In the latter example, we might have said **magnā cum audāciā.** Note the position of **cum** in this phrase.

VOCABULARY

aeger, -gra, -grum, sick
appropinquō, *I,* approach
audācia, -ae, *f.,* boldness, daring, courage
bellicōsus, -a, -um, warlike
bonus, -a, -um, good
cum, *prep. w. abl.,* with
dīligentia, -ae, *f.,* carefulness, diligence
fēmina, -ae, *f.,* woman
gaudium, -dī, *n.,* joy
lātus, -a, -um, broad, wide
laudō, *I,* praise
lēgātus, -ī, *m.,* envoy, legion-commander
līber, -bera, -berum, free

magnus, -a, -um, large, great
meus, -a, -um,[2] my, mine
multus, -a, -um, much
multī, -ae, -a, many
noster, -tra, -trum, our
parvus, -a, -um, small, little
pulcher, -chra, -chrum, beautiful
quod, *conj.,* because
Rōmānus, -ī, *m.,* Roman
schola, -ae, *f.,* school
socius, -cī, *m.,* ally, comrade
tuus, -a, -um, your, yours (*referring to singular*)
validus, -a, -um, strong, sturdy
vester, -tra, -trum, your, yours (*referring to plural*)

[2] Voc. sing. masc., **mī.**   **Ō mī fīlī,** *O my son.*

EXERCISE A

(1) Parvae puellae; hortī vestrī; dōnōrum meōrum; agricolās bonōs.
(2) Carrīs magnīs; in agrō parvō; in silvīs pulchrīs. (3) Magnō
studiō; sociōs validōs; agricolae aegrō. (4) Fīliī meī; dōna nostra;
parvā cum dīligentiā. (5) Lēgātum bellicōsum; gladī longī; nautās
validōs.

EXERCISE B

1. Servī vestrī sunt aegrī.
2. Agricolaene bella longa probant?   Nōn probant.
3. Bellicōsī erant Gallī et cum audāciā pugnābant.
4. Rōmānī, virī līberī, magnō studiō pugnāvērunt.
5. Caprī tuī in hortum nostrum errāvērunt.
6. Magnum erat in Italiā gaudium, quod Rōmānī Gallōs super-
āverant.
7. Gallōrum lēgātī ad oppidum appropinquābant.
8. Sunt stellae nātūrā flammeae.
9. In prōvinciīs nostrīs sunt multae et pulchrae fēminae.
10. Rōmānī bonum agricolam laudābant.
11. Appia est viārum longārum rēgīna.
12. Segesta est magnum oppidum in Siciliā.

EXERCISE C

(1) My sons; the good farmer's sick friend. (2) Warlike men
and beautiful women; with boldness; with little joy. (3) Were the
Romans good sailors? (4) The poet Horace loved the great forests
and broad fields of Apulia. (5) Where are your books? (6) With
great diligence, the boys and girls carry (their) books to school.
(7) Men and women love and praise the books of the poets. (8) Many
large horses were wandering in the farmer's field. (9) Many[3] joyfully approach[4] the temples.

[3] Observe that in English the adjective may be used as a noun. The same
is true of Latin in an even greater degree. Thus, in military writers, the adjective **nostrī** is extensively used to designate *our men* or *our soldiers*, as opposed
to those of the enemy. Similarly, **bona** (n. pl.) means *goods* or *good things*;
malum, *an evil*; **amīcus**, *a friend*.

[4] **Appropinquāre** is an intransitive verb. You must, therefore, say "to (**ad**)
the temples," or use the dative.

Indicative Passive of *Amō*—Present Infinitive and Participle—Ablative of Agent

103. Personal endings of the passive.—

	SINGULAR	PLURAL
1.	-or	-mur
2.	-ris (-re)	-minī
3.	-tur	-ntur

104. Indicative passive of *amō*.—

	SINGULAR	PLURAL
	PRESENT	
1.	am-or (contracted from amā-or)	amā-mur
2.	amā-ris (-re)	amā-minī
3.	amā-tur	ama-ntur
	IMPERFECT	
1.	amā-ba-r	amā-bā-mur
2.	amā-bā-ris (-re)	amā-bā-minī
3.	amā-bā-tur	amā-ba-ntur
	FUTURE	
1.	amā-b-or	amā-bi-mur
2.	amā-be-ris (-re)	amā-bi-minī
3.	amā-bi-tur	amā-bu-ntur

Note that **amor** can mean not only *I am loved* but *I am being loved*; **amābar** not only *I was loved* but *I was being loved* or *used to be loved*.

The passive forms are made by adding the *passive* personal endings to the appropriate tense stems.[1] These stems, as you have already learned, are: present, **amā-**; imperfect, **amābā-**; future, **amābi-**. Note carefully the following points:

---

[1] Tense stems are really the present stem + tense signs.

(a) *Present tense.*—In the first person, **amā-or** becomes **amor**, just as **amā-ō** becomes **amō** in the active; **a** is *short* in the third person plural. See sec. **75**, obs. 2(3).

(b) *Imperfect tense.*—**O** of the personal ending is lost after **ā** of the tense stem. **A** is *short* in the first person singular and the third person plural.

(c) *Future tense.*—**I** of the tense stem disappears before **o** of the personal ending in the first person singular. Cf. the active, **amābō**. In the second person singular, it changes to **e**. In the third person plural, it changes to **u**, as in the active. Cf. **amābunt**.

105. Present infinitives of *amō.*—

	ACTIVE	PASSIVE
PRESENT	amā-re, *to love*	amā-rī, *to be loved*

106. Present participle of *amō.*—

	ACTIVE
PRESENT	amā-ns, *loving*

107. Ablative of the agent.—The person by whom an action is performed is indicated by the ablative case after the preposition **ā (ab)**.

Ā Gallīs laudātur; culpātur *ā Rōmānīs.*
He is praised by the Gauls, censured by the Romans.

VOCABULARY

ā, ab, *prep. w. abl.,* by
amīcitia, -ae, *f.,* friendship
arō, *I,* plough
aurum, -ī, *n.,* gold
crās, *adv.,* tomorrow
dēsīderō, *I,* desire, long for
fortiter, *adv.,* bravely
frūmentum, -ī, *n.,* grain
Graecia, -ae, *f.,* Greece
hodiē, *adv.,* today
incola, -ae, *c.,*[2] inhabitant
līberī, -ōrum, *m.,* children

lūna, -ae, *f.,* moon
maximē, *adv.,* especially
minimē, *adv.,* very little, not at all, no
miser, misera, miserum, poor, wretched, unfortunate
pīrāta, -ae, *m.,* pirate
possum, I can, am able (to), *used with infinitive*
Rōmānus, -a, -um, Roman
saepe, *adv.,* often
vexō, *I,* harass, molest

[2] Common gender; see end of sec. **47.**

EXERCISE A

1. Amābuntur, laudābiminī, vocāris, vocāminī.
2. Vexantur, incitābantur, probābitur, amābāminī.
3. Gallōrum oppida saepe ā Germānīs vexābantur.
4. Multa templa in oppidō aedificābantur.
5. In silvā diū et fortiter pugnābāmus.
6. Nostra rēgīna ā līberīs maximē amābātur.
7. Agrī ab agricolīs arābuntur.
8. In Graeciā sumus hodiē; crās in Italiam portābimur.
9. Poētae amīcitia ā multīs dēsīderātur.
10. Lūna stellaeque ab astrologīs spectantur.
11. Miserī īnsulārum incolae saepe ā pīrātīs vexantur.
12. Cūr Rōmam properāvistis?
13. Aeger sum. Rōmam properāre nōn possum.
14. Possum-ne hodiē in hortō labōrāre?

EXERCISE B

(1) They have carried; we are being called; you (*pl.*) are over-come. (2) It will be built; he was being aroused; are they praised? (3) Grain was being transported into the town by means of wagons and placed in the temples by slaves. (4) Will the war be approved by the farmers? No, but by the sailors. (5) The girl was praised by (her) friend. (6) Our country house is being built on an island. (7) We praise the poet because (his) books are loved by many chil-dren. (8) Provinces were often overcome by gold. (9) I can carry grain into the town by-means-of a wagon. (10) Can I be won (overcome) by friendship?

1 he will be commended.
2 You all were being loved.
3 the towns of the Gauls were often raided by the Germans.
4 Many temples were being built in the town
6 Our queen was loved especially by the children

Beātī sunt pācificī quoniam fīliī Deī vocābuntur.

Blessed are the peace-makers, for they shall be called the sons of God.

—ST. MATTHEW, V, 9

LESSON IX

Indicative Passive of *Amo* (Concluded)— Periphrastic Conjugations

108. To form the perfect, pluperfect, and future perfect passive tenses of **amō**, the perfect passive participle **amātus** is used, and to it are added, respectively, the present, imperfect, and future of the auxiliary verb **sum**. The participle **amātus**, being a verbal adjective, is declined like the adjective **bonus**, and agrees with the subject in gender, number, and case, according to the rule for the agreement of the predicate adjective (**101**).

SINGULAR	PLURAL
PERFECT	
1. amāt-us (-a, -um) **sum**	amāt-ī (-ae, -a) **sumus**
2. amāt-us (-a, -um) **es**	amāt-ī (-ae, -a) **estis**
3. amāt-us (-a, -um) **est**	amāt-ī (-ae, -a) **sunt**
PLUPERFECT	
1. amāt-us (-a, -um) **eram**	amāt-ī (-ae, -a) **erāmus**
2. amāt-us (-a, -um) **erās**	amāt-ī (-ae, -a) **erātis**
3. amāt-us (-a, -um) **erat**	amāt-ī (-ae, -a) **erant**
FUTURE PERFECT	
1. amāt-us (-a, -um) **erō**	amāt-ī (-ae, -a) **erimus**
2. amāt-us (-a, -um) **eris**	amāt-ī (-ae, -a) **eritis**
3. amāt-us (-a, -um) **erit**	amāt-ī (-ae, -a) **erunt**

Rēgīnae laudātae erant.   *The queens had been praised.*
Gallī superātī sumus.   *We Gauls have been defeated.*
Aurum dēmōnstrātum erit.   *The gold will have been pointed out.*

57

109. Just as **amātus** is used in combination with three tenses of **sum,**[1] there are two other participles which can be combined with these same tenses to form the so-called periphrastic conjugations.[2] These are the future active (**amātūrus, -a, -um**) and future passive (**amandus, -a, -um**) participles.

Amātūrus, -a, -um means "going to love," or "about to love," or "intending to love." Combined with **sum, eram,** and **erō** it forms the first or active periphrastic conjugation.

> **Amātūrī sumus.**   *We are about to love.*
> **Properātūra erat.**   *She was about to hurry.*

110. Amandus, -a, -um, the future passive participle means "about to be loved," or "worthy or fit to be loved," or "that should be loved." It is also called the *gerundive.* Combined with **sum** in various tenses, it forms the so-called *second* or *passive periphrastic conjugation.*

> **Gallī** *superandī sunt.*
> *The Gauls **are to be overcome** (i.e., **must be overcome**).*

> **Quod** (rel. pron. meaning *which*) **erat dēmōnstrandum. (Q.E.D.)**
> *Which was to-be-proved (i.e., the thing which had to be proved).*

Observation.—With the second or passive periphrastic conjugation, agency is expressed by the *dative.*

> **Gallī** *Rōmānīs* **superandī sunt.**
> *The Gauls **are for the Romans** to conquer (i.e., **must be conquered by the Romans**).*

VOCABULARY

ager, agrī, *m.,* field
deus, -ī, *m.,* god *or* God
dōnum, -ī, *n.,* gift

nāvigō, *I,* sail
superō, *I,* overcome, conquer

---

[1] **amātus** is also combined with **esse** to form the perfect passive infinitive, *to have been loved.*

[2] Periphrastic is an adjective derived from a Greek word *periphrasis,* meaning "a round-about way of speaking"; it is exactly parallel to the Anglicized Latin word *circumlocution.*

Transitive verb last

EXERCISE A

1. Via mōnstrāta erat.
2. Prōvinciae superātae erant.
3. Agrī arātī erunt.
4. Rōmam properātūrī sumus.
5. Dōna in templīs collocāta erant.
6. Agrī agricolīs arandī sunt.
7. Ā rēgīnā laudātī sumus.
8. Multa templa in oppidō aedificāta sunt.
9. In Britanniā sunt hodiē; crās in Galliam nāvigātūrī sunt.
10. Ad Galliam nāvigāre hodiē nōn possum.

EXERCISE B *all*

(1) You (*pl. masc.*) have been overcome; we (*fem.*) had been praised; towns will have been built. (2) Our country houses have not been built in the province but on an island. (3) They (*masc.*) are about to fight in Italy. (4) The stars will have been pointed out to the queen's daughter. (5) The horses have been given to the legion-commanders. (6) I cannot build my house without[3] money.

to build not / amabile are.

---

[3] sine + abl.

Nōn omnēs quī habent citharam sunt citharoedī.

Not all who own a harp are harpists.
"Not all are hunters who wind the horn."

—VARRO, *dē Rē Rūsticā*, II, 1, 3

LESSON X

Second Conjugation: Indicative, Infinitives, and Participles

111. Second conjugation: *monēre, to warn.*—

PRINCIPAL PARTS
moneō, monēre, monuī, monitum

ACTIVE

SINGULAR	PLURAL

PRESENT

1. mone-ō	monē-mus
2. monē-s	monē-tis
3. mone-t	mone-nt

(a) The verbs of the second conjugation are known as ē-verbs, because the long ē characterizes their stem. The present stem of **moneō** is **monē-**. Review the notes on the active of **amō** in sec. **79**. Note that, in the first person singular of the present of **moneō**, the stem vowel is not dropped as in **amō**, but merely shortened.

112. Using the imperfect and future active of **amō** (**79**) as a model and substituting **monē-** for **amā-**, write out in full the imperfect and future active of **moneō**. Write out in full the same tenses of **habeō**.

113. Using the conjugation of **sum** (**78**) as a model and substituting for **fu-** the stem **monu-** (seen in the third of the principal parts),

60

write out in full the perfect, pluperfect, and future perfect active of
moneō. Write out the same tenses of **videō.**

114. The perfect stem.—Only a few verbs of this conjugation
form their perfect stem regularly—i.e., by adding **v** to the present
stem—as does **amō.** Most second-conjugation verbs are irregular
in the perfect, and the principal parts must therefore be learned
one by one from the vocabularies.

> REGULAR: **compleō, complēre, complēvī, complētum,** *fill.*
> IRREGULAR: **videō, vidēre, vīdī, vīsum,** *see.*

Other variations occur. **Moneō** is given in the paradigm because
many verbs of the second conjugation are of this type.

115. The passive of moneō.—

	SINGULAR	PLURAL
	PRESENT	
1.	mone-**or**	monē-**mur**
2.	monē-**ris** (-**re**)	monē-**minī**
3.	monē-**tur**	mone-**ntur**

(a) Review the notes on the passive of **amō** in sec. **104.** Notice
the retention of **e** in the first person singular of the present. Cf.
active of **moneō.**

(b) Referring to sec. **104** and using **monē-** for **amā-**, write out the
imperfect and future passive of **moneō.**

(c) Using the perfect passive participle **monitus** (derived from the
fourth of the principal parts), write out the three perfect passive
tenses of **moneō,** i.e., perfect, pluperfect, and future perfect. Compare your work with Appendix **42.**

116. The infinitives and participles of moneō.—

INFINITIVES

	ACTIVE	PASSIVE
PRESENT	monē-**re**	monē-**rī**
FUTURE	monit-**ūrus esse**	(monit-**um īrī**)[1]
PERFECT	monu-**isse**	monit-**us esse**

---

[1] Disregard this rare form for the present.

PARTICIPLES

	ACTIVE	PASSIVE
PRESENT	monē-ns	——
FUTURE	monit-ūrus, -a, -um	mone-ndus, -a, -um
PERFECT	——	monit-us, -a, -um

VOCABULARY

annus, -ī, *m.*, year

arma, -ōrum, *n. pl.*, arms (*of war*)

bene, *adv.*, well

cessō, *I*, stop, cease from

clārus, -a, -um, clear; famous, distinguished

commoveō,[2] -movēre, -mōvī, -mō-tum, move, stir, excite

compleō, -plēre, -plēvī, -plētum, fill up, finish

cōnsilium, -lī, *n.*, plan

Corinthus, -ī, *f.*, Corinth

dēleō, dēlēre, dēlēvī, dēlētum, destroy

doleō, dolēre, doluī, dolitum,[3] be in pain (*intr.*); grieve for (*tr.*)

Graecus, -a, -um, Greek

habeō, -ēre, -uī, -itum, have, hold; consider

lacrima, -ae, *f.*, tear

magister, -trī, *m.*, master

maneō, manēre, mānsī, mānsum, stay, remain

moveō, movēre, mōvī, mōtum, move

nefārius,[4] -a, -um, wicked

neque, *conj.*, and . . . not; nor

oppidānus, -ī, *m.*, townsman

pertinācia, -ae, *f.*, obstinacy

Poenus, -a, -um, Carthaginian

potest, *3rd. pers. sing. of* possum, he, she, *or* it is able, can (*with infin.*)

praeceptum, -ī, *n.*, maxim, rule, precept

sententia, -ae, *f.*, opinion

teneō, tenēre, tenuī, ——, hold

terreō, -ēre, -uī, -itum, frighten

toga, -ae, *f.*, toga (*outer garment worn by a Roman citizen*)

umquam, *adv.*, ever

undique, *adv.*, on *or* from all sides

videō, vidēre, vīdī, vīsum, see; *in passive often means* seem

EXERCISE A

1. Vīsī sunt; vidēbant; vidēbuntur; vident.
2. Habēbātis; habuit; terrēmur; monitae erant.
3. Aurīgam videō. Equōs tenēre nōn potest.
4. Britannia undique aquā continētur.
5. Lacrimīs nōn movētur. Praedam habeō.

---

[2] Compound verbs formed by the prefixing of prepositions to simple verbs are far commoner than the simple verbs.

[3] See sec. **119.** [4] *Adjectives* in -ius do *not* contract in the gen. sing.

6. Maximē ā poētīs agrī cultūra laudātur.

7. Clārus fuit Ti. Gracchus et in armīs et in togā.

8. Magnā pertināciā in sententiā mānsit.

9. Bene philosophōrum praecepta monent.

10. Catilīna Manlium et Cethēgum cōnsiliōrum nefāriōrum sociōs[5] habuit.

11. Oppidum ā Gallīs dēlētum[6] Rōmānī maximē dolēbant.

12. Nostrī[7] ā Pyrrhī elephantīs terrērī vidēbantur. *multa bella*

13. Multa memoriā tenent[8] oppidānī et domestica et externa bella.

14. Magister noster multōs complēvit annōs neque umquam in studiō cessāvit.

EXERCISE B

(1) Have you seen Corinth, the famous town of the Greeks? (2) They were being terrified; I have been seen; it had been destroyed; we shall be advised. (3) Cethegus was considered Catiline's friend and associate. (4) Mummius had to destroy Corinth.[10] (5) We were affected (moved) with great joy. (6) With many tears the Greeks grieved (for) the destruction of[9] (their) temples. (7) The Carthaginians seemed to be sturdy.

[5] (as) partners in crime

[6] The participle is freely used as an adjective: **oppidum dēlētum** means *the town destroyed,* or better *the destruction of (their) town.*

[7] adj. used as noun, *our men*   [8] i.e., *remember*   [9] Cf. A 11 above.

[10] See sec. **110.** *C. had to be destroyed by M.*

Cethegus of Catiline the friend and associate was considered.

Ō lentē, lentē currite noctis equī.

Run slowly, slowly, horses of the night.

—OVID, *Ars Amātōria*, I, 13, 40

LESSON XI

Imperative Mood
Use of Principal Parts—Review

117. Imperative mood.—
(a) Personal endings of the imperative:

	ACTIVE	PASSIVE
SING.	——	-re
PLUR.	-te	-minī

(b) The imperative mood is formed by adding these endings to the present stems, **amā-**, **monē-**, etc., as follows:

	ACTIVE	PASSIVE
SING.	amā	amā-**re**
PLUR.	amā-**te**	amā-**minī**
SING.	monē	monē-**re**
PLUR.	monē-**te**	monē-**minī**

(1) The singular active is identical with the present stem. No personal ending is added.

(2) Notice that the singular passive is identical in form with the present active infinitive.

(3) The plural passive is identical in form with the second person plural of the present indicative passive.

(c) **Es** and **este** are the imperatives singular and plural of **sum**.

118. Prohibitions (negative imperative).—**Nōlī**, *be unwilling* (sing.), and **nōlīte**, *be unwilling* (plur.), are used before the present infinitives of other verbs to express negative commands, requests, etc.

> *Nōlī, mī fīlī, īrā commovērī.*
> **Be unwilling,** *my son,* **to be moved** *with anger* (i.e., *Do not be angry*).
> *Nōlīte* in arma *properāre,* Rōmānī.
> *Romans,* **do not rush** *to arms.*

Nōlī and **nōlīte** are present imperatives of the irregular verb **nōlle**, *to be unwilling,* the full conjugation of which will be given later. See sec. **190c.**

119. Principal parts and their use.—If the rules of conjugation are known, all forms of the verb can be built up from four forms of the verb, the so-called *principal parts.* What are the names of these four parts? See sec. **45b.** All verbs, however, do not possess these four parts. Some verbs, like **teneō**, have neither supine nor future active participle. As we proceed, we shall find verbs that are more defective still. Such verbs we have in English, e.g., *ought. Ought* is past tense in form. It is sometimes referred to present *owe.* It has no future. We cannot say "I shall ought" or even "owe" to express the idea that I must do something in the future, but must employ some periphrastic expression, such as "I shall have to," or "I shall be under obligation to."

It is essential to commit to memory the principal parts of each new verb, for from these parts are derived the three key stems upon which the whole conjugation is based. Thus:

vocō	vocā-**re,**	vocāv-**ī,**	vocāt-**um**
videō,	vidē-**re,**	vīd-**ī,**	vīs-**um**

give, respectively:

vocā-	vocāv-	vocāt-
vidē-	vīd-	vīs-

The following scheme shows how the several moods and tenses already familiar to you are derived from these three stems.

From the present stems **vocā-, vidē-:**

	ACTIVE		PASSIVE	
PRES. IMPERAT.	vocā	vidē	vocā-re	vidē-re
PRES. PART.	vocā-ns	vidē-ns	——	——
FUT. PART.	——	——	voca-ndus	vide-ndus[1]
PRES. INFIN.	vocā-re	vidē-re	vocā-rī	vidē-rī
PRES. INDIC.	voc-ō	vide-ō	voc-or	vide-or
IMPERF. INDIC.	vocā-bam	vidē-bam	vocā-bar	vidē-bar
FUT. INDIC.	vocā-bō	vidē-bō	vocā-bor	vidē-bor

From the perfect stems **vocāv-**, **vīd-**:

ACTIVE

PERF. INFIN.	vocāv-isse	vīd-isse
PERF. INDIC.	vocāv-ī	vīd-ī
PLUP. INDIC.	vocāv-eram	vīd-eram
FUT. PERF. INDIC.	vocāv-erō	vīd-erō

From the stems **vocāt-**, **vīs-**:

PASSIVE

PERF. PART.	vocāt-us	vīs-us
PERF. INFIN.	vocāt-us esse	vīs-us esse
FUT. INFIN.	vocāt-um īrī	vīs-um īrī
PERF. INDIC.	vocāt-us sum	vīs-us sum
PLUP. INDIC.	vocāt-us eram	vīs-us eram
FUT. PERF. IND.	vocāt-us erō	vīs-us erō

ACTIVE

FUTURE PART.	vocāt-ūrus	vīs-ūrus
FUTURE INFIN.	vocāt-ūrus esse	vīs-ūrus esse

When you later study the subjunctive mood, you will see that its
tenses also may be grouped about these same three stems.

EXERCISE A

1. Longa via est; properā.
2. Ab amīcīs, mī fīlī, monēre.
3. Nōlīte, oppidānī, templum dēlēre.
4. Tacē.

---

[1] The future participle passive is usually called the gerundive.

5. Nōlī terrērī, parve.
6. Dā pecūniam servīs.
7. Terram cum studiō arāte.

EXERCISE B

(1) Stay[2] in the forum. (2) Do[3] not incite the Gauls to[4] war. (3) Do[2] not grieve. (4) Carry[3] the grain into the town. (5) Children, do not wander into the woods. (6) Do[2] not be moved by tears.

EXERCISE C

Using the verbs **laudō** and **deleō**, draw up a scheme similar to that given for **vocō**, etc., giving the meaning of each form derived from the three stems of each verb.

---

[2] sing.   [3] plur.   [4] ad

Magna dī cūrant, parva neglegunt.

The gods are concerned with important things; trifles they ignore.

—CICERO. *dē Nātūrā Deōrum*, II, 66

LESSON XII

Verbs of the Third Conjugation

120. Third conjugation: *regō, I rule*.—

PRINCIPAL PARTS

reg-ō,   rege-**re**,   rēx-ī,   rēct-**um**

The present stem is **regĕ-**, but this stem appears in that form in only a few places in the conjugation. The characteristic short ĕ undergoes so many changes that it will be more profitable for the beginner to commit the paradigm directly to memory than to attempt its analysis. Note, however, that the base **reg-** is invariable in the present system, and that the personal endings are the same as in the first two conjugations, with the exception that the first person singular of the future has **-m** instead of **-ō**. The tense sign **-bā-** is used to designate the imperfect, but note that the future tense sign **-bi-** belongs only to the first and second conjugations. The paradigm:

INDICATIVE

ACTIVE		PASSIVE	
SINGULAR	PLURAL	SINGULAR	PLURAL
PRESENT			
1. reg-ō	regi-**mus**	reg-**or**	regi-**mur**
2. regi-**s**	regi-**tis**	rege-**ris** (**-re**)	regi-**minī**
3. regi-**t**	regu-**nt**	regi-**tur**	regu-**ntur**

(a) Imperfect: **regē-bam, -bās**, etc., exactly like **monē-bam**. Note the lengthening of the -e- of the stem.

FUTURE

1. rega-m   regē-mus   rega-r   regē-mur
2. regē-s   regē-tis   regē-ris (-re)   regē-minī
3. rege-t   rege-nt   regē-tur   rege-ntur

(b) Note -a- instead of -e- in the first person singular.
(c) Write out the three perfect tenses in full.

IMPERATIVE

PRESENT

2. rege   regi-te   rege-re   regi-minī

INFINITIVES

PRESENT	rege-re	regī
FUTURE	rēct-ūrus esse	rēct-um īrī
PERFECT	rēx-isse	rēct-us esse

PARTICIPLES

PRESENT	regē-ns	——
FUTURE	rēct-ūrus	rege-ndus
PERFECT	——	rēct-us

(d) The present infinitive *passive* is formed by substituting -ī for the -ere of the active.

121. -iō verbs of the third conjugation: *capiō, I take.*—

PRINCIPAL PARTS

capi-ō,   cape-re,   cēp-ī,   capt-um

The present stem is **capie-**. The i before the final e of the stem appears in the first person singular and third person plural of the present indicative, in all the forms of the imperfect and future indicative, in the present participle, and in the future passive participle. In all other respects, the paradigm is the same as that of **regō**. The student should carefully compare for himself the corresponding forms of the two verbs. The paradigm:

INDICATIVE

	ACTIVE		PASSIVE	
SINGULAR	PLURAL		SINGULAR	PLURAL

PRESENT

1.	capi-ō	capi-mus	capi-or	capi-mur
2.	capi-s	capi-tis	cape-ris (-re)	capi-minī
3.	capi-t	capiu-nt	capi-tur	capiu-ntur

IMPERFECT

1.	capiē-bam	capiē-bāmus	capiē-bar	capiē-bāmur
2.	capiē-bās	capiē-bātis	capiē-bāris (-re)	capiē-bāminī
3.	capiē-bat	capiē-bant	capiē-bātur	capiē-bantur

FUTURE

1.	capia-m	capiē-mus	capia-r	capiē-mur
2.	capiē-s	capiē-tis	capiē-ris (-re)	capiē-minī
3.	capie-t	capie-nt	capiē-tur	capie-ntur

(a) Note the long ē of the imperfect and future.   Cf. **regō.**
(b) Write out the perfect tenses in full.

IMPERATIVE

PRESENT

2.	cape	capi-te	cape-re	capi-minī

INFINITIVE

PRESENT	cape-re	capī
FUTURE	capt-ūrus esse	capt-um īrī
PERFECT	cēp-isse	capt-us esse

PARTICIPLES

PRESENT	capiē-ns	——
FUTURE	capt-ūrus	capie-ndus
PERFECT	——	capt-us

(c) On the present infinitive *passive*, see sec. **120d.**

VOCABULARY

animus, -ī, *m.*, mind, mood, spirit, feeling

atque, *conj.*, and

capiō, capere, cēpī, captum, take, seize, capture

concilium, -lī, *n.*, assembly, meeting, council

dīcō,[1] dīcere, dīxī, dictum, say, tell

dīmittō, dīmittere, dīmīsī, dīmissum, send away, dismiss

dūcō,[1] dūcere, dūxī, ductum, lead

emō, emere, ēmī, ēmptum, buy

fābula, -ae, *f.*, tale, story; play

faciō,[1] facere, fēcī, factum, do, make

fossa, -ae, *f.*, ditch

gerō, gerere, gessī, gestum, manage, carry on; wage

iaciō, iacere, iēcī, iactum, throw

imperium, -rī, *n.*, supreme power, sovereignty; empire

īra, -ae, *f.*, anger, passion

mittō, mittere, mīsī, missum, send

nārrō, I, tell, relate; describe

nunc, *adv.*. now, at this moment

per, *prep. w. acc.*, through, throughout; by means of

prō, *prep. w. abl.*, for, in behalf of

regō, reger rēxī, rēctum, rule, govern, control

rumpō, rumpere, rūpī, ruptum, break, burst

sapientia, -ae, *f.*, wisdom, good sense

scrībō, scrībere, scrīpsī, scrīptum. write

temperō, I, control, curb

terra, -ae, *f.*, earth; land, country

ventus, -ī, *m.*, wind

verbum, -ī, *n.*, word

vincō, vincere, vīcī, victum, conquer

vīnum, -ī, *n.*, wine

EXERCISE A

1. Vinceris, vincēris, vincēbat, dūcent.
2. Gessit, mittuntur, mittere (*give three meanings*).
3. Multam dē (*from*) pīrātīs praedam cēpimus.
4. Fābulam līberīs nārrāte.
5. Sapienter (*wisely*) vītam īnstituit.
6. Concilium lēgātīs dīmittendum est.
7. Librōs dē (*about, concerning*) bellō Pūnicō scrīpsit Naevius poēta.
8. Dīc clārē.
9. Cibus vīnumque in forō ā servīs ementur.
10. Viam per Gallōs magnā audāciā rūpit.
11. Ōceanus ventīs magnā īrā excitābātur.
12. Prō Haeduīs Dīviciācus verba fēcit.

---

[1] The imperatives singular active of dīcō, dūcō, and faciō shorten to dīc, dūc, and fac respectively; so do all their compounds, except those in -ficiō. For passive of faciō see 216.

13. Dē sapientiā et dīximus multa et saepe dīcēmus; nunc librum ad Atticum amīcum dē amīcitiā mittimus.

14. Vītam regit fortūna, nōn sapientia.

15. Saepe aurō prōvinciam vincere potes.[2]

16. Vīnum in templō emī nōn potest.[2]

EXERCISE B

(1) Anger must be controlled.   (2) Much[3] has been written about the Roman empire.   (3) The Roman people waged many wars in foreign lands.   (4) We shall be conquered by words, not the sword.[4] (5) Lead (*sing.*) the troops to Rome.   (6) The envoys of the Persians were thrown into a ditch by the angry Greeks.   (7) I shall tell the children a story about the Romans.   (8) My son seems to have taken much booty in the wars.   (9) A king cannot rule without wisdom.

[2] **potes, potest,** the 2nd and 3rd pers. sing., respectively, of the pres. indic. of **possum,** *I am able, can* (with infinitive).

[3] Say *many things,* n. pl. of adj. **multus.**   [4] Use plural.

Lesson XIII

Verbs of the Fourth Conjugation— Ablative of Place from Which

122. Fourth conjugation: *audiō, I hear.*—

PRINCIPAL PARTS *add✓ I was hearing*

audi-ō,   audī-re,   audīv-ī,   audīt-um

The present stem is **audi-**. In early Latin, the imperfect was audī-**bam**, and the future audī-**bō**; but, perhaps on the analogy of **capiō**, an **ē** crept in after the **ī** of the stem in the imperfect,[1] making the form audi-**ē-bam**, while the future became audi-**am**, audi-**ēs**, etc. In the same way, **u** crept in after the **i** of the stem in the third person plural of the present indicative, audi-**u-nt**. Cf. **capiunt**.
The paradigm:

INDICATIVE

ACTIVE		PASSIVE	
SINGULAR	PLURAL	SINGULAR	PLURAL

PRESENT

1. audi-ō	audī-**mus**	audi-**or**	audī-**mur**
2. audī-**s**	audī-**tis**	audī-**ris** (-**re**)	audī-**minī**
3. audi-**t**	audi-**u-nt**	audī-**tur**	audi-**u-ntur**

(a) The imperfect and the future are exactly like those of **capiō** (**121**). Write out these tenses of **audiō**.
(b) Write out the three perfect tenses.

IMPERATIVE

PRESENT

2. audī	audī-**te**	audī-**re**	audī-**minī**

---

[1] Also in the present participle, audi-**ē-ns**, and in the future participle passive, audi-**e-ndus**.

73

INFINITIVES

PRESENT	audī-**re**	audī-**rī**
FUTURE	audīt-**ūrus esse**	audīt-**um īrī**
PERFECT	audīv-**isse**	audīt-**us esse**

PARTICIPLES

PRESENT	audi-**ē-ns**	——
FUTURE	audīt-**ūrus**	audi-e-**ndus**
PERFECT	——	audīt-**us**

123. Place from which.—A noun denoting the place *from which* a thing or person moves stands in the *ablative case* and is preceded by the prepositions **ā** (**ab**), **dē**, or **ē** (**ex**). Before names of cities and towns,[2] no preposition is used. Review sec. **94.**

> Rōmam *ā vīllā* vēnit.   *Ex out of*
> *He came **from** his country house to Rome.*

> *Corinthō* Ephesum nautae Graecī saepe nāvigābant.
> *Greek sailors often sailed **from** Corinth to Ephesus.*

> Gallī saxa *dē locīs ēditīs* in Rōmānōs iēcērunt.
> *From high places the Gauls threw rocks onto the Romans.*

VOCABULARY

ā, (ab), *prep. w. abl.,* from; away from

audiō, audīre, audīvī, audītum, hear, listen to

castra, castrōrum, *n.* (*plural with sing. meaning*), camp

cōnficiō, cōnficere, cōnfēcī, cōnfectum, complete, execute, accomplish

dē, *prep. w. abl.,* from; concerning

deus, -ī, *m.,* god (*Appendix 2b*)

ē (ex), *prep. w. abl.,* from; out of

excēdō, excēdere, excessī, excessum, withdraw from, go out

fugiō, fugere, fūgī, fugitum, flee

idōneus, -a, -um, suitable

interim, *adv.,* meanwhile

iubeō, iubēre, iussī, iussum, order, bid, command

locus, -ī, *m.,* (*in plural,* **loca, locōrum,** *n.*), place

littera, -ae, *f.,* letter (*of the alphabet*); *in plural,* letters; literature

maximus, -a, -um, very great, greatest

mora, -ae, *f.,* delay

mūniō, mūnīre, mūnīvī, mūnītum, build; fortify

pōnō, pōnere, posuī, positum, place, set, put

---

[2] And **domus** and **rūs.**

praeclārus, -a, -um, famous, distinguished
proelium, -lī, *n.*, battle
reperiō, reperīre, repperī, repertum, find
sciō, scīre, scīvī (sciī), scītum,
   know

sine, *prep. w. abl.*, without
tabula, -ae, *f.*, tablet, record
undique, *adv.*, from all sides
vallum, -ī, *n.*, rampart
veniō, venīre, vēnī, ventum, come

EXERCISE A

1. Vēnī, vīdī, vīcī.
2. Lēgātī in castra veniunt. Audīvī et crēdō.
3. Litterās Graecās scīmus.
4. Ti. Gracchum audīte, Rōmānī.
5. Marius bellum in Āfricā maximum cōnfēcit.
6. Gallī Macedoniam vexābant; agricolae ex agrīs undique in oppida fūgērunt.
7. Castra sine morā vāllō fossāque mūnīrī iubet.
8. Aurīgae interim ex proeliō excēdunt.
9. Multa Rōmānīs dē nātūrā deōrum dīxit poēta noster.
10. Multīs cum lacrimīs incolae miserī lēgātōrum verba audīvērunt.
11. In castrīs Helvētiōrum tabulae repertae sunt litterīs Graecīs cōnfectae.
12. Castra nostra in locō idōneō pōnenda sunt.
13. Inveniēmus viam aut faciēmus.
14. Castra sine vallō fossāque mūnīrī nōn possunt.
15. Ex agrīs in oppidum fugere nōn potestis.[3]

EXERCISE B

(1) Many envoys came to Rome. (2) As the Gauls were about to withdraw[4] from the battle, they were captured by our soldiers.* (3) Fortify the camp without delay. (4) Records were found made out[5] in Greek letters. (5) In terror[6] the Greeks fled to the towns. (6) Gold is found in many places. (7) The Appian way reaches from Rome to Brundisium. (8) We can[3] come to Corinth today. (9) Many are able[3] to find gold in California (*same word*).

---

[3] possumus, potestis, possunt, *we, you* (pl.), *they are able* or *can* (with infinitive).
[4] "The about-to-withdraw Gauls were captured."
[5] Use conficio. Cf. sentence A 11.   [6] Say "terrified."
* nostrī

Lesson XIV

Personal and Demonstrative Pronouns: *Ego*, *Tū*, *Is*, *Hic*, *Ille*—Ablative of Accompaniment

124. Pronouns.—Though the subject of a Latin sentence or clause is often to be found already contained in the verb, e.g., **laudābimus**, *we-shall-praise*, there are separate forms for *I*, *you*, *he*, *she*, *it*, etc., and their plurals. These are used either (1) for emphasis, in sentences like "*I* do this, but *you* do that," or (2) for oblique cases (i.e., cases other than the nominative and vocative), in sentences like "We give *them* a book," or "I see *you*," etc.*

125. Personal pronouns (9).—

FIRST PERSON

	SINGULAR	PLURAL
NOM.	ego	nōs
GEN.	meī	nostrum, nostrī
DAT.	mihi	nōbīs
ACC.	mē	nōs
ABL.	mē	nōbīs

SECOND PERSON

	SINGULAR	PLURAL
NOM.	tū	vōs
GEN.	tuī	vestrum, vestrī
DAT.	tibi	vōbīs
ACC.	tē	vōs
ABL.	tē	vōbīs

THIRD PERSON

Lacking. See **is, ea, id** in secs. **127, 128.**

(a) **Nōs** is often used for **ego** in grave or official language. Cf. the royal and editorial "we" in English.

(b) Of the genitive plural forms, **nostrum** and **vestrum** are partitive, and **nostrī** and **vestrī**, objective,[1] genitives. The terms "parti-

---

[1] **Nostrī** and **vestrī** have also a collective use, *e.g.*, **Animus est pars melior** *nostrī*, *Our mind is the better part of us.*

* See *app.* **29** for the adjectives meus, tuus, etc., which are used instead of the genitive of the personal pronouns.

tive" (genitive of the whole, sec. **148**) and "objective" (sec. **182**) will be explained later.

126. Order; agreement of verb with different persons.—Latin, unlike the politer English idiom, puts the first person before the second or third where both are mentioned together: e.g., **ego et tū**, *you and I;* even **ego et rēgīna mea**, *my queen and I.*

Where two different persons are used, the verb agrees with the first rather than the second or third, and the second rather than the third; i.e., the person of lower number predominates.

Ego et tū philosophī sumus.	*You and I (we) are philosophers.*
Ego et Tullia valēmus.	*Tullia and I (we) are in good health.*
Tū et Galba Rōmānī estis.	*You and Galba are Romans.*

127. Demonstrative pronouns.—Since the personal pronouns of the third person—*he, she, it,* and *they*—are lacking in Latin, a demonstrative is often used to take their place. These demonstratives are also used, as in English, to point out (**dē-mōnstrō**) a person or thing for special attention, either with nouns as adjectives, or alone as pronouns; e.g., *He* or *that man, she* or *that woman, it* or *that thing.*

Among the most common are **is, hic,** and **ille.** They are declined in three genders like adjectives, as follows:

	M.	F.	N.
		SINGULAR	
NOM.	is	ea	id
GEN.	eius	eius	eius
DAT.	eī	eī	eī
ACC.	eum	eam	id
ABL.	eō	eā	eō
		PLURAL	
NOM.	eī, iī	eae	ea
GEN.	eōrum	eārum	eōrum
DAT.	eīs, iīs	eīs, iīs	eīs, iīs
ACC.	eōs	eās	ea
ABL.	eīs, iīs	eīs, iīs	eīs, iīs

	M.	F.	N.

SINGULAR

Nom.	hic	haec	hoc
Gen.	huius	huius	huius
Dat.	huic	huic	huic
Acc.	hunc	hanc	hoc
Abl.	hōc	hāc	hōc

PLURAL

Nom.	hī	hae	haec
Gen.	hōrum	hārum	hōrum
Dat.	hīs	hīs	hīs
Acc.	hōs	hās	haec
Abl.	hīs	hīs	hīs

	M.	F.	N.

SINGULAR

Nom.	ille	illa	illud
Gen.	illīus	illīus	illīus
Dat.	illī	illī	illī
Acc.	illum	illam	illud
Abl.	illō	illā	illō

PLURAL

Nom.	illī	illae	illa
Gen.	illōrum	illārum	illōrum
Dat.	illīs	illīs	illīs
Acc.	illōs	illās	illa
Abl.	illīs	illīs	illīs

(a) The **i** in **eius** and **huius** is consonantal (**71**).

(b) The second **i** in **illīus** is long, an exception to the general rule that a vowel before another vowel is short.

128. Meanings of *is, hic,* and *ille*.—Is means *this* or *that*, but it is weaker, more colorless, and less emphatic than **hic** and **ille**. For this reason it supplies the lack of a personal pronoun of the third person—*he, she,* or *it*. It also often supplies the lack of the definite article.

Hic means *this*, referring to that which is near the speaker in place, time, or thought.

Ille means *that*, or *that yonder*, referring to that which is remote from the speaker in place, time, or thought. It often indicates admiration, e.g., **Sulla ille**, *that famous Sulla* (*whom you have all heard about*). Another meaning is *the former*, as opposed to **hic**, *the latter*.

129. Accompaniment.—Accompaniment is expressed by the preposition **cum**, governing the ablative case.

> **Fīlius tuus *cum lēgātīs* in Graeciam missus erat.**
> *Your son had been sent to Greece **with the envoys.***

> **Servōs *mēcum* dūcam.**
> *I shall bring (my) slaves **with me.***

(a) This construction is also used with verbs signifying contention or fighting.

> **Rōmānī saepe *cum Gallīs* pugnābant.**
> *The Romans often fought **with the Gauls.***

The meaning here is not that the Romans fought side by side *with* the Gauls, but *with them in rivalry*, i.e., *against* them.

(b) Note that **cum** follows and is joined with the ablatives **mē**, **tē**, **nōbīs**, **vōbīs**: e.g., **mēcum**, *with me;* **tēcum**, *with you*, etc. So also with **sē**, **quō**, **quā**, **quibus**.

VOCABULARY

contendō, contendere, contendī, contentum, fight, contend; hasten

dēlectō, *I*, delight (*tr.*), *pass.*, take pleasure in

cotīdiānus, -a, -um, daily

nihil (*indeclinable*), nothing

nūntiō, *I*, report, announce

relinquō, -linquere, -līquī, -lictum, leave behind

valdē, *adv.*, strongly; exceedingly, very much

vix, *adv.*, scarcely

EXERCISE A

1. Tē vocō. Et tū, Brūte! Is sum.
2. Venīte mēcum.
3. Ego Marius ille sum.

4. Ego maneō, tū excēdēs.

5. In hāc sententiā semper manēbimus.

6. Hoc praeceptum nōbīs magnā dīligentiā tenendum est.

7. Fānum vidēsne[2] hoc?

8. Nōs nihil dē eō reperiēbāmus.

9. Haec ā multīs eī nūntiāta erant. *These feat had been related*

10. Alexander ille hīs studiīs valdē dēlectābātur. *to kindly many*

11. Hāc viā Caesar, Pompeius illā properābat.

12. Germānī cum Gallīs cotīdiānīs proeliīs contendunt et eōrum agrōs vexant.

13. Et pecūniam et frūmentum eīs dedistis.

14. In haec loca nōbīscum mittēminī.

15. Id oppidum appellābātur Ephesus.

16. Ēmistīne dē eō hanc vīllam ubi nunc habitās? Ēmī atque argentum dedī.

17. Nōs patriam fugimus.

18. Crās fābulam cum amīcō spectātūrus sum.

19. Corinthī vestīgium[3] vix relictum est.

EXERCISE B

(1) Come with me, my son. (2) This book belongs to me. (3) The inhabitants of that island over there are always being molested by pirates. (4) This man rules by words; that one, by arms. (5) She and her[4] friend were hurrying to the temple. (6) Is this your daughter?

[2] The effect of the word order is: "This temple here—do you see it?"
[3] *trace*　　[4] **eius**

Est profectō deus quī quae nōs gerimus audit et videt.

There is assuredly a God who hears and sees what we do.

Lesson XV

Relative Pronoun

130. The relative pronoun *quī*.—

	M.	F.	N.
		SINGULAR	
Nom.	quī	quae	quod
Gen.	cuius[1]	cuius	cuius
Dat.	cui	cui	cui
Acc.	quem	quam	quod
Abl.	quō	quā	quō
		PLURAL	
Nom.	quī	quae	quae
Gen.	quōrum	quārum	quōrum
Dat.	quibus	quibus	quibus
Acc.	quōs	quās	quae
Abl.	quibus	quibus	quibus

131. Use of the relative.—In English, we often omit the relative; e.g., "The man I saw yesterday," for "The man whom I saw yesterday." In Latin, we must always insert the relative. It is declined in all three genders, and agrees with its antecedent in gender, number, and person. The *case* in which it is to stand will be determined, however, by its use in its own clause, i.e., the clause which it introduces.

Alexandrō equus erat *quem* Būcephalum appellāvit.

*Alexander had a horse **which** he called Bucephalus.*

---

[1] The i in **cuius** is consonantal. Cf. **huius** and **eius.**

Question: Who called?   *Answer: He* called.

Question: Called whom or *which?* *Which* is therefore in the accusative case, **quem**, and masculine singular to agree with its antecedent, **equus.**

Another way to find the proper case, gender, number, and person of the relative is to take it away and put the antecedent in its place; thus instead of:

> *Boadicea is a queen whom the Britons love,*

we have:

> *Boadicea is a queen; the Britons love (her).*
> **Boudicēa est rēgīna; Britannī eam amant.**

Now we put back the relative pronoun in the same case, gender, number, and person as **eam**, and we have:

> **Boudicēa est rēgīna *quam* Britannī amant.**
> *Boadicea is a queen **whom** the Britons love.*
>
> **Dīcēbās ea *quae* sentiēbās.**
> *You used to say **what** you felt.*
>
> **Ubi est puer *cui* librum dedistī?**
> *Where is the boy **to whom** you gave the book?*

Observation.—Where antecedent and relative are in the same case, **quī** without **is** will express *he who.*

> ***Quī* haec vidēbant flēbant.**
> ***Those who** saw this wept.*
> *(The onlookers wept.)*

VOCABULARY

ante, *adv.,* before, previously
auxilium, -lī, *n.,* help; *in pl.,* reinforcements
dē, *prep. w. abl.,* about, concerning
emō, emere, ēmī, ēmptum, buy
factum, -ī, *n.,* deed
Haeduus, -ī, *m.,* a Haeduan (*member of a Gallic tribe*)
Hispānia, -ae, *f.,* Spain
ibi, *adv.,* there

medicus, -ī, *m.,* doctor
numquam, *adv.,* never
prō, *prep. w. abl.,* for; on behalf of
saepe, *adv.,* often
ubi, *adv.,* where?
ūnā, *adv.,* together
vehō, vehere, vēxī, vectum, carry
vēndō, vēndere, vēndidī, vēnditum, sell

EXERCISE A

1. Eōs saepe quōs numquam vīdimus amāmus.
2. Ubi sunt eī quōrum facta laudāre possumus?
3. Patriam relīquit prō quā saepe pugnāverat.
4. Litterās accēpī tuās quās Cornificius mihi dedit.
5. Ibi frūmentum quod ex Hispaniā vēxerat relīquit.
6. Petent castra quae capta sunt.
7. Hic medicus est cuius fīlius vulnerātus est.
8. Erat ūnā cum cēterīs Dumnorīx Haeduus, dē quō ante ā nōbīs dictum est.[2]
9. Equī quōs mihi ēmistī iam vēnditī sunt.
10. Auxilia ex Britanniā, quae contrā Galliam posita est, postulāvērunt.

EXERCISE B

1. The horse which was bought for me was sold by you.
2. Boadicea is the queen who sent help to the Gauls.
3. The farmers whom we saw today and whose grain we bought are not our friends.
4. The sailors with whom we wage war are inhabitants of Gaul.
5. Where are the men the doctor saved yesterday?

SELECTION FOR READING

Nūper[3] erat medicus, nunc est vispillo[4] Diaulus:
  Quod vispillo facit, fēcerat et medicus.
                                            —Martial, I, 47.

---

[2] an impersonal use, mention has been made   [3] recently
[4] undertaker, nominative case

Urbānus et īnstructus

A gentleman and a scholar (*A medieval description of Isaiah*)

—MIGNE, *Patrologia Latīna*, 79, c. 356

Lesson XVI

Interrogative Pronoun and Adjective—Ablative of Separation—Dative with Adjectives

132. The interrogative pronoun **quis, quid**, *who?*, *what?*, is declined as follows:

	SINGULAR		PLURAL
	M. & F.	N.	
Nom.	quis	quid	(Like the relative
Gen.	cuius	cuius	throughout)
Dat.	cui	cui	
Acc.	quem	quid	
Abl.	quō	quō	

Quid exspectās?
What are you waiting for?

Cui dōnō lepidum novum libellum?
To whom do I give my nice, new book?

Sed tū quī eum dēfendis *quid* dīcis?
But, you who are defending him, what do you say?

133. The interrogative adjective **quī**, *what?* or *what kind of?*, is declined throughout in exactly the same way as the relative.

Quam prōvinciam tenuistis ā pīrātīs līberam? *Quem* socium dēfendistis?

What province have you kept free from pirates? What ally have you protected?

Sed quis ego sum? Aut *quae* est in mē sapientia?
But who am I? Or what wisdom is there in me?

84

134. Ablative of separation.—The ablative case is used following verbs and adjectives implying *want, absence, deprivation, freedom,* and cognate ideas, sometimes with and sometimes without the prepositions ā (ab), dē, or ē (ex).

> abstinēre *iniūriā*
> *to refrain from wrong*
>
> oppidum vacuum *ā praesidiō*
> *a town empty of* (i.e., *bereft of*) *its garrison*
>
> Britannī, Rōmānōs *ab ōrīs vestrīs* prohibēte.
> *Britons, keep the Romans from your shores.*

135. Dative with certain adjectives.—The dative is used in dependence on the following adjectives, and with others which will be found with a special comment to this effect in subsequent vocabularies:

amīcus, -a, -um, *friendly* (*to*)
inimīcus -a, -um, *hostile* (*to*)
idōneus, -a, -um, *suitable* (*for*)
grātus, -a, -um, *pleasing* (*to*)
proximus, -a, -um, *nearest* (*to*), *next* (*to*)

īnfestus, -a, -um, *hostile* (*to*), *dangerous* (*to*), *troublesome* (*to*)
propinquus, -a, -um, *near* (*to*)
fīnitimus, -a, -um, *neighboring* (*to*)
molestus, -a, -um, *annoying, detestable* (*to*)

Tribūnī *nōbīs* sunt amīcī.
Dōnec grātus eram *tibi.*
Castrīs idōneus locus.

The tribunes are friendly to us.
While still I pleased thee.
A place suitable for a camp.

VOCABULARY

cārus, -a, -um, dear
continenter, *adv.*, continuously
grātus, -a, -um, pleasing, acceptable
incolō, -colere, -coluī, ——, inhabit, dwell in; live
incommodum, -ī, *n.*, inconvenience
īnfestus, -a, -um, hostile, troublesome
irrumpō, -rumpere, -rūpī, -ruptum, break into; invade

lībero, *I*, free
molestus, -a, -um, irksome, annoying
pecūnia, -ae, *f.*, money
praeceptum, -ī, *n.*, maxim, rule
prohibeō, -hibēre, -hibuī, -hibitum, prevent, keep from (e.g., somebody, *acc.*, from something, *abl.*)
Rhēnus, -ī, *m.*, the Rhine
trāns, *prep. w. acc.*, across

EXERCISE A

1. Quid fēcī?   Quem vidēs?   Quid agit?   Quod verbum audiō?
2. Fuitne hic tibi amīcus?
3. Cārus fuit Āfricānō noster Ennius.
4. Multīs ex hīs incommodīs pecūniā nōs[1] līberāmus.
5. Irrūpērunt in Galliam quae Rōmānīs īnfesta erat.
6. Helvētiī proximī sunt Germānīs quī trāns Rhēnum incolunt, quibuscum[2] continenter bellum gerunt.
7. Quae[3] praecepta!   Quae[3] sapientia!
8. Caesar frūmentō diū ab Helvētiīs prohibēbātur.
9. Quis est dux ā quō dūcēminī?
10. Laudārī, id quod multīs grātum est, mihi est molestum.

EXERCISE B

(1) He has broken; we were breaking into; I shall be deprived of; keep (*pl.*) them out! what have you done?   (2) You (*sing.*) will be sent; the camp was pitched; these things had been written; it had been bought and sold.   (3) I came, I saw, I conquered.   (4) Whom will you send?   My son.   (5) From what inconveniences will they set us free by means of money?   (6) The Gauls are neighbors of[4] the Germans, who live across the Rhine.

---

[1] nōs is acc., *us*, i.e., *ourselves*.

[2] The preposition **cum** follows the relative pronoun. Cf. **mēcum, tēcum, vōbīscum, nōbīscum.**

[3] The interrogative often has an exclamatory force. Cf. English *What weather!*

[4] Say *to*.

Obsequium amīcōs, vēritās odium parit.

Flattery wins friends, the truth unpopularity.

—TERENCE, *Andria* I, i, 41

LESSON XVII

Third Declension: Mute Stems— Ablative of Time

Review the classification of mutes in **72a.**

136. Third declension.—The largest and most heterogeneous of the declensions is the third. The nouns of this declension are conveniently classified by their stems rather than by the ending of the nominative singular, for the latter shows too great apparent variety and irregularity. The stem of a third declension noun is best found by dropping off the ending -**is** from the genitive singular.

There is, furthermore, no comprehensive rule for the gender of these nouns, such as exists for nouns of the first and second declensions. For this reason, the student must learn the nominative singular, the genitive singular, and the gender of each noun as it is encountered in the vocabularies. For certain aids in determining gender, see sec. **144.**

137. Case endings of the third declension.—

	SINGULAR	PLURAL
NOM.	(*irregular*)	-ēs (*m., f.*), -a (*n.*)
GEN.	-is	-um
DAT.	-ī	-ibus
ACC.	-em (*m., f.*) (*neut., like nom.*)	-ēs (*m., f.*), -a (*n.*)
ABL.	-e	-ibus

138. Mute stems.—Mute stems form the nominative singular by the addition of -**s** in the case of masculines and feminines. The vowel before the mute often undergoes modification.

(a) *Labial mute stems.*—Before -**s** of the nominative singular, a labial mute (**p, b**) remains unchanged.

prīnceps, m., *chief;* stem, **prīncip-**

87

	SINGULAR	PLURAL
Nom.	prīncep-s	prīncip-ēs
Gen.	prīncip-is	prīncip-um
Dat.	prīncip-ī	prīncip-ibus
Acc.	prīncip-em	prīncip-ēs
Abl.	prīncip-e	prīncip-ibus

(b) *Dental mute stems.*—A dental (lingual) mute (**t, d**) is dropped before **-s** of the nominative singular.

mīles, m., *soldier;* stem, **mīlit-**

Nom.	mīle-s	mīlit-ēs
Gen.	mīlit-is	mīlit-um
Dat.	mīlit-ī	mīlit-ibus
Acc.	mīlit-em	mīlit-ēs
Abl.	mīlit-e	mīlit-ibus

(c) *Guttural mute stems.*—A guttural (palatal) mute (**c, g**) combines with **-s** of the nominative singular to form **-x.**

rēx, m., *king;* stem, **rēg-**

Nom.	rēx (rēg-s)	rēg-ēs
Gen.	rēg-is	rēg-um
Dat.	rēg-ī	rēg-ibus
Acc.	rēg-em	rēg-ēs
Abl.	rēg-e	rēg-ibus

(d) Nearly all the nouns of the third declension having mute stems are masculine or feminine. A few are neuter. The nominative singular of the neuters is the simple stem, sometimes with vowel modification. Stems ending in two consonants drop the final mute.

cor, n., *heart;* **cord-**   **caput,** n., *head;* stem, **capit-**

	SINGULAR	PLURAL	SINGULAR	PLURAL
Nom.	cor	cord-a	caput	capit-a
Gen.	cord-is	(cord-um)[1]	capit-is	capit-um
Dat.	cord-ī	cord-ibus	capit-ī	capit-ibus
Acc.	cor	cord-a	caput	capit-a
Abl.	cord-e	cord-ibus	capit-e	capit-ibus

[1] Not found.

139. Ablative of time.—A noun denoting *the time at which* or *within which* some act or event takes place stands in the ablative case.

Eō annō <u>condita est</u> *Rōma.*
In this year Rome *was founded.*

Prīmā lūce mīlitēs ē somnō excitāvit.
At dawn he aroused the soldiers from sleep.
   (prīmā lūce—literally, *at the first light*)

Hominum *memoriā.*
Within the memory of man.

VOCABULARY

auctōritās, auctōritātis, *f.*, influence, prestige

cīvitās, cīvitātis, *f.*, clan, state

cognōscō, cognōscere, cognōvī, cognitum, learn (by inquiry), find out

condō, condere, condidī, conditum, found

cōnfirmō, *I*, establish; declare

expellō, expellere, expulī, expulsum, drive out

hōra, -ae, *f.*, hour

incrēdibiliter, *adv.*, extraordinarily, unbelievably

occīdō, occīdere, occīdī, occīsum, kill

lūx, lūcis, *f.*, light

mors, mortis, *f.*, death

pāx, pācis, *f.*, peace

pellō, pellere, pepulī, pulsum, drive, beat, rout

permoveō, permovēre, permōvī, permōtum, move thoroughly, affect, influence

perveniō, pervenīre, pervēnī, perventum, come to, arrive

pēs, pedis, *m.*, foot

prīmus, -a, -um, first

prīncipium, -pī, *n.*, beginning

prīnceps, prīncipis, *m.*, first or leading man, chief

sex, *indecl. adj.*, six

somnus, -ī, *m.*, sleep

voluptās, voluptātis, *f.*, pleasure

EXERCISE A

1. Pellētur, occīsae sunt, repperērunt, mitteris, vidēns.
2. Victūrī sumus, dīcēbātur, fueris, iēcisse, capiēmur.
3. Ad rēgem in castra vēnērunt cuius ad pedēs dōna posuērunt.
4. Prīncipiō huius annī lēgātī, quī in Aetōliam et Macedoniam missī erant, ad rēgem Perseum pervēnērunt.
5. Lūcius Cassius occīsus est mīlitēsque eius ab Gallīs pulsī sunt.
6. Veniō nunc ad voluptātēs agricolārum, quibus ego incrēdibiliter dēlector.

7. Rēgnō est expulsus Ariobarzānēs rēx, socius populī Rōmanī atque amīcus.

8. Auctōritāte Orgetorīgis permōtī, cum proximīs cīvitātibus pācem et amīcitiam cōnfīrmābant.

9. Cognōscit ea quae in Italiā geruntur.

10. In fugā foeda mors est; in victōriā glōriōsa.

11. Paucīs annīs Gallī ex Galliā pellentur.

12. Animam meam cūrīs expedīvī.

13. Paucī veniunt ad senectūtem.

14. Veniunt ad ea loca quae numquam anteā vīdērunt.

15. Pāx vōbīscum!

16. Prīncipēs prō victōriā pugnant, comitēs prō prīncipe.

EXERCISE B

(1) They threw great stones upon the soldiers' heads. (2) Come to me within-six-hours. (3) Do not arouse her from sleep. (4) The pirates were killed at dawn by the soldiers. (5) The chieftains of these clans were unfriendly to the Germans.

SELECTIONS FOR READING

(1) Caelum nōn animum mūtant quī trāns mare currunt.

—Horace, *Epistles*, I, xi, 27.

(2) Silent lēgēs inter arma.

—Cicero, *pro Milone*, iv, 10.

Deus quī nōbīs vītam eōdem tempore et lībertātem dedit, quae ambae hominum vī dēlērī sed nūllō modō disiungī possunt.

The God who gave us life gave us liberty at the same time; the hand of force may destroy but cannot disjoin them.

—THOMAS JEFFERSON

LESSON XVIII

Third Declension: Liquid and Nasal Stems

Review section **72b** and **c**.

140. Nouns whose stems end in a liquid (*l*, *r*) or a nasal (*n*).— These use for their nominative singular the simple stem:

cōnsul; gen., cōnsulis; stem, cōnsul-

Some undergo slight modifications, as follows:
(a) Stems in -ōn- drop **n**:

legiō; gen., legiōnis; stem, legiōn-

(b) Stems in -din- and -gin- drop **n** and change **i** to **ō**, possibly after the analogy of the nouns in (a) above:

multitūdō; gen., multitūdinis; stem, multitūdin-

(c) Stems in -in- (other than -din- and -gin-) retain **n** and change **i** to **e**:

nōmen; gen., nōminis; stem, nōmin-

(d) Stems in -tr- insert **e** between **t** and **r**:

pater; gen., patris; stem, patr-

(e) Most neuter stems in -er- and -or- have -us in the nominative:

tempus; gen., temporis; stem, tempor-

The paradigms:

cōnsul, m., *consul;* stem, cōnsul-	multitūdō, f., *crowd;* stem, multitūdin-	legiō, f., *legion;* stem, legiōn-

SINGULAR

Nom.	cōnsul	multitūdō	legiō
Gen.	cōnsul-is	multitūdin-is	legiōn-is
Dat.	cōnsul-ī	multitūdin-ī	legiōn-ī
Acc.	cōnsul-em	multitūdin-em	legiōn-em
Abl.	cōnsul-e	multitūdin-e	legiōn-e

PLURAL

Nom.	cōnsul-ēs	multitūdin-ēs	legiōn-ēs
Gen.	cōnsul-um	multitūdin-um	legiōn-um
Dat.	cōnsul-ibus	multitūdin-ibus	legiōn-ibus
Acc.	cōnsul-ēs	multitūdin-ēs	legiōn-ēs
Abl.	cōnsul-ibus	multitūdin-ibus	legiōn-ibus

pater, m., *father;* stem, patr-	nōmen, n., *name;* stem, nōmin-	tempus, n., *time;* stem, tempor-

SINGULAR

Nom.	pater	nōmen	tempus
Gen.	patr-is	nōmin-is	tempor-is
Dat.	patr-ī	nōmin-ī	tempor-ī
Acc.	patr-em	nōmen	tempus
Abl.	patr-e	nōmin-e	tempor-e

PLURAL

Nom.	patr-ēs	nōmin-a	tempor-a
Gen.	patr-um	nōmin-um	tempor-um
Dat.	patr-ibus	nōmin-ibus	tempor-ibus
Acc.	patr-ēs	nōmin-a	tempor-a
Abl.	patr-ibus	nōmin-ibus	tempor-ibus

VOCABULARY

augeō, augēre, auxī, auctum, increase (tr.); enrich, honor

Belgae, -ārum, m., Belgae, Belgians

celeritās, celeritātis, f., speed

cōnsul, cōnsulis, m., consul

corpus, corporis, n., body

dux, ducis, m., leader, commander, general

frāter, frātris, m., brother

hiemō, I, spend the winter

homō,[1] hominis, m., human being, man

honor (honōs),[2] honōris, m., distinction, honor; dignity, office

mōs,[2] mōris, m., custom, precedent

multitūdō, multitūdinis, f., large number, crowd

novus, -a, -um, new, novel, strange

ōrātor, ōrātōris, m., orator

per, prep. w. acc., through, throughout; over, through, by means of

praesidium, praesidī, n., garrison, guard; protection

prōveniō, -venīre, etc., come forward

quot, (1) interrog. adj., indecl., how many?

(2) rel. adj., indecl., as many (as)

repellō, repellere, reppulī, repulsum, drive back, repel

salūs, salūtis, f., safety, welfare

—— salūtem dīcere, to send greeting (to)

sōlitūdō, sōlitūdinis, f., desolation, solitude

stultus, -a, -um, foolish

tēlum, -ī, n., weapon, missile

tempus, temporis, n., time, occasion

tot, adj., indecl., so many

tot . . . quot, as many . . . as

virtūs, virtūtis, f., manliness, valor; pl. good qualities, virtues

EXERCISE A

1. Accēpit condiciōnem.

2. Ex quō tempore hōc morbō affectus es?

3. Cōnsulēs Rōmānī salūtem dīcunt Pyrrhō rēgī.

4. Caesar cum eīs legiōnibus quae in Italiā hiemāverant magnā cum celeritāte in Belgās contendit.

5. In oppidō captō praesidium collocāvit.

6. Eō annō quō M. Cicerō et C. Antōnius cōnsulēs fuērunt interfectus est Cethēgus.

7. Per patrum frātrumque corpora properābant Belgae quōs nostrī multitūdine tēlōrum reppulērunt.

---

[1] An exception to **140c.**

[2] An exception to **140**; many stems in **r** have nom. in **s**. Their stem originally ended in **s**, which was changed by rhotacism (Greek **rho**), a process by which **s** between vowels changes to **r**.

8. Ille cārus est cordī meō. *mine*

9. Frūstrā tantus labor sūmēbātur.

10. Ubi sōlitūdinem faciunt pācem appellant.

11. Ō tempora, ō mōrēs. *O times, O Customs*

12. Leōnum animī index[3] cauda.

13. In pāce leōnēs, in proeliō cervī.[4] *deers*

14. Eō tempore rēgis honōre et nōmine auctus est.[5]

He was invested in the rank and title of king

EXERCISE B

(1) The Belgae drove out the Gauls who inhabit these places.
(2) The courage of the soldiers should be praised.*   (3) Lead the
legions against the clans that are hostile to us.   (4) Caesar to Pompey, greeting.   (5) At dawn a large number of the Belgae came to
Caesar's camp.

SELECTIONS FOR READING

(1) Quot hominēs, tot sententiae.

—Terence, *Phormio*, II, iv, 14.

(2) Ducis in cōnsiliō posita est[6] virtūs mīlitum.

—Publilius Syrus, *Sententiae*.

(3) Carmine dī superī plācantur, carmine Mānēs.

—Horace, *Epistles*, II, i, 138.

---

[3] Supply **est**.   **Cauda** is subject; **index** is predicate noun.
[4] Supply **sunt**.   [5] *Was invested with the rank and title*, etc.
[6] *Depends on*, a frequent meaning of the passive of **pōnō**.
* See sec. 110.

Ille dolet vērē quī sine teste dolet.

He truly grieves who grieves when none is there.

—MARTIAL, I, 33

LESSON XIX

Third Declension: *I*-Stems

141. Some nouns of the third declension have stems ending in -i. These are:

(a) *Masculines and Feminines*—

(1) Ending in -is or -ēs in the nominative singular, with the same number of syllables in the genitive as in the nominative (parisyllabic), e.g., **cīvis**, gen. **cīvis**, c., *citizen;* **nūbēs**, gen. **nūbis**, f., *cloud.* Among the commonest exceptions are **canis**, m., *dog,* and **iuvenis**, m., *young man* (see vocabulary).

(2) Nouns in -s or -x in the nominative singular, in which -is of the genitive is preceded by two consonants, e.g., **nox**, gen., **noctis**, f., *night;* **cliēns**, gen., **clientis**, m., *dependent.*

(3) A few other words whose peculiarity in this respect will be noted as they are encountered, e.g., **mūs**, gen., **mūris**, m., *mouse;* **līs**, **lītis**, *strife;* **nix**, **nivis**, *snow;* **fax**, **facis**, *torch;* **plēbs**, **plēbis**, *people;* **trabs**, **trabis**, *beam;* **fraus**, **fraudis**, *wrong;* **dōs**, **dōtis**, *dowry* (all feminine); **os**, **ossis**, n., *bone;* and others (see vocabulary).

These nouns differ from the consonant stems in declension in having -ium in the genitive plural and -īs or -ēs in the accusative plural.

What is the ending of the *consonant* stems in these cases?

(b) *Neuters.*—These end in the nominative singular in -e, -al, -ar, and differ from the neuter *consonant* stems in having -ī in the ablative singular; -ia in the nominative and accusative plural; -ium in the genitive plural.

What are the endings of the neuter *consonant* stems in these cases?

142. The few exceptions to the rules above stated, such as masculines and feminines with ablative singular in -ī and the still rarer

95

accusative singular in **-im**, e.g., **turris**, *tower;* **sitis**, *thirst;* **tussis**, *cough;* **fēbris**, *fever;* **secūris**, *axe;* **puppis**, *ship's stern* (all feminine), and others (see vocabulary), will be commented upon as they occur in the exercises and vocabularies.

143. Paradigms of typical *i*-stems.—

	cīvis, c., *citizen;* stem, **cīv(i-)**	**nūbēs**, f., *cloud;* stem, **nūb(i-)**	**urbs**, f., *city;* stem, **urb(i-)**
		SINGULAR	
Nom.	cīvis	nūbēs	urbs
Gen.	cīvis	nūbis	urbis
Dat.	cīvī	nūbī	urbī
Acc.	cīvem	nūbem	urbem
Abl.	cīve	nūbe	urbe
		PLURAL	
Nom.	cīvēs	nūbēs	urbēs
Gen.	cīvium	nūbium	urbium
Dat.	cīvibus	nūbibus	urbibus
Acc.	cīvīs (-ēs)	nūbīs (-ēs)	urbīs (-ēs)
Abl.	cīvibus	nūbibus	urbibus

	cohors, f., *cohort;* stem, **cohort(i-)**	**mare**, n., *sea;* stem, **mar(i-)**	**animal**, n., *animal;* stem, **animāl(i-)**
		SINGULAR	
Nom.	cohors	mare	animal
Gen.	cohortis	maris	animālis
Dat.	cohortī	marī	animālī
Acc.	cohortem	mare	animal
Abl.	cohorte	marī	animālī
		PLURAL	
Nom.	cohortēs	maria	animālia
Gen.	cohortium	——	animālium
Dat.	cohortibus	maribus	animālibus
Acc.	cohortīs (-ēs)	maria	animālia
Abl.	cohortibus	maribus	animālibus

VOCABULARY

aestās, aestātis, *f.*, summer
appellō, *I*, name, call by name
centuriō, centuriōnis, *m.*, centurion
cīvis, cīvis (cīvium),[1] *c.*, citizen
cohors, cohortis (cohortium), *f.*, cohort
collis, collis (collium), *m.*, hill
dēfēnsor, dēfēnsōris, *m.*, defender, protector
dēfessus, -a, -um, tired out, exhausted
eques, equitis, *m.*, trooper, cavalryman; knight
explōrātor, explōrātōris, *m.*, scout
fīnis, fīnis (fīnium), *m.*, end; boundary, limit, border (*pl. also* territory); frontier
hostis, hostis (hostium), *m.*, enemy; the enemy (*usually pl.*)
imperātor, imperātōris, *m.*, commander-in-chief, general

intrā, *prep. w. acc.*, within, inside; into
lapis, lapidis, *m.*, stone
mare, maris (maria),[2] *n.*, sea
mōns, montis (montium), *m.*, mountain; mountain range
mūrus, -ī, *m.*, wall
nāvis, nāvis (nāvium), *f.*, ship
nūbēs, nūbis (nūbium), *f.*, cloud
nūdō, *I*, strip, uncover, strip bare
nūntius, nūntī, *m.*, messenger
ob, *prep. w. acc.*, on account of, for
patria, -ae, *f.*, native land, country
pedes, peditis, *m.*, foot-soldier, infantryman
pīlum, -ī, *n.*, heavy javelin, pike
reportō, *I*, bring back; win (a victory)
tuba, -ae, *f.*, trumpet
urbs, urbis (urbium), *f.*, city

EXERCISE A

1. Nāvis portat mīlitēs.
2. Mōns Iūra intrā fīnēs Sēquanōrum est.
3. In quā urbe vīvimus?
4. Sex cohortēs in hostium mūrum lapidēs ac tēla iēcērunt.
5. Mox mūrus dēfēnsōribus nūdātus est.
6. Haec urbs est Thēbae.
7. Cibum captāmus ē marī.
8. Cicerō pater patriae ā populō Rōmānō appellātus est.
9. Id Caesarī per explōrātōrēs nūntiātum est.
10. Eā aestāte imperātor ob victōriam quam dē Poenīs reportāvit appellātus est Āfricānus.
11. Equitēs peditēsque nostrī cīvīs cēpērunt quī in urbe hostium erant.

---

[1] i-stem nouns will be indicated in all vocabularies by thus printing their genitive plural in parentheses.

[2] Thus shown because the *genitive* plural is not found.

12. Tubā incitātī, mīlitēs dēfessī pīla in hostēs iēcērunt multōsque occīdērunt.

13. Prīmae cohortis centuriō hostium nāvīs quae in marī nāvigābant ducī suō dēmōnstrābat.

EXERCISE B

(1) Do not disturb the animals. (2) They were throwing javelins down from the walls of that city. (3) In the summer of that year the consuls sent messengers to King Pyrrhus. (4) He carried[3] a wall from the frontiers of the Helvetians to the Jura mountains.[4] (5) The ships of the Carthaginians were destroyed by the Roman consul.

[3] Use dúcō.   [4] Use the singular.

Prīma est ēloquentiae virtūs perspicuitās.

The first requisite of mastery of language is clarity.

—QUINTILIAN, *Institutio Oratoria*, II, 3, 8

LESSON XX

Third Declension: Gender and Review— Irregular Nouns

144. Gender in the third declension.—The gender of most third declension nouns must be learned by practice. The principles laid down in sec. **96** will apply: e.g., **soror**, f., *sister;* **uxor**, f., *wife;* **frāter**, m., *brother;* **Hannibal**, m., *Hannibal.* In addition the following rules will be helpful:

Masculines are nouns in	Feminines are nouns in
-or; gen., -ōris	-tās
-ex; gen., -icis	-ūs; gen., -ūtis, -ūdis
-es; gen., -itis	-dō, -gō; gen., -inis
	-iō (abstract and collective)

Neuters are nouns in

-e, -al, -ar, -us, -men

145. The declensions of the following show special peculiarities:

senex, m., *old man*   **vīs**, f., *strength*

SINGULAR

NOM.	senex	vīs
GEN.	senis	(vīs)
DAT.	senī	(vī)
ACC.	senem	vim
ABL.	sene	vī

99

PLURAL

Nom.	senēs	vīrēs
Gen.	senum	vīrium
Dat.	senibus	vīribus
Acc.	senēs	vīrīs (-ēs)
Abl.	senibus	vīribus

iter, n., *march*   **Iuppiter**, m., *Jupiter, Jove*

SINGULAR

Nom.	iter	Iuppiter
Gen.	itineris	Iovis
Dat.	itinerī	Iovī
Acc.	iter	Iovem
Abl.	itinere	Iove

PLURAL

Nom.	itinera
Gen.	itinerum
Dat.	itineribus
Acc.	itinera
Abl.	itineribus

Only verb forms 28

REVIEW EXERCISE A

Locate and translate the following forms:

fuerātis	multitūdinis	dēlectātur	veniēbātis
portābuntur	fīliābus	rēgum	regēmus
proelī	quid?	eī	mē
cuius	scīverit	prohibērī	nostra
pellī	parābitis	vocābar	dūc
nautīs	frātrum	corpore	ēmī
complēvisse	cohortium	contendētis	maximō
occīsae sunt	permōvī	mī	cōpiārum
huius	hominem	grātae	illud
conciliō	dēlēte	quō	aquā
cui	sunt	nāvī	bonō
audīminī	maria	illīus	librum
duce	dedistī	gladiō	nōminī

capita	emī *[hand written]*	haec	excessūrus
posuistī	incoluerant	vidērī	armīs
carēbis	equitēs	homō	prīncipī
potes	mōrum	tempora	regī

REVIEW EXERCISE B

Write the Latin equivalents for the following: *adj follows noun [handwritten]*

long ships (*abl.*)   a pleasing gift (*nom.*)
the good citizen (*acc.*)   these foot-soldiers (*dat.*)
a captured town (*abl.*)   many enemies (*gen.*)
a good sailor (*acc.*)   large clouds (*acc.*)
a famous general (*dat.*)   our shores (*acc.*)
great states (*dat.*)   forced (**magnus**) marches (*abl.*)
first cohort (*gen.*)   great strength (*abl.*)
that old man (*gen.*)   found gold (*nom.*)

REVIEW EXERCISE

(a) Make a list of the various uses of the dative case that you have studied up to this point. Illustrate each use by (1) a sentence selected from the exercises and (2) a sentence of your own composition.

(b) Make a list of the prepositions so far encountered that govern the accusative case. Illustrate each in a simple sentence of your own composition. See appendix **24**.

(c) List the prepositions governing the ablative case. Notice that some of these **ā** (**ab**), **dē**, **cum**, are capable of more than one meaning. Make a separate list of those ablative constructions that require no preposition. Illustrate all the uses of the ablative in the two ways suggested above for the dative.

Animal hoc prōvidum, sagāx, multiplex, acūtum, memor, plēnum ratiōnis et cōnsilī quem vocāmus hominem . . .

This practical, intelligent, keen-witted animal; this complex organism with the ability to remember, reason, and plan that we call Man . . .

—CICERO, *de Legibus*, I, 22

LESSON XXI

Adjectives of the Third Declension— Genitive of the Whole

146. Adjectives of the third declension.—These are like the nouns of the third declension, except that they regularly have -ī in the ablative singular; -ium in the genitive plural; -ia in the neuter nominative and accusative plural; and -īs or -ēs in the masculine and feminine accusative plural.[1]

They may be grouped as follows:

(a) Adjectives that, in the nominative singular masculine, end in -x or -s (except those in -is) have one ending for all genders of the nominative singular. This class includes the present participle of all verbs.

(b) Those ending in -is in the nominative singular masculine have two endings in the nominative case, is (m. and f.), and -e (n.).

(c) Those ending in -er (with very few exceptions) have three endings in the nominative singular, -er (m.), -is (f.), and -e (n.). But observe that most adjectives in -er belong to the first-second declension.

---

[1] The commonest exceptions are **dīves**, *rich;* **pauper**, *poor;* **vetus**, *old;* all comparatives except **plūs**, and adjectives used as nouns, e.g., **sapiēns**, *a wise man.*

147. Paradigms.—

audāx, *bold*

	SINGULAR		PLURAL	
	M. AND F.	N.	M. AND F.	N.
Nom.	audāx		audāc-ēs	audāc-ia
Gen.	audāc-is		audāc-ium	
Dat.	audāc-ī		audāc-ibus	
Acc.	audāc-em	audāx	audāc-īs (-ēs)	audāc-ia
Abl.	audāc-ī (-e)		audāc-ibus	

capiēns, *taking*

	M. AND F.	N.	M. AND F.	N.
Nom.	capiēns		capient-ēs	capient-ia
Gen.	capient-is		capient-ium	
Dat.	capient-ī		capient-ibus	
Acc.	capient-em	capiēns	capient-īs (-ēs)	capient-ia
Abl.	capient-ī (-e)		capient-ibus	

Like **capiēns** are declined all present participles, e.g., **amāns, amantis,** *loving;* **monēns, monentis,** *warning;* **regēns, regentis,** *ruling;* and **audiēns, audientis,** *hearing,* as well as adjectives like **ingēns, ingentis,** *huge.*

Observation.—For the use of the ablative singular form **in -e** of present participles, see sec. **237,** *obs.* 5.

omnis, *all*

	SINGULAR		PLURAL	
	M. AND F.	N.	M. AND F.	N.
Nom.	omn-is	omn-e	omn-ēs	omn-ia
Gen.	omn-is		omn-ium	
Dat.	omn-ī		omn-ibus	
Acc.	omn-em	omn-e	omn-īs (-ēs)	omn-ia
Abl.	omn-ī		omn-ibus	

ācer, *sharp*

	M.	F.	N.	M. AND F.		N.
NOM.	ācer	ācr-is	ācr-e	ācr-ēs		ācr-ia
GEN.		ācr-is	ācr-is		ācr-ium	
DAT.		ācr-ī	ācr-ī		ācr-ibus	
ACC.		ācr-em	ācr-e	ācr-īs (-ēs)		ācr-ia
ABL.		ācr-ī	ācr-ī		ācr-ibus	

148. Genitive of the whole (partitive genitive).—Words denoting a part are followed by the genitive of the whole to which the part belongs. This genitive follows (among other words): **aliquid,** *something;* **quantum,** *how much;* **satis,** *enough;* **nimis,** *too much;* **parum,** *too little;* **quid,** *any;* **nihil,** *nothing;* **tantum,** *so much;* **mīlia,** *thousands;* **multum,** *much;* **plūs,** *more;* **minus,** *less;* **pars,** *part;* **plūrimum,** *plenty of.*

> **Nostrī magnam *hostium* partem interfēcērunt.**
> *Our soldiers put-to-death a great part **of the enemy**.*

> **Prīncipiō *huius annī*.**   *At the beginning **of this year**.*
> **Satis *verbōrum*.**   *Enough (of) words.*

Observation 1.—With cardinal numerals and certain other words expressing number, such as **multī, nēmō, quīdam, paucī,** and **perpaucī, ex** or **dē** with the ablative is often used in place of a genitive. Where the whole is a numeral or contains a numeral or adjective expressing number or quantity, the preposition is always used.

> ***Ūnus ē* multīs.**   ***One** of the crowd.*

> ***Perpaucī ex* omnī numerō Rōmam pervēnērunt.**
> ***Very few** of the whole number reached Rome.*

Observation 2.—Note also: **Nōs omnēs** *all (of) us, (we all).* Because all is not a part, **omnēs** is in apposition to **nōs.** See also Exercise B, sentence 8, where **quī** and **paucī** denote the same persons.

Observation 3.—Note the idioms: **summus, medius, īmus mōns;** *the top of, half way up, the foot of the mountain.*

VOCABULARY

ācer, ācris, ācre, *adj.,* piercing, sharp; fierce
ambulō, *I,* walk
audāx, *adj.,* (*gen.* **audācis**), bold, daring
condūcō, -dūcere, *etc.,* bring together, conduct
cōnstituō, -stituere, -stituī, -stitū-tum, set up; appoint, set; decide, determine
ēloquentia, -ae, *f.,* eloquence
gravis, grave, *adj.,* heavy; serious
immortālis, immortāle, *adj.,* immortal
iter facere, to make a march, to march
iūdicium, iūdicī, *n.,* trial, court; judgment

mundus, -ī, *m.,* world
numerus, -ī, *m.,* number
pars, partis (partium), *f.,* part; direction
parum, *adv. and indecl. noun,* little, too little
poena, -ae, *f.,* punishment, penalty
satis, *adv. and indecl. noun,* enough
sōl, sōlis, *m.,* sun
solvō, solvere, solvī, solūtum, loosen; pay
persolvō, *etc.,* pay in full; suffer
tollō, tollere, sustulī, sublātum, raise up, lift; take away
vīta, -ae, *f.,* life
vulnus, vulneris, *n.,* wound

EXERCISE A

1. Patrēs nostrī magna et gravia bella gessērunt.
2. Hunc ego hominem tam ācrem, tam audācem ex cīvitāte expulī.
3. Cōnsuētūdinis magna vīs est.
4. Is nāvem atque omnia perdidit in marī.
5. Tū multum labōris meā causā[2] capis.
6. In hōc expōnēmus librō dē vītā excellentium imperātōrum.
7. Parum est auctōritātis in fābulā.
8. Senectūs nōs omnibus ferē voluptātibus prīvat.
9. In Britanniā nihil est neque aurī neque argentī.
10. Agrī relīquit eī nōn magnum modum.[3]

EXERCISE B

1. Caesarī erat in animō iter in Helvētiōrum fīnīs facere.
2. Sōlem ē mundō tollere videntur eī quī amīcitiam ē vītā tollunt.
3. Gallōs victōs et in omnīs partīs fugientīs nostrī equitēs cēpērunt.

---

[2] *on my account*　　　[3] *amount*

4. Xerxēs maria ambulāvit terramque nāvigāvit.

5. Catilīnae erat satis ēloquentiae, sapientiae parum.

6. Cum barbarīs aeternum omnibus Graecīs bellum est eritque.

7. Iūstitia omnium est domina et rēgīna virtūtum.

8. Haec omnia vīdērunt equitēs quī paucī[4] aderant.

9. Hōrā cōnstitūtā Orgetorīx omnīs amīcōs, quōrum magnum numerum habēbat, ad iūdicium condūxit.

10. Cōnsiliō deōrum immortālium, quae pars cīvitātis Helvētiae legiōnēs pepulerat ea prīnceps[5] poenās persolvit.

EXERCISE C

(1) He sent food enough to the infantry. (2) All these things were completed within six hours. (3) The soldier was overcome[6] by a serious wound. (4) It is my intention[7] to hurry to Rome. (5) Catiline made-pledges-of[8] friendship with Manlius, a daring centurion. (6) The enemy hurled spears at our men as-they-were-marching[9] through the woods.

[4] *of whom a few*
[5] as adj., *first.* In translating, take this order: **ea pars quae . . . prīnceps.**
[6] Use **cōnficiō.**   [7] Cf. Exercise B, sentence 1.   [8] Use **cōnfīrmō.**
[9] Use the present participle.

Quantum enim Graecī praeceptīs valent, tantum Rōmānī, quod est maius, exemplīs.

Strong as the Greeks are in moral theory, the Romans are just as strong in the more important matter of putting those theories into practice.

—QUINTILIAN, *Institutio Oratoria*, XII, 2, 30

LESSON XXII

Fourth and Fifth Declensions—Ablative of Specification—The Verb *Eō*

149. Nouns of the fourth declension.—

	passus, m., *pace*		cornū, n., *horn*	
	SINGULAR	PLURAL	SINGULAR	PLURAL
NOM.	passus	passūs	cornū	cornua
GEN.	passūs	passuum	cornūs	cornuum
DAT.	passuī (-ū)	passibus	cornū	cornibus
ACC.	passum	passūs	cornū	cornua
ABL.	passū	passibus	cornū	cornibus

150. Gender.—Fourth declension nouns ending in -us are masculine. The commonest exceptions are **domus,** *house;* **manus,** *hand;* **acus,** *needle;* **tribus,** *tribe;* **quercus,** *oak;* **Īdūs,** *Ides,* (all feminine). Nouns ending in -ū are neuter and are rare.

151. Declension of *domus,* f., *house*.—Domus has variant forms, in certain cases, belonging to the second declension. It is declined as follows:

	SINGULAR	PLURAL
NOM.	domus	domūs
GEN.	domūs,[1] domī[2]	domōrum, domuum
DAT.	domuī, domō	domibus
ACC.	domum	domōs, domūs
ABL.	domō, domū	domibus

---

[1] The form more commonly used precedes.
[2] For **domī** meaning *at home,* see sec. **192.**

107

152. Nouns of the fifth declension.—

rēs, f., *thing*   diēs, m., *day*

	SINGULAR	PLURAL	SINGULAR	PLURAL
Nom.	rēs	rēs	diēs	diēs
Gen.	reī	rērum	diēī	diērum
Dat.	reī	rēbus	diēī	diēbus
Acc.	rem	rēs	diem	diēs
Abl.	rē	rēbus	diē	diēbus

(a) The genitive and dative singular have -eī after a consonant, -ēī after a vowel.

(b) Very few are declined in the plural.

153. Gender.—Nouns of the fifth declension are feminine, except **diēs**, which is usually masculine. But **diēs** is feminine in certain expressions, e.g., **diē cōnstitūtā**, *on the appointed day*.

154. The irregular verb *eō, I go*.—

PRINCIPAL PARTS: **eō, īre, (īvī) and iī, itum**
PRESENT: **eō, īs, it, īmus, ītis, eunt**
IMPERFECT: **ībam, ībās**, etc. FUTURE: **ībō, ībis**, etc.
IMPERATIVE: **ī** (sing.), **īte** (plur.)
PRESENT PARTICIPLE: **iēns, euntis** (gen.)

(a) Wherever -iī occurs before **s**, it is regularly contracted to -ī, e.g., **īsse**.

Conjugate **eō** in the perfect system. What is the future active participle?

155. Ablative of specification.—A noun in the ablative case is used to specify that in respect to which a statement is true.

Belgae reliquōs Gallōs *virtūte* praecēdunt.
The Belgae surpass the other Gauls in valor.

VOCABULARY

aciēs, aciēī, *f.*, line of battle
aditus, aditūs, *m.*, approach
agō, agere, ēgī, āctum, drive
brevis, breve, *adj.*, short

cōgō, cōgere, coēgī, coāctum, bring
    together, collect; force, compel
cōnātus, cōnātūs, *m.*, attempt
cōnsultum, -ī, *n.*, decree

dēiciō, dēicere, dēiēcī, dēiectum, throw down; disappoint

dēsistō, dēsistere, dēstitī, dēstitum, abandon, cease

diēs, diēī, *m.*, day

domus, -ūs, *f.*, house, home

exercitus, -ūs, *m.*, army

flūmen, flūminis, *n.*, river

ita, *adv.*, so, thus, in this way

manus, manūs, *f.*, hand

opus, operis, *n.*, work, task

pōns, pontis, (pontium), *m.*, bridge

rēs, reī, *f.*, thing; rēs pūblica, republic, commonwealth

sentiō, sentīre, sēnsī, sēnsum, be aware of, feel; think

senātus, -ūs, *m.*, senate

similis, simile, *adj.*, like, similar (to)

speciēs, speciēī, *f.*, appearance

spēs, speī, *f.*, hope

trādūcō, *etc.*, lead across, transport

vehemēns, *adj.*, (*gen.*, vehementis) violent, impetuous; drastic

EXERCISE A

1. Ībō ad portum. Tempestās abiit.
2. Rem omnem ā prīncipiō audiēs.
3. Habeō opus magnum in manibus.
4. Cūr tū abīs ab illā?
5. Mittuntur dē hīs rēbus ad Caesarem lēgātī.
6. Haec animālia speciē et colōre et figūrā taurīs sunt similia.
7. Amīcīs abeuntibus vīnum dedit.
8. Posterō diē lūce prīmā movet castra.
9. Cūrā quae iussī atque abī.
10. Sex legiōnēs brevī tempore ex Italiā coēgit.

EXERCISE B

1. Habēmus senātūs cōnsultum in tē, Catilīna, vehemēns et grave.
2. Helvētiī, eā spē dēiectī et tēlīs repulsī, hōc cōnātū dēstitērunt.
3. Interim proeliō ācrī inter aciēs contendēbātur.[3]
4. Pontem in flūmine Rhēnō sex diēbus cōnfēcit atque ita diē cōnstitūtā exercitum trādūxit.
5. Quid dē rē pūblicā sentīs?
6. Hīs rēbus permōtī, pontem quī in eō flūmine erat dēlērī iussērunt.
7. Agricolae domum[4] ex agrīs taurōs labōre cōnfectōs agēbant.

---

[3] Literally *it was fought;* impersonal use of intransitive verb used in passive. English has no parallel; translate with proeliō ācrī, *fierce fighting occurred.*

[4] See sec. **94**. **Domus** follows the rule for names of towns and cities.

8. Multōs mīlitēs Caesaris exercitūs autumnī[5] pestilentia[5] in Italiā cōnsūmpsit; multī domum discessērunt; multī sunt relictī in continentī.[5]

9. Mors misera nōn est; aditus[6] ad mortem est miser.

EXERCISE C

(1) We shall go; they went; go! (*sing.*); to have gone; going (*gen. pl.*). (2) The bridge was destroyed by the violence of the river. (3) The soldiers of the first cohort completed this short march within six days. (4) Cicero went from Rome to Capua by the Appian Way. (5) She is like Diana in appearance. (6) The storm has passed over (gone away).

SELECTIONS FOR READING

(1) Amīcus certus in rē incertā cernitur.

—Ennius, ap. Cic., *Lael.*, xvii, 64.

(2) Nōn vīribus aut vēlōcitātibus aut celeritāte corporum rēs magnae geruntur, sed cōnsiliō, auctōritāte, sententiā.

—Cicero, *dē Senect.*, vi, 17.

---

[5] Same in English.   [6] *approach, the going towards*

Rēs ardua vetustīs novitātem dare, novīs auctōritātem, obsolētīs nitōrem, obscūrīs lūcem, fastīdītīs grātiam, dubiīs fidem, omnibus vērō nātūram, et nātūrae suae omnia.

It is an uphill task to bring freshness to what is ancient, prestige to what is new, to re-illumine with its first brightness that which is now dim, to shed light on what is obscure or charm on what is hackneyed, to lend conviction to what is doubtful, in effect to restore to everything its first significance and in each instance every aspect of that significance.

—PLINY THE ELDER, Preface to the *Natural History*, 15

LESSON XXIII

Some Common and Useful Nouns— Review Exercises

animus, -i, *m.*, spirit, soul, mind, feeling

auctōritās, -tātis, *f.*, authority, influence, prestige

bellum, -ī, *n.*, war; **b. gerere,** wage war, **b. indīcere,** declare w.

cīvis, cīvis, *gen. pl.* **cīvium,** *c.*, citizen

cīvitās, -tātis, *f.*, citizenship, state

cōnsilium, -lī, *n.*, counsel, plan, judgment

cōnsul, -is, *m.*, consul

diēs, diēī, *m.*, *often f.*, day; *sec. 153*

domus, -ūs, *f.*, house, home; **domī,** at home; *sec. 151*

eques, -itis, *m.*, horseman; *pl.*, cavalry

hostis, hostis, *gen. pl.* **hostium,** *m.*, enemy

iūs, iūris, *n.*, justice, right, rights; the law

legiō, -iōnis, *f.*, legion

locus, -ī, *m.; pl.* **loca, locōrum,** *n.*, place

mīles, -itis, *m.*, soldier

modus, -ī, *m.*, manner, amount, measure

mūnītiō, -iōnis, *f.*, fortification

nātiō, -iōnis, *f.*, tribe, clan, people, race, nation

nāvis, nāvis, *gen. pl.* **nāvium,** *f.*, ship

nēmō, *acc.* **nēminem,** *m., and f.* (**nullīus, nūllī, nūllō, -ā, -ō** *supply gen. dat. abl. respectively*) no man, no one

nōmen, -inis, *n.*, name

nōx, noctis, *gen. pl.* **noctium,** *f.*, night

obses, -idis, *m.*, hostage, pledge

opīniō, -iōnis, *f.*, notion, thought, reputation

oppidum, -ī, *n.*, town

ops, opis, *f.*, help; *pl.*, riches, wealth

opus, operis, *n.*, work (*concrete as opposed to* opera, -ae, assistance, help)

parēns, parentis, *c.*, parent

pater, patris, *m.*, father

pāx, pācis, *f.*, peace

pecūnia, -ae, *f.*, money

perīculum, -lī, *n.*, danger, trial

possessiō, -iōnis, *f.*, possession

praedō, -dōnis, *m.*, robber

praetor, -ōris, *m.*, judge, praetor

prīnceps, -ipis, *m.*, leading man, prime mover; chief, first

prōvincia, -ae, *f.*, province

quaestiō, -iōnis, *f.*, investigation, inquiry, trial, court

ratiō, -iōnis, *f.*, reason, account, manner, theory

regiō, -iōnis, *f.*, quarter, region

sanguis, sanguinis, *m.*, blood

sēdēs, sēdis, *gen. pl.* sēdum, *f.*, seat, abode, home

senātor, -ōris, *m.*, senator

senātus, -ūs, *m.*, senate

sermō, -mōnis, *m.*, conversation, talk, speech

societās, -tātis, *f.*, alliance, partnership, company

tempus, -poris, *n.*, time, occasion

timor, -ōris, *m.*, fear

turris, turris (turrium), *f.*, tower

urbs, urbis (urbium), *f.*, city

vectīgal, -is (vectīgālium), *n.*, revenue, tax, toll

vīs, vīs, *pl.* vīrēs, vīrium, *f.*, force, violence; *pl.* strength, forces

Any or all of the following examples will be found useful in reviewing principles of syntax already studied. Consult the general vocabulary for unfamiliar words not explained in text or footnotes.

REVIEW EXERCISE A

1. Ego mē dō historiae.

2. Hannibal imperātor tribus* annīs omnīs nātiōnēs Hispāniae bellō superāvit; Sāguntum vī expugnavit.

3. Ex Āfricā servī exspectantur.

4. Dēpōnendae tibi sunt urbānitātēs;[1] rūsticus Rōmānus factus es.

5. Nostrae nāvēs tempestātibus dētinēbantur.

6. Nōn magnum in rē mīlitārī ūsum habēbāmus.

7. Īrācundiam quī vincit hostem superat maximum.

---

[1] *city ways*

* three; for declension see sec. **171**

8. Mihi enim līber esse nōn vidētur quī nōn aliquando nihil agit.
9. Quī nōn est hodiē aptus, crās minus erit.
10. Ab iīs quī eum maximē timuērunt maximē dīligētur.

REVIEW EXERCISE B

1. Equum mīsit, quem optimum habēbat.[2]
2. Libenter quod nēsciō discō et doceō quod didicī.
3. In hōc palātiō[3] tot sunt ostia[4] quot in annō diēs computantur.
4. Voluntās reputābātur[5] prō factō.
5. Nōn habēmus rēgem nisi Caesarem.
6. Nōn vitium nostrum sed virtūs nostra nōs afflīxit.
7. Collocābat in fronte suās et Iubae legiōnēs.
8. Ex Siciliā exercitum trānsportāverat.
9. In eā nāvī captus est P. Vestrius, eques Rōmānus.
10. Nōn nōvit virtūs calamitātibus cēdere.

REVIEW EXERCISE C

1. Omnium animī ad laetitiam excitantur.
2. Militadēs, Cimōnis fīlius, Athēniēnsis erat.
3. Perpaucae nāvēs ex omnī numerō noctis interventū[6] ad terram pervēnērunt.
4. Paucīs annīs omnēs Gallī ex Galliae fīnibus pellentur atque omnēs Germānī Rhēnum trānsībunt.
5. Sedūnī ā fīnibus Allobrogum et lacū Lemannō ad summās Alpēs pertinent.
6. At tuba terribilī sonitū "Taratantara" dīxit.
7. Ante Carthāginem dēlētam populus et senātus Rōmānus placidē modestēque inter sē rem pūblicam tractābant neque glōriae neque dominātiōnis certāmen inter cīvīs erat; metus hostium in bonīs artibus cīvitātem retinēbat.

---

[2] **optimum quem habēbat**   [3] *palace*   [4] *doors*   [5] *was taken for*
[6] *coming up, arrival*

8. In hōc prīncipe[7] nihil sordidi[8] erat, nihil turpe,[9] nihil humile; parum doctrīnae, ingenī satis, ēloquentiae nōn nihil; multum prūdentiae, probitātis[10] plūrimum[11] et cōnstantiae.

---

[7] *emperor*   [8] *mean, petty*

[9] The genitive of third declension adjectives is rarely used partitively.

[10] *honesty*   [11] as noun *plenty*

Dulcis et alta quiēs placidaeque simillima mortī.

Sweet and profound repose most like to quiet death.

—VERGIL, *Aeneid*, VI, 522

LESSON XXIV

Comparison of Adjectives—Declension of the Comparative—Ablative of Comparison

156 Regular comparison of adjectives.—Adjectives are compared in three degrees:

POSITIVE	COMPARATIVE	SUPERLATIVE
lāt-**us**	lāt-**ior**	lāt-**issimus**
clār-**us**	clār-**ior**	clār-**issimus**
cār-**us**	cār-**ior**	cār-**issimus**
long-**us**	long-**ior**	long-**issimus**
brev-**is**	brev-**ior**	brev-**issimus**
audāx (audāc-)	audāc-**ior**	audāc-**issimus**
amāns (amant-)	amant-**ior**	amant-**issimus**

The positive is the adjective itself expressing the quality; the comparative expresses a greater degree, the superlative expresses the greatest degree of the quality.

The comparative is formed by substituting **-ior**, the superlative by substituting **-issimus**, for the final **-ī** or **-is** of the genitive singular of the positive.

(**a**) Adjectives ending in **-er** in the positive form the superlative by adding **-rimus** to the nominative singular masculine of the positive.

POSITIVE	COMPARATIVE	SUPERLATIVE
pulcher (pulchr-)	pulchr-**ior**	pulcher-**rimus**
miser	miser-**ior**	miser-**rimus**
ācer (ācr-)	ācr-**ior**	ācer-**rimus**

115

(b) Six adjectives ending in **-lis** form their superlative by substituting **-limus** for the **-is** of the nominative singular masculine of the positive:

POSITIVE	COMPARATIVE	SUPERLATIVE
facil-**is**	facil-**ior**	facil-**limus**
difficil-**is**	difficil-**ior**	difficil-**limus**
simil-**is**	simil-**ior**	simil-**limus**
dissimil-**is**	dissimil-**ior**	dissimil-**limus**

The other two are **gracilis**, *slender,* and **humilis,** *lowly.* Other adjectives in **-lis** have the regular superlative, e.g., **nōbilissimus** from **nōbilis**, *renowned.*

157. Declension of the comparative.*

	SINGULAR		PLURAL	
	M. AND F.	N.	M. AND F.	N.
NOM.	melior	melius	meliōr-**ēs**	meliōr-**a**
GEN.	meliōr-**is**		meliōr-**um**	
DAT.	meliōr-**ī**		meliōr-**ibus**	
ACC.	meliōr-**em**	melius	meliōr-**ēs**	meliōr-**a**
ABL.	meliōr-**e**		meliōr-**ibus**	

Viā breviōre **equitēs praemīsī.**
*I sent the cavalry ahead **by a shorter road.***

(a) Compare this paradigm with the paradigms of **audāx**, **ācer**, etc. Wherein does it differ?

(b) **Plūs,** the comparative of **multus,** is used in the singular only as a *neuter noun.* It is declined as follows:

	SINGULAR	PLURAL	
	N.	M. AND F.	N.
NOM.	plūs	plūr-**ēs**	plūr-**a**
GEN.	plūr-**is**	plūr-**ium**	
DAT.	——	plūr-**ibus**	
ACC.	plūs	plūr-**ēs** (-**īs**)	plūr-**a**
ABL.	plūr-**e**	plūr-**ibus**	

---

* For **melior,** *better* and **plūs,** *more* see sec. **160.**

158. Meaning of the comparative and the superlative.—Comparative forms may often be translated by *rather*, *somewhat*, or *too*, followed by the simple adjective, e.g.:

Breviōrem fēcit ōrātiōnem.
He made a rather short speech.

Senectūs est nātūrā *loquācior*.
Old age is by nature somewhat garrulous.

Similarly the superlative may often be rendered by *very* plus the adjective, e.g.:

Vir fuit *praeclārissimus*.   *He was a very famous man.*

Note the idiomatic use of **quam** with the superlative.

Quam plūrimōs servāvit.
He saved as many as possible.

159. Ablative of comparison.—The comparative degree is often followed by an ablative of comparison, signifying *than*, when two persons or things are directly compared.

Aestāte *diēs noctibus* longiōrēs sunt.
In summer, the days are longer than the nights.

Dux mīlitum *vītam victōriā* cāriōrem habēbat.
The general held the life of his soldiers dearer than victory.

Instead of the ablative of comparison in the foregoing examples, **quam**, *than*, might have been used, as follows:

Aestāte *diēs* longiōrēs quam *noctēs* sunt.
Dux mīlitum *vītam* cāriōrem quam *victōriam* habēbat.

Note that when **quam** is used the things compared are in the same case.

Observation.—**Quam** may be omitted (without affecting the construction) between **plūs, amplius, minus, longius** and a word of number or measure, as follows:

Plūs duo mīlia mīlitum periērunt.
More than two thousand soldiers were killed.

VOCABULARY

altus, -a, -um, high; steep
argentum, -ī, n., silver; money
gēns, gentis (gentium), f., race; clan, tribe
gignō, gignere, genuī, genitum, produce, breed
grātia, -ae, f., favor, gratitude; esteem, influence
grātiās agere, (with dat.), to thank
grātiam habēre, (with dat.), to feel grateful (toward)

mel, mellis, n., honey
mēns, mentis (mentium), f., mind
perīculum, -ī, n., trial; risk, danger, peril
potēns, adj. (gen., **potentis**), powerful
rēs gestae, achievements; history
sagāx, adj. (gen., **sagācis**), sage, wise
sapiēns, adj. (gen., **sapientis**), wise
somnus, -ī, m., sleep

EXERCISE A

1. Patria mihi vītā meā est cārior.
2. Sceledre, Sceledre, quis in terrā tē est audācior?
3. Illa tua praeclārissima et sapientissima verba audīvī.
4. Summus mōns[1] ā maximā multitūdine Helvētiōrum tenēbātur.
5. Difficillimum erat exercitum trāns flūmina altissima et lātissima trādūcere.
6. Nihil est mortī tam simile quam somnus.
7. Quem clāriōrem in Italiā Pompeiō vīdistī, quem potentiōrem?
8. Lūce sunt clāriōra nōbīs tua cōnsilia omnia.
9. Ex eius linguā melle dulcior fluēbat ōrātiō.
10. Vōbīs omnīs[2] nostrōrum imperātōrum, omnīs[2] exterārum gentium potentissimōrumque populōrum, omnīs clārissimōrum rēgum rēs gestās nārrāvī.
11. Vōs quī multās perambulāstis[3] terrās ecquam[4] cultiōrem Italiā vīdistis?
12. Vīlius[5] argentum est aurō, virtūtibus aurum.

EXERCISE B

1. On the wings were the horsemen whom Caesar had sent with Labienus.
2. The soldiers of the first legion drove the enemy from the higher ground into the river.

---

[1] *the top of the mountain*   [2] Supply **rēs gestās.**
[3] Contracted from **perambulāvistis.**   [4] Fem. sing. acc. of **ecqui?** *any?*
[5] **vīlis, vīle,** adj., cheap

3. Of all these tribes, the Germans are the bravest.

4. Nothing was more pleasing to the citizens than the words of Cicero, a very famous orator.

5. The Gauls were more in number than the Romans, but inferior[6] in courage.

[6] Use **minor**.

Sōlem enim ē mundō tollere videntur quī amīcitiam ē vītā tollunt quā nihil ā dīs immortālibus melius habēmus, nihil grātius.

Life without friendship would be as gloomy as a world without its sun; heaven has granted us no finer, no more blessed boon.

—CICERO, *de Amicitia*, XIII, 47

LESSON XXV

Irregular Comparison of Adjectives—Formation and Comparison of Adverbs—Ablative of Degree of Difference

160. Irregular comparison.—The following adjectives are irregular in comparison (cf. Eng. *good, better, best*):

POSITIVE	COMPARATIVE	SUPERLATIVE
bonus	melior	optimus
malus	peior	pessimus
parvus	minor	minimus
magnus	maior	maximus
multus	plūs	plūrimus

(a) The following commonly used adjectives are partially irregular, and some are defective in the positive and comparative degrees:

POSITIVE	COMPARATIVE	SUPERLATIVE
exterus, *outside*	exterior, *outer*	extrēmus, extimus, *outermost*
īnferus, *under*	īnferior, *lower*	īnfimus, īmus, *lowest*
posterus, *following*	posterior, *later*	postrēmus, postumus, *last*
superus, *upper*	superior, *higher*	suprēmus, summus, *highest*
——	citerior, *hither*	citimus, *hithermost*
——	interior, *inner*	intimus, *inmost*
——	ulterior, *farther*	ultimus, *farthest, last*
——	prior, *former*	prīmus, *first*
——	propior, *nearer*	proximus, *nearest, next*
novus, new	——	novissimus, *newest, last*
fīdus, *faithful*	——	fīdissimus, *most faithful*

120

(b) Adjectives in -eus, -ius, and -uus (but not -quus) are generally compared with the adverbs **magis**, *more*, and **maximē**, *most,* e.g.:

POSITIVE	COMPARATIVE	SUPERLATIVE
idōneus, *suitable*	magis idōneus	maximē idōneus

161. Formation of adverbs.—Many adverbs are formed from adjectives:

(a) In the first-second declension, by substituting -ē for -a of the nominative singular feminine:

longē lātēque,	*far and wide*
miserē,	*wretchedly*
pulchrē,	*beautifully*

(b) From most third declension adjectives, by substituting -ter for -s of the nominative singular feminine:

sapienter,	*wisely*
breviter,	*briefly*
ācriter,	*fiercely*
audācter,	*boldly* (from **audāx** = audāc-s)

(c) *Irregulars.*—Often the adverb is the accusative or ablative singular of the neuter adjective, e.g., **multum, multō,** *much,* from **multus; facile,** *easily,* from **facilis.** For other irregular terminations, see sec. **164** and the vocabularies.

162. Comparison of adverbs.—

(a) The comparative is the accusative singular of the neuter of the corresponding comparative adjective, e.g., **longius.**

(b) The superlative is formed by substituting -ē for the final -us of the superlative of the adjective, e.g., **longissimē.**

POSITIVE	COMPARATIVE	SUPERLATIVE
longē	longius	longissimē
miserē	miserius	miserrimē
pulchrē	pulchrius	pulcherrimē
sapienter	sapientius	sapientissimē
breviter	brevius	brevissimē
ācriter	ācrius	ācerrimē
audācter	audācius	audācissimē
facile	facilius	facillimē

163. Irregular comparison (160) has corresponding forms in adverbs:

POSITIVE	COMPARATIVE	SUPERLATIVE
bene, *well*	melius	optimē
male, *badly, ill*	peius	pessimē
parum, *not enough*	minus	minimē
magnopere, *greatly*	magis	maximē
multum, *much*	plūs	plūrimum

164. Note the following irregularly formed adverbs:

POSITIVE	COMPARATIVE	SUPERLATIVE
diū, *long* (in time)	diūtius	diūtissimē
saepe, *often*	saepius	saepissimē
——	prius	prīmum
prope, *near, nearly, almost*	propius	proximē

165. The ablative of degree of difference is used with comparatives and sometimes with superlatives and words implying comparison.

Pater *pede* altior est quam fīlius.
*The father is **a foot** taller than his son.*

Hieme noctēs *paucīs hōrīs* longiōrēs sunt quam diēs.
*In winter the nights are longer than the days **by a few hours**.*

VOCABULARY

celeriter, *adv.,* swiftly, rapidly
coniciō, -icere, -iēcī, -iectum, hurl, throw, cast; put
cornū, cornūs, *n.,* horn; wing (*of an army*)
crūdēliter, *adv.,* cruelly
dēfendō, dēfendere, dēfendī, dēfēnsum, ward off, repel, defend, protect
deinde, *adv.,* thereupon, then, next
dexter, dextra, dextrum, right

equitātus, equitātūs, *m.,* cavalry
fortis, forte, *adj.,* powerful, brave, manly
fuga, -ae, *f.,* flight
impetus, impetūs, *m.,* attack, charge
līberē, *adv.,* freely
maiōrēs, maiōrum, *m. pl.,* ancestors
manus, manūs, *f.,* hand
prīmum, *adv.,* first, in the first place
prōiciō, -icere, *etc.,* throw forward

quam, (1) *conj.*, than
 (2) *adv. w. superl.*, as . . .
 as possible
scūtum, -ī, *n.*, shield
servō, *I*, save, preserve, maintain,
 guard
sinister, sinistra, sinistrum, left

superbē, *adv.*, proudly, arrogantly
valeō, valēre, valuī, valitūrus, be
 strong, be in good health, have
 influence
plūrimum valēre, to be very powerful
vehementer, *adv.*, strongly

EXERCISE A

1. Dīcit līberius atque audācius.
2. Sōl multīs partibus maior est quam lūna.
3. Saepissimē haec Catōnis verba audīvimus: dēlenda est Carthāgō.
4. Mōs maiōrum dīligentius nōbīs est servandus.
5. Nerviī equitātū plūrimum valent.
6. Magis tē quam oculōs meōs amō.
7. Erat multō īnferior numerō nāvium Brūtus.
8. Quam[1] maximīs itineribus in Hispāniam citeriōrem contendit.
9. Dux parvum fīlium dextrā manū ex urbe quam[1] celerrimē dūcēbat.
10. Vehementius tuā miseriā quam meā commoveor.

EXERCISE B

1. Quid melius est quam virtūs?
2. Quid est in homine sagācī ac bonā mente melius?
3. Nōbīs ea loca quae superiōra erant castrīs magis idōnea vīsa sunt.
4. Mīlitēs pīlīs ē locō superiōre missīs hostium aciem fugāvērunt.
5. Haec praecepta vōbīs summā dīligentiā tenenda sunt.
6. Hīs perīculīs coāctī itinere dēstitērunt et proximā viā in Italiam iērunt.
7. Magnās Iovī Optimō Maximō grātiās ob victōriam ēgērunt quam dē exterīs gentibus Scīpiō reportāvit.
8. Ex agricolīs et virī fortissimī et mīlitēs strēnuissimī[2] gignuntur.
9. Oppidum Avāricum erat maximum mūnītissimumque in fīnibus Biturīgum.

---

[1] See sec. **158**. [2] An exception to **160b**.

EXERCISE C

(1) Our ancestors, very brave men, very often fought with the Carthaginians. (2) Scipio defended us rather bravely with his shield. (3) The pike of the Roman soldier was a few feet longer than (his) sword. (4) Ariovistus, King of the Germans, ruled too arrogantly and too cruelly in Gaul. (5) They gave thanks to Jove, best and greatest, for[3] the victory which Caesar had won[4] over the Gauls. (6) He hurried home as quickly as possible.

---

[3] Use **ob** + acc.   [4] Use **reportō dē** + abl.

Est amāns suī virtūs.

Virtue is fond of itself.

—CICERO, *dē Amīcitiā, 98*

LESSON XXVI

Reflexive Pronouns

166. Reflexive pronouns.—In the first and second persons, these are supplied by the oblique cases of the personal pronouns **ego** and **tū**, to which the appropriate case of **ipse** (**201, 202**) is sometimes added.

Tē (ipsum) amās.	*You love **yourself**.*
Eum ad *mē* vocāvī.	*I called him to **me** (**myself**).*

The reflexive pronoun of the third person is declined as follows:

GEN.	suī, *of himself, herself, itself, themselves*
DAT.	sibi
ACC.	sē, sēsē
ABL.	sē, sēsē

By its very nature, no reflexive pronoun can have a nominative. The possessive pronominal adjective corresponding to **sē** is **suus, -a, -um**, meaning *his, her, its, their (own)*.

167. Use of *sē* and *suus*.—These are used as reflexives of the third person only. Sē can be used in any gender or number.

168. *Sē* and *suus* in simple sentences.—The person whom **sē** and **suus** denote is the same as the grammatical subject of the sentence in which they occur, i.e., the same as the nominative to the verb. This is called the *direct reflexive*.

Brūtus *sē* *suō* gladiō interfēcit.
*Brutus killed **himself** with **his own** sword.*

Caesar eum ad *sē* vocāvit.
*Caesar called him to **himself** (i.e., Caesar summoned him into **his** presence).*

Notice that **eum** refers to someone else (not Caesar), whereas **sē**, the reflexive, refers to the subject, Caesar.

Observation 1.—Where no ambiguity is likely to arise, **suus** is usually omitted.

> **Pater fīlī mortem dolēbat.**
> *The father mourned his son's death.*

Observation 2.—In the sentence **Dux mīlitēsque *eius* fūgērunt**, *The general and **his** soldiers fled*, **eius** and not **suus** is used because **dux mīlitēsque eius** is the subject; **eius** does not refer back to the subject, but is part of it. But in the sentence **Dux mīlitēs *suōs* dīmīsit**, *The general disbanded **his** soldiers*, **suus** is used because it does refer back to the subject **dux** and is not part of it, but of the object. If **eius** were used in the place of **suōs** in this sentence, it would mean: *The general disbanded his (someone else's) soldiers*. But **suōs** would ordinarily be omitted (see Obs. 1).

169. Use of *sē* and *suus* in complex sentences.—Sē and **suus** may *not* be used in a principal clause referring to the subject of a subordinate clause. Therefore we must say:

> **Sī hoc faciet, amīcī *eius* nōn probābunt.**
> *If **he** intends to do this, **his** friends will not approve.*

(**a**) In adjectival clauses **sē** generally refers to the subject of the verb in its own clause, i.e., it is used (as in all the above instances) as a *direct* reflexive:

> **Mīlitēs quī *sē suaque* omnia hostibus trādiderant laudāre nōluit.**
> *He would not praise the soldiers who had surrendered **themselves** and all **their belongings** to the enemy.*

(**b**) Although the reflexive pronoun may always be used to refer to the subject of its own clause, yet in most subordinate clauses which express the words or thoughts of the subject of the *principal* clause, **sē** and **suus** generally refer to the subject of the *principal* clause, where that subject is in the third person; they do *not* refer to the subject of their *own* clause. This is called the *indirect* reflexive; its use will be considered later as it arises (cf. **228**).

VOCABULARY

dēportō, *I*, carry away

expetō, -petere, -petīvī or -petiī, -petītum, seek out

prō-iciō, -icere, -iēcī, -iectum, hurl; sē prōicere, jump

restituō, -stituere, -stituī, -stitū-tum, restore

EXERCISE A

1. Tē tuaque omnia dēdis.
2. Sua dēportābant omnia sēque in proximum oppidum recipiē-bant.
3. Rēx cōpiās quās sibi comparāverat contrā hostēs dūxit.
4. Nōbīscum tribus diēbus redībis.   *Reflex (for himself)*
5. Horātius poēta vīllam sibī in Āpūliā aedificāvit.
6. Sē ad pedēs Caesaris multīs cum lacrimīs prōiēcērunt.
7. Centuriō, vir fortissimus, sē ex nāvī* in mare prōiēcit.
8. Hannō praefectūram urbis fīliō suō dedit.
9. Amīcitia ex sē† et propter sē est expetenda.
10. Huic hominī Caesar prō eius virtūte atque in sē benevolentiā maiōrum locum restituerat.
11. Ipse nārrāvit omnia quae sibi acciderant.[1]

EXERCISE B

(1) They have built themselves a very large country house in Gaul.   (2) He had wounded himself with the sword he was carrying. (3) We do not blame ourselves for[2] the war which is being waged against the Germans.   (4) The pirate is defending himself rather bravely with his shield.   (5) Wisdom should be sought for its own sake.

[1] *happen*   [2] **ob** + acc.
* sometimes used for **nāve**
† *of itself*, i.e., *apart from other considerations*

Quid vērō histōriae dē nōbīs ad annōs DC[1] praedicāverint?

I wonder what will be the verdict of history on me a thousand years from now.

—CICERO, *ad Atticum*, II, 5

LESSON XXVII

Numerals—Accusative of Extent

170. Numerals.—

		CARDINALS	ORDINALS
1	I	ūnus, -a, um	prīmus, -a, -um
2	II	duo, duae, duo	secundus (alter)
3	III	trēs, tria	tertius
4	IIII	quattuor	quārtus
5	V	quīnque	quīntus
6	VI	sex	sextus
7	VII	septem	septimus
8	VIII	octō	octāvus
9	VIIII	novem	nōnus
10	X	decem	decimus
11	XI	ūndecim	ūndecimus
12	XII	duodecim	duodecimus
13	XIII	tredecim	tertius decimus
14	XIIII	quattuordecim	quārtus decimus
15	XV	quīndecim	quīntus decimus
16	XVI	sēdecim	sextus decimus
17	XVII	septendecim	septimus decimus
18	XVIII	duodēvīgintī	duodēvīcēsimus
19	XVIIII	ūndēvīgintī	ūndēvīcēsimus
20	XX	vīgintī	vīcēsimus
21	XXI	vīgintī ūnus	vīcēsimus prīmus
		ūnus et vīgintī	ūnus et vīcēsimus

---

[1] Although literally 600, **sescentī** is often used idiomatically (as here) to denote an indefinitely large number.

		CARDINALS	ORDINALS
22	XXII	vīgintī duo duo et vīgintī[2]	vīcēsimus secundus alter et vīcēsimus
30	XXX	trīgintā	trīcēsimus
40	XXXX	quadrāgintā	quadrāgēsimus
50	L	quīnquāgintā	quīnquāgēsimus
60	LX	sexāgintā	sexāgēsimus
70	LXX	septuāgintā	septuāgēsimus
80	LXXX	octōgintā	octōgēsimus
90	LXXXX	nōnāgintā	nōnāgēsimus
100	C	centum	centēsimus
200	CC	ducentī, -ae, -a	ducentēsimus
300	CCC	trecentī	trecentēsimus
400	CCCC	quadringentī	quadringentēsimus
500	D	quīngentī	quīngentēsimus
600	DC	sescentī	sescentēsimus
700	DCC	septingentī	septingentēsimus
800	DCCC	octingentī	octingentēsimus
900	DCCCC	nōngentī	nōngentēsimus
1000	M	mīlle	mīllēsimus
2000	MM	duo mīlia	bis mīllēsimus

Whenever four identical symbols occur together, a variant (e.g., IV) is often used, the smaller number preceding and being subtracted from the larger. Cf. also XIX, XL, MCM, etc.

171. Declension of numerals.—Cardinals are indeclinable, except **ūnus, duo, trēs,** the hundreds above **centum,** and the plural **mīlia,** which are declined as follows:

ūnus, -a, -um, like **tōtus** (see sec. **173**)

	M.	F.	N.	M. AND F.	N.
NOM.	duo	duae	duo	trēs	tria
GEN.	duōrum	duārum	duōrum	trium	trium
DAT.	duōbus	duābus	duōbus	tribus	tribus
ACC.	duōs (-o)	duās	duo	trēs (trīs)	tria
ABL.	duōbus	duābus	duōbus	tribus	tribus

Like **duo** is declined **ambō, ambae, ambō,** *both,* except that it retains its original long **-ō.**

---

[2] Compare English *"four and twenty blackbirds."*

The hundreds, above **centum**, are declined like the plural of **bonus**. All ordinals are declined like **bonus**.

Mīlle, in the singular, is an indeclinable adjective, e.g., **mīlle passūs**, *a thousand paces* (i.e., *one mile*). In the plural, it is a noun, followed by a genitive of the whole, e.g., **duo mīlia** *passuum*, *two thousand(s)* (*of*) *paces* (i.e., *two miles*). It is declined as follows:

	SINGULAR	PLURAL
Nom.	mīlle	mīlia
Gen.	mīlle	mīlium
Dat.	mīlle	mīlibus
Acc.	mīlle	mīlia
Abl.	mīlle	mīlibus

172. Accusative of extent.—Extent of time or of space is expressed by the accusative case.

> **Rōmulus septem et trīgintā rēgnāvit** *annōs*.
> *Romulus reigned (for) thirty-seven* **years**.

> **Flūmen** *ducentōs pedēs* **lātum est.**
> *The river is* **two hundred feet** *wide.*

VOCABULARY

aetās, -tātis, *f.*, age, period of life
campus, -ī, *m.*, plain, field, prairie
circiter, *adv.*, about, approximately
genus, generis, *n.*, origin; class, kind

mēnsis, mēnsis (**mēnsium**), *m.*, month
portus, -ūs, *m.*, harbor
vix, *adv.*, with difficulty; barely, scarcely

EXERCISE A

1. Trēs iam mēnsēs abest.
2. Ambō accūsandī sunt.
3. Germānōrum mīlia hominum quattuor et vīgintī ad Ariovistum vēnērunt.
4. Ab hīs castrīs oppidum Rēmōrum nōmine Bibrax aberat mīlia passuum octō.
5. Castra nōn amplius quīnque mīlia passuum aberant.
6. Ducentī nōnāgintā duo equitēs ad Marcellum contendērunt.

7. Hunc librum annō quārtō et nōnāgēsimō aetātis suae scrīpsit Īsocrates, cuius ā morte hic tertius et trīcēsimus est annus.

8. Ipse ab hostium castrīs nōn longius mīlle et quīngentīs passibus aberat.

9. Cohortēs duās in Nantuātibus collocāvit; ipse cum octō reliquīs eius legiōnis cohortibus in vīcō quī appellābātur Octodūrus hiemābat.

10. In eō proeliō ex[3] equitibus nostrīs interficiuntur quattuor et septuāgintā, in hīs vir fortissimus Pīsō Aquitānus.

11. Quod iter Helvētiī diēbus vīgintī vix cōnfēcerant, id Caesar ūnō diē fēcit.[4]

12. Circiter CCXX nāvēs eōrum omnī genere armōrum parātissimae ex portū nāvigāvērunt.

13. Duo-dē-quadrāgintā annōs tyrannus Syrācūsānōrum fuit Dionȳsius.

14. Ōrātiōnum Cicerōnis duodecim quae cōnsulārēs nōminantur[5] tertiam dē Othōne habuit, quārtam prō Rabīriō, quīntam dē prōscrīptōrum fīliīs,[6] sextam eō diē quō prōvinciam dēposuit,[7] septimam cum[8] Catilīnam ēmīsit, octāvam habuit ad[9] populum, nōnam in contiōne,[10] decimam in senātū Nōnīs Decembribus.[11]

EXERCISE B

(1) The plains extended sixteen miles. (2) Caesar stationed the fourth legion on-this-side-of[12] the river. (3) Twenty-two of the soldiers were wounded. (4) For fifteen days they marched through the province without-committing-any-outrage.[13] (5) I am now living[14] my eighty-fourth year. (6) The whole state (of) Helvetia is divided into four parts. (7) Tell me, Atticus, about the twelve

---

[3] With cardinal numerals, **dē** or **ex** and the ablative are regularly used in place of the genitive of the whole.

[4] Take in this order: **C. ūnō diē fēcit id iter quod H.**, etc.

[5] *Are named consular* because all delivered (**habitae**) in 63 B.C., the year of Cicero's consulship.

[6] The sons of the proscribed were children of the victims of the political assassinations ordered by the dictator Sulla, years before.

[7] Cicero declined the governorship of the province of Macedonia, which he would normally have accepted after his year as consul.

[8] **Cum** is here a conjunction meaning *when*.

[9] *before*   [10] *public meeting*

[11] *The Nones of D.* represent our date *Dec. 5.*

[12] **citrā** + acc.   [13] *without injury*   [14] **agō**

speeches of Cicero which he delivered (while) consul. (8) Did he
deliver the ninth in a public meeting on that day on which the Gallic
tribe which is called the Allobroges gave evidence?[15]

---

[15] indicō, *I*

Fortūna multīs dat nimis, satis nūllī.

Fortune gives many too much, but enough to none.

—MARTIAL, XII, 67

LESSON XXVIII

Adjectives with Genitive in *-īus*

173. The following adjectives have the genitive in **-īus** and dative in **-ī**. Otherwise, with the exception of **alius**, which has neuter nominative and accusative singular **aliud**, they are regulars of the first-second declension:

ūnus, -a, -um,	*one*	**alter, altera, alterum,**	*the other*
tōtus, -a, -um	*whole*	**uter, utra, utrum,**	*which (of two)?*
sōlus, -a, -um	*alone*	**neuter, -tra, -trum,**	*neither*
ūllus, -a, -um,	*any*	**uterque, utraque, utrumque,**	
nūllus, -a, -um,	*no*		*each (of two), both*
alius, alia, aliud,	*another*		

	SINGULAR			SINGULAR		
	M.	F.	N.	M.	F.	N.
NOM.	tōtus	tōta	tōtum	alius	alia	aliud
GEN.	tōtīus	tōtīus	tōtīus		*See note (b)*	
DAT.	tōtī	tōtī	tōtī	aliī	aliī	aliī
ACC.	tōtum	tōtam	tōtum	alium	aliam	aliud
ABL.	tōtō	tōtā	tōtō	aliō	aliā	aliō

(a) The plural is regular, like **bonus**.

(b) **Alterīus** is commonly used in place of the rare **alīus** as the genitive of **alius**; sometimes the adj. **aliēnus** is used:

> **Suum perīculum in *aliēnā* videt virtūte cōnstāre.**
> *He perceives his own safety (danger) to depend on the courage of another.*

133

(c) **Uterque** (like **nēmō**) is used with the genitive of pronouns, but in apposition with substantives:

> *Vestrum* uterque
> Fīlius *uterque*

174. Some idiomatic uses of adjectives in 173:

> **nōnnūllī, nōnnūllōrum,** etc., *some*
>
> *Aliī* **Caesarem,** *aliī* **Pompeium laudant.**
> *Some praise Caesar,* **others** *Pompey.*
>
> **Aliī alia sentiunt.**
> *Some think one thing, some another.*
>
> **Alia atque anteā sentit.**
> *He feels different from before.* (*His feelings have changed.*)
>
> **uterque parēns**
> *each parent* (i.e., *both father and mother*)
>
> **Uter utrō audācior est?**
> *Which* (*man*) *is bolder than which?*
> Better: *Which of the two is bolder?*

EXERCISE A

1. Dē vīgintī restābam sōlus.
2. Is sōlus[1] ad summum montem pervēnit.
3. Ibi Orgetorīgis fīlia atque ūnus ē fīliīs captus[2] est.
4. Neuter quod sibi sed quod alterī contigerat dolēbat.
5. Duae sunt sorōrēs quārum alteram ille amat, ego alteram.
6. Aliī in aliās partēs fūgērunt.
7. Ex ūnō oppidō sōlō haec omnis praeda exportāta est.
8. Nōnnūllī eōrum annōs vīgintī in disciplīnā permanent.
9. Utra tibi hārum puellārum pulchrior esse vidētur?
10. Corinthus, tōtīus Graeciae glōria, dēlēta est.
11. Multī illam magnō ē Latiō tōtāque petēbant Ausoniā.[3]
12. Aliī bellō, agrīcultūrā aliī dēlectantur.
13. Hōc proeliō bellum Venetōrum tōtīusque ōrae maritimae cōnfectum est.

---

[1] *He was the only one who,* etc.   [2] Verb agrees with the nearer subject.
[3] From Vergil's *Aeneid* VII, 54. **Ausonia** is an old name for **Italia.**

14. Eōdem diē uterque imperātor ex castrīs ā flūmine exercitum suum ēdūcit, Pompēius clam et noctū, Caesar palam atque interdiū.

15. Venetī[4] eōrum locōrum ubi bellum gestūrī erant vada, portūs, īnsulās nōvērunt; ac longē alia est nāvigātiō[5] in conclūsō marī atque[6] in vāstissimō atque apertissimō Ōceanō.

16. Hannibal trēs exercitūs maximōs comparāvit. Ex hīs ūnum in Āfricam mīsit, alterum cum frātre Hasdrubale in Hispāniā relīquit, tertium in Italiam sēcum dūxit.

EXERCISE B

(1) Each of the two commanders led his legions back into camp. (2) Caesar sent Curio into Sicily with three legions and all the cavalry. (3) People's feelings differ (use sentio + alius). (4) Neither grieves (for) what is happening[7] to himself but (for what) is happening to the other. (5) One[8] of the brothers was consul, the other[8] praetor. (6) He said one thing (but) did another.

[4] **Venetī,** a Gallic tribe
[5] *navigation*
[6] For alia . . . atque see sec. **174.**
[7] **contingit**
[8] **alter** . . . **alter**

Prospera omnēs sibi vindicant; adversa ūnī imputantur.

All are eager to lay claim to successes; disasters are laid at one man's door.

—TACITUS, *Agricola*, 27

LESSON XXIX

Ablative of Cause—Ablative and Genitive of Description—*Ferō* and Its Compounds

175. Ablative of cause.—The ablative with or without one of the prepositions **ā** (**ab**), **dē**, and **ē** (**ex**) is found denoting cause and is to be translated by *on account of* or *because of*.

Dumnorīx *grātiā* plūrimum poterat.
*Dumnorix was very powerful **because of his popularity**.*

Iam vīrēs *itinere* dēficiēbant.
*Now their strength began to fail **on account of the march**.*

Dēlīrat *timōre*.
*He is mad **with fear** (**from** or **because of fear**).*

Note the following idiomatic expressions:

pecūniae causā,	*for the sake of money*
multīs dē causīs,	*for many reasons*

sīve *cāsū* sīve *cōnsiliō*
*whether **by accident** or **design***

176. Genitive and ablative of description or quality.—A noun in the genitive case *modified by an adjective* may be used to describe a person or thing. The ablative is also used in this way with no difference in meaning, and is much more common than the genitive. Where, however, the description is a *measurement*, the genitive is always used.

136

mulier *eximiā pulchritūdine,*	*a woman of rare beauty*
eius modī cōnsilium,	*a plan of this sort*
vir *summā scientiā,*	*a man of great learning*
diērum vīgintī supplicātiō,	*a twenty-day thanksgiving*
mūrus *sēdecim pedum,*	*a sixteen-foot wall*
spatium *decem annōrum,*	*a ten-year interval*
mīlle colōribus arcus,	*the many-colored rainbow*

177. *Ferō* and some of its compounds.—

PRINCIPAL PARTS: **ferō, ferre, tulī, lātum,** *bear*

INDICATIVE

	ACTIVE		PASSIVE	
	SINGULAR	PLURAL	SINGULAR	PLURAL
PRES.	ferō	ferimus	feror	ferimur
	fers	fertis	ferris	feriminī
	fert	ferunt	fertur	feruntur
IMPERF.	ferēbam		ferēbar	
FUT.	feram, ferēs, *etc.*		ferar, ferēris (-re), *etc.*	

(a) In the present tense the personal endings are added directly to the verb stem **fer-** except before **m** and **n**. Future and imperfect are regular.

(b) Write out the three perfect tenses of **ferō** active and passive.

IMPERATIVE

PRES.	fer[1]	ferte	ferre	feriminī

INFINITIVES

PRES.	ferre	ferrī
FUT.	lātūrus esse	(lātum īrī)
PERF.	tulisse	lātus esse

PARTICIPLES

PRES.	ferēns		——
FUT.	lātūrus	(GERUNDIVE)	ferendus
PERF.	——		lātus

---

[1] Cf. **dīcō, dūcō, faciō,** which give **dīc, dūc, fac** as imperatives.

178. Some common compounds of *ferō* similarly conjugated:

afferō, afferre, attulī, allātum, *bring to, present*
auferō, auferre, abstulī, ablātum, *carry off*
cōnferō, cōnferre, contulī, collātum, *bring together, collect; compare*
dēferō, dēferre, dētulī, dēlātum, *bring or carry down; hand over*
differō, differre, distulī, dīlātum, *differ; postpone*
efferō, efferre, extulī, ēlātum, *carry away; elate*
īnferō, īnferre, intulī, illātum, *bear into; import; inflict*
offerō, offerre, obtulī, oblātum, *bring before; offer, give*
praeferō, praeferre, praetulī, praelātum, *place before, esteem above; prefer to*
prōferō, prōferre, prōtulī, prōlātum, *bring forth or out, produce*
sufferō, sufferre, sustulī,[2] sublātum,[2] *undergo, bear, endure*
trānsferō, trānsferre, trānstulī, trānslātum, *carry or bring over*

VOCABULARY

dēfessus, -a, -um, tired out
dēmulceō, dēmulcēre, dēmulsī, dēmulctum, stroke
dissentiō, dissentīre, dissēnsī, dissēnsum, disagree
diūturnitās, diūturnitātis, *f.*, long duration
exanimātus, -a, -um, rendered breathless; terrified
ferō, ferre, tulī, lātum, bear; bring
folium, folī, *n.*, leaf
heri, *adv.*, yesterday
improbitās, improbitātis, *f.*, wickedness

incrēdibilis, incrēdibile, unbelievable
īnfirmus, -a, -um, weak, feeble
interclūdō, interclūdere, interclūsī, interclūsum, shut or cut off
lēnitās, lēnitātis, *f.*, smoothness, gentleness
lingua, linguae, *f.*, tongue
nix, nivis (nivium), *f.*, snow
sīve, *conj.* (sī, if + ve, or) or if, or
taceō, tacēre, tacuī, tacitum, be silent
valētūdō, valētūdinis, *f.*, condition of health
vitium, vitī, *n.*, vice

EXERCISE A

1. Multās iniūriās servī ferunt. Hiems fert nivēs.
2. Diūturnitāte pugnae hostēs dēfessī erant.
3. Erat Catilīna vitiīs atque improbitāte omnibus nōtus.
4. Haec silva iter[3] novem diērum patet.

[2] Sustulī and sublātum also supply the perfect and participle of the verb tollō, to lift, take away.   [3] See sec. **172.**

2. they were exhausted by the fight.
3. Cataline was known to everyone because of his weaknesses.

5. Leō hominis exanimātī metū manūs linguā dēmulcēbat.

6. Hī omnēs linguā, īnstitūtīs, lēgibus inter[4] sē differunt.

7. Vīs ventī folia arboris omnia abstulit.

8. Id flūmen erat incrēdibilī lēnitāte.

9. Gallī nōndum bonō animō in populum Rōmānum esse vidē-bantur.

10. Nūntius hanc epistulam mihi heri attulit.

11. Tulit hoc vulnus graviter Cicerō.

12. Erat illō tempore īnfirmā valētūdine Cluentius.

13. Agricolae bellō perterritī sua omnia ex agrīs in oppida cōn-ferunt.

14. Ferte citī[5] ferrum, date tēla, ascendite mūrōs. Hostis adest.

15. Hic vir fortissimus frātrī interclūsō ab hostibus auxilium tulit.

16. Taceō nōn timōre sed dolōre.

17. P. Africānus et Tiberius Gracchus dissēnsērunt dē rē pūblicā et eā sīve quā aliā rē nōn amīcī fuērunt.

EXERCISE B

(1) Britain is an island of no great size. (2) Exhausted because of wounds, the soldier could not bring back the message. (3) Deer with huge horns wander through the forests. (4) My father and his father disagreed about politics and for that reason were not friendly. (5) The garden is surrounded by a ten-foot wall.

[4] *"among themselves,"* i.e., from each other. This idiom supplies the lack of the reciprocal pronoun in Latin.

[5] **Citus** means *swift*, but adjectives modifying pronominal or unexpressed subjects are best translated by adverbs.

Ubi īra dominātur ratiō nihil valet.

Where passion rules reason is of no avail.

Lesson XXX

Deponent and Semi-Deponent Verbs

179. Deponent verbs.—Certain verbs, having lost their active forms, are conjugated only in the passive. But these passive forms have laid aside (**dē-pōnō**) their passive meanings and have assumed active meanings. More than half of them are of the first conjugation.

	INDIC. PRES.	INFIN.	PERF. INDIC.
Conjugation:	I—**cōnor** (*try*),	**cōnārī,**	**cōnātus sum**
	II—**vereor** (*fear*),	**verērī,**	**veritus sum**
	III—**sequor** (*follow*),	**sequī,**	**secūtus sum**
	—**patior** (*suffer*),	**patī,**	**passus sum**
	IV—**experior** (*try*),	**experīrī,**	**expertus sum**

(**a**) The gerundive (future passive participle) retains its passive meaning.

(**b**) The following active forms are retained: present participle, future participle, future infinitive, supine (see **241**), and gerund (see **238**).

180. Semi-deponent verbs.—A few verbs, regular in the present system, lack the active forms of the perfect system (perfect, pluperfect, and future perfect) and therefore use the passive with active meaning. These verbs are called semi-deponent.

> **fīdō**[1] (*trust*), **fīdere, fīsus sum**
> **audeō** (*dare*), **audēre, ausus sum**
> **gaudeō** (*rejoice*), **gaudēre, gāvīsus sum**
> **soleō** (*be wont, be accustomed*), **solēre, solitus sum**

181. The following five deponent verbs govern the *ablative* case in place of the accusative of the direct object:

---

[1] with its compounds **cōnfīdō, diffīdō**

potior (*get possession of*),   fruor (*enjoy*), fruī, fructus sum
   potīri, potītus sum   fungor (*perform*), fungī, functus sum
ūtor (*use*), ūtī, ūsus sum   vēscor (*feed on*), ——, ——

Scythae *corporibus* hominum *vēscī* dīcuntur.
*The Scyths are said **to feed on** human flesh.*

Ariovistus *linguā Gallicā multā ūtēbātur*.
*Ariovistus **spoke** the **language of the Gauls** fluently.*

VOCABULARY

apud, *prep. w. acc.*, among, in the works of
audeō, audēre, ausus sum, dare
cōnor, *I*, try
ēgredior, ēgredī, ēgressus sum, go out
experior, experīrī, expertus sum, try
fleō, flēre, flēvī, flētum, weep, lament
Hippomenēs, Hippomenis, *m.*, Hippomenes
Homērus, -ī, *m.*, Homer
hortor, *I*, urge, encourage
ignis, ignis (ignium), *m.*, fire

loquor, loquī, locūtus sum, speak, talk
mentior, *IV*, lie, tell lies
morior, morī, mortuus sum, die
moror, *I*, delay, linger
proficīscor, proficīscī, profectus sum, start, depart
sequor, sequī, secūtus sum, follow
soleō, solēre, solitus sum, be wont, be accustomed (to)
suppliciter, *adv.*, as a suppliant, beseechingly
tamquam, *adv.*, as if, like
ūtor, ūtī, ūsus sum, use; enjoy
valētūdō, -dinis, *f.*, state of health
vereor, verērī, veritus sum, fear

EXERCISE A

1. Cōnābar; patiēmur; secūtī erant; ūtuntur; verēbitur.
2. Sequentēs; audēs; nāscitur; ausus es; loquēminī.
3. Quis hīc loquitur?   Turpe est mentīrī.
4. Cūr es ausus mentīrī mihi?
5. Rem tenē; verba sequentur.
6. Ēgredere ex urbe; patent portae; proficīscere.
7. Solēbam haec ego puer apud Homērum legere.
8. Difficile est, sed experiar.
9. Multae rēs ad hoc cōnsilium Gallōs hortābantur.
10. Semper bonā valētūdine sum ūsus.

EXERCISE B

1. Hippomenē,[2] properā! Nunc vīribus ūtere tōtīs.

2. Sē ad pedēs Caesaris prōiēcērunt suppliciterque locūtī flentēs pācem petīvērunt.

3. Eā quae secūta est hieme Germānī magnā multitūdine hominum flūmen Rhēnum trānsiērunt.

4. Prīmā nocte ē castrīs Helvētiōrum ēgressī ad Rhēnum fīnēsque Germānōrum contendērunt.

5. In hōc sumus sapientēs quod Nātūram, optimam[3] ducem, tamquam deum sequimur.

6. Nōn aquā, nōn ignī[4] in locīs plūribus[5] ūtimur quam amīcitiā.

EXERCISE C

(1) Why are you delaying in Italy all the winter? Tomorrow we shall set out for Greece. (2) Born in the province of Sicily, he did not dare lie to me. (3) The ships, after delaying in harbor for three days, sailed to Sardinia. (4) Our men soon got possession of the enemy's camp. (5) He was a brave officer (**dux**), but he did not enjoy[6] good health. (6) We usually[7] rose[8] before (it was) light.

---

[2] *O Hippomenes* (who raced with Atalanta for his life and her love)
[3] **Dux** is here feminine because it is in apposition with the feminine **Nātūrām** (sec. **47**).   [4] Abl. of **ignis**; see sec. **142**.   [5] *on more occasions*   [6] **ūtor**
[7] Use **soleō**.   [8] **surgō**

Tendēbantque manūs rīpae ulteriōris amōre.

And they stretched out their hands in passionate yearning for the farther shore.

—VERGIL, *Aeneid*, VI, 314

LESSON XXXI

Objective Genitive

182. The objective genitive.—This common use of the genitive case indicates a person or thing affected by the feeling or action expressed by certain nouns, adjectives, and participles as adjectives, all of which reveal a transitive force. Latin frequently uses such a genitive where English uses a preposition between two substantives, e.g., desire *for* fame, freedom *from* anxiety, skill *in* archery, devotion *to* duty, love *of* money. Latin usages of the objective genitive:

(a) With nouns:

spēs *victōriae,*	*hope of victory.*
formīdine *calamitātis* līberātī,	*set free from the dread of disaster.*
quōrum ratiō habenda est,	*of which account must be taken.*
Scientiā atque ūsū *rērum nauticārum* cēterōs antecēdunt.	*They surpass everybody else in the theory and practice of seamanship.*
Capit odium *meī.*	*She is conceiving a dislike for me.*
hiemis perfugium,	*a shelter from winter.*
dolōris remedium,	*a remedy against pain.*

(b) With adjectives:[1]

cupidus *laudis,*	*desirous of praise.*
memor *nostrī,*	*mindful of us.*

---

[1] They denote desire, knowledge, memory, fullness, power, sharing, and their opposites, and include present participles used as adjectives.

immemor *beneficiī,*	*ungrateful.*
litterārum **studiōsus,**	*devoted to literature,*
	with a passion for literature.
homō imperītus *mōrum,*	*a man without experience of the*
	world.

Note that in such an expression as **amor patriae,** it is implied that **aliquis** (*somebody*) **amat patriam.** Since **patriam** is the object of **amat,** the term *objective genitive* becomes self-explanatory.

(c) With participles:

amantissimus meī,	*most devoted to me.*
oblītus suī,	*forgetful of self.*

(d) With verbs of remembering and forgetting, which often govern an objective genitive:

Quid est homō quod recordāris *eius*?
What is man that Thou art mindful of him?

(e) With **potior** (see sec. **181**), which often governs an objective genitive in place of the ablative.

VOCABULARY

contentiō, -iōnis, *f.,* strife, argument

cupiditās, -tātis, *f.,* desire

cupidus, -a, -um, desirous

ignōminia, -ae, *f.,* disgrace

memor, *adj.* (*gen.* **memoris**), mindful

merces, mercēdis, *f.,* pay, hire, reward

oblītus, -a, -um, forgetful

obliviscor, obliviscī, oblītus sum, forget

perītus, -a, -um, skilled (in), experienced

EXERCISE A

1. Ōrātōrēs contentiōnis quam vēritātis cupidiōrēs esse solent.

2. Nūllam virtūs aliam mercēdem labōrum perīculōrumque dēsīderat praeter hanc laudis[2] et glōriae.

3. Habētis ducem memorem vestrī,[3] oblītum suī.

4. Quis est Caesare optimārum artium studiō praestántior?

---

[2] **laudis** (*consisting of*) renown

[3] For the special objective (and collective) genitives **vestrī, nostrī,** from **vōs** and **nōs** respectively, see sec. **125b**.

5. Utrōsque[4] et laudis cupiditās et timor ignōminiae ad virtūtem excitābat.

6. Multārum rērum īnscius es quārum dēbēs esse perītus.

7. Cūra rērum aliēnārum difficilis est.

EXERCISE B

(1) Born in the distant province of Bithynia, he was eager for renown. (2) You are a rich man, Crassus, but you have no knowledge of the science of warfare. (3) Patriotism has more weight with[5] him than the fear of death. (4) Immoderate[6] desires for riches, glory, and absolute power[7] over others are diseases of the mind. (5) Socrates represented[8] himself (as) ignorant of almost everything.

[4] In the plural uterque often means *those on both sides.*
[5] plūs valet apud   [6] immēnsus   [7] dominātiō in + acc.   [8] fingō

Nōn tam praeclārum est scīre Latīnē quam turpe nescīre.

It is not so much a distinction to know Latin as a disgrace not to know it.

—CICERO, *Brutus* 140

LESSON XXXII

Infinitive as Subject—Predicate Genitive—Infinitive as Object

183. Infinitives of *amō, moneō, regō, capiō, audiō*.—

	ACTIVE	PASSIVE
PRES.	amā-re, *to love*	amā-rī, *to be loved*
FUT.	amāt-ūrus esse, *to be going to love*	(amāt-um īrī, *to be going to be loved*)
PERF.	amāv-isse, *to have loved*	amāt-us esse, *to have been loved*
PRES.	monē-re	monē-rī
FUT.	monit-ūrus esse	(monit-um īrī)
PERF.	monu-isse	monit-us esse
PRES.	rege-re	regī
FUT.	rēct-ūrus esse	(rēct-um īrī)
PERF.	rēx-isse	rēct-us esse
PRES.	cape-re	capī
FUT.	capt-ūrus esse	(capt-um īrī)
PERF.	cēp-isse	capt-us esse
PRES.	audī-re	audī-rī
FUT.	audīt-ūrus esse	(audīt-um īrī)
PERF.	audīv-isse	audīt-us esse

184. Infinitive as subject.—The infinitive is a neuter noun and may be used in the nominative[1] case as the subject of a finite verb.[2] Read secs. **40** and **41**.

> *Scīre* est difficillimum.
> *To know* (*Knowledge*) *is very difficult.* Or,
> *It is very difficult to know.*

Note that *it* does not appear in the Latin, but is merely a device of English to postpone the logical subject of the sentence.

185. Verbal characteristics of the infinitive-noun.—Since the infinitive is a *verbal* noun, it may retain its power, as a verb, in the following instances:

(**a**) To govern a case:

> Scīre *litterās Latīnās* difficillimum est.
> *It is very difficult to know Latin literature.*

(**b**) To be modified by an adverb:

> *Bene* scīre litterās Latīnās difficillimum est.
> *It is very difficult to know Latin literature well.*

(**c**) To have a subject of its own. Where it occurs, this subject must be in the accusative case.

> *Mē* bene scīre litterās Latīnās difficillimum est.
> *It is very difficult for me to know Latin literature well.*

186. Verbs that have the infinitive as subject.—The use of the infinitive[3] as subject is confined to **est** (and the other tenses of **sum** in the third singular), to impersonal verbs like **oportet**, *it is fitting* or *necessary*, and to verbs used impersonally, such as **dēlectat**, *it delights, it is a pleasure*, and **vīsum est**, *it seems good, it was decided.*

> *Nihil agere* mē dēlectābat.
> *Doing nothing delighted me.*

---

[1] The infinitive is indeclinable and is used only in the nominative and accusative cases.

[2] The infinitive in the nominative case may also be used in apposition with the subject and as a predicate nominative.

[3] usually a *present* infinitive

Mē hoc facere oportet.
It is necessary that I do this (I ought to do this).

Praestat *aliquid superesse* quam *dēesse.*
It is better that there be too much than not enough.

In such instances it is really the whole "infinitive clause," i.e., the infinitive + subject accusative + adjuncts, that is the subject of the finite verb.

187. Subject infinitive and predicate genitive.—A subject infinitive is frequently modified by a predicate genitive, which is really a variety of the possessive genitive (sec. 85). In this idiom the genitive conveys such ideas as *the duty of, the mark of, the characteristic of,* e.g.:

Stultī erat spērāre, suādēre *impudentis.*
It was the mark of a fool to hope, of a scoundrel to plead.

or:

It was folly to hope, brazen impudence to plead.

Nihil est tam *parvī animī* quam amāre dīvitiās.
Nothing is so characteristic of a petty mind as to love riches.

or:

Nothing is so small-minded, etc.

Grātēs[4] persolvere dignās nōn *opis* est *nostrae.*
It lies not in our power to return fitting thanks.

Observation 1.—This usage does not extend to personal pronouns; here the neuter of the possessive is used:

Meum est (not meī) hoc facere.
It is my duty to do this.

Observation 2.—Since Latin abhors ambiguity, this use of the genitive (with or without an infinitive) is specially useful in the case of adjectives of one termination like sapiēns.

Sapiēns est might mean not only *It is wise,* but *He is a wise man.* Therefore, Sapientis est (hoc facere) is the expression used when it is desired to convey the meaning *It is the sign of a wise man, It is the part of wisdom,* etc.

---

[4] variant of grātiās

188. Infinitive as object,—

(a) *Where the subject of the infinitive does not exist or is not expressed.*
The use of the infinitive as the exact equivalent of the accusative of a noun is rare, but an infinitive which is virtually an object infinitive is used with such verbs as **volō, mālō, nōlō, cupiō**, and others. It is customary and practical to class such object infinitives without subjects as complementary infinitives (see sec. **189**); but a real distinction exists between the infinitive in *Īre* possum, *I am able to go,* and that in *Scīre* cupiō, *I desire to know* (*I desire knowledge*).

A rough working rule to enable the beginner to distinguish the objective from the complementary infinitive is that the objective infinitive has a subject accusative (usually different from that of the main verb), whereas the complementary infinitive has *no* subject accusative because its subject is the same as the nominative subject of the verb on which the infinitive depends.

> Volō *dīcere.* *I wish to speak.*
> *Fugere* mālō quam servus *manēre.* *I prefer to* (i.e., *would rather*) *run away than stay a slave.* (*I prefer flight to a continuation of servitude.*)

Observation.—Note that in (a) the predicate noun **servus** agrees in case with the *nominative* subject of the main verb **mālō** (**ego** understood); see sec. **101.**

(b) *Where subject of infinitive is expressed.*—The verbs listed in (a), and others such as **cōgō**, *compel;* **sinō**, **patior**, *allow;* **prohibeō**, *prevent;* **iubeō**, *order;* **vetō**, *forbid, order not to,* etc., may take as object an "infinitive clause," which has a subject in the accusative case. Verbs of saying, thinking, etc., which also govern this construction, are separately treated in Lesson XXXVI.

> Sine *mē esse consulem,* *Allow me to be consul.*
> Cupiō *mē esse clēmentem,* *I desire (myself) to be lenient.*
> *Tē scīre* voluī. *I wished you to know.*

Observation.—Note that with the infinitive in (b) a predicate noun, e.g., **cōnsulem**, agrees in *case*, and that a predicate adjective, e.g., **clēmentem**, agrees in *gender, number,* and *case,* with the (accusative) subject of the infinitive; see sec. **101.**

VOCABULARY

careō, carēre, caruī, caritum, be without, be deprived of (w. abl.)
cēlō, I, hide
certus, -a, -um, certain
cōnsistō, cōnsistere, cōnstitī, ——, stand, halt; become motionless
facinus, facinoris, n., misdeed, misdemeanor
glaciēs, glaciēī, f., ice
māter, mātris, f., mother

medius, -a, -um, middle, middle of
parricīdium, -dī, n., parricide, murder of near relative
pontus, -ī, m., sea
prope, adv., almost
scelus, sceleris, n., crime
verberō, I, whip, lash
vērus, -a, -um, true
vinciō, vincīre, vīnxī, vīnctum, bind
voluptās, voluptātis, f., pleasure

EXERCISE A

1. Mihi est in animō Rōmam īre.
2. Mātre carēre miserrimum est.
3. Hās rēs nūntiārī nōlēbat.
4. Ars est cēlāre artem.
5. Sēsē tōtōs voluptātibus trādidērunt.
6. Laudārī, id quod multīs grātissimum est, mihi est molestissimum.
7. Quid enim stultius est quam incerta prō certīs habēre, falsa prō vērīs?
8. Facinus est vincīre cīvem Rōmānum; scelus verberāre; prope parricīdium necāre.
9. Vīdimus ingentem glaciē cōnsistere⁵ pontum.
10. Rēgem esse⁶ difficillimum est.
11. Temporī⁷ cēdere semper sapientis est habitum.

EXERCISE B

(1) I wish you to be friendly to me. (2) Work is prayer. (3) You are unwilling that all these things be announced. (4) He ordered Crassus to go into Aquitania with a large number of cavalry. (5) It will be an easy thing (for) you to draw up your line of battle in this plain. (6) He wished his mother to come to Rome.

⁵ freeze solid
⁶ Esse, the subject of est, has a subject of its own (185c). This subject is not expressed but is understood. The understood subject, if expressed, would be in the accusative case, e.g., aliquem, anyone. The predicate noun rēgem, therefore, stands in the accusative.
⁷ circumstances; or, taken together, temporī cēdere = to temporise.

Malum est cōnsilium quod mūtārī nōn potest.

It is a poor plan that cannot be changed.

—PUBLILIUS SYRUS, *Sententiae*

LESSON XXXIII

Infinitive as Complement—*Possum*— *Volō, Nōlō, Mālō*

189. Infinitive as complement.—We have seen that usually[1] the objective infinitive has a subject accusative different from that of the main verb. There are, however, some verbs used with an infinitive which can have no subject accusative whatever. In such a case the infinitive completes or carries out the meaning of the main verb, for the latter implies another action of the same subject to complete its meaning. The sense of the verb is usually such that it cannot stand alone; together with the infinitive it practically supplies a fresh mood to the verb. Such infinitives are called *complementary.* Compare English *can, be able (to), must, ought (to), seem (to), am compelled (to), am allowed (to),* etc. Among such Latin verbs are: **possum,** *I can, am able to;* **dēbeō,** *I ought;* **properō,** *I hasten,* and the passives **videor,** *I seem;* **cōgor,** *I am compelled;* **prohibeor,** *I am prevented;* **sinor,** *I am allowed,* etc.

Potesne hoc *facere*?	*Can you **do** this?*
Dēbēmus *esse* bellicōsī.	*We ought **to be** warlike.*
Timēre vidēris.	*You seem **to be afraid.***
Domō *exīre* prohibētur.	*He is prevented **from going out of** the house.* (lit., ***to go***)
Cupiō *esse* rēx.	*I desire **to be** king.*

Contrast this with:

Cupiō *tē esse rēgem.*	*I desire **you to be** king.*

[1] But not necessarily; cf. **Cupiō mē** esse *clēmentem.*

151

190. Conjugation of *possum, volō, nōlō, mālō*.—

PRINCIPAL PARTS

possum,	posse,	potuī,	——,	*can, be able*
volō,	velle,	voluī,	——,	*wish, be willing*
nōlō,	nōlle,	nōluī,	——,	*be unwilling*
mālō,	mālle,	māluī,	——,	*prefer*

INDICATIVE

PRES.	pos-**sum**	volō	nōlō	mālō
	pot-**es**	vīs	nōn vīs	māvīs
	pot-**est**	vult	nōn vult	māvult
	pos-**sumus**	volumus	nōlumus	mālumus
	pot-**estis**	vultis	nōn vultis	māvultis
	pos-**sunt**	volunt	nōlunt	mālunt
IMPERF.	pot-**eram**	volēbam	nōlēbam	mālēbam
FUT.	pot-**erō**	volam	nōlam	mālam

Write the three perfect tenses of each of these verbs.

INFINITIVES AND PARTICIPLES

INFIN. PRES.	posse	velle	nōlle	mālle
INFIN. PERF.	potuisse	voluisse	nōluisse	māluisse
PART. PRES.	potēns	volēns	nōlēns	——

(a) **Possum** is a compound of **sum** and **potis**, *able* (stem, **pot-**). Wherever in the conjugation the final **t** of **pot-** comes before **s**, it is itself assimilated to **s**. **Potēns** is used as an adjective meaning *powerful*.

(b) **Nōlō** is compounded of **nōn** and **volō**; **mālō**, of **magis** and **volō**.

(c) **Nōlō** has imperatives **nōlī** (s.), **nōlīte** (pl.). See sec. **118**.

191. Possum (and **valeō**, *am strong*) may be followed by the neuter accusative singular of **multus, parvus, omnis**, and similar adjectives, and the neuter noun **nihil**. In this usage the verbs mean *to be powerful* and the accusatives denote the degree of the power. In practice these neuter accusatives do duty as adverbs, e.g., **Quantum poterō**, *To the best of my ability*.

VOCABULARY

certē, *adv.*, certainly, at least

cupiō, cupere, cupīvī, cupītum, long for, be eager for, desire

dēbeō, dēbēre, dēbuī, dēbitum, owe; *w. infin.*, ought, must

incipiō, incipere, incēpī, inceptum, begin

īnstruō, īnstruere, īnstrūxī, īnstrūctum, draw up, marshal

inveniō, invenīre, invēnī, inventum, come upon, find

pār, *adj.* (*gen.*, **paris**), equal, like

plānitiēs, plānitiēī, *f.*, plain, level ground

propter, *prep.*, *with acc.*, because of, on account of

timeō, timēre, timuī, ——, fear, be afraid

timor, timōris, *m.*, fear, state of dread

vel . . . vel, either . . . or

vērō, *adv.*, truly, indeed; however; **iam vērō,** moreover

EXERCISE A

I wish to be king.
1. Cupiō esse rēx.

Death seems to me to be a bad thing.
2. Malum[2] mihi vidētur esse mors.

3. Propter hanc causam minus facile in hostēs impetum facere potuit. *For this reason he was less able to make an attack on the enemy.*

I can no longer abide in this fear.
4. Diūtius in hōc timōre esse nōn possum.

I am not stirred by that hatred as I ought to be.
5. Nōn eō odiō commoveor quō dēbeō (commovērī).

What greater thing is able to be given to a man than fame & glory
6. Quid hominī potest darī maius quam glōria et laus?

What speech can be found to equal the valor of Cn. P.
7. Iam vērō virtūtī Cn. Pompeī quae potest ōrātiō pār invenīrī?

He who does not know how to bluff does not know how to rule
8. Quī nescit dissimulāre nescit rēgnāre.

A brave man will either begin to wish for death or
9. Homō fortis mortem vel optāre incipiet vel certē timēre dēsistet. *at least cease to fear it*

Because of the enemies cavalry he was not able to set up his battle line in the middle of the plane.
10. Propter hostium equitātum aciem mediā[3] in plānitiē īnstruere nōlēbat.

He preferred to be the companion of a fleeing queen than to be the
11. Antōnius fugientis rēgīnae quam pugnantis mīlitis[4] suī comes esse māluit. *comrad of his own fighting soldiers.*

EXERCISE B

(1) I begin to be friendly to you. (2) You do not wish to hear all these things. (3) We ought not to have[5] ordered him to go.

---

[2] **Malum** (neuter) is used as predicate noun; *a bad thing.*

[3] *in the middle of*

[4] Translate *soldiers*; **mīles** is often used in the collective sense of "soldiery."

[5] Latin will use the perfect tense of **dēbeō** with the present infinitive.

1. Tibi amicus esse incipio.

2. Omnes has res audire non vis. *Haec omnia*

3. Eum ire iubere debuimus

(4) I can say only this, I do not like you. (5) They had learned the most difficult of all things, to be silent and to listen.

SELECTIONS FOR READING

(1) Nōn amo tē, Sabidī, nec possum dīcere quārē:[6]
Hoc tantum[7] possum dīcere, nōn amo tē.

—Martial, I, 32.

(2) Dīmidium[8] dōnāre Linō quam crēdere[9] tōtum
Quī māvult, māvult perdere[10] dīmidium.

—Martial, I, 75.

---

[6] *why*   [7] *only*   [8] *half*   [9] *entrust, lend*   [10] *lose*

4. Hoc tantum possum dicere, non amo te.

5. Res difficillimas omnium rerum didecerant tacere et audire.

Semper aut discere aut docēre aut scrībere dulce habuī.

I have always considered it a pleasure to learn, to teach, or to write.

—THE VENERABLE BEDE, *Historia Ecclēsiastica Gentis Anglōrum*, V, 24

And gladly wolde he lerne, and gladly teche.

—CHAUCER, Prologue to the *Canterbury Tales*, 308

LESSON XXXIV

Vocabulary Review

The following are among the commonest verbs in Latin. Note the special irregularities of those marked with an asterisk.

accipiō, accipere, accēpī, acceptum, receive, suffer, learn, get

*****agō, agere, ēgī, āctum,** do, act; treat, plead; *pass.*, be at stake

arbitror, *dep.***, arbitrārī, arbitrātus sum,** think, judge, suppose

audiō, audīre, audīvī, audītum, hear; hear of, listen (to)

cognōsco, cognōscere, cognōvī, cognitum, learn by inquiry, ascertain; *in the perfect,* know, be aware of

cōnstituō, cōnstituere, cōnstituī, cōnstitūtum, establish; determine, decide

crēdō, crēdere, crēdidī, crēditum, trust, entrust, believe

dēbeō, dēbēre, dēbuī, dēbitum, owe, be bound, ought (*w. infin.*)

dēfendō, dēfendere, dēfendī, dēfēnsum, ward off, defend

dīco, dīcere, dīxī, dictum, say, tell

*****dō, dare, dedī, datum,** give, grant

faciō, facere, fēcī, factum, make, do

*****ferō, ferre, tulī, lātum,** carry, bring, say

gerō, gerere, gessī, gestum, carry, carry on, manage; *pass.*, go on

habeō, habēre, habuī, habitum, have, hold, consider, regard

*****inquam, inquis, inquit, inquiunt,** *defective verb found most often in 1, 2, 3, sing. and 3 plural pres. indic.,* I say, you say, he says, they say, *used only with direct quotations and following one or more words of quotation.*

intellegō, intellegere, intellēxī, intellēctum, understand, see

iūdicō, *I*, judge, adjudge, estimate

licet, licēre, licuit, *or* licitum est, *impersonal*, it is permitted, may
  (*w. dat. and infin.*)

mittō, mittere, mīsī, missum, send (*in compounds*, put *or* let)

oportet, oportēre, oportuit, *impersonal*, ought (*w. acc. and infin.*,
  e.g., Mē hoc facere oportet.)

petō, petere, petīvī, *or* petiī, petītum, aim at, make for, attack, ask,
  seek; be a candidate for

pōnō, pōnere, posuī, positum, place, put, lay

*possum, posse, potuī, can, be able, have power (*w. infin.*)

putō, *I*, think, reckon, imagine

quaerō, quaerere, quaesīvī, *or* quaesiī, quaesītum, search for, ask,
  investigate (*used w.* ā, dē, *or* ē *w. abl. of pers. asked*)

relinquō, relinquere, relīquī, relictum, leave behind, abandon

sciō, scīre, scīvī, scītum, know

soleō (*semi-dep.*), solēre, solitus sum, be accustomed (*w. infin.*)

*sum, esse, fuī, futūrus, be, exist

teneō, tenēre, tenuī, tentum, hold, keep; *pass.*, be caught

*tollō, tollere, sustulī, sublātum, raise, put out of the way, destroy

ūtor, *dep.*, ūtī, ūsus sum, use, enjoy, employ (*w. abl.*)

veniō, venīre, vēnī, ventum, come

videō, vidēre, vīdī, vīsum, see; *pass.*, seem (*w. infin.*)

*volō, velle, voluī, wish, will (*w. infin.*)

Any or all of the following examples will be found useful in reviewing principles of syntax already studied.   Consult the general vocabulary for unfamiliar words not explained in text or footnotes.

REVIEW EXERCISE A

1. Audācem eam faciēbat amor.
2. Huic reī quod satis esse vīsum est mīlitum relīquit.
3. Cotta perterritus ex Sardiniā in Āfricam fūgit.
4. Ignis aurum probat, miseria fortēs virōs.
5. Sed haec minōra sunt.
6. Mea Terentia, fīdissima atque optima uxor, et mea cārissima
fīliola, et spēs reliqua nostra, Cicerō, valēte.
7. Ad[1] contumēliam omnia accipit.
8. Trēs ūnō diē ā tē accēpī epistulās, ūnam brevem, duās plēniōrēs.

---

[1] *as*

Like so many mice we are always eating other peoples food.

9. Quasi[2] mūrēs semper edimus aliēnum cibum.

10. Hōrum Germānōrum prīmō circiter mīlia XV Rhēnum trānsiērunt; nunc sunt in Galliā ad centum et vīgintī mīlium numerum.

REVIEW EXERCISE B

1. Litterās Graecās senex didicī.
2. Taleae[3] pedem longae tōtae in terram īnfodiēbantur.[4] *Foot long stakes in their entirety were driven into the earth.*
3. Fēminīs lūgēre honestum est, virīs meminisse. *For women it is proper to grieve, for the men to remember.*
4. Ēmisse tē praedium vehementer gaudeō, fēlīciterque tibi rem istam ēvenīre cupiō. *I am glad that you have bought an estate, and I desire that the purchase will turn out happily for you.*
5. Vārus cum legiōnibus īnstābat iamque cīvēs pulverem venientium vidēbant. *V. was pressing on with his legions and already the citizens were beholding the dust of the oncoming men.*
6. Rēs didicerant rērum omnium difficillimās, tacēre audīreque.
7. Commodissimum esse statuit omnēs nāvēs subdūcī. *He decided that it was most convenient for all the ships to be beached.*
8. Ibi permānsērunt atque agrōs colere coepērunt.
9. Nēmō dēbet bis pūnīrī prō ūnō dēlictō.[5] *No man ought to be punished twice for the same offence.*
10. Epistulārum genera multa esse nōn ignōrās.

REVIEW EXERCISE C

1. Beātus esse sine virtūte nēmō potest.
2. Hīc vōbīs bellum et pācem portāmus; utrum placet sūmite.
3. Culpā caret is quī scit sed prohibēre nōn potest.
4. Nūllō labōre aut corpus eius fatīgārī aut animus vincī poterat.
5. Ego minus saepe ad vōs dō litterās quam possum.
6. Ex altō[6] sē aestus incitat. Hoc accidit semper hōrārum duodecim spatiō.
7. Nōn queō[7] plūra iam scrībere; impedit maeror.
8. Nostrī mīlitēs summā vī trānscendere in hostium nāvēs contendēbant.
9. Aliud[8] est epistulam, aliud[8] historiam, aliud amīcō, aliud omnibus[9] scrībere.
10. Nōn omne quod nitet[10] aurum est.

REVIEW EXERCISE D

1. Germānī per vim[11] nāvibus flūmen trānsīre[11] cōnantur.

---

[2] *just as, like*   [3] *wooden stakes*   [4] *were driven into*   [5] *offense*
[6] Cf. English, *the deep.*   [7] *same meaning as* **possum**
[8] *one thing . . . another*   [9] i.e., the general reader, *the public*   [10] *glisten*
[11] *force a passage*

2. Esse quam vidērī mālēbat.

3. Hōc ex portū brevissimus in Britanniam trāiectus est, circiter mīlium passuum XXX ā continente.[12]

4. Eī quī in classe erant proficīscī properābant.

5. Aequē secundum[13] Nātūram est morī ac nāscī.

6. Vincere scīs, Hannibal; victōriā ūtī nescīs.

7. Meminī etiam quae volō; oblīvīscī nōn possum quae volō.

8. Dulce et decōrum est prō patriā morī.

9. Cuius nōn audeō dīcere nōmen?

10. Summae est dēmentiae[14] haec spērāre.

REVIEW EXERCISE E

1. Id factum graviter tulit Antōnius, suam grātiam inter suōs minuī.

2. Aurum et argentum omne pūblicum prīvātumque ad sē iubet dēferrī.

3. Scīpiōnis cōnsiliō atque virtūte Hannibal in Āfricam redīre atque Italiā dēcēdere coāctus est.

4. Lympha cadit, fugit hōra rapāx; bibe, carpe fugācem.

5. Ego tē quam prīmum, mea vita, cupiō vidēre et in tuō complexū ēmorī.

6. Paulum legiōnēs Caesar quās prō vallō cōnstituerat prōmovērī iubet.

7. Neque frūctum ūllum labōris meī exspectō, et cōgor nōnnumquam hominēs non optimē dē mē meritōs dēfendere.

8. Nōn minus est imperātōris cōnsiliō superāre quam gladiō.

REVIEW EXERCISE F

the horses of their own accord hurry. Tis hard to hold them back

1. Equī sponte suā properant; labor est inhibēre volentēs.[15]

2. Est difficilius Fābricium ab honōre quam sōlem ā cursū vertere.

in their eagerness

3. Magister Pȳthagoras discipulōs tempus certum tacēre iussit, nōn omnēs idem sed aliōs aliud tempus; sed nōn minus quisquam[16] tacuit quam biennium.

---

[12] used as a noun, *the continent (of Europe)*
[13] *in accordance with;* cf. "It is as natural to die as to be born"—Francis Bacon.
[14] *madness*   [15] *in their willingness, eagerness*
[16] nōn quisquam, *not a single one*

Both on account of the wounds of the soldiers and burial of the dead

4. Et propter vulnera mīlitum et propter sepultūram occīsōrum nostrī Helvētiōs sequī nōn potuērunt.

our soldiers were not able to pursue the Helvetians

5. Nōnne ēmorī per virtūtem praestat[17] quam vītam miseram atque inhonestam[18] per dēdecus[19] āmittere?

6. "Perterritum," inquit, "hostem vidēs, Cūriō; cūr dubitās ūtī hāc opportūnitāte?"

7. Nerviī lātissimum flūmen trānsīre, altissimās rīpās ascendere, inīquissimum locum subīre ausī sunt; quae facilia ex[20] difficillimīs animī magnitūdō redēgerat.

---

[17] **Nōnne praestat,** *is it not better?*   [18] *dishonorable*   [19] *in disgrace*
[20] *instead of*

Quod nōn opus est, asse cārum est.

What is not needed is dear at a farthing.

—CATO, quoted in Seneca, *Epistulae*, 94, 28

LESSON XXXV

Locative Case—Genitive of Indefinite Value— Ablative of Price—Genitive with Verbs of Accusing, Condemning, and Acquitting

192. Locative case.—In addition to the six cases already learned, Latin has a case called the *locative* (**locus**, *place*) to denote *at, in,* or *on.* It survives only in a few common expressions (**domī**, *at home;* **rūrī**, *in the country;* and a few others) and in names of towns.

In the first and second declensions, the locative corresponds in the singular to the genitive, and in the plural to the ablative. In the third declension it corresponds usually to the ablative, sometimes to the dative.[1]

> **Rōmae**, *at Rome* (nom., **Rōma**)
> **Athēnīs**, *at Athens* (nom. pl., **Athēnae**)
> **Carthāginī**[1] (**-e**), *at Carthage* (nom., **Carthāgō**)
> **Corinthī**, *at Corinth* (nom., **Corinthus**)
> **Philippīs**, *at Philippi* (nom., **Philippī**)

(a) For *place where* with other nouns, see sec. **87.**

(b) For the omission of the preposition in expressing place to which and place from which with names of towns and cities, **domus** (*home*), and **rūs** (*country*), see secs. **94** and **123.**

(c) In accounts of naval and military affairs the names of towns and cities will often appear preceded by the prepositions **ad** and **ab**

---

[1] Some of the proper names in which this form is frequently retained are **Carthāginī, Lacedaemonī, Sicyōnī;** it appears also in nouns used adverbially such as **herī**, *yesterday;* **rūrī**, *in the country;* **temperī**, *in time;* **vesperī**, *in the evening;* **lūcī**, *in the daytime;* **forīs**, *out of doors,* and others. All are used without a preposition.

to indicate position near and motion to or from the neighborhood
of. This is a logical exception, for a fleet, at least, cannot sail all
the way into a town or small island.

(d) Note the following idiomatic usages:

> *In Āfricam* Carthāginem vēnī.
> *I came to Carthage in Africa.*
> Nēmō *tōtā Capuā* est.
> *There isn't a soul in the whole of Capua.*
> domī meae, *at my house*

(e) The functions of the locative in its extended use as the case
expressing notions of the value or price *at which* a thing is held,
bought, or sold were soon absorbed by the genitive and ablative.
See following sections.

193. Genitive of indefinite value.—Closely related to such locatives as **Corinthī**, *at Corinth*, are the so-called genitives (really old
locatives) of value, **magnī, parvī, tantī, quantī, plūris, minōris, plū-
rimī, maximī, minimī**; and expressions of utter worthlessness like
floccī (*at a straw's value*), **assis** (*at the value of an* as[2]), and **nihilī**.
These are found in conjunction with **sum** and such verbs as **habeō,
aestimō, faciō, dūcō**, and **pendō** in the sense of *reckon, value,* or *esteem.*

> Rem pūblicam *maximī* habet, salūtem suam *nihilī.*
> *He sets the highest value on the national interest, none on his
> personal safety.*

194. Ablative of price.—The ablative (a type of the instrumental)
is used to express the actual price for which a thing is bought or sold.
It is frequently found in conjunction with the verbs **sum** and **stō**
(in the sense of *cost*) with or without a dative of the person concerned.

> *Multō sanguine* et *vulneribus* ea Poenīs victōria stetit.
> *That victory cost the Carthaginians much bloodshed and many
> casualties* (many bloody casualties).
> Trīticī modius erat *dēnāriīs quīnque.*
> *A bushel of wheat cost five denarii.*
> Hoc signum *parvō* (*pretiō*) vēndidit.
> *He sold this statue at a low price.*

---

[2] **As,** a Roman copper coin corresponding roughly to a cent.

Observation.—Such apparent exceptions as the ablatives **parvō, magnō, plūrimō, minimō, dīmidiō, vīlī** are to be explained by supplying the word **pretiō.** Note the use of the word **grātīs** (for **grātiīs,** as opposed to **praemiō**), i.e., *for thanks, free;* and the idioms **bene emere,** *to buy cheap;* **bene vēndere,** *to sell dear.*

195. Genitive with verbs of accusing, condemning, and acquitting.

—With verbs like **accusō,** *accuse;* **arguō,** *prove guilty;* **condemnō,** *condemn;* **absolvō,** *acquit,* a genitive of the charge is often found, explained perhaps by the omission of the word **crīmine,** *on the charge,* or **nōmine,** *under the heading (of).*

> **Mē ipse *inertiae nēquitiaeque* condemnō.**
> *I condemn myself for* ⎱
> *I find myself guilty of* ⎰ *criminal neglect.*
> **Prōditiōnis accusātus est.**
> *He was accused of treason.*
> **Fūrtī condemnāberis.**
> *You will be found guilty of theft.*

Observation.—The ablative of the charge and punishment is a common alternative.

> **Eum *dē vī* reum fēcī.**
> *I have brought an action against him for assault.*
> **Exsiliō multātus est.**
> *He was sentenced to exile.*

VOCABULARY

adulēscēns, adulescentis (adulēscentium), *m.,* young man (*seventeen and over*)
aliquot, *indecl. adj.,* some, a few, several
Athēnae, -ārum, *f. pl.,* Athens
cēnō, *I,* dine
congredior, congredī, congressus sum, meet with, meet in battle
cōnstituō, cōnstituere, cōnstituī, cōnstitūtum, decide, determine
cotīdiē, *adv.,* daily
doctor, doctōris, *m.,* teacher

Genava, -ae, *f.,* Geneva
Lutētia, -ae, *f.,* Lutetia, *site of modern Paris*
Pindarus, -ī, *m.,* Pindar, *Greek lyric poet*
Prisciānus, -ī, *m.,* Priscian, *celebrated grammarian, fl.* 512 A.D.
rūs, rūris, *n.,* countryside
Sēquana, -ae, *f.,* Seine (River)
talentum, -ī, *n.,* talent, *Greek unit of money* = $1,000.
Thēbae, -ārum, *f. pl.,* Thebes, *city in Greece*

EXERCISE A

1. Domī erō. Saepe domī nōn es.
2. Tē cotīdiē plūris faciō. Quantī mē facis?
3. Hoc Thēbās nūntiābitur.
4. Pindarus poēta Thēbīs nātus est.
5. Labiēnus ad Genavam trīs diēs morātus, quārtō diē cum exercitū profectus est.
6. Athēnīs, praeclārā in urbe[3] Graecōrum, adulēscēns multōs audīvī philosophōs.
7. Aliquot amīcī cōnstituērunt eā nocte domī nostrae cēnāre.
8. Prisciānus nostrō tempore Cōnstantīnopolī doctor fuit.
9. Centum talentīs ea rēs Graecīs stetit.
10. Rōmā ā patre discessī.
11. Hannibal quotiēnscumque[4] cum populō Rōmānō congressus est in Italiā semper discessit superior.[5]
12. Cum quattuor legiōnibus Lutētiam profectus est. Id est oppidum Parīsiōrum positum in īnsulā flūminis Sēquanae.

EXERCISE B

(1) I ordered the cavalry to leave Sicily. (2) Do you value these things very highly? (3) My brother bought that man's property (bona) for two thousand sesterces. (4) Brutus values his life very cheap. (5) At Philippi he was accused of treason and condemned to death. (6) The ships, after delaying[6] ten days at Syracuse, set off for Carthage. (7) We have stayed at home three days; tomorrow we shall go to the country.

---

[3] *In Athens, the famous city*   [4] *as often as*   [5] Cf. English *"came off best."*
[6] Use perfect participle for "after delaying."

Īnsānus omnēs furere crēdit cēterōs.

"Everyone's queer but me and thee, and even thee's a little queer."

Lesson XXXVI

Indirect Statement—Tenses of the Infinitive

196. Indirect statement.—In the English sentence

> *"I shall go to Rome," says he*

the words within the quotation marks are the actual words of the speaker. This is called *direct statement* (**ōrātiō rēcta**). The Latin will be:

> **"Rōmam," inquit, "ībō."**

In the English sentence

> *He says (that) he will go to Rome*

the words introduced by *that* are not the actual words of the speaker. This is called *indirect statement* (**ōrātiō oblīqua**). The Latin prefers this way of reporting a statement, thought, or feeling:

> **Dīcit sē Rōmam itūrum esse.**

Note:

(a) That an indirect statement in Latin is never introduced by a conjunction such as the English *that*.

(b) That the dependent verb is in the infinitive mood instead of the indicative.

(c) That the subject of this infinitive is in the accusative case (cf. sec. **185c**).

(d) That any predicate noun will agree with this subject in case, while a predicate adjective (including the participial element of the

164

future active and perfect passive infinitives) will agree in gender, number, and case (cf. secs. **101, 188b**).

(e) That **sē** (**suus**) when used as the subject of a verb in the infinitive refers to the subject of the verb on which the infinitive verb depends.

197. Verbs introducing indirect statement.—Any verb meaning *say, know, perceive, think, feel, believe,* and essentially similar ideas, may govern the above construction in Latin. Among these, of those you have already encountered, are **dīcō,** *say;* **sciō,** *know;* **cognōscō,** *learn;* **audiō,** *hear;* **videō,** *see;* **moneō,** *warn;* and **sentiō,** *feel.* This construction is not entirely foreign to English.

> *I perceive **him to be** a brave man.*
> *He declared **us to be** enemies.*

Note the infinitives and also the case of *him* and *us.*

Some common verbs and expressions introducing indirect statement (**ōrātiō oblīqua**) with its typical *accusative and infinitive construction*:

1. Telling:	**dīcō, negō, nūntiō, referō, polliceor, prōmittō, certiōrem faciō, certior fīō** (sec. **216**).
2. Thinking:	**putō, exīstimō, arbitror, cēnseō, habeō** (*regard*), **dūcō, iūdicō, crēdō.**
3. Knowing:	**cognōscō, sciō, nesciō, compertum habeō** (*ascertain*), **intellegō.**
4. Perceiving:	**sentiō** (*be aware*), **comperiō** (*find out*), **videō, cernō, audiō** (*hear that*).
5. Remembering:	**memoriā teneō, reminīscor, meminī.**

198. Tenses of the infinitive.—

(a) The present infinitive denotes time *contemporaneous with* that of the verb on which it depends, in whatever tense that verb may be:

Dīcit sē librum *legere.*
*He says that he **is reading** the book.* (Contemporary)
"I am reading the book," says he.

Dīxit sē librum *legere.*
*He said that he **was reading** the book.* (Contemporary)
"I am reading the book," said he.

(**b**) The perfect infinitive denotes time *earlier than* that of the verb on which it depends:

> Dīcit sē librum *lēgisse.*
> *He says that he* **has read** *the book.* (Prior)
> "*I* **have read** *the book,*" *says he.*

> Dīxit sē librum *lēgisse.*
> *He said that he* **had read** *the book.* (Prior)
> "*I* **have read** *the book,*" *said he.*

(**c**) The future infinitive denotes time *later than* that of the verb on which it depends:

> Dīcit sē librum *lēcturum esse.*
> *He says that he* **will read** *the book.* (Later)
> "*I* **shall read** *the book,*" *says he.*

> Dīxit sē librum *lēcturum esse.*
> *He said that he* **would read** *the book.* (Later)
> "*I* **shall read** *the book,*" *said he.*

Observation 1.—Note (**196d**) that the participial part of the infinitive (**lēcturus** and **lēctus**) is declined like any other adjective of the second declension, and must, therefore, agree in gender, number, and case with the (accusative) subject of the infinitive, e.g.:

> Dīcit *librōs lēctōs* esse.
> *He says that* **the books have been read.**
> "**The books have been read,**" *says he.*

Observation 2.—Dīcō is never followed by a negative; in such cases negō (*I say that not*) is used. In accordance with this principle negō . . . umquam, negō . . . ūllum, etc. take the place of dīcō . . . nunquam, dīcō . . . nūllum:

> Ita rescrīpsērunt *nihil umquam* sē lēgisse melius.
> *Accordingly they wrote back that they had* **never** *read* **anything** *better.*

> Negābō *mē umquam* anteā hominem vīdisse.
> *I shall say that I have* **never** *seen the fellow before.*

VOCABULARY

accipiō, -cipere, *etc.*, accept, receive

armō, *I*, arm, equip

cōnsuētūdō, cōnsuētūdinis, *f.*, custom, practice

discrīmen, discrīminis, *n.*, crisis, danger

exīstimō, *I*, estimate, think, consider

fēlīcitās, fēlīcitātis, *f.*, happiness; luck

fingō, fingere, finxī, fictum, feign, pretend

hīc, *adv.*, here, in this place

iaceō, iacēre, iacuī, ——, lie, rest

immineō, imminēre, ——, ——, project, hang over; threaten

intellegō, intellegere, intellēxī, intellēctum, understand; know; realize; learn

metus, metūs, *m.*, fear

nōndum, *adv.*, not yet

oportet, oportēre, oportuit, ——, it is fitting, it is necessary

perniciēs, perniciēī, *f.*, ruin, destruction

scientia, -ae, *f.*, knowledge

spērō, *I*, hope, anticipate

vāstō, *I*, make desolate

vigilō, *I*, be awake, be on guard

vīvō, vīvere, vīxī, vīctum, live

vōx, vōcis, *f.*, voice

EXERCISE A

1. Cīvem Rōmānum sē esse dīcēbat.
2. Fingunt cīvem Atticam esse hanc.
3. Negāvit sē mihi pecūniam dedisse.
4. Videt mē suam amīcitiam velle.
5. Aedificāre tē scrībis.
6. Scrībis grātās tibi fuisse litterās meās.
7. Videō adhūc duās esse sententiās.
8. Dolōrem exīstimō maximum malōrum omnium.
9. Spērat adulēscēns diū sē vīctūrum.
10. Aetātem meam scīs? Sciō esse magnam.
11. Id fore (= futūrum esse) spērat.
12. Videō enim esse hīc in senātū nōnnūllōs sociōrum tuōrum.

EXERCISE B

1. Intellegis multō mē ācrius ad salūtem quam tē ad perniciem reīpūblicae vigilāre.
2. Cicerō ad haec ūnum modo respondet: nōn esse cōnsuētūdinem populī Rōmānī accipere ab hoste armātō condiciōnem.
3. Ego enim sīc exīstimō: in summō imperātōre quattuor hās

rēs inesse oportēre—scientiam reī mīlitāris, virtūtem, auctōritātem, fēlīcitātem.

4. Quam multās exīstimātis īnsulās esse vāstātās? quam multās aut metū[1] relictās aut ā pīrātīs captās urbīs sociōrum?

5. Ego enim sīc exīstimō: Maximō, Marcellō, Scīpiōnī, Mariō, et cēterīs magnīs imperātōribus nōn sōlum propter virtūtem, sed etiam propter fortūnam saepius imperia mandāta atque exercitūs esse commissōs.

6. Rārō (*rarely*) quemquam[2] alium patriam, exsiliī causā relinquentem, tam maestum abīsse ferunt (= dicunt) quam Hannibalem ex hostium terrā excēdentem.

EXERCISE C

(1) I do not think that I have seen a more beautiful city than Rome. (2) Caesar remembered that L. Cassius, a consul, had been killed and his army captured by the Helvetians. (3) He told me many things about himself: he had been a soldier for many years; he did not like the city and had no friends there; he would return to his home in Gaul[3] as soon as possible.

SELECTIONS FOR READING

(1) Pudōre et līberālitāte līberōs
    Retinēre satius[4] esse crēdō quam metū.

            —Terence, *Adelphi*, 57–8.

(2) Homō sum: hūmānī nihil ā mē aliēnum putō.

            —Terence, *Heaut.*, I, i, 25.

---

[1] abl. of cause: *through fear*   [2] acc. of **quisquam**, *anyone*
[3] **in Galliam domum suam**   [4] equals **melius**

Quī stultīs vidērī ērudītī volunt stultī ērudītīs videntur.

Those who would seem learned to fools seem fools to the learned.

—QUINTILIAN, *Institutio Oratoria*, X, 7, 22

Lesson XXXVII

The Pronouns *Īdem, Ipse, Iste,* and *Quīdam*

199. Declension of *īdem* (pron. and adj.), same.—

SINGULAR

	M.	F.	N.
Nom.	īdem	eadem	idem
Gen.	eiusdem	eiusdem	eiusdem
Dat.	eīdem	eīdem	eīdem
Acc.	eundem	eandem	idem
Abl.	eōdem	eādem	eōdem

PLURAL

	M.	F.	N.
Nom.	eīdem	eaedem	eadem
Gen.	eōrundem	eārundem	eōrundem
Dat.	eīsdem	eīsdem	eīsdem
Acc.	eōsdem	eāsdem	eadem
Abl.	eīsdem	eīsdem	eīsdem

(a) Compare this paradigm with that of **is** (sec. **127**), from which **īdem** is derived.

(b) **Iīdem** and **īdem** are also found in the nominative plural, masculine; and **iīsdem** and **īsdem** in the dative and ablative plural.

200. Use of *īdem*.—Īdem may be used as a pronoun:

Omnibus in causīs *idem* valēbit.
The same will hold good in all cases.

169

or as an adjective:

> **eōdem** tempore, *at the **same** time.*

(a) With **quī** it expresses *the same . . . as*:

> **Eadem** est *quae* semper fuit.
> *She is the **same as** she always was.*

(b) **Īdem** is sometimes best translated adverbially as *also*:

> **Ego vir fortis, īdem**que **philosophus.**
> *I am a brave man and **also** a philosopher.*

201. Declension of *ipse* (pron.), *self*.—

SINGULAR

	M.	F.	N.
Nom.	ipse	ipsa	ipsum
Gen.	ipsīus	ipsīus	ipsīus
Dat.	ipsī	ipsī	ipsī
Acc.	ipsum	ipsam	ipsum
Abl.	ipsō	ipsā	ipsō

PLURAL

	M.	F.	N.
Nom.	ipsī	ipsae	ipsa
Gen.	ipsōrum	ipsārum	ipsōrum
Dat.	ipsīs	ipsīs	ipsīs
Acc.	ipsōs	ipsās	ipsa
Abl.	ipsīs	ipsīs	ipsīs

202. Use of *ipse*.—The intensive pronoun **ipse** may be used alone or in apposition to any case of a noun or pronoun. It is used either to give additional emphasis or to indicate sharp contrast. Such emphasis is often best translated by *just, very, mere,* etc.

> ***Ipse** ībō.   I will go **myself** (i.e., in person).*

> **Eaque *ipsa* causa bellī fuit.**
> *And that was the cause **itself** (the actual or real cause) of the war.*

Ipse eum vīdī. *With my own eyes I saw him.*
illō *ipsō* diē, *on that very day.*

Observation.—Distinguish carefully the intensive and the reflexive uses of *himself* in the following examples:

Ipse veniet. *He will come* **himself** (intensive).
Sē laudābit. *He will praise* **himself** (reflexive).

203. *Iste* (pron. and adj.) is declined exactly like **ille** (see appendix **31**). It is a strong demonstrative and means *that, that of yours*. Iste often implies antagonism, contempt, or even deliberate insult.

Dē *istīs* rēbus exspectō tuās litterās.
I am awaiting your letter about **those** *affairs* **of yours.**

Quae tua est *ista* vīta?
What sort of life is **that of yours?**

204. Declension of *quīdam* (pron. and adj.), *certain, a certain (one).*—

SINGULAR

	M.	F.	N.
Nom.	quīdam	quaedam	quiddam (quoddam)
Gen.	cuiusdam	cuiusdam	cuiusdam
Dat.	cuidam	cuidam	cuidam
Acc.	quendam	quandam	quiddam (quoddam)
Abl.	quōdam	quādam	quōdam

PLURAL

	M.	F.	N.
Nom.	quīdam	quaedam	quaedam
Gen.	quōrundam	quārundam	quōrundam
Dat.	quibusdam	quibusdam	quibusdam
Acc.	quōsdam	quāsdam	quaedam
Abl.	quibusdam	quibusdam	quibusdam

(a) Compare this paradigm with the paradigm of **quī (130)**. In the neuter, **quiddam** is substantive and **quoddam** is adjective.

(b) **Use of *quīdam*.**—*As pronoun:*

> *Quīdam* mihi dīxit . . . *A certain (**man**) said to me* . . .
> *Quaedam* mihi dīxit . . . *A certain (**woman**) said to me* . . .

As adjective:

> *Quāsdam* suspīciōnēs audīvī.
> *I have heard **certain** suspicions.*

Observation.—In expressions meaning *certain of*, **quīdam** is followed by an ablative of separation (with a preposition) rather than by the genitive of the whole; compare the construction used with cardinal numerals, e.g.:

> Quīdam *ex Gallīs*   *Certain of the Gauls*

VOCABULARY

dēligō, dēligere, dēlēgī, dēlectum, choose

iaceō, iacēre, iacuī, ——, lie

morbus, -ī, *m.*, disease

nōndum, *adv.*, not yet

ostendō, ostendere, ostendī, ostentum, show, reveal

societās, societātis, *f.*, kinship, affinity

vulnerō, *I*, wound

EXERCISE A

1. Dīcet prō mē ipsa virtūs.
2. Est elephantīs cum genere hūmānō quaedam societās.
3. Sed ego quī tē confirmō ipse mē confirmāre nōn possum.
4. Senectūs ipsa est morbus. Ipsa suā Dīdō[1] concidit ūsa manū.
5. Īdem sum quī semper fuī.
6. Rēmī īsdem lēgibus quibus Suessiōnēs ūtī solēbant.
7. Ipsa sē virtūs satis ostendit.
8. Videō hīc in senātū quōsdam quī tēcum ūnā fuērunt.
9. Haec eōdem tempore in eādem prōvinciā tū ipse fēcistī.
10. Ille erat ūnus timendus ex istīs omnibus.
11. In ipsā Scīpiōnis Āfricānī vīllā iacēns haec tibi scrībō.

---

[1] **Dido**, queen of Carthage, deserted by Aeneas in Vergil's epic.

12. Caesar mīlitibus dīxit eundem Ariovistum superiōre annō populī Rōmānī amīcitiam petīvisse.

13. Spērat adulēscēns diū sē vīctūrum, quod spērāre idem senex nōn potest.

14. Satis mihi multa verba fēcisse videor.

15. Nōn dīcam id quod probāre difficile est.

16. Idōneum quendam hominem dēlēgit ex iīs quōs sēcum habēbat.

17. Quōs gladiīs interficī oportet, eōs nōndum vōce vulnerō.

EXERCISE B

(1) He is his own enemy.[2]   (2) We think our country dearer than our very selves.   (3) You told me, Terentia, that you would be in the city at the same hour.   (4) Of-their-own-accord,[3] the horses returned home.   (5) By his mere arrival he reassured[4] the citizens.   (6) There is a sort of affinity between[5] the elephant and man.

SELECTION FOR READING

Difficilis facilis, iūcundus acerbus es īdem:
Nec tēcum possum vīvere, nec sine tē.

—Martial, XII, 46.

[2] Say *himself is unfriendly to himself.*   [3] Use **ipse.**   [4] cōnfirmō
[5] Say *to elephants with.*

hortatory - Lets go.
Optative - wish
deliberative - what are we to do

Faciāmus dē necessitāte virtūtem.

Let us make a virtue of necessity.

—QUINTILIAN, *Institutio Oratoria*, I, 4, 22

LESSON XXXVIII

Introduction to the Subjunctive Mood

205. Subjunctive of *sum*.—

PRESENT		IMPERFECT	
SINGULAR	PLURAL	SINGULAR	PLURAL
si-m	sī-mus	esse-m	essē-mus
sī-s	sī-tis	essē-s	essē-tis
si-t	si-nt	esse-t	esse-nt

Int + ending

PERFECT		PLUPERFECT	
fu-erim	fu-erīmus	fuisse-m	fuissē-mus
fu-erīs	fu-erītis	fuissē-s	fuissē-tis
fu-erit	fu-erint	fuisse-t	fuisse-nt

(a) The imperfect subjunctive is formed by adding the personal endings to the present active infinitive. This is true of all verbs, e.g., amāre-m (act.), amāre-r (pass.); regere-m, regere-r; velle-m, etc.

(b) The perfect subjunctive active of all verbs is formed like fu-**erim** by adding -erim, -erīs, etc. to the perfect stem, e.g., amāv-**erim**, rēx-**erim**, volu-erim, etc.

(c) The pluperfect subjunctive active is formed by adding the personal endings to the perfect active infinitive: fuisse-**m**. So also, amāvisse-**m**, rēxisse-**m**, voluisse-**m**, etc.

174

206. Subjunctive of the four conjugations.—

utinam *would that*

ACTIVE

PRESENT

SINGULAR

I	II	III	III	IV
1. am-e-m	mone-a-m	reg-a-m	capi-a-m	audi-a-m
2. am-ē-s	mone-ā-s	reg-ā-s	capi-ā-s	audi-ā-s
3. am-e-t	mone-a-t	reg-a-t	capi-a-t	audi-a-t

PLURAL

1. am-ē-mus	mone-ā-mus	reg-ā-mus	capi-ā-mus	audi-ā-mus
2. am-ē-tis	mone-ā-tis	reg-ā-tis	capi-ā-tis	audi-ā-tis
3. am-e-nt	mone-a-nt	reg-a-nt	capi-a-nt	audi-a-nt

PASSIVE

PRESENT

SINGULAR

1. am-e-r	mone-a-r	reg-a-r	capi-a-r	audi-a-r
2. am-ē-ris,	mone-ā-ris,	reg-ā-ris,	capi-ā-ris,	audi-ā-ris,
(-re)	(-re)	(-re)	(-re)	(-re)
3. am-ē-tur	mone-ā-tur	reg-ā-tur	capi-ā-tur	audi-ā-tur

PLURAL

1. am-ē-mur	mone-ā-mur	reg-ā-mur	capi-ā-mur	audi-ā-mur
2. am-ē-minī	mone-ā-minī	reg-ā-minī	capi-ā-minī	audi-ā-minī
3. am-e-ntur	mone-a-ntur	reg-a-ntur	capi-a-ntur	audi-a-ntur

(a) The present subjunctive of the first conjugation is formed by changing final ō of the first principal part to **e** and adding the personal endings.

(b) The present subjunctive of the second, third, and fourth conjugations is formed by changing final ō of the first principal part to **a** and adding the personal endings.

(c) Write out the imperfect subjunctive active and passive of these verbs according to the rule given in **205** (a).

(d) Write out the perfect and pluperfect subjunctive active of these verbs according to the rules in **205** (b) and (c).

Just as the perfect and pluperfect indicative passive are formed by adding the present and imperfect indicative, respectively, of **sum** to the perfect passive participle, so the perfect and pluperfect subjunctive passive are formed by adding the present and imperfect subjunctive, respectively, of **sum** to the same participle.

PERFECT: **amātus sim**, etc.
PLUPERFECT: **amātus essem**, etc.

(e) Write the perfect and pluperfect subjunctive passive of the five model verbs.

(f) There is no future or future perfect subjunctive.

(g) No precise meanings can be assigned to the forms in the paradigms for the reason that the uses of the subjunctive are many and various. The subjunctive mood is used most extensively in dependent clauses, and the exact translation of any verb form will be determined by the nature of the clause in which it stands. These clauses will be treated in the subsequent lessons.

207. The subjunctive of the irregular verbs *eō, volō, nōlō, mālō*.—

PRESENT

eam	eās	eat	eāmus	eātis	eant
velim[1]	velīs	velit	velīmus	velītis	velint
nōlim[1]	nōlīs	nōlit	nōlīmus	nōlītis	nōlint
mālim[1]	mālīs	mālit	mālīmus	mālītis	mālint

Write the imperfect, perfect, and pluperfect subjunctive of these verbs.

208. The subjunctive mood in Latin.—As stated in secs. **39** and **206g**, no one meaning can be assigned to cover all uses of the subjunctive mood, and any attempt at an accurate definition will break down when tested by actual usage, yet an understanding of the use of the subjunctive is so essential to the reading of this language (and of its daughters, the Romance languages) that it may fairly be claimed that he who has mastered the Latin subjunctive has mastered Latin. English usage will prove a treacherous guide,

---

[1] **Velim, mālim**, and **nōlim**, when used independently, have the idiomatic meanings of *I would like, I would rather, I would rather not*, respectively.

for, as our language has grown simpler in structure, indicative and subjunctive forms have become almost identical until the subjunctive now has an archaic flavor and survives chiefly in the speech and writing of purists. Most surviving usages can be and usually are replaced by alternative expressions. Here are a few examples of the English subjunctive, with alternatives which avoid its use:

*I urge that this resolution **be** adopted.*
I urge the adoption of this resolution.

*If I **were** you, I should remain silent.*
In your position I should remain silent.

*Though he **slay** me, yet will I love him.*
In spite of all he may do to me, I will continue to love him.

*God **bless** you!*
I wish you God's blessing.

***Come** what may.*
In spite of any misfortune.

*Someone **tell** us what to do.*
Won't someone tell us what to do?

These alternatives show that English is usually content with the indicative or ingenious substitutes for a true mood such as the modal auxiliaries *may, might, could, should, would,* or imperatives like *let* + infinitive, just as in the use of nouns it avoids the necessity for case forms in most instances by an equally ingenious use of prepositions.

Latin, however, in a great variety of instances regards the **modus subjunctīvus** or **coniunctīvus**[2] as necessary to express many of those **inclīnātiōnēs animī** (39) which Priscian mentions in his definition of mood, even where English usage does not give us the slightest inkling of such necessity. Consider the following, in all of which Latin requires a subjunctive for the words in boldface type:

1. I was so tired that **I fell asleep.**
2. It happened that **there was** a full moon.
3. He was never one **to betray** a confidence.

---

[2] In older grammars the subjunctive used independently is often called the *conjunctive.*

4. You are afraid **he will** not **return.**
5. We came **to see** your house.
6. They never doubted **they would succeed.**
7. We wondered whether **he had seen** us.
8. The mountains are too high **to climb.**
9. One of them said that the Athenians knew what **was right** but were unwilling to practise it.
10. She persuaded us **to hear** her story.

Nor is the mood confined to subordinate clauses. It is far more probable that the dependent uses of the subjunctive have developed from the independent, as may be shown from the following:

Quamvīs *sit* validus eum nōn timeō.
Although he is strong I do not fear him.

This use developed from the independent use of **sit** in the sense of:

Let him be as strong as you wish—I do not fear him.

So it comes about that the Latin subjunctive is used to express, not facts which we indicate, but such things as events which owe their existence to preceding events (i.e., results), conceptions and fancies of the mind, images of the twilight world of the imagination, hypothetical cases, desires, fears, purposes, hopes for the future, regrets for what might have been, unfulfilled obligations (like Macbeth's "She should have died hereafter," **Posteā** *morerētur*), exhortations, statements or reasons put forward on authority other than our own, subordinate clauses in indirect statement, as well as "thoughts hardly to be packed into a narrow act." Study of all such usages, elusive at first acquaintance, will yield a rich reward in revealing the full meaning of the literature we read. First let us consider the independent subjunctive.

Nōmina dēclīnāre et verba in prīmīs puerī sciant.

First of all let youngsters know how to decline nouns and conjugate
verbs.

—QUINTILIAN, *Institutio Oratoria*, 1, 4, 22

LESSON XXXIX

Independent Uses of the Subjunctive: Jussive, Deliberative, Optative, and Concessive

209. Independent subjunctive.—The subjunctive mood is used
in independent sentences as follows:

(a) *Jussive subjunctive* (**iubeō**, perf. part. **iussus**, *order*).—The
present subjunctive is used in all three persons[1] to express a command
or exhortation. With the first person, this usage is often called
the *hortatory* (**hortor**, *urge*) subjunctive. Where a negative is required, **nē** is used.

Rōmam *eāmus*.	*Let us go to Rome.*
Nē **hōc cōnātū *dēsistāmus*.**	*Let us not give up this attempt.*
Sīs fēlīx.	*Be happy.*
Interficiantur **pīrātae.**	*Let the pirates be put to death.*

(b) *Deliberative subjunctive.*—The present and imperfect subjunctive may be used in independent questions that imply either doubt
or impossibility. Such questions are not asked for information,
but are uttered in perplexity and hesitation. Often they imply a
negative answer. The negative to be used with them is **nōn**.

---

[1] To express commands the second person of the present subjunctive seems to
be used in prose less frequently than the imperative. Where the second person
subjunctive does occur in this use, its subject is indefinite and the tone is more
polite and informal.

Quid *agam?*	*What **am I** to do?*
Quid *dīceret?*	*What **was** he **to say?*** (i.e., there was nothing for him to say).
Maneamne ūsque ad noctem?	*Am I to wait until night?*

(c) *Optative subjunctive* (**optō**, *wish*).—The present, imperfect, and pluperfect subjunctive may be used in independent sentences introduced by **utinam** to express a wish.

(1) The present expresses a wish for the future.

> **Utinam** id *sit* quod spērō.
> *Would that what I hope **may be.***

(2) The imperfect denotes a regret for the present or a present wish unfulfilled.

> **Utinam** virōrum fortium cōpiam tantam *habērētis.*
> *Would that you **had** [but you have not] so great a supply of brave men.*
> **Utinam** adhūc *vīveret.*
> *Would that he **were** still **alive.***

(3) The pluperfect denotes an unfulfilled wish in past time, i.e., a regret for the past.

> **Utinam, Pompeī,** cum C. Caesare societātem aut numquam *coīssēs* aut numquam *dirēmissēs.*
> *Pompey, would that **you had** either never **entered into** a partnership with Caesar or **had** never **dissolved** it.*

Observation.—The negative is **nē,** occasionally **nōn.**

(d) *In concessions, with or without* **ut** *(negative* **nōn**):

> Haec *sint* falsa sānē.
> *Granting this to be quite untrue.*
> Ut *nōn* omnis perītissimus *sim* bellī, cum Rōmānīs certē bellāre didicī.
> *Though I may not be highly skilled in every type of warfare, I have certainly learned how to wage war with the Romans.*

VOCABULARY

caveō, cavēre, cāvī, cautum, be on one's guard

ēloquor, ēloquī, ēlocūtus sum, speak out

ēmptor, -tōris, *m.*, buyer

improbus, -a, -um, wicked, dishonest

iūdex, iūdicis, *m.*, juryman

pereō, perīre, periī, peritum, die, be lost

rogō, *I*, ask

sēcernō, sēcernere, sēcrēvī, sēcrētum, keep apart

sinō, sinere, sīvī, situm, allow

taceō, tacēre, tacuī, tacitum, be silent

uxor, uxōris, *f.*, wife

EXERCISE A

1. Caveat ēmptor. Eāmus in forum. Nē errēs. Quem ego rogem?
2. Quid[2] ego tibi commendem eum quem tū ipse dīligis?
3. Taceant quī patriā carent.
4. Auxilium petās ab omnibus etiam ab īnfimīs.
5. Ēloquar an taceam?
6. Utinam frāter meus veniat.
7. Gāī et Gāia, fēlīx vīvās. Ūtāre istō bonō.
8. Ad clārās Asiae volēmus urbēs.
9. Ego dem hanc pecūniam iūdicibus?
10. Pereant quī ante nōs nostra dīxērunt.

EXERCISE B

1. Utinam nē pecūniae tam cupidus fuissem.
2. Postrēmus loquāris; prīmus taceās.
3. Discēdant improbī ex urbe nostrā; sēcernant sē ā bonīs; ūnum in locum cōgantur.
4. Utinam lēx esset eadem virō quae est uxōrī.
5. Quid ego nunc faciam? Domum īre cupiō, sed uxor nōn sinit.
6. Ut dēsint vīrēs, tamen laudanda est voluntās.
7. Sanctificētur nōmen Tuum; adveniat rēgnum Tuum; fīat[3] voluntās Tua.
8. Utinam līberōrum nostrōrum mōrēs nōn ipsī perderēmus.

---

[2] *Quid* often carries the same meaning as *cūr*. [3] See sec. **216.**

EXERCISE C

1. Would that my father were living!
2. Let us buy bread and wine in the market.
3. Let the sick boys be sent to the country.
4. Am I to wait here all day?
5. Let them not think that we are foolish.
6. Thy will be done.

SELECTIONS FOR READING

(1) . . . Moriāmur et in media arma ruāmus.
    Ūna salūs victīs nūllam spērare salūtem.
                                        —Vergil, *Aeneid*, II, 353–4.

(2) Omnia vincit amor: nōs et[4] cēdāmus amōrī.
                                        —Vergil, *Eclogues*, X, 69.

(3) Crās amet quī numquam amāvit quīque amāvit crās amet.
                                        —*Pervigilium Veneris*, 1.

(4) (*Atalanta loquitur*)
        Utinam dēsistere vellēs;
    Aut, quoniam[5] es dēmēns, utinam vēlōcior essēs.
                                        —Ovid, *Metamorphoses*, X, 629–30.

---

[4] For **et nōs**, word order due to meter. Translate "*Let us, too,*" etc.
[5] *since*

Hōrae quidem cēdunt et diēs et mēnsēs et annī, nec praeteritum tempus umquam revertitur, nec quid sequātur scīrī potest.

Hours, days, months and years pass; the past never returns; we cannot know what is to be.

—CICERO, *de Senectute*, 20

LESSON XL

Questions: Direct and Indirect—Subjunctive in Indirect Questions—Sequence of Tenses

210. Direct questions.—A direct question is put in the exact words of the speaker.

> **Ubi sunt?**   *Where are they?*

Direct questions, as you have already learned, are introduced by interrogative words like **ubi?**, **cūr?**, **quis?**, **an?**, or are indicated by the enclitic **-ne** (see Vocabulary, Lesson I). In addition, note the following:

(a) The interrogative particle **nōnne** introduces a question that expects the answer *Yes.*

> **Nōnne potes?**   *You can, can't you?*

(b) The interrogative particle **num** introduces a question that expects the answer *No.*

> **Num potes?**   *You can't, can you?*

(c) Double (disjunctive) questions are introduced by **utrum** or **-ne . . . an(nōn)**, *(whether) . . . or (not).*

> **Utrum manēbis, an excēdēs?** ⎱ *Will you stay, or will you*
> **Manēbisne, an excēdēs?**   ⎰ *depart?*
>
> **Utrum manēbis, annōn?**   ⎱
> **Manēbisne, annōn?**   ⎰ *Will you stay, or not?*

183

211. Indirect questions.—An indirect question quotes the substance of a direct question, adapting it to the form of the sentence in which it is quoted. It is a subordinate *noun* clause dependent on a verb or some other expression of asking, knowing, doubting, wondering, or any verb or expression capable of suggesting the interrogative idea.

DIRECT: *Did you go?* **Iistī-ne?**

INDIRECT: *Tell me **whether you went**.* **Dīc** mihi *num ierīs*.

Note the following:

(a) The verb of the indirect question is in the *subjunctive*.

(b) An indirect question must be introduced by an interrogative word like **num, quis,** etc.[1] **Num** in indirect questions means merely *if* or *whether*, and has no negative force as in direct questions.

Observation.—Where **ánnōn** is used in direct questions, **necne** is used in indirect.

Dī utrum sint *necne* sint quaeritur.

*It is asked whether the gods exist **or** do **not** exist.*

Notice that in syntax the indirect question is a *substantive* clause, being the object or (as above) the subject of the verb of asking.[2] The *indirect* reflexive (sec. **169b**) is used.

212. Sequence of tenses.—Review the definitions of *primary* and *secondary* (*historical*) tenses in sec. **34.** Note that the Latin perfect (usually secondary) may sometimes be a primary tense, i.e. **dūxī** may be translated *I led* (secondary) or *I have led* (primary). The primary tenses of the subjunctive mood are the *present* and *perfect*; the secondary, the *imperfect* and *pluperfect*.

In general, a primary tense in a main clause will be followed by a primary tense in a subordinate clause, and a secondary by a secondary. This principle is known as the *sequence of tenses*. In primary sequence, the present subjunctive is used to denote time contemporary with or subsequent to that of the main verb, and the perfect subjunctive to indicate time prior to that of the main verb. In secondary sequence, the imperfect denotes contemporary or subsequent time; the pluperfect time prior. This principle may be illustrated by the following table and examples:

---

[1] such as **quō,** *whither;* **quid,** *what;* **ubi,** *where;* **quibus auxiliīs,** *by what means;* **cūr,** *why;* **quōmodō,** *how;* **quando,** *when?*

[2] or in apposition to a noun or pronoun

PRIMARY SEQUENCE

INDICATIVE   SUBJUNCTIVE

PRESENT
FUTURE   ⎱⎧PRESENT (contemporary, subsequent)
(PERFECT)   ⎰⎩PERFECT (prior)
FUTURE PERFECT

SECONDARY SEQUENCE

IMPERFECT   ⎱⎧IMPERFECT (contemporary, subsequent)
PERFECT   ⎰⎩PLUPERFECT (prior)
PLUPERFECT

(1) **Rogō num librum *legat*.**
 *I ask whether he **is reading** the book.*   (Primary-contemporary)
 *I ask, "**Is** he **reading** the book?"*

(2) **Rogō num librum *lēgerit*.**
 *I ask whether he **has read** the book.*   (Primary-prior)
 *I ask, "**Has** he **read** the book?"*

(3) **Rogāvī num librum *legeret*.**
 *I asked whether he **was reading** the book.*(Secondary-contemporary)
 *I asked, "**Is** he **reading** the book?"*

(4) **Rogāvī num librum *lēgisset*.**
 *I asked whether he **had read** the book.*   (Secondary-prior)
 *I asked, "**Has** he **read** the book?"*

 (a) Though in primary sequence the present and in secondary sequence the imperfect subjunctive often look toward the future, in the case of *indirect questions* time *subsequent* to that of the main verb is expressed by the active periphrastic forms (see sec. **109**) -ūrus sim, etc., in primary sequence; -ūrus essem, etc., in secondary sequence.

(5) **Rogō num librum *lēctūrus sit*.**
 *I ask whether he **will read** the book.*   (Primary-subsequent)
 *I ask, "**Will** he **read** the book?"*

(6) **Rogāvī num librum *lēctūrus esset*.**
 *I asked whether he **would read** the book.*   (Secondary-subsequent)
 *I asked, "**Will** he **read** the book?"*

The following diagram summarizes these rules:

	Contemp.	Prior	Subsequent
PRIM.	Pres. Subj.	Perf. Subj.	A. & P. Periph. + sim
SEC.	Impf. Subj.	Ppf. Subj.	A. & P. Periph. + essem

213. Indirect questions and relative clauses distinguished.—
Since the pronouns *who, which* and *what* may be either interrogative
or relative, an indirect question may closely resemble a relative
clause. The following distinctions should be noted:

(a) Clauses introduced by relative pronouns or adverbs always
have an antecedent expressed or understood in the main clause.
The whole relative clause is never the subject or object of the main
verb, whereas indirect questions are regularly so used.

(b) An interrogative clause involves a direct question; a relative
clause does not.

(c) A relative clause always asserts or assumes something as a
fact with no accessory notion.

The following example illustrates the difference between the two
constructions:

> *This is the officer **who chose the route**.* (Relative)
> *The general asked **who chose the route**.* (Indirect Question)

VOCABULARY

ancilla, -ae, *f.*, maid-servant
arbitror, *I*, think, believe; decide
captīvus, -ī, *m.*, captive, prisoner
clam, *adv.*, secretly
conventus, conventūs, *m.*, a coming together, assembly
convocō, *I*, call together, assemble
dēserō, -serere, -seruī, -sertum, abandon, desert, forsake
doceō, docēre, docuī, doctum, show, teach, instruct, inform

ignōrō, *I*, not know, be ignorant
nesciō, nescīre, *etc.*, not to know, be unaware
obses, obsidis, *c.*, hostage
ostendō, -tendere, -tendī, -tentum, present, show; declare
recipiō, -cipere, -cēpī, -ceptum, take *or* get back, recover
rogō, *I*, ask
tum, *adv.*, then

EXERCISE A

1. Servusne es an līber?
2. Nōnne dīxī esse hoc futūrum?
3. Num barbarōrum Rōmulus rēx fuit?

4. Utrum prō ancillā mē habēs an prō fīliā?

5. Sciō quid cōnēre.

6. Ego quid nārrēs nesciō.

7. Loquere quid velīs.

8. Ego quid agās nesciō.

9. Mīror unde sit.

10. Quaesīvērunt ā mē ubi esset pecūnia.

11. Rogant mē servī quō crās itūrus sim.

12. Deōs nōn cūrāre opīnor quid agat hūmānum genus.

13. Omnēs nōs scīmus quam miserē hanc amāverit.

14. Quid āctūrus esset scīvī.

15. Nōn quaerō ā tē quārē Sex. Roscius patrem occīderit; quaerō quō modō occīderit.

EXERCISE B

1. Tē nōn nōvimus; nescīmus quis sīs; numquam tē ante vīdimus.

2. Quis sim sciēs ex eō quem ad tē mīsī.

3. Quaerēs ā nōbīs cūr hōc homine dēlectēmur.

4. Quid superiōre nocte ēgerīs, ubi fuerīs, quōs convocāverīs, quid cōnsilī cēperīs, quem nostrum ignōrāre arbitrāris?

5. Quaesīvī ā Catilīnā utrum in nocturnō conventū fuisset necne.

6. Tum ostendī litterās Lentulō, et quaesīvī num cognōsceret manum.

7. Nōnne in Hispāniā rēs gestās Caesaris audīvistis? duōs pulsōs[3] exercitūs, duōs superātōs ducēs, duās receptās[3] prōvinciās?

8. Vōsne vērō L. Domitium, an vōs Domitius dēseruit? Nōnne sibi clam salūtem fugā petīvit?

9. Ibi ex captīvīs cognōscit quae apud Cicerōnem gerantur quantōque in perīculō rēs sit.

EXERCISE C

(1) Tell me why you came to Rome and what you are doing here.
(2) He told us that he was a-leading-man[4] among the Gauls, that he had gathered together many troops, and would lead them against the Germans. (3) We asked them who they were, where they had been, and why they had left (their) friends at home. (4) I wonder when[5] we shall see the city of Athens.

[3] Supply esse. Where the future active and perfect passive infinitives are used in an indirect statement, esse is often omitted.

[4] princeps   [5] When in indirect questions is rendered by quando.

Vertere Graeca in Latīnum veterēs nostrī ōrātōrēs optimum iūdicābant.

Our orators of earlier days considered it an excellent practice to translate passages of Greek into Latin.

—QUINTILIAN, *Institutio Oratoria*, X, 5, 2

LESSON XLI

Review Exercises on Subjunctive and Infinitive*

EXERCISE A

1. Alexandrīae dē Pompeī morte cognōscit.
2. Omnēs alacrēs et fīdūciae plēnī ad Alesiam proficīscuntur.
3. Et quid agās quidque agātur certior fīerī (pass. infin. of **faciō**) volō.
4. Utinam ita velint superī (= deī).
5. Cautus sīs, mī Tīrō. (*Tiro, Cicero's secretary.*)
6. Capiat quī capere potest. (*Catch as catch can.*)
7. Nūllam crēdō mulierem mē miseriōrem vīvere.
8. Ego rūs mē abitūram hinc esse cum tuō dēcrēvī patre.
9. Faciam quod vultis ut (*so far as*) poterō.
10. Abī intrō ac mē vēnisse nūntiā.
11. Nēmō plūs iūris in alium trānsferre potest quam ipse habet.

EXERCISE B

1. Caesar intellēxit frūstrā tantum labōrem sūmī.
2. Cicerō Pompeium habēre magnum ūsum in rē mīlitārī sciēbat.
3. Equitēs ex Cyprō dēcēdere iussī.
4. Accipere quam facere iniūriam praestat.
5. Nihil tibi dulcius esse dēbet quam patria.
6. Omnibus Gallīs idem est faciendum quod Helvētiī fēcērunt.
7. Quae ego vīdī Athēnīs! Quae aliīs in urbibus Graeciae!
8. Putātisne vōs illīs rēbus fruī posse?

---

* For unfamiliar words, consult general vocabulary.

9. Tē inimīcum mihi esse arbitror.

10. Quae quidem rēs Caesarī non minōrem quam ipsa victōria voluptātem attulit.

11. Mē parum patriae amantem esse exīstimant.

EXERCISE C

1. Nōn possumus eius imperia diūtius sustinēre.

2. Equidem soleō ante lūcem surgere.

3. Helvētiōs in fīnēs suōs unde erant profectī revertī iussit.

4. In animō habeō exīre domō.

5. Hoc certē Tullia tē facere nōn vult.

6. Bellum mē gerere cum Iugurthā iussistis.

7. Nōn satis mē nōvistī quālis sim.

8. Quid dē vītā, quid de ingeniō Cicerōnis sentiam audīvistī.

9. Mīlitēs ā centuriōnibus rogant ubi castra pōnenda sint.

10. Quid sī (*if*) nōn veniet? Maneamne ūsque ad noctem?

11. Ipse iubet mortis tē meminisse deus.

EXERCISE D

1. Druidēs quid deī velint scīre profitentur.

2. Quis sit aut unde nesciō.

3. Quam prīmum intellegere volō utrum apud vōs pudor an timor plūs valeat.

4. In utram partem fluat flūmen iūdicārī nōn potest.

5. Intellegō quantō cum perīculō id fēcerīs.

6. Ad tē quid scrībam nesciō.

7. Eius reī quae causa esset mīrātus ex ipsīs quaesiit.

8. Nōn quā viā sententia eius possit mūtārī sciō.

9. Quae agat, quibuscum loquātur scīre volō.

10. Huic utinam aliquandō grātiam referre possīmus! (Grātiam) habēbimus quidem semper.

11. Iamne oblītus es quid inter nōs sit dictum?

EXERCISE E

1. Perterritī, vōce et vultū cōnfessī sunt sē epistulās accēpisse, sed (eās) excidisse in viā.

2. Huius operā Gallī, ut anteā dēmōnstrāvimus, fidēlī atque
ūtilī superiōribus annīs erat ūsus in Britanniā Caesar.

3. Rōmam erat nūntiātum cum paucīs inermibus perterritīs metū
frāctō animō fūgisse Antōnium.

4. Sē suōsque omnēs in officiō futūrōs[1] neque ab amīcitiā populī
Rōmānī dēfectūrōs cōnfīrmāvit.

5. Certīs ex aquā mēnsūrīs (i.e., *water clock*) breviōrēs esse quam
in continentī noctēs vidēbāmus.

6. Is sine hāc iūrābat (*swear*) sē ūnum numquam vīctūrum diem.

7. Utinam Catilīna omnēs sēcum suās cōpiās ēdūxisset.

8. Dīcere solitus est sē Athēnīs, praeclārā in urbe Graecōrum,
adulēscentem multōs audīvisse philosophōs.

9. Quī sēcum loquī poterit sermōnem alterīus nōn requīret.

10. Initiō hiemis in Illyricum profectus est, quod (*because*) eās
quoque nātiōnēs adīre et regiōnēs cognōscere volēbat.

11. Caesar Dumnorīgem sēcum habēre cōnstituerat quod eum
cupidum rērum novārum, cupidum imperī cognōverat.

EXERCISE F

1. Magnō (pretiō) illa eī cūnctātiō[2] stetit,[3] nam fīlium intrā
paucōs diēs āmīsit.

2. Hiemis enim nōn avāritiae perfugium māiōrēs nostrī in sociōrum tectīs esse voluērunt.

3. Reī frūmentāriae magna vīlitās cōnsecūta est, ūnīus hominis
spē ac nōmine.

4. Aliae nātiōnēs servitūtem patī possunt; populī Rōmānī est
propria lībertās.

5. Numquam ante hoc tempus exercitus populī Rōmānī Galliae
prōvinciae fīnibus ēgressus est.

6. Ex innocentiā nāscitur dignitās; ex dignitāte honor; ex honōre
imperium; ex imperiō lībertās.

7. Neque sum nescius quantīs oneribus premāris susceptārum
rērum.

8. Exspectāvit si[4] trānsīrent.

9. Ego dē tē ad Caesarem quam dīligenter scrīpserim tūte[5] scīs;
quam saepe, ego.

---

[1] *remain loyal*   [2] *delay*   [3] *cost*
[4] With expressions of trying, hoping, or expecting, a single indirect question
may be introduced by **sī**.   [5] an intensive form of **tū**

10. Caesar reperīre non poterat:
    ubi hostēs castra pōnerent.
    ubi hostēs castra posuissent.
    ubi hostēs castra positūrī essent.

EXERCISE G

1. Nōn arbitror esse praetermittendum quem ad modum exercitūs utrīusque fuerint in aciem īnstructī.

2. Ariovistus, rēx Germānōrum, in eōrum fīnibus cōnsēdit terti-amque partem agrī Sēquanī, quī est optimus tōtīus Galliae, occupāvit, et nunc dē alterā parte tertiā Sēquanōs dēcēdere iubet.

3. Caesar, Aegyptō atque Alexandrīā potītus, rēgēs cōnstituit quōs Ptolemaeus testāmentō scrīpserat.

4. At nōbīs est domī inopia, forīs aes aliēnum; mala rēs, spēs multō asperior; dēnique quid reliquī habēmus praeter miseram animam?

5. Per explōrātōrēs Caesar certior factus est trēs iam partēs cōpiārum Helvētiōs id flūmen trādūxisse.[6]

6. Arcessītōs sociōrum lēgātōs interrogāvit cūr in tālī tempore et sē[7] dēserere et ipsōrum[8] lībertātem prōdere vellent.

---

[6] **Trādūxisse** has, besides its accusative subject **Helvētiōs**, two accusative objects, one belonging to **dūxisse**, the other governed by the **trā-(trāns)** of the compound verb.

[7] indirect reflexive   [8] to avoid ambiguity

Est ūnus quisque faber ipse fortūnae suae.

Every single man is the fashioner of his own destiny.

—APPIUS CLAUDIUS

Lesson XLII

Indefinite Pronouns *Quis, Aliquis, Quisquam, Quisque*

214. Indefinite pronouns.—

quis, *anyone, anything, any* (without emphasis)

	PRONOUN		ADJECTIVE		
	M. AND F.	N.	M.	F.	N.
NOM.	quis	quid	quī	qua	quod
ACC.	quem	quid	quem	quam	quod

In the other cases, singular and plural, the indefinite is like the relative, except that **qua** is used in the neuter nominative and accusative plural.

Quis is most commonly used with **sī, nisi, nē,** and **num** (*if, unless, lest, whether*), and the comparatives **quō,** *in proportion,* and **quantō,** *in exact proportion.* It cannot begin a sentence. **Quis** often appears for **quī.**

Rogāvī num *quem* vīdisset.
*I asked whether he had seen **anyone.***

Quō *quis* honestior, eō beātior.
*The more honorable **a man** is, the happier he is.*

Sī *quid* cognōvistī, loquere.
*If you have learned **anything,** speak.*

aliquis, *someone, something, some*

192

	M.	F.	N.
Pron.	aliquis	aliquis	aliquid (Declined like **quis**, above.)
Adj.	aliquī	aliqua	aliquod (Declined like **quī**, above.)

Note: **Aliquis** often appears for **aliquī**.

When *someone* may be substituted for *anyone* in the English without altering the sense, **aliquis** may be used.

> **dīxerit aliquis** *some one will say*
> **Nēmō est sine *aliquā* virtūte.**   *No one is without **some** good quality.*

But:

> **sine *ūllā* virtūte**   *without **any** good quality*

> **quisque,** *each, each by himself*

	M.	F.	N.
Pron.	quisque	quisque	quidque
Adj.	quīque	quaeque	quodque

Declined like the interrogative adjective and pronoun, secs. **132, 133.** It is used in the singular only and is usually postpositive.

> **Quod *cuique* obtigit, id *quisque* teneat.**
> *Let **each** man retain what has fallen to his lot.*

In short, **quis, aliquis,** and **quisque** are inflected like the interrogative pronoun and adjective except that **quis** and **aliquis** have **qua** in nominative feminine singular of the adjective and in nominative and accusative neuter plural of adjective and pronoun.

Observation.—Note the idiomatic use of **quisque** with superlatives, **optimus quisque,** *all the best men;* **tertiō quōque verbō,** *at every other word.*

215. Quisquam, *anyone at all* (with emphasis)—

	M. AND F.	N.	NO PLURAL
Pron.	quisquam	quicquam *or* quidquam	

It is declined like **quis,** above, except that the entire ablative singular is supplied by **ūllus, -a, -um,** which is used also as the adjective corresponding to **quisquam.**

Quisquam is used chiefly in sentences which are negative or virtually negative, i.e., which imply some sort of negation. These fall into three main types:
   (a) Questions expecting the answer 'no.'

> **Potest *quicquam* esse absurdius?**
> *Can **anything** be more absurd?*
> = **Nihil potest esse absurdius.**

   (b) Sentences containing such words as **vix** (*hardly*), **aegrē** (*scarcely*), **paene** (*nearly, almost*):

> ***Vix quisquam* hoc negāre potest.**
> *Hardly anyone can deny this.*

Compare English:

> *Hardly a man is now alive*
> *Who remembers that famous day and year.*

   (c) Sentences containing comparatives:

> **Fidēlior es quam *quisquam* tuōrum.**
> *You are more faithful than **any** of your countrymen.*

VOCABULARY

absurdus, -a, -um, absurd
avāritia, -ae, *f.,* greed, avarice
concertō, *I,* strive
conflīgō, -flīgere, -flīxī, -flīctum, struggle
diūturnus, -a, -um, lasting, enduring

extrēmus, -a, -um, final, having an end
illūstris, -e, bright, dazzling
ineptus, -a, -um, silly
prūdenter, wisely, shrewdly
senīlis, -e, of old age, pertaining to an old man

EXERCISE A

1. Negāvērunt sē quemquam audīvisse.
2. Haec optimus quisque sentit.
3. Audīvistīne aliquid novī?
4. Īs saepius cum hostibus cōnflīxit quam quisquam cum inimīcīs concertāvit.

5. Fortissima quaeque cōnsilia tūtissima sunt.
6. Sūmat sibi quisque quod grātum est animō.
7. Omnēs in medium[1] dabant quod quisque pecūniae habēbat.
8. Fortior fuit lēgātus quam quisquam[2] mīlitum.
9. Sōlis candor[3] illūstrior est quam (candor) ūllīus ignis.
10. Mīror quōmodō tam ineptum quicquam tibi venīre in mentem potuerit.

EXERCISE B

1. Nōn sine aliquō metū ad leōnem appropinquābāmus.
2. Iūris praecepta sunt haec: honestē vīvere, alterum nōn laedere, suum cuique tribuere.
3. Avāritia vērō senīlis quid sibi velit nōn intellegō; potest enim quicquam esse absurdius quam, quō viae minus restat, eō plūs viāticī[4] quaerere?
4. Num igitur aliquis (= aliquī) dolor post mortem est?
5. Ūnus quisque Hannibalī adulēscentī aliquid, fraudāns[5] sē ipse vīctū suō, contulit.
6. Nōn perfectum est quidquam quō melius est aliud.
7. Nēmō unquam[6] ad ūllam eiusmodī virtūtem sine dīvīnō aliquō afflātū[7] pervēnit.
8. Vēnī Athēnās neque[8] mē quisquam ibi agnōvit.[9]
9. Tempus est pars quaedam aeternitātis.
10. Ut enim adulēscentem in quō est senīle aliquid, sīc senem in quō est aliquid adulēscentis probō.

EXERCISE C

(1) We can say that we haven't seen a soul. (2) She has gone away from Thebes and no one can find her. (3) If anyone at all is afraid, I am he. (4) Each man sought his own safety. (5) They returned to the country as soon as possible, but could not find anyone

[1] In medium, lit. *into the midst, out into the open,* in this context means *to a common fund.*
[2] The negation here implied is that none of his soldiers was as brave as he.
[3] *brightness*   [4] viāticum, -ī, *n.,* journey money   [5] fraudō, *I,* cheat, deprive
[6] Latin prefers this to numquam quisquam.   [7] afflātus, -ūs, *m., inspiration*
[8] Neque quisquam is preferred to et nēmō; but nēmō and nihil are preferred to nōn quisquam and nōn quicquam.   [9] agnōscō, *recognize*

at home.   (6) Some philosophers think that the soul is immortal.
(7) Not without some tears did the boy leave his mother.   (8) Without a sign of (ūllus) fear, the two centurions drew close to (approached) the enemy's camp.

Vae, putō, deus fīō.

Dear me, I think I'm turning into a god.

—THE EMPEROR VESPASIAN *on his death-bed*

LESSON XLIII ⟨start⟩

Irregular Verb *Fīō*—Subordinate Clauses in Indirect Statement

216. Conjugation of *fīō, be made, become, happen.*—This verb serves also as the passive of **faciō and is conjugated as follows:

PRINCIPAL PARTS: **fīō, fierī, factus sum**

		INDICATIVE		SUBJUNCTIVE	
		SINGULAR	PLURAL	SINGULAR	PLURAL
PRES.	1.	fīō	——	fīam	fīāmus
	2.	fīs	——	fīās	fīātis
	3.	fit	fīunt	fīat	fīant
IMP.		fīēbam, etc.		fierem, fierēs, etc.	
FUT.		fīam, fīēs, fīet, etc.		—— ——	
PERF.		factus sum, etc.		factus sim, etc.	
PLUP.		factus eram, etc.		factus essem, etc.	
FUT. PERF.		factus erō, etc.			

	IMPERATIVE		INFINITIVES	
PRES.	fī	fīte	PRES.	fierī
			FUT.	(factum īrī)
			PERF.	factus esse

PARTICIPLES

PERF. factus   FUT. (GERUNDIVE)   faciendus

Observation.—The prepositional compounds of **faciō**, e.g., **cōnficiō**, **afficiō**, etc., have the regular passive forms of the third conjugation -**iō** verbs like **capiō**.

197

217. The verb of a clause that is a subordinate part of an "infinitive clause" in indirect statement is generally in the subjunctive mood.

DIRECT

Mōns quem ā Labiēnō occupārī *voluit* ab hostibus tenētur.

*The mountain which he **wished** to be seized by Labienus is held by the enemy.*

INDIRECT

Dīcit montem quem ā Labiēnō occupārī *voluerit* ab hostibus tenērī.

*He says that the mountain which he **wished** to be seized by Labienus is held by the enemy.*

VOCABULARY

certiōrem faciō (*pass.* **certior fīō**), inform (*pass.* be informed)
dēnique, *adv.*, finally
dēvincō, dēvincere, dēvīcī, dēvictum, conquer thoroughly
discēdō, discēdere, discessī, discessum, go away, depart
frōns, frontis (frontium), *f.*, forehead
fulmen, fulminis, *n.*, lightning
incognitus, -a, -um, unknown
inquam, I say, *defective verb*
īnscrībō, īnscrībere, īnscrīpsī, īnscrīptum, write on, inscribe
īnstitūtum, -ī, *n.*, established practice, custom

inūtilis, -e, useless
magnitūdō, -tūdinis, *f.*, size
mercātor, -tōris, *m.*, merchant
nōtus, -a, -um, known
obses, obsidis, *m.*, hostage
palūs, palūdis, *f.*, marsh, swamp
polliceor, pollicērī, pollicitus sum, promise
praeter, *prep. with acc.*, beyond, past; except
temerē, *adv.*, rashly, without good reason
timidus, -a, -um, afraid
ūsus, -ūs, *m.*, practice, practical experience *or* skill

EXERCISE A

1. Fīat lūx!
2. Plūrima aestāte fīunt fulmina.
3. Certior per mē iīs dē omnibus rēbus.
4. Sī[1] quis est timidus, is ego sum.

[1] *if*

5. Quaerō utrum aliquid āctum sit an nihil.

6. Dēfendat² quod quisque sentit.

7. Exspectābam aliquem meōrum.

8. Neque ex castrīs Catilīnae quisquam omnium discesserat.

9. Ex eā rē quid fīat vide.

10. Caesarem certiōrem faciunt sēsē nōn facile ab oppidīs vim hostium prohibēre.

11. Sit dēnique īnscrīptum in fronte unīus cuiusque quid dē rē-pub-līcā sentiat.

12. Pollicitus iīs sum mē omnia quae vellent esse factūrum.

13. Dīxit Haeduōs, quī plūrimum ante in Galliā potuissent, iam coāctōs esse Sēquanīs obsidēs dare.

14. Inveniēbat ex captīvīs Nerviōs omnēs mulierēs et eōs quī per aetātem ad pugnam inūtilēs vidērentur in palūdēs collocāvisse.

15. Ennius tria corda habēre sēsē dīcēbat, quod loquī Graecē et Oscē et Latīnē scīret.

16. "Nōlī," inquit, "exīstimāre, Pompeī, hunc esse exercitum quī Galliam Germāniamque dēvīcerit."

17. Sati'n sānus es?³ Ego novus marītus⁴ annō dēmum quintō et sexāgēsimō fīam atque ānum⁵ dēcrepitam dūcam⁶?

EXERCISE B

(1) The merchants informed the general about the harbors of Britain. (2) The sailors tell us that there is in the ocean an island which is called Britain. (3) Lucius said that the book which he was reading was written by a famous philosopher. (4) These animals cannot be captured by anyone. (5) Let each one of you buy for himself a small field.

SELECTION FOR READING

Britannia īnsula omnibus ferē Gallīs erat incognita neque enim temerē praeter mercātōrēs illō⁷ adībat quisquam neque hīs ipsīs quicquam praeter ōram maritimam atque eās regiōnēs quae sunt contrā Galliam nōtum erat.

---

² Quisque is in sense the subject of both verbs.
³ *Are you crazy?* Satis-ne sānus = īnsānus. ⁴ *bridegroom* ⁵ *old woman*
⁶ *lead (to the altar), marry* ⁷ illō, *to that place*

Caesar neque quanta esset īnsulae magnitūdō, neque quae aut quantae nātiōnēs incolerent, neque quem ūsum bellī habērent aut quibus īnstitūtīs ūterentur, neque quī essent idōneī portūs reperīre poterat.

—Adapted from Caesar, *de Bello Gallico*, IV, 20.

Imperat aut servit collecta pecūnia cuique.

To each man money is either master or slave.

—HORACE, *Epistles* I, x, 47

LESSON XLIV

Dative with Verbs

218. Dative with certain intransitive verbs.—Several Latin verbs take a dative where their English equivalents take a direct object. The following, given here for reference, are the commonest:

> **crēdō, crēdere, crēdidī, crēditum,** *entrust to, believe*
> **faveō, favēre, fāvī, fautum,** *be favorable to, favor*
> (**fīdō, fīdere, fīsus sum**) See sec. **180.**
> **cōnfīdō,** etc., *have faith in, trust;* **diffīdō,** *distrust*
> **grātulor,** *I, congratulate*
> **ignōscō, ignōscere, ignōvī, ignōtum,** *make excuses for, forgive*
> **imperō,** *I, give orders to, command*
> **indulgeō, indulgēre, indulsī,** ——, *be kind to, indulge*
> **īrāscor, īrāscī, īrātus sum,** *be angry with*
> **noceō, nocēre, nocuī, nocitum,** *be injurious to, harm*
> **nūbō, nūbere, nūpsī, nūptum,** *take the veil for, marry* (said of the woman)
> **parcō, parcere, pepercī, parsum,** *spare*
> **pāreō, pārēre, pāruī,** ——, *be obedient to, obey*
> **placeō, placēre, placuī, placitum,** *be pleasing to, please*
> **resistō, resistere, restitī,** ——, *be opposed to, resist*
> **serviō,** *IV, be slave to, serve*
> **studeō, studēre, studuī,** ——, *be eager for, desire*
> (**suādeō, suādēre, suāsī, suāsum**)
> **persuādeō,** etc., *make acceptable to, advise, persuade*

(a) Like all intransitive verbs in Latin, the above cannot be used in the passive except impersonally.

Omnēs *tibi* favent.   *All men favor you.*

Tibi ab omnibus *favētur*.   *Favor is shown you by all (i.e.,*
          you are favored by all).

(b) This impersonal passive of intransitive verbs, a usage entirely
foreign to English, is most characteristic of Latin and should be
studied in the following expressions:

Pugnātum est.   *Fighting occurred.*

Sīc *ītur* ad astra.   *Such is the path to the stars.*

Tōtīs castrīs *trepidātur*.   *There is confusion all over the*
          camp.

Quoniam ad hunc locum *perventum est*.
Since we have reached this point (in our narrative).

Pervenīrī ad summa nisi ex principiīs *nōn potest*.
You cannot attain the heights unless you begin with fundamentals.

219. Dative with verbs compounded with preposition.—Many
verbs when compounded with certain prepositions take a dative
where the force of the preposition requires a word to complete the
sense.   These fall into two classes:

(a) *Intransitive.*—Where the simple verb, like **sum** or **veniō**, can
by itself govern no case whatever, it will, when compounded with the
preposition, govern a dative only.

Legiōnī *praesum*.   *I am over a legion (i.e., I am in com-*
          mand of a legion).

Tibi *sub*veniō.   *I come up under you (i.e., I support,*
          or help, you).

Multa petentibus *dē*sunt multa.
To those who seek much, much is lacking.

(b) *Transitive.*—Where the simple verb can, like **faciō**, govern a
direct object (accusative), it will, when compounded with the preposition, retain its direct object and govern a dative in addition.

Tē legiōnī *prae*fēcī.   *I placed you in command of a legion.*

Bellum *Gallīs* inferimus.   *We make war upon the Gauls.*

Bellum *Gallīs* indīcimus.   *We declare war upon the Gauls.*

Even with the passive, this dative is retained:

Tū *legiōnī* ā mē praefectus es.

You were placed in command of a legion by me.

Nōbīs nihil *obicī* potest.

We are open to no reproach.

Observation.—It will be noticed that in the instances above the force of the preposition requires a word to complete the sense. Several compounds of simple verbs are *transitive*, and take an accusative which is the direct object of the simple verb. In such compounds the prefix governs no noun but has merely an adverbial force. Consider the following list:

cōnscrībō, *enroll*
cōnsequor, *follow up, overtake*
convocō, *call together, assemble*
interclūdō, *shut off, hinder*

interficiō, *kill*
praemittō, *send ahead*
prohibeō, *prevent*
sustineō, *uphold, withstand, endure*

Note that the *general* vocabulary, by references to sec. **219**, indicates which intransitive and which transitive verbs govern the dative when compounded with prepositions.

VOCABULARY

antepōnō, -pōnere, -posuī, -positum, prefer

cōnsuētūdō, -dinis, *f.*, custom, precedent

dēsum, dēesse, dēfuī, dēfutūrus, be lacking, fail

intersum, interesse, interfuī, interfutūrus, take part in, be present at

praesum, praeësse, praefuī, praefutūrus, be in command of

praestō, praestāre, praestitī, praestitum, be superior to, excel

prūdentia, -ae, *f.*, prudence, foresight

tener, tenera, tenerum, tender, young

ūtilitās, -tātis, *f.*, usefulness, expediency

vetus, *adj.* (*gen.* veteris), old

EXERCISE A

1. Nihil est, mihi crēde, virtūte pulchrius.
2. Decimae legiōnī Caesar maximē cōnfidēbat.
3. Hūmānī generis est bonīs[1] aliēnīs invidēre.
4. Hīs rēbus nōn interfuit sōlum sed praefuit.
5. Maiōrēs nostrī prūdentiā cēterīs gentibus praestitērunt.

---

[1] What is the gender of bonīs?

6. Labiēnum rogāvit num omnibus Caesaris proeliīs interfuisset.

7. Praeceptīs tuīs pārēre cupiō.

8. Maiōrēs nostrī semper in pāce cōnsuētūdinī, in bellō ūtilitātī pārēbant.

9. Negāvit sē umquam nōbīs esse nocitūrum.

10. Omnibus hīs, ōrātiōnibus resistitur.

11. Antepōnātur omnibus Pompeius.

12. Equīs veteribus tenerōs anteponere solēmus: amīcī veterēs novīs sunt antepōnendī.

13. Cōnsul reī pūblicae sē nōn dēfutūrum[2] pollicētur.

14. Omnēs nunc in eīs locīs intellegunt nōn sine causā maiōrēs suōs servīre populō Rōmānō quam imperāre aliīs māluisse.

EXERCISE B

(1) I used to ask him why men were superior to other animals. (2) You have been put in charge of this city. Why do you attempt to hurt us? (3) He said that Pompey would not fail the common-wealth. (4) For three hours we resisted the charges of the cavalry. (5) The scouts informed the tribunes that the higher places had been seized by the enemy.

SELECTIONS FOR READING

(1) Ōdī[3] et amō. Quārē id faciam fortasse[4] requīris.
 Nescio, sed fierī sentiō et excrucior.[5]

—Catullus, 85.

(2) Nōn ignāra[6] malī, miserīs succurrere discō.[7]

—Vergil, *Aeneid*, I, 630.

(3) Victrīx[8] causa deīs placuit, sed victa Catōnī.

—Lucan, *Pharsalia*, I, 128.

---

[2] Supply esse.   [3] *I hate* (see appendix **54**)   [4] *perhaps*   [5] *am in agony*
[6] *without knowledge (of)*   [7] *I learn*   [8] *victorious*

Nam verbōrum proprietās ac differentia omnibus quī sermōnem cūrae habent dēbet esse commūnis.

As for precise meanings and nice distinctions between words, they should be a subject of study common to all who have any regard for language.

—QUINTILIAN, *Institutio Oratoria* I, Prooemium, 16

LESSON XLV

Datives of Purpose and Reference

220. Dative of reference.—The dative is frequently used in dependence, not on any particular word, but on the general meaning of the sentence, to indicate the *person* (rarely the *thing*) *concerned or interested.* Compare the English, "Villain, I say, knock **me** at this gate and rap **me** well."—*The Taming of the Shrew*, I, 2, 11–12. "*Heat* **me** *these irons hot.*"—*King John*, IV, I, 1.

> **Laudāvit** *mihi* **frātrem.** *He praised* **me** *my brother* (i.e., *he praised my brother* **out of regard for me**).

221. Dative of purpose.—The dative is used to express *purpose* or *tendency.* It is commonly used in the predicate after **sum**, meaning *to serve as.*

> **Hoc mihi** *gaudiō* **est.** *This is* (*serves as*) *a joy to me.*

It is also frequent in such expressions as **auxiliō, subsidiō,** etc., in combination with verbs like **mittō** and **veniō.**

> **Caesar trēs legiōnēs** *auxiliō* **urbis dēfēnsōribus mīsit.**
> *Caesar sent three legions* (*to serve*) *as an aid to the defenders of the city.*

This dative is frequently used in connection with the dative of reference. Note **mihi** and **dēfēnsōribus** above and **Rōmānīs** in the example below.

Observation 1.—The dative of purpose or predicative dative is found in the singular only and almost always in conjunction with the adjectives of quantity **magnus, maior, maximus, tantus,** and **quantus.** Only when this dative is used with **sum** does any adjective modify it.

Observation 2.—**Odiō esse,** *to be an object of hatred to,* forms a passive voice to the defective verb **ōdī,** *I hate.* Thus Hannibal said at the close of his life

Ōdī *odiōque* **sum Rōmānīs.**
*I hate the Romans and **am hated** by them.*

VOCABULARY

adimō, adimere, adēmī, adēmptum, take away, remove
adversus, *prep. w. acc.,* against
classis, -is, *f.,* fleet
Crētēnsis, -e, of Crete, Cretan
dēditiō, -ōnis, *f.,* surrender
ērudiō, *IV,* teach, instruct
habeō fidem + *dat.,* have confidence in
immisceō, immiscēre, immiscuī, immixtum, mix in; **sē imm.,** concern one's self (with, *dat.*)
impedīmentum, -ī, *n.,* hindrance
īnsignis, -e, marked, conspicuous

iuventūs, -tūtis, *f.,* youth, young-manhood
mūnus, mūneris, *n.,* gift, boon
Pamphȳlius, -a, -um, Pamphylian
pertineō, pertinēre, pertinuī, ——, belong, have reference to
praecipuē, *adv.,* especially
praesidium, -dī, *n.,* garrison, protection
Rhodius, -a, -um, of Rhodes, Rhodian
subsidium, -dī, *n.,* assistance
Syria, -ae, *f.,* Syria

EXERCISE A

1. Mihi impedīmentō estis.
2. Ex Gallīs eī maximam fidem Caesar habēbat.
3. Nōn ego Gallīs sed Gallī mihi bellum intulērunt.
4. Haec pars cīvitātis Helvētiae īnsignem calamitātem populō Rōmānō intulerat.
5. Haec rēs summae mihi voluptātī est.
6. Quid huius audāciae et scelerī poterat oppōnī?
7. Decimae legiōnī Caesar et indulserat praecipuē et propter virtūtem cōnfīdēbat maximē.
8. Pompeius Crētēnsibus spem dēditiōnis nōn adēmit obsidēsque imperāvit.

9. Is P. Āfricānō vim attulisse existimātus est.
10. Clāmor post tergum pugnantibus exstitit.[1]

EXERCISE B

1. Hīs difficultātibus duae rēs erant subsidiō: scientia atque ūsus mīlitum.
2. Equitātum cum legiōne ūnā praesidiō castrīs relīquit.
3. Neque dēesse neque superesse reī pūblicae volō.
4. Praefuit paucīs nāvibus quās ex Syriā iussus erat in Asiam dūcere, iīsque adversus Rhodiōrum classem in Pamphȳliō marī cōnflīxit.
5. Quod mūnus reī pūblicae adferre maius meliusve possumus, quam sī docēmus atque ērudīmus iuventūtem?
6. Culpa est immiscēre sē reī ad sē nōn pertinentī.
7. Omnēs hominēs nātūrā lībertātī student et condiciōnem servitūtis ōdērunt.
8. Graecia capta ferum victōrem cēpit et artēs
   Intulit agrestī Latiō.

—Horace, *Epistles*, II, i, 156–7.

9. Quī parentem meum interfēcērunt, eōs in exilium[2] expulī iūdiciīs[3] lēgitimīs[4] ultus[5] eōrum facinus,[6] et posteā bellum īnferentīs reī pūblicae vīcī bis aciē.

—*Rēs Gestae Dīvī Augustī*, I, 2.

EXERCISE C

(1) The third legion was sent to our assistance. (2) You are a hindrance to us. (3) You ought to leave the cavalry together with three cohorts as a protection to the camp. (4) It was thought that he (*he was thought to have*) envied his brother. (5) A great uproar arose[7] at our backs as we were fighting.

---

[1] *broke out, arose*   [2] **exilium, -lī,** *exile*   [3] *trial*   [4] *legal*
[5] **ulcīscor, ulcīscī, ultus sum,** *punish*   [6] *deed, evil deed, crime*
[7] **exsistō;** see Exercise A, sentence 10.

Ōrandum est ut sit mēns sāna in corpore sano.

The thing to pray for is a healthy mind in a healthy body.

—JUVENAL, *Satires*, x, 356

LESSON XLVI

Subjunctive in Purpose Clauses— Indirect Commands

222. Adverbial clauses of purpose ("final" clauses).—Clauses introduced by the conjunction **ut** (or its negative **nē**), followed by the subjunctive mood, express the *purpose* or *end in view* (**fīnis**).

Tenses.—Since purposes and intentions are always directed toward the future, i.e., toward a time subsequent to that of the main verb, it is obvious by the principle stated in sec. **212** that only the *present* and *imperfect* tenses of the subjunctive will be used in final clauses, the present in primary sequence and the imperfect in secondary.

English idiom follows the same sequence:

I come in order that I **may** *see you.*	**Veniō ut tē videam.**
I came in order that I **might** *see you.*	**Vēnī ut tē vidērem.**

Observation 1.—Unlike English, Latin does not use the infinitive to express purpose:

We eat **to live**; *we do not live* **to eat**.

To *live* and *to eat* would be translated **ut vīvāmus** and **ut edāmus**.

Observation 2.—The negative **nē** is like the English *lest*. It is more usually translated *so as not, to avoid being*.

Pugnō *nē* **vincar.** $\begin{cases} \textit{I fight } \textbf{lest } \textit{I be defeated.} \\ \textit{I fight } \textbf{so as not } \textit{to be defeated.} \\ \textit{I fight } \textbf{in order that } \textit{I may } \textbf{not } \textit{be defeated.} \\ \textit{I fight } \textbf{to avoid being } \textit{defeated.} \end{cases}$

208

Observation 3.—**Nē quis** is translated *that no one* (lit., *lest anyone*).

Portae clausae sunt *nē quis* urbem relinqueret.
*The gates were closed **in order that no one** might leave the city.*

Similarly, **nē ūllus** means *in order that no;* **nē umquam,** *in order that never.* If two or more negative final clauses are connected in English by *and*, the conjunction **nēvē (neu)** is used in Latin.[1]

Observation 4.—The approach of a purpose clause is often, signalled by an adverb or adverbial expression in the main clause, such as **ideō, idcircō.**

223. Relative clauses of purpose.—The relative pronoun **quī, quae, quod** is often used instead of **ut**, the clause being then *adjectival* and modifying the antecedent of the relative. Relative clauses of purpose are more common than the adverbial type.[2]

Equitēs praemīsit *quī* hostēs sequerentur.
He sent horsemen ahead to follow the enemy (lit., **who were to follow**).

Quī is here equivalent to **ut eī.**

Similarly, in the place of **ut**, the neuter ablative of the relative, **quō** (a variety of the ablative of degree of difference), is regularly used with a comparative adjective or adverb to express *in order . . . the more.*

Dux pontem fēcit *quō facilius* exercitum trāns flūmen trādūceret.
*The general built a bridge **in order to** lead his army **the more easily** across the river.*

Observation.—**Quō magis** in this construction is the exact parallel to the **quōminus** of sec. **272.**

224. Substantive clauses of purpose (indirect commands).—Clauses introduced by **ut** and **nē**, with their verbs in the subjunctive mood, are used as subject or object of verbs like **imperō,** *I order;* **hortor,** *I urge;* **persuādeō,** *I persuade;* and **rogō,** *I ask.* This construction is really an indirect command, and is parallel to indirect

---

[1] Or if one positive and one negative are joined.

[2] They are not often used in connection with the subject of an active verb.

statement and indirect questions, inasmuch as it represents not the
original order as given but a report of it.

DIRECT COMMAND

Discēdite.	*Depart!*
Nōlī hoc facere.	*Don't do this.*

INDIRECT COMMAND

Vōbīs imperō ut *discēdātis.*	*I order you to depart.*
	(*I give orders that you depart.*)
Tē moneō *nē* hoc *faciās.*	*I warn you not to do this.*
	(*I warn you lest you do this.*)

Compare also English subjunctive in

> *I move that the meeting be adjourned.*

225. Such substantive clauses of purpose or fact may also stand
in apposition to a word implying command, decision, etc., or to an
expression like **eō cōnsiliō,** e.g.:

> **Hoc *eō cōnsiliō* fēcit *nē* vīs aquae pontī *nocēret.***
> *He did this with the intention that the force of the water might
> not damage the bridge.*

> **Dīcuntur etiam ab nōnnūllīs *sententiae ut* lēgātī ad Caesarem
> mittantur.**
> *Yet by some is voiced the opinion that envoys should be sent
> to Caesar.*

226. The subjunctive is used without a preceding *ut* particularly
in clauses depending on the verbs **volō, nōlō, mālō, faciō, licet,
oportet, necesse est,** e.g.:

> **Volō *veniās.*   *I wish you would come.***

> **Fac *cōgitēs* in quantā calamitāte sīs.**
> *Kindly consider how desperate your situation is.*

> **Caesar Labiēnō mandat Rēmōs reliquōsque Belgās *adeat*
> atque in officiō *contineat.***
> *Caesar orders Labienus to visit the Remi and the rest of the
> Belgians and keep them loyal.*

Necesse est multōs *timeat* quem multī timent.

One whom many fear is bound to fear many.

Such clauses may be regarded as the objects of **volō, mālō, nōlō, faciō,** and as the subjects of **licet, oportet, necesse est.**

227. The verbs *iubeō,* command, and **vetō,** *forbid,* govern an accusative and an infinitive (see sec. **188**). In the place of **iubeō nōn,** the verb **vetō** is found.

228. Indirect reflexive.—In all purpose clauses (adverbial, relative, or substantive) the reflexive pronoun, **sē** or adjective, **suus** is regularly used to refer to the person whose purpose the clause expresses, usually the subject of the *main* verb. This is the *indirect* reflexive; for examples, see sentences 3 and 5 of Exercise A.

VOCABULARY

arbor, arboris, *f.,* tree
colloquium, -quī, *n.,* interview
commeātus, -ūs, *m.,* supplies, provisions
cūstōs, cūstōdis, *m.,* guard, spy
dētrīmentum, -ī, *n.,* harm, loss
ēnītor, ēnītī, ēnīsus sum, strive
impediō, *IV,* hinder, prevent, delay
interclūdō, -clūdere, -clūsī, -clūsum, shut off from
obiciō, obicere, obiēcī, obiectum, throw against, place opposite, expose
postulō, *I,* demand, request, ask
praecipiō, -cipere, -cēpī, -ceptum, instruct, order

praemittō, -mittere, *etc.,* send ahead
propius, *prep. with acc.,* nearer
prōpōnō, -pōnere, -posuī, -positum, set before, suggest to
prōsum, prōdesse, prōfuī, prōfutūrus, be of service to, help
reficiō, reficere, *etc.,* repair; allow to rest
rūrsus, *adv.,* again
saeclum, saeclī, *n.,* century, generation
succīdō, -cīdere, -cīdī, -cīsum, cut down, fell
ultrā, *prep. w. acc.,* beyond, on the far side of
voluntās, -tātis, *f.,* will; wish, desire

EXERCISE A

1. Audī ut sciās.
2. Nē errētis, hoc vobis dīcam.
3. Petunt atque ōrant ut sibi[3] parcat.
4. Rōmam rediit ut hanc rem vōbīs nārrāret.
5. Lēgātōs rūrsus ad Crassum mittunt sēque in dēditiōnem ut accipiat petunt.

---

[3] Sibi refers to the subject of the main verbs **petunt** and **ōrant.**

6. Properat Caesar ut proeliō intersit.

7. Rēx supplicem monuit ut sibi[4] cōnsuleret.

8. Tē iubet ā patriā discēdere Caesaris īra.

9. Lēgātī ad Caesarem mittuntur quī voluntātem senātūs eī prōpōnant.

10. Haec nōn ut vōs excitārem locūtus sum.

EXERCISE B

1. Vōs hortor ut amīcitiam omnibus rēbus hūmānīs antepōnātis.

2. Agricola bonus arborēs serit quae alterī saeclō prōsint.

3. Quō facilius fīnitimōrum equitātum impedīrent tenerās arborēs succīdērunt.

4. Videant cōnsulēs nē quid rēs pūblica dētrīmentī capiat.

5. Lēgem brevem esse oportet quō facilius teneātur.

6. Caesar in campīs exercitum reficit, nē dēfessum proeliō obiciat.

7. Dominus meus mē ā portū praemīsit[5] domum ut haec uxōrī suae nūntiem.

8. Tum Ariovistus praeter castra Caesaris suās cōpiās trādūxit, et mīlibus passuum duōbus ultrā eum castra fēcit eō cōnsiliō ut frūmentō commeātūque Caesarem interclūderet.

9. Quam ob rem placuit Caesarī ut ad Ariovistum lēgātōs mitteret, quī ab eō postulārent ut aliquem locum medium utrīusque[6] colloquiō dēligeret.

10. Patrēs cōnscrīptī, Micipsa, pater meus, moriēns praecēpit ut rēgnum Numidiae exīstimārem meum; simul ēnīterer domī mīlitiaeque[7] quam maximō ūsuī esse populō Rōmānō.

EXERCISE C

(1) Come with me to see[8] Cicero's house. (2) I warned him not to expose his men to danger. (3) We left the city at dawn so that nobody might see us. (4) The general sent ahead three scouts to

---

[4] With verbs of *advising*, *exhorting*, etc. sē and **suus** generally refer to the subject of the *subordinate* verb, as the person *in whose interest* the advice is given.

[5] A true perfect (see sec. **31**).   Which sequence?   [6] *some neutral spot*

[7] *in war*   [8] Use 1st pl. of verb.

find out what was going on in the enemy's camp.   (5) Let us beseech
him not to harm the prisoners.

SELECTION FOR READING

(1) Exigis ut nostrōs dōnem tibi, Tucca, libellōs:
nōn faciam, nam vīs vēndere, nōn legere.

—Martial, VII, 77.

Mihi ille dētur puer quem laus excitet, quem glōria iuvet, quī victus fleat.

Give me a boy whose greatest incentive is praise, who delights in success, and is mortified by failure.

—QUINTILIAN, *Institutio Oratoria*, I, 3, 6

LESSON XLVII

Subjunctive in Result and Characteristic Clauses

229. Adverbial clauses of result—consecutive clauses (cōnsequor). —Clauses introduced by the conjunction **ut** (or its negative **ut nōn**), followed by the subjunctive mood, express the result of the main verb. Older English used "that" in a way exactly parallel to **ut** to express result.

"And right so he smote his father Arthur with his sword
. . . on the side of the head *that* the sword pierced the
helmet and the brain-pan."
—Sir Thomas Malory, *Le Morte d'Arthur*, ch. 4.

Tenses.—Since a result logically follows or is at most contemporary with its cause, it is obvious by the principle stated in sec. **212** that the present and imperfect tenses of the subjunctive will be used in result clauses: the present in primary sequence, and the imperfect in secondary sequence. But the perfect subjunctive will sometimes be found in secondary sequence.

Observation 1.—The subjunctive in a result clause is generally to be rendered by the English indicative.

Observation 2.—**Ut nēmō** means *with the result that no one;* **ut nūllus,** *with the result that no;* **ut numquam,** *with the result that never.* Contrast **nē quis, nē ūllus,** and **nē umquam** in final clauses (sec. **222**, Obs. 3).

Observation 3.—The approach of a result clause is often signaled by demonstrative adverbs such as **tam,**[1] **ita, sīc,**[2] **adeō,**[3] all meaning

---

[1] Tam modifies adjectives and adverbs.
[2] Ita usually modifies verbs, sometimes modifies adjectives; sīc modifies verbs.
[3] Adeō modifies adjectives, adverbs, and verbs.

so; or adjectives such as **tantus,** *so great;* **tālis,** *of such a sort;* **tot** (indeclinable) *so many,* in the main clause.

> **Non est *ita* stultus *ut* haec *dīcat.***
> *He is not so foolish as to say this.*
>
> ***Tantus* erat eōrum timor *ut* omnēs domī *manērent.***
> *So great was their fear that they all stayed home.*
>
> **Portās clausit *ut* nēmō urbem *relinqueret.***
> *He closed the gates with the result that no one left the city.*

Nē quis in place of **ut nēmō** in this sentence would mean *so that no one might leave the city,* or *to prevent any one's leaving,* in other words would give the *purpose* of **clausit** instead of the result.

Observation 4.—Closely allied with the consecutive is the *limiting* force of **ut.**

> **Huius ingenium ita laudō *ut nōn* pertimēscam.***
> *I admire his ability without fearing it.*

230. Relative clauses of characteristic.—Closely related to result clauses are clauses with their verbs in the subjunctive mood and introduced by the relative pronoun. Consider the following examples:

> **Sunt *quī dīcant* ā mē in exsilium ēiectum esse Catilīnam.**
> *There are those **who say** (i.e., of such a character that they say) that Catiline was driven into exile by me.*
>
> **Quis inveniētur *quī* haec *crēdat?***
> *Who will be found* { *who will believe this?*
> *of such a nature as to believe this?*
> *to believe this?* }
>
> **Hīc nihil est *quod edam.***
> *There is nothing here for me to eat.*

Such clauses as **quī dīcant, quī haec crēdat** and **quod edam** are called *relative clauses of characteristic* or *characterizing clauses,* because their express purpose is to complete the sense of the main clause by characterizing the antecedent, i.e., by indicating the *type* of person or thing to which the antecedent belongs. Common among such antecedents are the following:

Is est (quī) . . .	*He is the (sort of) man who or to*
Nēmo est (quī) . . .	*There is no one who*
Nihil est (quod) . . .	*There is nothing which*
Quis est (quī) . . . ?	*Who is there who?*
Sunt (quī) . . .	*There are people who*
Dignus est (quī) . . .	*He is worthy to*

These clauses are treated with result clauses because they express some natural consequence or result arising from the character of the antecedent.

Notice that the antecedent is general, vague, indefinite, and, except for the characterizing clause, usually undefined. In the case of **sunt quī** . . . , the antecedent is not even expressed. It is for this reason that the weak, colorless pronoun **is** (*a man, a person, one*) is so often used as the antecedent to the relative in such clauses.

> **Nōn *is* sum quī mortis perīculō terrear.**
> *I am not **one** to be terrified by the risk of death.*

Observation 1.—With comparatives a similar construction is found.

> **Maior sum quam *cui possit* Fortūna nocēre.**
> *I am too great **for fate to harm.***
> (*I am greater than the type of person whom fate can harm.*)

231. *Is quī* with indicative and *is quī* with subjunctive.—The difference between **is quī** with an indicative and **is quī** with a subjunctive must be carefully noticed, for it is one which English often fails to mark.

(a) When **is** and **quī** denote identity, the indicative is always used.

> **Is sum *quī fēcī*.**
> *I am the man **who did this**.*

Is and **quī** are here co-extensive.

(b) When the **quī** clause is used "characteristically" or generically and denotes the larger class to which we say the person (**is**) belongs, the subjunctive is used.

Nōn is sum *quī haec faciam.*

I do not belong to the larger class of men who do this, i.e., *I am*

not the $\begin{cases} sort \\ or \\ type \end{cases}$ *of man to do this.*

VOCABULARY

acerbus, -a, -um, harsh

adventus, -ūs, *m.*, arrival

āmittō, -mittere, -mīsī, -missum, lose

antecellō, -cellere, ——, ——, excel

antīquus, -a, -um, former, old, ancient

aperiō, aperīre, aperuī, apertum, open; reveal

calamitās, -tātis, *f.*, disaster

cernō, cernere, crēvī, crētum, distinguish; perceive

commūtātiō, -iōnis, *f.*, change

concēdō, -cēdere, -cessī, -cessum, grant

coörior, -orīrī, -ortus sum, arise, spring up

cursus, -ūs, *m.*, running; course, career

dignus, -a, -um, worthy, deserving

famēs, famis, *f.*, hunger

fertilis, -e, fertile

fīrmus, -a, -um, strong, firm

flōreō, flōrēre, flōruī, ——, be in flower, flourish

frūctus, -ūs, *m.*, fruit; reward

impōnō, -pōnere, -posuī, -positum, place upon; impose

iterum, *adv.*, a second time, again

oculus, -ī, *m.*, eye

opīmus, -a, -um, rich

perdō, perdere, perdidī, perditum, destroy

perturbō, *I*, disturb

poena, -ae, *f.*, penalty

prōsum, prōdesse, prōfuī, prōfutūrus, be of use to

redintegrō, *I*, renew

restituō, -stituere, -stituī, -stitūtum, renew, restore

status, statūs, *m.*, state, condition

tantus, -a, -um, so great

tolerō, *I*, endure; relieve

trahō, trahere, trāxī, trāctum, drag, draw

tūtus, -a, -um, safe

EXERCISE A

1. Hic locus tam fīrmum habuit praesidium ut tūtus esset.

2. Hōrum adventū tanta rērum commūtātiō est facta ut nostrī proelium redintegrārent.

3. Tanta tempestās subitō coörta est ut nūlla nāvium cursum tenēre possit.

4. Verrēs Siciliam ita perdidit ut restituī in antīquum statum nōn iam possit.

5. Nēmō est cui crēdere possim.

6. Domī nihil erat quō famem tolerārent.

7. Omnia sīc aperiam ut ea cernere oculīs videāminī.

8. Ita sum perturbātus ut omnia timērem.

9. Nōn is est quī dē inimīcī morte gaudeat.

10. Adsunt quī haec nōn probent.

11. Quem fugiam habeō; quem sequar nōn habeō.

12. Sunt ita multī ut eōs[4] carcer capere (*hold*) nōn possit.

EXERCISE B

1. Quae lēx tam acerba est quae hās poenās impōnat?

2. Asia tam opīma est ac fertilis ut varietāte frūctuum facile omnibus terrīs antecellat.

3. Nunc enim quis est quī nōn probet, quī nōn laudet?

4. Nēmō erit tam inimīcus Cluentiō quī hoc eī nōn concēdat.

5. Hae fābulae nōn satis dignae sunt quae iterum legantur.

6. Nōn enim possunt ūnā in cīvitāte multī rem ac fortūnās āmittere ut nōn plūrēs sēcum in eandem trahant calamitātem.

7. Dīcere solēbat nūllum librum tam malum esse quī nōn aliquā ex parte prōdesset.

8. Huius locī haec erat nātūra ut ex locīs superiōribus in lītus tēlum adicī posset.

9. Quī omnia ā sē ipsīs petunt iīs nihil potest malum vidērī quod nātūrae necessitās afferat.

10. Philippus omnia castella expugnārī posse dīcēbat in quae modo[5] asellus[6] onustus[7] aurō posset ascendere.

EXERCISE C

(1) So great a storm had arisen that all the sailors were terrified. (2) He has done this in-such-a-way[8] that we do not praise him. (3) I have not one to trust. (4) There were some who could run faster. (5) They say that he died of wounds. (6) The queen of France (*of the Gauls*) was not one to rejoice at[9] the death of a personal enemy.

---

[4] The reflexive *cannot* stand here, for the subordinate clause does not express the words or thought of the subject of the main verb.

[5] *only, merely*   [6] *a little donkey*   [7] *laden*, adj. from **onus**   [8] **ita**   [9] **dē**

Quid eī potest vidērī magnum in rēbus hūmānīs cui aeternitās omnis,
tōtīusque mundī nōta sit magnitūdō?

How can anything of this world seem impressive to one who is familiar
with all eternity and the vast expanse of the entire heavens?

—CICERO, *dē Nātūrā Deōrum*

LESSON XLVIII

Substantive Clauses of Result—Review

232. Substantive clauses of result.—

(a) Clauses introduced by **ut** and **ut nōn**, with their verbs in the
subjunctive mood, are used as the *subjects* of verbs like **fit**, *it happens
(that), the result is (that)* . . . , **restat**, *it remains (that)* . . . , **fierī
potest**, *it is possible (that)* . . . , **accidit**, *it happens (that)* . . . ,
etc.

> **Restat *ut* dē hīs quoque rēbus *loquar*.**
> *It remains **for me to speak** (lit., **that I speak**) of these matters
> also.*

Such substantive clauses may occur as predicates or appositives
with expressions like **mōs est, cōnsuētūdō est**; nouns such as **negōtium** and **sententia**, and the neuter pronouns **hoc** and **illud**.

> **Est mōs hominum *ut nōlint* eundem plūribus rēbus excellere.**
> *It is the way of men **not to wish** (lit., **that they do not wish**)
> the same person to excel in more things (than one).*

(b) A type of clause usually classified as "substantive clause of
result" is found as object of **faciō** and **efficiō**. It should be noted,
however, that these verbs are frequently followed by *nē* to introduce
a negative clause.

> **Fac *ut sciam*.**
> *Let **me know** (lit., make or bring it about **that I know**).*

219

Efficiō *nē* cui molestī *sint* mīlitēs.

*I am bringing it about **that** the soldiers **be not** a nuisance to anyone.*

REVIEW EXERCISE A

1. Potest, haec mala timēns, esse quisquam beātus?
2. Hannibal trāns palūdēs elephantō vectus est quō altius ab aquā exstāret.
3. Accidit ut Athēniēnsēs Chersonēsum[1] colōnōs vellent mittere.
4. Quō facilius hostēs prohibēre posset, praesidia dispōnit.[2]
5. Quaesō ut ūnā mēcum ad mātrem virginis eās, Mīciō.
6. Eādem nocte accidit ut esset plēna lūna.
7. Dat negōtium Senōnibus ūtī ea quae apud Belgās gerantur cognōscant sēque dē hīs rēbus certiōrem faciant.
8. Ea quī cōnficeret C. Trebōnium lēgātum relīquit.
9. Equitēs in expedītiōnem mīsit ut eōs quī fūgerant persequerentur.
10. Labiēnō scrībit ut quam plūrimās possit nāvēs īnstituat.[3]

REVIEW EXERCISE B

1. Prīmō vēre ēdīco (ut) adsītis.
2. Hortātus sum ut ea quae scīret sine timōre indicāret.
3. Nēmō tam humilis erat cui nōn aditus ad rēgem patēret.
4. Adhūc nēminem cognōvī poētam quī sibi nōn optimus vidērētur.
5. Haec ad tē plūribus verbīs scrīpsī quam soleō nōn ōtī abundantiā sed amōris ergā tē.
6. Brevī tempore factum est ut plēna essent omnia timōris.
7. Nūllus dolor est quem nōn longinquitās temporis minuat ac molliat.
8. Sōl efficit ut omnia flōreant.

REVIEW EXERCISE C

1. Et tamen faciam ut intellegās quid hī dē tē sentiant.

---

[1] *to the Chersonese,* today known as the peninsula of Gallipoli
[2] An historical present, used as the graphic equivalent of a past tense. It may introduce either primary or, as here, secondary sequence.
[3] *start building, lay the keels for*

2. Erant itinera duo quibus itineribus domō exīre possent.

3. Obsidēs ut inter sēsē dent perficit.

4. Factum est ut ab Arvernīs mercēde arcesserentur.

5. Quārē Iānuāriō mēnse, ut cōnstituistī, cūrā ut Rōmae sīs.

6. Atticus sīc Graecē loquēbātur ut Athēnīs nātus esse vidērētur.

7. Ego vērō iam tē nec hortor nec rogō ut domum redeās.

8. Tē aut Capuae aut Rōmae cūrā ut videāmus.

9. Dīviciācō ut idem cōnārētur persuāsit.

10. Monet ut in reliquum tempus omnēs suspīciōnēs vītet.

REVIEW EXERCISE D

1 Cum suō mōre conclāmāvērunt utī aliquis ex nostrīs ad colloquium prōdīret.

2. Cēnsēsne tē posse reperīre ūllam mulierem quae careat culpā?

3. Quid tam inaudītum quam equitem Rōmānum triumphāre? Quid tam inūsitātum quam ut eques Rōmānus ad bellum maximum prō cōnsule mitterētur?

4. Eō circiter hominum sēdecim mīlia expedīta cum omnī equitātū Ariovistus mīsit, quae cōpiae nostrōs perterrērent et mūnītiōne prohibērent.

5. Nē ignōrēs quid ego in tuīs litterīs desīderārim, scrībam apertē sīcut et mea nātūra et nostra amīcitia postulat.

6. Inter castra rēgis et Caesaris iter flūmen intercēdēbat angustum, altissimīs rīpīs, quod in Nīlum īnfluēbat, aberat autem ab rēgis castrīs mīlia passuum circiter VII.

7. Sunt autem post discessum ā mē tuum rēs dignae litterīs nostrīs, sed nōn committendae eius modī perīculō ut aut interīre aut aperīrī aut intercipī possint.

8. Haec habuī dē senectūte quae dīcerem, ad quam utinam perveniātis, ut ea quae ex mē audīvistis rē expertī probāre possītis.

REVIEW EXERCISE E

1. XXV iūdicēs ita fortēs fuērunt ut vel perīre māluerint quam perdere omnia.

2. Senātus cōnsulibus negōtium dederat ut cūrārent nē quid rēs pūblica dētrīmentī caperet.

3. Dā hoc patriae tuae ut operā et cōnsiliō tuō ūtī possit.

4. Hoc idem fac ante oculōs tibi prōpōnās.

5. Fac aliquandō intellegāmus adversam fortūnam quoque tē aequē ferre posse.

6. Stīpitēs praeustī[4] dēmittēbantur ita ut nōn amplius digitīs quattuor ex terrā ēminērent.

7. Nōlī committere ut quisquam tē putet nōn tam fīliam quam reī pūblicae tempora lūgēre.

8. Servus exceptus ā centuriōne nec pretiō nec minīs ut dominum prōderet potuit addūcī.

9. Ūnus ego sum ex omnī cīvitāte Haeduōrum quī addūcī non potuerim ut iūrārem.

10. Hīs rēbus fīēbat ut et minus lātē vagārentur et minus facile fīnitimīs bellum īnferre possent.

REVIEW EXERCISE F

1. Ōrat ut suae salūtis ratiōnem habeant neu sē hostibus dēdant.

2. Hīs persuādērī ut diūtius morārentur nēve suīs auxilium ferrent nōn poterat.

3. Catilīna, dēmissō voltū, vōce supplicī, postulāre ā patribus coepit nē quid dē sē temerē crēderent.

4. Hāc ex rē dīxit futūrum esse ut[5] tōtīus Galliae animī ā sē āverterentur.

5. Magnam in spem veniēbat futūrum esse ut pertināciā dēsisterēs.

6. Sed eā celeritāte atque eō impetū mīlitēs iērunt ut hostēs impetum legiōnum atque equitum sustinēre non possent, rīpāsque relinquerent ac sē fugae mandārent.

7. Relinquēbātur ut nōn longius ab agmine legiōnum discēdī[6] ab equitibus Caesar paterētur.

8. Iūs est bellī ut quī vīcerint eīs quōs vīcerint quem ad modum velint imperent. (**Velint**, subjunctive by attraction. Translate as indicative.)

9. Ariovistus tantōs sibi spīritūs, tantam arrogantiam sūmpserat ut ferendus non vidērētur.

10. Post Orgetorīgis mortem nihilōminus Helvētiī id quod cōnstituerant facere cōnātī sunt, ut ē fīnibus suīs exīrent.

---

[4] *stakes charred at the tip*   [5] *the result would be that*
[6] Intransitive verb used impersonally in the passive: *"did not allow the cavalry to go away,"* lit. *"a departure to be made by the cavalry."*

REVIEW EXERCISE G

1. Helvētiī Allobrogibus vel persuadēbunt vel vī cōgent ut per suōs fīnēs eōs (i.e., Helvētiōs) īre patiantur.

2. Fuit tantā vigilantiā quī suō tōtō cōnsulātū somnum nōn vīderit.

3. Equitēs hostium cum equitātū nostrō in itinere cōnflīxērunt, ita tamen ut nostrī superiōrēs fuerint atque eōs in silvās collēsque compulerint.

4. Cīvibus victīs ut parcerētur labōrāvī.

5. Mihi persuadētur eum nōn meam grātiam repudiātūrum.

6. Habeō senectūtī magnam grātiam, quae mihi sermōnis aviditātem auxit, potiōnis et cibī sustulit.

7. Animadvertit Caesar ūnōs ex omnibus Sēquanōs nihil eārum rērum facere quās cēterī facerent sed tristēs, capite dēmissō, terram intuērī.

8. Sed opprimor interdum et vix resistō dolōrī, quod (*because*) ea mē sōlācia dēficiunt quae cēterīs quōrum mihi exempla prōpōnō similī in fortūnā nōn dēfuērunt.

9. Ego iam tē nec hortor nec rogō ut domum redeās; quīn[7] hinc ipse ēvolāre cupiō et aliquō pervenīre ubi nec eōrum nōmen nec facta audiam.

10. Vōs quī aequī estis omnibus, quī ut quisque crūdēlissimē oppugnātur, eum lēnissimē sublevātis, cōnservāte A. Cluentium . . . amīcīs reddite. Vestrum est hoc, iūdicēs, vestrae dignitatis, vestrae clēmentiae; rēctē hoc repetitur ā vōbīs ut virum optimum hīs calamitātibus līberētis.

11. Ac mē quidem diū cōgitantem ratiō ipsa in hanc potissimum sententiam dūcit ut exīstimem sapientiam sine ēloquentiā parum prōdesse cīvitātibus, ēloquentiam vērō sine sapientiā nimium obesse plērumque, prōdesse numquam.

SELECTION FOR READING

No Excuse for Not Writing

Ōlim[8] mihi nūllās epistulās mittis. "Nihil est," inquis, "quod scrībam." At[9] hoc ipsum scrībe, nihil esse quod scrībās, vel sōlum illud unde incipere

---

[7] *indeed, nay rather*

[8] **Ōlim**, like **iam diū**, is used with the present tense in this idiom. Translate *for some time past you have sent*, etc.

[9] **At** answers the objections raised by another person, *well, then*.

priōrēs[10] solēbant: "Sī valēs, bene est; ego valeō."[11]   Hoc mihi sufficit;
est enim maximum.   Lūdere[12] mē putās?   Sēriō[13] petō.   Fac (ut) sciam
quid agās, quod sine sollicitūdine summā nescīre nōn possum.   Valē.

                                        —Pliny, *Epistulae*, I, 11.

---

[10] **priōrēs**, *those who went before*, i.e., *"the old-timers"*
[11] This sentence was the regular formula for starting a letter in the generation
before Pliny.   It was even abbreviated to **S.V.B.E.V.**
[12] **lūdō**, play, jest, fool   [13] adverb, *in all seriousness*

Croesus Halyn penetrāns magnam pervertet opum vim.

By crossing the Halys river Croesus will overthrow a mighty realm.

—AN ORACLE quoted in Cicero's *de Divinatione* ii, 115

LESSON XLIX

Participles and Their Use

233. Participles.—The participle expresses in adjective form the action of the verb, but retains its verbal nature to the extent that it indicates tense and may govern a case. Its very name **participium** shows that as a verbal adjective it partakes of (**partem + capiō**) the nature of both verb and adjective. Read secs. **40** and **44**.

Every transitive verb in Latin has four participles: two active (present[1] and future), and two passive (perfect and future). Deponents have three participles with active meanings (present, future, and perfect), and one with a passive meaning (future passive). The future passive participle is called the gerundive. We have already met it in the passive periphrastic conjugation and shall meet it again in Lesson 51. Until then we shall confine our attention to the present, future active, and perfect participles.

234. Examples of participles of the four conjugations and a deponent verb.—

	ACTIVE	PASSIVE
PRESENT	amāns *loving*	——
	monēns	——
	dūcēns	——
	capiēns	——
	audiēns	——
	sequēns	——

---

[1] For the present participle and its declension, see sec. **147**.

225

	ACTIVE	PASSIVE
FUTURE	**amātūrus, -a, -um,** *about to love*	**amandus, -a, -um,** *about* or *fit to be loved* or, *that should be loved*
	monitūrus, -a, -um	**monendus, -a, -um**
	ductūrus, -a, -um	**dūcendus, -a, -um**
	captūrus, -a, -um	**capiendus, -a, -um**
	audītūrus, -a, -um	**audiendus, -a, -um**
	secūtūrus, -a, -um	**sequendus, -a, -um**
PERFECT	——	**amātus, -a, -um,** *loved, having been loved*
	——	**monitus, -a, -um**
	——	**ductus, -a, -um**
	——	**captus, -a, -um**
	——	**audītus, -a, -um**
	secūtus,[2] **-a, -um** *having followed*	——

235. Tenses and uses of the participle.—

Nostrī Gallōs *iter facientēs* **vexant.**

LITERAL: *Our men harass the* **marching** *Gauls.*

BETTER: *Our men harass the Gauls* **as they march.**

The participle **facientēs** modifies **Gallōs** as an adjective; it indicates time contemporary with the main verb **vexant**; and it governs a direct object **iter**.

Tenses of the participle.—In general, the present participle indicates *time contemporary with* the main verb; the perfect, *prior time*, and the future, *subsequent time*.

(1) **Haec dīxit** *moriēns.*

     He said this (**as he was**) *dying.* (Contemporary.)

(2) **In oppidō** *captō* **praesidium collocāvit.**

     He placed a garrison in the town (**that had been**) *captured.*

                                   (Prior.)

(3) **Plūra** *locūtūrōs* **dīmīsit.**

     He sent them away (**when they were**) *going to say* more.

                               (Subsequent.)

---

[2] Passive in form, active in meaning. Deponent perfect participles will prove useful in constructions to be discussed later.

236. Translation of the participle.—The Latin participle is frequently equivalent to, and is therefore often to be translated by, a subordinate clause in English. The participle may thus express *time, cause, occasion, condition, concession, manner, means, attendant circumstance,* and other similar relations.

> **Restitimus semper *lacessītī*.**
> *We have always resisted if we were attacked.* (Condition.)
>
> **Hīs etiam *repugnantibus* parcere dēbēmus.**
> *We ought to spare these men, even though they resist us.* (Concession.)
>
> **Haec *scrībēns* interpellātus sum.**
> *I was interrupted while I was writing this.* (Time, occasion, attendant circumstances.)

Observation.—Often the participle is equivalent to a coördinate clause in English.

> **Prīncipēs *captōs* Rōmam mīsit.**
> *He sent the captured chieftains to Rome* (i.e., *he captured the chieftains and then sent them to Rome*).
>
> **Pīla *intercepta* remittēbant.**
> *They kept catching the javelins and throwing them back.*

Review the use of the future participles in the periphrastic conjugations (secs. **109, 110**). For other uses of the gerundive, see Lesson 51.

VOCABULARY

carcer, carceris, *m.*, prison
catēna, -ae, chain
clāmitō, *I*, call out loudly
dēmēns, *adj.* (gen. dēmentis), insane
expetō, -petere, -petiī, -petītum, seek
funditor, -tōris, *m.*, slinger
incēnātus, -a, -um, supperless
inopia, -ae, *f.*, lack
opera, -ae, *f.*, assistance
pluvia, -ae, *f.*, rain

prehendō, prehendere, prehendī, prehēnsum, seize, arrest
resolvō, -solvere, -solvī, -solūtum, loosen, melt
retrahō, -trahere, -trāxī, -trāctum, drag back
revocō, *I*, recall, call back
rīdeō, rīdere, rīsī, rīsum, laugh (at)
sagittārius, sagittārī, *m.*, archer
silentium, silentī, *n.*, silence
vigilia, -ae, *f.*, a watch, *one of four equal divisions of the night*

EXERCISE A

1. Vēnit ad mē clāmitāns.   Audentēs deus ipse iuvat.
2. Dormīmus incēnātī.   Occīsus est ā cēnā rediēns.
3. Dionȳsius tyrannus, Syrācūsīs expulsus, Corinthī puerōs docēbat.
4. Hostēs item suās cōpiās ex castrīs ēductās īnstrūxērunt.
5. Nix iacet et iactam[3] nec sōl pluviaeque resolvunt.
6. Eum frūstrā vocantem auxilium rīsērunt.
7. Cōnantēs dīcere prohibuit et in catēnās coniēcit.
8. Ad tē adveniō, spem, salūtem, cōnsilium, auxilium expetēns.
9. Labiēnus, silentiō ē castrīs tertiā vigiliā ēgressus, eōdem quō vēnerat itinere ad oppidum pervēnit.
10. Deinde eōs pollicitōs operam suam domum dīmīsit.

EXERCISE B

1. Caesar Catōnem prehendī loquentem et in carcerem dūcī iussit.
2. Nōn tam sum dēmēns ut nesciam quid sentiātis.
3. Helvētiī, omnium rērum inopiā adductī, lēgātōs dē dēditiōne ad Caesarem mīsērunt.
4. Post eum diem quīdam L. Tarquinius ad senātum adductus erat quem ad Catilīnam proficīscentem ex itinere retrāctum dīcēbant.
5. Alexandrīae dē Pompeī morte cognōvit atque ibi prīmum ē nāve ēgrediēns clāmōrem mīlitum audīvit.
6. Equitēs nostrī cum funditōribus sagittāriīsque flūmen trānsgressī cum hostium equitātū proelium commīsērunt.
7. Dumnorīx autem revocātus resistere ac sē manū (*violently*) dēfendere coepit, saepe clāmitāns līberum sē līberaeque[4] esse cīvitātis.
8. Hostēs impedītōs nostrī in flūmine aggressī magnum numerum eōrum occīdērunt; per[5] eōrum corpora reliquōs audācissimē trānsīre cōnantēs multitūdine tēlōrum reppulērunt.
9. Invidentiam esse dīcunt aegritūdinem susceptam[6] propter alterīus rēs secundās quae nihil noceant invidentī.   Misericordia est aegritūdō ex[7] miseriā alterīus iniūriā labōrantis.[8]

---

[3] *when it has fallen*   [4] Supply **cīvem.**   [5] *over*   [6] *contracted*
[7] *arising from*   [8] *suffering undeservedly*

EXERCISE C

(1) She died in her sleep.   (2) We found the horse and led him back home again.   (3) (If) asked why you are doing this, answer that Caesar ordered you to do it.   (4) I was caught while trying to bring help to your friends.   (5) Although frightened and exhausted, the child warned us of the approach of the enemy.   (6) After returning to the top of the hill, the scout caught sight of the forces of the Gauls as they were advancing across the plain.

Quid rīdēs? Mūtātō nōmine dē tē fābula nārrātur.

What are you laughing at? Just change the name and the story applies to you.

—HORACE, *Satires*, I, 1, 69–70

LESSON L

Ablative Absolute

237. Ablative absolute.—This construction corresponds to the nominative absolute, a construction which is tending to disappear in English, e.g., *This being the case, I shall not go.* The phrase *this being the case* has no grammatical connection with the rest of the sentence and is therefore called absolute (**ab-solvō**, *free from*), but logically it is an adverbial modifier of the verb *shall go*, the whole being equivalent practically to *Since this is the case, I shall not go.* The clause *since this is the case* is an adverbial clause of *cause.* The absolute construction may also express *time, condition, concession, attendant circumstance*, and other ideas.

In Latin, a noun or pronoun with a participle[1] in agreement may be put in the ablative case to express these relations. This construction is called the *ablative absolute.* Since there is no present participle of the verb **sum**, two nouns, or a noun and a pronoun, or a noun and an adjective, may be used in this way with the force of the participle *being* understood. Even in English the participle *being* is sometimes omitted in the absolute construction, e.g.:

> "For the poor wren,
> The most diminutive of birds, will fight—
> *Her young ones in her nest*—against the owl."
> —*Macbeth*, Act IV, Scene 2, 9–10

The ablative absolute, like the English nominative absolute, though grammatically unconnected with the rest of the sentence, is in thought an adverbial modifier of the verb.

---

[1] Most commonly a present or perfect participle.

230

(1) *Hāc ōrātiōne habitā,* concilium dīmīsit.

This speech made,

When this speech had been made, } *he dismissed the meeting.*

After making this speech,

Having made this speech,

(2) *Tē duce,* nōn timēmus.

You (being) leader,

If you are leader, } *we do not fear.*

With you as leader,

(3) *M. Tulliō et C. Antōniō cōnsulibus,* Catilīna coniūrā- tiōnem fēcit.

Cicero and Antonius (being) consuls, } *Catiline formed a conspiracy.*

When Cicero and Antonius were consuls,

In the consulship of Cicero and Antonius,

Observation 1.—In the above examples, the first translation in each instance, though literal, is usually to be avoided on the score of good English usage. The third translation in each case is perhaps better than the second, although the Latin ablative absolute will frequently be best rendered in English by a clause.

Observation 2.—A noun representing the subject or object of the main verb must not be used in the ablative absolute, but instead the participle must be used in direct agreement with the subject or object. For example, the Latin for

Caesar, after capturing the chieftains, sent them to Rome.

is *not*

Prīncipibus captīs, Caesar eōs Rōmam mīsit.

but

Caesar *prīncipēs captōs* Rōmam mīsit.

Observation 3.—In translating into Latin such sentences as *Having done these things, the envoys departed,* the ablative absolute is used to avoid the difficulty arising from the fact that Latin has no perfect active participle. The sentence must, therefore, be turned into the passive:

These things (having been) done, the envoys departed.
Hīs rēbus factīs, lēgātī abiērunt.

In the case of deponent verbs, however, this difficulty does not arise, for the perfect participle of deponents is active in meaning. Hence,

Having spoken these things, he departed.

will be translated:

Haec *locūtus,* **abiit.**

But if **dīcō** be used instead of **loquor**, then, of course, the sentence will be rendered as above:

Hīs rēbus dictīs, abiit.

Observation 4.—This does not mean that the ablative absolute construction is impossible with deponent verbs.

Equō lāpsō, concidit.   *His horse stumbled and he fell.*

Observation 5.—When the present participle singular is used in an ablative absolute, the ablative form in **-e** is employed. See paradigm of **capiēns**, sec. **147.**

Deō *volente, God willing,* or *If God is willing.*
Aestū *minuente, At the ebb-tide.*

VOCABULARY

aegrē, *adv.,* with difficulty
anima, -ae, *f.,* soul
antīquitus, *adv.,* in ancient times
āvolō, *I,* fly away
castellum, -ī, *n.,* fort
citō, *I,* set in rapid motion, spur
dēspērō, *I,* give up hope
dēvorō, *I,* devour
Druidēs, -um, *m. pl.,* the Druids, *priests in Gaul and Britain*
ēlābor, -lābi, -lāpsus sum, slip away, escape

expugnō, *I,* take by storm
exūrō, -ūrere, -ussī, -ustum, burn up
facultās, -tātis, *f.,* chance, opportunity
hīberna, -ōrum, *n. pl.,* for **hīberna castra,** winter camp, winter quarters
ibi, *adv.,* there
intereō, -īre, -iī, -itum, perish, die
interscindō, -scindere, -scidī, -scissum, cut through, destroy

invītus, -a, -um, against one's wish *or* will, unwilling(ly)
praegredior, -gredī, -gressus sum, go before, precede, lead the way
ratis, ratis (ratium), *f.*, raft

reliquus, -a, -um, remaining, rest of
stabilis, -e, firm, steady
statuō, statuere, statuī, statūtum, decide
tamquam, *adv.*, just as; as if; like

EXERCISE A

1. Factā facultāte discessit. Mē invītō hoc fēcit.
2. Citātīs equīs, Rōmam āvolant.
3. Mūnītīs castrīs, duās ibi legiōnēs relīquit.
4. P. Scaevolā et L. Pīsōne cōnsulibus, Ti. Gracchus rēgnum occupāre cōnātus est.
5. Hī, cognitō hostium adventū, suās nāvēs ex portū ēdūcunt.
6. Ibi hostēs, locīs superiōribus occupātīs, itinere exercitum prohibēre cōnantur.
7. Huic mandat Caesar ut, explōrātīs omnibus rēbus, ad sē quam prīmum revertātur.
8. Germānicō bellō cōnfectō, multīs dē causīs Caesar statuit sibi Rhēnum esse trānseundum.
9. Fēcērunt id servī, neque imperante neque sciente dominō.
10. Barbarī dīcēbantur antīquitus omnēs gentēs, exceptīs Graecīs.

EXERCISE B

1. Sōlis occāsū suās cōpiās Ariovistus, multīs et inlātīs et acceptīs vulneribus, in castra redūxit.
2. Persuādēbant fīnitimīs suīs ut, eōdem ūsī cōnsiliō, oppidīs suīs[2] exustīs, ūnā cum eīs[2] proficīscerentur.
3. Eōdem tempore, clāmōre audītō, dat tubā signum suīs Vercingetorīx atque ex oppidō ēdūcit.
4. Tum elephantī per[3] stabilem ratem tamquam viam, praegredientibus fēminīs,[4] āctī sunt.
5. In prīmīs[5] hoc Druidēs docent, nōn interīre animās, sed ab aliīs post mortem trānsīre ad aliōs; atque hōc maximē ad virtūtem excitārī[6] putant, metū mortis neglēctō.

---

[2] This suīs refers to the **fīnitimī**. When the reflexive refers to the *subordinate* subject, the demonstrative (**eīs**) refers to the *principal* subject.
[3] *on to*   [4] *cow-elephant*   [5] lit., *among the first*, i.e., *especially*
[6] impersonal; *it is stirred up, there is a stirring up.* Say *men are stirred up.*

6. Illī aegrē ad noctem oppugnātiōnem sustinent; nocte ad ūnum[7] omnēs, dēspērātā salūte, sē ipsī interficiunt. Paucī ex proeliō ēlāpsī incertīs itineribus per silvās ad T. Labiēnum lēgātum in hīberna perveniunt, atque eum dē rēbus gestīs certiōrem faciunt.

7. Ibi, vadīs repertīs, partem suārum cōpiārum trādūcere cōnātī sunt, eō cōnsiliō ut castellum cui praeerat Q. Titūrius lēgātus expugnārent pontemque interscinderent.

EXERCISE C

(1) On hearing this, my brother Quintus decided to leave the city. (2) The Romans thought that, while Hannibal lived (*H. living*), they would never be free from danger. (3) A great calm having followed, we soon reached land. (4) In the consulship of Hirtius and Pansa, Octavian led his army into Cisalpine Gaul to attack Antony. (5) Having started at daybreak, she reached Rome in three hours.

SELECTION FOR READING

Mīlle tibī nummōs[8] hesternā[9] lūce rogantī
     in sex aut septem, Caeciliāne, diēs
"Nōn habeō" dīxī: sed tū causātus[10] amīcī
     adventum lancem[11] paucaque vāsa[12] rogās.
Stultus es? an stultum mē crēdis, amīce? negāvī
     mīlle tibī nummōs, mīlia quīnque dabō?

                                            —Martial, IV, 15.

---

[7] *to a man*
[8] **nummus, -ī, m.**, *sestertius*, a Roman coin worth about five cents
[9] adj. from adv. **heri,** *yesterday*   [10] **causor, I,** *plead, offer as an excuse*
[11] **lanx, lancis, f.,** *silver plate*   [12] **vāsa, -ōrum, n.,** *dishes*

Nec tamen, ut vērum fatear tibi, nostra tenērī
Ā compōnendō carmine Mūsa potest.

And yet (if I must strictest truth rehearse)
My Muse cannot be stopped from making verse.

—OVID, Tristia v, xii, 59–60

LESSON LI

Gerund—Gerundive

238. The gerund.—This is a verbal noun derived from the present stem of the verb and identical in form with the neuter of the gerundive or future passive participle. The gerund is active in meaning and, therefore, not confined to transitive verbs. It is declined in the singular only, and the existence of the nominative is not generally recognized. The gerund corresponds to the English verbal noun in *-ing*, e.g., *loving, going, using, speaking*.

GEN.	amandī	eundī	ūtendī	loquendī
DAT.	amandō	eundō	ūtendō	loquendō
ACC.	amandum	eundum	ūtendum	loquendum
ABL.	amandō	eundō	ūtendō	loquendō

The gerund, though a noun, retains its verbal nature to the extent that it is modified by adverbs and may, if necessary, govern the case governed by the verb from which it is derived.

Docendō discimus.	*We learn by teaching.*
ars rēctē *scrībendī.*	*the art of writing correctly.*
Inimīcīs *parcendō* vincit.	*He conquers by sparing his enemies.*

(a) A common construction to express purpose is **ad** followed by the accusative of the gerund,[1] or **causā** (sometimes **grātiā**) preceded by the genitive of the gerund.

---

[1] The accusative of the gerund is used only when governed by a preposition.

parātus *ad proficīscendum.*
ready for **departing** (i.e., *ready to depart*).

Diem *ad dēlīberandum sūmam.*
I shall take time **to think.**

Ad persuādendum cīvibus vēnit.
He came **to persuade the citizens.** (*He came for* **persuading**
the citizens.)

Cīvibus *persuādendī causā vēnit.*
He came **to persuade** *the citizens.*
He came **for the sake of persuading** *the citizens.*

Observation.—This construction is more usual with intransitive
verbs. Verbs governing the accusative case generally take the
gerundive construction.

239. The gerundive.—This is a verbal adjective, derived from
the present stem of the verb. It is the future passive participle, and
is used in the following constructions:

(**a**) In the second or passive periphrastic conjugation (**110**) as
one of the commonest ways of expressing duty, necessity, or obligation.

Dēlenda est Carthāgō.
Carthage **must be destroyed.**

(**b**) In intransitive verbs and transitive verbs used absolutely
(i.e., intransitively) a neuter gerundive may be used impersonally
in the second periphrastic conjugation. As in (**a**) it expresses duty,
necessity, or obligation. As in (**a**) the person upon whom the
obligation rests is in the dative case.

Domī mihi manendum est.
I must remain at home.

Dē gustibus nōn disputandum est.
There's no accounting for tastes.

Nōbīs vincendum est.
We must win the day.

This usage belongs properly to the lesson on impersonal verbs, and is similar to such constructions of the perfect passive participle as:

Diū et ācriter pugnātum est,
There was long and bitter fighting, or
A long and fiercely contested engagement was fought.

With verbs that govern a dative or ablative, an object may be expressed in the appropriate case, e.g.:

Occāsiōne utendum fuit.
The opportunity *should have been used.*

Hostibus parcendum est.
The enemy *should be spared.*

(c) In constructions involving transitive verbs, where, instead of employing a gerund with a direct object, Latin generally uses a gerundive phrase, e.g.:

Neque eīs data est *Massiliae līberandae* **facultās.**
And they were not given the opportunity of liberating Massilia.

Latin prefers this to:

Massiliam līberandī facultās.

240. Other examples of this use of the gerundive.—Thus we find the gerundive:

(a) In agreement with a noun or pronoun in the accusative case after **ad** or in the genitive case preceding **causā** to express purpose.

Ad eās rēs cōnficiendās Orgetorīx dēligitur.
For the completion of these plans, *Orgetorix is chosen.*
(For these things to-be-completed, etc.)

(b) In agreement with nouns and pronouns in the genitive, dative, and ablative cases in a variety of constructions.

spēs *capiendī oppidī*
a hope of taking the town
(*a hope of the town to-be-taken*)   (Objective genitive.)

reī pūblicae bene gerendae cupidī
desirous of administering the government well
(*desirous of the government to-be-administered well*)
(Objective genitive.)

Dē imperātōre dēligendō dīcāmus.
Let us speak about the choice of a general.
(*Let us speak about a general to-be-chosen.*)
(Ablative with preposition dē.)

Senectūti celebrandae et ornandae quid honestius potest esse
perfugium quam iūris interpretātiō?
*For the purpose of conferring distinction on old age what more
honorable avocation can there be than the expounding of the law?*
(Dative of purpose.)

Bellō trahendō vincēs.
You will conquer by dragging-on the war.
(*You will conquer by the war to-be-dragged-on.*)
(Ablative of means.)

Note that Latin deals reluctantly in abstractions and wherever possible avoids recourse to them. English speaks of "the choosing (or choice) of a general," Latin of "the general that-is-to-be-chosen."

(c) In agreement with the direct object of verbs like **cūrō**, *see to*, *take care of*, **trādō**, *hand over*, and similar verbs.

Pontem faciendum cūrāvit.
He had a bridge made.
(*He took care of a bridge to-be-made*, i.e., *of the making of a bridge.*)

Observation 1.—A working rule for translating the Latin gerundive construction is:
   (i) Turn the Latin gerundive into the English gerund.
   (ii) Make the Latin noun which the gerundive modifies the object of the English gerund.
Observation 2.—Exceptions such as

ars vēra ac falsa *dīiūdicandī*
the art of distinguishing truth from falsehood

may often be explained by the fact that, to the Latin ear, jingles like
vērōrum ac falsōrum dīiūdicandōrum were offensive and to be avoided
except for deliberate effect. Even where there is no jingle to be
avoided the genitive of the gerund will often take a direct object,
especially a neuter pronoun or adjective, e.g. **aliquid *agendō, by*
doing** *something*, and sentence 8, Exercise A. This avoids ambiguity.

VOCABULARY

cavō, *I*, make hollow

cōnservō, *I*, save, preserve

cōnsistō, -sistere, -stitī, -stitum,
stand, keep a footing

dēsiliō, -silīre, -siluī, ——, leap
down from

discō, discere, didicī, ——, learn

fluctus, -ūs, *m.*, wave

gutta, -ae, *f.*, drop

iūdicō, *I*, judge, decide

lapis, lapidis, *m.*, stone

legō, legere, lēgī, lēctum, read

maleficium, -ficī, *n.*, wrong-doing

negōtium, -tī, *n.*, business; trouble,
difficulty

ordō, ordinis, *m.*, rank, class of
society

patior, patī, passus sum, allow;
endure

prōcurrō, -currere, -currī, -cursum,
run forward

pūrgō, *I*, clear, excuse, exonerate

repentē, *adv.*, -suddenly

trīstis, -e, sad

vīvus, -a, -um, alive

vulgō, *adv.*, commonly, popularly

EXERCISE A

1. In hīs locīs Caesar nāvium parandārum causā morātur.

2. Caesarī omnia ūnō tempore erant agenda.

3. Nōlī igitur in cōnservandīs bonīs virīs dēfatīgārī.

4. Agrōs Rēmōrum populēmur, quī magnō hostibus ūsuī ad belium
gerendum sunt.

5. Locus prō castrīs ad aciem īnstruendam nātūrā idōneus est.

6. Nēmō timendō ad summum pervēnit locum.

7. Omnēs ordinēs ad cōnservandam rem pūblicam mente, volun-
tāte, vōce consentiunt.

8. Lēgātīs multa pollicendō persuādet[2] ut rēgem sibi vīvum trā-
derent.

9. Ea quae sunt ūsuī ad armandās nāvēs ex Hispāniā apportārī
iubet.

[2] The present indicative, in Latin as in English, is often used for added vivid-
ness to represent past action as going on now. The tense when so used is called
the *historical present* or present of vivid narration and frequently introduces a
secondary sequence.

10. Philosophī Graecī Rōmānīs artem bene disserendī trādidērunt.

11. Ab eīs quī ad condūcendōs hominēs facultātēs habēbant vulgō rēgna occupābantur.

12. Gutta cavat lapidem nōn vī sed saepe cadendō.

13. Suī pūrgandī causā adsunt.

14. Multī metū moriendī moriuntur.

EXERCISE B

1. Omnibus hībernīs Caesaris oppugnandīs hic est dictus diēs, nē qua legiō alterī legiōnī subsidiō venīre posset.

2. Prīmum mihi vidētur dē genere bellī, deinde dē magnitūdine, tum dē imperātōre dēligendō esse dīcendum.

3. Ita nostrī ācriter in hostēs impetum fēcērunt, itaque hostēs repente celeriterque prōcurrērunt ut spatium pīla in hostēs coniciendī nōn darētur.

4. Dolor trīstis rēs est et ad patiendum difficilis.

5. Flūmen est Arar, incrēdibilī lēnitāte, ita ut oculīs in utram partem fluat iūdicārī nōn possit.

6. Quae illī audīre aut legere solent, eōrum partem vīdī, alia egomet[3] gessī; quae illī litterīs, ea ego mīlitandō didicī.

7. Neque enim illae sunt sōlae virtūtēs imperātōriae quae vulgō exīstimantur—labor in negōtiīs, fortitūdō in perīculīs, industria in agendō, celeritās in cōnficiendō, cōnsilium in prōvidendō.

8. Neque hominēs inimīcō animō, datā facultāte per prōvinciam itineris faciendī, temperātūrōs ab iniūriā et maleficiō exīstimābat.

9. Mīlitibus simul et dē nāvibus dēsiliendum et in flūctibus cōnsistendum et cum hostibus erat pugnandum.

10. Nerviōs hortātur nē suī[4] līberandī occāsiōnem dīmittant.

EXERCISE C

(1) They promised a large number of ships to carry the army across. (2) By reading and by listening we learn many things. (3) Our cavalry gave the enemy no chance to recover.[5] (4) In order to ascertain the nature of the place, Caesar sent ahead a legion-commander in a warship. (5) We had to return home.

---

[3] Emphatic for ego; translate *I actually.*
[4] a *direct* reflexive, common with such verbs as hortor
[5] sē colligere

Spectātum veniunt, veniunt spectentur ut ipsae.

They come to see and to be seen.

—OVID, *Ars Amatoria,* I, 99 (*on Roman ladies at the theatre*)

LESSON LII

The Supine

241. The supine.—This verbal (the fourth principal part of the verb and identical in form with the nominative singular neuter of the perfect passive participle where that occurs) is found in two cases, the accusative and the ablative.

ACC.	amātum	dictum	locūtum	audītum
ABL.	amātū	dictū	locūtū	audītū

(a) The accusative of the supine is used with verbs of motion like **eō, veniō, mittō,** etc., to denote purpose.

Abiit *piscātum* (*piscor,* I, *fish*).
He went off **to fish.**
Eam vēnī *quaesītum.*
I have come **to look for** *her.*

(b) The ablative of the supine is used with a few adjectives as an ablative of specification (see sec. **155**).

perfacile *factū,*	*very easy* **to do** (i.e., **in the doing**).
mīrābile *dictū,*	*wonderful* **to relate** (i.e., **in the telling**).
peracerba *gustātū,*	*very bitter* **to taste** (i.e., **in the tasting**).

242. The future passive infinitive in *-um īrī.*—By (a) above, the sentence

It urbem captum

means

241

He goes (for) to capture the city.

If the verb of this sentence is turned into the impersonal passive:

Ītur urbem captum,

the meaning becomes

(Literally) *It is gone (there is a going) (for) to capture the city.*
Somebody goes (for) to capture the city.
or
The city is going to be captured.

Quoting this last after a verb of saying and making the necessary change of **ītur** to the infinitive, we have

Dīcit urbem captum īrī.

(Literally) *He says that there is a going (for) to capture the city.*
He says that the city will be captured.

This somewhat clumsy expression (supine in **-um** + impersonal passive infinitive of **eō, īre**) is what Latin uses for the future passive infinitive. The construction, however, is usually avoided in favor of the **futūrum esse ut** construction.

243. Futūrum esse ut (fore ut).—Like the expressions **potest fierī ut** and **fit ut** is the expression **est ut . . .** , *the situation is that. . . .*

Erit ut urbs capiātur.
The situation will be that the city will be captured.

Quoted after a verb of saying, this becomes:

Primary

Dīcit futūrum esse ut urbs capiātur.
He says (that it will be) that the city will be captured.

Secondary

Dīxit futūrum esse ut urbs caperētur.
He said (that it would be) that the city would be captured.

The substantive clauses **ut capiātur** and **ut caperētur** are subjects of the infinitive **futūrum esse.**

This construction is regularly employed in indirect statement in place of the so-called future passive infinitive in **-um īrī.** The form **fore** is frequently used for **futūrum esse.**

VOCABULARY

aestus, -ūs, *m.,* tide
Apollō, Apollinis, *m.,* the god Apollo
cōnsulō, cōnsulere, cōnsuluī, cōn-sultum, consult
Delphī, -ōrum, *m.,* Delphi, *a town of Phocis, Greece*
dēsiliō, dēsilīre, dēsiluī, dēsultum, leap down from
dominor, *I,* be lord and master
Druentia, -ae, *f., name of a river, the modern* Durance
essedum, -ī, *n.,* two-wheeled war chariot

frūmentor, *I,* forage
habitō, *I,* live
hinc, *adv.,* from here
īnficiō, -ficere, -fēcī, -fectum, stain, dye
magistrātus, -ūs, *m.,* magistrate
migrō, *I,* depart
potissimum, *adv.,* chiefly, principally
seges, segetis, *f.,* crop
spoliō, *I,* strip, despoil
vāstus, -a, -um, desolate

EXERCISE A

1. Migrās rūs habitātum.
2. Perfacile factū esse illīs probat[1] cōnāta perficere.
3. Lēgātōs ad Caesarem mīsērunt ōrātum nē sē in numerō hostium dūceret.[2]
4. Hinc Hannibal invictus[3] patriam dēfēnsum revocātus est.
5. Ex iīs dēlēctī Delphōs dēlīberātum missī sunt quī cōnsulerent Apollinem quō potissimum duce ūterentur.
6. Quīnque cohortēs frūmentātum in proximās segetēs mittit.
7. Omnēs vērō sē Britannī vitrō[4] īnficiunt, atque hōc horribiliōrēs sunt in pugnā aspectū.
8. Druentia flūmen longē omnium Galliae flūminum difficillimum trānsitū est.
9. Bellō Helvētiōrum cōnfectō, tōtius ferē Galliae lēgātī ad Caesarem grātulātum convēnērunt.

---

[1] *proves*   [2] *consider*   [3] The participle has here a concessive force.
[4] *woad,* a blue vegetable dye

10. Rōmam ad senātum vēnī auxilium postulātum.

11. Nūlla virtūs commodior hominī est patientiā, ac nūlla adeō aspera est fortūna quam[5] prūdenter patiendō vir fortis nōn vincat.

EXERCISE B

1. Summa erat, vāstō atque apertō marī, magnīs aestibus, rārīs ac prope nūllīs portibus, difficultās nāvigandī.

2. Statuit exspectandam classem esse.

3. Dīxit eōs et ūsū rērum necessāriārum et dignitāte spoliātum īrī.

4. Cum illō ego tē dominandī cupiditāte cōnferre possum; cēterīs vērō rēbus nūllō modō comparandus es.

5. Equitēs nostrī hostibus neque suī colligendī neque cōnsistendī aut ex essedīs dēsiliendī facultātem dedērunt.

6. Saepe ipsa plēbs, aut dominandī studiō permōta aut superbiā magistrātuum, armāta ā patribus[6] sēcessit. At nōs nōn imperium neque dīvitiās petimus, quārum rērum causā bella atque certāmina omnia inter mortālēs sunt, sed lībertātem quam nēmō bonus nisi cum animā simul āmittit.

EXERCISE C

(1) We have come to see the gardens of Lucullus. (2) A soldier came to announce the arrival of Pompey. (3) They thought that by this they would be more terrifying to behold in battle. (4) This river was by far the hardest to cross in the whole of Spain. (5) I am always lending[7] you money; you are always borrowing[8] it.

SELECTIONS FOR READING

(1) Neque enim potest exercitum is continēre imperātor, quī sē ipse nōn continet, neque sevērus esse in iūdicandō, quī aliōs in sē sevērōs esse iūdicēs nōn vult.

—Cicero, *pro Leg. Man.*, XIII, 38.

---

[5] = **ut eam**, a relative clause of result
[6] i.e., the senate. The plebs seceded in 494, 449, and 287 B.C.
[7] **ūtendam dare**　　[8] **ūtendam petere, rogāre, accipere**

(2)   *Dē eō quī prīmum Rōmam librōs advexit*

Rōmae prīmus librōrum cōpiam advexit Aemilius Paulus, Perseō
Macedonum rēge dēvictō; deinde Lūcullus ē Ponticā praedā. Post hōs
Caesar dedit Mārcō Varrōnī negōtium quam maximae bibliothēcae cōn-
struendae. Prīmum autem Rōmae bibliothēcās pūblicāvit[9] Polliō,
Graecās simul atque Latīnās, additīs auctōrum imāginibus[10] in ātriō,
quod dē manubiīs[11] magnificentissimum[12] īnstrūxerat.

—Isidorus, *Origines,* VI, v.

_____

[9] **pūblicō,** *I, open to the public*   [10] **imāgō, imāginis,** f., *bust, portrait*
[11] **manubiae, -ārum,** f. pl., *spoils of war, plunder*   [12] *on a most lavish scale*

Certa āmittimus dum incerta petimus.

A bird in the hand is worth two in the bush.

—PLAUTUS

LESSON LIII

Subordinate Clauses: Some Conjunctions Taking the Indicative Mood—Substantive *Quod*-Clauses

244. Subordinate clauses.—It has already been stated, in secs. **236** and **237**, that the ideas expressed in English by subordinate clauses of *time, cause, concession,* and *condition* are often conveyed by the Latin participle and ablative absolute. Latin has, however, like English, special subordinating conjunctions to introduce clauses that express these ideas.

245. Some temporal conjunctions followed by the verb in the indicative mood.—

(a) **ubi,** *when.*—

Ubi ea diēs *vēnit* et lēgātī ad eum *revertērunt,* negat sē posse iter ūllī per prōvinciam dare.

When the day came and the envoys returned to him, he said that he could not (literally, *says that he cannot*) *grant passage through the province to anyone.*

(b) **postquam,** *after, when.*—

Eō *postquam* Caesar *pervēnit,* obsidēs et arma poposcit.

After Caesar had arrived there, he demanded arms and hostages.

(c) **simul ac (atque),** *as soon as.*—

Lūcius Clōdius[1] *simul atque intrōductus est,* rem cōnficit.

---

[1] When a noun or pronoun is the subject of *both* clauses, it precedes the subordinate conjunction.

246

As soon as he was brought in, Lucius Clodius *finished* (lit., *finishes*) *the business.*

or,

No sooner was he brought in than, etc.

In the same way are used **ut prīmum** and **cum prīmum,** *when . . . first, as soon as.*

Observation 1.—Notice that Latin uses the *perfect* tense with these conjunctions, whereas English often requires the *pluperfect.*

Observation 2.—When a definite interval is stated, **postquam** is often found with the *pluperfect* after an accusative or ablative of time, and is divided **post . . . quam.**

Pugnātum est *post quārtum diem quam pervēnerat.*
The battle was fought **four days** *after he arrived.*

(d) **dum,** *while* (i.e., *within the time during which*), is followed by the *present* indicative at all times.

Dum **haec** *geruntur,* **Caesarī nūntiātum est. . .**
While this **was being done** *(these things* **were being done***),
it was reported to Caesar. . . .*

(e) **dum,** *as long as, while* (i.e., *all the time during which*), is usually followed by the same tense as is used in the main clause.

Vīvet **eius memoria** *dum erit* **haec cīvitas.**
His memory **will live as long as** *this state* **exists** *(will exist).*

Observation.—Like **dum** in this latter sense are **dōnec, quoad, quamdiū,** all meaning *as long as.*

Quoad **in urbe** *fuit* **Catilīna, eius cōnsiliīs** *obstitī.*
As long as **(while)** *Catiline* **was** *in the city,* **I stood in the way of** *his plans.*

Meum parvum fīlium *quamdiū āfuī* **nēmō nisi lacrimantem vīdit.**

All the time I was away **no one** *saw* **my little son** *when he was not crying.*

246. *Quamquam, although,* introducing an admitted fact in concessive clauses, is followed by a verb in the indicative mood.

Rōmānī, *quamquam* itinere et aestū fessī *erant, tamen* hostēs aggressī sunt.

The Romans, **although** *they* **were** *tired from marching and from the heat,* **nevertheless** *attacked the enemy.*

247. *Ut, as.*—Ut, with this meaning, introduces parenthetical clauses, which may be removed from the sentence without affecting the essential meaning. The verb is in the indicative.

Gallia sub septentriōnibus, *ut ante dictum est,* posita est.
Gaul, **as has been said before,** *is situated in the north.*

248. Substantive *quod*-clauses.—Quod, meaning *that, namely that, the fact that, as regards the fact that,* introduces substantive clauses with the verb in the indicative.

Illud praetereō, *quod Caesarem occīdērunt.*
This I pass over—the fact that they killed Caesar.
I pass over the fact that they killed Caesar.

In this sentence the **quod**-clause is in apposition with **illud**, which may be omitted in translation. Such clauses are used also as subject or object of the verb. A frequent use is as the subject of **accēdit**, *it is added:*

Accēdēbat *quod erat senex.*
There was the additional fact **that he was an old man.**

Such clauses often approximate in meaning an infinitive clause or **ut** + subjunctive in a substantive clause of purpose or fact.

VOCABULARY

accēdō, -cēdere, -cessī, -cessum, come to, approach; be added
adequitō, *I,* ride up to

colligō, -ligere, -lēgī, -lēctum, collect, gather
colloquium, -quī, *n.,* conference

colloquor, -loquī, -locūtus sum, converse

dēcrētum, -ī, *n.*, decree

dispergō, -pergere, -persī, -persum, scatter (*tr.*)

dubitō, *I*, hesitate

fera, -ae, *f.*, wild beast

initium, -tī, *n.*, beginning

iuvenis, iuvenis, *m.*, young man

moenia, moenium, *n. pl.*, city walls

praetereō, -īre, -iī, -itum, pass by

statim, *adv.*, at once

tumulus, -ī, *m.*, mound, hill

EXERCISE A

1. Hominēs dum docent discunt.

2. Ut prīmum potuit, urbem relīquit.

3. Vīxit, dum vīxit, bene.

4. Gaudeāmus igitur iuvenēs dum sumus.

5. Abīte, dum est facultās, vōsque ad legiōnem recipite.

6. Ubi neutrī transeundī initium faciunt,[2] Caesar suōs in castra redūxit.

7. Hanc dum nostrī colligunt praedam dīligentius, rēx ipse ē manibus effūgit.

8. Quamdiū quisquam erit quī tē dēfendere audeat, vīvēs.

9. Hōc ūnō praestāmus ferīs, quod inter nōs colloquimur.

10. Ubiī, quamquam sunt eiusdem generis, sunt cēterīs Germānīs hūmāniōrēs.

11. Sub[3] occāsum sōlis sequī dēstitērunt sēque in castra, ut erat imperātum, recēpērunt.

12. Postquam Pompeius ex aciē effūgit, mīlitēs eius statim dispersī sunt.

EXERCISE B

1. Hāc ex parte est Hibernia, dīmidiō minor, ut exīstimant, quam Britannia.

2. Nam ut prīmum ex puerīs excessit Archiās, sē ad scrībendī studium contulit.

3. Ille erat ūnus timendus ex istīs omnibus, sed tam diū dum urbis moenibus continēbātur.

4. Habētis eum cōnsulem quī et pārēre vestrīs dēcrētīs nōn dubitet, et ea quae cōnstitueritis, quoad vīvet, dēfendere possit.

5. Dum haec in colloquiō geruntur, Caesarī nūntiātum est equitēs

[2] See footnote 2, Lesson 51.   [3] *toward*

Ariovistī propius[4] tumulum accēdere et ad nostrōs adequitāre, lapidēs tēlaque in nostrōs conicere.

6. Tū quidem, Cicerō, ut homō[5] vīxistī, ut ōrātor[5], dīxistī, ut philosophus[5] scrīpsistī.

7. Hūc ubi rediit rēx factus est annō secundō et vicēsimō postquam imperātor fuerat.

EXERCISE C

(1) As soon as they saw us, they went away.   (2) While Pompey delayed in Rome, (his) enemies were gathering their forces against him.   (3) When I went to Corinth, I saw your father.   (4) On the eleventh day after I left you, I arrived in the country.   (5) Although our friends are here, we shall not be able to see them.

SELECTIONS FOR READING

(1) Ubi lībertās cecidit[6] audet līberē nēmō loquī.

—Publilius Syrus, *Sententiae.*

(2) Dum vītant stultī vitia, in contrāria currunt.

—Horace, *Sermones,* I, ii, 24.

(3)* Omnīnō[7] quī reī pūblicae praefutūrī sunt, duo Platōnis praecepta teneant: ūnum ut ūtilitātem cīvium tueantur,[8] ut quaecumque[9] agunt ad eam referant, oblītī commodōrum suōrum; alterum, ut tōtum corpus reī pūblicae cūrent, nē, dum partem aliquam tuentur, reliquās dēserant.

—Cicero, *de Officiis,* I, xxv, 85.

---

[4] used as prep. with acc., *nearer*   [5] Supply vīvit, dīcit, scrībit.
[6] Ubi here is equal to cum iterative, i.e., with the meaning *whenever.*
[7] *in general*   [8] tueor, tuērī, tūtus sum, *protect, guard*
[9] quī- (quae-, quod-) cumque, *whoever, whatever*
* Hints on the translation of (3): praecepta has two appositives, ūnum (praeceptum) and alterum (praeceptum). In apposition with ūnum is the indirect command ut . . . tueantur; in apposition with alterum is the indirect command ut . . . cūrent. Ut . . . referant is a purpose clause dependent upon tueantur; nē . . . dēserant is a purpose clause dependent upon cūrent.

Crassus ille Dīves cum Asiae praeesset quīnque Graecī sermōnis diffe-rentiās tenuit.

When Crassus, surnamed the Rich, was governor of the province of Asia, he acquired a mastery of five different Greek dialects.

—QUINTILIAN, *Institutio Oratoria*, XI, 2, 50

LESSON LIV

Clauses Introduced by the Conjunction *Cum*

249. The functions of the subordinating conjunction **cum** may be divided under three heads:

1. **Cum**-temporal, *when, as, after; whenever.*
2. **Cum**-causal, *since, because.*
3. **Cum**-concessive, *although.*

250. *Cum*-temporal.—

(a) *Present and future time.*—**Cum** meaning *when*, in a clause referring to present or future time, is followed by a verb in the *indicative* mood.

Dē hīs rēbus, *ōtiōsī cum erimus,* loquēmur.
We shall speak of these things, when we are (shall be) at leisure.

Rōmae videor esse, *cum tuās litterās legō.*
I seem to be at Rome, when I am reading your letter.

Cum vēneris, cognōscēs.
When you come⎫ *(will have come), you will find out.*
After you come⎭

With the future or future perfect indicative **cum** replaces **postquam**.

(b) *Past time.*—

(1) *Cum* meaning *when*, in a sentence referring to past time, is followed by a verb in the *indicative* mood when the clause merely

251

dates the action of the main verb or is strictly contemporaneous with it.

> **Cum Caesar in Galliam vēnit, alterīus factiōnis prīncipēs erant Haeduī, alterīus Sēquanī.**
>
> *When Caesar came into Gaul, the Haedui were leaders of one faction, the Sequani of the other.*
>
> **Tum, cum ex urbe Catilīnam ēiciēbam, putābam. . . .**
> *At the time when I was expelling Catiline from the city, I was thinking. . . .*

Observation 1.—In sentences of this sort, the verb of the main clause is often modified by some such word or phrase as **tum**, *then;* **tum dēmum**, *then at last, then and not till then;* **eō tempore**, *at that time;* and the like. (French *alors* supplies an exact parallel: "Un jour de 14 juillet, *alors* qu'il faisait sa tournée habituelle en ville, il trouva les boutiques fermées.")

Observation 2.—The indicative is used also in the so-called "inverted cum clause," a rare type in which for literary effect the principal action is stated in the subordinate clause. **Cum** here = *"when suddenly."*

> **Vix iter incēperāmus cum ut consisterēmus imperātum est.**
> *We had scarcely begun our march, when we were ordered to halt.*

(2) But **cum** meaning *when*, referring to past time and, instead of merely dating the event, describing the circumstances under which it took place (**cum**-circumstantial), is followed by a verb in the *subjunctive* mood. The difference between mere time and circumstance is not always easy to determine, for **cum**, like English *since*, is first temporal, then causal. The subjunctive after **cum** in past time is much more frequent than the indicative. Caesar, for example, uses the indicative only once. The tenses used are the imperfect and the pluperfect, the former representing action contemporary with, the latter, action prior to, that of the main verb.

Here, in contrast to the inverted **cum** clause of Obs. 2 above, the principal action is stated in the principal clause, the **cum** clause merely describing the situation in which it happened.

Cum essem ōtiōsus in Tusculánō, accēpī tuās litterās.
*I received your letter **when** (**as, while**) I was taking my ease in my Tusculan villa.*

Cum id nūntiātum esset, mātūrāvit.
***When this had been reported,** he hurried.*

To understand the first example, it is helpful to apply the test of a condition. "Had I not been there, should I have received your letter?" No. Therefore the connection between subordinate and principal clause is not *merely* temporal.

Cum-circumstantial is often equivalent to the English *as*, e.g.:

> "*As* I was going to St. Ives,
> I met a man with seven wives"

or to a present participle:

> *Cum intellegeret* omnēs fere Gallōs novīs rēbus studēre . . .
> *Realizing (**as he did**) that almost all the Gauls were eager for a change of government . . .*

Cum + the pluperfect subjunctive is a common substitute for the ablative absolute, especially with intransitive verbs like **veniō**, and **appropinquō** (where the ablative absolute is impossible except in the present and future participles).

(c) **Cum** meaning *whenever*, and referring to present time, is regularly followed by a verb in the *perfect indicative*, the verb of the main clause being *present;* referring to past time, it is followed by the *pluperfect indicative*, the main verb being *imperfect*.

> Eō *cum vēnit,* locō dēlectātur.
> ***Whenever he comes** there, he is [always] delighted with the place.*

> Eō *cum vēnerat,* locō dēlectābātur.
> ***Whenever he came** there, he used-to-be-delighted with the place.*

> Ēvigilō *cum libuit.*
> *I wake up **whenever I like** (it pleases me).*

251. *Cum*-causal.—**Cum** meaning *since* or *because* is always followed by a verb in the *subjunctive* mood. Any tense required by the meaning may be used.

Perfacile est, *cum* virtūte omnibus *praestēmus,* tōtīus Galliae imperiō potīrī.

It is easy to get control of the whole of Gaul, **since we surpass** *all in valor.*

Quae *cum* ita essent. . . .

Since this **was** *so. . . .   This being the case. . . .*

252. *Cum*-concessive.—Cum meaning *although* is always followed by a verb in the *subjunctive* mood.   Any tense required by the meaning may be used.   It is often balanced by a **tamen** in the main clause; see Exercise A, sentence 6.

Ille Catō, *cum esse* Tusculī *nātus,* in populī Rōmānī cīvitātem susceptus est.

The famous Cato, **though he was born** *at Tusculum, was received into the citizenship of the Roman people.*

Observation.—Note the word order.   In common with several other conjunctions, **cum** is placed *after* the subject of its clause in cases where the subject is the same as that of the main clause; cf. fn. 1, Lesson 53.

VOCABULARY

anteā, *adv.,* formerly

at, *conj.,* but, at least

beātus, -a, -um, blessed, happy

coepī, *defective verb,* **coepisse, coeptum,** began

concidō, concidere, concidī, concisum, fall utterly, collapse

cōnfiteor, -fitērī, -fessus sum, confess

cōnsīderō, *I,* consider, ponder

cōnsulātus, -ūs, *m.,* consulship

continuō, *adv.,* immediately, forthwith

dēmum, *adv.,* at length, at last, finally

extimēscō, -timēscere, -timuī, ——, dread; be afraid

fidēs, fideī, *f.,* trust; credit

lūdus, -ī, *m.,* sport; *pl.* (organized) games

mentiō, -ōnis, *f.,* mention

nam, *conj.,* for

orbis, orbis (orbium), *m.,* ring, circle; orbis terrārum, the world

plēbs, plēbis (plēbium), *f.,* populace, common people

sapiō, sapere, sapīvī, ——, be wise, have sense

solūtiō, -ōnis, *f.,* payment

tamen, *adv.,* yet, nevertheless, however

trānsfīgō, -fīgere, -fīxī, -fīxum, pierce through

vectīgal, vectīgālis (vectīgālium), *n.,* tax; *pl.* revenues

EXERCISE A

1. Illa cum audīsset, Capuam vēnit.
2. Cum pugnābant maximē, ego tum fugiēbam maximē.
3. Eō cum vēnisset Caesar, Rēmī ad eum lēgātōs mīsērunt.
4. Fuistī saepe, crēdō, cum Athēnīs essēs, in scholīs philosophōrum.
5. Cum id posset negāre, subitō praeter[1] opīniōnem omnium cōnfessus est.
6. Cum centuriōnēs hostium trānsfīxī pīlīs cecidissent, tamen ācerrimē reliquī resistēbant.
7. Tarentī lūdī forte erant cum illūc vēnit.
8. At iī quī in castrīs erant relictī, cum proelium commissum audīssent, subsidiō suīs iērunt.
9. Tum dēmum beātus terrārum orbis erit cum aut sapientēs rēgnāre aut rēgēs sapere coeperint.
10. Cum vōs cōnsīderō, mīlitēs, et cum facta vestra aestimō, magna mē spēs victōriae tenet.

EXERCISE B

1. Cum aut scrībō ad vōs aut vestrās epistulās legō, cōnficior lacrimīs sīc ut ferre nōn possim.
2. Interim cum lēgātī saepe ultrō citrōque[2] inter eōs mitterentur, Ariovistus postulāvit nē quem peditem ad colloquium Caesar addūceret.
3. Anteā cum erat ā tribūnō plēbis[3] mentiō lēgis agrāriae facta, continuō quī agrōs pūblicōs tenēbant, extimēscēbant.
4. Nam in cēterīs rēbus cum venit calamitās, tum dētrīmentum accipitur; at in vectīgālibus nōn sōlum adventus malī, sed etiam metus ipse affert calamitātem.
5. Nam tum cum in Asiā permultī rēs āmīsērunt scīmus Rōmae, solūtiōne impedītā, fidem concidisse.

EXERCISE C

(1) When I see you, I shall tell you everything. (2) When I had

---

[1] *contrary to*   [2] *back and forth*   [3] *tribune of the people, a Roman magistrate*

said this in the senate, I returned home. (3) Were you consul at
the time when I was in Asia? (4) Since such were the circumstances,
he no longer hesitated to send us help. (5) Although I could not
see him, yet I knew that he was not far away.

SELECTIONS FOR READING

(1) Quem recitās meus est, ō Fīdentīne, libellus:
  sed male cum recitās, incipit esse tuus.

            —Martial, I, 38.

(2) Vīvāmus, mea Lesbia, atque amēmus,
  rūmōrēsque senum sevēriōrum[4]
  omnēs ūnius aestimēmus assis.[5]
  Sōlēs occidere et redīre possunt:
  nōbīs, cum semel[6] occidit[7] brevis lūx,
  nox est perpetua ūna dormienda.[8]

          —Catullus, V, ll. 1–6.

(3) Themistoclem illum, summum Athēnīs virum, dīxisse aiunt[9] cum
ex eō quaererētur quod ācroāma[10] aut cuius vōcem libentissimē[11] audīret:
eius ā quō sua virtūs optimē praedicārētur.[12]

        —Cicero, *Archias*, IX, 20.

(4) Equidem[13] beātōs putō quibus deōrum mūnere[14] datum est aut
facere scrībenda aut scrībere legenda, beātissimōs vērō[15] quibus utrumque.[16]

        —Pliny, *Epistulae*, VI, 16.

(5) Facile omnēs cum valēmus rēcta cōnsilia aegrōtīs damus.
        —Terence, *Andria*, **309.**

---

[4] *gossip of old fogies* [5] **ūnius assis,** *at a single farthing* (gen. of price)
[6] *once* [7] **occidō, occidere, occidī, occāsum,** *fall down; set*
[8] **dormiō,** *IV, sleep* [9] *they say* [10] *entertainer* [11] **libenter,** *gladly*
[12] **praedicō,** *I, proclaim*
[13] = **ego quidem,** *I, for my part,* cf. French *quant à moi . . . je.* Also supply
at this point **eōs esse.**
[14] **mūnus, mūneris,** n., *gift;* here means *bounty.* [15] Supply **eōs esse (putō).**
[16] Supply **datum est.**

(6) Maiōrēs nostrī . . . virum bonum cum laudābant, ita laudābant—bonum agricolam bonumque colōnum. Amplissimē laudārī exīstimābātur quī ita laudābātur.

—Cato, *de Re Rustica, praefat.*, 2.

apr. 26 Quiz

1. Cum ācerrima esset, *sickone superlitive (very)* ergo Romam venire non potuit.

2. Cum ad montes ex urbe me recepi, felix semper fio.

3. Cum soror mea adsit, tamen eam videre non potero.

4. Cum ea patrem suum vidisset, ad maritum *husband* suum rediit.

5. Cum in urbem veneram, huic puellae flores semper dabam.

6. Ubi manebas tum cum ruri manebam?

7. Cum in villa eius iacerem, libros multos legi.

8. Cum haec ita essent, ergo diu ibi non mansimus.

9. Cum domum eum misissem multo melior factus sum *(I felt)*

10. Cum eam video, puellae flores do.

Modo liceat vīvere, est spēs.

While there's life there's hope.

—TERENCE, *H. T.* V, ii, 28

LESSON LV

Temporal Conjunctions That Take Either the Indicative or the Subjunctive— Clauses of Proviso

253. Dum, dōnec, and quoad, meaning until.—
(a) When no idea but that of *time* is involved, **dum, dōnec,** and **quoad** are followed by a verb in the *indicative* mood.

> **Rōmae fuērunt** *quoad* **L. Metellus in prōvinciam** *profectus est.*
> *They were at Rome **until** Lucius Metellus **set out** for the province.*

Observation.—The *until*-clause answers the question, *How long were they in Rome?*

(b) When, in addition to mere time, some further idea of *expectancy, anticipation,* or, especially, *purpose* is involved, **dum, dōnec,** and **quoad** are followed by a verb in the *subjunctive* mood.

> **Proeliō abstinuit** *dum reliquae cōpiae adīrent.*
> *He refrained from battle **until** the rest of the troops **should arrive.***

Observation.—The *until*-clause answers the question, *How long and why* did he refrain from battle?

254. Clauses of proviso.—Dum (sometimes **dum modo,** or **modo** alone) meaning *if only* or *provided that* is followed by a verb in the *subjunctive* mood. When these proviso clauses are negative, **nē** is used.

> **Ōderint** *dum metuant.*
> *Let them hate, **provided that they fear.***

255. Priusquam, antequam (*prius . . . quam, ante . . . quam*), meaning *before.*—

(a) Denoting mere *time*, **priusquam** and **antequam** are followed by a verb in the *indicative* mood.

> **Abiī** *antequam vēnit.*
> *I left before he came.*   (*I left.   Then he came.*)

Observation.—The *before*-clause answers the question, **When did I leave?**

(b) When some further idea of *purpose, end in view,* or *result prevented* is involved, **priusquam** and **antequam** are followed by a verb in the *subjunctive* mood.

> **Abiī** *antequam venīret.*
> *I left before he could come* (i.e., I didn't care to meet him).

Observation.—The *before*-clause answers the question, **When and why** *did I leave?*

> **Priusquam** rēs **perficerētur**, nox intervēnit.
> *Before the task could be completed, night intervened.*
> (*Night intervened, so that the task was not completed.*)

Observation.—The *before*-clause answers the question, **When and with what result** *did night intervene?*

VOCABULARY

abdō, abdere, abdidī, abditum, hide

addūcō, -dūcere, -dūxī, -ductus, induce, influence

canis, canis, *c.,* dog

cōgitō, *I,* think (of), plan

conveniō, -venīre, -vēnī, -ventum, assemble

cotīdiē, *adv.,* daily

dēsinō, -sinere, -siī, ——, cease

īnsidiae, -ārum, *f. pl.,* ambush

meminī, *defective,* remember

neglegentia, -ae, *f.,* carelessness

noctū, *adv.,* by night

perfuga, -ae, *m.,* deserter

praeceps, *adj.* (*gen.* **praecipitis**), headlong

vertō, vertere, vertī, versum, turn

EXERCISE A

1. Nec prius fugā dēstitērunt quam[1] in cōnspectum castrōrum vēnērunt.

---

[1] **Nec prius . . . quam** is to be translated *not until.*

into the view of the camp they came

2. Pervēnit Caesar priusquam Pompeius sentīre posset.

3. Priusquam tēlum conicī posset aut nostrī propius accēderent omnis aciēs terga vertit. — *retreated*

4. Dum reliquae nāvēs convenīrent ad hōram nōnam exspectāvit.

5. Dum litterae veniant morābor. *for something to happen*

6. Exspectāvit dum dormīret canis.

7. Nostrī hostēs reppulērunt neque fīnem sequendī fēcērunt quoad eōs praecipitēs[2] ēgērunt.

8. Ego hīc cōgitō commorārī quoad mē reficiam.

9. Meminī Catōnem annō antequam est mortuus mēcum disserere.

10. Sōl, antequam sē abderet, fugientem vīdit Antōnium.

EXERCISE B

1. Dē Carthāgine vererī nōn ante dēsinam quam illam dēlētam esse cognōverō.

2. Magnō mē metū līberābis dum modo inter mē atque tē mūrus intersit.

3. Vercingetorīx, priusquam mūnītiōnēs ab Rōmānīs perficerentur, cōnsilium cēpit omnem ab sē equitātum noctū dīmittere.

4. Caesar interim, dē īnsidiīs Labiēnī ex perfugīs certior factus, paucōs diēs morātus est dum hostēs cotīdiē idem faciendō in neglegentiam addūcerentur.

EXERCISE C

(1) There was silence until he returned. (2) Wait at Rome until you have received my letter. (3) Provided my brother is-in-good-health, we shall set out tomorrow. (4) My mother left the city before I could speak with her. (5) I am waiting for him to come.

SELECTIONS FOR READING

(1) Nīl recitās et[3] vīs, Māmerce, poēta vidērī:
    Quidquid vīs estō,[4] dummodo nīl recitēs.
                                    —Martial, II, 88.

---

[2] **Praecipitēs** is here used predicatively; translate *drove the enemy into headlong flight.*

[3] **Et** here means *and yet.*   [4] imperative, *be*

(2) "Dīc vērum mihi, Mārce, dīc, amābō;[5]
nīl est quod magis[6] audiam libenter."
Sīc et cum recitās tuōs libellōs,
et causam quotiēns agis clientis,
ōrās, Gallice, mē rogāsque semper.
Dūrum est mē tibi quod petis negāre.
Vērō[7] vērius ergo quid sit audī:
vērum, Gallice, nōn libenter audīs.

—Martial, VIII, 76.

(3) *Scenery on the Roman Comic Stage*

Haec urbs Epidamnus est, dum haec agitur fābula;
quandō alia agētur, aliud fīet oppidum.

—Plautus, *Menaechmi,* 72–3.

---

[5] idiom meaning *please!*   [6] **magis libenter** = **libentius**
[7] **vērō**, the abl. sing. of **vērum** used as a noun, *the truth*

Hannibal in sē ac suum ipsīus caput exsecrātus est quod nōn cruentum ab Cannēnsī victōriā mīlitem Rōmam duxisset.

Hannibal called down curses on his own head for not having led his troops, still bloody from their victory at Cannae, straight on to Rome.

—LIVY XXX, 20, 7

LESSON LVI

Indicative and Subjunctive in Causal and Concessive Clauses

256. Causal clauses (adverbial).—

(a) **Cum**-causal is aways followed by a verb in the subjunctive mood (see sec. **251**).

(b) Subordinate clauses of cause may also be introduced by **quod (proptereā quod), idcircō . . . quod; quia (proptereā quia), quoniam**, and **quandō.**[1]

(1) These conjunctions are followed by a verb in the *indicative* mood when the reason stated is a *known fact*, or is stated on the authority of the speaker or writer.

> **In hīs locīs, *quod* omnis Gallia ad septentriōnēs *vergit*, mātūrae sunt hiemēs.**
> *In these parts the winters are early, **because** Gaul as a whole lies toward the north.* (That Gaul lies toward the north is a generally known fact.)

> **Cūr igitur pācem nōlō?** **Quia turpis *est*.**
> *Why do I not desire peace?* **Because it is** disgraceful.
> (The speaker is Cicero. The reason given is Cicero's.)

(2) They are followed by a verb in the *subjunctive* mood when the reason given is quoted or assigned on the authority of another.

---

[1] In the authors commonly read, it will be found that a reason introduced by **quia, quoniam,** or **quandō** is a *fact*. These conjunctions are, therefore, nearly always followed by the *indicative*.

Supplicātiō ā senātū dēcrēta est, *quod* urbem *līberāssem*.

*A thanksgiving was decreed by the senate, **because** (as they said)
I had liberated the city.*

(The speaker is Cicero. The reason given is the senate's.)

**Dumnorīx omnibus precibus petere contendit ut in Galliā
relinquerētur, *quod* īnsuētus nāvigandī mare *timēret*.**

*Dumnorix begged most earnestly to be left in Gaul **on the pretext that,** unaccustomed as he was to sailing, **he was afraid of
the sea.***

(The writer is Caesar. The reason given is that of Dumnorix.)

257. Causal clauses (adjectival or relative).—A clause implying
cause is sometimes introduced by a relative pronoun. The verb
is in the *subjunctive* mood. This clause is a variety of the relative
clause of characteristic.

**O fortūnāte adulēscēns, *quī* tuae virtūtis Homērum praecōnem
invēnerīs.**

*O fortunate youth, **because you have found** (to have found)
a Homer (lit., who have found a Homer) to be the herald of
your valor.*

Stulta ego *quae* cum hōc īnsānō *fābuler*.

*Foolish woman **that I am to talk** with this madman.*

258. Concessive clauses (adverbial).—

(a) **Quamquam,** *although,* is always followed by a verb in the indicative mood (sec. **246**).

(b) **Cum,** *although,* is always followed by a verb in the subjunctive
mood (sec. **252**).

(c) **Quamvīs** (quam vīs, *as you please,* hence, *however much, although*) is generally followed by a verb in the *subjunctive* mood.

Agricola, *quamvīs sit senex,* serit.

*A farmer, **although he be old** (however old he may be),
continues to plant.*

(d) **Ut** and **licet,** *although, granting that, supposing,* are followed
by the *subjunctive.*

Ut *sit* fortis, tamen est crūdēlissimus.

Although he is brave, yet he is very cruel.

Ut maximē *cupiam,* venīre nōn possum.
I cannot come, much as I wish to.

259. Concessive clauses (adjectival or relative).—A relative clause with its verb in the *subjunctive* may be used with a concessive force. Compare the causal relative (sec. **257**).

Cethēgus, *quī* ante *respondisset,* repente conticuit.
*Cethegus, **though he** (literally, **who**) **had replied** previously, suddenly became silent.*

Observation.—**Quī,** in relative clauses of *cause* and *concession,* is equivalent to **cum ego, tū, is,** etc. *since I, you, he, although I, you, he,* etc. Compare **quī** in the relative final clauses (sec. **223**), where it is equivalent to **ut is,** *in order that he.*

VOCABULARY

aliēnus, -a, -um, of another; foreign, irrelevant
cēnseō, cēnsēre, cēnsuī, cēnsum, decide
contineō, -tinēre, -tinuī, -tentum, keep in
cultus, -ūs, *m.,* civilization
expōnō, -pōnere, -posuī, -positum, set forth, explain
exstinguō, -tinguere, -tīnxī, -tīnctum, quench; put out
hūmānitās, -tātis, *f.,* refinement
īnfīrmitās, -tātis, *f.,* unsteadiness, fickleness
ingenium, -ī, *n.,* talent
intercēdō, -cēdere, -cessī, -cessum, come between
īrāscor, īrāscī, īrātus sum, be angry (*w. dat.*)
laetitia, -ae, *f.,* joy

lūmen, lūminis, *n.,* light
maestus, -a, -um, dejected, sad
mōbilis, -e, easily moved, unreliable
neglegō, -legere, -lēxī, -lēctum, disregard, neglect
perscrībō, -scrībere, -scrīpsī, -scrīptum, write out
plērumque, *adv.,* generally
praeditus, -a, -um, endowed, gifted
prōpōnō, -pōnere, -posuī, -positum, relate, explain
prōsequor, -sequī, -secūtus sum, pursue
Quirītēs (Quirītium), *m. pl.,* Roman citizens
simulō, I, pretend; feign
tālis, -e, such, of such a kind
vereor, verērī, veritus sum, fear, dread

EXERCISE A

1. Longius prōsequī veritus est quod silvae palūdēsque intercēdēbant.

2. Noctū ambulābat in pūblicō Themistoclēs, quod somnum capere nōn posset.

3. Catō sapiēns putābātur quia multārum rērum ūsum habēbat.

4. Et quoniam nōndum est perscrīptum senātūs cōnsultum, ex memoriā vōbīs, Quirītēs, quid senātus cēnsuerit expōnam.

5. Eum semper prō amīcō habuī quem sciam meī esse amantissimum.

6. Omnēs mē laudābant quī fīlium habērem tālī ingeniō praeditum.

7. Mihi īrāscitur quod eum neglēxerim.

8. Maestus erat quamvīs laetitiam simulāret.

9. Q. Cicerō, quī omnēs superiōrēs diēs mīlitēs in castrīs continuisset, septimō diē quīnque cohortēs frūmentātum mīsit.

10. Bene est mihi, quia tibi bene est.

EXERCISE B

1. Lēgātī quod erant appellātī[2] superbius, Corinthum patrēs vestrī, totīus Graeciae lūmen, exstīnctum esse voluērunt.

2. Quoniam ad hunc locum perventum est,[3] nōn aliēnum esse vidētur dē Galliae Germāniaeque mōribus et quo[4] differant hae nātiōnēs inter sēsē prōpōnere.

3. Vīnum Germānī omnīnō ad sē importārī nōn patiuntur quod eā rē ad labōrem ferendum remollēscere hominēs atque effēminārī arbitrantur.

4. Quod salūs sociōrum summum in perīculum ac discrīmen vocātur, quō tandem animō ferre dēbētis?

5. Caesar īnfirmitātem Gallōrum veritus est quod sunt in cōnsiliīs capiendīs mōbilēs et novīs plērumque rēbus student.

6. Dīcēbant sibi esse in animō sine ūllō maleficiō iter per prōvinciam facere, proptereā quod aliud iter habērent nūllum.

---

[2] *spoken to*
[3] Impersonal use. Translate *this point has been reached.*
[4] Quō is an abl. of specification, *in what respect(s).*

7. Caesar, quod memoriā tenēbat Cassium occīsum esse ab Helvētiīs, concēdendum[5] nōn putābat.

8. Hōrum omnium fortissimī sunt Belgae, proptereā quod ā
cultū atque hūmānitāte prōvinciae longissimē absunt.

9. Miser quī nōn sentiās illō iūdiciō tē nōn absolūtum sed ad
aliquod sevērius iūdicium ac maius supplicium reservātum!

EXERCISE C

(1) Since you have heard this, you ought to announce it to all.
(2) This being the case, no one was willing to remain. (3) They
did this because (as they said) they wished the city to be safe. (4)
He was blamed on-the-ground-that he had taken the money. (5)
However tired you may be, you must make this journey to the
emperor.

SELECTIONS FOR READING

(1) Magnus est in rē pūblicā campus, ut sapienter dīcere Crassus
solēbat, multīs apertus[6] cursus[7] ad laudem.

—Cicero, *Philippics*, XVI, vi, **17.**

(2) Trahimur omnēs studiō laudis, et optimus quisque[8] maximē glōriā
dūcitur. Ipsī illī philosophī, etiam in eīs libellīs quōs dē contemnendā[9]
glōriā scrībunt, nōmen suum īnscrībunt.

—Cicero, *Archias*, xi, 26.

---

[5] Supply **esse** and translate *concessions should not be made.*
[6] **apertus, -a, -um,** *open*   [7] Here translate by *career.*
[8] literally, *"each best,"* regular idiom for *all the best (men)*
[9] **contemnō, -temnere, -tempsī, -temptum,** *despise*

Utque aliōs industria ita hunc ignāvia ad fāmam prōtulerat.

—TACITUS, *Annals* XVI, 18, on Petronius

Most men toil for it, but this man loitered into fame.

—HELEN WADDELL

LESSON LVII

Review Exercises on Subordinate Clauses and Conjunctions Introducing Them

REVIEW EXERCISE A

1. Dum fēlis dormit, mūs gaudet et exsilit antrō.[1]
2. Cum sciam quō diē ventūrus sim faciam ut sciās.
3. Ut[2] heri mē salūtāvit Rōmam profectus est.
4. Annō post consul prīmum fuerat quam ego nātus sum.
5. Vercingetorīx, ubi dē Caesaris adventū cognōvit, oppugnātiōne dēstitit.
6. Servum meum, hominem fidēlem, domum remīsī quod valētūdine oculōrum impedītur.
7. Multaque ut[3] ēripiat, multō mihi plūra relinquet.
8. Quod tē vīvum ac valentem reppererim vehementer gaudeō.
9. Cum ē Graeciā in Italiam redīrēmus et Brundisium īrēmus ēgressīque ē nāvī in terram in portū illō spatiārēmur, fascēs librōrum vēnālium[4] expositōs vīdimus.

REVIEW EXERCISE B

1. Dum vīxī, bibī libenter; bibite vōs quī vīvitis.[5]
2. Cum perspexerō voluntātēs nōbilium, scrībam ad tē.

---

[1] exsilit, *jumps;* antrum, *cave* or *hole*   [2] Here ut = ut prīmum.
[3] ut concessive; see sec. 258d.   [4] vēnālis, *for sale*
[5] Epitaph of a toper; it runs in a lively trochaic meter.

3. Sit dīvus dum nōn sit vīvus.[6]

4. Pāret aegrē, incūsatque sē quod mē morētur.

5. Ipse, equō vulnerātō dēiectus, quoad potuit fortissimē restitit.

6. Ego ad nāvem cum cēterīs opperiar (*wait*) dum Eurylochus reversus sit.

7. Ego minus saepē ad vōs dō litterās quam possum proptereā quod omnia mihi tempora[7] sunt misera.

8. Hannibal annō tertiō postquam domō profūgerat, L. Cornēliō, Q. Minūciō cōnsulibus, cum quīnque nāvibus Āfricam accessit.

9. Quī cum Caesarem in itinere convēnissent sēque ad pedēs eius proiēcissent, flentēsque pācem petīssent, atque eōs in eō locō quō tum essent[8] adventum exspectāre iussisset, pāruērunt.

REVIEW EXERCISE C

1. O miser, quī apud tālīs virōs tam impudenter loquāre.

2. Graviter eōs incūsat quod ab eīs nōn sublevētur.

3. Ubi[9] ex lītore aliquōs singulārēs[10] ex nāvī ēgredientēs cōnspexerant, eōs adoriēbantur, plūrēs paucōs circumsistēbant.

4. Haec dēcrēvī brevī (spatiō) ad tē perscrībere, nōn quō[11] (ea) tē fugere (*escape your notice*) exīstimem sed quod forsitan[12] dolōre impedītus minus ea perspiciās.

5. Dīc, hospes, Spartae (*Sparta*) nōs tē hīc vīdisse iacentēs dum sānctīs patriae lēgibus obsequimur (*obey*).

6. O miserum senem[13] quī mortem contemnendam esse in tam longā aetāte nōn vīderit!

7. Ardentīsque (*spirited*) āvertit equōs in castra priusquam pābula gustāssent (*taste*) Trōiae Xanthumque (*Xanthus River*) bibissent.

8. Dum elephantī trāiciuntur[14] interim Hannibal Numidās equitēs quīngentōs ad castra Rōmāna mīserat speculātum ubi et quantae copiae essent et quid parārent.

9. Quīdam sapiēns querēbātur quod omnibus in rēbus hominēs dīligentiōrēs essent quam in amīcīs ēligendīs.

---

[6] Caracalla's remark after killing Geta   [7] *circumstances*
[8] subjunctive by attraction   [9] **cum,** *whenever*   [10] *individuals*
[11] **nōn quō,** *not because;* used to introduce a *rejected* reason
[12] **fors-sit-an,** *it may chance that, perhaps*
[13] accusative of exclamation   [14] *ferry across*

10. Dum ea geruntur, ūnā legiōne ex cōnsuētūdine (*as was customary*) frūmentātum missā quae appellābātur septima, iī quī prō portīs castrōrum in statiōne erant Caesarī nūntiāvērunt pulverem maximum in eā parte vidērī quam in partem legiō iter fēcisset.

REVIEW EXERCISE D

1. Nihil tam asperum neque tam difficile est quod nōn cupidissimē (*eagerly*) factūrī sīmus dum ea rēs cīvitātem nostram aere aliēnō (*debt*) līberet.

2. Subitō praeter spem omnium exortus Octāviānus prius cōnfēcit (*raise*) exercitum quem furōrī M. Antōnī oppōneret quam quisquam hoc eum cōgitāre sūspicārētur.

3. Caesar nōn exspectandum sibi statuit dum, omnibus fortūnīs (*property*) sociōrum cōnsūmptīs, in Santonōs Helvētiī pervenīrent.

4. Haeduī veniēbant questum quod paene in cōnspectū exercitūs Rōmānī agrī vastārentur, līberī in servitūtem abdūcerentur, oppida expūgnārentur.

5. Sed eā celeritāte atque eō impetū mīlitēs iērunt, cum capite sōlō ex aquā exstārent, ut hostēs impetum legiōnum atque equitum sustinēre nōn possent.

6. Hāc rē statim Caesar per speculātōrēs cognitā, īnsidiās veritus, quod quā dē causā hostēs discēderent nōndum perspexerat, exercitum equitātumque castrīs continuit.

7. Nerviī increpitābant (*taunt*) atque incūsābant reliquōs Belgās quī sē populō Rōmānō dedissent patriamque[15] virtūtem prōiēcissent.

8. Mīrārī Catō sē aiēbat (= dīcēbat) quod nōn rīdēret haruspex (*soothsayer*) haruspicem cum vīdisset.

9. Cicerō, quī[16] omnēs superiōrēs diēs praeceptīs[17] Caesaris summā dīligentiā mīlitēs in castrīs continuisset ac nē cālōnem (*soldier's servant*) quidem quemquam extrā mūnītiōnem ēgredī passus esset, quīnque cohortēs frūmentātum in proximās segetēs mittit.

10. Iam ad urbem appropinquābant cum[18] novās cōpiās advēnisse nūntiātum est.

---

[15] **patriam,** here used as f. s. of **patrius,** adjective, *traditional*
[16] See sec. **259.**   [17] *in accordance with Caesar's orders*
[18] See sec. **250b. 1,** *obs.* 2.

Mūtōs enim nāscī (hominēs) et egēre omnī ratiōne satius fuisset quam prōvidentiae mūnera in mūtuam perniciem convertere.

Better had it been for mankind to be born dumb and devoid of reason than to pervert the gifts of providence to their mutual destruction.

—QUINTILIAN, *Institutio Oratoria*, XII, 1,2

LESSON LVIII

Conditional Sentences

260. Conditional conjunctions.—Though Latin often uses the participle and the ablative absolute construction to convey the sense of a conditional clause (see secs. **236** and **237**), it also has special conjunctions to introduce clauses of condition. These are **sī**, *if;* **nisi**, *if not, unless;* **quod sī, sīn**, *but if;* and **etsī, tametsī**, and **etiamsī**, *even if (though).* They are frequently preceded by such words as **ita, eā condiciōne.**

261. Protasis and apodosis.—In the sentence *If it rains tomorrow, I shall not go out*, the adverbial clause of condition, introduced by the conjunction *if*, is called the *protasis;* the main clause containing the conclusion, *I shall not go out*, is called the *apodosis.*

262. Moods in conditional sentences.—Verbs in conditional sentences are found in both the indicative and subjunctive moods, in most cases the same mood being found in both the protasis and apodosis. The choice of mood is determined by the class to which the condition belongs.

Conditions fall into two main classes.

263. Class I: Open conditions; both verbs in the indicative.— In conditions of this class, nothing is implied as to the truth or falsity of the statement contained in the protasis. The attitude of the speaker is entirely detached and objective. Such conditions are found in present, past, and future time. The verb of the protasis is always in the indicative mood, and the verb of the apodosis in the indicative or imperative (or the subjunctive in its hortatory or jussive uses, which are equivalent to an imperative).

(1) **Sī valēs, bene est.**
If you are in good health, it is well.

(2) **Sī hoc fēcistī, stultus erās (or fuistī).**
If you did this, you were foolish.

(3) **Sī hoc fēceris, dolēbis.**
If you do (will have done) this, you will be sorry.

(4) **Venīte, sī vultis.**
Come, if you wish.

(5) **Veniant, sī volunt.**
Let them come, if they wish.

264. Class II: Conditions in which a negative is implied; both verbs in the subjunctive.—In conditions of this class is implied the *impossibility* or, as in (b) below, the *improbability* of the state of things expressed in the protasis, with a corresponding impossibility or improbability in the apodosis. The attitude of the speaker is here subjective; he is giving play to his imagination. These conditions, like those of Class I, are found in past, present, and future time.

(a) *Past and present time.*—The implied negative is here so strong that these conditions may definitely be characterized as "contrary-to-fact."

(1) *Present time.*—Both verbs in the *imperfect.*

Sī adesset, eum vidērēs.
If he were here [now] (but he is not here), you would see him (but you do not).

(2) *Past time.*—Both verbs in the *pluperfect.*

Sī adfuisset, eum vīdissēs.
If he had been here (but he was not here), you would have seen him (but you did not).

Note.—This protasis may be in past time (*pluperfect*), while the apodosis is in present time (*imperfect*).

Sī vīllam abhinc annōs XV *vēndidissem,* hodiē dīves *essem.*
*If I **had sold** my house fifteen years ago, **I should be** rich today.*

(b) *Future time.*—Both verbs in the *present.* Here the implied negative is not nearly so strong. It usually indicates a feeling on the part of the speaker that the statement contained in the protasis is unlikely, or, weaker still, it indicates an unwillingness on the part of the speaker to admit that the statement contained in the protasis is probable, even though he may hope it is. The term "contrary-to-fact" is not applicable to conditions of this type, because, from the very nature of futurity, we cannot say with certainty[1] whether the statement contained in the protasis will be true or not.

These conditions are characterized in English by the words *should* or *were to* in the protasis, and *would* (*should* in the first person) in the apodosis.

> **Sī veniat, gaudeās.**
> *If he should come,* ⎫
> *If he were to come,* ⎬ *you would be glad.*

English also allows *If he came, you would be glad.*

These conditions are sometimes called "future less vivid" in contrast to the future conditions of Class I, which are called "future more vivid."

265. A working rule for distinguishing conditions in their English form.—Conditions of Class I can be recognized in English by the fact that the apodosis makes complete sense, even when isolated from the protasis. For example, in sec. **263**, *It is well, You were foolish, You will be sorry, Come,* and *Let them come* all express thoughts complete in themselves.

In Class II, however, the apodosis leaves the hearer unsatisfied. For example, in sec. **264**, *You would see him, You would have seen him, I should be rich today,* and *You would be glad* do not express thoughts complete in themselves, but leave the hearer with a feeling that something has been suppressed or remains to be stated, i.e., the protasis.

266. Apparent exceptions to Class II.—Instead of the subjunctive, the indicative is often found in the apodosis of conditions of Class II

---

[1] Except, possibly, where the protasis is past and only the apodosis future. Sentences of this kind reveal the *"contrary-to-fact"* aspect of the so-called *"should-would"* or *"future less vivid"* conditions. "If I had not lost all my money (but I have), I should be going to Europe next summer (but I [most probably] shall not)."

when a modal auxiliary, e.g., an expression meaning *can, may, might, ought,* or *must,* is used. The reason for this is that the modal auxiliary has already given the principal verb all the modification it needs and is equivalent in sense to a subjunctive.

Antōnī gladiōs *potuit contemnere,* sī sīc omnia *dīxisset.* . . .
He (Cicero) **might have scorned** *the swords of Antony, if he* **had expressed** *everything thus.* . . .

267. Conditions in indirect statement.—After a verb introducing indirect statement, the verbs of all protases will stand in the subjunctive mood, in accordance with the rule stated in sec. 217, while the verbs of all apodoses[2] will stand in the infinitive mood (sec. 196b).

DIRECT

Sī pācem populus Rōmānus cum Helvētiīs *faciet,* in eam partem *ībunt* . . . Helvētiī ubi eōs tū cōnstitueris. . . .
If the Roman people **make** *peace with the Helvetians, the Helvetians* **will go** *into the section that you (Caesar) decide (lit., shall have decided).* . . .

INDIRECT

(Dīxit) sī pācem populus Rōmānus cum Helvētiīs *faceret,* in eam partem *itūrōs* . . . Helvētiōs ubi eōs Caesar cōnstituisset[3]. . . .
(He said) that if the Roman people **would make** *peace with the Helvetians, the Helvetians* **would go** *into the section that Caesar should decide (should have decided).*

VOCABULARY

aberrō, *I,* wander away, go astray
aevum, -ī, *n.,* age; an age, an eternity
concēdō, -cēdere, -cessī, -cessum, give up, yield
coniūrātus, -ī, *m.,* conspirator

convincō, -vincere, -vīcī, -victum, prove; prove guilty
dēcēdō, -cēdere, -cessī, -cessum, go from, withdraw
dēdūcō, -dūcere, -dūxī, -ductum, lead down *or* away

---

[2] Except verbs standing in the imperative or jussive subjunctive. These become or remain subjunctive.   [3] See sec. **217.**

exiguus, -a, -um, short, small
hūc, *adv.*, to this place
impetrō, *I*, obtain one's request
Latīnē, *adv.*, in Latin
mātūrus, -a, -um, early
mentior, mentīrī, mentītus sum,
　lie, tell lies
nōbilis, -e, noted; *as noun*, man of
　noble birth

numquam, *adv.*, not ever, never
quīcumque, quaecumque, quod-
　cumque, whoever, whatever
redarguō, redarguere, redarguī, re-
　dargūtum, disprove, refute
remūneror, *I*, reward
resideō, residēre, resēdī, resessum,
　remain, remain behind
uxor, uxōris, *f.*, wife

EXERCISE A

1. Sī vīs, potes.
2. Dīcam, sī poterō, Latīnē.
3. Num negāre audēs? Quid[4] tacēs? Convincam, sī negās.
4. Redargue mē, sī mentior.
5. Etiamsī tacent, satis dīcunt.
6. Sī id scīssem, numquam hūc tulissem pedem.
7. Nātūram sī sequēmur ducem, numquam aberrābimus.
8. Sī esset in terrīs, rīdēret Dēmocritus.
9. Sī taceās, loquar.
10. Sī quem interrogēs, respondeat.
11. Errās, sī id crēdis.
12. Quae si vidērēs, lacrimās nōn tenērēs.

EXERCISE B

1. Haec sī tēcum patria loquātur, nōnne impetrāre dēbeat?

2. Sī tē interficī iusserō, residēbit in rē pūblicā reliqua coniūrā-
tōrum manus.

3. Nisi dēcēdēs atque exercitum dēdūcēs ex hīs regiōnibus, tē
nōn prō amīcō sed prō hoste habēbō.

4. Quod sī tē interfēcerō, multīs nōbilibus prīncipibusque populī
Rōmānī grātum (*a favor*) faciam.

5. Quod sī dēcesseris et līberam possessiōnem Galliae mihi trādi-
deris, magnō tē praemiō remūnerābor et quaecumque bella gerī volēs
sine ūllō tuō labōre et perīculō cōnficiam.

6. Caesar, etsī in hīs locīs mātūrae sunt hiemēs, tamen in Britanniam proficīscī contendit.

---

[4] *Why?*

7. Sī sine uxōre possēmus vīvere, Quirītēs, omnēs eā molestiā carērēmus.

8. Unum quidem certē nēmō erit tam inimīcus Cluentiō quī mihi nōn concēdat: sī doceō nōn ab Cluentiō hoc esse factum, vincō⁵ ab Oppiānicō⁶; sī ostendō⁶ ab Oppiānicō, pūrgō Cluentium.

9. Sī computēs annōs, exiguum tempus;⁷ sī vicēs rērum,⁸ aevum (*an age*) putēs.

10. Sī causae⁹ ipsae prō sē loquī possent, nēmō adhibēret ōrātōrem.

EXERCISE C

(1) If he should say this, he would be wrong.   (2) If I give you money, I shall be sorry.   (3) If you had been here, my daughter would not have died.   (4) Although¹⁰ Caesar knew this, he yet called the envoys to him.   (5) If Caesar were now living, would he be speaking Latin?

SELECTIONS FOR READING

(1)   *Retort of Quintus Fabius to a Roman General*

General: Meā operā, Q. Fabī, Tarentum recēpistī.
Fabius: Certē; nam, nisi tū āmīsissēs, numquam recēpissem.
                                        —Cicero, *de Senectute*, iv, **11.**

(2) Nīl mihi dās vīvus; dīcis post fāta¹¹ datūrum.
      Sī nōn es stultus, scīs, Maro, quid cupiam.
                                        —Martial, XI, 67.

(3) Aestāte puerī sī valent, satis discunt.
                                        —Martial, X, 62.

(4) Perfēcit opus suum Phīdiās, etiamsī nōn vēndidit.
                                        —Seneca, *de Beneficiis*, II, 33.

(5) Dōnec eris fēlīx multōs numerābis amīcōs;
      Tempora si fuerint nūbila, sōlus eris.
                                        —Ovid, *Tristia*, I, ix, 5–6.

---

⁵ **Vincō** here means *win a point, prove.*   ⁶ Supply **hoc esse factum.**
⁷ Supply **putēs.**   ⁸ **vicēs rērum,** *changes, vicissitudes, ups and downs*
⁹ **causae,** *law suits, briefs*   ¹⁰ Use **etsī.**
¹¹ *death,* see vocab.   With **datūrum** supply **tē.**

Nōn vereor nē quid timidē, nē quid stultē faciās, sī ea dēfendēs quae ipse rēcta esse sentiēs.

I am not afraid that you will show timidity or stupidity in anything, if only you stand up for what you yourself feel to be right.

—CICERO, *ad Familiares*, II, 7, to the Tribune Curio in 51 B.C.

LESSON LIX

Subjunctive with Expression of Fearing— Historical Infinitive

268. Expressions of fearing.—Vereor, timeō, metuō,[1] and phrases such as **perīculum est** and **metus est**, all of which connote fear, have a construction of their own—the subjunctive verb introduced by **nē** and **nē nōn** (= ut).

Verbs of fearing can, of course, take a direct object, just as they can in English, e.g., **Timeō Danaōs**, *I fear the Greeks*, or an infinitive, e.g., **Equitēs intrāre fūmum timēbant**, *The horsemen were afraid to enter the smoke;* but where such verbs introduce a clause, the subjunctive with **ut** or **nē** must be used.

This use of **nē** corresponds to the use of the English *lest.*

> **Vereor** *nē veniat.*
> *I fear lest he come.*
> *I fear that he will come.*

Ut (**nē nōn**) is in such clauses equal to *lest . . . not.*

Nē nōn usually replaces **ut** where the verb of fearing is itself negatived.

> **Vereor ut** *veniat.*
> *I fear lest he come not.*
> *I fear that he will not come.*

---

[1] **Vereor** expresses a feeling of respect, awe, or dread; **timeō** a feeling of fear so strong that one wishes to fly; **metuō** a mere feeling or premonition of danger.

Observation.—In such sentences, clauses like **nē veniat** and **ut veniat** are substantive clauses, objects of the verb of fearing, **vereor.** The *indirect* reflexive is usual.

269. The usual rules for the sequence of tenses hold good.

PRIMARY: **Vereor nē servus *effugiat.***
          *I fear that the slave **will escape.***

          Vereor nē servus *effūgerit.*
          *I fear that the slave **has escaped.***

SECONDARY: **Verēbar nē servus *effugeret.***
          *I feared that the slave **would escape.***

          Verēbar nē servus *effūgisset.*
          *I feared that the slave **had escaped.***

270. It looks at first sight as if **nē** and **ut** in these clauses were inverted from their usual meanings. This is really not the case. These clauses are developed from an optative (see sec. **209c**). Originally, the wish must have been an independent sentence to which was added an independent or parenthetical verb of fearing. E.g., *May the slave **not** escape* (**nē effugiat servus**). *However, I fear it* (**timeō**). In other words, *I fear that the slave **will escape.*** Similarly, *May he come* (**ut veniat**). *However, I am afraid.* In other words, *I fear that he **will not** come.*

271. Historical infinitive.—Frequently, in Caesar and other authors, an infinitive will be found which does not stand in indirect statement and is not a complementary infinitive, *e.g.,*

Gallī ex omnibus partibus *dēcurrere,* lapidēs tēlaque in vāllum *conicere.*
*The Gauls **rushed down** from all sides and **hurled** stones and weapons against the rampart.*

Initiō, quāle ubīque, silentium noctis; dein *concutī* ferrum, vincula *movērī:* ille nōn *tollere* oculōs, nōn *remittere* stīlum, sed *offirmāre* animum auribusque *praetendere:* tum *crēbēscere* fragor, *adventāre,* et iam ut in līmine, iam ut intrā līmen *audīrī:* respicit, videt agnoscitque nārrātam sibi effigiem.

—Pliny, *Epistolae,* VII, 27.

At first, as everywhere else, the silence of the night: then **came the clanking** *of iron,* **the rattle** *of chains. He neither* **raised** *his eyes nor* **laid** *down his pen but* **concentrated** *more intently so as to make himself deaf to the sounds. Then the din* **began to grow louder, kept coming closer** *till it* **sounded** *first at the threshold then within the room. He looked back; he saw and recognized the ghost of which they had told him.*

Here the infinitive is styled *"historical."* It is often so used for the imperfect indicative in narration and description. Its subject stands in the *nominative* case. In this idiom, only the present tense of the infinitive is used, and the idiom is usually found only in main clauses. For purposes of the sequence of tenses, the historical infinitive is a *secondary* tense.

VOCABULARY

apportō, *I,* bring
circumveniō, -venīre, -vēnī, -ventum, surround
inermis, -e, unarmed
integer, -gra, -grum, whole; unimpaired, fresh

metuō, metuere, metuī, metūtum, fear
perfidia, -ae, *f.,* treachery
premō, premere, pressī, pressum, press hard, attack
supportō, *I,* bring up

EXERCISE A

1. Deōs et amō et metuō.
2. Hominēs quem metuunt ōdērunt.
3. Nōn vereor invidiam.
4. Timeō nē maleficia mea sint inventa omnia.
5. Vereor nē quid malī puella apportet.
6. Nōn timēbant nē ab hoste circumvenīrentur.
7. Caesar timēbat tantae magnitūdinis flūminī exercitum obicere.
8. Ut possim metuō. Vereor nē molestus videar.
9. Dē rē pūblicā valdē timeō. 9a. Verēbātur nē hostēs dē suīs cōnsiliīs certiōrēs fierent.
10. Quamquam omnia sunt timenda, nihil magis quam perfidiam timēmus.
11. Quōs ōlim inermēs sine causā timuistis, hōs posteā armātōs ac victōrēs superāvistis.
12. Timuit ut satis commodē supportārī posset rēs frūmentāria.
13. Aurum quod condidī metuō ut possim recipere.

14. Verērī videntur nōn nūllī ut habeam satis praesidī.

(15.) Nostrī prīmō integrīs vīribus fortiter pugnāre[2] neque ūllum frūstrā tēlum ex locō superiōre mittere,[2] et quaecumque pars castrōrum nūdāta dēfēnsōribus premī vidēbātur, eō currere[2] et auxilium ferre.[2]

(16.) Vereor ut hoc tibi prōfutūrum sit.[3]

EXERCISE B

(1) You are not afraid to do this, are you? (2) I fear you have not spoken the truth. (3) We are afraid that he will see us. (4) Fearing[4] that the enemy would pursue them, they set out at dawn. (5) He feared we would not reach the camp before sunset.

---

[2] See sec. **271**.

[3] Where a sense of *likelihood* is introduced, the equivalent of a *future* subjunctive may be used.   [4] Use **veritus** (see appendix **46a**).

Quis dubitet quīn in virtūte dīvitiae sint?

Who would doubt that it pays to be good?

—CICERO, *Paradoxa*, 48

LESSON LX

Subjunctive with *Quōminus* and *Quīn*—Verbs of Preventing and Refusing—Verbs of Doubting

272. Verbs of preventing and refusing.—The conjunction **quōminus** equals **quō minus**, literally, *by which the less*. It is analogous to expressions like **quō magis** and **quō facilius**, which introduce relative clauses of purpose (sec. **223**). It introduces what is in effect a purpose or result clause, and serves as an equivalent to **ut eō minus**, *in order that* (or *so that*) *by this the less*. The verb of such a clause will naturally stand in the subjunctive.

> **Tempestās nāvēs *dēterruit quōminus* cursum *tenērent.***
> *A storm prevented the ships from keeping to their course.*
> (Lit., *a storm prevented the ships so that by this the less they kept to their course.*)

The commonest verbs that govern this construction are: **impediō**, *hinder;* **dēterreō**, *prevent;* **obstō**, *stand in the way of;* **temperō**, *restrain (oneself) from;* **teneō**, *keep (from);* **retineō**, *restrain;* and **recūsō**, *refuse, object.*

Observation 1.—**Prohibeō**, *prevent*, and **vetō**, *forbid*, are followed by the infinitive (sec. **225**, obs.).

> **Eōs *regredī* prohibuit.**
> *He prevented them from returning.*

Observation 2.—**Nē** is often found in place of **quōminus** when the main clause containing the idea of prevention, or the like, is affirmative.

Quīn is often found in place of **quōminus** when the main clause containing the idea of prevention, or the like, is negative.

> **Plūra** *nē dīcam* **tuae mē lacrimae** *impediunt.*
> *Your tears **hinder** me **from saying** more.*
>
> **Nihil impedīre** potest *quīn* **tibi** *cōnsulās.*
> *Nothing can **prevent** you **from consulting** your own interest.*

Observation 3.—All the above constructions follow the regular rule for the sequence of tenses (sec. **212**).

Observation 4.—Note the idiom

> **Per tē (mē, etc.) stetit** *quōminus vincerēmus.*
> *You were the cause **of our not winning.***

273. Verbs of doubting.—

(a) **Dubitō num ventūrus sit**
    I doubt whether he will come

is a perfectly normal indirect question of the type of primary sequence which looks toward the future (sec. **212a**). The subjunctive is the natural mood; the dependent (noun) clause is introduced by **num**.

(b) *Nōn dubitō quīn* **ventūrus sit**
    *I do **not doubt that** he will come,*

   Nōn dubium est quīn **ventūrus sit**
   *There is no **doubt that** he will come,*

   Nōn dubitārī potest quīn **ventūrus sit**
   *It cannot be **doubted that** he will come,*

   Quis dubitat (i.e. *nēmō dubitat*) *quīn* **ventūrus sit?**
   *Who doubts (i.e. **no one doubts**) **that** he will come?*

all illustrate the construction with **quīn** which verbs and expressions of doubting govern when they are negative or virtually negative. An example of the virtual negative is the rhetorical question **quis dubitat?**, which is the equivalent of **nēmō dubitat**.

These constructions all follow the regular rule for the sequence of tenses. Since doubts (like fears) more frequently refer to the future, the use of the active periphrastic with **sim** and **essem** is prevalent. (Sec. **212a**.) **Dubitō,** *hesitate,* takes the infinitive.

274. *Quīn*: **other uses.**—In addition to its uses with verbs of preventing, negatived verbs, and expressions of doubting, **quīn** appears in certain constructions where it is equivalent to **quī** (or **quae** or **quod**) **nōn.**

> *Nūlla* **nāvis est** *quīn* **tempestāte laesa sit (quīn = quae nōn).**
> *There is* **no** *ship that* **has not** *been hurt by the storm.*

The use of the subjunctive in such clauses may be explained in the light of relative clauses of characteristic or result (sec. **230**).

Quīn may even stand for **quī, quae,** or **quod nōn** in oblique cases.

> *Nūllum* **patiēbātur esse** *diem quīn* **in forō dīceret.**
> *He did* **not** *let a* **day** *pass* **without** *making a speech in the market place.*

In this example, **quīn = quō nōn = ut eō nōn =** *so that on it (he did) not.*

Observation 1.—A **quīn** which is the equivalent of **quod** or **quō nōn** followed by the subjunctive is found in causal clauses where a negative reason is introduced only to be rejected.

> **Nōn** *quīn* **parī virtūte et voluntāte aliī** *fuerint,* **sed tantam causam nōn habuērunt.**
> *Not that there were not* *others of equal courage and good will, but they had not so strong a reason.*

Observation 2.—**Quīn** may sometimes stand for a direct interrogative = **quī nōn =** *by which not =* *why not?* and be joined with any mood.

> **Quīn abīs?** *Why don't you go away?*

VOCABULARY

auferō, auferre, abstulī, ablātum, carry off
columna, -ae, *f.,* column
cōnstantia, -ae, *f.,* firmness
extrīnsecus, *adv.,* on the outside
inaurātus, -a, -um, gilded
intermittō, -mittere, -mīsī, -missum, let slip
īnsequor, -sequī, -secūtus sum, pursue

introeō, -īre, -iī, -itum, go into
modus, -ī, *m.*, way
perpetuus, -a, -um, continuous, unbroken
recūsō, *I*, refuse
servitūs, -tūtis, *f.*, slavery

solidus, -a, -um, solid
temperō, *I*, stop (oneself), refrain
from
ventitō, *I*, come repeatedly, visit
vetō, vetāre, vetuī, vetitum, forbid

EXERCISE A

1. Dubitāsne, Catilīna, abīre?
2. Amīcum meum hoc facere prohibēbō.
3. Nēmō est quīn saepe peccet.
4. Hannibal flūmen Rhodanum trānsīre nōn dubitāvit.
5. Nūllum tempus intermīsērunt quīn trāns Rhēnum lēgātōs mitterent.
6. Quis nāvigāvit quīn sē aut mortis aut servitūtis perīculō committeret?
7. Nūllō modō introīre possum quīn mē videant.
8. Diēs ferē nūllus est quīn hic homō domum meam ventitet.
9. Recūsāmus quōminus perpetuō sub Sēquanōrum imperiō sīmus.
10. Multae nāvēs ventō tenēbantur quōminus in portum venīre possent.

EXERCISE B

1. Hannibal columnam auream quae in fānō Iūnōnis erat auferre voluit sed dubitāvit utrum ea solida esset an extrīnsecus inaurāta.
2. An quod ad diem amīcī vestrī nōn vēnērunt, dē eōrum fidē cōnstantiāque dubitātis?
3. Nūllum ferē tōtīus hiemis tempus intercessit quīn Caesar aliquem dē cōnsiliīs Gallōrum nūntium acciperet.
4. Hominēs tam ferī ac barbarī nōn sibi temperābunt quīn in prōvinciam exeant atque inde in Italiam contendant.
5. Caesar equitātum subsidiō labōrantibus celeriter mīsit et hostēs quōminus ācriter nostrōs īnsequerentur terruit.
6. Tū vel auctōritāte tuā, vel exercitū, vel nōmine populī Rōmānī dēterrēre potes nē magna multitūdō Germānōrum Rhēnum trādūcantur.[1]

[1] A "sense construction"; multitūdō G. is treated as a plural.

7. Nōn, quōminus perpetua cum Gallīs amīcitia esset, per populum Rōmānum stetit.

8. Nōn potes mihi nocēre quīn[2] tibi ipsī noceās.

EXERCISE C

(1) The storm prevented our arriving promptly.　(2) We shall
never refuse to obey our emperor.　(3) My friends never hesitate to
tell me the truth.　(4) I doubt whether my wife will allow me to go
to the forum today.　(5) You did not doubt that Pompey had been
defeated, ~~did you~~?

[2] **quīn noceās,** *without injuring*

[handwritten annotations:]

1. the storm prevented quominus to theday
we arrived (imp. sub)   Perf   ad diem

2. never shall we refuse quin we obey
(numquam)   fut. indic   (pres sub)
our emperor

3. Friends my to me the truth to
dat.   acc.
tele never hesitate.   numquam

4. dubito num wife my going to
is — pres sub
non sing fem (sine participle)   ad   acc.
allow   forum.
me today into
forum to go is
going to allow
perf indic

5. (Negitive) Num doubt quin
pp. sub pass.
Pompey had been defeated (vinco)

Ego tēcum tanquam mēcum loquor.

I talk to you as though to myself.

—CICERO, *ad Atticum*

LESSON LXI

Clauses of Comparison

275. When a comparative clause is meant to state an actual fact, its verb is in the indicative.

> **Perinde ac meritus est, poenās persolvit.**
> *He was punished, exactly as he deserved.*

Words commonly introducing this construction are **sīcut, ita ut,** *just as;* **prō eō ac,** *in accordance with;* **proinde ac, perinde ac,** *in the same manner as;* **aequē ac,** *as much as;* **aliter ac,** *otherwise than;* **alius ac,** *different from;* **īdem ac,** *the same as.* **Idem quī** is also used; cf. sec. **200a.**

276. When a comparative clause expresses a purely imaginary and unreal comparison, its verb is in the subjunctive.

> **Pugnābat *velut* salūs cīvitātis in sē ūnō *pōnerētur*.**
> *He fought **as if** the safety of the state **depended** on him alone.*

The reason for the subjunctive is that we are here dealing with a condensed form of the sentence:

> **Pugnābat *velut* (*pugnāret sī*) salūs cīvitātis in sē ūnō pō-nerētur.**
> *He fought **as** (**he would fight if**) the safety of the state depended on him alone.*

This type of comparative clause is really a species of Class II condition, sec. **264,** the apodosis of which has been suppressed.

285

Words commonly introducing this construction are **velut, velut sī, quasi, ut sī, ac sī, tamquam sī,** *as if;* **perinde ac, proinde ac,** *just as.*
277. Where both moods are used in a single passage, the effect deliberately aimed at is that of contrast:

> **Rem pūblicam administrat** *nōn sīcut rēs postulat* **sed** *quasī* **cēterīs ipse** *futūrus esset* **exemplō.**
> *He governs the state,* **not as circumstances demand,** *but* **as if he were destined to set** *in his person an example to the rest of mankind.*

Observation.—**Quī** plus the subjunctive is often found after comparatives followed by **quam.**

> **Haec beneficia** *maiōra* **sunt** *quam* **quibus grātiam referre** *possim.*
> *These favors are* **greater than I can** *repay* (*too great for me to repay*).

EXERCISE A

1. Nostrī victī sunt sīcut ego praedīxī.
2. Numquam secus[1] habuī illam ac sī ex mē nāta esset.
3. Nōn aliter stupuī quam quī Iovis ignibus ictus[2] vīvit et est vītae nēscius ipse suae.
4. Fortior erat Caesar quam quī mortem timēret.
5. Animum tuum, Cicerō, ex librīs nōscere mihi nōn aliter quam sī tēcum vīxissem videor.
6. Hoc accidit nōn perinde atque ego putāveram.
7. Vidēre aliud est ac crēdere.
8. Proinde age ac sī domī sīs tuae.
9. Fortūna iam adversa erat, et Hannibal in proelium iniit quasi hoc ipse nōn ignōrāret.
10. Metus Patrēs cēpit velut sī iam ad portās hostēs essent.
11. Sīc eum amēs velim[3] ut sī frāter esset tuus.
12. In proximō monte cōpias ostendit Caesar velut sī ibi castra positūrus esset.
13. Disce ut semper vīctūrus; vīve ut crās moritūrus.

---

[1] *otherwise*　　　[2] from the irregular verb **feriō, ferīre, percussī, ictus,** *strike*
[3] *I should like you to,* etc.

EXERCISE B

(1) You keep turning round[4] as if some one were following you.
(2) We ought to treat[5] others just as we wish them to treat us. (3)
They dreaded the cruelty of Ariovistus in-his-absence[6] just as if he
had been present.[7] (4) You (*pl.*) have acted in-accordance-with
your duty.[8] (5) They were punished deservedly (as they deserved).

---

[4] Use the reflexive **sē convertere.** [5] **ūtor** [6] **absens**
[7] Use the imperfect. [8] **prō eō ac + dēbeō**

Taedet caelī convexa tuērī.

—VERGIL, Aeneid, IV, 451

Compare:

Hateful is the dark-blue sky,
Vaulted o'er the dark-blue sea.

—TENNYSON, The Lotos-Eaters

LESSON LXII

Impersonal Verbs

278. Certain verbs, because of their meaning, are found only in the third person singular, the infinitive, and occasionally in the participles; and have the word *it* for their apparent nominative in English: as **licet,** *it is permitted;* **pluit,** *it is raining.* These are called impersonal verbs because they have no personal subject. The passive of many intransitive verbs is used in the same way; cf. secs. **218a** and **b.**

279. The commonest impersonal verbs are the following, all of which are of the second conjugation and are found only in the third person singular of the finite verb and in the infinitive mood:

decet, decēre, decuit	*it is suitable* or *seemly*
dēdecet, etc.	*it is unsuitable, unseemly*
oportet, etc.	*it is proper*
libet,[1] etc.	*it is pleasing* (with dative)
licet,[1] etc.	*it is lawful* or *permissible* (with dative)
placet, etc.	*it is acceptable* or *agreeable* (with dative)
liquet,[2] etc.	*it is clear* or *apparent* (with dative)

miseret, piget, taedet, paenitet, pudet; *it moves to: pity, disgust, boredom, repentance,* and *shame* (with accusative and genitive)

---

[1] The older forms **libitum** and **licitum est** sometimes appear.

[2] **Nōn liquet,** "*Not proven,*" was one of the three verdicts possible under Roman (and today Scots) law.

280. A number of completely conjugated verbs are used impersonally. Thus **iuvō**, *help*, and **dēlectō**, *charm, give pleasure to*, have **iuvat** and **dēlectat** meaning respectively *it is beneficial* and *it is delightful*. Note the following intransitive verbs which can be used impersonally:

(**a**) with **ut** and subjunctive or **quod** and indicative:

accēdit, -cēdere, -cessit	*it is added, there is the added fact* (that)
accidit, -cidere, -cidit	*it happens, chances* (that), often of what is undesirable

(**b**) with **ut** and subjunctive:

fit, fierī, factum est	*it comes about, the result is* (that)
ēvenit, -venīre, -vēnit	*it turns out* (that), for good or bad as result of previous circumstances
est ut (see sec. **243**)	*it is the case, there is reason* (that)

(**c**) with accusative and infinitive like **iuvat** and **dēlectat**:

cōnstat, -stāre, -stitit	*it is well known* (that)
praestat, -stāre, -stitit	*it is preferable*
fallit, fallere, fefellit ⎱ ⎰ *it eludes one,*	
fugit, fugere, fūgit ⎰ ⎱ *it escapes one's notice*	

(**d**) with the dative and infinitive:

expedit, -pedīre, -pedīvit	*it is advantageous*
contingit, -tingere, -tigit	*it happens* (by a natural process, usually of something desirable)

281. Other impersonals:

(**a**) Verbs denoting change of weather:

pluit, *it rains*	**fulminat**, *it lightens*
tonat, *it thunders*	**ningit**, *it snows*

(**b**) Other phrases:

necesse est, *it is absolutely* or *logically necessary*, with infinitive plus either accusative or dative; also with **ut**[3] and the subjunctive.

    quod ad mē attinet,   *so far as it concerns me*

  (c) Intransitive verbs, which include all verbs that govern only a dative, are used impersonally in the passive. They can be used in the passive only in this way.

Faveō tibi.	*I favor you.*
Ā mē tibi favētur.	*You are favored by me.*
Undique concurritur.	*A crowd forms.*
Huic culpae ignoscī potest.	*This fault can be forgiven.*

282. Construction of impersonals in 279 and 280 illustrated.

  (a) **Decet, dēdecet, oportet, dēlectat, iuvat** of the impersonals mentioned in sec. **279** are used with an accusative and an infinitive:

    Abīre mē **oportet.**   *I ought to go away.*

The "infinitive clause" **mē abīre** is the subject of **oportet.** Within that clause, **mē** is the subject of the infinitive **abīre.**

  (b) **Miseret, piget, taedet, paenitet,** and **pudet** are regularly found with an objective genitive of the person or thing that arouses the feeling concerned in addition to the accusative of the person so affected.

Miseret *mē tuī.*	*I am sorry **for you.***
Taedet *eam vītae.*	***She** is weary **of life.***
suī **paenitēre**[4]	*self-reproach*

  (c) **Libet, licet, liquet, placet, expedit, contingit,** are found with a dative:

Dīxit *sibi* **liquēre.**	*He said it was clear **to him.***
Licetne *mihi* **Anglicē loquī?**	*May **I** speak English?*
sibi **placēre**	*complacency, smugness*

Licet is found also with a subjunctive sometimes introduced by **ut;** see fn. 3.

    Licet pauca *dēgustēs.*   *You **may taste** a few samples.*

---

  [3] **Ut** is often omitted, especially before a second person singular subjunctive; cf. licet.

  [4] This form of idiom will often express the nom. and acc. of English abstract nouns for which Latin has no exact equivalent.

(d) Where the subjunctive with **ut** is found with **licet, accidit, accēdit, ēvenit** and other verbs and expressions, it forms a substantive result clause which takes the place of a subject to the impersonal verb concerned.

> **Accidit** *ut esset* **plēna lūna.**   *It happened **that** the moon **was** full.*
>
>   *(**That** the moon **was** full happened.)*

283. *Rēfert* and *interest*[5]; their special construction.—Both these impersonals mean *it concerns* or *it is the concern of*. Both take a genitive of the person and are often found with an infinitive or an **ut** clause with the subjunctive. But instead of the pronoun genitives **meī, tuī, nostrī, vestrī,** and **suī,** the ablative forms **meā, tuā, nostrā, vestrā,** and **suā** are used; with each the ablative form **rē** is understood.

> **Nec *Caesaris* nec *nostrā* interest ut veniās.**
>
> *It is of importance neither **to Caesar** nor **to us** that you should come.*

EXERCISE A

1. Hanc scīre oportet fīlia tua ubi sit.
2. Cicerōnem proficīscī oportuit.[6]
3. Mē stultitiae tuae miseret.
4. Mē culpārum meārum paenitet.
5. Paupertātis eum pudēbat.
6. Nōs hoc facere pudet.
7. Eōs hoc fēcisse paenitet.
8. Cōnstat aditūs īnsulae mūnītōs esse.
9. Tuā interest pācem cum illīs esse.[7]
10. Cito scrībendō nōn fit ut bene scrībātur; bene scrībendō fit ut cito.

EXERCISE B

1. Nostrā interest ut[7] pāx cum illīs sit.
2. Hoc Caesaris parvī rēfert.

---

[5] **Interest** follows the model of **rē-fert**. **Meā rē fert** is a type of ablative of accordance; *it bears on my advantage*.

[6] The tense is expressed by the modal verb, not the infinitive; *Cicero ought to have started.*

[7] Here, as often, the infinitive and **ut** + subjunctive constructions are virtually interchangeable.

3. "Putāsne," inquit imperātor, "mē hoc facere oportuisse?"

4. Nōn longius ab agmine legiōnum discēdī ab equitibus Caesar patiēbātur.

5. Culpam fateāris necesse est.

6. Aliīs licet ignāvīs[8] esse; vōbīs necesse est virīs fortibus esse.

7. Paenituit iūrāvisse patrem.

8. Eum puduit. Dīxit sē pudēre.

9. Nōn fierī potuit ut effugerēmus.

10. Nōn cuivīs[9] hominī contingit adīre Corinthum.

EXERCISE C

1. In hīberna perventum esse certior factus est.

2. Licet nēminī contrā patriam dūcere exercitum.

3. Miseret tē aliōrum; tuī nec miseret nec pudet.

4. Petiērunt ut sibi concilium tōtīus Galliae in diem certam indīcere licēret.

5. Post diem quārtum quam est in Britanniam ventum, nāvēs XVIII dē quibus suprā dēmōnstrātum est ex portū lēnī ventō solvērunt.

6. Sed quid mihi īrāscuntur sī id optō ut paeniteat eōs suī factī?

7. Nē id accideret Caesar exīstimābat magnopere sibi praecavendum[10] esse.

8. Prīmō ita pugnātum est ut ācrius nōn posset ex utrāque parte pugnārī.

9. Nōn tam interfuit meā quam reī pūblicae.

10. Expedit esse deōs; et, ut expedit, esse putēmus.

11. Themistoclem ūnum intrā annum optimē locūtum esse Persicē[11] cōnstat.

12. Mē vīxisse nōn paenitet quoniam ita vīxī ut nōn frūstrā mē nātum exīstimem.

EXERCISE D

(1) You pity others; for yourself you feel neither pity nor shame.
(2) We should have come[12] yesterday. (3) Bitter fighting took place on both sides[13] until evening. (4) It is necessary for me to return to Athens immediately. (5) They asked for permission to see their children again.

[8] *cowardly;* note case of predicate complements.
[9] dative of **quīvīs**, *anyone you please* [10] *take precautions* [11] *in Persian*
[12] Use **oportet**. [13] **utrimque**

Certë, sī nihil animus praesentīret in posterum, et sī quibus regiōnibus vītae spatium circumscrīptum est eīsdem omnīs cōgitātiōnēs termināret suās, nec tantīs sē labōribus frangeret neque tot cūrīs vigiliīsque angerētur.

If the soul had no presentiment of what comes after and if it narrowed the scope of its imagination to the same limits as those within which our span of life is confined, surely it would never exhaust itself in such great efforts or torture itself with such sleepless anxiety.

—CICERO, *pro Archia*, XI

LESSON LXIII

A Common and Idiomatic Use of the Relative—Proleptic Relative

284. One of the commonest turns of expression to be found in idiomatic Latin prose is that in which the relative pronoun comes before its grammatically normal antecedent. By thus placing the relative clause first and the demonstrative pronoun in the other (or principal) clause afterwards, the force of demonstratives like is **quī**, **hic quī**, and parallel combinations is emphasized. English rarely exhibits this peculiarity, using it only for unusual effects or in archaic language, e.g.:

*"Silver and gold have I none; but **what** I have, **that** will I give thee."*—Acts III, 6.

Quod habeō, *id* dō (instead of **Dō** id quod habeō.)

What things I know, **those** I know well.

*"**Whose** bread I eat, **his** song I sing."*

Le renard est fameux par ses ruses;
ce que le loup ne fait que par force,
il le fait par adresse.
The fox is well known for his artful dodges;
what the wolf can do only by violence,
that the fox does by craftiness.

285. Consequently, in translation, the simplest method is to re-arrange the Latin word order to conform to English usage, then translate it; for example:

Sed potius *quae* aliīs tū praecipere solēs *ea* tū tibi subice
becomes, when rearranged,
Sed potius tū tibi subice *ea quae* aliīs tū praecipere solēs.

But rather apply to your own case the maxims which you are in the habit of preaching to others.

EXERCISE AND REVIEW

Rearrange in Latin then translate the following, which will be found to review many constructions including the idiomatic relative. The groups increase slightly in difficulty, but any one group will prove adequate for the purpose of practice in this particular word order.

EXERCISE A

1. Quī tum tē dēfendit is hodiē accūsat.
2. Quod est eō decet[1] ūtī.
3. Quae minimē vīsa pars firma est hūc concurritur.
4. Quī ōlim terrārum orbī imperāvimus iī hodiē servīmus.
5. Sed ego quae mente agitāvī[2] ea omnēs iam anteā dīversī[3] audīstis.
6. Sed tamen quī semel verēcundiae fīnīs[4] trānsierit eum bene et nāviter[5] oportet esse impudentem.
7. Tamen quae in praesentiā[6] in mentem mihi vēnērunt dēcrēvī brevī[7] ea ad tē perscrībere.
8. Uter eōrum vītā superāvit[8] ad eum pars utrīusque pervenit.
9. Quī ex hīs secūtī nōn sunt (eī) in dēsertōrum ac prōditōrum[9] numerō dūcuntur.
10. Haec quī facit nōn ego eum cum summīs virīs comparō sed simillimum deō iūdicō.

---

[1] *it is proper, fitting*   [2] intensive form of **agō**, *turn over, ponder*
[3] *severally*   [4] *the bounds of modesty*
[5] *well and thoroughly*, cf. *"good and proper"*   [6] *at the time*
[7] Supply **spatiō**. *briefly*.   [8] *the survivor*   [9] *traitors*

EXERCISE B

1. Virī quantās pecūniās ab uxōribus dōtis nōmine[10] accēpērunt tantās ex suīs bonīs, aestimātiōne factā, cum dōtibus commūnicant.[11]

2. Ut enim nōn omne vīnum sīc nōn omnis nātūra vetustāte[12] coacēscit.[13]

3. Pugnandum tamquam contrā morbum sīc contrā senectūtem.

4. Quod cuīque temporis ad vīvendum datur, eō dēbet esse contentus.

5. Quī imperāre cōnsuēram nunc alterīus imperiō obsequor.[14]

6. Quae gravissimē afflīctae erant nāvēs eārum māteriā[15] atque aere ad reliquās reficiendās ūtēbātur.

7. Cuius autem aurēs vēritātī clausae sunt ut ab amīcō vērum audīrī nequeat,[16] huius salūs dēspēranda est.

8. Quod igitur adulēscentēs (et eī quidem nōn sōlum indoctī[17] sed etiam rūsticī) contemnunt, id doctī senēs extimēscent?

9. Quod[18] salūs sociōrum summum in perīculum ac discrīmen vocātur,[19] quō id tandem animō[20] ferre dēbētis?

10. Īsdem temporibus Rōmae Lentulus quōscumque mōribus aut fortūnā novīs rēbus idōneōs crēdēbat, (eōs) aut per sē aut per aliōs sollicitābat.

EXERCISE C

1. Quārē in quā urbe imperātōrēs prope armātī poētārum nōmen coluērunt in eā nōn dēbent togātī[21] iūdicēs ā poētārum salūte abhorrēre.[22]

2. Ut enim Rōmae cōnsulēs, sīc Carthāgine quotannis[23] annuī[24] bīnī[25] rēgēs creābantur.

3. Neāpolitānōs crēdō, quod scaenicīs artificibus[26] largīrī[27] solēbant, id huic summā ingenī praeditō glōriā noluisse.

4. Nam ferē[28] quem quisque vīvus pugnandō locum cēperat eum, āmissā animā, corpore tegēbat.

5. Deinde quod nōs eadem Asia atque īdem iste Mithridātēs initiō bellī Asiāticī docuit, id quidem certē calamitāte doctī memoriā retinēre dēbēmus.

---

[10] *under the head of dowry* [11] *add to* [12] *age* [13] *becomes acid or sour*
[14] *obey* [15] *timbers* [16] *same as* **nōn possit** [17] *uneducated*
[18] *the fact that* [19] *is involved* [20] *attitude* [21] *civilians* [22] *hesitate to help*
[23] *each year* [24] *for a year* [25] *two kings* [26] *stage hands* [27] *bestow*
[28] *generally, almost without exception*

6. Genus hoc cōnsōlātiōnis[29] miserum atque acerbum[30] est quia per quōs ea cōnficī[31] dēbet, propinquōs ac familiārēs, iī parī molestiā afficiuntur.

7. Quārē quis tandem mē reprehendat sī, quantum cēterīs ad suās rēs obeundās[32] concēditur temporum tantum mihi egomet ad haec studia recolenda[33] sūmpserō?

8. Quod sī haec vōx, huius hortātū[34] conformāta, nōnnūllīs aliquando salūtī fuit, ā quō id accēpimus quō cēterīs opitulārī[35] possēmus huic profectō ipsī, quantum est situm in nōbīs, et opem et salūtem ferre dēbēmus.

[29] *condolence in general*　　[30] *sad and heart-rending*　　[31] *offered*　　[32] *transact*
[33] *survey*　　[34] *encouragement*　　[35] *help, assist*

Maximē autem et glōria paritur et grātia dēfēnsiōnibus, eōque maior sī quandō accidit ut eī subveniātur quī potentis alicuius opibus circumvenīrī urgērīque videātur.

But most of all a lawyer's successful defense wins him renown and influence, which is all the greater if he ever happens to come to the rescue of one who seems to be suffering unfairly as the victim of some wealthy and powerful opponent.

—CICERO, *de Officiis* II, 51

LESSON LXIV

Review of the Subjunctive—Subjunctive of Polite Statement and Subjunctive by Attraction

286. It is by now apparent that the use of the subjunctive mood in Latin is "constant and manifold," especially in dependent clauses. It should, however, be noted that its dependent uses developed from an earlier stage of language in which an independent subjunctive construction was used in connection with a main statement, e.g.:

Quīn rogem? *Why shouldn't I ask?* **Nūlla causa est.** *There is no reason.*

becomes

Nūlla causa est quīn rogem. *There is no reason why I shouldn't ask.*

Quamvīs sit senex. *He may be as old as you please (ever so old).*

Arborēs serit. *He goes on planting trees.*

becomes

Quamvīs sit senex arborēs serit. *However old he may be, he goes on planting trees.*

A similar development from a paratactic to a syntactic form of expression can be traced in clauses of fearing, condition, etc. We shall now consider two more instances of the use of the subjunctive.

One is an old form slightly disguised; the other is closely related to a form already discussed.

287. Use of the independent subjunctive in polite or hesitating statements.—This use is confined chiefly to the present, imperfect, and perfect tenses[1] and is paralleled in English by a verb plus the auxiliaries *may, might, would, can, could,* and *should.*

> Facile crēdiderim.   *I can well believe it.*
> Quis crēderet umquam?   *Who would ever believe?*
> Velim adsīs.   *I wish you were here.*

Notice in the last example that the polite form of a wish, when that wish is applied to another person, is joined with another (substantive clause of desire or indirect command) without **ut.**

> Hoc faciās velim.   *I wish you would do this.*
>   (*Please do this.*)

In the second person this polite form often acquires an indefinite meaning.

> Putēs.   *You* (i.e. *anyone*) *would think.*

In all these cases we may supply a suppressed protasis such as "If you should ask me," etc. Therefore, this use is not really a new one but merely a variety of condition (Class II).

288. Subjunctive by attraction.—This use, which is also known as "subjunctive of the integral part," frequently occurs in clauses the meaning of which is intimately and essentially connected with another subjunctive clause or infinitive upon which they are dependent. The verbs of such dependent clauses are attracted into the mood of their context. Such attraction or assimilation is not invariable, but will often explain unexpected subjunctives. It is closely connected with the use of the subjunctive in subordinate clauses in ōrātiō oblīqua.

> Reliquās cīvitātēs sollicitant ut in eā lībertāte quam ā maiōribus *accēperint* permanēre malint.
> *They worked upon the feelings of* (*importuned*) *the rest of the states to prefer to remain in that free way of life which* **they had inherited** *from their forefathers.*

---

[1] Cicero has the pluperfect, **Nē poposcissēs,** *You shouldn't have asked.*

REVIEW EXERCISE A

1. Nescīre autem quid antequam nātus sīs acciderit, id est semper esse puerum.

2. Ego vērō mē minus diū senem esse māllem quam esse senem ante quam essem.

3. Quid prōfēcerim faciās mē velim certiōrem.

4. Caesar Labiēnō scrībit ut quam plūrimās possit iīs legiōnibus quae sint apud eum nāvēs īnstituat.[2]

5. Cōnsīderēs[3] quid tuae ratiōnēs[4] postulent.

6. Utinam Iuppiter mihi annōs praeteritōs referat.

7. Quae rēs est quae cuiusquam animum in hāc causā dubium facere possit?

8. Itaque cum longinqua ā[5] domō īnstet mīlitia incertumque sit quandō domōs vestrās vīsūrī sītis, sī quis vestrum suōs invīsere[6] vult, commeātum dō.

9. Sī ex Latīnīs scrīptōribus nēminem habērēmus praeter Cicerōnem, Vergilium, Senecam, Līvium, Plīnium, Tacitum—et cōnstat multōs esse aliōs quī in idem album[7] referrī[8] queant (= possint)—sed sī eōs sōlōs habērēmus, iūsta tamen mihi causa vidērētur cūr ad eōs intellegendōs linguam Latīnam avidē[9] discerēmus.

REVIEW EXERCISE B

1. Ego vērō, Servī, vellem in meō gravissimō cāsū adfuissēs.

2. Veniāmus ad Graecōs ut videāmus quid forte dē Deō sentiant.

3. Quotus quisque est quī epistulam paulō graviōrem ferre possit nisi eam perlectiōne relevārit (= relevāverit).

4. Concēdātur vērum esse ut bonōs bonī dīligant.

5. Itaque maiōribus nostrīs in Āfricam ex hāc prōvinciā Siciliā gradus[10] imperī factus est; neque enim tam facile opēs Carthāginis tantae concidissent nisi illud reī frūmentāriae subsidium nōbīs patēret.

6. Conclāmant equitēs iūre iūrandō[11] cōnfīrmārī oportēre nē quis tēctō recipiātur quī nōn bis per agmen hostium perequitārit.[12]

---

[2] *start building, lay the keels for*   [3] jussive subjunctive   [4] *best interests*
[5] an exception, *from the general region of*   [6] *visit*   [7] *list*   [8] *included*
[9] *eagerly*   [10] *stepping stone*   [11] *oath*   [12] *ride through*

7. Tanta vīs probitātis[13] est ut eam vel in eīs quōs numquam vīdimus[14] dīligāmus.

8. Mīlitēs mīsit ut eōs quī fūgerant[15] persequerentur.

9. Quae ipse intellegat, quae cīvitās querātur prōpōnit; monet ut in reliquum tempus omnēs sūspīciōnēs vītet; praeterita sē condōnāre[16] dīcit.

10. Ā miser Hippomenē,[17] nōllem tibi[18] vīsa fuissem.

REVIEW EXERCISE C

1. Nihil est prūdentiā dulcius quam, ut cētera auferat, adfert certē senectūs.

2. Ut in pauca cōnferam, testāmentō factō, mulier moritur.

3. Lutātius Catulus, cum ā Cimbrīs magnō dētrīmentō pulsus esset, ūnam spem salūtis habēbat sī flūmen trānsīsset[19] cuius rīpam hostēs tenēbant.

4. Caesar in eam spem vēnerat sē sine pugnā et sine vulnere suōrum rem cōnficere posse, quod rē frūmentāriā adversāriōs interclūsisset. Cūr etiam secundō proeliō aliquōs ex suīs āmitteret? Cūr vulnerārī paterētur optimē meritōs dē sē mīlitēs? Cūr dēnique Fortūnam perīclitārētur,[20] praesertim cum nōn minus esset imperātōris cōnsiliō superāre quam gladiō?

—Caesar, *Bellum Cīvīle* 1, 72.

5. Quisquis amat valeat; pereat quī nescit amāre.
   Bis tantō[21] pereat quisquis amāre vetat.—*An inscription*

---

[13] *integrity*

[14] Here the verb of the subordinate clause is *not* attracted into the subjunctive mood. Some grammarians explain this on the ground that "it gives special prominence to the fact stated."

[15] Again no attraction, perhaps because **quī fūgerant** is purely adjectival and equivalent to **fugitīvōs.**

[16] *forgive*   [17] *Ah poor Hippomenes*

[18] A *dative* of personal agent often used with perfect passive participles in poetry.

[19] **Trānsīsset** stands for **trānsierō** in the ōrātiō rēcta or direct speech. His actual thought was **Ūna spēs salūtis mihi est sī flūmen trānsierō,** etc.

[20] **perīclitor,** *I,* *hazard, make trial of*   [21] *twice as much*

Scīre tuum nihil est nisi tē scīre hoc sciat alter.

Your knowing something means nothing without the other fellow's knowing that you know.

—PERSIUS, I, 1, 27

A Note on Hendiadys

289. **Hendiadys**, a word derived from the Greek ἓν διὰ δυοῖν ("one by means of two"), is a term applied to the use of two nouns connected by a conjunction to express in Latin what is expressed in English by a combination of adjective (or adjectival phrase) and noun. This figure of speech is far commoner than is at first apparent. Consider the following examples:

carrī impedīmentaque	*baggage carts*
frūmentum commeātusque	*grain supply*
ratiōne et cōnsiliō	*by well-planned strategy*
furor atque āmentia	*mad folly*
iter immēnsum Alpēsque	*the long march across the Alps*
in timōre et fugā	*in panic-stricken flight*
vōcibus ac timōre	*by means of cowardly remarks*
in labōre atque itinere	*in their toilsome march*
proeliīs calamitātibusque frāctī	*their morale shattered **by disastrous defeats***
inertia nēquitiaque	*criminal neglect*
vīta ac spīritus	*the breath of life*
Gallōrum *immānitāte multitūdineque*	***by a savage horde** of Gauls*
ad amplitūdinem et ad glōriam	*for the enhancement of his reputation*
per angustiās et fīnēs	*through a narrow frontier pass*
cursū ac lassitūdine exanimātī	*out of breath **because of their exhausting charge***
aestuāria ac palūdēs	*marshy estuaries*
cursū et vīribus	*by running at full speed*
vīs et minae	*threats of violence* or *violent threats*
mercēs atque onera	*cargoes of merchandise*

summum *perīculum et discrīmen*   *a very **dangerous** crisis*
Catilīna, *vir imprōvidus et*   *the **unscrupulous** eloquence of*
  fācundus   *Catiline*
flūctūs tempestātēsque   *stormy waves*
vīs et contumēlia   *violent buffeting*
sōlitūdinēs et silvae   *lonely forests*
ā cultū atque hūmānitāte provin-   Supply suitable translations for
  ciae (longissimē absunt)   the remaining examples.
inter se fidem[1] et iūs iūrandum
  dant
in contentiōne et certāmine
auxiliō salūtīque fuit
in eō genere studī litterārumque
fūmō atque ignibus
vīcīs aedificiīsque
Rutulī somnō vīnōque solūtī
sine maleficiō et iniūriā
in fidem[2] et potestātem populī
  Romani
quōrum ad arbitrium iūdiciumque
summa omnium rērum
  cōnsiliōrumque
unīus hominis spē ac nōmine

---

[1] *loyalty*   [2] *protection*

THE CUSTOMS OF THE GAULS AND THE GERMANS

(Caesar, *B.G.*, VI, xi–xxviii)

Quibus rebus cognitis,

PRINCIPES BRITANNIAE

qui post proelium ad Caesarem
convenerant, inter se locuti

cum equites et frumentum Romanis deesse intellegerent
et paucitatem militum ex castrorum exiguitate cognoscerent,

quae hoc erant etiam angustiora quod sine impedimentis Caesar
legiones transportaverat,

optimum factu esse DUXERUNT,

rebellione facta, rem in hiemem producere

quod his superatis aut reditu interclusis
neminem postea belli inferendi causa in Britanniam
transiturum confidebant.

Caesar, B.G. IV,30

Learning of this,

THE BRITISH CHIEFS

who after the battle had met
before Caesar, after conferring with each other,

realizing that the Romans were short of both cavalry and grain
and ascertaining the small number of troops from the smallness of the camp,

(a camp made) even smaller because of the fact that Caesar had
brought his legions across
without heavy baggage,

THOUGHT (that) the best thing to do was,

after stirring up a revolt, to drag things on into the winter

because, when the present invaders had been beaten or cut off,
they felt sure that no one thereafter would cross over
into Britain for the purpose of making war upon it.

NOTE

IN THE sixth book of his *Commentaries on the Gallic War*, Caesar digresses for eighteen chapters on the social, religious, and political institutions of the Gallic and Germanic tribes against whom he had been campaigning since he came out to Gaul as military governor in 58 B.C. These chapters are inserted into the account of the second invasion of Germany in 53 B.C.

About one hundred and fifty years later, another Roman wrote a short treatise on Germany called the *Germānia*. It bore the subtitle *dē orīgine, sitū, mōribus ac populīs Germānōrum*. This writer was the brilliant historian Publius Cornelius Tacitus.

It is interesting to contrast the treatment of the same subject by two such different personalities. Caesar had scanty information, which he presents simply and directly—with a distinct touch of humor, if Chapter XXVII of the sixth book is really his work. Tacitus seems to some deliberately to idealize the simple life and character of the "noble savage" in order that he may by contrast excoriate the weaknesses of contemporary Roman society. "Though he admires their bravery, loyalty, purity, hospitality, and simplicity of life, he does not overlook their faults like drunkenness, gaming, and unpunctuality in attending popular assemblies." The information at his disposal was far more accurate and trustworthy than that which Caesar was able to acquire.

11. Quoniam ad hunc locum perventum est, nōn aliēnum esse vidētur dē Galliae Germāniaeque mōribus et quō differant hae nātiōnēs inter sēsē prōpōnere.

In Galliā nōn sōlum in omnibus cīvitātibus atque in omnibus pāgīs
5 partibusque, sed paene etiam in singulīs domibus factiōnēs sunt, eārumque factiōnum prīncipēs sunt quī summam auctōritātem eōrum iūdiciō habēre exīstimantur, quōrum ad arbitrium iūdiciumque summa omnium rērum cōnsiliōrumque redeat.

Idque eius reī causā antīquitus īnstitūtum vidētur, nē quis ex plēbe
10 contrā potentiōrem auxilī egēret; suōs enim quisque opprimī et circumvenīrī nōn patitur, neque, aliter sī faciat, ūllam inter suōs habeat auctōritātem. Haec eadem ratiō est in summā tōtīus Galliae; namque omnēs cīvitātēs dīvīsae sunt in duās partēs.

The Political Situation Which Caesar Found in Gaul, 58 B.C.

12. Cum Caesar in Galliam vēnit, alterīus factiōnis prīncipēs

---

Chapter 11

5. singulī, -ae, -a, single, separate, individual

7. arbitrium, arbitrī, *n.,* decision, discretion, judgment

8. summa, -ae, *f.,* main point; control

 redeō, redīre, rediī, reditum, go back; be referred

10. egeō, egēre, eguī, be in need of (*with genitive*)

 opprimō, opprimere, oppressī, oppressum, press down; oppress

11. circumveniō *has here the special meaning of* defraud, cheat

 aliter, *adv.,* otherwise

12. ratiō, ratiōnis, *f.,* design, plan, system

Chapter 11

2. quō: *in what respect*

3. inter sēsē: English idiom requires *from each other.*

7. quōrum refers to (eī) quī . . . **exīstimantur,** and is equivalent to **ut ad eōrum arbitrium,** *so that to their decision and judgment is referred, etc.* For the mood of **redeat,** see sec. **230.**

9. Id īnstitūtum [esse] vidētur, *That practice seems to have become established.* eius reī is explained by nē . . . egēret.

12. Haec . . . Galliae, *This same system exists throughout the whole of Gaul.*

erant Haeduī, alterīus Sēquanī. Hī cum per sē minus valērent, quod summa auctōritās antīquitus erat in Haeduīs magnaeque eōrum erant clientēlae, Germānōs atque Ariovistum sibi adiūnxerant eōsque ad sē magnīs iactūrīs pollicitātiōnibusque perdūxerant. 5

Proeliīs vērō complūribus factīs secundīs, atque omnī nōbilitāte Haeduōrum interfectā, tantum potentiā antecesserant, ut magnam partem clientium ab Haeduīs ad sē trādūcerent obsidēsque ab eīs prīncipum fīliōs acciperent, et pūblicē iūrāre cōgerent, nihil sē contrā Sēquanōs cōnsilī initūrōs, et partem fīnitimī agrī per vim occupātam 10 possidērent Galliaeque tōtīus prīncipātum obtinērent. Quā necessitāte adductus Dīviciācus, auxilī petendī causā Rōmam ad senātum profectus, īnfectā rē redierat.

Adventū Caesaris factā commūtātiōne rērum, obsidibus Haeduīs redditīs, veteribus clientēlīs restitūtīs, novīs per Caesarem comparā- 15 tīs, quod eī quī sē ad eōrum amīcitiam aggregāverant meliōre condi-

---

4. clientēla, -ae, *f.*, dependant, vassal

    adiungō, -iungere, -iūnxī, -iūnctum, join to, attach

5. iactūra, -ae, *f.*, loss, sacrifice (*cf.* iaciō, throw)

    pollicitātiō, -ōnis, *f.* (polliceor, promise), promise, offer

    perdūcō, -dūcere, -dūxī, -ductum (dūcō, lead), bring over, win over

6. complūrēs, -a and ia, *adj.*, several, many

    nōbilitās, -tātis, *f.* (nōbilis), nobility, the nobles

7. potentia, -ae, *f.* (potēns, powerful), power

    antecēdō, -cēdere, -cessī, -cessum, excel, surpass

9. pūblicē, *adv.*, publicly; on behalf of the state

10. ineō, -īre, -iī, -itum (eō, go), go into; enter upon, begin; inīre cōnsilium, form a plan

11. possideō, -sidēre, -sēdī, -sessum (sedeō, sit), take possession of, seize

    prīncipātus, -ūs, *m.* (prīnceps, chief), chief place, leadership

    obtineō, -tinēre, -tinuī, -tentum (teneō, hold), acquire, obtain

    necessitās, -tātis, *f.*, necessity, need

13. īnfectus, -a, -um (in- + factus, done), not done; rē īnfectā, without accomplishing (his) purpose

15. comparō, *I* (parō, prepare), get ready; acquire

---

2. Hī: *The latter.* Throughout this chapter, translate pronouns like eī, etc., by proper nouns for the sake of clarity. Minus: *too little.*

    valērent: for mood, see sec. 251.

14. commūtātiōne: i.e., through Caesar's defeat of Ariovistus.

ciōne atque aequiōre imperiō sē ūtī vidēbant, reliquīs rēbus eōrum grātiā dignitāteque amplificātā, Sēquanī prīncipātum dīmīserant.

20 In eōrum locum Rēmī successerant; quōs quod adaequāre apud Caesarem grātiā intellegēbātur, eī quī propter veterēs inimīcitiās nūllō modō cum Haeduīs coniungī poterant sē Rēmīs in clientēlam dicābant. Hōs illī dīligenter tuēbantur; ita et novam et repente collēctam auctōritātem tenēbant. Eō tum statū rēs erat ut longē prīncipēs habērentur Haeduī, secundum locum dignitātis Rēmī 25 obtinērent.

13. In omnī Galliā eōrum hominum quī aliquō sunt numerō atque honōre genera sunt duo; nam plēbēs paene servōrum habētur locō, quae nihil audet per sē, nūllī adhibētur cōnsiliō. Plērīque, cum aut

---

Chapter 12

16. aggregō, *I* (ad + grex, flock), unite in a flock; join, attach

17. aequus, -a, -um, equal; impartial, just; favorable

18. dignitās, -tātis, *f.* (dignus, worthy), dignity, position, rank

amplificō, *I* (amplus, large, + faciō, make), extend, enlarge, increase

19. succēdō, -cēdere, -cessī, -cessum (sub + cēdō, go), come up to; succeed, take the place of

adaequō, *I* (aequō, make equal), be equal to

20. inimīcitia, -ae, *f.* (inimīcus, unfriendly), enmity

21. coniungō, -iungere, -iūnxī, -iūnctum (iungō, join), join with, unite

22. dicō, *I*, proclaim

Chapter 13

2. plēbēs, -eī, *f.* (a fifth-declension form of plēbs, plēbis), common people

3. adhibeō, -hibēre, -hibuī, -hibitum (ad + habeō, have), have in, bring to; admit

plērīque, -aeque, -aque, *adj.*, very many; *as noun*, a great many

4. aes, aeris, *n.*, bronze; money; aes aliēnum, another's money, *i.e.*, debt

tribūtum, -ī, *n.*, tribute, tax

Chapter 12

17. ūtī: *enjoyed*
18. dīmīserant, *had let slip, lost*
19. Quōs adaequāre is the subject of intellegēbātur: *since it was understood that they (the Remi) stood equally high in Caesar's favor.*
21. sē . . . dicābant: *they proclaimed themselves dependencies of the Remi.*
24. secundum, *second*

Chapter 13

1. quī . . . numerō: *who are of any account.* For the ablative, see sec. **176.**
2. locō: with this word, the prep. **in** is usually omitted.

aere aliēnō aut magnitūdine tribūtōrum aut iniūriā potentiōrum premuntur, sēsē in servitūtem dicant nōbilibus; quibus in hōs eadem omnia sunt iūra quae dominīs in servōs.

Sed dē hīs duōbus generibus alterum est druidum alterum equitum.

Illī rēbus dīvīnīs intersunt, sacrificia pūblica ac prīvāta prōcūrant, religiōnēs interpretantur; ad hōs magnus adulēscentium numerus disciplīnae causā concurrit, magnōque hī sunt apud eōs honōre. Nam ferē dē omnibus contrōversiīs pūblicīs prīvātīsque cōnstituunt et, sī quod est facinus admissum, sī caedēs facta, sī dē hērēditāte, dē fīnibus contrōversia est, īdem dēcernunt, praemia poenāsque cōnstituunt; sī quī aut prīvātus aut populus eōrum dēcrētō nōn stetit, sacrificiīs interdīcunt.

5. **premō, premere, pressī, pressum,** press; crush, burden

    servitūs, -ūtis, *f.* (**servus,** slave), slavery, servitude

6. **iūs, iūris,** *n.*, right; rights, power

8. **rēs dīvīnae,** *f. pl.*, religious matters

    sacrificium, -cī, *n.* (**sacer,** sacred, + **faciō,** make), sacrifice

    prīvātus, -a, -um, private, personal

    prōcūrō, *I* (**cūrō,** care), care for, attend to

9. **religiō, -ōnis,** *f.*, religion; *pl.*, questions of religion

    interpretor, *I*, interpret, explain

10. **concurrō, -currere, -currī, -cursum** (**currō,** run), run together; come, gather

11. **contrōversia, -ae,** *f.* (**contrā,** against, + **versus,** turned), dispute, quarrel

12. **admittō, -mittere, -mīsī, -missum** (**mittō,** send), admit; commit, incur

    caedēs, -is, *f.* (**caedō,** cut), murder

    hērēditās, -tātis, *f.* (**hērēs,** heir), inheritance

14. **stō, stāre, stetī, statum,** stand; abide by

15. **interdīcō, -dīcere, -dīxī, -dictum** (**dīcō,** say), prohibit, exclude

4. **potentiōrum:** *done by the more powerful,* subjective genitive
5. **quibus:** For the case, see sec. **93.**
    in hōs: *over them*
11. **ferē:** used with **īdem, reliquī, omnēs,** and **plērīque** to mean *almost* or *practically*
12. **quod:** *any,* the neuter of the indefinite adjective **quī;** this is always used with **sī** to denote *any.*
14. **quī:** *any,* the masculine form of the indefinite adjective. **Sī quī = quīcumque,** *whoever* (does not abide by). In this idiom the perfect has a present meaning. Compare **cum** + perfect indicative in sense of *whenever.*

Haec poena apud eōs est gravissima. Quibus ita est interdictum, hī numerō impiōrum ac scelerātōrum habentur, hīs omnēs dēcēdunt, aditum eōrum sermōnemque dēfugiunt, nē quid ex contāgiōne incommodī accipiant, neque hīs petentibus iūs redditur neque honōs 20 ūllus commūnicātur.

Hīs autem omnibus druidibus praeest ūnus, quī summam inter eōs habet auctōritātem. Hōc mortuō aut, sī quī ex reliquīs excellit dignitāte, succēdit, aut, sī sunt plūrēs parēs, suffrāgiō druidum, nōn numquam etiam armīs, dē prīncipātū contendunt.

25 Hī certō annī tempore in fīnibus Carnutum, quae regiō tōtīus Galliae media habētur, cōnsīdunt in locō cōnsecrātō. Hūc omnēs undique, quī contrōversiās habent, conveniunt eōrumque dēcrētīs iūdiciīsque pārent.

Disciplīna in Britanniā reperta atque inde in Galliam trānslāta 30 esse exīstimātur, et nunc, quī dīligentius eam rem cognōscere volunt, plērumque illō discendī causā proficīscuntur.

---

17. **impius, -a, -um,** wicked
   scelerātus, -a, -um, infamous; *as noun, m.,* criminal
18. **dēfugiō, dēfugere, dēfūgī,**
   ——, flee from, shun
   contāgiō, -ōnis, *f.,* contact
20. **commūnicō,** *I,* impart, bestow
22. **excellō, -cellere, -celluī,**
   ——, excel

23. **suffrāgium, -gī,** *n.,* vote
25. **Carnutēs, -um,** *m.,* the Carnutes, *a Gallic tribe*
26. **cōnsīdō, -sīdere, -sēdī, -sessum,** sit down together; hold a meeting
   cōnsecrō, *I,* consecrate
   hūc, *adv.,* to this place
29. **trānsferō, -ferre, -tulī, -lātum,** bring over

---

16. **Quibus** = Et eīs

Est interdictum: an impersonal use: *those on whom such excommunication has been passed.* Interdīcō is used here with the dative of the person (**quibus**) and the ablative of the thing (**sacrificiīs,** line 15). Verbs governing the dative can be used in the passive only *impersonally.*

17. **numerō:** as with **locō,** the preposition **in** is often omitted: *they are regarded as.*

   hīs: dative, sc. **dē viā,** *get out of their way:* translate *avoid them.*

18. **aditum eōrum:** subjective genitive, *their approach*
   quid . . . incommodī: genitive of the whole, *any harm*
   petentibus: The participle has a concessive force, *though they ask (for it).*

22. **Hōc mortuō:** ablative absolute, *on his death*
   quī, indefinite adjective modifying Druid understood. **Sī quī** = **quīcumque;** compare Ch. 13, line 14.

29. **reperta (esse):** *devised, originated*

Privileges Enjoyed by Druids: Their Method of Teaching: Their Theory of the Transmigration of Souls

14. Druidēs ā bellō abesse cōnsuērunt neque tribūta ūnā cum reliquīs pendunt, mīlitiae vacātiōnem omniumque rērum habent immūnitātem. Tantīs excitātī praemiīs et suā sponte multī in disciplīnam conveniunt et ā parentibus propinquīsque mittuntur. Magnum ibi numerum versuum ēdiscere dīcuntur. Itaque annōs 5 nōn nūllī vīcēnōs in disciplīnā permanent. Neque fās esse exīstimant ea litterīs mandāre cum in reliquīs ferē rēbus, pūblicīs prīvātīsque ratiōnibus, Graecīs litterīs ūtantur. Id mihi duābus dē causīs īnstituisse videntur, quod neque in vulgus disciplīnam efferrī velint, neque eōs quī discunt, litterīs cōnfīsōs, minus memoriae stu- 10 dēre, quod ferē plērīsque accidit ut praesidiō litterārum dīligentiam in perdiscendō ac memoriam remittant.

In prīmīs hoc volunt persuādēre, nōn interīre animās, sed ab aliīs

---

Chapter 14

1. cōnsuēscō, -suēscere, -suēvī, -suētum, become accustomed, be wont

2. pendō, pendere, pependī, pēnsum, pay out

    mīlitia, -ae, f., military service

    vacātiō, -ōnis, f., exemption

3. immūnitās, -ātis, f., freedom (from public burdens)

    sponte, abl. (of an obsolete nom. spōns), of one's own accord

4. propinquus, -ī, m., relative

5. versus, -ūs, m., verse

    ēdiscō, -discere, -didicī,

    ——, learn by heart

6. vicēnī, -ae, -a, num. adj., twenty each

9. vulgus, -ī, n., the common people

    efferō, efferre, extulī, ēlātum, bring out; spread abroad

12. perdiscō, -discere, -didicī,

    ——, learn thoroughly

    remittō, -mittere, -mīsī, -missum, relax

Chapter 14

1. cōnsuērunt = cōnsuēvērunt

7. cum: although

8. ratiōnibus, records

    Graecīs litterīs, i.e., the Gallic language written in Greek characters

9. quod . . . velint, subjunctive of a quoted reason

11. quod: because

13. hoc persuādēre: to convince men of this; in apposition with **hoc** are the infinitive clauses which follow.

post mortem trānsīre ad aliōs; atque hōc maximē ad virtūtem excitārī
15 putant, metū mortis neglēctō. Multa praetereā dē sīderibus atque
eōrum mōtū, dē mundī ac terrārum magnitūdine, dē rērum nātūrā,
dē deōrum immortālium vī ac potestāte disputant et iuventūtī
trādunt.

15. Alterum genus est equitum. Hī, cum est ūsus atque aliquod
bellum incidit (quod ferē ante Caesaris adventum quotannīs accidere
solēbat utī aut ipsī iniūriās īnferrent aut illātās prōpulsārent), omnēs
in bellō versantur, atque eōrum ut quisque est genere cōpiīsque
5 amplissimus ita plūrimōs circum sē ambactōs clientēsque habet.
Hanc ūnam grātiam potentiamque nōvērunt.

16. Nātiō est omnis Gallōrum admodum dēdita religiōnibus, atque,
ob eam causam, quī sunt affectī graviōribus morbīs quīque in proeliīs

Chapter 14

15. praetereā, *adv.*, besides
mōtus, -ūs, *m.*, movement, motion

17. potestās, -tātis, *f.*, power; sway
disputō, *I*, discuss, debate about

Chapter 15

2. incidō, -cidere, -cidī, -cāsum (**cadō,** fall), befall; happen, occur
quotannīs, *adv.*, every year, yearly

3. prōpulsō, *I*, drive back, ward off
4. versor, *I*, be engaged in
5. amplus, -a, -um, magnificent, illustrious
ambactus, -ī, *m.*, paid retainer

Chapter 16

1. admodum, *adv.* (**modus,** measure, limit), up to the limit; very much
dēdō, -dere, -didī, -ditum, give up *or* over
2. afficiō, -ficere, -fēcī, -fectum (**ad + faciō,** do), affect

Chapter 14

14. excitārī: Supply **hominēs** as subject: *that men are aroused.*
metū mortis neglēctō: *in spite of the fear of death.* How, literally?
16. terrārum = **orbis terrārum,** *the earth*
dē rērum nātūrā: a prosaic, practical, and typically Roman phrase. It is the title of the great poem of Lucretius.

Chapter 15

2. quod: *and this.* **utī . . . prōpulsārent** is in apposition with **quod.**
4. ut quisque . . . ita, etc.: lit., *according as each of them is . . . so.* Say: *the more distinguished any individual is, the more retainers he has,* etc.
6. Hanc ūnam . . . nōvērunt, *This is the only form of influence and power which they recognize.*

Chapter 16

1. dēdita religiōnibus: *superstitious*

perīculīsque versantur, aut prō victimīs hominēs immolant aut sē
immolātūrōs vovent, administrīsque ad ea sacrificia druidibus ūtuntur, quod, prō vītā hominis nisi hominis vīta reddātur, nōn posse 5
deōrum immortālium nūmen plācārī arbitrantur; pūblicēque eiusdem
generis habent īnstitūta sacrificia.

Aliī immānī magnitūdine simulācra habent, quōrum contexta
vīminibus membra vīvīs hominibus complent; quibus succēnsīs, cir-
cumventī flammā exanimantur hominēs.   10

Supplicia eōrum quī in fūrtō aut latrōciniō aut aliquā noxiā sint
comprehēnsī grātiōra dīs immortālibus esse arbitrantur; sed cum
eius generis cōpia dēfēcit etiam ad innocentium supplicia dēscendunt.

17. Deōrum maximē Mercurium colunt. Huius sunt plūrima

Chapter 16

victima, -ae, *f.*, victim

immolō, *I*, sacrifice

4. voveō, vovēre, vōvī, vōtum, vow

administer, -trī, *m.*, attendant, priest

6. nūmen, -inis, *n.*, divinity; divine will

8. immānis, -e, *adj.*, huge

simulācrum, -ī, *n.*, image, statue

contexō, -texere, -texuī, -textum, weave together; construct

9. vīmen, -inis, *n.*, osier, pliant twig

succendō, -cendere, -cendī, -cēnsum, set on fire below, burn

10. exanimō, *I* (deprive of breath), kill

11. supplicium, -cī, *n.*, punishment

fūrtum, -ī, *n.*, theft

latrōcinium, -nī, *n.*, highway robbery, brigandage

noxia, -ae, *f.*, crime, offense

12. comprehendō, -prehendere, -prehendī, -prehēnsum, seize, catch

13. innocēns, -entis, *adj.*, innocent

Chapter 17

1. colō, colere, coluī, cultum, worship

Mercurius, -rī, *m.*, *the god* Mercury

Chapter 16

3. sē: subject of immolātūrōs (esse). Hominēs is object of both immolant and immolātūrōs.

4. administrīs: *as officiating priests*

5. nisi, etc.: condition in indirect statement: see sec. **267.**

6. pūblicē, *on behalf of the state*

7. habent īnstitūta = īnstituērunt

9. quibus = et eīs

12. cum + perf. indic., *whenever the supply fails*

13. dēscendunt: *they resort*

simulācra; hunc omnium inventōrem artium ferunt, hunc viārum
atque itinerum ducem, hunc ad quaestūs pecūniae mercātūrāsque
habēre vim maximam arbitrantur; post hunc, Apollinem et Mārtem
5 et Iovem et Minervam.

Dē hīs eandem ferē quam reliquae gentēs habent opīniōnem:
Apollinem morbōs dēpellere, Minervam operum atque artificiōrum
initia trādere, Iovem imperium caelestium tenēre, Mārtem bella
regere.

10 Huic, cum proeliō dīmicāre cōnstituērunt, ea quae bellō cēperint
plērumque dēvovent; cum superāvērunt, animālia capta immolant
reliquāsque rēs in ūnum locum cōnferunt. Multīs in cīvitātibus
hārum rērum exstrūctōs tumulōs locīs cōnsecrātīs cōnspicārī licet;
neque saepe accidit ut neglēctā quispiam religiōne aut capta apud sē
15 occultāre aut posita tollere audēret, gravissimumque eī reī supplicium cum cruciātū cōnstitūtum est.

---

2. **inventor, -ōris,** *m.* (**inveniō,**
find), inventor, author

3. **quaestus, -ūs,** *m.* (**quaerō,**
seek), gain, profit, acquisition

    mercātūra, -ae, *f.,* trade

4. **Apollō, -inis,** *m.,* Apollo
    Mărs, -tis, *m.,* Mars, *god of
war*

5. **Minerva, -ae,** *f.,* Minerva,
goddess of wisdom and the (*domestic*)
arts

7. **dēpellō, -pellere, -pulī, -pul-
sum,** drive away

    artificium, -cī, *n.* (**ars,** art,
+ **faciō,** make), trade, handicraft

8. **caelestis, -e,** *adj.* (**caelum,**

heaven), heavenly; *as noun, m. pl.,*
the gods

10. **dīmicō,** *I,* fight

11. **dēvoveō, -vovēre, -vōvī, -vō-
tum,** vow away, consecrate
    immolō, *I,* sacrifice

13. **exstruō, -struere, -strūxī,
-strūctum,** build *or* pile up
    cōnspicor, *I,* observe, per-
ceive

14. **quispiam, quidpiam,** *indef.
pron.,* anyone, anything
    religiō, -ōnis, *f.,* scruple,
taboo

15. **occultō,** *I,* hide

16. **cruciātus, -ūs,** *m.* (**cruciō,**
torture; **crux,** cross), torture

Chapter 17

3. **ferunt:** *they say*

7. The infinitive clauses are in apposition with **opīniōnem** and explain it.

10. **cum . . . cōnstituērunt:** *whenever they decide.* So also with **superāvērunt**
in next line.

    cēperint: subjunctive in implied indirect statement introduced by **dēvovent**.
The direct statement would be future perfect.

18. Gallī sē omnēs ab Dīte patre prōgnātōs praedicant idque ab druidibus prōditum dīcunt. Ob eam causam spatia omnis temporis nōn numerō diērum, sed noctium fīniunt; diēs nātālēs et mēnsium et annōrum initia sīc observant ut noctem diēs subsequātur. In reliquīs vītae īnstitūtīs hōc ferē ab reliquīs differunt, quod suōs 5 līberōs, nisi cum adolēvērunt ut mūnus mīlitiae sustinēre possint, palam ad sē adīre nōn patiuntur, fīliumque puerīlī aetāte in pūblicō in cōnspectū patris assistere turpe dūcunt.

19. Virī, quantās pecūniās ab uxōribus dōtis nōmine accēpērunt, tantās ex suīs bonīs, aestimātiōne factā, cum dōtibus commūnicant.

Chapter 18

1. Dīs, Dītis, *m.*, Dis *or* Pluto, *god of the lower world*

prōgnātus, -a, -um [(g) nāscor, be born], descended, sprung (from)

2. prōdō, -dere, -didī, -ditum, hand on *or* down; reveal

3. fīniō, *IV*, limit; measure

nātālis, -e, *adj.* (nāscor, be born), pertaining to birth; diēs nātālis, birthday

4. observō, *I*, observe, keep, celebrate

subsequor, -sequī, -secūtus sum, follow closely, follow on

6. adolēscō, -olēscere, -olēvī, -ultum, grow up

7. palam, *adv.*, openly, publicly

puerīlis, -e, *adj.* (puer, child), childish

8. assistō, assistere, astitī, —— (ad + sistō, stand), stand by *or* near

dūcō, *regard*

Chapter 19

1. dōs, dōtis, *gen. pl.*, dōtium, *f.*, dowry

2. bona, -ōrum, *n. pl.*, goods, property

aestimātiō, -ōnis, *f.*, valuation

Chapter 18

1. patre: *as their father*

4. diēs, etc.: i.e., a day was reckoned from sunset to sunset, a month being from the night of new moon to the night of the next new moon. Compare also our "fortnight" (fourteen nights).

5. hōc: for the ablative, see sec. **155.**

ferē: to be taken with reliquīs, *almost all other (peoples)*. See note on Chap. **13**, line 11.

6. nisi: *except*

Chapter 19

1. Translate in this order: Virī commūnicant ex suīs bonīs tantās pecūniās quantās ab uxōribus dōtis nōmine accēpērunt. For quantās to *precede* its antecedent correlative tantās is typical Latin idiom.

Virī: *husbands*

dōtis nōmine: *as dowry*

Huius omnis pecūniae coniūnctim ratiō habētur frūctūsque servantur; uter eōrum vītā superāvit, ad eum pars utrīusque cum frūctibus superiōrum temporum pervenit.

Virī in uxōrēs, sīcutī in līberōs, vītae necisque habent potestātem; et cum pater familiae illūstriōre locō nātus dēcessit, eius propinquī conveniunt et, dē morte sī rēs in suspīciōnem vēnit, dē uxōribus in servīlem modum quaestiōnem habent et, sī compertum est, ignī atque omnibus tormentīs excruciātās interficiunt.

Fūnera sunt prō cultū Gallōrum magnifica et sūmptuōsa; omniaque quae vīvīs cordī fuisse arbitrantur in ignem īnferunt, etiam animālia, ac paulō suprā hanc memoriam servī et clientēs quōs ab eīs dīlēctōs esse cōnstābat, iūstīs fūnebribus cōnfectīs, ūnā cremābantur.

20. Quae cīvitātēs commodius suam rem pūblicam administrāre exīstimantur, habent lēgibus sānctum, sī quis quid dē rē pūblicā ā

---

3. **coniūnctim,** *adv.,* jointly
frūctus, -ūs, *m.,* fruit; profit, income
6. **nex, necis,** *f.,* death
sīcutī, *adv.,* as
7. **illūstris, -e,** *adj.,* distinguished
9. **servīlis, -e,** *adj.* (**servus,** slave), like a slave
quaestiō, -ōnis, *f.* (**quaerō,** inquire), inquiry, investigation
comperiō, -perīre, -perī, -pertum, discover, ascertain

10. **excruciō,** *I,* torture
11. **fūnus, -eris,** *n.,* funeral
sūmptuōsus, -a, -um, expensive, costly
13. **dīligō, -ligere, -lēxī, -lēctum,** love
14. **cōnstat,** *I, impersonal,* it is agreed, it is well known
iūstus, -a, -um, right, lawful
fūnebria, -rium, *n. pl.,* funeral rites
cremō, *I,* burn

Chapter 19

2. **commūnicant,** *put into the common fund,* add (*to the dowries*)
3. **ratiō habētur:** *an account is kept.*
4. **vītā:** See sec. **155.**
7. **cum . . . dēcessit,** *whenever* (*the head of a family*) *dies*
9. **compertum est:** impersonal, *if proof is found*
ignī: abl. of **ignis**
11. **prō:** *in view of*
12. **vīvīs cordī fuisse:** *were dear to them when alive.* **Cordī** is dative of purpose. See secs. **220** and **221.** The whole clause is subject of **cōnstābat.**
13. **suprā hanc memoriam:** *before our time*

fīnitimīs rūmōre aut fāmā accēperit, utī ad magistrātum dēferat nēve cum quō aliō commūnicet, quod saepe hominēs temerāriōs atque imperītōs falsīs rūmōribus terrērī et ad facinus impellī et dē summīs [5] rēbus cōnsilium capere cognitum est.

Magistrātūs, quae vīsa sunt, occultant, quaeque esse ex ūsū iūdicāvērunt, multitūdinī prōdunt. Dē rē pūblicā nisi per concilium loquī nōn concēditur.

21. Germānī multum ab hāc cōnsuētūdine differunt. Nam neque druidēs habent quī rēbus dīvīnīs praesint neque sacrificiīs student. Deōrum numerō eōs sōlōs dūcunt quōs cernunt et quōrum apertē opibus iuvantur, Sōlem et Vulcānum et Lūnam; reliquōs nē fāmā quidem accēpērunt. [5]

Vīta omnis in vēnātiōnibus atque in studiīs reī mīlitāris cōnsistit; ā parvīs labōrī ac dūritiae student.

Chapter 20

3. rūmor, -ōris, *m.*, hearsay, rumor

4. temerārius, -a, -um, rash, imprudent

5. imperītus, -a, -um, inexperienced, ignorant

impellō, -pellere, -pulī, -pulsum, drive *or* urge on

7. occultō, *I*, hide, keep secret

Chapter 21

3. apertē, *adv.*, obviously, manifestly

4. iuvō, iuvāre, iūvī, iūtum, aid, help

Vulcānus, -ī, *m.*, Vulcan, *the god of fire*

nē . . . quidem, *adv.*, not even

fāma, -ae, *f.*, rumor, report

6. vēnātiō, -ōnis, *f.* (vēnor, hunt), hunting

cōnsistō, -sistere, -stitī, ——, consist (in)

7. dūritia, -ae, *f.*, hardship

Chapter 20

3. utī . . . commūnicet is the object of **habent sānctum**, which is itself equivalent to **sānxērunt**. Translate **commūnicet** as *share*.

4. cum quō aliō, *with anyone else*

7. vīsa sunt: supply **occultanda**.

8. Dē rē pūblicā, *on politics*

9. nōn concēditur, used impersonally in the sense of *permission is not granted, one is not allowed*

Chapter 21

3. Deōrum numerō: Supply **in**.

5. nē . . . accēpērunt: *they have not even heard of*

7. ā parvīs: adjective used as noun, *from childhood*

22. Agrī cultūrae nōn student, maiorque pars eōrum vīctūs in
lacte, caseō, carne cōnsistit. Neque quisquam agrī modum certum
aut fīnēs habet propriōs; sed magistrātūs ac prīncipēs in annōs singulōs gentibus cognātiōnibusque hominum, quīque ūnā coiērunt, quan-
5 tum et quō locō vīsum est agrī, attribuunt, atque annō post aliō
trānsīre cōgunt.

Eius reī multās afferunt causās: nē, assiduā cōnsuētūdine captī,
studium bellī gerendī agrī cultūrā commūtent; nē lātōs fīnēs parāre
studeant, potentiōrēsque humiliōrēs possessiōnibus expellant; nē
10 accūrātius ad frīgora atque aestūs vītandōs aedificent; nē qua oriātur
pecūniae cupiditās, quā ex rē factiōnēs dissēnsiōnēsque nāscuntur;

Chapter 22

1. vīctus, -ūs, *m.* (**vīvō,** live),
living; food

2. lac, lactis, *n.*, milk
    caseus, -ī, *m.*, cheese
    carō, carnis, *f.*, flesh, meat

3. proprius, -a, -um, of one's
own

4. singulī, -ae, -a, one at a time;
each, every
    cognātiō, -ōnis, *f.* [**cō + (g)
nātus,** born], blood relationship;
clan
    coëō, -īre, -iī, -itum (**eō,** go),
come together, combine

5. attribuō, -tribuere, -tribuī,
-tribūtum (**ad + tribuō,** assign),
assign, allot
    aliō, *adv.*, to another place,
elsewhere

7. assiduus, -a, -um (**ad +
sedeō,** sit), continual, constant

8. commūtō, *I* (**mūtō,** change),
exchange

10. accūrātē, *adv.*, carefully
    frīgus, -oris, *n.*, cold; cold
season
    aedificō, *I*, build

11. cupiditās, -tātis, *f.* (**cupidus,**
eager), eagerness, desire
    dissēnsiō, -ōnis, *f.* (**dissentiō,**
think differently), disagreement

Chapter 22

3. in annōs singulōs: *each year*
4. quīque = et eīs quī
5. vīsum est: idiomatic use of the impersonal form of the word. Supply
eīs and translate *it seems good to them*.
    post, an adverb here
7. nē . . . **commūtent:** This and the succeeding clauses are substantive in
nature, standing in apposition with **causās.**
8. studium . . . **agrī cultūrā commūtent:** Where Latin idiom requires the
ablative with verbs of exchanging, English requires the dative, *for.*
    parāre: *acquire*
10. qua: indefinite adjective (see sec. **214.**)

ut animī aequitāte plēbem contineant, cum suās quisque opēs cum potentissimīs aequārī videat.

23. Cīvitātibus maxima laus est quam lātissimē circum sē, vāstātīs fīnibus, sōlitūdinēs habēre. Hoc proprium virtūtis exīstimant, expulsōs agrīs fīnitimōs cēdere, neque quemquam prope audēre cōnsistere; simul hōc sē fore tūtiōrēs arbitrantur, repentīnae incursiōnis timōre sublātō. 5

Cum bellum cīvitās aut illātum dēfendit aut īnfert, magistrātūs, quī eī bellō praesint et vītae necisque habeant potestātem, dēliguntur. In pāce nūllus est commūnis magistrātus, sed prīncipēs regiōnum atque pāgōrum inter suōs iūs dīcunt contrōversiāsque minuunt.

Latrōcinia nūllam habent īnfāmiam quae extrā fīnēs cuiusque 10 cīvitātis fīunt atque ea iuventūtis exercendae ac dēsidiae minuendae causā fierī praedicant. Atque ubi quis ex prīncipibus in conciliō

Chapter 22

12. aequitās, -tātis, *f.*, fairness; contentment

13. aequō, *I*, make even *or* equal, equalize

Chapter 23

4. fore, = fūtūrōs esse
    repentīnus, -a, -um, sudden
    incursiō, -ōnis, *f.* (incurrō, rush into), invasion, raid

9. iūs, iūris, *n.*, right, justice, law

10. latrōcinium, -nī, *n.* (latrō, robber), robbery, brigandage

11. minuō, -uere, -uī, -ūtum, lessen; put an end to
    īnfāmia, -ae, *f.*, discredit

11. minuō, -uere, -uī, -ūtum, lessen; put an end to

exerceō, -ercēre, -ercuī, -ercitum (ex + arceō, drive away), train, exercise
    dēsidia, -ae, *f.*, idleness, indolence

Chapter 22

12. ut . . . contineant: a positive reason in apposition with causās, like the preceding negative clauses

13. potentissimīs: adj. used as noun: *the most influential people.* Here, too, we have a condensed expression equal to **cum opibus potentissimōrum.**

Chapter 23

1. Cīvitātibus: For the case, see sec. **93.**
    quam . . . habēre: This is the subject of **est.**

2. proprium virtūtis, *a mark of valor*

3. expulsōs . . . cōnsistere: These infinitive clauses explain and are in apposition with **Hoc.**

5. sublātō: See tollō.

7. quī . . . praesint: purpose clause, *to be in charge of*

11. With this sentiment compare the views of the ancient Spartans.

dīxit sē ducem fore, quī sequī velint profiteantur, cōnsurgunt eī quī et causam et hominem probant suumque auxilium pollicentur atque
15 ā multitūdine collaudantur; quī ex hīs secūtī nōn sunt, in dēsertōrum ac prōditōrum numerō dūcuntur, omniumque hīs rērum posteā fidēs dērogātur.

Hospitem violāre fās nōn putant; quī quācumque dē causā ad eōs vēnērunt ab iniūriā prohibent, sānctōs habent, hīsque omnium
20 domūs patent vīctusque commūnicātur.

24. Ac fuit anteā tempus cum Germānōs Gallī virtūte superārent, ultrō bella īnferrent, propter hominum multitūdinem agrīque inopiam trāns Rhēnum colōniās mitterent. Itaque ea quae fertilissima Germāniae sunt loca, circum Hercyniam silvam, quam Eratosthenī

Chapter 23

13. profiteor, -fitērī, -fessus sum, declare openly; volunteer

cōnsurgō, -surgere, -surrēxī, -surrēctum, arise, stand up

15. collaudō, *I* (**cum** + **laudō,** praise), praise warmly, commend

dēsertor, -ōris, *m.* (**dēserō,** desert), deserter

16. prōditor, -ōris, *m.* (**prōdō,** betray), betrayer, traitor

17. dērogō, *I*, take away from, withdraw

18. hospes, -itis, *m., f.*, guest, friend

violō, *I*, do violence to, maltreat

19. sānctus, -a, -um, sacred, inviolable

20. commūnicō, *I*, make common; share

Chapter 24

3. colōnia, -ae, *f.*, colony, settlement

fertilis, -e, *adj.* (**ferō,** bear), fertile

4. Hercynius, -a, -um, Hercynian; **silva Hercynia,** the Hercynian Forest, *a forest in southern Germany and Austria which followed the Danube from its source eastward beyond modern Vienna to the Carpathian Mountains*

Eratosthenēs, -is, *m.*, Eratosthenes, *a Gʳeek geographer, mathematician, historian, and grammarian; librarian of the library at Alexandria; 276–196 B.C.*

Chapter 23

13. fore = **futūrum esse**
profiteantur: The subjunctive stands for the imperative of ōrātiō rēcta: Ego dux vester erō; quī mē sequī vultis profitēminī.
16. hīs: dative with a verb of taking away; this is really a dative of reference. Translate *from them*.
18. quī: Supply **eōs** before it.

Chapter 24

1. Cum is to be supplied with **īnferrent** and **mitterent.** In spite of **fuit anteā tempus,** the clauses introduced by **cum** are circumstantial.
3. trāns Rhēnum: Caesar is mistaken. The Gallic tribes in Germany were remnants of the people who originally came from lands east of the Rhine.

et quibusdam Graecīs fāmā nōtam esse videō, quam illī Orcyniam 5
appellant, Volcae Tectosagēs occupāvērunt atque ibi cōnsēdērunt;
quae gēns ad hoc tempus hīs sēdibus sēsē continet summamque habet
iūstitiae et bellicae laudis opīniōnem.

Nunc, quod in eādem inopiā, egestāte, patientiā quā ante Germānī
permanent, eōdem vīctū et cultū corporis ūtuntur, Gallīs autem 10
prōvinciārum propinquitās et trānsmarīnārum rērum nōtitia multa
ad cōpiam atque ūsūs largītur, paulātim assuēfactī superārī mul-
tīsque victī proeliīs, nē sē quidem ipsī cum illīs virtūte comparant.

25. Huius Hercyniae silvae, quae suprā dēmōnstrāta est, lātitūdō

Chapter 24

5. Orcynia, -ae, *f.,* Orcynia, *same place as* **(silva) Hercynia**

6. Volcae Tectosagēs, Volcārum Tectosagum, *m. pl.,* the Volcae Tectosages, *a branch of the Volcae, a Gallic tribe in Provence*

cōnsīdo, -sīdere, -sēdī, -sessum, sit down together, settle

7. sēdēs, -is, *gen. pl.* **sēdum,** *f.,* seat; residence, home

8. bellicus, -a, -um (**bellum,** war), of war, military

9. egestās, -tātis, *f.* (**egeō,** want), poverty

patientia, -ae, *f.* (**patior,** endure), endurance

11. propinquitās, -tātis, *f.* (**propinquus,** near), nearness

trānsmarīnus, -a, -um (**trāns,** across; **mare,** sea), from beyond the sea; foreign, imported

nōtitia, -ae, *f.* (**nōtus,** known), knowledge, acquaintance

12. largior, *IV,* give freely

paulātim, *adv.,* little by little

assuēfaciō, -facere, -fēcī, -factum, accustom, train

13. comparō, *I* (**pār,** equal), place on an equal status with, compare

Chapter 25

1. lātitūdō, -inis, *f.* (**lātus,** wide), width

Chapter 24

5. illī: the Greeks

7. ad hoc tempus: To us, 53 B.C.; to Caesar, "the seven-hundred-and-first year from the foundation of Rome," **annus septingentēsimus prīmus ab urbe conditā** (abbreviated to **annus DCCI A.U.C.**).

9. Quod is to be supplied with **ūtuntur** and **largītur.**

10. cultū corporis: *dress*

autem: *whereas,* a mild "but." The general sense is that because the Germans have stayed hardy, while the Gauls have become effeminate, the Gauls have become inferior.

12. ad cōpiam atque ūsūs: Translate *in abundance for common use.*

13. ipsī: *the Gauls*

VIIII diērum iter expedītō patet; nōn enim aliter fīnīrī potest, neque mēnsūrās itinerum nōvērunt. Oritur ab Helvētiōrum et Nemetum et Rauracōrum fīnibus, rēctāque flūminis Dānuviī regiōne pertinet 5 ad fīnēs Dācōrum et Anartium; hinc sē flectit sinistrōrsus dīversīs ā flūmine regiōnibus multārumque gentium fīnēs propter magnitūdinem attingit; neque quisquam est huius Germāniae quī sē aut adīsse ad initium eius silvae dīcat, cum diērum iter LX prōcesserit, aut quō ex locō oriātur accēperit; multaque in eā genera ferārum nāscī cōnstat

---

Chapter 25

2. **expedītus, -ī,** *m.* *(perf. pass. part. of* **expediō** *used as noun),* a man "travelling light" *or* unencumbered

fīniō, *IV* (**fīnis,** end), limit; measure

3. **mēnsūra, -ae,** *f.* (**mētior,** measure), measurement, way of measuring

Nemetēs, -um, *m.,* the Nemetes, *a Gallic tribe*

4. **Rauracī, -ōrum,** *m.,* the Rauraci, *a Gallic tribe*

rēctus, -a, -um, straight

Dānuvius, -vī, *m.,* the Danube

5. **Dācī, -ōrum,** *m.,* the Daci (*who lived in Dacia, modern Rumania*)

Anartēs, -ium, *m.,* the Anartes, *a German tribe*

flectō, flectere, flexī, flexum, bend (*transitive*)

sinistrōrsus, *adv.* (**sinister,** left + **versus,** *from* **vertō,** turn), to the left

7. **attingō, -tingere, -tigī, -tāctum,** touch *or* border on

9. **cōnstat;** *impersonal use of* **cōnstō,** it is certain (that), it is well known (that)

Chapter 25

2. **iter,** accusative of extent, modified by genitive of description **VIIII diērum**

3. **Oritur:** third conjugation like most other forms of **orior.** The subject of **nōvērunt** must be supplied, e.g., **hominēs.**

4. **rēctā . . . regiōne:** *in a course parallel with the river Danube:* ablative of manner without a preposition.

6. **dīversīs . . . regiōnibus:** *in a direction away from the river.* Latin idiom often requires a plural where English is content with a singular.

7. **neque quisquam: Quisquam** is usually used with a negative. Hence, *"neither anyone"* = *and no one.*

huius Germāniae: *of this (part of) Germany;* i.e., the western part near Gaul

8. **initium:** i.e., the eastern limit

dīcat: why subjunctive? See sec. 230.

cum is here concessive.

iter: Compare its use in line 2.

9. **multaque . . . nāscī:** This "infinitive clause" is the subject of **cōnstat.**

quae reliquīs in locīs vīsa nōn sint; ex quibus quae maximē differant 10
ā cēterīs et memoriae prōdenda videantur haec sunt.

26. Est bōs cervī figūrā, cuius ā mediā fronte inter aurēs ūnum
cornū exsistit, excelsius magisque dērēctum hīs quae nōbīs nōta sunt
cornibus; ab eius summō sīcut palmae rāmīque lātē diffunduntur.
Eadem est fēminae marisque nātūra, eadem fōrma magnitūdōque
cornuum.   5

27. Sunt item quae appellantur alcēs. Hārum est cōnsimilis
caprīs figūra et varietās pellium, sed magnitūdine paulō antecēdunt

---

Chapter 26

1. bōs, bovis, *gen. pl.* **boum,** *c.*,
ox *or* cow
    auris, auris, *gen. pl.* **aurium,**
f., ear
**2. exsistō, -sistere, -stitī, -sti-
tum,** stand forth, arise
    excelsus, -a, -um, high
    dērēctus, -a, -um, straight
3. summum, -ī, *n.*, tip, end
    sīcut, *adv.*, just as if, as it
were
    palma, -ae, *f.*, palm (*of hand*)
    rāmus, -ī, *m.*, branch

**diffundō, -fundere, -fūdī,
-fūsum,** spread out
4. mās, maris, *gen. pl.* **marium,**
m., male
    fōrma, -ae, *f.*, shape, appear-
ance

Chapter 27

1. alcēs, -is, *gen. pl.* **alcium,** *f.*,
elk, *i.e., the European elk, which
closely resembles the American moose*
    cōnsimilis, -e, *adj.*, very like
2. pellis, -is, *gen. pl.* **pellium,**
f., hide, skin
    paulō, *adv.*, a little, slightly

Chapter 25

**10. ex quibus quae = et ex eīs ea quae
Differant** and **videantur** are unusual subjunctives. They may perhaps be
explained as subjunctives in relative clauses of characteristic. This and other
peculiarities of style have given rise to the suspicion that Chapters 25, 26, 27,
and 28 were written by a hand other than Caesar's.

11. memoriae prōdenda: *worth mentioning.* How, literally?

Chapter 26

This chapter describes the reindeer.

1. cervī figūrā: The descriptive ablative (here, **figūrā**) is normally modified
by an adjective. It is here modified by **cervī**, a noun in the genitive case, which
is an adjective-equivalent (= **cervīnā**).

3. palmae: This means that the antlers are like the palm of the hand: flat and
with projecting points.

    diffunduntur: *spread.* The verb **diffundō** is transitive. To express an
intransitive idea, Latin uses either **sē diffundunt** or the passive voice, as here.

4. nātūra: *characteristics*

Chapter 27

2. varietās: "markings"
    caprīs: a short way of saying **figūrae caprōrum**
    antecēdunt: *They surpass (the reindeer).*

mutilaeque sunt cornibus et crūra sine nōdīs articulīsque habent,
neque quiētis causā prōcumbunt, neque, sī quō afflīctae cāsū con-
5 cidērunt, ērigere sēsē aut sublevāre possunt.

Hīs sunt arborēs prō cubīlibus; ad eās sē applicant, atque ita,
paulum modo reclīnātae, quiētem capiunt. Quārum ex vestīgiīs
cum est animadversum ā vēnātōribus quō sē recipere cōnsuērint,
omnēs eō locō aut ab rādīcibus subruunt aut accīdunt arborēs tantum
10 ut summa speciēs eārum stantium relinquātur. Hūc cum sē cōn-

---

Chapter 27

3. mutilus, -a, -um, broken, crumpled

  crūs, crūris, *n.*, leg

  nōdus, -ī, *m.*, knot, knee-cap

  articulus, -ī, *m.*, joint

4. quiēs, -ētis, *f.*, rest

  prōcumbō, -cumbere, -cubuī, ——, lie down

  cāsus, -ūs, *m.*, accident

  concidō, -cidere, -cidī, ——, fall down

5. ērigō, -rigere, -rēxī, -rēctum, lift *or* raise

  sublevō, *I*, raise, support

6. cubīle, -is, *n.* (**cubō,** lie down), bed, resting place

  applicō, *I*, apply; **sē appli-cāre,** lean

7. paulum, *adv.*, a little, slightly

  reclīnō, *I*. lean back

  vestīgium, -gī, *n.*, track, footprint

8. animadvertō, -vertere, -vertī, -versum (**animus,** mind + **ad** + **vertō,** turn), turn the mind to; notice

  cōnsuēscō, -suēscere, -suēvī, -suētum, become accustomed to, be wont

9. rādīx, -īcis, *f.*, root

  subruō, -ruere, -ruī, -rutum, cause to fall from beneath; dig under, undermine

  accīdō, -cīdere, -cīdī, -cīsum, cut into

Chapter 27

4. quō: abl. of the indefinite adj.
6. sunt prō: *serve as*
7. Quārum = et eārum
8. cum, *whenever* (**cum** iterative)
  quō . . . cōnsuērint: This indirect question is the subject of **est animad-versum.** (**Cōnsuērint** is a shortened or syncopated form of **cōnsuēverint.**)
9. eō locō: As usual in this phrase, the preposition **in** is omitted.
  ab: *at*
  accīdunt: *cut into*
  tantum . . . relinquātur: *just so far that the perfect appearance of them standing is left,* i.e., only so much that the trees still preserve the illusion that they are standing firmly upright.

suētūdine reclīnāvērunt, īnfirmās arborēs pondere afflīgunt atque ūnā ipsae concidunt.

28. Tertium est genus eōrum, quī ūrī appellantur. Hī sunt magnitūdine paulō īnfrā elephantōs, speciē et colōre et figūrā taurī. Magna vīs eōrum est et magna vēlōcitās, neque hominī neque ferae quam cōnspexērunt parcunt.

Hōs studiōsē foveīs captōs interficiunt. Hōc sē labōre dūrant adulēscentēs atque hōc genere vēnātiōnis exercent, et quī plūrimōs ex hīs interfēcērunt, relātīs in pūblicum cornibus quae sint testimōniō, magnam ferunt laudem. Sed assuēscere ad hominēs et mānsuēfierī nē parvulī quidem exceptī possunt.

Chapter 28

1. **ūrus, -ī,** *m.*, wild ox
3. **vēlōcitās, -tātis,** *f.* (**vēlox,** swift), swiftness, speed
4. **cōnspiciō, -spicere, -spexī, -spectum,** see, catch sight of
5. **studiōsē,** *adv.* (**studiōsus,** zealous, *from* **studium,** zeal, enthusiasm), eagerly
   fovea, -ae, *f.*, pitfall

5. **dūrō,** *I* (**dūrus,** hard), harden, toughen
7. **testimōnium, -nī,** *n.*, evidence, proof
8. **assuēscō, -suēscere, -suēvī, -suētum,** become accustomed
9. **mānsuēfīō** (*passive of* **mānsuefaciō**), be tamed
   parvulus, -a, -um (*diminutive of* **parvus**), small, tiny

---

Chapter 27

10. **Hūc** = **In hās arborēs**
11. **cum . . . reclīnāvērunt:** the same idiom as **cum . . . est animadversum** above, line 8
   cōnsuētūdine: *as their custom is;* ablative of accordance, a variety of ablative of manner

Chapter 28

1. **est eōrum:** *consists of those*
2. **speciē taurī** = **speciē taurīnā**   Cf. Chapter 26, line 1.
5. **captōs interficiunt:** As so often, a Latin perfect participle and main verb must be translated by *two main verbs,* the *first* of which translates the Latin participle as denoting something that happened *first.* Translate *they catch and kill them.* (They must be *first* caught, *then* killed.)
7. **quae sint:** = **ut haec sint**
   testimōniō: What dative?
8. **assuēscere ad hominēs:** *become domesticated*
9. **nē . . . exceptī:** *not even if very young when caught*
   mānsuēfīō: manus + suēscō + fīō

10   Amplitūdō cornuum et figūra et speciēs multum ā nostrōrum boum cornibus differt. Haec studiōsē conquīsīta ab labrīs argentō circumclūdunt, atque in amplissimīs epulīs prō pōculīs ūtuntur.

---

10. amplitūdō, -dinis, *f.* (**amplus,** large), size

11. conquīrō, -quīrere, -quīsīvī, -quīsītum, seek out, search for
    labrum, -ī, *n.,* lip; edge

12. circumclūdō, -clūdere, -clūsī, -clūsum (**claudō,** shut), encircle
    epulae, -ārum, *f.* (*used in plural only*), feast, banquet
    pōculum, -ī, *n.,* cup (drinking horn)

---

11. conquīsīta circumclūdunt: Compare note on line 5.
    ab labrīs: *at the rim*
12. circumclūdunt: *mount* (as in *a silver-mounted pipe*)

SELECTIONS FROM MEDIEVAL LATIN

To those who refer to Latin as a dead language we may fairly reply that it has been fifteen hundred years a-dying and in defiance of the dissolution eagerly awaited by its detractors can at this hour make a strong claim for use as an international language. For the first thousand years of its "death," those following the dethroning of Romulus Augustulus, last emperor of the West, in A.D. 476, Latin as the official tongue of the church was the one great linguistic bond amid a welter of barbarian tongues. Even after it ceased to be the everyday speech of any people, Latin survived as the universal literary language of civilization, that is to say "of church, state, school, society, and belles lettres," and, through the seventeen and a half centuries which elapsed between Ennius and Erasmus, remained far more homogeneous than English during the five centuries from Chaucer to Tennyson.

Not only in the liturgies, hymns, and sacred writings of the church did Latin survive. Histories, religious drama, correspondence, popular tales, state documents, treatises on all sorts of learned subjects, poetry most passionate, tender, and lyrical, were written in Latin, which was thus kept as a living tongue before the masses of the people. For its literary sources and its inspiration this vigorous Methuselah of a language drew on Roman, Greek, Hebrew, Persian, Sanskrit, German, Scandinavian, perhaps even Celtic and Arabic, and the popular speech of various nations, but the deepest source of what we call Medieval Latin is, to quote Helen Waddell, "in the pagan learning that flows like a sunken river through the medieval centuries."[1]

No view could be more misleading than that so commonly heard which represents Medieval Latin as a debased and corrupted form of classical literature. We should remind ourselves that Medieval Latin is not as definite a term as classical Latin. Its extremes are farther apart, and its vast range comprises hundreds of authors, styles, and types of subject matter. In certain periods and in certain authors, to be sure, it degenerates into the so-called "monks' Latin" and a style which reaches a pitifully low ebb; but in a host of other authors it is a delightful instrument of ever varying range and power, meeting with amazing adaptability the demands of new vocabulary and an enormous widening of the scope of human interests.

By a rare sympathy it was in the hands of these very medievalists

---

[1] *Mediaeval Latin Lyrics*, pref. v.

that the speech of Cicero revealed much of the "hidden romantic quality" that had shyly peeped from an occasional line of Lucretius or Vergil, that had less self-consciously emerged from the white-hot lyrics of Catullus, and that had revealed new possibilities and patterns of expression in writers like Apuleius. It was as though the rich ore of Old Latin, smelted in the furnace of the emotions of a later age, yielded metal of unsuspected lustre and richness; or, to change the metaphor, as though the sober verse of Ennius and the older poets were now revealed as

> "sketches rude and faint,
> But where a passion yet unborn perhaps
> Lay hidden as the music of the moon
> Sleeps in the plain eggs of the nightingale."

And, when they chose, many of these writers of the Middle Ages could "write like angels." Einhard chose Suetonius for his model; Petrarch, Seneca; and, in their letters, Gerbert (1003) and Lupus (862) chose Cicero. One of the ablest defenses of classical literature was written in the sixteenth century in Latin that would be a credit to Cicero by Muretus (Marc-Antoine Muret, 1526–1585), the teacher of Montaigne.

By another evolutionary paradox the magnificent Latin hymns, like those of Bernard of Cluny, which are among the glories of medieval Latin, are accentual like their remote ancestors in early Latin Saturnian verse. Even their rhyming quality had been anticipated in certain types of Augustan elegiacs.

The passages here chosen are so simple in vocabulary, sentence structure, and word order that they may well be used for sight reading as soon as the subjunctive mood has been introduced. Slightly adapted and simple as they are, they may serve as an introduction to fields too long kept closed to beginners, who are assured of many an hour of delightful exploration under the guidance of such poetic scholars and scholarly poets as Helen Waddell, whose *Mediaeval Latin Lyrics*, and its companion volume, *The Wandering Scholars*, are fragrant gardens in the realm of classical scholarship.

One of the first impressions we receive while reading a passage of Medieval Latin is that it is far closer to the structure and order of English than the classical Latin to which we have become accustomed in Caesar and Cicero. But we are apt to forget that even in classical times there existed side by side two distinct types of Latin. One was the formal, dignified, periodic Latin used by the literary aristocracy; the other was the *sermō plēbēius* or speech of the people, the character of which we can only infer from such sources as the comedies of Plautus or the *Satyricon* of Petronius. The language of the involved and highly polished orations of Cicero was as far removed from the *sermō plēbēius* as are Burke's speeches from a telephone conversation of today. Both types of Latinity survived down the centuries, each influencing the other to a varying degree. As the *sermō plēbēius* strayed further and further from its more "correct" and conservative sister, it blended with the various vernaculars to become the Romance languages of Gaul (France), Dacia (Rumania), Italy, and Spain. As soon as the great cohesive force of the church and its schools began to exert its influence upon this scattered group of tongues, a newer and more popular version of the *sermō plēbēius* emerged.

Another factor partially responsible for creating the divergence between what we have met before and what we now shall see in the following selections is the human one of the ignorant copyist. The texts now at our disposal are copies of copies of a much battered and frequently lost original. Those to whose patient but pedestrian industry we owe the manuscripts which we now enjoy were frequently men of far less education than the authors whose works they copied. And whereas the classics, in the almost definitive form in which we now read them, have been subjected to the careful emendation of generations of scholars who have removed a great proportion of the errors of copyists, the medieval authors by comparison have been almost neglected and denied such restoration. Errors from ignorance, errors from weariness, errors from sheer inability to decipher a blurred word or line, errors arising from an excess of zeal in "correcting" what had better have been left alone, and occasionally deliberate alterations of a word or a phrase by some forgotten and misguided zealot to make an author a posthumous and unwilling propagandist for the gospel—all these have to be taken into account before we pass judgment on the "purity" of the style of many a medieval writer.

As the limits of man's physical horizons and experience constantly withdrew, as the flights of his imagination soared and new discoveries shattered the confining walls of outworn theories, as the need grew for a new vocabulary and wider connotations, so, to meet that imperious demand, the gnarled but sound old tree of Latin put forth new shoots, and sent its roots still deeper and wider into its sustaining earth.

There could be no finer example than Medieval Latin of the truth that the tongue of a vigorous and intelligent people is an organism capable of miracles of growth and adaptation such as no artificial product like Esperanto could achieve, capable at the same time of preserving its essential integrity as a strong "basic," measured, and masterly medium of expression of the holy spirit of man, as it was in the old time and as it still is.

To the student interested in the further study of Medieval Latin the following books are suggested:

Mediaeval Latin, by Karl Pomeroy Harrington. New York: Allyn and Bacon, 1925.

A Primer of Mediaeval Latin, by Charles H. Beeson. New York: Scott, Foresman and Company, 1925.

The Oxford Book of Medieval Latin Verse, by Sir Stephen Gaselee. Oxford: Oxford University Press, 1928.

Anthology of Medieval Latin, chosen by Sir Stephen Gaselee. London: Macmillan, 1925.

A History of Later Latin Literature, by F. A. Wright and T. A. Sinclair. New York: The Macmillan Company, 1931.

Mediaeval Latin Lyrics, by Helen Waddell. London: Constable & Co. Ltd., 4th ed. rev., 1933.

The Wandering Scholars, by Helen Waddell. London: Constable & Co. Ltd., 6th ed. (rev. and enl.), 1932.

A Glossary of Later Latin to 600 A.D., by Alexander Souter. Oxford: Clarendon Press, 1949.

THE PROUD KING

Here is a story known as Tale No. LIX of the *Gesta Rōmānōrum*, a misleading title given to an amazing collection of medieval tales compiled at the end of the thirteenth century. The *Gesta* proved a mine for later writers like Gower, Chaucer, Bocaccio, La Fontaine, Shakespeare,[1] Schiller, Tennyson, William Morris, Longfellow, and Mark Twain. In spite of its title the collection is drawn from a number of sources besides the Roman. Sanskrit, Greek, Persian, and Arabic stories and fables all contributed their quota.

This story in particular reappears in many literatures: as a Hindu fairy legend current in Southern India and called *The Wanderings of Vicram Maharajah;* as an old French moralité entitled *L'Orgueil et Présumption de l'Empéreur Jovinien;* as an old English metrical romance, *Robert of Cysille;* as *The Proud King* in William Morris' *The Earthly Paradise;* and, most familiar of all, as *Robert of Sicily* in Longfellow's *Tales of a Wayside Inn.* Another tale of the *Gesta,* No. LXXXIV, was used by Longfellow in *The Student's Tale* or *The Falcon of Ser Federigo.*

There was, of course, no such ruler as Jovinian. The whole incident is conveniently fathered upon a fictitious emperor; the tale is full of anachronistic absurdities. It has been suggested that many of these fantastic tales were brought back from the East by returning crusaders. They may have been first collected by a pious monk. Whoever he was, he concludes each story with an edifying appendix singularly reminiscent of *Alice in Wonderland:* "And the moral of that is . . . " A less frivolous comment on the story echoes from the *Magnificat:*

> Dēposuit potentēs dē sēde
> Et exaltāvit humilēs.

ARGUMENT

A certain King, blinded by pride, thought that he was something more than man, if not equal to God; but such a judgment fell on him that none knew him for King, and he suffered many things, till in the end, humbling himself, he regained his Kingdom and honour.

—William Morris, *The Earthly Paradise.*

Dē Superbiā et Arrogantiā Imperātōris Ioviniānī

I

Ioviniānus imperātor rēgnāvit potēns valdē. Quī cum ōlim in

---

[1] As, for instance, the casket scene in *The Merchant of Venice,* or in *King Lear.*

lectō[1] suō iacēret, ēlevātum* est cor eius ultrā quam crēdī potest, et
dīcēbat in corde suō: "Estne alter Deus quam sum ego?" Hīs cōgi-
tātīs, dormīvit. Māne vērō surrēxit,[2] vocāvit mīlitēs suōs ac cēterōs
et ait: "Cārissimī, bonum est cibum sūmere, quia hodiē ad vēnandum[3]
volō pergere." Illī vērō parātī erant eius voluntātem implēre.[4]
Cibō sūmptō ad vēnandum perrēxērunt. Dum vērō imperātor
equitat, calor[5] intolerābilis* arripuit eum, ita ut vidērētur sibi moritūrus esse nisi in aquā frīgidā posset balneārī.[6] Respexit, procul
vīdit aquam lātam. Dīxit mīlitibus suīs: "Hīc remanēte dum ad
vos veniam." Percussit equum calcāribus[7] et ad aquam festīnanter
equitāvit. Dē equō dēscendit, omnia vestīmenta[8] dēposuit, aquam
intrāvit et tamdiū ibīdem remansit, dum ex tōtō[9] refrīgerātus* esset.

Dum vērō ibīdem[10] exspectat, vēnit quīdam eī omnibus similis, et
vultū et gestū,[11] et induit[12] sē vestīmentis eius, equum eius ascendit
et ad mīlitēs equitāvit. Ab omnibus sīcut persōna imperātōris est
receptus, quia nūllam suspīciōnem dē eō habēbant, nisi quod dominus
suus esset, quia omnibus eī similis erat. Lūdēbant; fīnītō lūdō, ad
palātium* cum mīlitibus equitābat.

II

Post haec Ioviniānus ex aquā exiit, nec vestēs neque equum invēnit.
Admīrābātur; contristātus est valdē,[13] quia nūdus erat et nēminem
vīdit. Cōgitābat intrā sē: "Quid faciam ego? Miserē sum minis-
trātus."[14] Tandem ad sē reversus dīcēbat: "Hīc prope manet mīles
quem ad mīlitiam prōmōvī.[15] Pergam ad eum et vestīmenta habēbō
et equum, et sīc ad palātium meum ascendam et vidēbō quōmodō et
ā quō ita sim cōnfūsus."[16]

Ioviniānus ex tōtō nūdus sōlus ad castrum[17] mīlitis iit; iānuam
pulsāvit.[18] Iānitor causam pulsātiōnis quaesiit. At ille: "Iānuam
aperī et vidē quis sim ego." Ille iānuam aperuit, et cum vīdisset
eum, ait:[19] "Quis es tū?" Et ille: "Ego sum Ioviniānus imperātor.
Vāde ad dominum tuum et imperā eī ut mihi vestēs mittat, quia
cāsū[20] vestes et equum perdidi." Quī ait: "Mentīris, pessime ribalde.[21] Paulō ante tē dominus meus imperātor Ioviniānus ad
palātium suum cum mīlitibus equitāvit, et dominus meus cum eō

---

* Like the English loan word   [1] *bed*   [2] *arose*   [3] *hunting*   [4] *carry out*
[5] *heat*   [6] *bathe*   [7] *spur*   [8] *clothes*   [9] *entirely*   [10] *in the same place*
[11] *bearing*   [12] *clothed*   [13] *was very sad*   [14] *served*
[15] *promoted to official rank*   [16] *embarrassed*   [17] *castle*   [18] *knocked at*
[19] *says*   [20] *by accident*   [21] *scoundrel of a practical joker*

equitāvit et rediit et iam in[22] mēnsā sedet. Sed quia imperātōrem
tē nōminās, dominō meō dēnuntiābō." Iānitor intrāvit et dominō
suō verba eius annuntiāvit. Ille haec audiēns praecēpit[23] ut intrō-
dūcerētur. Et sīc factum est. Mīles cum eum vīdisset nūllam
nōtitiam[24] eius habēbat; sed imperātor eum peroptimē cognōvit.
Ait eī mīles: "Dīc mihi, quis es tū, et quod est tibi nōmen?" At ille:
"Imperātor sum et Ioviniānus dīcor et tē ad mīlitiam prōmōvī tālī
diē et tālī[25] tempore." At ille: "Ō ribalde pessime, quā audāciā
audēs tē ipsum imperātōrem nōmināre? Iam dominus meus, imperātor Ioviniānus, ante tē ad palātium cum mīlitibus equitāvit, et
ego per viam eram eī associātus[26] et sum reversus. Verum est mē
tālī diē et hōrā factum esse mīlitem ā dominō meō imperātōre. Quia
ad tantam praesūmptiōnem dēvēnistī[27] ut tē ipsum imperātōrem
nōminēs, impūne nōn trānsībis." [28] Et statim iussit eum ēgregiē
verberārī[29] et posteā expellī.

III

Ille vērō sīc verberātus et expulsus flēvit amārē[30] et ait: "Ō mī
deus, quid hoc esse potest quod mīles, quem ad mīlitiam prōmōvī,
nōtitiam meī nōn habet et praetereā mē graviter verberāvit? Hīc
prope est quīdam dux cōnsiliārius meus.[31] Ad eum pergam et neces-
sitātem[32] meam eī ostendam; per quem poterō induī et ad palātium
meum pergere." Cum vērō ad iānuam ducis vēnisset, pulsābat.
Iānitor, pulsātiōne audītā, ostium aperuit, et cum hominem nūdum
vīdisset, admīrābātur et ait: "Quis es tū et quāre sīc ex tōtō nūdus
advēnistī?" At ille: "Rogō tē, fac negōtium meum[33] cum duce.
Ego sum imperātor et cāsū vestīmenta et equum perdidī[34] et ideō ad
eum vēnī, ut mihi in hāc necessitāte succurrat." Iānitor cum verba
eius audīsset admīrābātur, intrāvit et dominō suō adnuntiāvit quendam hominem nūdum in[35] portā esse quī dīceret sē imperātōrem esse
et introitum[36] peteret. Ait dux: "Cito eum intrōdūc, ut videāmus
quis sit quī praesūmat sē imperātōrem nōmināre." Iānitor vērō
ostium aperuit ac hominem intrōdūxit. Imperātor nōtitiam ducis
peroptimē habēbat, sed ille eius nōtitiam nūllam. Ait eī dux:
"Quis es tū?" Et ille: "Ego sum imperātor et tē ad honōrēs et ad

---

[22] at   [23] gave orders that   [24] knowledge   [25] such and such   [26] accompanied
[27] come to   [28] Compare the slang "You shan't get away with it."
[29] soundly thrashed   [30] bitterly   [31] member of my ducal council   [32] plight
[33] take my message to, lit. do my errand with   [34] lost   [35] at   [36] admittance

ducātum³⁷ prōmōvī et cōnsiliārium meum inter aliōs cōnstituī."
Ait dux: "Insānīs³⁸ miser; paulō ante tē perrēxī cum dominō meō
imperātōre versus palātium et reversus sum; et quia tālem gradum
tibi arrogāvistī,³⁹ impūne⁴⁰ nōn trānsībis." Iussit eum incarcerārī*
et aliquōs diēs pāne⁴¹ et aquā sustentārī.* Deinde ē carcere⁴² eum
extrāxit et ūsque ad effūsiōnem* sanguinis ēgregiē verberārī eum
iussit et ē suā terrā eum ēiēcit.

IV

Ille sīc dēiectus ultrā quam crēdī potest gemitūs⁴³ et sūspīria⁴⁴
ēmittēbat et ait intrā sē: "Heu mihi. Quid faciam? Cōnfūsus sum.
Sum enim opprobrium⁴⁵ hominum et abiectiō⁴⁶ plēbis. Melius est
mē ad palātium meum pergere, et meī dē cūriā⁴⁷ nōtitiam meī habē-
bunt.⁴⁸ Sī nōn illī, saltem⁴⁹ domina uxor mea nōtitiam meī habēbit
per certa signa." Sōlus ad palātium ex tōtō nūdus accessit, iānuam
pulsāvit. Audītā pulsātiōne, iānitor iānuam aperuit. Quem cum
vīdisset ait: "Dīc mihi, quis es tū?" Et ille: "Numquid nōn nōvistī
mē?"⁵⁰ Quī ait: "In nūllō." At ille: "Dē hōc admīror quia portās
meās vestēs."⁵¹ Quī ait: "Mentīris, quia vestēs dominī meī imperātōris portō." Et ille: "Ego sum ille. In signum huius rogō tē deī
amōre, ut ad imperātrīcem⁵² pergās et eī de adventū meō dīcas, ut
mihi celeriter vestēs mittat, quia aulam⁵³ intrāre volō. Sī vērō
dictīs tuīs nōn crēdet, imperā eī ut per ista signa et ista, quae nēmō
nōvit nisī nōs duo, tibi per omnia⁵⁴ crēdat!" Ait iānitor: "Nōn
dubitō quīn sīs īnsānus, quia iam dominus meus in mēnsā sedet et
imperātrīx iūxtā eum. Vērumtamen,⁵⁵ quia dīcis tē imperātōrem
esse, imperātrīcī nūntiābo et sine dubiō graviter propter hoc pūniē-
ris."

Iānitor ad imperātrīcem perrēxit,⁵⁶ flexīs genibus⁵⁷ omnia eī
rettulit. Illa nōn modicē cōntristāta ad dominum suum conversa,
iūxtā⁵⁸ quem sedēbat, ait: "O domine mī, audīte⁵⁹ mīrābilia! Signa
prīvāta inter nos saepius ācta quīdam ribaldus per iānitōrem mihi
recitat et dīcit sē imperātōrem esse et dominum meum." Ipse cum

---

³⁷ *dukedom*   ³⁸ *you are mad*   ³⁹ *taken upon you*   ⁴⁰ *without being punished*
⁴¹ *bread*   ⁴² *prison*   ⁴³ *groans*   ⁴⁴ *sighs*   ⁴⁵ *disgrace*   ⁴⁶ *scorn*
⁴⁷ *my courtiers*   ⁴⁸ i.e., *will recognize me*   ⁴⁹ *at least*
⁵⁰ *You don't mean to say you don't know me?*   ⁵¹ *wear my livery*
⁵² *empress*   ⁵³ *banquet hall*   ⁵⁴ *completely*   ⁵⁵ *nevertheless*
⁵⁶ perf. of **pergō,** *went*   ⁵⁷ *on bended knee*   ⁵⁸ *next to, by the side of*
⁵⁹ formal for **audī;** cf. French. *écoutez*

hoc audīsset, praecēpit[60] iānitōrī ut eum intrōdūceret in cōnspectum omnium.

V

Quī cum intrōductus esset ex tōtō nūdus, canis quīdam, qui anteā eum multum dīlēxit, ad guttur[61] saltāvit,[62] ut eum occīderet, sed ab hominibus prohibitus est eum laedere. Item quendam falcōnem* habēbat in perticā,[63] quī cum eum vidēret, ligātūram[64] frēgit et extrā aulam volāvit. Ait imperator omnibus in aulā, sedentibus in mensā, sīve stantibus: "Cārissimī," ait, "audīte mea verba, quae istī dīcam! Dīc mihi, cārissime, quis es tū et ob quam causam hūc vēnistī?" At ille: "Domine,[65] imperātor sum istīus imperiī et dominus istīus locī; et ideō hūc vēnī ut loquar cum imperātrīce." Ait imperātor omnibus circumstantibus: "Dīcite mihi per iūrāmentum[66] quod fēcistis, quis nostrum est imperātor et dominus?" At illī: "Ō domine, ista est quaestiō* mīrābilis. Per iūrāmentum quod fēcimus, numquam illum nēquam[67] vīdimus, quod[68] scīmus; sed tū es dominus noster et imperātor, quem ā iuventūte habuimus. Et ideō rogāmus ut pūniātur, ut omnēs exemplum capiant." Imperātor ille conversus ad imperātrīcem et ait: "Dīc, domina, mihi per fidem quā tenēris, nōstī tū istum hominem, quī dīcit sē imperātōrem et dominum tuum esse?" At illa: "O bone domine, cūr tālia ā mē quaeris? Nōnne plūs quam XXX annīs in societāte* tuā stetī et prōlem[69] per tē habuī? Sed ūnum est quod mīror, quōmodō ribaldus ille pervēnit ad nostra sēcrēta inter nos perpetrāta."[70] Imperātor ille dīxit eī: "Quia tam audāx fuistī ut tē imperātōrem nōminēs, dō prō iūdiciō ut ad caudām equī hodiē sīs trāctus. Et sī iam nunc[71] tālia audēs affīrmāre, turpissimā morte tē condemnābō!" Vocāvit satellitēs,[72] praecēpit eīs ut eum ad caudam equī traherent, ita tamen, ut nōn occīderētur. Et sīc factum est.

VI

Post haec vērō ultrā quam crēdī potest dolēbat et quasī dēspērātus dē sē ipsō ait intrā sē: "Pereat dies, quā nātus sum! Ā mē amīcī recessērunt; uxor mea nec fīliī nōvērunt mē." Dum haec dīcit, cōgitābat: "Hīc prope manet eremita,[73] cōnfessor meus. Vādam ad eum: forte ipse nōtitiam meī habēbit, quia saepius cōnfessiōnem meam audīvit." Perrēxit ad eremitam et fenestram[74] cellae* eius

---

[60] *ordered*   [61] *throat*   [62] *leaped*   [63] *perch*   [64] *fastening, bonds*   [65] *sir*
[66] *oath of allegiance*   [67] *worthless fellow* (indecl.)   [68] *so far as*   [69] *children*
[70] *done*   [71] *from this time forth*   [72] *attendants*   [73] *hermit*   [74] *window*

pulsāvit. At ille: "Quis est, quī ibi pulsat?" Quī dīxit: "Ego sum Ioviniānus imperātor. Aperī mihi fenestram, ut loquar tēcum!" Ille vero cum vōcem eius audīsset, aperuit fenestram, et cum eum vīdisset, statim cum impetū[75] fenestram clausit et ait: "Discēde ā mē, maledicte![76] Tū nōn es imperātor, sed diabolus[77] in speciē hominis." Ille haec audiēns ad terram prae[78] dolōre cecidit, crīnēs[79] capitis trāxit et barbae,[80] et lāmentātiōnēs ūsque ad caelum dedit et dīxit: "Heu mihi, quid faciam? Heu ego!" Hōc dictō recordātus est quōmodō quādam nocte in strātū[81] suō ēlevātum est cor eius et dīxit: "Estne alter deus quam ego?" Pulsāvit iterum fenestram eremitae et dīxit: "Amōre illīus quī pependit[82] in cruce,[83] audī cōnfessiōnem meam! Saltem, si nōnvīs fenestram aperīre, clausā audiās tamen, quōūsque fīnierō!"[84] At ille: "Mihi bene placet." Tunc dē tōtā vītā suā est cōnfessus, et praecipuē,[85] quōmodō sē contrā Deum ērēxisset negāns sē crēdere alium deum esse quam sē ipsum.

VII

Factā cōnfessiōne et absolūtiōne,* eremita fenestram aperuit et statim nōtitiam eius habēbat et ait: "Benedictus Altissimus! Iam nōtitiam tuī habeō. Paucās vestēs hīc habeō; cito[86] indue tē et ad palātium tuum perge! Ut[87] spērō, omnēs nōtitiam tuī habēbunt." Imperātor induit sē et ad palātium perrēxit. Iānuam pulsāvit. Iānitor ostium aperuit et eum satis honōrificē[88] salutāvit. At ille: "Numquid nōtitiam meī habētis?"[89] Quī ait: "Etiam[90] domine, peroptimē. Sed mīror quod totā diē hīc stetī nec vīdī vōs[91] exīre." Ille vērō aulam intrāvit, et ecce[92] omnēs capita inclīnābant.[93] Sed alius imperātor erat cum dominā in camerā.[94] Quīdam autem mīles ē camerā exiit et eum intimē respēxit, in cameram rediit et ait: "Domine mī, est quīdam homō in aulā cuī omnēs honōrem faciunt, qui ita assimilātur[95] tibi omnibus, ut quis vestrum sit imperātor penitus[96] ignōrēmus." Imperātor, hōc audītō, ait imperātrīcī: "Cārissima domina, exī forās[97] et mihi dīc sī nōtitiam eius habeās, et mihi renuntiā!" Illa vērō forās exiit, et cum eum vīdisset admīrābātur. Statim cameram intrāvit et ait: "Ō domine, in perīculō animae meae vōbīs ūnum dīco, mē quis vestrum sit dominus meus penitus

---

[75] *bang*   [76] *accursed*   [77] *the Devil*   [78] *because of*   [79] *hair*   [80] *beard*
[81] *bed*   [82] *hung*   [83] *cross*   [84] *make an end, finish*   [85] *especially*
[86] *quickly*   [87] *as*   [88] *respectfully*   [89] for **habēs**; cf. fn. 59   [90] *certainly*
[91] formal for **tē**   [92] *lo!*   [93] *bowed*   [94] *room*   [95] *resembles*   [96] *completely*
[97] *outside*

ignōrāre." At ille: "Quae cum ita sint, forās pergam et vēritātem
discutiam."[98]

VIII

Cum aulam intrāsset, eum per manum accēpit et iūxtā sē stāre
iussit et vocāvit omnēs nōbilēs quī in aulā tunc erant cum imperātrīce
et ait: "Per iūrāmentum quod fēcistis, dīcite quis nostrum est imperātor?" Imperātrīx prīmō respondit: "Domine, mihi incumbit[99]
prīmō respondēre. Testis est mihi Deus in caelīs, quis vestrum sit
dominus meus penitus ignōrō!" Et sīc omnēs dīxērunt. Tunc ait
ille quī dē camerā exiit: "Audīte mē! Iste homo est imperātor vester
et dominus; nam aliquō tempore sē contrā Deum ērēxit, unde omnis
nōtitia hominum ab eō recessit, quōūsque satisfactiōnem* Deō fēcit.
Ego vērō sum angelus* eius, custōs animae eius, quī imperium eius
custōdīvī, quamdiu[100] paenitentiam* sustinuit. Iam paenitentia est
complēta et prō dēlictīs[101] suīs satisfēcit quia, ut vīdistis, illum ad
caudam equī trahī iussī." Hīs dictīs ait, "Iam nunc este eī obēdi-
entēs.* Ad Deum vos recommendō." Statim ab oculīs eōrum
dispāruit.[102] Imperātor vērō grātiās Deō reddidit et post haec omne
tempus vītae suae in bonā pāce vīxit et spīritum Deō trādidit.

---

[98] *sift out* [99] *it devolves upon me, it is my duty* [100] *for such time as*
[101] *misdeeds* [102] *disappeared*

THE TREASURE

This selection is a story from the *Dolopathos sīve dē rēge et septem sapientibus* of Johannēs dē Altā Silvā, sometimes called Johannes de Alta Villa. Jean de Hauteseille, or Jean de Hauteville, to give him his French equivalent names, was perhaps an English monk or one educated in England, who flourished c. A.D. 1200. He was the client of Walter of Coutances, Bishop of Lincoln and Archbishop of Rouen.

The story, Johannes asserts, is based on oral tradition. The original of *The Seven Sages* seems to have been written in India, and eight oriental versions have survived (*Book of Sindibâd*). There are two versions of the *Dolopathos* in Western literature and at least forty of *The Seven Sages*—almost every European language is represented. Herodotus, in the Egyptian section of his *History*,[1] gives us his variant of the clever thief in the story of the treasure of King Rhampsinitus.[2]

The Treasure and the Thief

Fuit antīquō tempore rēx quīdam magnus et potēns. Quī, colligendī thēsaurōs[1] cupidissimus, magnae altitūdinis lātitūdinisque turrim[2] aurō, argentō pretiōsīsque* omnibus rēbus ūsque ad summum[3] replēverat. Habēbat autem hic mīlitem quem in multīs fidēlem expertus[4] erat, cui et clāvēs[5] suī commīsit thēsaurī. At mīles thēsaurum servandum suscipiēns, cum iam multīs annīs ēvolūtīs[6] labōre et senectūte frāctus esset nec posset iam tumultum cūramque cūriae[7] sustinēre, rēgem rogābat ut suae dēbilitātī[8] senectūtīque parcēns, clāvēs thēsaurī reciperet sēque[9] sineret propriam redīre domum licēretque[10] sibi inter fīliōs reliquum vītae suae tempus quiētum agere[11] et iūcundum. Rēx vērō, cum mīlitem optimē dē sē meritum[12] iūdicāret, eum magnīs dōnātum mūneribus maestus[13] tamen abīre sīvit. Receptīs igitur clāvibus, thēsaurum iterum aliī commīsit servandum. Mīles autem domum veniēns cūram sibi suaeque familiae sollicitus impendēbat.[14] Habēbat hic multōs fīliōs, quōrum prīmōgenitus[15] mīlitārī* iam balteō[16] cingēbātur. Quem cum pater

---

[1] II, 121   [2] Evidently the Greek equivalent of a Rameses.
* English gives the clue.   [1] *treasure*   [2] *tower*   [3] *the top*
[4] *had found (to be)*   [5] *keys*   [6] *rolled by*   [7] *court*   [8] *weakness*
[9] indirect reflexive, *him* (the soldier)   [10] *be given permission*   [11] *spend*
[12] *deserved well of him*   [13] *sad*, translate *sadly*.   [14] *devoted*
[15] *first-born, oldest*   [16] *belt*, i.e., was of military age

nimis tenerē[17] dīligeret, omnēs eī suās exposuit dīvitiās iussitque largē expendentem fāmam sibi et amīcōs dīvitiīs comparāre.[18] Ipse vērō, ex licentiā[19] paternīs līberius largiusque ūtēns rēbus, equōs, arma, vestēs, cēteraque quibus magis adulēscentium aetās[20] dēlectārī solet studuit comparāre, amīcōs multōs mūneribus emēns facile post mūnera ab amīcitiā recessūrōs. Brevī ergō tempore loculōs[21] patris minuit; exhaustā* pecūniā, ad patrem redit dīcitque sē pecūniās dēfēcisse.

II

Tunc dēmum pater recōgitāns sēcum paenitēnsque[22] factī: "Quoniam," inquit, "tē, fīlī, nimis et stultē dīlēxī, quicquid habēbam tuae subdidī[23] potestātī.[23] At tu cernēns frēnum[24] tibi laxātum,[24] temperantiae immemor ita omnia cōnsūmpsistī, ut nihil mihi praeter[25] sōlam domum relīquerīs. Quid ergō tibi magis faciam? Doleō quidem quod fāma nōmenque tuum in flōre iuventūtis dēperit,[26] sed unde tē sustentem[27] nōn habeō. Hoc tantum ūnum superest cōnsiliī, sed perīculōsum, ut sī eā largitāte quā prius[28] vīvere vīs, turrim in quā rēgis positī sunt thēsaurī sub obscūrae noctis silentiō adeāmus." Audītō hōc fīlius: "Nūllum," ait, "pater, quamvīs grave sit perīculum tēcum subīre refugiō, modo[29] nē dēsint dīvitiae, nē sī illae dēfēcerint, nōminis quoque meī glōria ēvānēscat."[30] Cōnsurgunt igitur ambō nocte, turrim adeunt, perforant[31] malleīs[32] ferreīs mūrum; intrat pater sublātāque magnā parte thēsaurī exit obstruitque[33] forāmen.[34] Revertuntur domum onustī[35] opibus[36] aliēnīs, et iuvenis iterum suā ūtitur largitāte. Quandōcumque[37] iterum opus erat[38] opibus ad thēsaurum sibi nōtum revertēbantur.

III

Contigit[39] autem ut rēx thēsaurum vidēre vellet, arcessītō[40] custōde intrat turrim videtque magnam thēsaurī partem sublātam[41] esse. Furōre ergō replētus, dissimulāns tamen ēgreditur venitque ad dēcrepitum* quendam senem, cōnsilium quaesītūrus. Fuerat hic

---

[17] *tenderly*   [18] *acquire*   [19] *permission*   [20] for **adulēscentēs**, *young men*
[21] *money bags*   [22] *regretting*   [23] *entrusted to your control*
[24] *given a free rein*   [25] *except*   [26] *withered away*   [27] *support*
[28] *on the magnificent scale on which you lived before*   [29] *provided only that*
[30] *disappear*   [31] *pierce through*   [32] *hammers*   [33] *stop up, block*   [34] *hole*
[35] *laden*   [36] *riches*   [37] *whenever*   [38] *there was need (of)*
[39] *it happened (that)*   [40] *send for*   [41] from **tollo**, *taken away*

senex aliquandō fāmōsissimus[42] latrō[43] quem comprehēnsum rēx
oculīs prīvāverat[44] eīque dē mēnsā suā cotīdiānōs[45] comparābat
cibōs. Hic rēgī cōnsilium saepe bonum et ūtile praebēbat, utpote
quī[46] multa vīderat et audierat suāque experientiā didicerat multa.
Nārrat eī rēx damnum[47] suum quaeritque quōmodō perdita recuperāre[48] possit. Cui senex tāle dat cōnsilium: "Sī," inquit, "ō rēx,
nōvisse cupis quis hoc an[49] tuus custōs an[49] alius ēgerit, iubē fascicu-
lum[50] herbae viridis[51] in turrim inferrī suppōnīque[52] ignem. Tū
autem, clausō ostiō,[53] turrim iterum atque iterum circumeās,[54] et
videās sī per aliquam mūrī rīmulam[55] fūmum* ēgredī vīderis. Hōc
factō, ad mē redeās cōnsilium acceptūrus quid post haec tibi agendum
sit." Rēx autem dictum[56] senis cito implērī[57] iubēns, clausit ostium
et coepit tacitus turris ambitum[58] circumīre. Ecce autem calōre[59]
ignis viridisque māteriae[60] hūmōre[61] fūmus permaximē excitātus
tōtam ūsque ad tēctum[62] replēvit turrim. Quī cum aliud spīrācu-
lum[63] nōn habēret, per locum forāminis illīus, eō quod lapide tantum[64]
sine caementō* obstrūctum erat, ēgreditur.

IV

Quibus vīsīs, rēx properāvit ad senem; ea quae vīderat nārrāvit.
Hōc audītō, senex: "Sciās," ait, "rēx, fūrēs[65] tibi tuōs per locum ubi
fūmus ēgreditur abstulisse thēsaurōs; quōs nisi aliquā arte cēperis,
quod superest[66] asportābunt.[67] Nōn enim cessābunt, quippe[68]
quibus adhūc prosperē cessit rēs,[68] dōnec tōtum thēsaurum ex-
hauserint. Meō igitur ūsus cōnsiliō damnum dissimulā[69] et preme
silentiō,[70] nē, rūmōre hōc per aurēs[71] populī discurrente, tuum fūribus
studium innotēscat.[72] Et tū interim cuppam[73] lātam et profundam
calentī[74] implē bitūmine, resā, pice et glūtine,[75] quam forāminī in-
trorsus[76] oppōnās, ut dum fūr mōre solitō sēcūrus nūllam dēcep-
tiōnem* sūspicāns ad assuētum[77] thēsaurum recurrit, repentē[78] in

---

[42] *notorious*   [43] *robber*   [44] *deprived of*   [45] *daily*
[46] *in view of the fact that he*   [47] *loss*   [48] *recover*   [49] *whether . . . or*
[50] *little bundle*   [51] *green grass*   [52] *placed beneath*   [53] *door*
[54] *walk round* (subjunctive for imperative, cf. **videās, redeās** later.)
[55] *crack*   [56] *instruction*   [57] *carry out*   [58] *path around*   [59] *heat*   [60] *stuff*
[61] *moisture*   [62] *roof*   [63] *breathing hole, vent*   [64] *only*   [65] *thieves*
[66] *is left over*   [67] *carry away*
[68] *seeing that thus far things have come off successfully for them*   [69] *conceal*
[70] *keep silent (about)*   [71] *ears*   [72] *become known*   [73] *cask*   [74] *boiling*
[75] *tar, resin, pitch, and glue*   [76] *on the inside*   [77] *accustomed*   [78] *suddenly*

cuppam corruat[79] captusque et colligātus[80] glūtine sē tibi, velit nolit,[81] crās manifestet."[82] Admīrātus rēx astūtum[83] senis cōnsilium cuppam īlicō[84] ferventī implētam glūtine oppōnit forāminī serrātōque[85] ostiō abscēdit. Ecce[86] autem fātālis illa diēs, quae nēminem bonum malumve praeterit,[87] miserum patrem cum fīliō eādem nocte ad turrim addūxit, remōtōque ā forāmine lapide, intrat pater, nihil dē praetēnsīs laqueīs[88] sūspicātus, dumque festīnat ut heri et nūdius tertius[89] in pavīmentum* salīre,[90] incautus miser, ut erat vestītus calceātusque,[91] in cuppam mentō tenus[92] īnsilit,[93] statimque vāllātus[94] glūtine redditur immōbilis, ita ut nec manum nec pedem movēre posset, exceptā linguā quae tantum ab hāc iniūriā lībera remānserat. Ingemīscēns[95] igitur īnfēlīx fīlium advocat, nārrat quibus laqueīs teneātur adstrīctus, ōrat ut sibi cito, antequam aliquis superveniat,[96] caput amputet* et abscēdat, nē forte per caput cognitus aeternam suō generī[97] māculam[98] īnferat et iactūram.[99] At vērō fīlius tōtīs vīribus patrem cōnātus extrahere, cum labōrem suum frūstrāri[100] vidēret, coepit anxiāri[101] et haesitāre quid dē duōbus ageret; hinc[102] etenim horrēbat suās nece[103] patris cruentāre[104] manūs, hinc[102] vērō metuēbat per faciem patris dēprehendī. Cum ergo eum ā nece retraheret amor, timor et necessitās urgēret, nēsciens quid ūtilius ad tempus ageret, caput patris cultrō[105] abscīsum[106] fugiēns asportāvit.

V

Postrīdiē autem rēx prīmā lūce dē lēctulō[1] surgēns intrāvit turrim cucurritque ad cuppam invēnitque mūrum perforātum et tōtam illam bitūminis superficiem[2] infectam[3] sanguine, fūrem quoque suum, sed truncātō[4] capite dēprehendit. Festīnāns ergō ad suum recurrit cōnsiliārium,[5] illum vidēlicet[6] senem, annuntiāns captum quidem fūrem, sed capite mutilātum. Quod cum audīsset senex, parumper[7] subrīdēns: "Mīror," ait, "huius latrōnis astūtiam. Quia enim nōbilis erat nec voluit sē vel genus suum prōdere, idcircō ā sociō sibi caput amputārī iussit. Unde et difficile vidētur mihi tē posse aut thēsau-

---

79 *fall*   80 *held fast*   81 *willy nilly*   82 *reveal*   83 *shrewd*   84 *at once*
85 *bolt*   86 *behold*   87 *pass by*   88 *snare spread before him*
89 *day before yesterday*   90 *leap*   91 *with clothes and shoes on*
92 *up to the chin* (prep. **tenus** follows its case)   93 *leaps in*   94 *enveloped*
95 *groaning*   96 *came on the scene*   97 *family*   98 *disgrace*   99 *loss*
100 *spent in vain*   101 *be distressed*   102 *on one hand . . . on the other hand*
103 *death*   104 *stain with blood*   105 *knife*   106 *cut off*   1 *bed*   2 *surface*
3 *stained, dyed*   4 *cut off*   5 *adviser*   6 *that is to say*   7 *a moment*

rum recuperāre aut cognōscere fūrem." Tunc rēx vehementer urgēbat senem ut daret cōnsilium, minimē dē thēsaurō perditō aiēns[3] sē cūrāre, sī tantummodō fūrem quis fuerit[9] agnōvisset.[10]   Cui senex: "Fac illum," inquit, "abstrāctum[11] dē cuppā, caudae equī fortissimī alligārī[12] trahīque per plateās[13] et vīcōs[14] cīvitātum rēgnī tuī.   Porrō[15] mīlitēs armātī subsequantur, capientēs sī quōs vīderint virōs vel mulierēs ad aspectum cadāveris[16] lacrimārī tibique eōs praesentent. Et sī fuerint ibi socius aut uxor aut fīliī, nēquāquam[17] poterunt ā lacrimīs temperāre."[18]

VI

Bonum rēx ratus[19] senis cōnsilium iubet festīnanter truncum equō fortissimō pedibus alligātum cum armātīs mīlitibus trahī per proximam cīvitātem.   Quī dum miser trahitur, contigit eum ante forēs[20] domūs suae dēvenīre.   Stābat autem ille fīlius eius māior, quī et eī in fūrtō[21] fuerat socius, ante ipsās forēs.   Quī cum vidēret patrem sīc miserābiliter trahī, flēre quidem nōn audēns, sed nec valēns[22] lacrimās prohibēre, occāsiōne repertā, cultellum[23] lignumque[24] arripit, quasī aliquid incīsūrus, sinistraeque manūs pollicem[25] dē indūstriā[26] sibi amputat.   Tunc vērō sub occāsiōne[27] pollicis vōcem ēmittit lūctuōsam,[28] ērumpunt lacrimae, accurrit māter, frātrēs et sorōrēs dīlacerant[29] manibus vestēs ōraque[30] et capillōs,[31] in persōnā fīliī patris miseriam lāmentantēs.*   Affuērunt īlicō mīlitēs quī eōs caperent dūcerentque ad rēgem.   At vērō rēx maximō adfectus gaudiō, spērāns sē perdita recuperāre posse, pollicēbātur illīs vītam et grātiam suam, sī scelus confitērentur redderentque thēsaurōs suōs.   Iuvenis autem ille ex metū et necessitāte audāciam sūmēns: "Nōn ideō," ait, "ō serēnissime rēx, ego aut meī, quia hic miser truncus ad nōs aliquid[32] pertineat, lacrimās effundimus, sed quia hic diēs nefāstus[33] mihi sinistrae manūs pollicem abstulit.   Ob hoc ergō lacrimae effūsae, exarātae[34] faciēs, capillī ēvulsī,[35] quia ego adhūc iuvenis hodiē ūnō et potiōre membrō dēbilitātus[36] sum."   Rēx vērō pollicem adhūc fluentem sanguine[37] certissimum vēritātis argumentum fore ratus, mōtus misericordiā propter fortūnam iuvenis: "Nōn est," ait,

---

8 *saying*   9-10 *know the thief who he was; know who the thief was.*
11 *have him taken out*   12 *tied*   13 *streets*   14 *lanes*   15 *furthermore*
16 *corpse*   17 *in no way*   18 *refrain*   19 *thinking*   20 *door*   21 *theft*
22 *able*   23 *small knife*   24 *piece of wood*   25 *thumb*   26 *on purpose*
27 *pretext*   28 *(howl) of pain*   29 *rend*   30 *faces*   31 *hair*
32 *at all*   33 *unlucky*   34 *scratched*   35 *torn out*   36 *maimed*   37 *blood*

"mīrum sī dolet cui male contigit. Vāde[38] in pāce et hunc diem male ōminātum[39] dē cēterō[40] praecavētō."[41] Sīc ergō ille astūtiā suā sē suōsque līberāns domum rediit, et rēx similitūdine dēlūsus[42] vēritātis redit ad senem cōnsilium acceptūrus.

VII

Senex vērō affirmābat rēgem vīx posse invenīre quod quaereret, suadēbat tamen ut cadāver iterum per eandem traherētur cīvitātem. Quod et factum est. Cumque ut prius ventum esset ad domum eius, fīlius, internum animī dolōrem nōn ferēns, fīlium parvulum in puteum[43] quī prō foribus erat clam[44] prōiēcit, tuncque vultum[45] unguibus[46] carpēns[47] vōce lacrimōsā populum quasī ad līberandum fīlium convocat. Accurrit iterum māter cum fīliīs, cingunt[48] puteum, lacrimantur, aliīque fūnibus[49] ad extrahendum puerulum in puteum sē dēmittunt[50] et aliī eōs iterum sursum[51] trahunt. Quid plūra? Capitur iterum ille sōlus dūciturque ad rēgem et interim cadāver per aliās cīvitātēs frūstrā trāctum ad rēgem vīx ossibus[52] et nervīs[53] cohaerēns* redūcitur. Porrō rēx vidēns hunc iterum captum quem anteā dīmīserat et nimium admīrātus: "Quid prōsunt," ait, "tibi callidae[54] dēceptiōnēs? Diī summī tē prōdunt,[55] fūrta tua et scelera tē accūsant. Redde ergō thēsaurum et iūrō tibi per meam magnīque Iovis potentiam nec tē vītā nec aliquō mē prīvātūrum membrō, sed sānum et integrum līberumque dīmissūrum." Tunc latrō calliditāte suā ūtēns, prōdūcta prīmō sūspīria[56] ab īmō pectoris trahit,[56] dēhinc tālem ēmittit vōcem: "Ō mē,[57] omnium infēlīcissimum hominum, quem tantō diī odiō persequuntur, ut nec sōlum mihi diem sine dolōribus et cruciātibus corporis et animī trānsīre permittant! Heri mihi diēs īnfēlīx pollicem abstulit; hic hodiē īnfēlīcior fīlium ūnicum dēmersit[58] in puteum, et ecce dē thēsaurō rēgis requīror." Tunc etiam lacrimīs falsīs, immō vērissimīs perfūsus,[59] "Magnum," ait, "ō rēx, beneficium sōlāciumque praestiteris miserō, sī mē ab hāc vītā quae omnī tormentō, omnī morte mihi gravior vidētur, subtrāxeris." Rēx autem cum iuvenem crēbrīs[60] perfundī lacrimīs mortemque locō[61] beneficiī quaerere vidēret audīretque eum vērē ipsō diē fīlium perdidisse hesternōque diē pollicem, miserātus homi-

---

[38] go   [39] (ill) omened   [40] in future   [41] beware of   [42] tricked   [43] well
[44] secretly   [45] face   [46] fingernails   [47] tearing   [48] surround   [49] ropes
[50] lower   [51] up   [52] bones   [53] sinews   [54] clever   [55] betray
[56] heaved a sigh   [57] acc. of exclamation   [58] plunged   [59] bathed
[60] constant, frequent   [61] instead of

nem abīre sīvit, centum eī argentī marcās[62] prō sōlāciō tribuēns.
Sīc iterum rēx dēceptus cōnsiliārium suum adiit, aiēns sē frūstrā
operam īnsūmpsisse.

VIII

Sed senex ad rēgem: "Ūnum," ait, "adhūc superest agendum, quō
nisī fūrem superstitem[63] cēperis, iam frūstrā ad alia tē convertēs:
ēlige[64] tibi mīlitēs fortissimōs quadrāgintā, quōrum vīgintī nigrīs
armīs nigrīsque equīs mūniantur[65] aliīque vīgintī albīs[66] equīs ar-
mīsque eiusdem colōris sint armātī. Hīsque cadāver lignō pedibus
suspēnsum nocte ac diē custōdiendum committās, vīgintī albīs hinc,[67]
inde[68] vīgintī nigrīs[69] circā ipsum ordinātīs. Hī profectō[70] sī vigi-
lanter custōdierint, tuum capient fūrem quia nōn patiētur ipse diūtius
pendēre[71] socium, etiam sī sciat sē mortem prōtinus[72] subitūrum."
Rēx autem, prout[73] dīxerat senex, mīlitēs nigrīs albīsque mūnītōs
armīs circā sūspēnsum cadāver ordināvit.[74] At vērō fūr ille, suum
patrisque opprobrium[75] ferre nōn valēns mālēnsque[76] semel morī
quam diū īnfēlīciter vīvere, cōnsilium cēpit quō aut patrem turpī
lūdibriō[77] subtraheret aut ipse cum eō pariter[78] morerētur. Subtilī
ergō ingeniō arma[79] partīta[80] fabricat,* tōta scīlicet[81] ab ūnā parte
alba et nigra ab alterā. Quibus armātus equum hinc albō, inde
nigrō pannō[82] coöpertum[83] ascendit, sīcque lūcente lūnā[84] per mediōs
trānsit mīlitēs, ut nigra pars armōrum eius vīgintī albōs dēlūderet et
alba pars dēciperet nigrōs, putārentque nigrī ūnum esse ex albīs et
albī ūnum ex nigrīs esse. Sīc ergō pertrānsiēns[85] vēnit ad patrem
dēpositumque ā lignō asportāvit. Factō[86] autem māne,[86] mīlitēs
videntēs fūrem fūrtim sublātum sibi, cōnfūsī rediērunt ad rēgem,
nārrantēs quōmodō sē mīles albīs nigrīsque armīs partītīs[87] dēcēpisset.
Dēspērāns ergō iam[88] rēx posse recuperārī perdita, et fūrem et thēsaurum cessāvit quaerere.

---

[62] *marks* (coins)   [63] *surviving*   [64] *choose*   [65] *equipped*   [66] *white*
[67] *on one side*.   [68] *on the other side*   [69] *black*   [70] *certainly*   [71] *hang*
[72] *immediately*   [73] *just as*   [74] *arranged*   [75] *shame*   [76] *preferring*
[77] *jest*   [78] *equally, by a similar death*   [79] *armor*   [80] *of two colors*
[81] *that is to say*   [82] *cloth*   [83] *covered*   [84] *in the moon-light*
[85] *passing through them*   [86] *at dawn*   [87] *i.e., half white, half black*
[88] *by this time; any longer*

BIOGRAPHICAL NOTES

BIOGRAPHICAL NOTES

Brief Notes on the Lives and Works of Authors Mentioned
in the Selections for Reading

ENNIUS

(Quintus Ennius, 239–169 B.C.)

Ennius is commonly known as the "father of Latin poetry." He was
born in 239 B.C. in an old Calabrian town in the heel of Italy. Other
poets had preceded him, but Ennius is preëminent in the dawn of Latin
literature as the author of a great epic (in hexameters, which he was the
first to introduce from Greece) of Rome's victory over Hannibal. Little
of his work survives, and most of that little has been preserved in the
form of quotations found in other writers. Hence we often find lines
of Ennius referred to as *Ennius apud Ciceronem*, i.e., Ennius, quoted
in the works of Cicero.

Besides being an epic poet, Ennius was a satirist and dramatist.
Though he wrote both tragedies and comedies, his genius lay rather in
the former.

In 169 B.C. he died, "the greatest figure in the serious thought of
Rome before the days of Lucretius and Cicero."

CATO

(Marcus Porcius Cato, 234–139 B.C.)

This typical old Roman conservative was orator and historian as
well. His rugged, cumbrous prose is the earliest that has come down
to us. Though his speeches are known only from a few fragments,
they enjoyed a great reputation in Cicero's day. His *de Re Rustica*,
or *de Agri Cultura*, has been preserved entire. It is a practical hand-
book for the farmer. On elements in this prosaic foundation, Vergil
later built the graceful structure of his *Georgics*.

Two of his most famous phrases are: "Carthage must be destroyed,"
Delenda est Carthago, and, "I marvel how a soothsayer can refrain from
laughter when he meets another soothsayer."

PLAUTUS

(Titus Maccius Plautus, 254–184 B.C.)

Plautus came from the little Umbrian town of Sarsina. He found his
way to Rome, where he drudged for years and, in the intervals of drudg-

ery, wrote comedies. Though he uses Greek originals, he displays a wonderful versatility and originality in the treatment of his material. Of his twenty-one extant comedies, Shakespeare used the *Menaechmi* (*The Brothers Menaechmus*) in the *Comedy of Errors*, and Molière, the *Aulularia* (*The Hidden Pot of Gold*) in *L'Avare*.

He shows us the typical characters of Roman comedy: sighing lovers, parasites, soldiers of fortune, and hard-hearted fathers who are outwitted by nimble-witted slaves scheming in the interests of "the young master"; yet the oft-repeated plots rarely fail to entertain. A strong Roman flavor is added to everything.

Plautus was a prime favorite with the Roman mob, who would soon tire of an over-subtle plot and desert the theatre to watch a tight-rope walker or a performing bear. His broad farce and rollicking humor have won him a greater number of readers than the more urbane and less virile plays of Terence can claim.

TERENCE

(Publius Terentius Afer, 195–159 B.C.)

Afer is the Latin for *African*. Its presence in the name of the writer of comedies usually known as "Terence" means that he belonged to some native tribe conquered by the Carthaginians. At Carthage he was born, and was either purchased from a Carthaginian master or kidnapped. Terentius Lucanus, a Roman senator, educated and manumitted him, that is, gave him his freedom. Through his powerful protector, he met the members of the "Scipionic circle," a literary group of Roman aristocrats of which the younger Scipio Africanus was the centre.

Six plays are all that we have of Terence's comedies. The plots of four are taken from Menander, the greatest Greek writer of "new" Comedy, or the Comedy of Manners, of the late fourth century B.C. In consequence, the spirit of Terence's work is Greek, the scene is always Athens, and we are seldom tempted to imagine ourselves in Rome. In this respect he offers a striking contrast to the earlier playwright Plautus, 254–184, who infused into his Greek originals a vigor, a rough humor, and a universality all his own. The culture and elegance of Terence did not appeal to the Roman mob as much as the qualities of Plautus. Though his characters are more subtle, more polished, and more humane than those of Plautus, what is gained in refinement is lost in virility. Caesar, in an epigram on Terence, acknowledges him to be among the greatest, but deplores his lack of forcefulness and vigor. "Terence was an artist; Plautus an untutored genius."

CICERO

(Marcus Tullius Cicero, 106–43 B.C.)

Cicero is the best known figure in Roman literature. He studied at Athens and Rhodes. We have more writings from his pen than from that of any other writer of antiquity. He wrote speeches, letters, philosophical essays, translations, rhetorical treatises, and a little verse. As a young criminal lawyer, he speedily gained reputation, wealth, and political advancement by his defense of his clients and by his impeachment of Verres, the extortionate governor of Sicily, in 70 B.C. When consul in 63 B.C., he crushed the Catilinarian conspiracy, but, having made many enemies by his sharp tongue and self-esteem, was banished soon after. In the struggle between Caesar and Pompey, he sided with the latter, but was allowed by Caesar to return to Rome in 47 B.C. His political career was now virtually at an end and he devoted himself almost entirely to literary work.

It is as the writer who shaped and moulded the stiff and unwieldy material of the Latin tongue into a plastic prose instrument that he deserves the greatest credit. He also did much for Roman thought by translating and interpreting the mature heritage of Greek philosophy into Latin. Two of his original philosophical essays are the *de Amicitia* (On Friendship) and the *de Senectute* (On Old Age). They are also called the *Laelius* and *Cato Maior*, respectively, since these persons take the principal part in the dialogue.

After Caesar's assassination in 44 B.C., Cicero burst once more into politics with a series of furious attacks on Antony styled "Philippics," in imitation of the tirades pronounced three centuries earlier by the Greek orator Demosthenes against Philip of Macedon, father of Alexander the Great. Antony retaliated by having Cicero put on the list of the "proscribed" and assassinated in 43 B.C.

His brother Quintus was one of Caesar's most brilliant officers in the Gallic War.

CAESAR

(Gaius Julius Caesar, 100–44 B.C.)

Caesar's is the best known name in Roman history. It is with his *Commentaries*, the dispatches of a general in the field describing his conduct of the Gallic War, that most of us start our reading of Latin. His language shows the same clearness and force that were revealed in the actions of his amazing life. As we follow his career, we feel that he was, up to the day of the death which he had with contemptuous indifference foreseen, like his great parallel Alexander, the chosen darling of the gods.

This statesman, author, poet, and soldier was a member of one of the proudest families in Rome. Early in his career he realized that the outworn and unwieldy mechanism of the republican regime must sooner or later collapse under the thrust of some ambitious proconsul returning from abroad after successful years as governor and general.

In 60 B.C., he formed a coalition, known as the First Triumvirate, with the millionaire Crassus and the great soldier Pompey. Crassus was killed in a disastrous campaign against the Parthians. Caesar and Pompey were left facing one another.

A clash was inevitable. Pompey's legions had been trained in the East in the Mithridatic and Pirate Wars. He was the Senate's champion; Caesar was the leader of the popular party. Caesar maneuvered for position; for ten years as governor of Gaul he hardened and trained a large body of troops to a high standard of discipline and an allegiance that proved distinctly personal, all under the pretext of subjugating a new and troublesome province for the Republic. At the end of his command, which had been prolonged by his partisans at home to ten years, he refused to disband his troops unless Pompey did the same. His jealous rival refused, and was crushed, together with the senatorial party, in a series of battles fought in Thessaly, Macedonia, Spain, Africa, Syria, and Asia Minor.

The Republic was dead. Now began the colossal task of reform and the laying of the foundations of the Empire. In the midst of his work, Caesar was assassinated by enemies, political and personal, on the Ides (the fifteenth) of March, 44 B.C.

In the case of a versatile genius like Caesar's, the man's writings are incidental to his life's work as soldier, statesman, and virtual founder of the Empire. There are the seven books *de Bello Gallico*, the three *de Bello Civili*, and letters to Cicero and others. The first two provide many of the examples found in the exercises of this book. The style is detached and impersonal. Even in the *Civil War*, he states, without comment, his offers of peace to the Pompeian Party, their cruelty and greed, and their final defeat at his hands. In the *Gallic War*, we are so influenced by the cold, terse, lucid chapters that we forget that they were written as subtle propaganda to convince the fickle Roman mob that their favorite was campaigning solely in the interests of Rome.

To some historians, Caesar has appeared a god; to others, an unscrupulous self-seeker. It is hard to strike an even balance of truth in the case of such a unique personality. It is perhaps safe to say that "he was a supreme maker of history . . . who exercises lasting influence on his country and the world."

PUBLILIUS SYRUS

(About 100–50 B.C.)

Publilius "the Syrian" was born at Antioch and flourished in the first half of the first century B.C. He was a writer of "mimes," a type of light drama or farce which "travestied contemporary life and personages through imitations of man, beast, and bird." A collection of short, pithy sayings or saws known as *Sententiae* was made from his mimes in the first century A.D. "As wisdom and morality in tabloid form, they were found useful to administer in school."

LUCRETIUS

(Titus Lucretius Carus, 99–55 B.C.)

This profound philosopher-poet was the exponent of Epicureanism. His early life was spent in the stormy years of almost incessant civil war which preceded the final collapse of the Republic and the birth of the Empire. Seeking for a creed that would free men's minds from crude superstition and fear of death, he built his poem, *de Rerum Natura*, "On the Nature of Things," on Greek philosophy—that of Epicurus in particular. Its six books of hexameter verse are still extant. They deal with such subjects as the atomic theory, the evolution of mankind, and the causes of natural phenomena like rain and lightning. In spite of the technical nature of such material, he exhibits the highest poetic power. One passage of great pathos was copied by Gray in his "Elegy Written in a Country Churchyard." In his later years, it is thought that his reason tottered. The story of his madness is beautifully told in Tennyson's poem, "Lucretius."

One critic has said that with Lucretius a sense of infinity came into Latin verse, which lost it again for centuries. "And even in Lucretius it is rather the infinite of negation, a space that the swiftest lightning leaves still in darkness; immortal Death to ease our mortal life."[1]

At his death, no less a person than Marcus Cicero superintended the publication of his work.

SALLUST

(Gaius Sallustius Crispus, 86–35 B.C.)

This historian was a partisan of Caesar, and after the Civil War was sent to Africa as proconsul. After accumulating a considerable fortune there, he returned to his famous gardens in Rome to spend the years of

---

[1] Helen Waddell, *The Wandering Scholars*, page 1.

his retirement in writing. His *Histories* have survived only in fragments, but we have two monographs: one on the war from 112 to 106 B.C. with Jugurtha, king of Numidia, and the other on the Catilinarian conspiracy of 63 B.C. While proconsul of Africa, a province which had been made out of the old Kingdom of Numidia, he made considerable researches in preparation for his *Jugurtha*, and even had translations made from original documents in the Carthaginian language. The work is an exciting story of a dramatic episode in Roman history. Against a North African background, we follow a gripping tale of craft, intrigue, sieges, and murders. Marius is the hero.

In style, Sallust is representative of the period of transition between the Ciceronian and Augustan ages.

CATULLUS

(Gaius Valerius Catullus, 84–54 B.C.)

Verona was the native town of Catullus, one of the greatest lyric poets of the world's literature. He was the child of a wealthy and distinguished family at whose table Julius Caesar often sat as a guest.

At twenty-five, while staying in Rome, he fell in love with Clodia, the wife of Caecilius Metellus Celer, Governor of Cisalpine Gaul. In his poems, he calls her Lesbia. The story of his infatuation, quarrels, reconciliations, fresh quarrels, fresh infatuation, and final revolt runs through his lyric verse, which echoes the most spontaneous feeling in Latin literature. Besides love poems, he wrote of many aspects of the world of fashion of his day and ridicules many of his contemporaries. One of his gems is a translation from Sappho, a Greek poetess of the late seventh century B.C. He wrote in a variety of meters, including his favorite hendecasyllabics (a light, tripping meter of eleven syllables). In certain short passages of his hexameters, he excels even Vergil in his melodious cadences and the sheer inspiration of his language.

VERGIL

(Publius Vergilius Maro, 70–19 B.C.)

This most famous of the Roman poets was born near Mantua more than two thousand years ago. He was educated at Mediolanum (Milan) and Naples. Thence he came to Rome, was taken up by Maecenas, and by him introduced to Augustus.

His earliest works were some light verse and ten *Eclogues* (a name which means *Selections*), also styled *Bucolics*, for their theme is the lives and loves of shepherds and herdsmen. For seven years he labored on the four *Georgics* (*geōrgos* is the Greek for *farmer*), which treat of the raising of crops, the breeding of cattle and horses, the care of bees, and the "growth of the soil." They are exquisitely wrought; it is said that they were composed at the rate of four lines a day. In them we see Vergil as the apostle of work and in deep sympathy with man, beast, and countryside. He had an ear for "the still, sad music of humanity." The *Georgics* were in his opinion his finest work.

His great epic, the *Aeneid*, in twelve books of hexameter verse, is based on the legend that the Trojan Aeneas, son of Venus and Anchises, was the founder of Rome. It was unfinished at Vergil's death. The political motive behind it is the concept of the Roman Empire and the unity of Italy with Rome. Because of the national spirit of the epic and the fact that it was encouraged by Augustus and Maecenas, Vergil claims the right to be regarded as the poet laureate of the Great Age.

The brooding sadness of the *Aeneid* is in amazing contrast to the unrelenting vigor of Homer's *Iliad*. Vergil follows the conventions of the epic tradition, but his heart is not in his battle scenes. Beyond the funeral pyre of the young warrior, he sees the grinning skeleton of death and the weeping parents. He is at his best in the splendid love story of Dido in the fourth book, the descent of Aeneas to the underworld in the sixth, and the immortal friendship of Nisus and Euryalus in the ninth.

HORACE

(Quintus Horatius Flaccus, 65–8 B.C.)

Born in Apulia on the borders of Lucania, Horace was given a sound education by his freedman father at Rome and Athens. He took the side of Brutus in the Civil War and fought at Philippi in 42 B.C. Fortunately, he made his peace with Augustus and was introduced by Vergil to Maecenas, patrons of letters and influential friend of the emperor.

His works include the *Satires*, written in a colloquial style; the *Epistles*, in which he reveals himself most intimately and one of which is the famous *Art of Poetry*; the *Odes*, in four books; and the *Epodes*. Of these, the *Odes* are his most widely read poems. They show his rare ability in adapting the stiff Latin tongue to a variety of Greek meters in which few or none (except Catullus) before him had experimented with success. His style is polished and urbane; his thought does not soar; his philosophy is the tolerant common sense of a successful student of the art of living.

A wide range of subjects is treated in the *Odes*. Some tell of the joys of life on his little Sabine farm. Many are addressed to friends like Maecenas, Vergil, or the lady of the hour, and deal with personal experiences or emotions. Others are "state" or official odes, written, in his capacity of court poet, to please Augustus and further his schemes of social and moral reform in the state. He did for Latin lyric verse what Cicero had done for Latin prose; that is, he made it a more plastic instrument for conveying thought, and introduced much that was Greek in meter, construction, and expression.

AUGUSTUS AND THE "MONUMENTUM ANCYRANUM"

(Imperator Caesar Divi Filius Augustus, 63 B.C.–A.D. 14)

Augustus, the first Roman emperor, was the great-nephew and heir of Julius Caesar.

The *Monumentum Ancyranum,* so-called because it was found at Ancyra (modern Angora) in Asia Minor, is one of several copies, set up at various places in the Empire, of a bronze inscription placed by the emperor's order on his tomb in Rome shortly after his death. Its Latin title is *Res Gestae divi Augusti,* "The achievements of the divine Augustus." It is autobiographical, giving coldly and dispassionately an account of his great stewardship of the Roman Empire. The inscription, which Mommsen calls "the queen of Latin inscriptions," records the struggles of the earlier years, the rise of Augustus to the principate, the establishment of law and order, the disbursement of largesses to veterans and citizens, and similar details.

PROPERTIUS

(Sextus Propertius, 49–15 B.C.)

This writer of love poems came to Rome from his native Assisi originally to study law. Like Catullus, he addressed much of the poetry of his *Elegies* to a lady, in this case, a certain Cynthia, whose real name was Hostia.

At Rome he was introduced to the circle of Maecenas, and became a warm admirer of Vergil. For his age, the production of the first book of the *Elegies,* written in a meter which even Catullus had used awkwardly, was an amazing achievement. His poetry was full of obscure allusions; he ranks among the most learned of the Augustan poets.

OVID

(Publius Ovidius Naso, 43 B.C.–A.D. 18)

Ovid was the most famous of a group of elegiac poets of the Augustan age. He was educated, like many young men of good family who were born in the country, at Rome and Athens. Soon he gave up the study of law and a public career for poetry. He was the friend of Horace, Propertius, and other men of letters, but appears only to have *seen* Vergil. Many of his verses are addressed to a certain Corinna. His fashionable love poetry was for years the rage in Roman society.

The *Metamorphoses* ("Transformations" or "Changeling Shapes"), in fifteen books of hexameters, is his great work. It is a treasury of famous myths and legends of antiquity (mostly Greek) like the story of Daedalus and Icarus, or Orpheus and Eurydice. He also wrote the *Fasti*, a calendar in verse, dealing with folklore, religion, festivals, anniversaries, and astronomy.

In A.D. 8 came an imperial order banishing Ovid to Tomi on the Black Sea in consequence of an intrigue in which he was involved at Rome. The emperor had disapproved of much of his erotic poetry, notably *The Art of Love*. At Tomi, afflicted with illness and the miserable climate, he wrote the *Tristia* ("Laments") and *Letters from Pontus* to his old set in Rome, and died in lonely exile at the age of sixty.

SENECA

(Lucius Annaeus Seneca, 4 B.C.–A.D. 65)

Seneca the philosopher was a native of Corduba (modern Cordova), in Spain, and the second son of Seneca the rhetorician. One of his brothers became, by adoption, Gallio, and was governor of Achaea in A.D. 51 to 52, when the apostle Paul was brought before his tribunal. Lucan was his nephew.

He was brought by his aunt to Rome and was there trained in rhetoric. Then followed some foreign travel which took him to Egypt. On his return, his career at the bar began. His brilliant success excited the jealousy of the emperor Caligula. The young pleader wisely turned to literature and philosophy. On the accession of Claudius, he was banished to Corsica on the charge of being involved in a court intrigue. After nine years of exile, he was recalled to be the tutor of Nero, the ten-year-old son of Agrippina the younger and stepson of Claudius. When his young pupil became emperor at the age of seventeen, Seneca and his friend Afranius Burrus, prefect of the Imperial Guards, became virtual administrators of the Empire. These were the first five good years of Nero's reign. Seneca became a very wealthy and influential man.

At last the reaction came. Nero chafed under such tutelage; Seneca was, in accordance with the fashion of that time, ordered to commit suicide. The pretext was his complicity in the conspiracy of Piso. Tacitus has recorded for us his last hours.

Seneca wrote treatises on ethics, moral letters, and writings on natural philosophy. His *De Beneficiis* is a philosophical treatise in seven books. The title may be rendered, *On Giving and Receiving Favors*. All his writings are tinged with the Stoic point of view. He was also a writer of tragedies. These, however, were so stilted and pedantic in their tone that they were unsuitable for acting and were soon forgotten.

QUINTILIAN

(Marcus Fabius Quintilianus, about A.D. 35–96)

A professor of rhetoric, the greatest Latin authority on education, a consul, an imperial tutor, and a highly successful lawyer and lecturer, Quintilian, like a surprisingly large number of distinguished literary figures of his times, was of Spanish origin. He was born about A.D. 35 at Calagurris, now Calahorra, on the Ebro River. Here in Spain, as Mommsen says,[1] Roman civilization gained ground earlier and more powerfully than in any other province. Perhaps he was educated there, and perhaps his father was a rhetor and supervised that education; most critics believe Quintilian went to Rome with Galba in 68 and taught rhetoric there for twenty years.

In 72 the emperor Vespasian, founder of the new Flavian dynasty, made Quintilian a state-endowed professor of rhetoric and official head of a recognized school of oratory with prestige sufficient to influence considerably the educational system of the day. It is to this appointment that Martial refers in his epigram:

> Quintiliane vagae moderator summe iuventae,
> Gloria Romanae, Quintiliane, togae.

In A.D. 93 Vespasian's son Domitian entrusted to the distinguished rhetorician the education of his heirs-apparent, two young boys,[2] the children of his niece; Quintilian was rewarded with the consular insignia. But the treacherous politics of those days later involved the princes' parents in disgrace; their father, Flavius Clemens, was executed, and they with their mother, Flavia Domitilla, were sent into exile. Perhaps the parents' crime had been that of becoming converts to Christianity, the new faith with which Quintilian himself may have come into contact.

In his middle life Quintilian had married a young girl, who bore him two sons before she was nineteen. It had been with the intention of providing an authority for the guidance not only of Geta (the son of his friend Marcellus Victorius) and later of his imperial charges, but of his

---

[1] *Provinces under Roman Empire*, I, p. 75.
[2] Domitian adopted them and renamed them Vespasian and Domitian.

own two sons that Quintilian had started, before A.D. 86, his greatest extant[3] work, the *Institutio Oratoria* or *Training of the Orator*. After the death of his wife, followed a few months later by that of his younger son, aged five, the widower continued his great task in the hope of bequeathing it as the best advice he could offer not merely to the princes but to his remaining son. But that son, too, died four years later after an illness of eight months. Quintilian's heart was breaking; in the touching proem to the sixth "book" of the *Institutio* we hear the cry of one whose "house is left unto him desolate." It echoes the grief of Cicero for his Tullia, and anticipates the words of many another stricken parent in the annals of literature. But Quintilian completed the work he had begun, asking indulgence for its imperfections and bequeathing it, like his patrimony, to others than those to whom he intended to leave it.

The most rewarding of the twelve parts or "books" are the first on the home training and school discipline which should precede the lessons of the rhetorician; the second on the primary exercises of the pupil in rhetoric, and the nature and object, the utility and dignity of the rhetorical art; the best-known tenth book, whose long first chapter is a roster of the greatest names in Greek and Latin literature with concise and often surprising notices of each; and the concluding twelfth, which, although hastily written and poorly organized, gives us the author's conception of the finished product, the picture of the ideal orator.

Rhetoric implied wealth of thought as well as words. A great orator and master of rhetoric was far more in Quintilian's eyes than a mere declaimer. He had to be *vir bonus, dicendi peritus*, his moral qualifications meeting as exacting a standard as his intellectual. He is very close to the ideal citizen. Throughout the *Institutio*, its author intimates how near Cicero comes to fulfilling this ideal; Quintilian refers to him in more than 450 passages, throughout reaffirming the excellence of a reputation that had been vigorously assailed for more than a generation. This defensive attitude towards the Ciceronian tradition does much to explain Quintilian's contempt for philosophers and his apparent hostility to Seneca. The fact is that there were two theories of education prevalent at the time, the "rhetorical" and the "philosophical." Both differed more in method and emphasis than in aim; but then, as now, both wrestled desperately "for the soul of the child."

Until the early fifteenth century the influence of Quintilian had been uneven and intermittent; for the first three centuries after his death, almost imperceptible. He had been studied by such men as Jerome and Cassiodorus; encylopedists like Isidore of Seville and Vincent of Beauvais; and the poet Petrarch. But when Poggio Bracciolini, the inquisitive and

---

[3] An earlier (lost) work was *de Causis Corruptae Eloquentiae*.

acquisitive Florentine, discovered in 1416 a complete MS. of the *Institutio* lying in the rubbish at the base of a tower of the Benedictine abbey of St. Gall in the Swiss Alps, there swept over the scholars of Europe a wave of enthusiasm, either real or simulated, that lasted a hundred and fifty years. Quintilian's views on education were now reflected in the writings of such men as Laurentius Valla, Pope Pius II, the German humanist Rudolph Agricola, Erasmus, the Spaniard Juan Luis Vives, whose *de Tradendis Disciplinis* is the greatest educational work of the sixteenth century, Luther, Melanchthon, Racine, La Fontaine, Du Bos, Lessing, Elyot, Ascham, Mulcaster, Ben Jonson, Milton, Pope, and Swinburne.

From the middle of the eighteenth century the influence of Quintilian ebbed rapidly until it sank to its present comparatively low level. This we may attribute to a corresponding decline in the interest in formal rhetoric, especially among English-speaking peoples. But in spite of the vicissitudes of literary criticism and the ever-changing fashions in the philosophy of education, the shadow of the wise and gentle Quintilian stretches far down eighteen hundred years of the living and thinking of educated Western man, and "broad and deep continueth greater than his knowing" the work of the great Latin Schoolmaster.

LUCAN

(Marcus Annaeus Lucanus, A.D. 39–65)

Lucan was born at Corduba, in Spain. Mela, brother of Seneca the philosopher, was his father. At the age of twenty-six, he was executed by the order of Nero for having taken part in the conspiracy of Piso to restore the Republic. His uncle, Seneca, was also involved and ordered to commit suicide.

He was far the most brilliant poet of his age. We have the ten books of his epic poem, the *Pharsalia* (also called in the MSS. *de Bello Civili*), which runs to eight thousand hexameters. Its theme is the war which broke out in 49 B.C. between Caesar and Pompey and was brought to an end by the decisive battle of Pharsalus in Thessaly, which left Caesar master of the Roman world. Throughout the poem, Lucan shows his strong republican tendencies in his sympathetic treatment of his hero, Cato, and of Pompey. He is highly rhetorical in style. Quintilian, one of the greatest literary critics of antiquity, says, "His style should be imitated more by orators than by poets."

MARTIAL

(Marcus Valerius Martialis, A.D. 40–105)

Like several other poets of the early Empire, Martial was a Spaniard who, as a young man, sought his fortune in Rome. Seneca and Lucan, fellow countrymen, introduced him to the society of the capital. There he was soon on familiar terms with Quintilian, the younger Pliny, Silius Italicus, and Juvenal. Soon came the realization that only a few of the crowd of poets besieging the doors of the rich could scrape a living. For years, he lived in obscurity in a backroom, up three flights of stairs.

On the occasion of the opening, by Titus, of the Flavian Amphitheatre (the Colosseum), Martial published his first collection of poems. Later came a collection of couplets intended to be used as mottoes for presents. Next came the twelve books of his *Epigrams* in a variety of meters, presenting us with an amazing fund of information on the society and life of his day. He is an unashamed spectator of all that goes on around him. Often his tongue is scathing; his satire cuts to the bone.

In his own words, he could write seriously, but preferred to write entertainingly. "Martial's function is to hold up the mirror to the manners of the day." The types represented in his pages range from the emperor Domitian down to the vilest scum of the streets. He is particularly fond of satirizing the dinner-hunter, fortune-hunter, and charlatans of all kinds.

Yet he is more than a sharp-tongued Spaniard with a flair for epigram. Throughout his work is many a touch of sheer poetry like his *viva et quies ponti*, "the live repose of the sea."

Martial's chief fame rests on his adaptation to his own purpose of the literary form known as the epigram, which reached Rome from Greece. He made of it "a short, independent verse composition, sacrificing poetic flavor to point, and most of all to the point that stings."

PLINY THE YOUNGER

(Gaius Plinius Caecilius Secundus, A.D. 61–115)

Pliny the Younger is so called in order that he may be distinguished from his maternal uncle, Pliny the Elder, a man of great energy and author of the *Natural History* in thirty-seven books. This uncle, who was at the time Admiral of the Fleet at Misenum, was killed in the summer of 79 as the result of the eruption of Vesuvius which his nephew has described. Pliny the Younger lived under the reigns of nine emperors: Nero, Galba, Otho, Vitellius, Vespasian, Titus, Domitian, Nerva, and Trajan. He studied under the great Quintilian.

Except Cicero, no Latin author is so well known to us. His *Letters* are a full self-revelation. Throughout his life, he corresponded with a large circle of friends. We have nine books of letters to a great number, including Tacitus and Suetonius, and know that he helped Martial financially and mourned his death. Juvenal, Statius, and Silius Italicus were his contemporaries. After Trajan had selected him (probably in A.D. 111) as governor of Bithynia and Pontus, he corresponded frequently with his imperial master on questions arising out of the administration of those provinces. This correspondence forms the tenth book of Pliny's letters, and contains a famous reference to the Christians. It is instructive to contrast his lengthy explanations and inquiries with the emperor's concise and admirably effective replies.

He bequeathed large sums for a school, baths, and a library to his native town of Comum, where the remains of a great inscription set up to his honor may still be seen. Two of his villas which overlooked Lake Como he called Tragedy and Comedy. He also owned country houses near the Apennine hills, at Tusculum, Tibur, and Praeneste, as well as a splendid villa on the seashore at Laurentum, seventeen miles from Rome. To this estate he would often drive after his day's work in the city was done. He has left us a long letter describing in detail its plan and grounds.

He is a writer of "Silver Latin" and a type of the successful and patriotic Roman gentleman of rank under the early Empire.

JUVENAL

(Decimus Junius Juvenalis, A.D. 60?–128)

Little is known of the life of Juvenal, but the scathing hexameters of his sixteen *Satires* have made him one of the most famous satirists of all time. He was born probably in Aquinum, a town in Latium; served as commander of a cohort; was banished at some time in his life for offending a favorite of the Emperor; and is repeatedly mentioned by Martial. During his exile, he may have travelled to Britain and Egypt.

Just as Tacitus has colored his presentation of the history of the early Empire with his own bitter prejudices, so Juvenal excoriates the social evils of the same period with the malignancy of a fiend. Exaggerated as both pictures are, they leave us with a conviction that the life of the Romans of the late first and early second centuries left a wide target for the shafts of political historian and social satirist.

The best known *Satires* are the third, which details the inconveniences of daily life in the narrow streets and stuffy lodgings of imperial Rome, and the tenth, on the vanity of human wishes, which treats of the futility of "the worldly hopes men set their hearts upon." Both were copied by Samuel Johnson: the third in his "London," and the tenth in his "Vanity of Human Wishes."

As he says of himself, "Facit indignatio versum."[1] He was bursting to stigmatize the pleasure-loving Roman mob ever demanding "panem et circenses,"[2] the *nouveau riche*, the fortune-hunter, the athletic woman, the harassed school-teacher, the complaisant husband, the obsequious Greek (Si dixeris, "Aestuo," sudat[3]), the horse-racing spendthrift, and the thug who cannot sleep at night without the satisfaction of having beaten some innocent wayfarer.

Here are some of the gibes and epigrams which have lent themselves to quotation for nearly two thousand years and even "reached the crowning honor of habitual misquotation:"

> Intolerabilius nihil est quam femina dives.[4]

> Maxima debetur puero reverentia.[5]

> Sed quis custodiet ipsos custodes?[6]

> Orandum est ut sit mens sana in corpore sano.[7]

ISIDORE OF SEVILLE

(Isidorus Hispalensis Episcopus, Died in A.D. 636)

This learned bishop of Seville, who lived in the early seventh century A.D., compiled from the lost treatises of Suetonius a great encyclopædia called *Origines*. It collected for the Middle Ages much of the learning of the Roman world. In one of the manuscripts[8] of this work, an early scholar or copyist has written these words:

> "This booke is a Scoolemaster to those that are wise,
> But not to fond fooles that learning despise,
> A Juwell it is, who liste it to reede,
> Within it are Pearells precious in deede."

---

[1] *Indignation makes my verse.*
[2] *bread and games*
[3] *If you say, "I am warm," he breaks into a sweat.*
[4] *Nothing is more unbearable than a wealthy woman.*
[5] *The highest degree of respect is due to a child.*
[6] *Who will watch the watchers themselves?*
[7] *The thing to pray for is a healthy mind in a healthy body.*
[8] Now in the library of Trinity College, Cambridge, England.

APPENDIX

Nē quis tamquam parva fastīdiat grammaticēs elementa.

Let no man look down on the rudiments of grammar as trifles unworthy
of his notice.

—QUINTILIAN, *Institutio Oratoria*, I, 4, 6

Appendix

NOUNS

1.   FIRST DECLENSION

porta, f., *gate*

	SINGULAR	PLURAL
Nom.	porta	portae
Gen.	portae	portārum
Dat.	portae	portīs
Acc.	portam	portās
Abl.	portā	portīs

(a) **Fīlia**, *daughter*, and a few other nouns, e.g., **dea**, *goddess*,
equa, *mare*, have the dative and ablative plural in **-ābus** (**fīliābus,
deābus, equābus**) to distinguish them from the corresponding cases
of **fīlius**, *son*, **deus**, *god*, and **equus**, *horse*.

2.   SECOND DECLENSION

equus, m., *horse*   **oppidum**, n., *town*

SINGULAR

	equus	oppidum
Nom.	equus	oppidum
Gen.	equī	oppidī
Dat.	equō	oppidō
Acc.	equum	oppidum
Abl.	equō	oppidō

PLURAL

Nom.	equī	oppida
Gen.	equōrum	oppidōrum
Dat.	equīs	oppidīs
Acc.	equōs	oppida
Abl.	equīs	oppidīs

caper, m.,	**signifer,** m.,	**vir,** m.,
goat	*standard-bearer*	*man*

SINGULAR

Nom.	caper	signifer	vir
Gen.	caprī	signiferī	virī
Dat.	caprō	signiferō	virō
Acc.	caprum	signiferum	virum
Abl.	caprō	signiferō	virō

PLURAL

Nom.	caprī	signiferī	virī
Gen.	caprōrum	signiferōrum	virōrum
Dat.	caprīs	signiferīs	virīs
Acc.	caprōs	signiferōs	virōs
Abl.	caprīs	signiferīs	virīs

fīlius, m.,	**Iūlius,** m.,	**cōnsilium,** n.,
son	*Julius*	*plan*

SINGULAR

Nom.	fīlius	Iūlius	cōnsilium
Gen.	fīlī	Iūlī	cōnsilī
Dat.	fīliō	Iūliō	cōnsiliō
Acc.	fīlium	Iūlium	cōnsilium
Abl.	fīliō	Iūliō	cōnsiliō

PLURAL

Nom.	fīliī	Iūliī	cōnsilia
Gen.	fīliōrum	Iūliōrum	cōnsiliōrum
Dat.	fīliīs	Iūliīs	cōnsiliīs
Acc.	fīliōs	Iūliōs	cōnsilia
Abl.	fīliīs	Iūliīs	cōnsiliīs

(a) **Equus** has the vocative **eque**; **fīlius**, the vocative **fīlī**; **Iūlius**, the vocative **Iūlī**, etc. Otherwise, the vocative in this declension, as in all the others, is like the nominative.

(b) The following are irregular:

locus, m. (in sing.), **deus**, m.,
n. (in plur.), *place*   *god*

SINGULAR

Nom.	locus	deus
Gen.	locī	deī
Dat.	locō	deō
Acc.	locum	deum
Abl.	locō	deō

PLURAL

Nom.	loca	deī (diī), dī
Gen.	locōrum	deōrum, deum
Dat.	locīs	(deīs, diīs) dīs
Acc.	loca	deōs
Abl.	locīs	(deīs, diīs) dīs

THIRD DECLENSION

3. Mute stems.—

	prīnceps, m., *chief*	**pēs**, m., *foot*	**dux**, m., *leader*	**cor**, n., *heart*	**caput**, n., *head*
			SINGULAR		
Nom.	prīnceps	pēs	dux	cor	caput
Gen.	prīncipis	pedis	ducis	cordis	capitis
Dat.	prīncipī	pedī	ducī	cordī	capitī
Acc.	prīncipem	pedem	ducem	cor	caput
Abl.	prīncipe	pede	duce	corde	capite
			PLURAL		
Nom.	prīncipēs	pedēs	ducēs	corda	capita
Gen.	prīncipum	pedum	ducum	(cordum)	capitum
Dat.	prīncipibus	pedibus	ducibus	cordibus	capitibus
Acc.	prīncipēs	pedēs	ducēs	corda	capita
Abl.	prīncipibus	pedibus	ducibus	cordibus	capitibus

4. Liquid and nasal stems.—

	ōrātor, m., orator	virgō, f., maiden	leō, m., lion

SINGULAR

Nom.	ōrātor	virgō	leō
Gen.	ōrātōris	virginis	leōnis
Dat.	ōrātōrī	virginī	leōnī
Acc.	ōrātōrem	virginem	leōnem
Abl.	ōrātòre	virgine	leōne

PLURAL

Nom.	ōrātōrēs	virginēs	leōnēs
Gen.	ōrātōrum	virginum	leōnum
Dat.	ōrātōribus	virginibus	leōnibus
Acc.	ōrātōrēs	virginēs	leōnēs
Abl.	ōrātōribus	virginibus	leōnibus

	frāter, m., brother	fulmen, n., thunderbolt	genus, n., kind

SINGULAR

Nom.	frāter	fulmen	genus
Gen.	frātris	fulminis	generis
Dat.	frātrī	fulminī	generī
Acc.	frātrem	fulmen	genus
Abl.	frātre	fulmine	genere

PLURAL

Nom.	frātrēs	fulmina	genera
Gen.	frātrum	fulminum	generum
Dat.	frātribus	fulminibus	generibus
Acc.	frātrēs	fulmina	genera
Abl.	frātribus	fulminibus	generibus

5. *I*-stems.—

	pestis, f., plague	nūbēs, f., cloud	nox, f., night

SINGULAR

Nom.	pestis	nūbēs	nox
Gen.	pestis	nūbis	noctis
Dat.	pestī	nūbī	noctī
Acc.	pestem	nūbem	noctem
Abl.	peste	nūbe	nocte

PLURAL

Nom.	pestēs	nūbēs	noctēs
Gen.	pestium	nūbium	noctium
Dat.	pestibus	nūbibus	noctibus
Acc.	pestīs, -ēs	nūbīs, -ēs	noctīs, -ēs
Abl.	pestibus	nūbibus	noctibus

| cliēns, m., | mare, n., | vectīgal, n., |
| client | sea | tax |

SINGULAR

Nom.	cliēns	mare	vectīgal
Gen.	clientis	maris	vectīgālis
Dat.	clientī	marī	vectīgālī
Acc.	clientem	mare	vectīgal
Abl.	cliente	marī	vectīgālī

PLURAL

Nom.	clientēs	maria	vectīgālia
Gen.	clientium	———	vectīgālium
Dat.	clientibus	maribus	vectīgālibus
Acc.	clientīs, -ēs	maria	vectīgālia
Abl.	clientibus	maribus	vectīgālibus

6. **Irregular.—**

| senex, m., | vīs, f., | iter, n., | Iuppiter, m., |
| old man | force | march | Jupiter |

SINGULAR

Nom.	senex	vīs	iter	Iuppiter
Gen.	senis	(vīs)	itineris	Iovis
Dat.	senī	(vī)	itinerī	Iovī
Acc.	senem	vim	iter	Iovem
Abl.	sene	vī	itinere	Iove

PLURAL

Nom.	senēs	vīrēs	itinera	*None*
Gen.	senum	vīrium	itinerum	
Dat.	senibus	vīribus	itineribus	
Acc.	senēs	vīrīs, -ēs	itinera	
Abl.	senibus	vīribus	itineribus	

7.   FOURTH DECLENSION

exercitus, m., *army*   **cornū**, n., *horn*

	SINGULAR	PLURAL	SINGULAR	PLURAL
Nom.	exercitus	exercitūs	cornū	cornua
Gen.	exercitūs	exercituum	cornūs	cornuum
Dat.	exerc ituī, -ū	exercitibus	cornū	cornibus
Acc.	exercitum	exercitūs	cornū	cornua
Abl.	exercitū	exercitibus	cornū	cornibus

(a) **Domus**, f., *house*, has forms of both the second and fourth declensions:

	SINGULAR	PLURAL
Nom.	domus	domūs
Gen.	domūs, domī	domuum, domōrum
Dat.	domuī, domō	domibus
Acc.	domum	domōs, domūs
Abl.	domō, domū	domibus

The alternative genitive form **domī** is used almost exclusively for the locative case.

(b) Many words of the fourth declension have dative and ablative plural in **-ubus** instead of **-ibus**, e.g., **lacus**, *m.*, lake; **tribus**, *f.*, tribe. **Senātus**, *senate*, sometimes has a genitive singular **senātī**.

8.   FIFTH DECLENSION

rēs, f.,   **diēs**, m. (f.),   **speciēs**, f.,   **fidēs**, f.,
thing   *day*   *appearance*   *faith*

SINGULAR

Nom.	rēs	diēs	speciēs	fidēs
Gen.	reī	diēī	speciēī	fideī
Dat.	reī	diēī	speciēī	fideī
Acc.	rem	diem	speciem	fidem
Abl.	rē	diē	speciē	fidē

PLURAL

Nom.	rēs	diēs	speciēs	*None*
Gen.	rērum	diērum	——	
Dat.	rēbus	diēbus	——	
Acc.	rēs	diēs	speciēs	
Abl.	rēbus	diēbus	——	

Only **diēs** and **rēs** are declined in full.   Most others lack the plural. A few have nominative and accusative plural only.

ADJECTIVES

9.   FIRST-SECOND DECLENSION

lātus, *wide*   **meus,** *my, mine*

	M.	F.	N.	M.	F.	N.

SINGULAR

	M.	F.	N.	M.	F.	N.
Nom.	lātus	lāta	lātum	meus[1]	mea	meum
Gen.	lātī	lātae	lātī	meī	meae	meī
Dat.	lātō	lātae	lātō	meō	meae	meō
Acc.	lātum	lātam	lātum	meum	meam	meum
Abl.	lātō	lātā	lātō	meō	meā	meō

PLURAL

	M.	F.	N.	M.	F.	N.
Nom.	lātī	lātae	lāta	meī	meae	mea
Gen.	lātōrum	lātārum	lātōrum	meōrum	meārum	meōrum
Dat.	lātīs	lātīs	lātīs	meīs	meīs	meīs
Acc.	lātōs	lātās	lāta	meōs	meās	mea
Abl.	lātīs	lātīs	lātīs	meīs	meīs	meīs

noster, *our, ours*

	M.	F.	N.

SINGULAR

	M.	F.	N.
Nom.	noster	nostra	nostrum
Gen.	nostrī	nostrae	nostrī
Dat.	nostrō	nostrae	nostrō
Acc.	nostrum	nostram	nostrum
Abl.	nostrō	nostrā	nostrō

---

[1] Vocative singular masculine—**mī.**

PLURAL

Nom.	nostrī	nostrae	nostra
Gen.	nostrōrum	nostrārum	nostrōrum
Dat.	nostrīs	nostrīs	nostrīs
Acc.	nostrōs	nostrās	nostra
Abl.	nostrīs	nostrīs	nostrīs

miser, *wretched*

         M.   F.   N.

SINGULAR

Nom.	miser	misera	miserum
Gen.	miserī	miserae	miserī
Dat.	miserō	miserae	miserō
Acc.	miserum	miseram	miserum
Abl.	miserō	miserā	miserō

PLURAL

Nom.	miserī	miserae	misera
Gen.	miserōrum	miserārum	miserōrum
Dat.	miserīs	miserīs	miserīs
Acc.	miserōs	miserās	misera
Abl.	miserīs	miserīs	miserīs

10. Adjectives with genitive in -*īus*.—

ūnus, -a, -um,	*one*	alter, altera, alterum,	*the other*
nūllus, -a, -um,	*no*	uter, utra, utrum,	*which (of two)*?
ūllus, -a, -um,	*any*	uterque, utraque, utrumque,	
sōlus, -a, -um,	*alone*		*each (of two)*, *both*
neuter, -tra, -trum,	*neither*	tōtus, -a, -um,	*whole*
		alius, alia, aliud,	*another*

The first letters of the adjectives above spell the Latin words
UNUS NAUTA.

SINGULAR

	M.	F.	N.	M.	F.	N.
Nom.	ūnus	ūna	ūnum	alter	altera	alterum
Gen.	ūnīus	ūnīus	ūnīus	alterīus	alterīus	alterīus
Dat.	ūnī	ūnī	ūnī	alterī	alterī	alterī
Acc.	ūnum	ūnam	ūnum	alterum	alteram	alterum
Abl.	ūnō	ūnā	ūnō	alterō	alterā	alterō

(a) The plural is regular, like that of **lātus (9)**. Usually, **ūnus** has none.[1]

THIRD DECLENSION

11. Adjectives with one termination in the nominative singular.—

	sagāx, *wise*		vetus, *old*[2]	
	M., F.	N.	M., F.	N.

SINGULAR

Nom.		sagāx	vetus	
Gen.		sagācis	veteris	
Dat.		sagācī	veterī	
Acc.	sagācem	sagāx	veterem	vetus
Abl.		sagācī, (-e)	vetere	

PLURAL

Nom.	sagācēs	sagācia	veterēs	vetera
Gen.		sagācium	veterum	
Dat.		sagācibus	veteribus	
Acc.	sagācīs, -ēs	sagācia	veterēs	vetera
Abl.		sagācibus	veteribus	

	pār, *equal*		dīves, *rich*[2]	
	M., F.	N.	M., F.	N.

SINGULAR

Nom.		pār	dīves	
Gen.		paris	dīvitis	
Dat.		parī	dīvitī	
Acc.	parem	pār	dīvitem	dīves
Abl.		parī	dīvite	

PLURAL

Nom.	parēs	paria	dīvitēs	(dītia)
Gen.		parium	dīvitum	
Dat.		paribus	dīvitibus	
Acc.	parīs, -ēs	paria	dīvitēs	(dītia)
Abl.		paribus	dīvitibus	

[1] Except in expressions like **ūna castra,** *one camp.*
[2] An exception, ablative in **-e.**

Observation.—Most adjectives of one termination are declined like **sagāx**. Note the irregularities of **vetus** and **dīves**. **Pauper,** *poor,* has the ablative singular in **-e**, the nominative and accusative plural neuter **paupera**, and the genitive plural **pauperum**. Like **dīves** are **locuples,** *rich*; **superstes,** *surviving.*

12. Adjectives of two terminations in the nominative singular.—

facilis, *easy*

	SINGULAR		PLURAL		
	M., F.	N.	M., F.		N.
Nom.	facilis	facile	facilēs		facilia
Gen.	facilis		facilium		
Dat.	facilī		facilibus		
Acc.	facilem	facile	facilīs, -ēs		facilia
Abl.	facilī		facilibus		

13. Adjectives of three terminations in the nominative singular.—

ācer, *sharp*

	SINGULAR			PLURAL	
	M.	F.	N.	M., F.	N.
Nom.	ācer	ācris	ācre	ācrēs	ācria
Gen.	ācris		ācris	ācrium	
Dat.	ācrī		ācrī	ācribus	
Acc.	ācrem		ācre	ācrīs, -ēs	ācria
Abl.	ācrī		ācrī	ācribus	

(a) There are very few adjectives in this group. Among the commonest are **alacer,** *brisk;* **volucer,** *swift;* **celeber,** *crowded, famous;* and the months **September, Octōber, November,** and **December,** which are really adjectives modifying the noun **mēnsis** (m.), *month.* Note that **celer,** *swift,* keeps the **-e** of the nominative singular masculine throughout, e.g., feminine **celeris,** neuter **celere.** **Celer** is further exceptional in having the genitive plural **celerum.**

14. The present participles of verbs.—These are all declined like the adjectives of one termination.

dūcēns, *leading*

	SINGULAR		PLURAL	
	M., F.	N.	M., F.	N.
NOM.	dūcēns		dūcentēs	dūcentia
GEN.	dūcentis		dūcentium	
DAT.	dūcentī		dūcentibus	
ACC.	dūcentem	dūcēns	dūcentīs, -ēs	dūcentia
ABL.	dūcentī, -e[1]		dūcentibus	

iēns, *going*

	M., F.	N.	M., F.	N.
NOM.	iēns		euntēs	euntia
GEN.	euntis		euntium	
DAT.	euntī		euntibus	
ACC.	euntem	iēns	euntīs, -ēs	euntia
ABL.	euntī, -e[1]		euntibus	

15. Declension of the comparative adjective.—

brevior, *shorter*

	SINGULAR		PLURAL	
	M., F.	N.	M., F.	N.
NOM.	brevior	brevius	breviōrēs	breviōra
GEN.	breviōris		breviōrum	
DAT.	breviōrī		breviōribus	
ACC.	breviōrem	brevius	breviōrēs,-īs	breviōra
ABL.	breviōre		breviōribus	

(a) **Plūs,** the comparative of **multus,** is used in the singular only as a neuter noun.   It is declined as follows:

	SINGULAR	PLURAL	
	N.	M., F.	N.
NOM.	plūs	plūrēs	plūra
GEN.	plūris	plūrium	
DAT.	——	plūribus	
ACC.	plūs	plūrīs, -ēs	plūra
ABL.	plūre	plūribus	

---

[1] See sec. **237,** *Obs.* 5.

COMPARISON OF ADJECTIVES

16. Regular comparison.—

Positive	Comparative	Superlative
altus, -a, -um	altior, altius	altissimus, -a, -um
beātus, -a, -um	beātior, beātius	beātissimus, -a, -um
parātus, -a, -um	parātior, parātius	parātissimus, -a, -um
dulcis, dulce	dulcior, dulcius	dulcissimus, -a, -um
sagāx	sagācior, sagācius	sagācissimus, -a, -um
potēns	potentior, potentius	potentissimus, -a, -um

17. Adjectives in -er and -lis.—

Positive	Comparative	Superlative
aeger, aegra, aegrum	aegrior, aegrius	aegerrimus, -a, -um
līber, -bera, -berum	līberior, līberius	līberrimus, -a, -um
celer, celeris, celere	celerior, celerius	celerrimus, -a, -um
facilis, etc.[1]	facilior, etc.	facillimus, etc.
difficilis	difficilior	difficillimus
similis	similior	simillimus
dissimilis	dissimilior	dissimillimus

Also **gracilis**, *slender*, and **humilis**, *lowly*; but other adjectives in -lis are regular:

nōbilis	nōbilior	nōbilissimus

18. The commonest irregulars.—

Positive	Comparative	Superlative
bonus	melior	optimus
malus	peior	pessimus
parvus	minor	minimus
magnus	maior	maximus
multus	plūs	plūrimus

---

[1] From this point, to save space, only the masculine form will be printed.

19. Other irregulars.—

POSITIVE	COMPARATIVE	SUPERLATIVE
exterus, *outside*	exterior, *outer*	extrēmus, extimus, *outermost*
īnferus, *under*	īnferior, *lower*	īnfimus, īmus, *lowest*
posterus, *following*	posterior, *later*	postrēmus, postumus, *last*
superus, *upper*	superior, *higher*	suprēmus, summus, *highest*
————	citerior, *hither*	citimus, *hithermost*
————	interior, *inner*	intimus, *inmost*
————	ulterior, *farther*	ultimus, *farthest, last*
————	prior, *former*	prīmus, *first*
————	propior, *nearer*	proximus, *nearest, next*
novus, *new*	——	novissimus, *last*
fīdus, *faithful*	——	fīdissimus, *most faithful*
vetus, *old*	vetustior	veterrimus

20. Adjectives in *-eus, -ius,* and *-uus.*—[1]

POSITIVE	COMPARATIVE	SUPERLATIVE
idōneus	magis idōneus	maximē idōneus

ADVERBS

21. Formation of adverbs.—

ADJECTIVE (*nom. sing. fem.*)	ADVERB
longa	longē
misera	miserē
pulchra	pulchrē
lībera	līberē
sapiēns	sapienter
brevis	breviter
celeris	celeriter
audāx (audāc-s)	audācter

But most adverbs formed from adjectives in **-x** have **-iter** instead of **-ter**:

sagāx, *wise*—sagāciter, *wisely*

———————

[1] But not—quus; propinquus, propinquior, propinquissimus.

(a) The accusative singular neuter of the adjective is often used as an adverb. Some adjective accusatives are regularly used in this way; e.g., **multum**, *much*, and **facile**, *easily*.

(b) Some adverbs are specialized ablatives; e.g., **multō**, (*by*) *much*. Among the commonest adverbs ending in -ō are:

falsō	falsely	**rārō**	rarely
cito	swiftly	**necessāriō**	necessarily
meritō	deservedly	**profectō**	certainly
prīmō	firstly, at first	**subitō**	suddenly
postrēmō	finally, at last	**continuō**	forthwith, uninterruptedly, without interval
vulgō	commonly	**tūtō**	safely
crēbrō	frequently		

COMPARISON OF ADVERBS

22. Regular comparison.—

POSITIVE	COMPARATIVE	SUPERLATIVE
longē	longius	longissimē
miserē	miserius	miserrimē
pulchrē	pulchrius	pulcherrimē
sapienter	sapientius	sapientissimē
breviter	brevius	brevissimē
ācriter	ācrius	ācerrimē
audācter	audācius	audācissimē
facile	facilius	facillimē

23. Adverbs from the adjectives in sec. 18.—

bene	melius	optimē
male	peius	pessimē
parum	minus	minimē
magnopere	magis	maximē
multum	plūs	plūrimum

(a) Other irregulars.—

diū	diūtius	diūtissimē
saepe	saepius	saepissimē
——	prius	prīmum
prope	propius	proximē

PREPOSITIONS

24. **(a) Governing the accusative.**—The great majority of Latin prepositions govern the accusative. The commonest are:

ad	*to, towards; at*	**extrā**	*outside (of)*
adversum	*towards, against, op-*	**īnfrā**	*below*
adversus	*posite*	**inter**	*between, among*
ante	*before*	**intrā**	*within, inside*
apud	*at, near, among; at the house of; in the works of*	**iūxtā**	*close to*
		ob	*on account of*
		per	*through*
circā	*around*	**post**	*after; behind*
circiter	*about, around (with numbers)*	**praeter**	*beside, beyond, past*
		prope	*near*
circum	*around*	**propter**	*on account of*
cis		**suprā**	*above*
citrā	*this side of*	**trāns**	*across*
contrā	*against*	**ultrā**	*beyond*

(b) Governing the ablative.—

ā (ab, abs)	*from, away from; by*	**ē (ex)**	*from, out of*
cōram	*in the presence of*	**prae**	*in front of; in comparison with*
cum	*with*		
dē	*from, down from; concerning*	**prō**	*in front of; in behalf of*
		sine	*without*

(c) Governing accusative or ablative according as they denote (1) limit or direction of motion (accusative) or (2) the mere place where a thing is or moves:

> **in** (acc.) into
> *in* hortum, *into the garden*
>
> **in** (abl.) in, on, at
> *in* hortō, *in the garden*
>
> **sub** (acc.) under
> Fēlis *sub mēnsam* coniecta est.
> *The cat was thrown **under the table**.*

sub (abl.) under

Fēlis *sub mēnsā* **dormiēbat.**

The cat was sleeping **under the table.**

25.   NUMERALS

ARABIC	ROMAN	CARDINALS	ORDINALS
1	I	ūnus, -a, -um	prīmus, -a, -um
2	II	duo, duae, duo	secundus (alter)
3	III	trēs, tria	tertius
4	IIII	quattuor	quārtus
5	V	quīnque	quīntus
6	VI	sex	sextus
7	VII	septem	septimus
8	VIII	octō	octāvus
9	VIIII	novem	nōnus
10	X	decem	decimus
11	XI	ūndecim	ūndecimus
12	XII	duodecim	duodecimus
13	XIII	tredecim	tertius decimus
14	XIIII	quattuordecim	quārtus decimus
15	XV	quīndecim	quīntus decimus
16	XVI	sēdecim	sextus decimus
17	XVII	septendecim	septimus decimus
18	XVIII	duodēvīgintī	duodēvīcēsimus
19	XVIIII	ūndēvīgintī	ūndēvīcēsimus
20	XX	vīgintī	vīcēsimus
21	XXI	vīgintī ūnus	vīcēsimus prīmus
		ūnus et vīgintī	ūnus et vīcēsimus
22	XXII	vīgintī duo	vīcēsimus secundus
		duo et vīgintī	alter et vīcēsimus
30	XXX	trīgintā	trīcēsimus
40	XXXX	quadrāgintā	quadrāgēsimus
50	L	quīnquāgintā	quīnquāgēsimus
60	LX	sexāgintā	sexāgēsimus
70	LXX	septuāgintā	septuāgēsimus
80	LXXX	octōgintā	octōgēsimus
90	LXXXX	nōnāgintā	nōnāgēsimus
100	C	centum	centēsimus

Arabic	Roman	Cardinals	Ordinals
200	CC	ducentī, -ae, -a	ducentēsimus
300	CCC	trecentī	trecentēsimus
400	CCCC	quadringentī	quadringentēsimus
500	D	quīngentī	quīngentēsimus
600	DC	sescentī	sescentēsimus
700	DCC	septingentī	septingentēsimus
800	DCCC	octingentī	octingentēsimus
900	DCCCC	nōngentī	nōngentēsimus
1000	M	mīlle	mīllēsimus
2000	MM	duo mīlia	bis mīllēsimus

For alternatives to IIII, VIIII, etc. see end of sec. **170.**

26. The ordinals are declined like **lātus (9).** For declension of **ūnus,** see **(10).**

<table>
<tr><td colspan="4" align="center">duo, two</td><td colspan="2" align="center">trēs, three</td></tr>
<tr><td></td><td>M.</td><td>F.</td><td>N.</td><td>M., F.</td><td>N.</td></tr>
<tr><td>Nom.</td><td>duo</td><td>duae</td><td>duo</td><td>trēs</td><td>tria</td></tr>
<tr><td>Gen.</td><td>duōrum</td><td>duārum</td><td>duōrum</td><td>trium</td><td>trium</td></tr>
<tr><td>Dat.</td><td>duōbus</td><td>duābus</td><td>duōbus</td><td>tribus</td><td>tribus</td></tr>
<tr><td>Acc.</td><td>duōs (-o)</td><td>duās</td><td>duo</td><td>trēs (trīs)</td><td>tria</td></tr>
<tr><td>Abl.</td><td>duōbus</td><td>duābus</td><td>duōbus</td><td>tribus</td><td>tribus</td></tr>
</table>

(a) Like **duo** is declined **ambō,** *both.*

PRONOUNS

27.

PERSONAL PRONOUNS

FIRST PERSON

	Singular	Plural
Nom.	ego	nōs
Gen.	meī	nostrum, nostrī
Dat.	mihi	nōbīs
Acc.	mē	nōs
Abl.	mē	nōbīs

SECOND PERSON

	SINGULAR	PLURAL
Nom.	tū	vōs
Gen.	tuī	vestrum, vestrī
Dat.	tibi	vōbīs
Acc.	tē	vōs
Abl.	tē	vōbīs

THIRD PERSON

Lacking. See **is, ea, id (33)**.

REFLEXIVE PRONOUNS

28. In the first and second persons, these have the same forms as the personal pronouns (**27**). By definition, the reflexive can have no nominative. The reflexive of the third person in all genders and numbers is:

Gen.	suī	Acc.	sē, sēsē
Dat.	sibi	Abl.	sē, sēsē

29.   POSSESSIVE PRONOUNS

1st pers. **meus, -a, -um,** *my*   **noster, -tra, -trum,** *our*
2nd pers. **tuus, -a, -um,** *your*   **vester, -tra, -trum,** *your*
         (of ownership by one)   (of ownership by more than one)
3rd pers. **eius,** *his, her, its*   **eōrum, eārum, eōrum,** *their*
     (when referring to ownership by someone or something other than the subject of the sentence)
3rd pers. **suus, -a, -um,** *his, her, its, their*
     (when referring to ownership by the subject)

Observation.—**Eius** is the genitive singular and **eōrum, eārum, eōrum** the genitive plural of **is, ea, id,** which supplies the personal pronoun of the third person. The other forms given above are more properly adjectives, and are declined in full like **lātus** and **noster (9)**.

DEMONSTRATIVE PRONOUNS

30.   hic, *this*

| | SINGULAR | | | PLURAL | | |
	M.	F.	N.	M.	F.	N.
Nom.	hic	haec	hoc	hī	hae	haec
Gen.	huius	huius	huius	hōrum	hārum	hōrum
Dat.	huic	huic	huic	hīs	hīs	hīs
Acc.	hunc	hanc	hoc	hōs	hās	haec
Abl.	hōc	hāc	hōc	hīs	hīs	hīs

31.   iste, *that, that of yours*[1]

| | SINGULAR | | | PLURAL | | |
	M.	F.	N.	M.	F.	N.
Nom.	iste	ista	istud	istī	istae	ista
Gen.	istīus	istīus	istīus	istōrum	istārum	istōrum
Dat.	istī	istī	istī	istīs	istīs	istīs
Acc.	istum	istam	istud	istōs	istās	ista
Abl.	istō	istā	istō	istīs	istīs	istīs

32. Ille, *that, that yonder,* is declined like **iste.**

33.   is, *this* (unemphatic), *he, she, it, the*

| | SINGULAR | | | PLURAL | | |
	M.	F.	N.	M.	F.	N.
Nom.	is	ea	id	eī, iī, ī	eae	ea
Gen.	eius	eius	eius	eōrum	eārum	eōrum
Dat.	eī	eī	eī	eīs, iīs, īs	eīs, iīs, īs	eīs, iīs, īs
Acc.	eum	eam	id	eōs	eās	ea
Abl.	eō	eā	eō	eīs, iīs, īs	eīs, iīs, īs	eīs, iīs, īs

34.   īdem, *the same*

| | SINGULAR | | | PLURAL | | |
	M.	F.	N.	M.	F.	N.
Nom.	īdem	eadem	idem	eīdem	eaedem	eadem
Gen.	eiusdem	eiusdem	eiusdem	eōrundem	eārundem	eōrundem
Dat.	eīdem	eīdem	eīdem	eīsdem	eīsdem	eīsdem
Acc.	eundem	eandem	idem	eōsdem	eāsdem	eadem
Abl.	eōdem	eādem	eōdem	eīsdem	eīsdem	eīsdem

[1] Iste is a demonstrative of the second person.

THE INTENSIVE PRONOUN

35. ipse, *self*

	SINGULAR			PLURAL		
	M.	F.	N.	M.	F.	N.
Nom.	ipse	ipsa	ipsum	ipsī	ipsae	ipsa
Gen.	ipsīus	ipsīus	ipsīus	ipsōrum	ipsārum	ipsōrum
Dat.	ipsī	ipsī	ipsī	ipsīs	ipsīs	ipsīs
Acc.	ipsum	ipsam	ipsum	ipsōs	ipsās	ipsa
Abl.	ipsō	ipsā	ipsō	ipsīs	ipsīs	ipsīs

36. THE RELATIVE PRONOUN

quī, *who*

	SINGULAR			PLURAL		
	M.	F.	N.	M.	F.	N.
Nom.	quī	quae	quod	quī	quae	quae
Gen.	cuius	cuius	cuius	quōrum	quārum	quōrum
Dat.	cui	cui	cui	quibus	quibus	quibus
Acc.	quem	quam	quod	quōs	quās	quae
Abl.	quō	quā	quō	quibus	quibus	quibus

(a) **Quīcumque, quaecumque, quodcumque,** *whoever* or *whatever,* is declined throughout like **quī, -cumque** being added to all the forms.

(b) **Quisquis** (*m. and f.*), **quicquid** or **quidquid,** (*n.*), *whoever* or *whatever,* is seldom found except in these forms and in the ablative singular **quōquō.**

37. THE INTERROGATIVE PRONOUN

quis, *who?*

	SINGULAR		PLURAL
	M. & F.	N.	
Nom.	quis	quid	(Like the relative throughout)
Gen.	cuius	cuius	
Dat.	cui	cui	
Acc.	quem	quid	
Abl.	quō	quō	

(a) The interrogative adjective **quī, quae, quod,** *what?* is declined like the relative (**36**).

38.   INDEFINITE PRONOUNS AND ADJECTIVES

PRONOUN	ADJECTIVE
quis, quis, quid, *anyone*	quī, qua (quae), quod, *any*
aliquis, aliquis, aliquid, *someone*	aliquī, aliqua, aliquod, *some*
quisque, quisque, quidque, *each*	quisque, quaeque, quodque, *each*
quīdam, quaedam, quiddam, *a certain man, woman, thing*	quīdam, quaedam, quoddam, *a certain*

39.   quīdam, *a certain (one)*

	M.	F.	N.
		SINGULAR	
Nom.	quīdam	quaedam	quiddam (quoddam)
Gen.	cuiusdam	cuiusdam	cuiusdam
Dat.	cuidam	cuidam	cuidam
Acc.	quendam	quandam	quiddam (quoddam)
Abl.	quōdam	quādam	quōdam
		PLURAL	
Nom.	quīdam	quaedam	quaedam
Gen.	quōrundam	quārundam	quōrundam
Dat.	quibusdam	quibusdam	quibusdam
Acc.	quōsdam	quāsdam	quaedam
Abl.	quibusdam	quibusdam	quibusdam

VERBS

40. The irregular verb *sum, be.*—

Principal Parts: sum, esse, fuī, futūrus

INDICATIVE		SUBJUNCTIVE	
		Present	
sum	sumus	sim	sīmus
es	estis	sīs	sītis
est	sunt	sit	sint

INDICATIVE		SUBJUNCTIVE	

IMPERFECT

eram	erāmus	essem	essēmus
erās	erātis	essēs	essētis
erat	erant	esset	essent

FUTURE

erō	erimus
eris	eritis
erit	erunt

PERFECT

fuī	fuimus	fuerim	fuerīmus
fuistī	fuistis	fuerīs	fuerītis
fuit	fuērunt, -ēre	fuerit	fuerint

PLUPERFECT

fueram	fuerāmus	fuissem	fuissēmus
fuerās	fuerātis	fuissēs	fuissētis
fuerat	fuerant	fuisset	fuissent

FUTURE PERFECT

fuerō	fuerimus
fueris	fueritis
fuerit	fuerint

IMPERATIVE

es	este

INFINITIVES		PARTICIPLES
PRESENT	esse	
FUTURE	futūrus esse, *or* fore	futūrus, -a, -um
PERFECT	fuisse	

For the compounds of **sum**, see below, secs. **48** and **49**.

REGULAR VERBS

41. First Conjugation

PRINCIPAL PARTS: **laudō, laudāre, laudāvī, laudātum,** *praise*

ACTIVE PASSIVE

INDICATIVE

PRESENT

laudō	laudāmus	laudor	laudāmur
laudās	laudātis	laudāris, -re	laudāminī
laudat	laudant	laudātur	laudantur

IMPERFECT

laudābam	laudābāmus	laudābar	laudābāmur
laudābās	laudābātis	laudābāris, -re	laudābāminī
laudābat	laudābant	laudābātur	laudābantur

FUTURE

laudābō	laudābimus	laudābor	laudābimur
laudābis	laudābitis	laudāberis, -re	laudābiminī
laudābit	laudābunt	laudābitur	laudābuntur

PERFECT

laudāvī	laudāvimus	laudātus sum	laudātī sumus
laudāvistī	laudāvistis	laudātus es	laudātī estis
laudāvit	laudāvērunt, -ēre	laudātus est	laudātī sunt

PLUPERFECT

laudāveram	laudāverāmus	laudātus eram	laudātī erāmus
laudāverās	laudāverātis	laudātus erās	laudātī erātis
laudāverat	laudāverant	laudātus erat	laudātī erant

FUTURE PERFECT

laudāverō	laudāverimus	laudātus erō	laudāti erimus
laudāveris	laudāveritis	laudātus eris	laudātī eritis
laudāverit	laudāverint	laudātus erit	laudātī erunt

	ACTIVE		PASSIVE

SUBJUNCTIVE

PRESENT

laudem	laudēmus	lauder	laudēmur
laudēs	laudētis	laudēris, -re	laudēminī
laudet	laudent	laudētur	laudentur

IMPERFECT

laudārem	laudārēmus	laudārer	laudārēmur
laudārēs	laudārētis	laudārēris, -re	laudārēminī
laudāret	laudārent	laudārētur	laudārentur

PERFECT

laudāverim	laudāverīmus	laudātus sim	laudātī sīmus
laudāverīs	laudāverītis	laudātus sīs	laudātī sītis
laudāverit	laudāverint	laudātus sit	laudātī sint

PLUPERFECT

laudāvissem	laudāvissēmus	laudātus essem	laudātī essēmus
laudāvissēs	laudāvissētis	laudātus essēs	laudātī essētis
laudāvisset	laudāvissent	laudātus esset	laudātī essent

IMPERATIVE

laudā	laudāte	laudāre	laudāminī

INFINITIVES

PRESENT	laudāre	laudārī
FUTURE	laudātūrus esse	laudātum īrī
PERFECT	laudāvisse	laudātus esse

PARTICIPLES

PRESENT	laudāns	———
FUTURE	laudātūrus	laudandus
PERFECT	———	laudātus

GERUND   SUPINE

	GERUND	SUPINE
GEN.	laudandī	———
DAT.	laudandō	———
ACC.	laudandum	laudātum
ABL.	laudandō	laudātū

(a) Some verbs of this conjugation form the perfect irregularly, e.g.,

> iuvō, iuvāre, iūvī, iūtum, *help*
> vetō, vetāre, vetuī, vetitum, *forbid*

Second Conjugation

42. A few verbs of this conjugation have regular principal parts:

> compleō, complēre, complēvī, complētum, *fill*

A common type is:

> moneō, monēre, monuī, monitum, *warn*

But many have an irregular perfect and an irregular supine:

PRINCIPAL PARTS: videō, vidēre, vīdī, vīsum, *see*

ACTIVE		PASSIVE	

dolēre

INDICATIVE

SING.	PRESENT		PL.
videō	vidēmus	videor	vidēmur
vidēs	vidētis	vidēris, -re	vidēminī
videt	vident	vidētur	videntur

IMPERFECT

vidēbam	vidēbāmus	vidēbar	vidēbāmur
vidēbās	vidēbātis	vidēbāris, -re	vidēbāminī
vidēbat	vidēbant	vidēbātur	vidēbantur

FUTURE

vidēbō	vidēbimus	vidēbor	vidēbimur
vidēbis	vidēbitis	vidēberis, -re	vidēbiminī
vidēbit	vidēbunt	vidēbitur	vidēbuntur

PERFECT

vīdī	vīdimus	vīsus sum	vīsī sumus
vīdistī	vīdistis	vīsus es	vīsī estis
vīdit	vīdērunt, -ēre	vīsus est	vīsī sunt

ACTIVE   PASSIVE

PLUPERFECT

vīderam	vīderāmus	vīsus eram	vīsī erāmus
vīderās	vīderātis	vīsus erās	vīsī erātis
vīderat	vīderant	vīsus erat	vīsī erant

FUTURE PERFECT

vīderō	vīderimus	vīsus erō	vīsī erimus
vīderis	vīderitis	vīsus eris	vīsī eritis
vīderit	vīderint	vīsus erit	vīsī erunt

SUBJUNCTIVE

PRESENT

videam	videāmus	videar	videāmur
videās	videātis	videāris, -re	videāminī
videat	videant	videātur	videantur

IMPERFECT

vidērem	vidērēmus	vidērer	vidērēmur
vidērēs	vidērētis	vidērēris, -re	vidērēminī
vidēret	vidērent	vidērētur	vidērentur

PERFECT

vīderim	vīderīmus	vīsus sim	vīsī sīmus
vīderīs	vīderītis	vīsus sīs	vīsī sītis
vīderit	vīderint	vīsus sit	vīsī sint

PLUPERFECT

vīdissem	vīdissēmus	vīsus essem	vīsī essēmus
vīdissēs	vīdissētis	vīsus essēs	vīsī essētis
vīdisset	vīdissent	vīsus esset	vīsī essent

IMPERATIVE

vidē	vidēte	vidēre	vidēminī

INFINITIVES

PRESENT	vidēre	vidērī
FUTURE	vīsūrus esse	vīsum īrī
PERFECT	vīdisse	vīsus esse

	ACTIVE	PASSIVE

PARTICIPLES

	ACTIVE	PASSIVE
PRESENT	vidēns	————
FUTURE	vīsūrus	videndus
PERFECT	————	vīsus

	GERUND	SUPINE
GEN.	videndī	———
DAT.	videndō	———
ACC.	videndum	vīsum
ABL.	videndō	vīsū

Third Conjugation

43. These verbs show great variety in the formation of the perfect, though many form it by adding **-s** to the present stem, often with modification of the root vowel, e.g., **regō, regere, rēxī (rēg-sī), rēctum.**

PRINCIPAL PARTS: **pōnō, pōnere, posuī, positum,** *place*

	ACTIVE	PASSIVE

INDICATIVE

SING.		PRESENT	PL.
pōnō	pōnimus	pōnor	pōnimur
pōnis	pōnitis	pōneris, -re	pōniminī
pōnit	pōnunt	pōnitur	pōnuntur

IMPERFECT

pōnēbam	pōnēbāmus	pōnēbar	pōnēbāmur
pōnēbās	pōnēbātis	pōnēbāris, -re	pōnēbāminī
pōnēbat	pōnēbant	pōnēbātur	pōnēbantur

FUTURE

pōnam	pōnēmus	pōnar	pōnēmur
pōnēs	pōnētis	pōnēris, -re	pōnēminī
pōnet	pōnent	pōnētur	pōnentur

ACTIVE		PASSIVE	

PERFECT

posuī	posuimus	positus sum	positī sumus
posuistī	posuistis	positus es	positī estis
posuit	posuērunt, -ēre	positus est	positī sunt

PLUPERFECT

posueram	posuerāmus	positus eram	positī erāmus
posuerās	posuerātis	positus erās	positī erātis
posuerat	posuerant	positus erat	positī erant

FUTURE PERFECT

posuerō	posuerimus	positus erō	positī erimus
posueris	posueritis	positus eris	positī eritis
posuerit	posuerint	positus erit	positī erunt

SUBJUNCTIVE

PRESENT

pōnam	pōnāmus	pōnar	pōnāmur
pōnās	pōnātis	pōnāris, -re	pōnāminī
pōnat	pōnant	pōnātur	pōnantur

IMPERFECT

pōnerem	pōnerēmus	pōnerer	pōnerēmur
pōnerēs	pōnerētis	pōnerēris, -re	pōnerēminī
pōneret	pōnerent	pōnerētur	pōnerentur

PERFECT

posuerim	posuerīmus	positus sim	positī sīmus
posuerīs	posuerītis	positus sīs	positī sītis
posuerit	posuerint	positus sit	positī sint

PLUPERFECT

posuissem	posuissēmus	positus essem	positī essēmus
posuissēs	posuissētis	positus essēs	positī essētis
posuisset	posuissent	positus esset	positī essent

IMPERATIVE

| pōne | pōnite | pōnere | pōniminī |

	ACTIVE	PASSIVE

INFINITIVES

	ACTIVE	PASSIVE
PRESENT	pōnere	pōnī
FUTURE	positūrus esse	positum īrī
PERFECT	posuisse	positus esse

PARTICIPLES

	ACTIVE	PASSIVE
PRESENT	pōnēns	——
FUTURE	positūrus	pōnendus
PERFECT	——	positus

	GERUND	SUPINE
GEN.	pōnendī	——
DAT.	pōnendō	——
ACC.	pōnendum	positum
ABL.	pōnendō	positū

44. Third conjugation, -iō type.—

PRINCIPAL PARTS: **iaciō, iacere, iēcī, iactum,** *throw*

INDICATIVE

SING.		PRESENT	PL.
iaciō	iacimus	iacior	iacimur
iacis	iacitis	iaceris, -re	iaciminī
iacit	iaciunt	iacitur	iaciuntur

IMPERFECT

iaciēbam	iaciēbāmus	iaciēbar	iaciēbāmur
iaciēbās	iaciēbātis	iaciēbāris, -re	iaciēbāminī
iaciēbat	iaciēbant	iaciēbātur	iaciēbantur

FUTURE

iaciam	iaciēmus	iaciar	iaciēmur
iaciēs	iaciētis	iaciēris, -re	iaciēminī
iaciet	iacient	iaciētur	iacientur

PERFECT

iēcī	iēcimus	iactus sum	iactī sumus
iēcistī	iēcistis	iactus es	iactī estis
iēcit	iēcērunt, -ēre	iactus est	iactī sunt

	ACTIVE		PASSIVE

SING.   PLUPERFECT   PL.

iēceram	iēcerāmus	iactus eram	iactī erāmus
iēcerās	iēcerātis	iactus erās	iactī erātis
iēcerat	iēcerant	iactus erat	iactī erant

FUTURE PERFECT

iēcerō	iēcerimus	iactus erō	iactī erimus
iēceris	iēceritis	iactus eris	iactī eritis
iēcerit	iēcerint	iactus erit	iactī erunt

SUBJUNCTIVE

PRESENT

iaciam	iaciāmus	iaciar	iaciāmur
iaciās	iaciātis	iaciāris, -re	iaciāminī
iaciat	iaciant	iaciātur	iaciantur

IMPERFECT

iacerem	iacerēmus	iacerer	iacerēmur
iacerēs	iacerētis	iacerēris, -re	iacerēminī
iaceret	iacerent	iacerētur	iacerentur

PERFECT

iēcerim	iēcerīmus	iactus sim	iactī sīmus
iēcerīs	iēcerītis	iactus sīs	iactī sītis
iēcerit	iēcerint	iactus sit	iactī sint

PLUPERFECT

iēcissem	iēcissēmus	iactus essem	iactī essēmus
iēcissēs	iēcissētis	iactus essēs	iactī essētis
iēcisset	iēcissent	iactus esset	iactī essent

IMPERATIVE

| iace | iacite | iacere | iaciminī |

INFINITIVES

PRESENT	iacere	iacī
FUTURE	iactūrus esse	iactum īrī
PERFECT	iēcisse	iactus esse

ACTIVE		PASSIVE

PARTICIPLES

PRESENT	iaciēns	——
FUTURE	iactūrus	iaciendus
PERFECT	——	iactus

	GERUND	SUPINE
GEN.	iaciendī	——
DAT.	iaciendō	——
ACC.	iaciendum	iactum
ABL.	iaciendō	iactū

(a) The commonest -iō verbs are **faciō, capiō**, and **iaciō**. They compound with nearly all the common prepositions. Note that in these prepositional compounds of all three verbs, the following changes take place:

(1) In the present system, -a becomes -i.

(2) In the supine, -a becomes -e.

Examples:

ad, *to* + **faciō**, *do* = **afficiō, afficere, affēcī, affectum**, *do (something) to, affect.*

ex, *out* + **capiō**, *take* = **excipiō, excipere, excēpī, exceptum**, *take out, except.*

dē, *down* + **iaciō**, *throw* = **dēiciō, dēicere, dēiēcī, dēiectum**, *throw down; disappoint.*

Observation.—In compounds of **iaciō**, the form -iciō was written instead of -iiciō. In other words, the **a** of **iaciō** was changed to the vowel **i**; the consonant **i** of **iaciō** was not written, although it was pronounced. Thus, **dēiciō** was pronounced as if it were written **dē-iiciō**.

Fourth Conjugation

45. Most verbs of this type are regular, like **audiō, audīre, audīvī, audītum**. But some have a perfect and a supine of irregular formation:

PRINCIPAL PARTS: **reperiō, reperīre, repperī, repertum,** *find*

ACTIVE   PASSIVE

INDICATIVE

PRESENT

SING.		PL.	
reperiō	reperīmus	reperior	reperīmur
reperīs	reperītis	reperīris, -re	reperīminī
reperit	reperiunt	reperītur	reperiuntur

IMPERFECT

reperiēbam	reperiēbāmus	reperiēbar	reperiēbāmur
reperiēbās	reperiēbātis	reperiēbāris, -re	reperiēbāminī
reperiēbat	reperiēbant	reperiēbātur	reperiēbantur

FUTURE

reperiam	reperiēmus	reperiar	reperiēmur
reperiēs	reperiētis	reperiēris, -re	reperiēminī
reperiet	reperient	reperiētur	reperientur

PERFECT

repperī	repperimus	repertus sum	repertī sumus
repperistī	repperistis	repertus es	repertī estis
repperit	reppererunt, -ēre	repertus est	repertī sunt

PLUPERFECT

reppereram	reppererāmus	repertus eram	repertī erāmus
reppererās	reppererātis	repertus erās	repertī erātis
reppererat	reppererant	repertus erat	repertī erant

FUTURE PERFECT

reppererō	reppererimus	repertus erō	repertī erimus
repipereris	reppereritis	repertus eris	repertī eritis
reppererit	reppererint	repertus erit	repertī erunt

SUBJUNCTIVE

PRESENT

reperiam	reperiāmus	reperiar	reperiāmur
reperiās	reperiātis	reperiāris, -re	reperiāminī
reperiat	reperiant	reperiātur	reperiantur

ACTIVE		PASSIVE	

SING.   IMPERFECT   PL.

reperīrem	reperīrēmus	reperīrer	reperīrēmur
reperīrēs	reperīrētis	reperīrēris, -re	reperīrēminī
reperīret	reperīrent	reperīrētur	reperīrentur

PERFECT

reppererim	reppererīmus	repertus sim	repertī sīmus
reppererīs	reppererītis	repertus sīs	repertī sītis
reppererit	reppererint	repertus sit	repertī sint

PLUPERFECT

repperissem	repperissēmus	repertus essem	repertī essēmus
repperissēs	repperissētis	repertus essēs	repertī essētis
repperisset	repperissent	repertus esset	repertī essent

IMPERATIVE

reperī	reperīte	reperīre	reperīminī

INFINITIVES

PRESENT	reperīre	reperīrī
FUTURE	repertūrus esse	repertum īrī
PERFECT	repperisse	repertus esse

PARTICIPLES

PRESENT	reperiēns	——
FUTURE	repertūrus	reperiendus
PERFECT	——	repertus

GERUND   SUPINE

GEN.	reperiendī	——
DAT.	reperiendō	——
ACC.	reperiendum	repertum
ABL.	reperiendō	repertū

DEPONENT VERBS

46. Deponent verbs are passive in form but active in meaning.
Note, however, that the future passive participle is passive in mean-

ing and that the following active forms exist, viz., the present participle, the future participle and infinitive, the gerund, and the supine.

PRINCIPAL PARTS: *I*—hortor, hortārī, hortātus sum, *urge*
                 II—vereor, verērī, veritus sum, *fear*
                 III—loquor, loquī, locūtus sum, *speak*
                 patior, patī, passus sum, *suffer, allow*
                 IV—experior, experīrī, expertus sum, *try, test*

INDICATIVE, SUBJUNCTIVE, IMPERATIVE

hortor like laudor (41); vereor like videor (42); loquor like pōnor (43); patior like iacior (44); experior like reperior (45).

INFINITIVES

PRES.	hortārī	verērī	loquī	patī	experīrī
FUT.	hortātūrus	veritūrus	locūtūrus	passūrus	expertūrus
	esse	esse	esse	esse	esse
PERF.	hortātus	veritus	locūtus	passus	expertus
	esse	esse	esse	esse	esse

PARTICIPLES

PRES.	hortāns	verēns	loquēns	patiēns	experiēns
FUT. ACT.					
	hortātūrus	veritūrus	locūtūrus	passūrus	expertūrus
FUT. PASS.					
	hortandus	verendus	loquendus	patiendus	experiendus
PERF.	hortātus	veritus	locūtus	passus	expertus

GERUND

GEN.	hortandī	verendī	loquendī	patiendī	experiendī
DAT.	hortandō	verendō	loquendō	patiendō	experiendō
ACC.	hortandum	verendum	loquendum	patiendum	experiendum
ABL.	hortandō	verendō	loquendō	patiendō	experiendō

SUPINE

ACC.	hortātum	veritum	locūtum	passum	expertum
ABL.	hortātū	veritū	locūtū	passū	expertū

SEMI-DEPONENT VERBS

(a) Semi-deponent verbs are deponent in the perfect system only. They are:

fīdō, fīdere, fīsus sum, *trust*
cōnfīdō, cōnfīdere, cōnfīsus sum, *trust*
diffīdō, diffīdere, diffīsus sum, *distrust*
audeō, audēre, ausus sum, *dare*
gaudeō, gaudēre, gāvīsus sum, *rejoice*
soleō, solēre, solitus sum, *be wont, accustomed*

(b) Perfect participles of deponents and semi-deponents which
are equivalent in meaning to present participles:

ausus, daring, venturing	**gāvīsus,** rejoicing
complexus, embracing	**mīrātus,** wondering
arbitrātus, thinking	**prōgressus,** advancing
commorātus, delaying	**secūtus,** following
cōnfīsus, trusting	**ūsus,** using
cōnsōlātus, comforting	**veritus,** fearing
diffīsus, distrusting	**ratus,** thinking (from **reor**)

The past participles of passive verbs used in a middle or reflexive
sense are similarly to be rendered by a present participle in English;
for example:

conversus	*turning (himself)*
prōiectus	*throwing (himself)*
humī prōvolūtus	*rolling (himself) on the ground*

The English "turning to his friends" will be either **cum ad suōs sē
convertisset** or **ad suōs conversus.**

IRREGULAR VERBS

47. *Dō, give.*—

PRINCIPAL PARTS: **dō, dare, dedī, datum**

ACTIVE		PASSIVE	
SING.	INDICATIVE		PL.
PRESENT	dō	damus	——[1]	damur
	dās	datis	daris, -re	daminī
	dat	dant	datur	dantur

---

[1] "I am given a book" is English idiom, but not Latin, which would turn it
Liber mihi datur.

	ACTIVE	PASSIVE	

INDICATIVE

IMPERF.	dabam	dabar
FUTURE	dabō	dabor
PERFECT	dedī	datus sum
PLUPERF.	dederam	datus eram
FUT. PERF.	dederō	datus erō

SUBJUNCTIVE

PRESENT	dem, dēs, det, *etc.*	——, dēris (-re), dētur, *etc.*
IMPERF.	darem	darer
PERFECT	dederim	datus sim
PLUPERF.	dedissem	datus essem

IMPERATIVE

	dā	date	dare	daminī

INFINITIVES

PRESENT	dare	darī
FUTURE	datūrus esse	datum īrī
PERFECT	dedisse	datus esse

PARTICIPLES

PRESENT	dāns	——
FUTURE	datūrus	dandus
PERFECT	——	datus

	GERUND	SUPINE
GEN.	dandī	——
DAT.	dandō	——
ACC.	dandum	datum
ABL.	dandō	datū

(a) **DŌ and its compounds.**—

Most* compounds of DŌ are of the third conjugation and exhibit the reduplication of the parent verb.   They are:

---

* Exceptions are: circum-, inter-, pessum-, satis-, super-, venum-, of first conjugation.   See also Supplementary Notes, ad loc.

abdō,	abdere,	abdidī,	abditum,	hide
addō,	addere,	addidī,	additum,	add
condō,	condere,	condidī,	conditum,	found, hide
crēdō,	crēdere,	crēdidī,	crēditum,	believe
dēdō,	dēdere,	dēdidī,	dēditum,	give up
ēdō,	ēdere,	ēdidī,	ēditum,	give forth
perdō,	perdere,	perdidī,	perditum,	lose
prōdō,	prōdere,	prōdidī,	prōditum,	betray
reddō,	reddere,	reddidī,	redditum,	restore
subdō,	subdere,	subdidī,	subditum,	substitute
trādō,	trādere,	trādidī,	trāditum,	deliver, hand across
vēndō,	vēndere,	vēndidī,	vēnditum,	give in sale, sell

48. Compounds of *sum*.—

adsum, adesse, affuī, affutūrus, *be at hand, be present*

dēsum, dēesse, dēfuī, dēfutūrus, *be lacking*

īnsum, inesse, ——, īnfutūrus, *be in*

intersum, interesse, interfuī, interfutūrus, *be among, take part in*

obsum, obesse, obfuī, obfutūrus, *be in the way of, hinder*

praesum, praeësse, praefuī, praefutūrus, *be before, be in command of*

(**praesum** has a present participle **praesēns** used as an adjective meaning *present*.)

subsum, subesse, ——, ——, *be under, be near*

supersum, superesse, superfuī, superfutūrus, *be over, be left, survive*

All of the above are conjugated exactly like **sum**, with the addition of the prefix.

(a) **Absum, abesse**, *be away, be absent*, loses **b** before **f** in the perfect and in the future participle: **āfuī, āfutūrus**. It also has the present participle **absēns**.

(b) **Prōsum**, *be for, be of advantage to*, inserts **d** before all forms of **sum** beginning with **e**.

PRINCIPAL PARTS: **prōsum, prōdesse, prōfuī, prōfutūrus**

	INDICATIVE		SUBJUNCTIVE
PRESENT	prōsum	prōsumus	prōsim
	prōdes	prōdestis	
	prōdest	prōsunt	
IMPERF.	prōderam		prōdessem
FUTURE	prōderō		
PERFECT	prōfuī		prōfuerim
PLUPERFECT	prōfueram		prōfuissem
FUT. PERF.	prōfuerō		

IMPERATIVE		INFINITIVES	PARTICIPLE
prōdes	prōdeste	PRES. prōdesse	FUT. prōfutūrus
		FUT. prōfutūrus esse	
		PERF. prōfuisse	

Observation.—All prepositional compounds of **sum** govern the dative except **absum (ab)** and **insum (in)**. Even **insum** takes the dative in Sallust:

> *Huic hominī* nōn minor vānitās *inerat* quam audācia.
> —*Cat.*, XXIII.

49. *Possum, be able.*—This is a compound of **pot-** and **sum**. Wherever **t** comes before **s** in the conjugation, it is changed to **s**. Note the irregular perfect **potuī**.

PRINCIPAL PARTS: **possum, posse, potuī**

	INDICATIVE		SUBJUNCTIVE
PRESENT	possum	possumus	possim
	potes	potestis	
	potest	possunt	
IMPERF.	poteram		possem
FUTURE	poterō		
PERFECT	potuī		potuerim
PLUPERF.	potueram		potuissem
FUT. PERF.	potuerō		

INFINITIVES	PARTICIPLE
PRES. posse	PRES. potēns, *adj.*, *powerful*
PERFECT potuisse	

50. *Ferō, bear.*—

PRINCIPAL PARTS: **ferō, ferre, tulī, lātum**

ACTIVE		PASSIVE	

INDICATIVE

PRESENT	ferō	ferimus	feror	ferimur
	fers	fertis	ferris, -re	feriminī
	fert	ferunt	fertur	feruntur
IMPERF.	ferēbam		ferēbar	
FUTURE	feram		ferar	
PERFECT	tulī		lātus sum	
PLUPERF.	tuleram		lātus eram	
FUT. PERF.	tulerō		lātus erō	

SUBJUNCTIVE

PRESENT	feram	ferar
IMPERF.	ferrem	ferrer
PERFECT	tulerim	lātus sim
PLUPERF.	tulissem	lātus essem

IMPERATIVE

	fer	ferte	ferre	feriminī

INFINITIVES

PRESENT	ferre	ferrī
FUTURE	lātūrus esse	lātum īrī
PERFECT	tulisse	lātus esse

PARTICIPLES

PRESENT	ferēns	——
FUTURE	lātūrus	ferendus
PERFECT	——	lātus

	GERUND	SUPINE
GEN.	ferendī	——
DAT.	ferendō	——
ACC.	ferendum	lātum
ABL.	ferendō	lātū

For the compounds of **ferō**, see sec. 177.

51. *Volō* and its compounds.—

PRINCIPAL PARTS: volō, velle, voluī, *be willing*
nōlō, nōlle, nōluī, *be unwilling*
mālō, mālle, māluī, *prefer*

INDICATIVE

PRESENT	volō	nōlō	mālō
	vīs	nōn vīs	māvīs
	vult	nōn vult	māvult
	volumus	nōlumus	mālumus
	vultis	nōn vultis	māvultis
	volunt	nōlunt	mālunt
IMPERF.	volēbam	nōlēbam	mālēbam
FUTURE	volam	nōlam	mālam
PERFECT	voluī	nōluī	māluī
PLUPERF.	volueram	nōlueram	mālueram
FUT. PERF.	voluerō	nōluerō	māluerō

SUBJUNCTIVE

PPESENT	velim	nōlim	mālim
IMPERF.	vellem	nōllem	māllem
PERFECT	voluerim	nōluerim	māluerim
PLUPERF.	voluissem	nōluissem	māluissem

IMPERATIVE

	——	nōlī nōlite	——

INFINITIVES

PRESENT	velle	nōlle	mālle
PERFECT	voluisse	nōluisse	māluisse

PARTICIPLES

PRESENT	volēns	nōlēns	——

52. Fīō, be made, become, happen.—This verb supplies the passive of **faciō**. (See Lesson 43, sec. **216**.)

PRINCIPAL PARTS: **fīō, fierī, factus sum**

	INDICATIVE		SUBJUNCTIVE
PRESENT	fīō	——	fīam
	fīs	——	
	fit	fīunt	
IMPERFECT	fīēbam		fierem
FUTURE	fīam		
PERFECT	factus sum		factus sim
PLUPERF.	factus eram		factus essem
FUT. PERF.	factus erō		

IMPERATIVE INFINITIVES PARTICIPLES

PRES.	fī, fīte	fierī	——
FUTURE	——	factum īrī	faciendus
PERFECT	——	factus esse	factus

53. Eō, go.—

PRINCIPAL PARTS: **eō, īre, iī, itum**

	INDICATIVE		SUBJUNCTIVE
PRESENT	eō	īmus	eam
	īs	ītis	
	it	eunt	
IMPERF.	ībam		īrem
FUTURE	ībō		
PERFECT	iī (īvī)		ierim
PLUPERF.	ieram		iissem or īssem
FUT. PERF.	ierō		

IMPERATIVE INFINITIVES PARTICIPLES

PRESENT	ī, īte	īre	iēns (gen., euntis)
FUTURE	——	itūrus esse	itūrus
PERFECT	——	īsse	——

	GERUND	SUPINE
GEN.	eundī	——
DAT.	eundō	——
ACC.	eundum	itum
ABL.	eundō	itū

DEFECTIVE VERBS

54. Meminī, *I remember,* **ōdī,** *I hate,* and **coepī,** *I have begun* are conjugated only in the perfect system. Notice that **meminī** and **ōdī**, while perfect in form, are present in meaning. Correspondingly, the pluperfect has the meaning of an imperfect and the future perfect of a future.

INDICATIVE

PERFECT	meminī	ōdī	coepī
	meministī, *etc.*	ōdistī, *etc.*	coepistī, *etc.*
PLUPERF.	memineram	ōderam	coeperam
FUT. PERF.	meminerō	ōderō	coeperō

SUBJUNCTIVE

PERFECT	meminerim	ōderim	coeperim
PLUPERF.	meminissem	ōdissem	coepissem

IMPERATIVE

SING.	mementō
PLUR.	mementōte

INFINITIVES

PERFECT	meminisse	ōdisse	coepisse
FUTURE	——	ōsūrus esse	coeptūrus esse

PARTICIPLES

PERFECT	——	ōsus	coeptus
FUTURE	——	ōsūrus	coeptūrus

(a) With a dependent passive infinitive, a passive form of **coepī** is used:

> Māteria *comportārī coepta est.*
> The material **began to be assembled.**

TRANSLITERATION AND TRANSLATION OF FRONTISPIECE

576 SCALAEIMPROVISO · SUBITUSQUEAPPARUITIGNIS ·
DISCURRUNTALIIADPORTAS · PRIMOSQUETRUCIDANT ·

* FERRUMALIITORQUENT · ETOBUMBRAT͟AETHERATELIS ·
IPSEINTERPRIMOS · DEXTRAMSUBMOENIATENDIT

580 AENEAS · MAGNAQUEINCUSATVOCELATINUM ·
TESTATURQUEDEOS · ITERUMSEADPROELIACOGI ·
BISIAMITALOSHOSTIS · HAECALTERAFOEDERARUMPI ·
EXORITURTREPIDOSINTERDISCORDIACIVES ·

URBEMALIIRESA͟RAREIUBENT · ETPANDEREPORTAS
DARDANIDIS · IPSUMQUETRAHUNTINMOENIAREGEM ·

* ARMAFERUNTALI ͟· ETPERGUNTDEFENDEREMUROS ·
INCLUSAS · UTCUMLATEBROSOINPUMICEPASTOR

* VESTIGAVITAPES · ETFUMOQUEIMPLEVITAMARO ·
ILLAEINTUSTREPIDAERERUM · PERCEREACASTRA

590 DISCURRUNT · MAGNISQUEACUUNTSTRIDORIBUSIRAS ·
VOLVITURATERODORTECTIS · TUMMURMURECAECO
INTUSSAXASONANT · VACUASITFUMUSADAURAS ·
ACCIDITHAECFESSISETIAMFORTUNALATINIS ·
QUAETOTAMLUCTUCONCUSSITFUNDITUSURBEM ·
REGINAUTTECTISVENIENTEMPROSPICITHOSTEM ·

* INĆESSIMUROS · IGNESADINTECTAVOLARE ·
NUSQUAMACIESCONTRARUTULAS · NULLAAGMINATURNI ·

* INFELIXPUGNAEIUVENEM · INCERTAMINACERDIT

* * *

Scalae improviso subitusque apparuit ignis:
discurrunt alii ad portas primosque trucidant,
ferrum alii torquent et obumbrant aethera telis.
ipse inter primos dextram sub moenia tendit
Aeneas, magnaque incusat voce Latinum

* Notice the errors, omissions, and erasures of the scribe who copied this more than fifteen centuries ago: v. 578, *obumbrat* for *obumbrant,* the *N* is added above; v. 584, *resarare* corrected above to *reserare;* v. 586, *ali* for *alii,* the other *I* is added above; v. 588, *vestigavit apes et fumoque* for *vestigavit apes fumoque,* or *vestigavit apes et fumo;* v. 596, *IN,* because it was written in error, is struck out; v. 598 *in certamina cerdit* wrongly copied for *in certamine credit.*

testaturque deos iterum se ad proelia cogi,
bis iam Italos hostis, haec altera foedera rumpi.
exoritur trepidos inter discordia cives:
urbem alii reserare iubent et pandere portas
Dardanidis ipsumque trahunt in moenia regem:
arma ferunt alii et pergunt defendere muros:
inclusas ut cum latebroso in pumice pastor
vestigavit apes fumoque implevit amaro,
illae intus trepidae rerum per cerea castra
discurrunt magnisque acuunt stridoribus iras;
volvitur ater odor tectis, tum murmure caeco
intus saxa sonant, vacuas it fumus ad auras.
Accidit haec fessis etiam fortuna Latinis,
quae totam luctu concussit funditus urbem,
regina ut tectis venientem prospicit hostem,
incessi muros, ignis ad tecta volare,
nusquam acies contra Rutulas, nulla agmina Turni,
infelix pugnae iuvenem in certamine credit
Aen., XII, 576–598

*   *   *

Scaling ladders unexpectedly appeared and flames suddenly flared up.
Some rushed to the different gates and cut down the defenders they met;
others hurled spears or darkened the skies with swarms of arrows.   In
the vanguard Aeneas raised a threatening hand to the walls and loudly
upbraided Latinus, calling heaven to witness that for a second time he
was being forced into a fight, that the Italians had twice now declared
their enmity and violated a second treaty.   Now arose a hot dispute
among the frightened citizens; one faction ordered their fellows to fling
the city gates wide open to let the Greeks enter and dragged their king
in person onto the battlements; the other armed themselves to defend
the walls.   They were like bees which a shepherd has craftily followed
to their home in a crannied rock and tried to smoke out; inside their
waxen fortress the bees, in confusion at their plight, rush distractedly
here and there, and with shrill and angry buzzing sharpen their stings.
A dark cloud of pungent smoke fills their hive; the rocks within re-echo
with a confused buzzing as the smoke rolls out into the open air.

One further stroke of misfortune hit the disheartened Latins, a stroke
which plunged the whole city in the depths of grief; for when the queen
from her palace roof saw the enemy approaching, saw the assault on the
walls, and the flames licking up to the houses with no sign of Turnus and
the Rutulian army to put up a defense, she thought, poor lady, that the
young warrior had fallen in battle. . . .

VOCABULARIES

Latin-English Vocabulary

A

ā (*before consonants*), **ab** (*before vowels and some consonants, but almost never before* **v** *and* **m**), **abs** (*before* **tē** *and in some compounds*), *prep. w. abl.*, from, away from; by (*followed by noun denoting agent*); *in some phrases denoting position,* at, in, on, on the side of

abdō, abdere, abdidī, abditum, hide

abdūcō, -dūcere, -dūxī, -ductum, lead away, carry off

abeō, abīre, abiī, abitum, go away, depart

aberrō, *I,* wander away, go astray

abhinc, *adv.,* from this time (backward), ago

abhorreō, abhorrēre, abhorruī, ——, shrink back from, be adverse to

abiciō, abicere, abiēcī, abiectum, throw out *or* away

abluō, abluere, abluī, ablūtum, wash away, purify; atone for

absolvō, absolvere, absolvī, absolūtum, set free from; acquit

abstineō, abstinēre, abstinuī, abstentum, refrain from

absum, abesse, āfuī, āfutūrus, be away from, be absent; be free from

absūmō, absūmere, absūmpsī, absūmptum, take away, waste, destroy

absurdus, -a, -um, absurd

abundantia, -ae, *f.,* abundance, plenty, surfeit

ac, *see* **atque**

accēdō, accēdere, accessī, accessum, come up to, reach, approach, be added; **accēdit,** it is added, there is added; **accēdit quod,** there is the additional fact that

accidō, accidere, accidī, ——, befall, happen, occur; **accidit ut** *and subj.,* it happens (*or* happened) that

accipiō, accipere, accēpī, acceptum, accept, receive

accūsō, *I,* accuse, bring a charge against in court

ācer, ācris, ācre, *adj.,* piercing, sharp, fierce

acerbus, -a, -um, harsh

aciēs, aciēī, *f.,* line of battle

ācriter, *adv.,* sharply, fiercely, vigorously, keenly

acūtus, -a, -um, sharp, keen, intelligent

ad, *prep. w. acc.,* to, toward; against

addō, addere, addidī, additum, add

addūcō, addūcere, addūxī, adductum, lead to, bring to; induce, influence

adeō, *adv.,* to such an extent, so much, so

adeō, adīre, adiī, aditum, go to, approach, visit; attack

adequitō, *I,* ride up to

adf-, *for all entries beginning with these letters see* **aff-**; *e.g., for* **adferō** *see* **afferō**

adhibeō, adhibēre, adhibuī, adhibitum, apply, bring to bear, bring in, employ; treat

adhūc, *adv.,* hitherto; up till now, as yet

adiciō, adicere, adiēcī, adiectum, throw *or* fling to

adigō, adigere, adēgī, adāctum, drive, thrust; hurl

adimō, adimere, adēmī, adēmptum, take away, remove

aditus, aditūs, *m.*, approach, avenue, passage

adiuvō, adiuvāre, adiūvī, adiūtum, help

administrō, *I*, administer, manage, control

admittō, -mittere, -mīsī, -missum, send to; let in; let go; permit; commit

admodum, *adv.*, very much

adorior, -orīrī, -ortus sum, attack, assail

adquiescō, adquiescere, adquiēvī, adquiētum, be still; feel satisfaction in; feel relieved by *or* at (*w. abl.*)

adrogāns, *see* arrogāns

adsum, adesse, affuī, affutūrus, be here, be present, attend

adulēscēns, adulescentis (adulēscentium), *m.*, young man

adulēscentulus, -ī, *m.*, youngster

advehō, advehere, advēxī, advectum, bring in

adveniō, advenīre, advēnī, adventum, come up to, arrive at, reach

adventus, adventūs, *m.*, arrival

adversus, -a, -um, opposite, hostile, contrary; *n., pl. as noun or fem. pl. with* rēs, disaster, misfortune

adversus, *adv. and prep. with acc.*, (facing) toward, against

aedificium, -cī, *n.*, building

aedificō, *I*, build

aeger, aegra, aegrum, sick

Aegīna, -ae, *f.*, Aegina, *an island near Athens*

aegrē, *adv.*, with difficulty

aegritūdō, aegritūdinis, *f.*, sickness, malady

aegrōtus, -a, -um, sick

Aegyptus, -ī, *f.*, Egypt

Aemiliānus, -ī, *m.*, Aemilianus, a Roman name

Aemilius, Aemilī, *m.*, Aemilius, *name of a Roman clan. In particular, Lucius Aemilius Paulus (Macedonicus), conqueror of the Macedonian king, Perseus, at Pydna, in 168 B.C.*

Aenēās, Aenēae, *m.*, Aeneas, *a Trojan, the son of Anchises and Venus; mythical ancestor of the Romans and hero of Vergil's "Aeneid"*

Aeolus, -ī, *m.*, Aeolus, *a god, king of the winds*

aequē, *adv.*, equally, impartially

aequō, *I*, make equal

aequus, -a, -um, *adj.*, equal, fair

aes, aeris, *n.*, copper, bronze; money; aes aliēnum, debt

aestās, aestātis, *f.*, summer

aestimō, *I*, estimate, value. reckon; think

aestus, aestūs, *m.*, heat; tide

aetās, aetātis, *f.*, age, period of life

aeternus, -a, -um, eternal, everlasting

Aetōlia, -ae, *f.*, Aetolia, *a district in the northwest of Greece*

aevum, -ī, *n.*, age, duration; life

afferō, afferre, attulī, allātum, (*sec. 219b*), bring, take, or carry to; report

afficiō, afficere, affēcī, affectum, do something to, work upon, treat, affect, aliquem dolōre, laetitiā, cause someone pain, joy, *etc.*

afflīgō, afflīgere, afflīxī, afflīctum,

strike down, dash to the ground; damage, ruin

Āfrica, -ae, *f.*, Africa, *a Roman province corresponding roughly to modern Tunis and Algiers*

Āfricānus, -a, -um, of Africa. *In particular, the agnomen of Publius Cornelius Scipio, the conqueror of Hannibal in 202 B.C.*

ager, agrī, *m.*, field, land; **agrī cultūra,** agriculture

agger, aggeris, *m.*, earthwork, causeway

aggredior, aggredī, aggressus sum, advance toward, attack

agitur, is at stake

agmen, agminis, *n.*, moving body; line, column on march; **novissimum agmen,** the rear guard

agō, agere, ēgī, āctum, set in motion, drive; do, transact, carry on; discuss; give (*w.* **grātiās**); plead (*w.* **causam**)

agrārius, -a, -um, agrarian

agrestis, agreste, *adj.*, rural, of the country; boorish

agricola, -ae, *m.*, farmer

agricultūra, -ae, *f.*, agriculture

Agrippa, -ae, *m.*, Agrippa, *a Roman cognomen. In particular,* Marcus Vipsanius Agrippa, *leading general and right-hand man of the Emperor Augustus (63–12 B.C.).*

aiō, *defective verb,* say, say "yes," assert

alacer, alacre, *adj.*, alert, brisk, eager, ready

Alesia, -ae, *f.*, Alesia, a Gallic town, now *Alise Sainte Reine, northwest of Dijon*

Alexander, Alexandrī, *m.*, Alexander the Great (*356–323 B.C.*)

Alexandrīa, -ae, *f.*, Alexandria, *the*

capital of Egypt under the Ptolemies, founded by order of Alexander 332 B.C.

aliēnus, -a, -um, foreign; out of place; irrelevant

aliquandō, *adv.*, on certain occasions (*opposed to* never); at some time; finally

aliquantum, -ī, *n.*, a good deal, not a little; somewhat

aliquō, *adv.*, to some place, somewhere

aliquot, *indecl. adj.*, some, a few, several

aliquis, aliquid, *and* **aliquī, aliqua, aliquod,** *indef. pron. and adj.*, someone, something, some; anyone, anything, any

aliter, *adv.*, otherwise

aliunde, *adv.*, from elsewhere

alius, alia, aliud, *gen.* **alīus,** *but more commonly* **alterīus,** *pron.* (*see sec. 173*), another, other; **aliī . . . aliī,** some . . . others

Allobrogēs, Allobrogum, *m. pl.*, the Allobroges, *a Gallic tribe*

alō, alere, aluī, altum (alitum), sustain, foster, nourish, encourage

Alpēs, Alpium, *f.*, Alps

alter, altera, alterum, *gen.* **alterīus,** *pron.*, (*see sec. 173*), the other (of two); second

altercō, *I*, quarrel, wrangle, dispute

Alpīnus, -a, -um, Alpine

altus, -a, -um, high; deep

amābō, please! (*final syllable often treated as short in verse*)

amārē, *adv.*, bitterly

ambō, ambae, ambō, both

ambulō, *I*, walk

amīcitia, -ae, *f.*, friendship

amīcus, -a, -um, friendly

amīcus, -ī, *m.*, friend

āmittō, āmittere, āmīsī, āmissum, send away; let go, lose

amnis, amnis, *gen. pl.* amnium, *m.*, river

amō, *I*, love; be in love

amor, amōris, *m.*, love

amplē, *adv.*, generously; *in comparisons*, more, further

amplius, *adv.*, more

amplus, -a, -um, spacious, abundant, great

an, *conj.*, or; *sometimes merely the sign of a question and best omitted in translation*

anceps, *adj.*, *gen.* ancipitis, doubtful

ancilla, -ae, *f.*, maidservant

ancora, -ae, *f.*, anchor

angustiae, angustiārum, *f. pl.*, narrow place, pass; difficulties

angustus, -a, -um, narrow, cramped; short; difficult

anima, -ae, *f.*, vital principle, breath (of life); soul

animadvertō, -vertere, -vertī, -versum, turn one's attention to, notice; punish *with* in *and accusative*

animal, animālis, *gen. pl.* animālium, *n.*, animal

animus, -ī, *m.*, rational soul, mind; mood, spirit, feeling, intention

annōn, *conj.*, or not (*used in direct questions. See sec. 211, Obs.*)

annus, -ī, *m.*, year

ante, *adv.*, before, previously; *prep. w. acc.*, before

anteā, *adv.*, formerly, before, previously; once

antecēdō, -cēdere, -cessī, -cessum, go before

antecellō, antecellere, ——, ——, excel

antepōnō, antepōnere, anteposuī, antepositum, place before; prefer (*w. acc. and dat., sec. 219b*)

antequam, ante . . . quam, *conj.*, before

antīquitus, *adv.*, from *or* in early *or* ancient times

antīquus, -a, -um, former, old *and no longer existing*

Antium, Antī, *n.*, Antium, *an ancient town in Latium*

Antōnius, Antōnī, *m.*, Antonius, Anthony, *name of a Roman clan. In particular, Marcus Antonius, the triumvir (died 30 B.C.)*

ānulus, -ī, *m.*, ring, signet ring

Aper, Aprī, *m.*, Aper, *a proper name*

aperiō, aperīre, aperuī, apertum, open, disclose; reveal

apertē, *adv.*, openly, frankly

apertus, -a, -um, open

Apollō, Apollinis, *m.*, Apollo, *god of light, of prophecy, of immortality*

appellō, *I*, name, call by name

Appia, *see* via

apportō, *I*, bring to, bring

appropinquō, *I*, *intr.*, approach (*used with* ad + *acc. or with dative*)

aptus, -a, -um, adapted, trained

apud, *prep. with acc.*, at, among; at the house of; in the works of

Āpūlia, -ae, *f.*, Apulia, *a district in the southeast of Italy*

aqua, -ae, *f.*, water

aquila, -ae, *f.*, eagle

Aquītānus, -ī, *m.*, Aquitanian, inhabitant of Aquitania (*southwest France*)

Arar, Araris, *acc.* **Ararim,** *m.,* Arar River, *now* Saône. *It rises in the Vosges Mts. and flows southward into the Rhone.*

arātor, arātōris, *m.,* ploughman

arbitror, *I,* think, form a personal judgment

arbor, arboris, *f.,* tree

arcessō, arcessere, arcessīvī, arcessītum, summon, send for; invite

Archiās, -ae, *m.,* *(Greek noun),* Archias, *a Greek poet of Antioch defended by Cicero*

arduus, -a, -um, difficult; *n. pl. as noun,* difficulty, tribulation

argentum, -ī, *n.,* silver

Ariobarzānēs, Ariobarzānis, *m.,* Ariobarzanes, *the name of a line of kings of Cappadocia. In particular, that king (93–63 B.C.) expelled by Mithridates and restored by Pompey.*

Ariovistus, -ī, *m.,* Ariovistus, *a German king*

arma, armorum, *n. pl.,* weapons, arms, armor *(whether for defense or offense)*

armātus, -a, -um, armed

Armenius, -a, -um, Armenian

armō, *I,* arm, equip

arō, *I,* plough

Arpīnās, -ātis, *adj.,* of Arpinum, *town in Latium, birthplace of Cicero and Marius*

arrogāns, *adj., gen.* **arrogantis,** haughty, presumptuous

arrogantia, -ae, *f.,* haughtiness, presumption

ars, artis, *gen. pl.* **artium,** *f.,* art; **optimae artēs,** culture; **bonae artēs,** good moral habits

Arvernī, Arvernōrum, *m. pl.,* the Arverni, a Gallic tribe *(Auvergnats)*

as, assis, *gen. pl.* **assium,** *m.,* as, *a Roman copper coin*

Asia, -ae, *f.,* Asia, *a Roman province corresponding roughly to the middle portion of the western part of Anatolia (also called Asia Minor)*

Asiāticus, -a, -um, of Asia

aspectus, -ūs, *m.,* aspect, appearance

asper, aspera, asperum, rough; hard, difficult, *in n. pl.* adversity, "rough going"

astrologus, -ī, *m.,* astrologer; astronomer

astrum, astrī, *n.,* star

at, *conj.,* but, at least

Athēnae, Athēnārum, *f.,* Athens, *a city-state of Greece*

Athēniēnsis, -e, *adj.,* Athenian

atque, *conj.,* and, and what is more; **īdem atque,** same as; *after a comparative it means* than

ātrium, atrī, *n.,* entrance room, hall; *the large reception and living room, next to the entrance, which formed one of the two principal parts into which a Roman house was divided*

Atticus, -a, -um, Athenian

Atticus, -ī, Atticus, *the agnomen of Titus Pomponius (Atticus), the intimate friend of Cicero*

attingō, attingere, attigī, attāctum, touch on, reach, arrive at

attrectō, *I,* touch, handle; meddle with

auctor, auctōris, *m.,* author, originator

auctōritās, auctōritātis, *f.,* influence, prestige, ascendancy; authenticity

audācia, -ae, *f.*, boldness, daring, courage

audācter, *adv.*, boldly, fearlessly

audāx, *adj.*, *gen.* audācis, bold, daring

audeō, audēre, ausus sum, dare, venture

audiō, *IV*, hear, listen to

auferō, auferre, abstulī, ablātum, carry off

augeō, augēre, auxī, auctum, increase (*tr.*); enrich, honor

aura, -ae, *f.*, breeze, air

aureus, -a, -um, golden

aurīga, -ae, *m.*, charioteer

auris, auris, *gen. pl.* aurium, *f.*, ear

aurum, -ī, *n.*, gold

aut, *conj.*, or; aut . . . aut, either . . . or

autem, *conj.*, (*never first word in sentence*), but; however; now; moreover

auxilium, auxilī, *n.*, help, assistance, aid

avāritia, -ae, *f.*, greed, avarice

avārus, -a, -um, greedy, covetous

avē, *imperative of* aveō, hail!

āvertō, āvertere, āvertī, āversum, turn away; *pass.*, be alienated (from)

aviditās, -tātis, *f.*, greed

āvolō, *I*, fly away

B

barbarus, -a, -um, foreign, uncivilized, barbarous; *as noun*, masc. pl., barbarians

beātus, -a, -um, blessed, happy

Belgae, -ārum, *m.*, Belgae, Belgians

bellē, *adv.*, well

bellicōsus, -a, -um, warlike

bellum, -ī, *n.*, war; bellum gerere, wage war; alicui indīcere, declare war on someone (*dative*)

bellus, -a, -um, pretty, handsome

bene, *adv.*, well

beneficium, -cī, *n.*, kind deed, service

benevolentia, -ae, *f.*, goodwill

bestia, -ae, *f.*, wild beast

bibliothēca, -ae, *f.*, library

bibō, bibere, bibī, ——, drink

biduum, -uī, *n.*, period of two days

bīnī, -ae, -a, *distrib. num. adj.*, two each, two at a time

bis, *adv.*, twice

Bīthynia, -ae, *f.*, Bithynia, *a province in Asia Minor*

blandus, -a, -um, flattering, smooth-tongued, agreeable

bonus, -a, -um, good; *comp.* melior, melius, better; *superl.* optimus, -a, -um, best

bōs, bovis, *m.*, ox

Boudicēa, -ae, *f.*, Boadicea, *Queen of the Iceni, a British tribe (died A.D. 61)*

brevis, breve, *adj.*, short; brevī, for brevī spatiō, concisely

breviter, *adv.*, briefly

Britannia, -ae, *f.*, Britain

Britannus, -a, -um, of Britain, British; *as noun, masc.*, Briton

Brundisium, -sī, *n.*, Brundisium, *town on S.E. coast of Italy, modern* Brindisi

Brūtus, -ī, *m.*, Brutus, *a Roman cognomen. In particular,* (1) *Marcus Junius Brutus (85–42 B.C.), a Roman politician and one of the assassins of Julius Caesar;* (2) *Lucius Junius Brutus (about 501 B.C.), a Roman patriot*

Būcephalus, -ī, *m.,* Bucephalus, *name of a horse of Alexander the Great*

C

C., *abbreviation for* **Gāius**

cadō, cadere, cecidī, cāsum, fall, fall in battle

Caeciliānus, -ī, *m.,* Caecilianus, *a Roman name*

Caediciānus, -ī, *m.,* Caedicianus, *a Roman name*

caedēs, caedis, *gen. pl.* **caedium,** *f.,* slaughter

caedō, caedere, cecīdī, caesum, cut, hack, kill

caelum, -ī, *n.,* sky, heaven; climate

Caesar, Caesaris, *m.,* Caesar, *Roman cognomen of the clan Julii. In particular, C. Julius Caesar (100–44 B.C.), general, author, statesman, and virtual founder of the imperial dynasty*

calamitās, calamitātis, *f.,* misfortune, disaster, calamity; ruin

cālō, cālōnis, *m.,* officer's servant

campus, -ī, *m.,* field, plain, prairie

candidus, -a, -um, white

canis, canis, *gen. pl.* **canum,** *c.,* dog

cantō, *I,* to sing *or* play

caper, caprī, *m.,* goat

capiō, capere, cēpī, captum, take, seize, capture; **cōnsilium capere,** resolve, take measures

captīvus, -ī, *m.,* captive, prisoner

captō, *I,* catch

Capua, -ae, *f.,* Capua, *a town in Italy*

caput, capitis, *n.,* head

carcer, carceris, *m.,* prison

careō, carēre, caruī, caritūrus, be without, be deprived of, lack, do without (*w. abl. of separation, sec. 134*)

carmen, carminis, *n.,* song; (lyric) poem

Carnūtēs, -um, *m.,* Carnutes, *a Celtic tribe between the Seine and the Loire; chief town Autricum, now Chartres*

carō, carnis, *f.,* flesh

Carpetānī, -ōrum, *m.,* Carpetani, *a tribe of northern Spain*

carpō, carpere, carpsī, carptum, pluck, pick, take; enjoy

carrus, -ī, *m.,* cart, wagon

Carthāgō, Carthāginis, *f.,* Carthage, *a city in northern Africa, Rome's principal enemy and rival in the third century B.C.*

cārus, -a, -um, dear

Cassius, -ī, *m.,* Cassius, *name of a Roman clan. In particular, L. Cassius Longinus, killed 107 B.C. by the Gauls.*

castē, *adv.,* chastely, purely

castellum, -ī, *n.,* redoubt, fort

castrum, -ī, *n.,* fort; *plural,* **castra, castrōrum,** camp

cāsus, -ūs, *m.,* event, accident

catēna, ae, *f.,* chain

Catilīna, -ae, *m.,* Catiline, *a Roman cognomen. In particular,* Lucius Sergius Catilina, *leader of a conspiracy in 63 B.C.*

Catō, Catōnis, *m.,* Cato, *a Roman cognomen. In particular,* (1) Marcus Porcius Cato, *censor, 184 B.C.;* (2) Marcus Porcius Cato, *95–46 B.C., member of the senatorial party against Caesar; he committed suicide after the battle of Thapsus.*

cauda, -ae, *f.,* tail

causa, -ae, *f.,* cause, reason; lawsuit; **causā,** *following genitive*, for the sake of, for the purpose of

causor, *I*, plead

cautus, -a, -um, cautious, prudent

caveō, cavēre, cāvī, cautum, be cautious, be on one's guard against (*with accusative*)

cavō, *I*, hollow out

cēdō, cēdere, cessī, cessum, go, go away; give way, retreat; yield

celer, celeris, celere, swift

celeritās, celeritātis, *f.*, speed

celeriter, *adv.*, swiftly, rapidly

cēlō, *I*, conceal, hide

cēna, -ae, *f.*, supper

cēnō, *I*, take a meal, dine

cēnseō, cēnsēre, cēnsuī, cēnsum, think, form and express a clear view or judgment

centum, *card. num.*, *indecl.*, hundred

centuriō, centuriōnis, *m.*, centurion, *non-commissioned officer in Roman army, commanding 60–100 men, a "century." (There were six centuries to a cohort.)*

cernō, cernere, crēvī, crētum, separate, distinguish; perceive, see clearly

certāmen, certāminis, *n.*, strife, struggle

certē, *adv.*, certainly, at least

certus, -a, -um, certain, reliable, sure, fixed; **certiōrem facere,** to inform (*acc. and inf.*); **certior fierī,** to be informed

cervīx, cervīcis, *f.*, neck

cervus, -ī, *m.*, stag, deer

cessō, *I*, stop, cease from, be lax, hesitate

cēterī, -ae, -a, *pron.*, the rest, the others; *adj.*, the remaining, the other, *m. and n. pl. as subst.*, everybody, everything else

Cethēgus, -ī, *m.*, Cethegus, *a Roman cognomen*

cibus, -ī, *m.*, food

Cicerō, Cicerōnis, *m.*, Cicero, *a Roman cognomen. In particular,* (1) M. Tullius Cicero (*106–43 B.C.*), *consul 63 B.C., distinguished author, lawyer, orator, and politician;* (2) Quintus Tullius Cicero, *brother of* (1), *and one of Caesar's officers in Gaul.*

circiter, *adv.*, about, approximately

circuitus, circuitūs, *m.*, circumference, circuit

circum, *prep. w. acc.*, around, about

circumcircā, *adv.*, all around, on every side

circumdō, -dare, -dedī, datum, put around, surround

circumeō, -īre, -iī, -itum, go around, visit

circummūniō, *IV*, wall around, enclose

circumsistō, -sistere, -stetī, — -, stand around; surround

circumveniō, circumvenīre, circumvēnī, circumventum, surround; ensnare, ruin

citerior, citerius, *comp. adj.*, hither, nearer; *superlative*, **citimus, -a, -um,** nearest

citimus, -a, -um, *see* **citerior**

citius, *compar. of the adv.*, **cito,** quickly

citō, *I*, set in rapid motion, spur

citrō, *adv.*, hither; **ultrō citrōque,** back and forth

cīvis, cīvis, *gen. pl.* **cīvium,** *c.*, citizen

cīvitās, cīvitātis, *f.*, clan; state; canton

clam, *adv.*, secretly

clāmitō, *I*, shout out, cry aloud, howl; *an intensive form of*

clāmō, *I*, shout

clāmor, clāmōris, *m.*, shouting, din

clārē, *adv.*, clearly, distinctly

clārus, -a, -um, clear; famous, distinguished

classis, classis, *gen. pl.* classium, *f.*, fleet; class

claudō, claudere, clausī, clausum, close, shut

clēmentia, -ae, *f.*, mercy

cliēns, clientis, *gen. pl.* clientium *and* clientum, *m.*, client, vassal, dependent

Clōdius, Clōdī, *m.*, Clodius, *a Roman name*

Cluentius, Cluentī, *m.*, Cluentius, *a Roman name*

Cn., *abbreviation for* Gnaeus

cōdicillī, -ōrum, *m.*, small tablets, note book, short note

coeō, -īre, -īvī *or* iī, -itum, go *or* come together, unite, ally oneself

coepī, *defective verb, see appendix 54*, began

cōgitō, *I*, consider, think; plan

cognōscō, cognōscere, cognōvī, cognitum, learn (by inquiry), find out; cognitus, -a, -um, known, acknowledged, approved

cōgō, cōgere, coēgī, coāctum, bring together, collect; force, compel

cohibeō, -hibēre, -hibuī, -hibitum, hold in, restrain, check

cohors, cohortis, *gen. pl.* cohortium, *f.*, cohort, *a body of 400–600 soldiers.* (*There were ten cohorts to a legion.*)

colligō, colligere, collēgī, collēctum, gather together, acquire

collis, collis, *gen. pl.* collium, *m.*, hill

collocō, *I*, place, set into place

colloquium, colloquī, *n.*, talking together, conference

colloquor, colloquī, collocūtus sum, speak with, converse

colō, colere, coluī, cultum, cultivate, worship, respect

colōnus, -ī, *m.*, farmer, countryman

color, colōris, *m.*, color; complexion

columna, -ae, *f.*, column

comes, comitis, *m.*, comrade, companion, retainer

commeātus, commeātūs, *m.*, supplies, provisions; furlough

commemorō, *I*, relate, tell of

committō, committere, commīsī, commissum, join; proelium committere, to join or begin battle; *w. acc. and dat.*, entrust (*a thing to a person*)

commodē, *adv.*, conveniently, suitably; well

commodum, -ī, *n.*, advantage

commodus, -a, -um, convenient, suitable

commoror, *I*, wait, stop

commoveō, commovēre, commōvī, commōtum, move, stir, excite

commūnicō, *I*, share, communicate (cum + *abl.*)

commūnis, commūne, *adj.*, common, general

commūtātiō, commūtātiōnis, *f.*, change

commūtō, *I*, change *or* alter completely; exchange

comparō, *I*, compare, set in pairs, liken (cum + pār); furnish; buy

compellō, -pellere, -pulī, pulsum, drive together, collect

comperiō, comperīre, comperī,

compertum, find out with certainty, discover, learn

compēscō, compēscere, compēscuī, ——, restrain, check, smother

compleō, complēre, complēvī, complētum, fill up; finish

complexus, -ūs, *m.,* embrace

complūrēs, complūra *or* **complūria,** *gen. pl.* **complurium,** several together, very many

compōnō, compōnere, composuī, compositum, put together

comportō, *I,* bring together; collect

comprobō, *I,* approve, sanction, justify

computō, *I,* reckon, calculate

cōnātum, -ī, *n.,* (*n. of* **cōnātus,** *perf. partic. of* **cōnor;** *here used with passive meaning*), attempt

cōnātus, cōnātūs, *m.,* attempt

concēdō, concēdere, concessī, concessum, retire, give up, yield; admit, concede

concertō, *I,* strive

concidō, concidere, concidī, ——, fall utterly, collapse

conciliō, *I,* win over, reconcile

concilium, concilī, *n.,* assembly, meeting, council

conclāmō, *I,* shout, call aloud

concurrō, -currere, -currī, -cursum, run together; run to the rescue

concursus, -ūs, *m.,* a running together; tumult

condemnō, *I,* pronounce guilty, condemn

condiciō, condiciōnis, *f.,* condition; terms

condō, condere, condidī, conditum, found; store away

condūcō, condūcere, condūxī, conductum, lead *or* bring together, assemble; hire

cōnferō, cōnferre, contulī, collātum, bring together, compare; *with* **sē,** betake oneself, apply oneself; employ

cōnfestim, *adv.,* promptly

cōnfertus, -a, -um, packed close together, in close order

cōnficiō, cōnficere, cōnfēcī, cōnfectum, complete, execute, make ready, accomplish; use up, exhaust; write; *in passive,* be exhausted, be overcome; *p.p.p. as adj.,* "done in," "done for," "done with"

cōnfīdō, cōnfīdere, cōnfīsus sum, trust completely, rely on (*w. dat., sec. 218*)

cōnfirmō, *I,* establish, reassure; affirm, declare

cōnfiteor, cōnfitērī, cōnfessus sum, confess

cōnflīgō, -flīgere, -flīxī, -flīctum, strike together; clash, struggle

congredior, congredī, congressus sum, meet with, meet in battle

coniciō, conicere, coniēcī, coniectum, hurl, throw, cast, put

coniungō, -iungere, -iūnxī, -iūnctum, join together

coniūrātiō, coniūrātiōnis, *f.,* conspiracy

coniūrō, *I,* conspire, plot

coniūrātus, -ī, *m.,* conspirator, plotter

cōnor, *I,* attempt, endeavor, try

conquīrō, conquīrere, conquīsīvī, conquīsītum, seek for carefully; hunt up, collect

cōnscīscere sibi mortem, to commit suicide

cōnscrībō, cōnscrībere, cōnscrīpsī, cōnscrīptum, levy, enrol, enlist; **patrēs cōnscrīptī,** the Senate

cōnsentiō, cōnsentīre, cōnsēnsī, cōnsēnsum, agree together, make an agreement; unite, combine

cōnsequor, cōnsequī, cōnsecūtus sum, follow up; overtake, attain

cōnservō, I, save, spare, protect; preserve, maintain

cōnsīderō, I, consider, ponder

cōnsīdō, -sīdere, -sēdī, -sessum, sit down, settle; encamp

cōnsilium, cōnsilī, n., plan; ability, counsel, advice, wisdom; eō cōnsiliō ut and subj., with the intention of . . .

cōnsistō, cōnsistere, cōnstitī, ——, take a stand, keep one's position, stop, halt; (of ships) ride at anchor

cōnspectus, cōnspectūs, m., sight, view; presence

cōnspiciō, cōnspicere, cōnspēxī, cōnspectum, get sight of, catch a glimpse of

cōnspicor, I, catch sight of, perceive

cōnstāns, adj., gen. constantis, steadfast, unswerving

cōnstantia, -ae, f., firmness, steadfastness, strength of mind

cōnstat, vb. used impersonally, it is agreed, it is evident (that), with acc. and inf.

cōnstituō, cōnstituere, cōnstituī, cōnstitūtum, set up; appoint, set; decide, determine

cōnstruō, cōnstruere, cōnstrūxī, cōnstrūctum, build up, put together

cōnsuēscō, cōnsuēscere, cōnsuēvī, cōnsuētum, become accustomed

cōnsuētūdō, cōnsuētūdinis, f., practice, custom, mode of life

cōnsul, cōnsulis, m., consul (title of the two chief magistrates of Rome, originally chosen annually)

cōnsulātus, cōnsulātūs, m., consulship

cōnsulō, cōnsulere, cōnsuluī, cōnsultum, consult (w. acc.); look out for, act in the interests of (w. dat.)

cōnsultum, -ī, n., decree; senātūs cōnsultum, decree of the senate

cōnsūmō, cōnsūmere, cōnsūmpsī, cōnsūmptum, take all at once; consume; use up; waste

contemnō, contemnere, contempsī, contemptum, despise

contendō, contendere, contendī, contentum, fight, contend, strive, hasten

contentiō, contentiōnis, f., striving, contest, dispute

conticēscō, conticēscere, conticuī, ——, become silent

continēns, continentis, f., mainland, continent; Europe (abl. -e and -ī)

continenter, adv., continuously

contineō, continēre, continuī, contentum, keep together, keep in, restrain; sē continēre with abl., to remain on or in

continuō, adv., immediately, forthwith

continuus, -a, -um, unbroken, uninterrupted

contrā, prep. w. acc., against

contrārius, -a, -um, contrary, opposite

contrōversia, -ae, f., dispute, quarrel

contumēlia, -ae, f., insult, affront, reproach

conveho, convehere, convexi, convectum, carry together, gather, collect

convenio, convenire, conveni, conventum, come together, meet

conventus, conventus, *m.,* a coming together, assembly

conversus, -a, -um, *perf. pass. partic.* of **converto,** turning around, wheeling about

converto, -vertere, -verti, -versum, turn around

convinco, convincere, convici, convictum; prove; prove guilty; refute

convoco, *I,* call together, summon, assemble

coörior, coöriri, coörtus sum, arise, spring up

copia, -ae, *f.,* fulness, material, wealth, supplies, abundance; *pl.* troops

cor, cordis, *n.,* heart

Corinthus, -i, *f.,* Corinth, *a seaport city of Greece*

cornu, cornus, *n.,* horn; flank, wing (*of an army*)

corpus, corporis, *n.,* body

corripio, corripere, corripui, correptum, seize, snatch

cotidianus, -a, -um, daily, of each day

cotidie, *adv.,* daily, each day

cras, *adv.,* tomorrow

Crassus, -i, *m.,* Crassus, *a Roman cognomen of the clan Licinii. In particular, M. Licinius Crassus (died, 53 B.C.), triumvir and capitalist.*

creber, crebra, crebrum, thick, frequent, close, at short intervals; numerous

credo, credere, credidi, creditum, believe (*w. dat., sec. 218*); entrust, lend (*acc. and dat.*)

Creta, -ae, *f.,* Crete, *an island in the S. E. Mediterranean, about the size of Long Island*

Cretensis, -e, *adj.,* Cretan, of Crete

cruciatus, -us, *m.,* torture, agony

crudeliter, *adv.,* cruelly *from* **crudelis**

cubiculum, -i, *n.,* bedroom

culpa, -ae, *f.,* blame, fault

culpo, *I,* blame

cultura, -ae, *f.,* cultivation; **agri cultura,** agriculture

cultus, cultus, *m.,* cultivation, care, attention to; civilization; respect; worship

cultus, -a, -um, cultivated

cum, *conj.,* when, as, while; after, as soon as; whenever (*with indic.*); since, because (*with subj.*); although (*with subj.*); **cum primum,** as soon as

cum, *prep. w. abl.,* with, together with (*secs. 102 and 136*)

cunctatio, -onis, *f.,* delay

cunctor, *I,* delay, hesitate (*from caution or indecision*)

cupiditas, cupiditatis, *f.,* desire

cupidus, -a, -um, desirous, eager

cupio, cupere, cupivi, cupitum, long for, be eager for; desire

cur, *interrog. adv.,* why?

cura, -ae, *f.,* care, worry

curo, *I,* take care of; *with gerundive,* have (*a thing*) done

curro, currere, cucurri, cursum, run

cursus, cursus, *m.,* course, career

custodiae, -arum, *f. pl.,* guard

custos, custodis, *m.,* guard, spy

Cyprus, -i, *f.,* Cyprus, *an island in the N.E. corner of the Mediterranean*

D

D sign for **quīngentī,** five hundred (*formed from half of M, sign for a thousand*)

damnum, -nī, *n.,* loss, injury

Danaī, -ōrum, *m. pl.,* the Greeks

dē, *prep. w. abl.,* from, down from; about, concerning

dēbeō, dēbēre, dēbuī, dēbitum, owe; *with infinitive,* ought, must; *passive,* be due

dēcēdō, dēcēdere, dēcessī, dēcessum, go from, withdraw

decem, *card. num. adj.,* ten

dēcernō, dēcernere, dēcrēvī, dēcrētum, decide; vote, decree

dēcertō, *I,* fight it out; struggle fiercely

decimus, -a, -um, *ord. num. adj.,* tenth

dēclīvis, -e, sloping down; steep

decōrus, -a, -um, suitable, fitting

dēcrētum, -ī, *n.,* decision, decree, order

dēcurrō, dēcurrere, dēcucurrī, dēcursum, run down

dēditiō, dēditiōnis, *f.,* surrender

dēdō, dēdere, dēdidī, dēditum, give up, abandon, surrender

dēdūcō, dēdūcere, dēdūxī, dēductum, lead down *or* away; *w.* **nāvem,** launch

dēfatīgō, *I,* tire out, exhaust, fatigue; *in passive,* grow weary

dēfectiō, -ōnis, *f.,* desertion, revolt

dēfendō, dēfendere, dēfendī, dēfēnsum, ward off, repel; defend, protect

dēfēnsor, dēfēnsōris, *m.,* defender, protector

dēferō, dēferre, dētulī, dēlātum, report, bestow, confer

dēfessus, -a, -um, tired out, thoroughly exhausted

dēficiō, dēficere, dēfēcī, dēfectum, fail, desert, fall away from those by whom I have hitherto stood (*with ab or acc.*), revolt

dēgō, dēgere, dēgī, ——, spend *or* pass (*of time*)

dēiciō, dēicere, dēiēcī, dēiectum, throw down; disappoint

deinde, *adv.,* thereupon, then, next

dēlectō, *I,* delight (*trans.*); *passive* (*w. abl.*), take pleasure (*in*)

dēleō, dēlēre, dēlēvī, dēlētum, destroy

dēlīberō, *I,* deliberate; take counsel

dēlictum, -ī, *n.,* fault, offense

dēligō, dēligere, dēlēgī, dēlēctum, pick out, choose

dēlīrō, *I,* act insanely, rave

Delphī, -ōrum, *m.,* Delphi, *a small town in Phocis, Greece, famous as the seat of Apollo's oracle*

dēmēns, *adj., gen.* **dēmentis,** insane

dēmittō, dēmittere, dēmīsī, dēmissum, let down, lower

Dēmocritus, -ī, *m.,* Democritus, *Greek philosopher (460–361 B.C.), founder of atomic theory*

dēmōnstrō, *I,* point out

dēmulceō, dēmulcēre, dēmulsī, dēmulsum, soothe, stroke; *with* **linguā,** lick

dēmum, *adv.,* at length, at last, finally

dēnārius, dēnārī, *m.,* Roman silver penny, *worth about seventeen cents*

dēnique, *adv.,* and then, thereupon, finally, at last; at least

dēpellō, dēpellere, dēpulī, dēpulsum, drive away

dēpōnō, dēpōnere, dēposui, dēpositum, lay aside; give up dēpopulō, *and* -or, *I*, lay waste, pillage; destroy

dēportō, *I*, carry away

dēprōmō, dēprōmere, dēprōmpsī, dēprōmptum, draw forth, take out

dērīdeō, dērīdēre, dērīsī, dērīsum, laugh at, make fun of, deride

dēscendō, dēscendere, dēscendī, dēscēnsum, go down; have recourse; resort

dēserō, dēserere, dēseruī, dēsertum, quit, desert, forsake; *p.p.p. as adj.*, deserted, solitary

dēsīderium, dēsīderī, *n.*, longing, desire

dēsīderō, *I*, miss, long for, desire

dēsiliō, dēsilīre, dēsiluī, dēsultum, leap down from

dēsinō, dēsinere, dēsiī, ——, cease, stop

dēsistō, dēsistere, dēstitī, dēstitum, abandon, cease, give up

dēsperō, *I*, give up hope; despair of

dēspiciō, dēspicere, dēspexī, dēspectum, look down upon, desire

dēsum, dēesse, dēfuī, dēfutūrus, fail to be present (*where presence is desirable or right*), be wanting, be lacking (*w. dat.*)

dēterreō, dēterrēre, dēterruī, dēterritum, frighten away; deter

dētrīmentum, -ī, *n.*, harm, loss

deus, -ī, *m.*, god, deity (*appendix, 2b*)

dēvehō, dēvehere, dēvēxī, dēvēctum, carry away, convey, transport

dēveniō, dēvenīre, dēvēnī, dēventum, come down; go, come

dēvincō, dēvincere, dēvīcī, dēvictum, conquer thoroughly

dēvorō, *I*, devour

dexter, dextra, dextrum, right

Diaulus, -ī, *m.*, Diaulus, *a man's name*

diciō, -ōnis, *f.*, rule, sway

dīcō, dīcere, dīxī, dictum, say, tell, speak

dictum, -ī, *n.*, saying

diēs, diēī, *m.* (*often f.*) day; ad diem, in time, promptly

differō, differre, distulī, dīlātum, *intr.*, be different, differ; *tr.*, scatter, spread; put off, postpone

difficilis, difficile, *adj.*, difficult

difficultās, difficultātis, *f.*, difficulty, trouble

diffīdō, diffīdere, diffīsus sum, distrust (*w. dat.*)

digitus, -ī, finger

dignitās, -tātis, *f.*, worthiness, dignity, position, rank

dignus, -a, -um, worthy, worthy of (*w. abl.*), *also followed by rel. cl. of characteristic*

dīligens, *adj.*, *gen.*, dīligentis, accurate, careful, economical

dīligenter, *adv.*, diligently; conscientiously

dīligentia, -ae, *f.*, carefulness, industry, diligence

dīligō, dīligere, dīlēxī, dīlectum, single out; esteem highly, be fond of (*with less warmth than* amō)

dīmicō, *I*, fight, struggle

dīmidium, dīmidī, *n.*, half

dīmittō, dīmittere, dīmīsī, dīmissum, send away, dismiss, disband

Diodōrus, Diodōrī, *m.*, Diodorus, *a Sicilian historian of Caesar's time.*

Dionȳsius, Dionȳsī, *m.*, Dionysius, *tyrant of Syracuse 405-367 B.C.*

dīrigo, -rigere, -rēxī, -rēctum, direct, guide

dirimō, dirimere, dirēmī, dirēmptum, break off, put an end to

dīripiō, -ripere, -ripuī, -reptum, tear apart

discēdō, discēdere, discessī, discessum, depart, go away, retire

discessus, -ūs, *m.*, departure

disciplīna, -ae, *f.*, training

discō, discere, didicī, ——, learn, be taught

discrīmen, discrīminis, *n.*, crisis, danger

dispergō, dispergere, dispersī, dispersum, scatter

displiceō, displicēre, displicuī, displicitum, displease (*dat.*)

dispōnō, dispōnere, disposuī, dispositum, place apart, distribute, station (at intervals)

dissentiō, dissentīre, dissēnsī, dissēnsum, disagree (ā + *abl*)

disserō, disserere, disseruī, ——, discuss

dissimilis, dissimile, *adj.*, unlike

dissimulō, *I*, dissimulate, pretend (*that a thing is not so*), dissemble

diū, *adv.*, for a long time

diūturnitās, diūturnitātis, *f.*, long duration

diūturnus, -a, -um, lasting, enduring

dīversus, -a, -um, different

dīves, *adj.*, *gen.* dīvitis, *abl.* dīvite; *gen. pl.* dīvitum, rich (*see app. 11*)

Dīviciācus, -ī, *m.*, Diviciacus, a *Haeduan chief*

dīvidō, dīvidere, dīvīsī, dīvīsum, divide, separate

dīvitiae, -ārum, *f. pl.*, riches

dīvus, -a, -um, divine; *masc. as noun,* a god

dō, dare, dedī, datum (*see app. 47*), give

doceō, docēre, docuī, doctum, show, teach, instruct, inform, demonstrate; *p.p.p. as adj.*, learned, wise

doctrīna, -ae, *f.*, learning, training

doleō, dolēre, doluī, dolitūrus, *intr.*, be in pain; *trans.*, grieve for

dolor, dolōris, *m.*, grief, distress, pain

domesticus, -a, -um, internal, domestic

domina, -ae, *f.*, mistress, lady

dominātiō, dominātiōnis, *f.*, mastery

dominor, *I*, be lord and master, rule

dominus, -ī, *m.*, master, owner

Domitius, Domitī, *m.*, Domitius, a *Roman name*

domus, domūs, *f.* (*declined in sec. 151*), home; domum, homeward; domī, at home

dōnec, *conj.*, until, while, as long as

dōnō, *I*, present, give

dōnum, -ī, *n.*, gift

dormiō, *IV*, sleep

Druentia, -ae, *f.*, a river of Gallia *Narbonensis, now* the Durance

Druidēs, Druidum, *m.*, Druids, *priests of the ancient Gauls and Britons*

dubitō, *I*, *intr.*, hesitate, delay; be uncertain, doubt (*see sec. 273*)

ducentī, -ae, -a, *card. num. adj.*, two hundred

dūcō, dūcere, dūxī, ductum, lead, bring; consider

dulcis, -e, *adj.*, sweet, pleasant

dum, *conj.*, while, as long as; until

dummodo, dum . . . modo, *conj.*, provided that (*with subjunctive*)

Dumnorīx, -rīgis, *m.*, Dumnorix, a *Haeduan chieftain*

duo, duae, duo, *card. num. adj.*, two

duodecim, *card. num. adj.*, twelve

duodecimus, -a, -um, *ord. num. adj.*, twelfth

duodēvīgintī, *card. num. adj.*, eighteen

duplex, *adj., gen.* duplicis, double, two-fold (duo *plus* plicō, fold)

dūrus, -a, -um, hard

dux, ducis, *m.*, leader, commander, general

E

ē (*only before consonants*), ex (*before vowels and some consonants*), *prep. w. abl.*, out of, from, away from; after, since; out of, because of

ecquī, ecquae, ecquod, *interrog. adj.*, any?

ēdīcō, ēdīcere, ēdīxī, ēdictum, declare, proclaim; order

ēditus, -a, -um, *adj.* (*p.p.p. of* ēdō), raised up, elevated, lofty

edō, ēsse, ēdī, ēsum, eat

ēdūcō, ēdūcere, ēdūxī, ēductum, lead out

effēminō, *I*, make womanish; make soft, enervate

efferō, efferre, extulī, ēlātum, carry away; elate

efficiō, efficere, effēcī, effectum, make, cause, bring about

effugiō, effugere, effūgī, ——, flee from *or* away, escape

ego, meī, *pers. pron.*, I; *pl.* nōs, we

egomet, *pers. pron.*, I, *emphatic for* ego, I myself; I (for my part)

ēgredior, ēgredī, ēgressus sum, go out

ēgregius, -a, -um, distinguished, remarkable, illustrious

ēiciō, ēicere, ēiēcī, ēiectum, cast *or* drive out, expel

ēlābor, ēlābī, ēlāpsus sum, slip away, escape

elephans, -ntis, *gen. pl.* elephantium, *m.*, elephant

elephantus, -ī, *m.*, elephant

ēligo, -ligere, -lēgī, -lectum, pick out, choose

ēloquentia, -ae, *f.*, eloquence

ēloquor, ēloquī, ēlocūtus sum, speak out

ēmineō, ēminēre, ēminuī, ——, project, jut out

emō, emere, ēmī, ēmptum, buy

ēmorior, ēmorī, ēmortuus sum, die away, die

ēmptor, ēmptōris, *m.*, buyer

enim, *conj.* (*never first word in sentence*), for

ēnītor, ēnītī, ēnīsus sum, strive, work one's way out with effort

Ennius, Ennī, *m.*, Quintus Ennius (*239–169 B.C.*), *styled the* "father of Roman poetry"

eō, īre, iī (*and* īvī), itum (*see appendix 53*), go

eō, *adv.*, thither, to that place

eōdem, *adv.*, to the same place

Ephesus, -ī, *f.*, Ephesus, *Ionian seaport on the west coast of Asia Minor*

Epidamnus, -ī, *f.*, Epidamnus, *a Greek city on the Adriatic*

epigramma, epigrammatis, *n.*, epigram

epistula, -ae, *f.*, letter, epistle

equa, -ae, *dat. and abl. pl.* equābus, *f.*, mare

eques, equitis, *m.*, trooper, cavalryman; knight

equidem, *adv.*, for my part, as far as I am concerned

equitātus, equitātūs, *m.*, cavalry

equus, -ī, *m.*, horse

ērādīcō, *I*, take up by the roots; destroy

ergā, *prep. with acc.*, toward (*of feelings*)

ergo, *conj.*, therefore

ērigō, ērigere, ērēxī, ērēctum, raise up

ēripiō, ēripere, ēripuī, ēreptum, snatch away from

errō, *I*, wander, roam; make a mistake

ērudiō, *IV*, instruct; *p.p.p. as adj.*, ērudītus, -a, -um, erudite, learned

essedārius, -rī, *m.*, charioteer

essedum, -ī, *n.*, two-wheeled (*war*) chariot (*of the Britons*)

et, *conj.*, and; et . . . et, both . . . and

etenim, et enim, *conj.*, for . . . you see

etiam, *conj.*, and also, also, even, yet; nōn modo . . . sed etiam, not only . . . but also

etiamsī, *conj.*, even if, although

etsī, *conj.*, even if, although

ēvādō, ēvādere, ēvāsī, ēvāsum, escape

ēveniō, ēvenīre, ēvēnī, ēventum, come out, turn out, happen; *used impersonally*, ēvenit, it happens (that) + ut + *subjunctive*

ēvolō, *I*, fly *or* rush forth

ex, *prep. w. abl.*, out of, from

exanimō, *I*, kill; *p.p.p. as adj.*, exanimātus, -a, -um, out of breath; lifeless

exanimis, -e, *adj.*, breathless; lifeless, dead

exardēscō, exardēscere, exarsī, exarsum, blaze out, flame up

excēdō, excēdere, excessī, exces-

sum, go out, withdraw, retire

excellēns, *adj., gen.* excellentis, eminent, distinguished

excidō, -cidere, -cidī, ——, *intr.*, fall out, drop, be lost, disappear

excipiō, excipere, excēpi, exceptum, receive; take out; except

excitō, *I*, arouse, waken

exclūdō, -clūdere, -clūsī, -clūsum, shut out

excrucior, *I*, be on the rack, be in pain

excūsātiō, -ōnis, *f.*, excuse, plea

excūsō, *I*, justify, excuse; sē exc., apologize; allege in excuse

exemplum, -ī, *n.*, example, precedent

exeō, exīre, exiī, exitum, go out, depart, leave

exerceō, exercēre, exercuī, exercitum, train, practise; manage, administer

exercitātiō, -ōnis, *f.*, training

exercitus, exercitūs, *m.*, army

exigō, exigere, exēgī, exāctum, demand; pass, spend

exiguē, *adv.*, sparingly; briefly

exiguus, -a, -um, short, small

exilium, *see* exsilium

eximius, -a, -um, exceptional

exīstimō, *I*, estimate, think, consider

exitium, -tī, *n.*, destruction, disaster, havoc

exitus, -ūs, *m.*, outcome, end

exorior, exorīrī, exortus sum, rise

exortus, -ūs, *m.*, a coming forth, rising, sōlis exortus, the east

expedio, *IV*, free, make free

expedītiō, -ōnis, *f.*, march *or* expedition

expellō, expellere, expulī, expulsum, drive out

experior, experīrī, expertus sum,
try, test, experience

expetō, expetere, expetīvī *or* **expetiī, expetītum,** seek out

explōrātor, explōrātōris, *m.,* scout

explōrō, *I,* find out, search

expōnō, expōnere, exposuī, expositum, put *or* set out; explain

exportō, *I,* carry out *or* away

expugnō, *I,* take by storm, overpower, sack

exsequor, exsequī, exsecūtus sum,
follow out, perform, execute

exsiliō, -īre, -siluī, -sultum, leap forth

exsilium, exsilī, *n.,* exile

exsistō, -sistere, -stitī, -stitum,
stand forth, appear; ensue

exspectō, *I,* wait for, wait

exstinguō, exstinguere, exstīnxī, exstīnctum, quench, destroy; put out

exstō, exstāre, ——, ——, stand out, rise above, project; appear

exstruō, -struere, -strūxī, -structum, pile up, build

extemplō, *adv.,* on this instant, at once (*from* **tempulum,** a diminutive of **tempus**)

externus, -a, -um, foreign, external

exterus, -a, -um, outside; *comp.*
exterior, exterius, outer, exterior; *superl.* **extrēmus, -a, -um, extimus, -a, -um,** outermost, farthest, extreme, last

extimēscō, extimēscere, extimuī, ——, dread; be afraid

extimus, -a, -um, *see* **exterus**

extrā, *adv. and prep. with acc.,*
outside, outside of, beyond

extrēmus, -a, -um, *see* **exterus**

extrīnsecus, *adv.,* on the outside

exūrō, -ūrere, -ussī, -ustum, burn up

F

faber, fabrī, *m.,* craftsman, fashioner

Fabius, Fabī, *m.,* Fabius, *name of a Roman clan. In particular,* Quintus Fabius Maximus (Cunctator), *dictator 217 B.C.*

fābula, -ae, *f.,* tale, story; play

facile, *adv.,* easily, readily

facilis, facile, *adj.,* easy

facinus, facinoris, *n.,* deed; misdeed

faciō, facere, fēcī, factum, do, make; **iter faciō,** march

factiō, factiōnis, *f.,* faction, political party

factum, -ī, *n.,* thing done; deed, achievement

facultās, facultātis, *f.,* opportunity

fācundus, -a, -um, eloquent

fallō, fallere, fefellī, falsus, cheat, deceive, escape the notice of

falsō, *adv.,* falsely, without foundation *or* reason

falsus, -a, -um, false

fāma, -ae, *f.,* rumor, report, reputation (good or bad)

famēs, famis, *f.,* hunger, starvation

familia, -ae, *f.,* household

familiāris, familiāre, *adj.,* belonging to the household, domestic, private; *as noun,* intimate friend; **rēs f.,** property, estate

fānum, -ī, *n.,* temple, shrine

fās, *n., indecl.,* right

fascis, fascis, *gen. pl.* **fascium,** *m.,* bundle

fatīgō, *I,* tire, wear out, exhaust

fātum, -ī, *n.,* fate; death (*especially in plural*)

faveō, favēre, fāvī, fautum, be fa-

vorable to, favor (*w. dat., sec.*
218)

fēlīcitās, fēlīcitātis, *f.,* luck; good
luck, fortune

fēlīciter, *adv.,* happily, luckily, successfully

fēlis, -is, *gen. pl.* **fēlium,** *f.,* cat

fēlix, *adj., gen.* **fēlicis,** lucky, fortunate

fēmina, -ae, *f.,* woman

fera, -ae, *f.,* wild animal

ferē, *adv.,* almost, nearly, more or
less, about

ferō, ferre, tulī, lātum, bear, bring;
bear, endure; bear news, tell,
report; **ferre pedem,** stir one's
foot, go *or* come

ferreus, -a, -um, of iron

ferrum, -ī, *n.,* iron

fertilis, -e, fertile

ferus, -a, -um, fierce, savage

fervēns, *adj., gen.* **ferventis,** hot

fessus, -a, -um, weary, tired

fidēlis, -e, faithful, trustworthy,
reliable, loyal

Fīdentīnus, -ī, *m.,* Fidentinus, *a
Roman name*

fidēs, fideī, *f.,* faith, trust, loyalty;
credit

fīdō, fīdere, fīsus sum, have faith
in, trust (*w. dat., sec. 218*)

fīdūcia, -ae, *f.,* confidence, trust,
reliance

fīdus, -a, -um, loyal, faithful;
comp., none; superl. **fīdissimus,
-a, -um,** most faithful

fīgō, fīgere, fīxī, fīxum, fasten;
pierce

figūra, -ae, *f.,* form, shape, figure

fīlia, -ae, *dat. and abl. pl.* **fīliābus,**
f., daughter

fīliola, -ae, little daughter (*diminutive of* **fīlia**)

fīlius, fīlī, *vocative* **fīlī,** *m.,* son

fingō, fingere, fīnxī, fictum, pretend, feign; fashion

fīniō, *I V,* set limits to, bound

fīnis, fīnis, *gen. pl.* **fīnium,** *m.,* end;
boundary, limit, border; *plural,
also* territory; frontier

fīnitimus, -a, -um, neighboring

fīō, fierī, factus sum, *passive of*
faciō (*see appendix 52*)

fīrmus, -a, -um, strong, firm

flamma, -ae, *f.,* flame

flammeus, -a, -um, fiery

fleō, flēre, flēvī, flētum, weep,
lament

flōreō, flōrēre, flōruī, ——, be in
flower, flourish

flōs, flōris, *m.,* flower

flūctus, -ūs, *m.,* wave

flūmen, flūminis, *n.,* river

fluō, fluere, flūxī, ——, flow

foedus, -a, -um, disgraceful, foul

foedus, foederis, *n.,* a treaty

folium, folī, *n.,* leaf

forās, *adv.,* towards the out-of-
doors; forth, out (*acc. form from
obsolete* **fora**)

forīs, *adv.,* abroad (*antonym of*
domī)

forma, -ae, *f.,* shape, beauty

formōsus, -a, -um, fair of form,
beautiful

fors, fortis, *f.,* chance, *abl.* **forte,**
as *adv.,* by chance, as it hap-
pened

forsitan, fors sit an, *adv.,* there
would be a chance that; perhaps

fortasse, *adv.,* perhaps, possibly

fortis, forte, *adj.,* powerful, brave,
manly

fortiter, *adv.,* bravely

fortitūdō, fortitūdinis, *f.,* bravery,
courage

fortūna, -ae, *f.,* luck, fortune, change

fortūnātus, -a, -um, blessed by fortune, lucky, fortunate

forum, -ī, *n.,* forum, marketplace, public square

fossa, -ae, *f.,* ditch, moat

frangō, frangere, frēgī, frāctum, to break

frāter, frātris, *m.,* brother

frēnō, *I,* furnish with a bridle, bridle; check

frīgus, frigoris, *n.,* cold

frōns, frontis, *gen. pl.* **frontium,** *f.,* forehead, front

frūctus, -ūs, *m.,* fruit; reward; revenue

frūgālis, -e, *adj.,* thrifty

frūmentārius, -a, -um, relating to grain, *esp.* res *f.,* grain supply

frūmentor, *I,* get grain, forage

frūmentum, -ī, *n.,* grain

fruor, fruī, frūctus sum (*used with ablative*), enjoy

frūstrā, *adv.,* in vain (*of the person who fails in his object*)

fuga, -ae, *f.,* flight

fugāx, *adj., gen.* **fugācis,** apt to flee; swift, fleeting, transitory

fugiō, fugere, fūgī, fugitūrus, *intr.,* flee, escape; *trans.,* flee from, escape from

fugō, *I,* put to flight, rout; chase

fulmen, fulminis, *n.,* lightning

funditor, -ōris, *m.,* slinger

fundō, fundere, fūdī, fūsum, pour out

fungor, fungī, fūnctus sum (*used with ablative*), perform, execute, discharge

fūnis, fūnis, *gen. pl.* **fūnium,** *m.,* rope, cable

furō, furere, furuī, ——, be mad, rave, be madly eager

furor, furōris, *m.,* fury, rage

G

Gāius, Gāī, *m.,* Gaius, *a Roman praenomen*

Galba, -ae, *m.,* Galba, *Roman cognomen. In particular,* the Emperor Galba (*A.D. 69*).

Gallia, -ae, *f.,* Gaul

Gallicus, -ī, *m.,* Gallicus, *a Roman name*

gallus, -ī, *m.,* cock

Gallus, -ī, *m.,* a Gaul, an inhabitant of Gaul

gaudeō, gaudēre, gāvīsus sum, be glad, rejoice

gaudium, gaudī, *n.,* joy

gemma, -ae, *f.,* bud; precious stone, jewel

gena, -ae, *f.* (*usually in plural*), cheek

Genava, -ae, *f.,* Genava, *a city of the Allobroges, now* Geneva

gēns, gentis, *gen. pl.* **gentium,** *f.,* race; clan, tribe

genus, generis, *n.,* origin, descent; class, family; kind

Germānia, -ae, *f.,* Germany, *in ancient times all the country east of the Rhine*

Germānus, -ī, *m.,* a German, an inhabitant of Germany

gerō, gerere, gessī, gestum, manage, carry on, wage (*war*)

gignō, gignere, genuī, genitum, beget, produce

glaciēs, glaciēī, *f.,* ice

gladius, gladī, *m.,* sword

glōria, -ae, *f.,* glory, renown, fame

glōriōsus, -a, -um, glorious

Gracchus, -ī, *m.,* Gracchus, *a Ro-*

man cognomen. In particular, the brothers Ti. *and* C. *Sempronius Gracchus, tribunes 133 and 121 B.C. respectively.*

gracilis, gracile, *adj.,* slender

gradus, gradūs, *m.,* step, pace; two and a half Roman feet *or* half a **passus**; course

Graecē, *adv.,* in Greek

Graecia, -ae, *f.,* Greece

Graecus, -a, -um, Greek, of Greece

Graecus, -ī, *m.,* a Greek, an inhabitant of Greece

grātia, -ae, *f.,* favor, gratitude, esteem, influence, popularity; **grātiās agere,** to thank; **grātiam habēre,** to feel grateful; **grātiam referre,** return a favor

grātulor, *I,* congratulate (*dat.*)

grātus, -a, -um, pleasing, acceptable

gravis, grave, *adj.,* heavy; serious

-gredior, -gredī, -gressus sum, *in compounds for* **gradior,** step *or* go

gubernātor, -ōris, *m.,* governor; pilot

gutta, -ae, *f.,* drop (*of a liquid*)

H

habeō, habēre, habuī, habitum, have, hold; hold, regard, consider; **ōrātiōnem habēre,** to deliver a speech

habitō, *I,* dwell, live, reside

Haeduus, -ī, *m.,* a Haeduan, a member of the Gallic tribe of Haedui

Hannibal, Hannibalis, *m.,* Hannibal, *a Carthaginian general in the second Punic war, 218–202 B.C., one of the greatest military leaders of all time*

Hannō, Hannōnis, *m.,* Hanno, *a Carthaginian*

haruspex, haruspicis, *m.,* soothsayer

hasta, -ae, *f.,* spear

Helvētia, -ae, *f.,* Helvetia, the country of the Helvetians

Helvētius, -a, -um, of the Helvetii, Helvetian; *masc. as noun,* one of the Helvetii

heri, *adv.,* yesterday

hesternus, -a, -um, of yesterday

hīberna, hībernōrum, *n.,* winter quarters

Hibernia, -ae, *f.,* Ireland

hic, haec, hoc, *gen.* **huius,** *dem. pron.* (*see secs. 127 and 128*), this (*near me*); he, she, it; *as correlative of* **ille,** the latter

hīc, *adv.,* here, in this place

hiemō, *I,* spend the winter

hiems, hiemis, *f.,* winter

hinc, *adv.,* hence

Hispānia, -ae, *f.,* Spain

historia, -ae, *f.,* history

hodiē, *adv.,* today

Homērus, -ī, *m.,* Homer

homō, hominis, *m.,* a human being, man

honestē, *adv.,* honorably

honestus, -a, -um, honorable

honor (honōs), honōris, *m.,* distinction, dignity, honor; office

hōra, -ae, *f.,* hour

Horātius, Horātī, *m.,* Horace, *name of a Roman clan. In particular,* the poet Horace (*65–8 B.C.*).

horribilis, -e, *adj.,* horrible

hortor, *I,* urge, encourage

hortus, -ī, *m.,* garden

hospes, hospitis, *m.,* guest; stranger

hospitium, -ī, *n.,* hospitality

hostis, hostis, *gen. pl.* hostium, *m.*, enemy, the enemy (*usually in pl.*)

hūc, *adv.*, to this place, hither

hūmānitās, hūmānitātis, *f.*, humanity, civilization; refinement

hūmānus, -a, -um, human, of man, civilized

humilis, humile, *adj.*, on the ground, low; lowly, meek

I

iaceō, iacēre, iacuī, ——, lie, rest

iaciō, iacere, iēcī, iactum, throw

iam, *adv.*, now, at this time already, by this time, at last; by and by; presently, nōn iam *or* iam nōn, neque iam, no longer

iam vērō, furthermore, and besides

Iānuārius, Iānuārī, *m.*, January

ibi, *adv.*, there, in that place

idcircō, *adv.*, for this reason, therefore

īdem, eadem, idem, *pron. and adj.* (*see sec. 199*), same

identidem, *adv.*, again and again, repeatedly

ideō, *adv.*, for this reason, therefore

idōneus, -a, -um, suitable

iēns, *gen.* euntis, *present participle of* eō

igitur, *conj.* (*never first word in sentence*), therefore, then, now, you see

ignārus, -a, -um, ignorant

ignis, ignis, *gen. pl.* ignium, *m.*, fire

ignōminia, -ae, *f.*, disgrace

ignōrō, *I*, not know, fail to make myself acquainted with (*opposed to* nōvī)

ignōscō, ignōscere, ignōvī, ignōtum, make excuses for, forgive (*w. dat., sec. 218*)

ille, illa, illud, *gen.* illīus, *dem. pron.* (*see secs. 127 and 128*), that (away from me), that yonder; he, she, it; *as postpositive*, the famous; *as correlative of* hic, the former

illō, *adv.*, thither, to that place

illūc, *adv.*, thither, to that place

illūstris, -e, bright; noble, distinguished, renowned

Illyricum, -ī, *n.*, Illyricum, *a country northwest of Greece along the Adriatic*

imāgō, imāginis, *f.*, copy, image, likeness; bust

imbēcillus, -a, -um, weak, feeble

immineō, imminēre, ——, ——, hang over; threaten

imitor, *I*, imitate

immisceō, -miscēre, -miscuī, -mixtum *or* mistum, mix in, blend; join, associate, intrude; sē immiscēre *with dative*, meddle in or with

immortālis, immortāle, *adj.*, immortal

impedīmentum, -ī, *n.*, hindrance

impediō, *IV*, hinder, prevent, delay

impendeō, -ēre, ——, ——, hang over, be near; threaten

impendō, impendere, impendī, impēnsum, pay to, give over to, devote (*w. acc. and dat., sec. 219b*)

imperātor, imperātōris, *m.*, commander-in-chief; general

imperātōrius, -a, -um, of a general

imperium, imperī, *n.*, military authority *or* power, supreme command; sovereignty, empire

imperō, *I*, *intr.*, command, order (*w. dat., sec. 218*); *tr.*, levy, assess (*a thing, acc., on a person, dat.*)

impetrō, *I*, obtain by entreaty, ask for and get

impetus, impetūs, *m.*, attack, charge

impōnō, impōnere, imposuī, impositum, place upon, impose (*w. acc. and dat., sec. 219b*)

importō, *I*, bring in, import

improbitās, improbitātis, *f.*, wickedness

improbus, -a, -um, unfair, unprincipled; *m. pl. as noun*, villains; obstructionists

impudenter, *adv.*, shamelessly, in a barefaced manner

īmus, -a, -um, *see* īnferus, -a, -um

in, *prep., w. abl.*, in, among, at, on; *w. acc.*, into, toward, against

inānis, ināne, *adj.*, empty, vain, idle

inaudītus, -a, -um, unheard of

inaurātus, -a, -um, gilded

incendium, -dī, *n.*, fire

incendō, -cendere, -cendī, -cēnsum, set fire to, burn, kindle

incēnātus, -a, -um (in + cēnō), unfed, without supper

incertus, -a, -um, uncertain; critical

incidō, -cidere, -cidī, -cāsum, fall into *or* upon; befall, happen

incipiō, incipere, incēpī, inceptum, begin

incitō, *I*, arouse, stir up

incognitus, -a, -um, unknown

incola, -ae, *c.*, inhabitant

incolō, incolere, incoluī, ——, inhabit, dwell in; live

incolumis, -e, *adj.*, unhurt, safe

incommodus, -a, -um, inconvenient, disagreeable; *neuter as noun*, inconvenience

incrēdibilis, incrēdibile, *adj.*, unbelievable, incredible

incrēdibiliter, *adv.*, extraordinarily, unbelievably

incūsō, *I*, tax with, charge with, find fault with (*informally*)

inde, *adv.*, thence, from that place

index, indicis, *m.*, pointer, mark, sign, proof

indīcō, indīcere, indīxī, indictum, proclaim publicly, appoint; bellum alicui ind., declare war on someone

indignor, *I*, be indignant

indulgeō, indulgēre, indulsī, ——, be kind to, indulge (*w. dat., sec. 218*)

industria, -ae, *f.*, diligence

ineō, inīre, iniī, initum, go into, enter upon, undertake; cōnsilium inīre, form a plan

ineptus, -a, -um, silly

inermis, inerme, *adj.*, unarmed

inertia, -ae, *f.*, idleness, indolence

inexōrābilis, inexōrābile, *adj.*, inexorable, implacable

īnferior, *see* īnferus

īnferō, īnferre, intulī, illātum, bear into, inflict, bellum īnferre alicui, to make war on someone

īnferus, -a, -um, low, under; *comp.* īnferior, īnferius, lower; *superl.* īnfimus, -a, -um, *or* īmus, -a, -um, lowest

īnfestus, -a, -um, hostile, dangerous, troublesome

īnficiō, -ficere, -fēcī, -fectum, work in; dye, stain

īnfimus, -a, -um, *see* īnferus

īnfīrmitās, īnfīrmitātis, *f.*, feebleness, unsteadiness, fickleness

īnfīrmus, -a, -um, weak, infirm

īnfluō, īnfluere, īnflūxī, īnflūxum, flow into

infodiō, -fodere, -fōdī, -fossum, dig or drive into

ingenium, ingenī, n., natural gifts (mostly intellectual), abilities

ingēns, adj., gen. **ingentis,** huge

ingrātus, -a, -um, unpleasant

inhibeō, -hibēre, -hibuī, -hibitum, hold in, restrain

iniciō, -icere, -iēcī, -iectum, throw into, place on; inspire, infuse (w. acc. and dat.)

inimīcus, -a, -um, unfriendly, hostile; masc. as noun, personal enemy

inīquus, -a, -um, uneven; unfair (not "on the level")

initium, initī, n., beginning

iniūria, -ae, f., wrong, injustice; outrage, injury; abl. as adv., wrongly, unfairly

innocentia, -ae, f., harmlessness, blamelessness, integrity, uprightness, disinterestedness (esp. as opposed to graft)

inopia, -ae, f., need, want, lack

inquam, inquis, inquit, inquiunt, defective verb (used only with direct quotations and following one or more words of the quotation), I say, you say, says he, they say

īnsānus, -a, -um, insane

īnscrībō, īnscrībere, īnscrīpsī, īnscrīptum, write on, inscribe (with acc. and dat.)

īnsequor, īnsequī, īnsecūtus sum, follow close upon, pursue

īnsidiae, -ārum, f. pl., ambush

īnsigne, īnsignis, gen. pl. **īnsignium,** n., mark, sign, token, symbol, decoration

īnsignis, -e, adj., distinguished, famous, remarkable

īnspērāns, adj., gen. **īnspērantis,** not hoping or expecting

īnsternō, -sternere, -strāvī, -strātum, cover over, spread over; saddle

īnstituō, instituere, īnstituī, īnstitūtum, arrange, order

īnstitūtum, -ī, n., fixed principle; habit, institution, custom

īnstō, -stāre, -stitī, ——, stand upon or near, be at hand; press on; threaten

īnstrūmentum, -ī, n., tool, equipment, appliance, engine

īnstruō, īnstruere, īnstrūxī, īnstrūctum, draw up

īnsula, -ae, f., island

īnsum, inesse, ——, īnfutūrus, be in, be present (w. in + abl.)

integer, integra, integrum, whole; unimpaired; fresh

intellegō, intellegere, intellēxī, intellēctum, understand, know, realize, learn

inter, prep. w. acc., among, between

intercēdō, intercēdere, intercessī, intercessum, come between, intervene

intercipiō, -cipere, -cēpī, -ceptum, catch between (one point and another), cut off, intercept

interclūdō, interclūdere, interclūsī, interclūsum, shut off from

interdīcō, -dīcere, -dīxī, -dictum, forbid, exclude, interdict

interdiū, adv., by day

interdum, adv., at times, now and then (more rarely than **nōnnumquam**)

intereā, adv., meanwhile

intereō, interīre, interiī, interitum, perish, die

interest, *impers. verb,* it concerns (*w. abl. fem. sing. of personal adj., like* **meā, tuā,** *etc.; otherwise genitive*)

interfector, -ōris, *m.,* killer, slayer

interficiō, interficere, interfēcī, interfectum, kill

interim, *adv.,* meanwhile, in the meantime

interior, interius, *comp. adj.,* inner, interior; *superl.* **intimus, -a, -um,** innermost

intermittō, intermittere, intermīsī, intermissum, send between; discontinue; let slip, leave alone *for a time*

interpellō, *I,* interrupt, interfere with

interventus, -ūs, *m.,* intervention, assistance

interrogō, *I,* ask

interscindō, interscindere, interscidī, interscissum, cut through, cut in two, destroy

intersum, interesse, interfuī, interfutūrus, lie between; be present at, take part in (*w. dat., sec. 219a*).

intervallum, -ī, *n.,* space between (walls); interval

intestīnus, -a, -um, inward; domestic, civil, personal

intimus, -a, -um, *see* **interior, interius**

intrā, *prep. w. acc.,* within, inside; into

intrō, *adv.,* within, inside

intrōdūcō, intrōdūcere, intrōdūxī, intrōductum, lead in

introeō, introīre, introiī, introitum, go into

intueor, -tuērī, -tuitum, look upon, gaze at, examine

inūsitātus, -a, -um, unusual, novel, extraordinary, unprecedented

inūtilis, inūtile, *adj,* useless

inveniō, invenīre, invēnī, inventum, come upon, find, meet with

invertō, invertere, invertī, inversum, reverse, turn over

invictus, -a, -um, unbeaten

invideō, invidēre, invīdī, invīsum, envy (*w. dat. sec. 218*)

invidentia, -ae, *f.,* envy

invidia, -ae, *f.,* envy, unpopularity

invītō, *I,* invite; persuade

invītus, -a, -um, against one's wish *or* will, unwilling(ly)

ipse, ipsa, ipsum, *self, gen.* **ipsīus** (*see secs. 201 and 202*)

īra, -ae, *f.,* anger, passion

īrācundia, -ae, *f.,* violent temper, wrath

īrāscor, īrāscī, īrātus sum, become angry (*w. dat. sec. 218*)

irrumpō, irrumpere, irrūpī, irruptum, break into, burst into, invade

is, ea, id, *gen.* **eius,** *weak dem. pron.* (*see secs. 127 and 128*), this, that; he, she, it; the

Īsocratēs, Īsocratis, *m.,* Isocrates, *celebrated Athenian orator, friend of Plato*

iste, ista, istud, *gen.* **istīus,** *dem. pron.,* that (of yours), *see appendix 31*

ita, *adv.,* so, thus, in this way; as follows; even so, yes

Italia, ae, *f.,* Italy, *in ancient times designating all of the peninsula of Italy and, in addition, sometimes Cisalpine Gaul*

itaque, *conj.,* and so, accordingly, therefore

item, *adv.,* likewise

iter, itineris, *n.*, journey; iter faciō, march

iterum, *adv.*, again, for a second time

Iuba, -ae, *m.*, Juba, *a king of Numidia*

iubeō, iubēre, iussī, iussum, order, bid, command

iūcundus, -a, -um, pleasant, causing joy *or* delight

iūdex, iūdicis, *m.*, judge, juryman

iūdicium, iūdicī, *n.*, trial, court; judgment, verdict

iūdicō, *I*, judge, determine, decide; think

iugum, -ī, *n.*, yoke

Iugurtha, -ae, *m.*, Jugurtha, *King of Numidia, taken prisoner by Marius, 106 B.C.*

Iūlius, Iūlī, *m.*, Julius, *name of a Roman clan*

iungo, iungere, iūnxi, iūnctum, join, unite

Iūnō, Iūnōnis, *f.*, Juno, *a Roman goddess, wife of Jupiter*

Iuppiter, Iovis, *m.*, Jupiter, *chief god of the Romans*

Iūra, -ae, *m.*, the Jura mountain range

iūre, *abl. of* iūs *used as adv.*, rightly, rightfully, deservedly, with justice

iūrō, *I*, take an oath, swear

iūs, iūris, *n.*, right; iūs iūrandum, iūris iūrandī, *n.*, oath

iūstitia, -ae, *f.*, justice

iūstus, -a, -um, honorable

iuvenis, iuvene, *gen. pl.* iuvenum, *adj.*, young; *as noun*, young man

iuventūs, iuventūtis, *f.*, youth, young manhood

iuvō, iuvāre, iūvī, iūtum, help

L

L., *abbreviation for* Lūcius

Labiēnus, -ī, *m.*, Labienus, *Caesar's most trusted officer in the Gallic war*

lābor, lābī, lāpsus sum, slip, slide; sink, fall

labor, labōris, *m.*, labor, toil; effort, hardship

labōrō, *I*, work; be in trouble, be hard pressed

lacessō, lacessere, lacessīvī, lacessītum, rouse; annoy; provoke

lacrima, -ae, *f.*, tear

lacus, -ūs, *m.*, lake

Laeca, -ae, *m.*, Laeca, *a Roman name*

laedō, laedere, laesī, laesum, hurt (*governs accusative*)

Laelius, Laelī, *m.*, Laelius, *name of Roman clan. In particular, C. Laelius (Sapiens), consul 140 B.C., friend of Scipio the younger and principal interlocutor in Cicero's dialogue "de Amicitia."*

laetitia, -ae, *f.*, joy, rejoicing

laetor, *I*, be glad

laetus, -a, -um, joyful

lanx, lancis, *gen. pl.* lancium, *f.*, silver plate, dish

lapis, lapidis, *m.*, stone; milestone

lātē, *adv.*, widely, extensively

Latīnē, *adv.*, in Latin

Latīnus, -a, -um, Latin

Latium, Latī, *n.*, Latium, *a district in Italy*

lātus, -a, -um, broad, wide

latus, lateris, *n.*, side, flank

laudō, *I*, praise

laus, laudis, *f.*, praise, credit, glory, excellence, reputation

lēctiō, -ōnis, *f.*, a gathering; reading

lēgātiō, -ōnis, *f.,* office of ambassador, embassy

lēgātus, -ī, *m.,* envoy; legion-commander

legiō, legiōnis, *f.,* legion (*unit of army organization, in theory 6000 men, in practice about 4000, divided into ten cohorts*)

lēgitimus, -a, -um, lawful, legal

legō, legere, lēgī, lēctum, read

lēnis, -e, *adj.,* gentle, mild; slow

lēnitās, lēnitātis, *f.,* smoothness, gentleness

lēniter, *adv.,* gently

Lentulus, -ī, *m.,* Lentulus, *Roman cognomen of clan Cornelii. In particular,* Publius Cornelius Lentulus Sura, *consul 71 B.C., one of the Catilinarian conspirators.*

leō, leōnis, *m.,* lion

lepidus, -a, -um, charming, pleasing, neat

Lesbia, -ae, *f.,* Lesbia, *name of a Roman lady*

levis, leve, *adj.,* light, slight, trifling

lēx, lēgis, *f.,* law

libellus, -ī, *m.,* little book

libenter, *adv.,* gladly

liber, librī, *m.,* book

līber, lībera, līberum, free

līberālitās, līberālitātis, *f.,* generosity, frankness

līberē, *adv.,* freely, without restraint

līberī, līberōrum, *m.,* children

līberō, I, set free

lībertās, lībertātis, *f.,* liberty, freedom

licet, licēre, licuit, *and* **licitum est,** *impersonal,* it is lawful, permitted (*w. dat., sec. 218*)

Lilybaeum, -aeī, *n.,* Lilybaeum, *a town on the south coast of Sicily*

lingua, ae, *f.,* tongue; language, speech

Linus, -ī, *m.,* Linus, *a Roman name*

littera, -ae, *f.,* letter (*of the alphabet*); *plural,* letter, epistle; *also* "letters," *i.e.* literature

lītus, lītoris, *n.,* shore, beach

locus, -ī, *m.* (*pl.* **loca, locōrum,** *n.*), place, situation, rank

longē, *adv.,* far

longinquitās, -tātis, *f.,* length

longinquus, -qua, -quum, distant, remote

longus, -a, -um, long

loquāx, *adj., gen.* **loquācis,** talkative, garrulous

loquor, loquī, locūtus sum, speak (*informally*)

lōrum, -ī, *n.,* thong, strap, lash

Lūcius, Lūcī, *m.* (*abbrev.* **L**) Lucius, *a Roman praenomen*

Lūcullus, -ī, *m.,* Lucullus, *Roman cognomen of the clan Licinii. In particular,* L. Licinium Lucullus, *consul 74 B.C., famed for his victories over Mithridates, his great wealth, and his patronage of the arts.*

lūdus, -ī, *m.,* sport; plural (organized) games

lūgeō, lūgēre, lūxī, lūctum, mourn

lūmen, lūminis, *n.,* light

lūna, -ae, *f.,* moon

lūx, lūcis, *f.,* light; **prīma lūx,** dawn

lympha, -ae, *f.,* water

M

M., abbreviation for **Mārcus**

Macedō, Macedonis, *m.,* a Macedonian, *inhabitant of Macedonia*

Macedonia, -ae, *f.,* Macedonia, *in*

ancient times a country north of Greece

maeror, -ōris, *m.*, grief, sorrow

maestus, -a, -um, dejected, sad

magister, magistrī, *m.*, master, teacher

magistrātus, -ūs, *m.*, magistrate, office of magistrate; magistrate

magnificus, -a, -um, gorgeous, magnificent (*comparative* **magnificentior**)

magnitūdō, magnitūdinis, *f.*, size

magnopere, *adv.*, especially, greatly, exceedingly, earnestly

magnus, -a, -um, large, big, great; *comp.* **maior, maius,** larger, greater; *superl.;* **maximus, -a, -um,** largest, greatest

maior, maius, *see* **magnus**

maiōrēs, maiōrum, *m. pl.,* ancestors

male, *adv.,* badly, ill, adversely

maleficium, maleficī, *n.,* wrongdoing

mālō, mālle, māluī, ——, wish *or* would more *or* rather; prefer

malus, -a, -um, bad, evil; *comp.* **peior, peius,** worse; *superl.* **pessimus, -a, -um,** worst

Māmercus, -ī, *m.,* Mamercus, a Roman name

mandātum, -ī, *n.,* order

mandō, *I,* order; entrust, commit

māne, *adv.,* in the morning

maneō, manēre, mānsī, mānsum, remain, stay

Mānēs, Mānium, *m., pl.,* the Manes, the souls of the dead

Mānlius, Mānlī, *m.,* Manlius, *name of a Roman clan*

mānō, *I,* flow, trickle; spread, spread abroad

manubiae, -ārum, *f. pl.,* spoils of war, plunder

manus, manūs, *f.,* hand; handful, band

Marcellus, -ī, *m.,* Marcellus, *a Roman name*

Mārcus, -ī, *m.,* (*abbrev.* **M.**), Marcus, *a Roman praenomen*

mare, maris (*gen. pl. not found*), *n.,* sea

maritimus, -a, -um, of the seacoast, maritime

Marius, Marī, *m.,* Marius, *name of a Roman clan. In particular,* C. Marius (*157–86 B.C.*), *distinguished general and seven times consul.*

marmor, marmoris, *n.,* marble

Marō, Marōnis, *m.,* Maro, *a Roman name. In particular,* Publius Vergilius Maro, *epic poet, author of the Aeneid, 70–19 B.C.*

māter, mātris, *f.,* mother

māteria, -ae, *f.,* material; wood

mātūrō, *I,* hurry

mātūrus, -a, -um, early

mātūtīnus, -a, -um, belonging to the (early) morning

maximē, *adv.,* especially

maximus, -a, -um, *see* **magnus**

Maximus, -ī, *m.,* Maximus, *a Roman name*

medicus, -ī, *m.,* doctor, physician

mediocris, -cre, middle, average

medius, -a, -um, middle, middle of; **in mediō colle,** half-way up the hill

Megara, -ae, *f.,* Megara, *a city in Greece*

mel, mellis, *n.,* honey

melior, melius, *see* **bonus, -a, -um**

Melita, Melitae, *f.,* the island of Malta

meminī, *defective verb,* **meminisse,**

memineram, remember; *see appendix 54*

memor, *adj., gen.* **memoris,** mindful

memoria, -ae, *f.,* memory

mēns, mentis, *gen. pl.* **mentium,** *f.,* mind

mēnsis, mēnsis, *gen. pl.* **mēnsium,** *m.,* month

mēnsūra, -ae, *f.,* measurement

mentiō, mentiōnis, *f.,* mention

mentior, mentīrī, mentītus sum, lie, tell lies

mercātor, mercātōris, *m.,* merchant

mercēs, mercēdis, *f.,* pay, hire, reward

mereō, *and* **mereor, merēre, meruī, meritum,** deserve; earn; earn pay *or* **stīpendia m.,** serve as a soldier; **bene merērī dē,** deserve well of

merīdiēs, merīdiēī, *m.,* noon, midday; South

meritum, -ī, *n.,* that which one deserves, service, benefit, worth; *pl.* deserts

Metellus, -ī, *m.,* Metellus, *cognomen of a Roman family in the clan Caecilii*

metuō, metuere, metuī (metūtum), fear, have a sense of danger causing one to take precautions

metus, metūs, *m.,* fear

meus, mea, meum, my, mine

micō, *I,* shine, glitter

migrō, *I,* wander

mīles, mīlitis, *m.,* solidier

mīlitāris, mīlitāre, *adj.,* military

mīlitia, -ae, *f.,* soldiering, military service, warfare, campaign

mīlitō, *I,* serve as a soldier

mīlle, *indecl., adj.,* thousand; **mīlle passūs,** one mile; *n. pl. as noun,* **mīlia,** *gen.* **mīlium,** thousands,

usually followed by genitive of the whole; **duo mīlia passuum,** two miles

Milō, Milōnis, *m.,* Milo, *a celebrated athlete of Southern Italy*

mina, -ae, *f.,* threat

minimē, *adv.,* least, very little; not at all, no

minimus, -a, -um, *see* **parvus, -a, -um**

minor, minus, *see* **parvus, -a, -um**

minuō, minuere, minuī, minūtum, diminish, lessen, mitigate

mīrābilis, mīrābile, *adj.,* wonderful

mīrificus, -a, -um, (**mīrus** *and* **faciō**), wonderful, marvelous, extraordinary, astonishing

mīror, *I,* wonder; wonder at

mīrus, -a, -um, strange, astonishing

miser, misera, miserum, miserable, poor, wretched, unfortunate

miserē, *adv.,* wretchedly

miseria, -ae, *f.,* misery, wretchedness

misericordia, -ae, *f.,* pity

Mithridātēs, Mithridātis, *m.,* Mithridates VI, *King of Pontus, 120–63 B.C., finally defeated by Pompey*

mittō, mittere, mīsī, missum, send

mōbilis, mōbile, easily moved, fickle

modestē, *adv.,* discreetly

modestia, -ae, *f.,* discretion; self-restraint; sense of honor, propriety of conduct

modo, *adv.,* only, just now, recently; **nōn modo . . . sed etiam,** not only . . . but also

modō, *adv.,* in the manner of, like (*often follows genitive case*)

modus, -ī, *m.,* measure, limit; manner, method

moenia, moenium, *n.p.*, city walls

molestia, -ae, *f.*, annoyance, nuisance

molestus, -a, -um, irksome, annoying

molliō, *IV*, soften

moneō, monēre, monuī, monitum, warn, advise

mōns, montis, *gen. pl.* montium, *m.*, mountain; mountain range

mōnstrō, *I*, show

monumentum, -ī, *n.*, tomb, memorial

mora, -ae, *f.*, delay

morbus, -ī, *m.*, disease

morior, morī, mortuus sum, die (*fut. act. part.* moritūrus)

moror, *I*, delay; hinder; tarry

mors, mortis, *gen. pl.* mortium, *f.*, death

mōs, mōris, *m.*, custom, precedent; *in pl.*, manners; character

mōtus, -ūs, *m.*, commotion, turmoil, uprising

moveō, movēre, mōvī, mōtum, move, set in motion

mox, *adv.*, soon, presently

mulier, mulieris, *f.*, woman, wife

multitūdō, multitūdinis, *f.*, crowd, large number

multō, *adv.*, by far, much

multum, *adv.*, much, very, greatly, especially; (plūs, plūrimum *are comp. and superl. respectively*)

multus, -a, -um, much; *pl.* many; *comp.* plūs (*noun, only in sing.; for declension, see sec. 157b*) more; *superl.* plūrimus, -a, -um, most; multā nocte, late at night

Mummius, Mummī, *m.*, Mummius, *name of a Roman clan. In particular* Lucius Mummius, *Roman*

general who destroyed Corinth 146 B.C.

mundus, -ī, *m.*, world

mūniō, *IV*, build; fortify

mūnītiō, mūnītiōnis, *f.*, fortification

mūnus, mūneris, *n.*, gift, bounty; duty, task

Mūrēna, -ae, *m.*, Murena, *a Roman name*

mūrus, mūrī, *m.*, wall

mūs, mūris, *gen. pl.* mūrium, *c.*, mouse

Mūsa, -ae, *f.*, Muse

mūtō, *I*, change

mūtuus, -a, -um, mutual, reciprocal; mūtuās pecūniās sūmere ab aliquō, borrow money of someone; m. p. dare, lend money

N

Naevius, Naevī, *m.*, Naevius, *a Roman epic and dramatic poet 274-204 B.C.*

nam, *conj.*, for; namque, *conj.*, an *emphatic* nam, for truly, for indeed

nancīscor, nancīscī, nactus sum, obtain (*often without effort*) by circumstances or chance

nārrō, *I*, tell; relate; describe

nāscor, nāscī, nātus sum, be born; spring up

nātiō, nātiōnis, *f.*, race, tribe, people, nation

nātūra, -ae, *f.*, nature

nauta, -ae, *m.*, sailor

nāvigō, *I*, sail, cruise

nāvis, nāvis, *gen. pl.* nāvium, *f.*, ship

nāvita, -ae, *m.*, sailor

-ne, *enclitic, indicates a question to*

*which the answer may be "yes"
or "no"*

nē, (1) *conj. with subj.,* that . . .
not, in order that . . . not, lest
(*see secs. 222 and 268–270*);
(2) *adv.,* not, *with hortatory and
jussive subjunctive* (*see sec. 209*),
(3) **nē** . . . **quidem** (*inclosing
the emphatic word*), not even

nec, *conj., see* **neque**

necesse, *indecl. adj.,* necessary, un-
avoidable

necne, *conj.,* or not (*used in indirect
questions. See sec. 211, Obs.*)

necō, *I,* kill

nefārius, -a, -um, wicked

neglegentia, -ae, *f.,* carelessness,
negligence

**neglegō, neglegere, neglēxī, neglēc-
tum,** not heed, disregard, neglect

negō, *I,* say no, refuse, deny; say
. . . not

negōtium, negōtī, *n.,* concern, business; trouble, difficulty

nēmō, *acc.* **nēminem,** *m. and f.,*
(**nūllīus, nūllī,** *and* **nūllō, -ā** *supply the genitive, dative, and ablative respectively*), no man, no
one

neque, nec, *conj.,* neither, and . . .
not; **neque (nec)** . . . **neque
(nec),** neither . . . nor

Nerviī, Nerviōrum, *m.pl.,* the
Nervii, *a Gallic tribe*

**nesciō, nescīre, nescīvī (-iī), nes-
cītum,** not know; be absolutely
ignorant of

nescius, -a, -um, ignorant

neu, *see* **nēve**

neuter, neutra, neutrum, *gen.* **neu-
trīus,** neither

nēve, neu, *conj.,* and not, nor (*see
sec. 222*)

Nīcomēdia, -ae, *f.,* Nicomedia, *a
city in Bithynia*

nihil, *or* **nīl,** *indecl. noun, n.,* nothing; *w. gen.,* no, none of

nihilōminus, *adv.,* none the less,
notwithstanding

nihilum, -ī, *n.,* nothing

Nīlus, -ī, *m.,* the Nile

nimis, *adv.,* too much

nimium, *adv.,* too much

nisi, *conj.,* if not, except, unless

nix, nivis, *gen. pl.* **nivium,** *f.,* snow

nō, *I,* swim, float

nōbilis, nōbile, *adj.,* well known,
distinguished; of noble birth; *as
noun,* nobleman

noceō, nocēre, nocuī, nocitum, in-
jure, hurt (*w. dat., sec. 218*)

noctū, *adv.,* by night

nocturnus, -a, -um, nocturnal

nōlō, nōlle, nōluī, ——, be unwilling

nōmen, nōminis, *n.,* name

nōn, *adv.,* not; **nōn sōlum** (*or* **nōn
modo**) . . . **sed etiam,** not only
. . . but also

nōnāgēsimus, -a, -um, ninetieth

nōnāgintā, *card. num. adj.,* ninety

nōndum, *adv.,* not yet

nōnne, *interrog. participle, sign of
question expecting answer "yes"*
(*see sec. 210a*)

nōnnūllus, -a, -um, *gen.* **nōnnūllīus,**
some

nōnus, -a, -um, *ord. num. adj.,*
ninth

nōs, *see* **ego**

nōscō, nōscere, nōvī, nōtum, learn
(*perfect means* know; *pluperfect
means* knew.)

noster, nostra, nostrum, our, ours;
nostrī, nostrōrum, *m.,* our soldiers

nota, -ae, *f.,* mark, sign, brand

nōtus, -a, -um, known, well-known

novem, *card. num. adj.,* nine

novitās, -tātis, *f.,* newness, novelty

novus, -a, -um, new, novel, strange; *no comp.; superl.* **novissimus, -a, -um,** newest; **novissimum agmen,** rear guard

nox, noctis, *gen. pl.* **noctium,** *f.,* night

nūbēs, nūbis, *gen. pl.* **nūbium,** *f.,* cloud

nūbilus, -a, -um, cloudy, overcast

nūdō, *I,* strip, strip bare

nūdus, -a, -um, bare, naked

nūllus, nūlla, nūllum, *gen.* **nūllīus,** not any, no; **nōnnūllus, -a, -um,** some

num, (1) *interrog. particle, sign of question expecting answer "no" (see sec. 210b);* (2) *conj.,* if *or* whether *(introducing an indirect question)*

numerō, *I,* count, enumerate

numerus, -ī, *m.,* number

nummus, -ī, *m., Roman coin worth about five cents*

numquam, *adv.,* not ever, never

nunc, *adv.,* now, this actual moment

nūntiō, *I,* report, announce

nūntius, nūntī, *m.,* messenger; message

nūper, *adv.,* recently, lately

O

Ō! *exclam., sign of vocative,* O!

ob, *prep. w. acc.,* on account of, for

obeō, -īre, -iī, -itum, go to meet; **diem suum obīre,** to die; visit, attend to

obiciō, obicere, obiēcī, obiectum, throw against; place opposite,

expose *someone, acc.,* to *something, dat. (see sec. 219b)*

oblīquus, -a, -um, slanting, indirect

oblītus, -a, -um, forgetful

oblīvīscor, oblīvīscī, oblītus sum, forget, *w. gen.*

obsequium, -quī, *n.,* compliance, obedience

observō, *I,* watch closely

obses, obsidis, *c.,* hostage

obsideō, -sidēre, -sēdī, -sessum, besiege

obstō, obstāre, obstitī, obstitum, stand in way of, oppose *(w. dat., see sec. 219b; w.* **quōminus** *plus subjunctive, see sec. 272)*

obsum, obesse, obfuī, obfutūrus, be in the way of, hinder *(w. dat.)*

obtestor, *I,* call to witness; entreat

obtineō, -tinēre, -tinuī, -tentum, hold fast, obtain

obviam, *adv.,* in the way; **īre obviam** *plus dative,* to meet

occāsio, -ōnis, *f.,* opportunity

occāsus, occāsūs, *m.,* falling down, setting; *with* **sōlis,** sunset, West

occidō, occidere, occidī, occāsum, fall down, set *(used of the sun)*

occīdō, occīdere, occīdī, occīsum, cut down, kill *(with a weapon)*

occultō, *I,* hide

occultus, -a, -um, hidden, secret

occupō, *I,* seize

occurrō, occurrere, occurrī, occursum, go to meet, fall in with

Ōceanus, -ī, *m.,* the ocean, *i.e.,* the Atlantic

octāvus, -a, -um, *ord. num. adj.,* eighth

octō, *card. num. adj.,* eight

octōgintā, *card. num. adj.,* eighty

oculus, -ī, *m.,* eye

ōdī, *defective verb* (*see appendix 54*), hate

odium, odī, *n.*, hatred, prejudice, unpopularity

offendō, -fendere, -fendī, -fēnsum, strike against, hurt; **animum off.**, hurt the feelings

offerō, offerre, obtulī, oblātum, bring before; offer, give

officium, officī, *n.*, duty; **in officiō esse,** remain loyal

ōlim, *adv.*, formerly (*lit.* at that time, at some time)

Olympia, -ae, *f.*, Olympia, *a sacred region in Elis, Greece, where the Olympic games were held*

omnīnō, *adv.*, wholly, altogether; in all, at all; in general

omnis, omne, *adj.*, every, every kind of; *pl.* **omnēs, omnia,** all without exception (*as opposed to* **ūnus**)

onus, oneris, *n.*, burden

opera, -ae, *f.*, aid, help

opīmus, -a, -um, rich

opīniō, opīniōnis, *f.*, way of thinking, impression; reputation; expectation

opīnor, *I*, think, conjecture

oportet, oportēre, oportuit, ——, *impersonal verb*, it is necessary *or* proper

Oppiānicus, -ī, *m.*, Oppianicus, *a Roman name*

oppidānus, -ī, *m.*, townsman

oppidum, -ī, *n.*, town, walled town

oppōnō, -pōnere, -posuī, -positum, place in the path of (*sec. 219b*)

opportūnus, -a, -um, coming at the right time, suitable

opprimō, -primere, -pressī, -pressum, press down, oppress; overwhelm, fall upon

oppugnātiō, oppugnātiōnis, *f.*, storming, assault, attack

oppugnō, *I*, attack, assault

ops, opis, *f.*, help; *pl.* riches, wealth, resources

optimē, *adv.*, in the best way, fortunately

optimus, -a, -um, *superl. of* **bonus,** best; **optimī virī,** gentlemen

optō, *I*, wish for, welcome

opus, operis, *n.*, work, task

ōra, -ae, *f.*, shore, coast

ōrātiō, ōrātiōnis, *f.*, oration, speech; **ōrātiōnem habēre,** to make a speech; **ōrātiō rēcta,** direct speech; **ōrātiō oblīqua,** indirect speech

ōrātor, ōrātōris, *m.*, orator

orbis, orbis, *gen. pl.* **orbium,** *m.*, ring, circle; **orbis terrārum,** the world

ōrdō, ordinis, *m.*, rank, order, station, class (of society)

Orgetorīx, Orgetorīgis, *m.*, Orgetorix, *a chief of the Helvetii*

orior, orīrī, ortus sum, rise (*fut. act. part.* oritūrus)

ōrō, *I*, pray, ask

Oscē, *adv.*, in Oscan (*an Italic dialect*)

ostendō, ostendere, ostendī, ostentum, present, show, reveal; declare

ōtiōsus, -a, -um, at leisure

ōtium, -ī, *n.*, leisure

P

P., *abbreviation for* **Pūblius**

pābulor, *I*, forage, go foraging

pābulum, -ī, *n.*, fodder; pasturage

pācō, *I*, make peaceful, subdue

paene, *adv.*, nearly almost

paenitet, -ēre, -ituit, *impers.*, it

causes regret, makes one repent, (*acc. of person plus gen. of thing*)

pāgus, -ī, *m.*, district; canton

palam, *adv.*, openly

palma, -ae, *f.*, palm of hand

palūs, palūdis, *f.*, marsh, swamp

pandō, pandere, pandī, passum, spread *or* stretch out, extend

pār, *adj.*, *gen.* **paris,** equal, like, similar, a match for (*see app. 11*)

parātus, *see* **parō**

parcō, parcere, pepercī, parsum, spare (*w. dat., sec. 218*)

parēns, parentis, *c.*, parent

pāreō, pārēre, pāruī, ——, appear; obey (*w. dat., sec. 218*)

pariō, parere, peperī, partum, produce, create; procure, win

parō, *I*, prepare, make ready, furnish *or* provide what is necessary; equip, *hence perf. part. passive,* **parātus,** *as adj.,* ready, equipped

parricīdium, parricīdī, *n.*, parricide

pars, partis, *gen. pl.* **partium,** *f.*, part; direction

parturiō, *IV*, be in travail

parum, *adv. and indecl. noun,* little, too little; not enough

parvus, -a, -um, little, small; *comp.* **minor, minus,** less; *superl.* **minimus, -a, -um,** least

passim, *adv.*, in every direction, widespread, at random, indiscriminately

passus, passūs, *m.*, pace, five Roman feet, two **gradūs; mīlle passūs,** mile; **mīlia passuum,** miles

pateō, patēre, patuī, ——, lie *or* be open; extend

pater, patris, *m.*, father; **patrēs cōnscriptī,** senators

patientia, -ae, *f.*, patience

patior, patī, passus sum, allow, put up with

patria, -ae, *f.*, native land, country

paucī, -ae, -a, few; *as noun,* few, a few

paulātim, *adv.*, little by little

paulisper, *adv.*, for a little while

paulum, *adv.*, a little, somewhat, slightly

Paulus, -ī, *m.*, Paulus, *name of a Roman family, see* **Aemilius**

pauper, *adj.*, *gen.* **pauperis,** *abl.* **paupere,** *gen. pl.* **pauperum,** poor

pavīmentum, -ī, *n.*, pavement

pax, pācis, *f.*, peace

peccō, *I*, do wrong

pecūnia, -ae, *f.*, money

pecus, pecoris, *n.*, cattle

pedes, peditis, *m.*, foot-soldier, infantryman

peior, peius, *see* **malus**

pellō, pellere, pepulī, pulsum, drive, beat, rout

pendō, pendere, pependī, pensum, pay; consider, regard

per, *prep. w. acc.*, through, throughout; over; through, by means of

perambulō, *I*, wander through

perdō, perdere, perdidī, perditum, bring to nothing, ruin; lose

peregrīnātiō, -ōnis, *f.*, wandering abroad, travel

pereō, perīre, periī, peritum, perish, die, be lost

perfacilis, perfacile, *adj.*, very easy

perficiō, perficere, perfēcī, perfectum, complete, finish

perfidia, -ae, *f.*, treachery

perfuga, -ae, *m.*, deserter

perfugium, -ī, *n.*, refuge, shelter from

perīculum, -ī, *n.*, trial; risk, danger, peril

perimō, perimere, perēmī, perēmp-
tum, destroy, kill

perītus, -a, -um, experienced, skilled

perlēctiō, -lōctiōnis, f., a reading
through, perusal

permaneō, permanēre, permānsī,
permānsum, stay through to the
end, continue; persist

permittō, permittere, permīsī, per-
missum, allow, permit (w. dat.
sec. 219b)

permoveō, permovēre, permōvī,
permōtum, move thoroughly, affect, influence

permultī, -ae, -a, very many

perniciēs, perniciēī, f., ruin, destruction

perpetior, -petī, -pessus sum, bear
patiently, endure

perpetuō, adv., continuously; for-
ever

perpetuus, -a, -um, perpetual, continuous, unbroken

perrumpō, perrumpere, perrūpī,
perruptum, break through, force
a passage

persequor, persequī, persecūtum,
pursue, chase, hunt down

Persa, -ae, m., a Persian

perscrībō, perscrībere, perscrīpsī,
perscrīptum, write out

Perseus, Perseī, m., Perseus, the
last king of Macedonia, defeated
by Aemilius Paulus at Pydna in
168 B.C.

persolvō, persolvere, persolvī, per-
solūtum, pay in full, suffer
(punishment)

perspiciō, perspicere, perspēxī, per-
spectum, look into, at; examine,
inspect; perceive, observe

persuādeō, persuādēre, persuāsī,
persuāsum, convince (w. dat.,

sec. 218); with acc. & dat., convince a person (dat.) of a thing
(acc.); inculcate

pertemptō, I, make trial of, test

perterreō, -terrēre, -terruī, -terri-
tum, frighten thoroughly

pertinācia, -ae, f., obstinacy, per-
sistence, perseverance

pertineō, -tinēre, -tinuī, -tentum,
reach, belong, affect, concern,
suit

perturbō, I, disturb, upset

perveniō, pervenīre, pervēnī, perventum, come to, arrive

pēs, pedis, m., foot

pessimus, -a, -um, see malus, -a,
-um

petō, petere, petīvī or petiī, petītum,
seek, aim at

Petrus, -ī, m., Peter

Phīdiās, Phīdiae, m., Phidias, famous Greek sculptor, architect, and
painter, born 500 B.C.

Philippī, Philippōrum, m., Philippi,
a town in Macedonia

philosophus, -ī, m., philosopher

Philūmena, -ae, f., a girl's name

pietās, pietātis, f., devotion to duty;
character; filial love

pīlum, pīlī, n., heavy javelin, pike

Pindarus, -ī, m., Pindar, a famous
Greek lyric poet (522–442 B.C.)

Pīraeus, -ī, m., Piraeus, the port of
Athens

pīrāta, -ae, m., pirate

piscor, I, fish

Pīsō, Pīsōnis, m., Piso, a Roman
name

placeō, placēre, placuī, placitum,
be pleasing to, please (w. dat.,
sec. 218)

placidē, adv., calmly

plācō, I, appease

plānitiēs, plānitiēī, *f.*, plain, level ground

Platō, Platōnis, *m.*, Plato, *pupil of Socrates and most famous of Greek philosophers, 427-347 B.C.*

plēbs, plēbis, *f.*, populace, common people

plēnus, -a, -um, full

plērīque, *nom. pl. of adj. as noun*, the greater part, the majority

plērumque, *adv.*, generally, usually; for the most part; very often

plūrimus, -a, -um, *superl. of* multus, -a, -um

plūs, *comp. of* multus, -a, -um; *also of* multum (*adv.*)

pluvia, -ae, *f.*, rain

poena, -ae, *f.*, punishment, penalty, requital

Poenus, -ī, *m.*, a Carthaginian, an inhabitant of Carthage

poēta, -ae, *m.*, poet

pol, *interjection*, by Pollux; indeed; I declare

polliceor, pollicērī, pollicitus sum, promise

Polliō, Polliōnis, *m.*, Pollio, *Roman cognomen. In particular,* C. Asinius Pollio (*76 B.C.- A.D. 4*), *orator, poet, and historian of the Augustan age, patron of Vergil and Horace*

Pompeius, Pompeī, *m.*, Pompey, *name of a Roman clan. In particular,* Cn. Pompeius Magnus (*106-48 B.C.*), *general and statesman, leader of the senatorial party and Caesar's opponent.*

pondus, ponderis, *n.*, weight

pōnō, pōnere, posuī, positum, place, set, put, pitch (*camp*)

pōns, pontis, *gen. pl.* pontium, *m.*, bridge

Ponticus, -a, -um, Pontic, belonging to Pontus, *a district in Asia Minor*

pontus, -ī, *m.*, sea

populor, I, devastate, ravage, lay waste

populus, -ī, *m.*, people

porta, -ae, *f.*, city gate, gate

portō, I, carry

portus, portūs, *m.*, harbor, port

poscō, poscere, poposcī, ——, demand

possessiō, possessiōnis, *f.*, possession

possum, posse, potuī, ——, can, am able; plūrimum posse, to have great influence, be very powerful

post, *prep. with acc.* after (*of time*); behind (*of space*)

posteā, *adv.*, later, after this, afterwards

posteāquam, *conj.*, after

posterum, *neut. of adj. used as noun;* the following; in posterum, in *or* for the future

posterus, -a, -um, following, next, after; *comp.* posterior, posterius, further back; *superl.* postrēmus, -a, -um, postumus, -a, -um, last

postquam, post . . . quam, *conj.*, after, when

postrēmus, -a, -um, *see* posterus, -a, -um

postrīdiē, *adv.*, on the day after, next day

postulō, I, demand, claim (*in accordance with, or as though in accordance with, what is right*)

postumus, -a, -um, *see* posterus

potēns, *adj.*, (*gen.* potenis), powerful

potestās, -tātis, *f.*, legal *or* legitimate authority *or* power; possibility, opportunity

pōtiō, -ōnis, *f.*, drink

potior, potīrī, potītus sum (*w. abl. or gen., sec. 181*), become master of, obtain, capture

potissimum, *adv.*, most preferably, chiefly, most of all, especially

potius, *adv.*, rather

pōtō, *I*, drink, carouse

praebeō, praebēre, praebuī, praebitum, offer, furnish, display, exhibit

praecēdō, praecēdere, praecessī, praecessum, go before; surpass, excel

praeceps, *adj., gen.* praecipitis, headlong

praeceptum, -ī, *n.*, maxim, rule, precept

praecīdō, praecīdere, praecīdī, praecīsum, cut off, cut short, destroy

praecipiō, praecipere, praecēpī, praeceptum, instruct, advise, order

praecipue, *adv.*, especially, particularly

praeclārus, -a, -um, famous, distinguished (*strengthened form of* clārus)

praecō, praecōnis, *m.*, crier, herald

praeda, -ae, *f.*, booty, plunder, spoil

praedicō, *I*, proclaim

praeditus, -a, -um, gifted, endowed

praedium, -dī, *n.*, farm, estate

praedor, *I*, plunder, spoil, rob

praefectūra, -ae, *f.*, position of authority, command

praefectus, -ī, *m.*, one set in charge, commander

praeficiō, praeficere, praefēcī, prae-

fectum, put in command of (*w. acc. and dat. sec. 219b*)

praegredior, praegredī, praegressus sum, go in front

praemittō, praemittere, praemīsī, praemissum, send ahead

praemium, praemī, *n.*, reward

praesēns, *adj., gen.* praesentis, present, in person

praesentia, -ae, *f.*, presence

praesertim, *adv.*, especially, particularly

praesidium, praesidī, *n.*, garrison, guard, protection; stronghold; help

praestans, *adj., gen.* praestantis, outstanding

praestō, *adv.*, at hand, ready

praestō, praestāre, praestitī, praestitum, *or* praestātum, (1) *trans.*, show, supply, furnish; (2) *intrans.*, be superior to, excel (*w. dat. sec. 219a*)

praesum, praeesse, praefuī, praefutūrus, be over, in command of (*w. dat. sec. 219a*)

praeter, *prep. with acc.*, beyond, past; contrary to, in addition to; besides, except

praetereā, *adv.*, besides this, moreover

praetereō, praeterīre, praeteriī, praeteritum, go beyond, pass by, omit

praeteritus, -a, -um, bygone, past

praetermittō, praetermittere, praetermīsī, praetermissum, send by, pass by, omit (*undesignedly*)

praetor, -ōris, *m.*, praetor, *a senior Roman magistrate in charge of administration of justice*

praeustus, -a, -um, burnt at the end

prehendō, prehendere, prehendī, prehēnsum, seize, arrest

premō, premere, pressī, pressum, press, oppress; force in

pretium, -tī, *n.*, price, cost, value

prex, precis, *f.*, prayer

prīdiē, *adv.*, on the day before

prīmārius, -a, -um, prominent, distinguished

prīmum, *adv.*, first, at first, in the first place, for the first time; quam prīmum, as early as possible; ut prīmum, when first, as soon as

prīmus, -a, -um, first; in prīmīs, especially, chiefly

prīnceps, prīncipis, *m.*, first or leading man, chief

prīncipātus, -ūs, *m.*, leadership

prīncipium, prīncipī, *n.*, beginning

prior, prius, *comp. adj.*, former, prior; *superl.* prīmus, -a, -um, first

prīstinus, -a, -um, former, original

prius, *adv.*, before, sooner, previously

priusquam, prius . . . quam, *conj.*, sooner than, before; *after negatives*, until

prīvātus, -ī, *m.*, a private individual *as opposed to a magistrate*

prīvō, *I*, deprive

prō, *prep. w. abl.*, before, in front of; for (in place of); for (in behalf of)

probō, *I*, approve; prove

proboscis, -idis, *f.*, nose, trunk

prōcēdō, -cēdere, -cessī, -cessum, move forward, advance

procul, *adv.*, at a distance, far from; from afar

prōcurrō, -currere, -currī, -cursum, run forward, charge

prōdeō, -īre, -iī, -itum, go or come forth, advance

prōdō, -dere, -didī, -ditum, give forth, reveal; give away; betray; hand down

prōdūcō, -dūcere, -dūxī, -ductum, lead forth; prolong

proelior, *I*, do battle

proelium, proelī, *n.*, battle

profectiō, -ōnis, *f.*, a setting out, start, departure

profectō, *adv.*, certainly, doubtless

prōficiō, prōficere, prōfēcī, prōfectum, forge ahead, make progress

proficīscor, proficīscī, profectus sum, set out, start, depart

profiteor, -fitērī, -fessus sum, declare publicly, profess

profugiō, -fugere, -fūgī, -fugitum, flee, run away, escape

prohibeō, prohibēre, prohibuī, prohibitum, debar, prevent, keep from, *e.g. somebody* (acc.) *from something* (abl.). *See also sec. 272, Obs. 1.*

prōiciō, prōicere, prōiēcī, prōiectum, throw forward *or* away; give up

prōmittō, prōmittere, prōmīsī, prōmissum, promise

prōmoveō, -movēre, -mōvī, -mōtum, move forward, advance (*tr.*)

prōnūntiō, *I*, declare, proclaim; relate

prōpāgō, *I*, extend, spread; prolong; preserve

prope, (1) *prep. with acc.*, near, close to; (2) *adv.*, almost, nearly, recently

properō, *I*, hasten

propinquitās, -tātis, *f.*, nearness; relationship

propinquus, -a, -um, near

propior, propius, *comp. adj.*, nearer;

superl. **proximus, -a, -um,** nearest, next

propius, *prep. with acc.,* nearer

prōpōnō, -pōnere, -posuī, -positum, put forward, present, offer; propose, expose

propter, *prep. with acc.,* because of, on account of

proptereā, *adv.,* on this account; *with* **quod,** because, inasmuch as

prōsequor, prōsequī, prōsecutus sum, pursue

prosperus, -a, -um, favorable, fortunate; *n. plu. as noun,* good fortune

prōsum, prōdesse, prōfuī, prōfutūrus, (*app. 48b*), be of advantage (*w. dat., sec. 219a*)

prōtinus, *adv.,* at once

prōvehō, prōvehere, prōvesī, prōvectum, carry forward, carry out; *passive,* ride, sail

prōveniō, prōvenīre, prōvēnī, prōventum, come forward; grow; be produced, yield (*of grain*)

prōvideō, prōvidēre, prōvīdī, prōvīsum, foresee, care for, provide

prōvincia, -ae, *f.,* province

proximus, -a, -um, nearest, next; last

prūdēns, *adj., gen.* **prūdentis,** sage, wise, foreseeing

prūdenter, *adv.,* discreetly, intelligently

prūdentia, -ae, *f.,* prudence, foresight, good sense

Ptolemaeus, -ī, *m.,* Ptolemy, *one of twelve of this name who were Kings of Egypt from 323–48 B.C.*

pūblicō, *I,* make public

pūblicus, -a, -um, public

Pūblius, Pūblī, *m.,* Publius, *a Roman praenomen*

pudor, pudōris, *m.,* shame, sense of shame *or* decency

puella, -ae, *f.,* girl

puer, puerī, *m.,* boy, slave

pugna, -ae, *f.,* fight, battle

pugnō, *I,* fight

pulcher, pulchra, pulchrum, beautiful

pulchrē, *adv.,* beautifully

pulchritūdō, pulchritūdinis, *f.,* beauty

pulvis, pulveris, *m.,* dust

Pūnicus, -a, -um, Punic, Carthaginian

pūniō, *IV,* punish

puppis, puppis, *gen. pl.* **puppium,** *f.,* stern of ship; ship

pūrgō, *I,* clear, excuse, exonerate

putō, *I,* think, consider, believe

Pȳrēnaeus, -a, -um, of the Pyrenees

Pyrrhus, -ī, *m.,* Pyrrhus, *King of Epirus (d. 272 B.C.)*

Q

Q. *abbreviation for* **Quīntus**

quā, *adv.,* by what way, where

quadrāgintā, *card. num. adj., indecl.,* forty

quārē, *adv.,* wherefore, and therefore

quadrīga, -ae, *f.,* four-horse chariot

quaerō, quaerere, quaesīvī *or* **quaesiī, quaesītum,** see, look for, inquire (*with* **ā** *and ablative*), ask

quaesō, *an older form of* **quaerō**

quaestor, -ōris, *m.,* quaestor, junior Roman magistrate in charge of revenues

quālis, quāle, *adj.,* of what kind

quam, *conj.,* than, as; **quam** *with superl.,* as . . . as possible; how

quamdiū, *adv.,* as long as

quamquam, *conj.,* although

quamvīs, (1) *adv.,* however, however much; (2) *conj.,* although

quandō, *conj.,* because, since; when; (*use in indir. quest. see fn. 5 on Lesson XL*)

quantum, *adv.,* how much?, *rel.,* as much as

quantus, -a, -um, how great

quāre, *adv.,* why, wherefore

quārtus, -a, -um, *ord. num. adj.,* fourth

quasī (**quam sī**) *adv. and conj.,* as if, as it were

quattuor, *card. num. adj.,* four

quattuordecim, *card. num. adj.,* fourteen

-que, *enclitic,* and

queō, quīre, quīvī, quitum, be able

queror, querī, questus sum, complain

quī, qua, quod, *indef. adj.,* (*see sec. 214*), any

quī, quae, quod, *rel. pron.* (*see secs. 130 and 131*), who, which, what, that

quī, quae, quod, *interrog. adj.* (*see sec. 132*), what? which? what kind of?

quia, *conj.,* because, since

quīcumque, quaecumque, quodcumque, *indef. pron.,* whoever, whatever

quīdam, quaedam, quiddam (**quoddam**), *indef. pronoun and adj.,* a certain one, someone

quidem, *adv.,* indeed, at any rate; on the other hand; **nē . . . quidem,** not even

quies, quiētis, *f.,* quiet

quiētus, -a, -um, quiet, at rest

quīn, *conj.,* that not, but that. (*For construction, see Lesson LX.*)

quīndecim, *card. num. adj.,* fifteen

quīngentī, -ae, -a, five hundred

quīnquāgintā, *card. num. adj.,* fifty

quīnque, *card. num. adj.,* five

quīntus, -a, -um, *ord. num. adj.,* fifth

Quīntus, -ī, *m.,* Quintus, *a Roman praenomen*

Quirītēs, *gen. pl.* **Quirītium,** *m.,* Roman citizens (*usually found in plural only*)

quis, quis, quid, *interrog. pron.* (*see sec. 133*), who? what?, **quid,** *as adv.* why?

quis, quis, quid, *indef. pron.* (*see sec. 214*), anyone, anything

quisquam, quidquam *or* **quicquam,** *indef. pron.,* any, anyone

quisque, quidque, *and* **quīque, quaeque, quodque,** *indef. pron. and adj.,* each one, each; everyone, all

quisquis, quicquid, *or* **quidquid,** *indef. rel. pron.,* whoever, whatever

quō, (1) *interrog. adv.,* where? whither?; (2) *rel. adv.,* where, to what place; (3) **quō,** *in idiom* **nōn quō . . . sed quod,** *adv.,* for the reason that; *used to introduce a rejected reason*

quoad, *adv.,* as long as, as far as; until

quod, *conj.,* because; that, the fact that, as to the fact that; **quod sī,** but if

quōminus, *conj.,* by which the less, so that not; from. (*For construction see Lesson LX*)

quondam, *adv.,* at one time, once, formerly; at times; someday

quoniam, *conj.,* since, because

quoque, *adv.,* also

quot, (1) *interr. adj., indecl.;* (2) *rel.*

adj. indecl. (1) how many?;
(2) as many (as); **quot . . . tot,**
as many . . . as
quotiēns, *adv. and conj.,* how many
times, as many times; as often
as, whenever
quotiēns cumque, *adv.,* how often
soever, as often as
quotus, -a, -um, which in order,
quota hōra est, what o'clock is
it?; **quotus quisque,** how few

R

rapāx, *adj.,* apt to snatch, grasping,
greedy
rapiō, rapere, rapuī, raptum, snatch,
seize
rārus, -a, -um, scattered, far apart,
in small detachments, a few at a
time
ratiō, -ōnis, *f.,* reckoning; interest;
consideration; plan; reason; the-
ory, system (*see dictionary*)
ratis, ratis, *gen. pl.,* **ratium,** *f.,*
raft
Ravenna, -ae, *f.,* Ravenna, *a seaport on N. E. coast of Italy*
**recēdō, recēdere, recessī, reces-
sum,** go back, move back; retreat; recede, vanish
recēns, *gen.* recentis, fresh, new
recipiō, recipere, recēpī, receptum,
take *or* get back, recover; *with*
sē, retreat; recover oneself
recitō, *I,* read aloud
recreō, *I,* refresh
rēctē, *adv.,* rightly, correctly
rēctus, -a, -um, right, correct
recuperō, *I,* regain, get back
recūsō, *I,* refuse
**redarguō, redarguere, redarguī, re-
dargūtum,** disprove, refute

reddō, reddere, reddidī, redditum,
give back, restore; render
redeō, redīre, rediī, reditum, go
back, return
redigō, redigere, redēgī, redāctum,
drive back; reduce, render
redintegrō, *I,* renew
**redūcō, redūcere, redūxī, reduc-
tum,** lead *or* bring back
referō, referre, rettulī, relātum,
bring back; report
reficiō, reficere, refēcī, refectum,
repair; allow to rest
rēgīna, -ae, *f.,* queen
regiō, regiōnis, *f.,* region, part of
the world, district, direction
rēgius, -a, -um, kingly, of the king,
royal
rēgnō, *I,* reign, rule
rēgnum, -ī, *n.,* kingdom, kingly
power
regō, regere, rēxī, rēctum, rule,
direct, control
regredior, regredī, regressus sum,
go back, return
relevō, *I,* lift up, raise; make
lighter
religiō, -ōnis, *f.,* scruple; superstition; religious feeling
**relinquō, relinquere, relīquī, relic-
tum,** leave, leave behind, abandon
reliquus, -a, -um, remaining, the
rest of; **reliquum tempus,** the
future
Rēmī, Rēmōrum, *m.,* The Remi,
a Gallic tribe
remittō, -mittere, -mīsī, -missum,
send back; slacken, relax
remollēsco, remollēscere, ——,
——, soften, become feeble
remūneror, *I,* reward
rēmus, -ī, *m.,* oar
renovō, *I,* renew

repellō, repellere, reppulī, repul-
sum, drive back, repel
repente, *adv.*, suddenly
repentīnus, -a, -um, sudden, hasty,
unexpected
reperiō, reperīre, repperī, repertum,
find
repetō, repetere, repetīvī, repetī-
tum, seek *or* ask again, ask back;
poenās rep. ab aliquō, inflict
punishment on someone
reportō, *I,* bring back; **victōriam**
reportāre dē aliquō, win a victory over someone
repudiō, *I,* reject
reputō, *I,* reckon
requīrō, requīrere, requīsīvī *or* **re-**
quisiī, requīsītum, ask, look for,
miss
rēs, reī, *f.,* thing (*variously translated according to context*); **rēs**
familiāris, property; **rēs frū-**
mentāria, grain supply; **rēs mīli-**
tāris, warfare; **rēs pūblica,** commonwealth; **rēs gestae,** history,
achievements; **rēs novae,** revolu-
tion; **rēs secundae,** prosperity
rescindō, rescindere, rescidī, re-
scissum, cut down, destroy
reservō, keep back, save up
resideō, residēre, resēdī, resessum,
remain, remain behind; rest
resistō, resistere, restitī, ——, be
opposed to, resist (*w. dat. sec.*
218)
resolvō, resolvere, resolvī, resolū-
tum, loose, melt
respiciō, respicere, respēxī, re-
spectum, look back, take notice
of, consider, regard
respondeō, respondēre, respondī,
respōnsum, reply, answer
restituō, restituere, restituī, resti-

tūtum, set up again; renew,
restore
restō, restāre, restitī, ——, stand
firm, withstand; be left
retineō, retinēre, retinuī, retentum,
control, restrain, keep in check
(*for construction, see sec. 272*)
retrahō, retrahere, retrāxī, re-
trāctum, drag back
(revertō, revertere) revertī, re-
versum, turn back, return; *in*
present system regularly deponent
revertor, *see above*
revocō, *I,* recall; retrace
rēx, rēgis, *m.,* king
Rhēnus, -ī, *m.,* the Rhine
Rhodanus, -ī, *m.,* the Rhone, *a*
river in Gaul
Rhodus, Rhodī, *f.,* Rhodes, *an island off the S. W. coast of Asia*
Minor
rīdeō, rīdēre, rīsī, rīsum, laugh;
laugh at
rīdiculus, -a, -um, ridiculous
rīpa, -ae, *f.,* bank of a river
rogō, *I,* ask, request, beg
Rōma, -ae, *f.,* Rome
Rōmānus, -a, -um, Roman, *i.e.,*
pertaining to Rome; *masc. as*
noun, a Roman
Rōmānus, -ī, *m.,* Roman citizen
Rōmulus, -ī, *m.,* Romulus, *leg-
endary founder and first king of
Rome*
Rōscius, Rōscī, *m.,* Roscius, *a famous Roman actor of the first
century B.C.*
Rūfus, -ī, *m.,* Rufus, *a Roman name*
rūmor, rūmōris, *m.,* hearsay, report, rumor
rumpō, rumpere, rūpī, ruptum,
break
ruō, ruere, ruī, ruitūrus, rush

rūrsus, *adv.*, again

rūs, rūris, *n.*, country; rurī, in the country

rūsticus, -a, -um, of the country

S

Sabidius, Sabidī, *m.*, Sabidius, *a Roman name*

sacer, sacra, sacrum, sacred, holy

saeculum (saeclum), -ī, *n.*, age, century

saepe, *adv.*, often

saepissimē, *adv., superlative of above*, very often

sagax, *adj., gen* sagācis, shrewd

sagitta, -ae, *f.*, arrow

sagittārius, -ārī, *m.*, archer

salūs, salūtis, *f.*, safety, welfare; salūtem dīcō *and indir. obj.*, I send greeting to

salūtō, *I*, greet, salute

salveō, salvēre, ——, ——, be well; *imperative as common salutation*, hail!; how are you?

sanciō, sancīre, sānxī, sānctum, make sacred, ordain; *past participle as adj.*, holy, solemn

sānus, -a, -um, healthy

sapiēns, *adj., gen.* sapientis, wise

sapienter, *adv.*, wisely

sapientia, -ae, *f.*, wisdom, good sense

sapiō, sapere, sapīvī, ——, be wise, have sense

satis, *adv. and indecl. noun*, enough

saxum, -ī, *n.*, rock, stone

Scaevola, -ae, *m.*, Scaevola, *a Roman name*

scelus, sceleris, *n.*, crime; an offense against a fellow creature

-scendō, -scendere, -scendī, -scēnsum, *combining* form of scendō, climb

schola, -ae, *f.*, school

scientia, -ae, *f.*, knowledge

sciō, *IV,* know; *with infin.*, know how to

Scīpiō, Scīpiōnis, *m.*, Scipio, *a Roman name*

scrībō, scrībere, scrīpsī, scrīptum, write

scītō, *imperative of* sciō, be assured (that)

scūtum, -ī, *n.*, shield

sēcēdō, -cēdere, -cessī, -cessum, go away, withdraw; revolt, secede

sēcernō, sēcernere, sēcrēvī, sēcrētum, keep apart, separate

secundus, -a, -um, favorable, prosperous; rēs secundae, prosperity

secus, *adv.*, otherwise, differently

sed, *conj.*, but; nōn modo . . . sed etiam, not only . . . but also

sēdecim, *card. num. adj.*, sixteen

sedeō, sedēre, sēdī, sessum, sit

seges, -etis, *f.*, growing grain, field of grain, crop

semel, *adv.*, once

semper, *adv.*, always

senātus, senātūs, *m.*, senate

senectūs, senectūtis, *f.*, old age

senex, senis, *m.*, old man; *also adj.*, old (*declined, sec. 145*)

senīlis, -e, aged, senile

senior, *compar. adj.*, older

sententia, -ae, *f.*, feeling, opinion; decision

sentiō, sentīre, sēnsī, sēnsum, be aware of, feel; think; realize

septem, *card. num. adj.*, seven

septendecim, *card. num. adj.*, seventeen

septentriōnēs, septentriōnum, *m.*, *pl.*, *the seven stars of the constellation Great Bear; hence*, north septimus, -a, -um, *ord. num. adj.*, seventh

septuāgintā, *card. num. adj.*, seventy

sepultūra, -ae, *f.*, burial

Sēquana, -ae, *f.*, the Seine river

Sēquanus, -a, -um, of the Sequani; *pl. as noun*, the Sequani, *a Gallic tribe*

sequor, sequī, secūtus sum, follow, pursue

serēnus, -a, -um, calm

sermō, sermōnis, *m.*, talk, conversation

serō, serere, sēvī, satum, sow, plant

serviō, *IV*, be slave to, serve (*w. dat., sec. 218*)

servitūs, servitūtis, *f.*, slavery, servitude

servō, *I*, save, preserve, maintain, guard

servus, -ī, *m.*, slave, servant

sēstertius, sēstertī, *m.*, sestertius, *small silver coin worth about five cents*

seu, *see* sīve

sevērus, -a, -um, strict, severe, impartial

sex, *card. num. adj.*, six

sexāgintā, *card. num. adj.*, sixty

sextus, -a, -um, *ord. num. adj.*, sixth

sī, *conj.*, if; quod sī, but if

sīc, *adv.*, thus

sīcut, *adv.*, even as, just as

Sicilia, -ae, *f.*, Sicily

siccus, -a, -um, dry

sīcut, *adv.*, so as; just as, as; just as if

sīdus, sīderis, *n.*, star

significō, *I*, show, express, intimate, report

signum, -ī, *n.*, mark, sign, signal

silentium, -ī, *n.*, silence

sileō, silēre, siluī, ——, be silent

silva, -ae, *f.*, wood, forest

similis, simile, *adj.*, like, similar

simul ac *or* simul atque, *conj.*, as soon as, as well as

simulō, *I*, pretend to be (*what one is not*); feign

sīn, sī nōn, *conj.*, but if, if however

sine, *prep. w. abl.*, without

singulāris, -e, singular; extraordinary, remarkable

singulī, -ae, -a, *distrib. num. adj.*, one each; one at a time, separate

sinō, sinere, sīvī, situm, allow

sinister, sinistra, sinistrum, left

sitis, -is, *f.*, thirst

sīve (*or* seu) *conj.*, or if; sīve . . . sīve, if, or if; whether . . . or; either . . . or

sōbrius, -a, -um, sober

societās, -tātis, *f.*, fellowship; alliance; affinity

socius, socī, *m.*, ally, comrade

sōl, sōlis, *m.*, sun

sōlācium, -cī, *n.*, solace, comfort, consolation

soleō, solēre, solitus sum, be wont, be accustomed

solidus, -a, -um, solid

sōlitūdō, sōlitūdinis, *f.*, desolation, solitude

sollicitō, *I*, rouse, shake, incite

sollicitūdō, sollicitūdinis, *f.*, anxiety

sōlum, *adv.*, only

sōlus, -a, -um, *gen.* sōlius, alone, only; the only

solūtiō, solūtiōnis, *f.*, payment

solvō, solvere, solvī, solūtum, loosen, untie; pay, perform; nāvem s., set sail somnus, -ī, *m.*, sleep

sonitus, -ūs, *m.*, sound

soror, sorōris, *f.*, sister

Sōsia, -ae, *m.*, Sosia, *a name in Roman comedy*

spargō, spargere, sparsī, sparsum, scatter; spread

speciēs, speciēī, *f.*, appearance

spectō, *I*, look long at, watch as a spectacle

spatior, *I*, stroll

spatium, -tī, *n.*, space, distance; period

speculātor, -ōris, *m.*, spy

speculor, *I*, spy

spērō, *I*, hope, hope for, anticipate

spēs, speī, *f.*, hope

-spiciō, -spicere, -spēxī, -spectum, *combining form of* speciō, look

spīritus, -ūs, *m.*, spirit, breath of life; high spirit, arrogance

spoliō, *I*, despoil, strip, rob

sponte, *f.* (*abl. from obsolete* spōns, *from* spondeō), of one's own accord, voluntarily

stabilis, -e, *adj.*, voluntarily firm, steady

stadium, -dī, *n.*, stadium, racecourse

statim, *adv.*, at once, immediately

statiō, -ōnis, *f.*, post, guard; in statiōne esse, be on guard

statuō, statuere, statuī, statūtum, decide

status, -ūs, *m.*, standing, condition, state, status

stella, -ae, *f.*, star

stīpendium, -dī, *n.*, tax, tribute, pay; *in pl.*, military service

stīpes, stīpitis, *m.*, log, post, treetrunk

stō, stāre, stetī, statum, stand; *with abl. of price*, cost

strēnuus, -a, -um, active, vigorous

stringō, stringere, strinxī, strictum, draw out, draw

structūra, -ae, *f.*, structure, building

studeō, studēre, studuī, ——, be eager for, desire, engage in (*w. dat. sec. 218*)

studium, studī, *n.*, zeal, enthusiasm; study, literary pursuit

stultus, -a, -um, foolish

suādeō, suādēre, suāsī, suāsum, make acceptable to, advise, persuade (*w. dat. sec. 218*)

suāvis, suāve, sweet, pleasant

sub, *prep. w. acc. and abl.*, (1) *with acc.* (a) *w. verbs of motion*, under; up to (b) *of time*, about (2) *with abl.* (a) *of position*, under, near to (b) *of time*, during, at (*see app. 24c*)

subdūcō, -dūcere, -dūxī, -ductum, bring up to, *w.* navis, beach

subeō, -īre, -iī, -itum, go under, come up to; undergo, endure

subiciō, subicere, subiēcī, subiectum, throw *or* set beneath, place under (*w. acc. and dat., sec. 219b*)

subitō, *adv.*, suddenly

sublevō, *I*, lift from beneath; raise up, support, assist

subsequor, subsequī, subsecūtus sum, follow close after

subsidium, -dī, *n.*, reserve force, help, aid

subsisto, subsistere, substitī, ——, halt, hold out, last, continue

subveniō, subvenīre, subvēnī, subventum, come *or* go to help; aid, succor (*w. dat. sec. 219b*)

succēdō, succēdere, successī, successum, go *or* come under; come up to, advance, approach; be next to, succeed

successus, successūs, *m.,* success

succīdō, succīdere, succīdī, succīsum, cut down, fell

succurrō, succurrere, succurrī, succursum, run up under, run to assist, help (*w. dat., sec. 219a*)

Suēbī, Suebōrum, *m., pl.,* Suebi, Swabians, *a tribe of central Germany*

Suessiōnēs, Suessiōnum, *m., pl.,* Suessiones, *a Gallic tribe*

sufferō, sufferre, sustulī, sublātum, undergo, endure, suffer

suī, sibi, sē *or* **sēsē,** *reflex. pron. of third person,* himself, herself, itself, themselves

Sulla, -ae, *m.,* Sulla, *a Roman cognomen. In particular,* L. Cornelius Sulla (Felix), *138–78 B.C., Roman dictator and general*

sum, esse, fuī, futūrus, be, exist

summa, -ae, *f.,* main thing, total, whole; general management

summus, -a, -um, *see* **superus**

sūmō, sūmere, sūmpsī, sūmptum, take, assume; *with* **supplicium,** inflict punishment; **dē aliquō,** on someone

superbē, *adv.,* proudly, arrogantly

superbia, -ae, *f.,* pride, haughtiness

superior, superius, *see* **superus**

superō, *I,* overcome

supersum, -esse, -fuī, -futūrus, be left over, remain, survive (*w. dative*)

superus, -a, -um, over, above; *comp.* superior, superius, higher; former; previous; *superl.* **suprēmus, -a, -um, summus, -a, -um,** highest

supplicātiō, supplicatiōnis, *f.,* thanksgiving

suppliciter, *adv.,* as suppliants, humbly

supplicium, -cī, *n.,* punishment

supporto, *I,* bring up

suprā, *adv. and prep. w. acc.,* above, beyond

suprēmus, -a, -um, *see* **superus, -a, -um**

surgō, surgere, surrēxī, surrectum, arise, get up

suscēnseō, -ēre, -uī, -um, be angry (*w. dat.*)

suscipiō, suscipere, suscēpī, susceptum, undertake, take up, receive; adopt

suspīciō, suspīciōnis, *f.,* suspicion

suspicor, *I,* suspect

sustineō, -tinēre, -tinuī, -tentum, hold out; hold up, withstand, check

suus, -a, -um, *reflex. pronom. adj. referring to subject,* of *or* belonging to himself, herself, *etc.,* his own, their own; his, hers, its, theirs. *In nom. pl. masc.* **suī,** one's own people, party, troops.

Syrācūsae, -ārum, *f. pl.,* Syracuse, *the largest city in Sicily*

Syrācūsānus, -a, -um, Syracusan, of Syracuse

T

T., *abbreviation for* Titus

tabellārius, -rī, *m.,* letter carrier

tabernāclum (tabernāculum) -ī, *n.,* tent

tabula, -ae, *f.,* tablet, record

taceō, tacēre, tacuī, tacitum, be silent

talentum, -ī, *n.,* a talent, *a sum*

equal to 6000 denarii or about 1000 dollars

tālis, tāle, adj., such; **tālis . . . quālis,** such . . . as

tam, adv., so, so greatly

tamen, adv., yet, nevertheless; however

tamquam, adv., just as, like; as if

tandem, adv., at last; in questions, pray?

tangō, tangere, tetigī, tāctum, touch; hit, strike

tantopere, adv., so greatly, so much

tantum, adv., so much, so far; only, merely

tantus, -a, -um, so much, so great, so powerful, such

tardō, I, make late or slow, check

tardus, -a, -um, late

Tarentum, -ī, n., Tarentum, a Greek city in southern Italy

taurus, -ī, m., bull

tēctum, -ī, n., covered place, dwelling, house

tegō, tegere, tēxī, tēctum, cover

tēlum, -ī, n., weapon; missile, dart

temerē, adv., without good reason, rashly

temperō, I, control, curb; stop (**sibi temperāre,** stop oneself; see sec. 272)

tempestās, tempestātis, f., weather; storm, tempest

templum, -ī, n., temple

temptō, I, make an attempt upon; try, test; try to win over

tempus, temporis, n., time, occasion

tendō, tendere, tetendī, tentum, stretch, stretch out, extend

teneō, tenere, tenuī, ——, hold, possess, keep; seize, grasp, understand; prevent (see sec. 272)

tener, tenera, tenerum, tender, young

Terentia, -ae, f., Terentia, wife of Cicero

tergum, -ī, n., back; **tergum vertere,** to flee (lit., to turn the back)

terra, -ae, f., earth, land, country

terreō, terrēre, terruī, territum, frighten

tertius, -a, -um, ord. num. adj., third

testāmentum, -ī, n., will

testimōnium, -nī, n., evidence, proof

testis, testis, gen. pl. **testium,** m., witness

testūdō, -dinis, f., tortoise; shed; protective formation composed of men with shields upheld over their heads

Thēbae, Thēbārum, f., Thebes, a town in Boeotia, Greece

Themistocles, Themistoclī, or **is,** m., Themistocles (B.C. 514-449), Athenian statesman and founder of Athenian naval power

Ti, abbreviation for **Tiberius**

Tiberius, Tiberī, m. (abbrev. **Ti**), Tiberius, a Roman praenomen. In particular, the Roman Emperor (A.D. 14-37).

Tigrānēs, Tigrānis, m., Tigranes, a king of Armenia

Tigurīnus, -ī, m., Tigurinus, a canton or division of the Helvetians

timeō, timēre, timuī, ——, fear, be afraid, dread (so as to wish to fly)

timidus, -a, -um, afraid

timor, timōris, m., fear

tīrō, tīrōnis, m., recruit, young soldier

Titūrius, Titūrī, *m.,* Titurius, *a Roman name*

toga, -ae, *f.,* toga (*outer garment worn by a Roman citizen*)

tolerābilis, -e, *adj.,* bearable

tolerō, *I,* bear, endure; sustain, relieve

tollō, tollere, sustulī, sublātum, raise up; take away

tonō, *I,* thunder

tot, *adj., indecl.,* so many; **quot . . . tot, tot . . . quot,** as many . . . as

tōtus, -a, -um, *gen.* **tōtīus,** the whole, the whole of; entire, all

tractō, *I,* handle, manage, treat; conduct

trādō, trādere, trādidī, trāditum, hand over, give up

trādūcō, trādūcere, trādūxī, trāductum, lead across, transport

trahō, trahere, trāxī, trāctum, draw, attract

Trāiānus, -ī, *m.,* Trajan, *Roman cognomen. In particular, the Roman Emperor* (*A.D. 98–117*).

trāiciō, -icere, -iēcī, -iectum, hurl across; transfer, cause to go over

tranquillitās, -tātis, *f.,* calmness, stillness; a calm

trāns, *prep. w. acc.,* across, over

trānseō, trānsīre, trānsiī, trānsitum, go across, cross

trānsferō, -ferre, -tulī, -lātum, carry or bring over

trānsfīgō, trānsfīgere, trānsfīxī, trānsfīxum, pierce through

trānsitus, -ūs, *m.,* way across, crossing

trānsportō, *I,* carry across, ferry

Trānsrhēnānus, -a, -um, from across the Rhine

tredecim, *card. num. adj.,* thirteen

trēs, tria, *card. num. adj.* (*gen.* **trium**), three

tribūnus, -ī, *m.,* (1) civil tribune, *a Roman magistrate;* (2) military tribune, *a junior officer in the legion*

tribuō, tribuere, tribuī, tribūtum, assign; grant; render

trīcēsimus, -a, -um, thirtieth

triennium, -nī, *n.,* period of three years

trīgintā, *card. num. adj.,* thirty

trīstis, trīste, *adj.,* sad

triumphō, *I,* triumph, celebrate a triumph

tū, tuī, *pers. pron.,* you; *pl.* **vōs**

tuba, -ae, *f.,* trumpet

Tucca, -ae, *m.,* Tucca, *a Roman name*

tueor, tuērī, tūtus *or* **tuitus sum,** watch, guard, protect

Tullia, -ae, *f.,* Tullia, *a Roman feminine name. In particular the daughter of* (*M. Tullius*) *Cicero.*

tum, *adv.,* then

tumultus, -ūs, *m.,* uprising

tumulus, -ī, *m.,* mound, hill

turpis, turpe, disgraceful, shameful

turpiter, *adv.,* disgracefully

turris, turris, *gen. pl.* **turrium,** *acc. s.* **turrim,** *abl. s.* **turrī,** *f.,* tower

Tusculānus, -a, -um, Tusculan, of *or* appertaining to Tusculum, *a town of Latium*

Tusculum, -ī, *n.,* Tusculum

tūtus, -a, -um, safe

tuus, -a, -um, your, yours (*sing.*)

tyrannus, -ī, *m.,* tyrant

U

ubi, *adv., and conjunction,* (1) *of place* (*adv.*), where? where; (2) *of* *time* (*conj.*), when, whenever

Ūbiī, Ubiōrum, *m. pl.*, the Ubii, *a German tribe*

ulcīscor, ulcīscī, ultus sum, avenge; punish, take vengeance on

ūllus, -a, -um, *gen.* **ūllīus,** a single, any; *it serves as the adjective of* **quisquam**

ulmus, -ī, *f.*, elm

ulterior, ulterius, *comp. adj.*, farther, more remote; *superl.*, **ultimus, -a, -um,** farthest

ultimus, -a, -um, *see* **ulterior, ulterius**

ultrā, *prep. with acc.*, beyond, on the farther side of

ultrō, *adv.*, on the farther side; of one's own accord; besides; **ultrō citrōque,** back and forth

umerus, -ī, *m.*, shoulder

umquam, *adv.*, ever, at any time

ūnā, *adv.*, together

unda, -ae, *f.*, wave

unde, (1) *interrog. adv.*, whence?; (2) *rel. adv.*, whence, from where

ūndecim, *card. num. adj.*, eleven

ūndecimus, -a, -um, *ord. num. adj.*, eleventh

ūndēvīgintī, *card. num. adj.*, nineteen

undique, *adv.*, from all sides

ūniversus, -a, -um (turned into one), all as a body, as one man, en masse

ūnus, -a, -um, *gen.* **ūnīus,** *card. num. adj.*, one; single, alone; the only one

urbs, urbis, *gen. pl.* **urbium,** *f.*, city (*often means* Rome)

ūsque, *adv.*, all the way to, as far as; up to, till; **usque ad,** *adv.*, all the way up to (jusqu'à); **usque adeō,** *adv.*, so true is it

that (*lit.* all the way, to such a degree)

ūsus, ūsūs, *m.*, use; practice, experience; service

ut *and* **utī,** *adv., and conj. with indicative:* (1) as, just as; (2) when, after; **ut prīmum,** when first, as soon as; *with subj.:* (1) that, so that (2) that, in order that, to; (3) *after verbs of fearing,* that . . . not

uter, utra, utrum, *gen.* **utrīus,** which (of two)?

uterque, utraque, utrumque, *gen.* **utrīusque,** each (of two); both; **utrīque,** both sides

utī, *see* **ut**

ūtilis, -e, *adj.*, useful

ūtilitās, ūtilitātis, *f.*, advantage, expediency

utinam, *adv.*, if only, would that (*followed by subjunctive; see sec. 209c*)

ūtor, ūtī, ūsus sum (*used with ablative*), make use of, employ; enjoy

utrum, *coni.*, whether; **utrum . . . an** (whether) . . . or; **utrum . . . annōn** (whether) . . . or not; **utrum . . . necne,** whether . . . or not (*in indirect questions*)

uxor, uxōris, *f.*, wife

V

vacō, *I*, be empty; be free from, be idle, have leisure for

vacuus, -a, -um, empty; bereft of

vadum, -ī, *n.*, ford, shallow place

vāgīna, -ae, *f.*, scabbard, sheath

vagor, *I*, wander, roam

valdē, *adv.*, strongly; exceedingly, very much

valeō, valēre, valuī, valitūrus, be

strong, be in good health, have influence; **plūrimum valēre**, to be very powerful; *imperative* **valē, valēte**, farewell! good-bye!

valētūdō, valētūdinis, *f.*, condition of health, poor health, weak condition

validus, -a, -um, strong, sturdy, robust

vāllum, -ī, *n.*, rampart, earthwork, parapet

varietās, varietātis, *f.*, diversity, variety

Varrō, Varrōnis, *m.*, Varro, *Roman cognomen of the clan of the Terentii. In particular*, Marcus Terentius Varro (*116–27 B.C.*), *scholar, antiquary, and author*

vāsa, vāsōrum, *n. pl.*, dishes

vāstō, *I*, lay waste, devastate

vāstus, -a, -um, shapeless; waste, desolate

vectīgal, vectīgālis, *gen. pl.* **vectīgālium**, *n.*, tax; *pl.* revenues

vehemēns, *adj.*, *gen.* **vehementis**, violent, impetuous; drastic

vehementer, *adv.*, violently

vehō, vehere, vēxī, vectum, carry

vel, *conj.*, or; **vel . . . vel**, either . . . or; *adv.*, even

vēlōcitās, vēlōcitātis, *f.*, speed

vēlum, -ī, *n.*, sail

velut, *adv.*, just as

vēndō, vēndere, vēndidī, vēnditum, sell

veneror, *I*, respect, venerate

veniō, venīre, vēnī, ventum, come

ventitō, *I*, come repeatedly, visit

ventus, -ī, *m.*, wind

vēr, vēris, *n.*, spring

verberō, *I*, lash

verbum, -ī, *n.*, word

Vercingetorīx, Vercingetorīgis, *m.*,

Vercingetorix, *chief of the Averni, commander of the united Gallic revolt against Caesar in 52 B.C.*

vēre, *adv.*, truly

vereor, verērī, veritus sum, fear; look on with respect *or* awe

Vergilius, Vergilī, *m.*, Vergil, *Roman poet (70–19 B.C.)*

vergō, vergere, ——, ——, turn, slope; lie, be situated

vēritās, vēritātis, *f.*, truth

vērō, *adv.*, truly, indeed; however; **iam vērō**, moreover

Verrēs, Verris, *m.*, Verres, *Roman cognomen. In particular*, C. Cornelius Verres, *propraetor in Sicily in 73 B.C., prosecuted for extortion by Cicero.*

versor, *I*, turn oneself, be, remain, engage in

vertō, vertere, vertī, versum, turn (*tr.*)

versus, *adv., and prep.*, towards, *follows its case, which is the acc.*

vērus, -a, -um, true

vescor, vescī, —— (*used with ablative*), feed on

vester, vestra, vestrum, your, yours (*pl.*)

vestis, vestis, *gen. pl.* **vestium**, *f.*, clothing

veterānus, -ī, *m.*, veteran

vetō, vetāre, vetuī, vetitum, forbid

vetus, *adj., gen.* **veteris**, *abl. sing.* **vetere**, *gen. pl.* **veterum**, old and existing, *comparative* **vetustior**, *superlative* **veterrimus** (*see app. 11*)

vexō, *I*, molest, harass

via, -ae, *f.*, road, street, way, journey; **via Appia**, the Appian Way, *a great road which ran from Rome to Brindisi by way of Capua.*

*started by Appius Claudius Cae-
cus, censor 312 B.C.*
vicis, *gen. (no nom.), nom. and acc.
pl.,* **vicēs,** *f.,* changes, vicissitudes
victor, victōris, *m.,* conqueror
victōria, -ae, *f.,* victory
victrīx, *adj., gen.* **victrīcis,** conquering
vīctus, -ūs, *m.,* sustenance, food
vīcus, -ī, *m.,* village
videō, vidēre, vīdī, vīsum, see; *in
passive, often,* seem
vigeō, vigēre, viguī, ——, flourish,
prosper
vigilantia, -ae, *f.,* vigilance, watchfulness
vigilia, -iae, *f.,* a watch, one of the
four equal divisions of the night
vigilō, *I,* be awake, be on one's
guard
vīgintī, *card. num. adj.,* twenty
vīlis, vīle, *adj.,* cheap
vīlitās, tātis, *f.,* cheapness, cheap
price
vīlla, -ae, *f.,* countryhouse, farmhouse
vinciō, vincīre, vīnxī, vīnctum, bind
vincō, vincere, vīcī, victum, conquer
vīnum, -ī, *n.,* wine
violentia, -ae, *f.,* violence
vir, virī, *m.,* man (*of distinction or
honor*), warrior, hero; **vir optimus,** gentleman
virga, -ae, *f.,* rod, switch
virgō, virginis, *f.,* girl, young
woman
virtūs, virtūtis, *f.,* manliness, valor,
merit, worth, courage, virtue;
strength; *pl.* good qualities

vīs, vīs (*pl.* **vīrēs, vīrium**), *f.,* force,
strength, violence, power; *pl.*
strength, force
vispillō, vispillōnis, *m.,* undertaker
vīta, -ae, *f.,* life
vitium, vitī, *n.,* fault; flaw (*marking
imperfection*)
vītō, *I,* avoid
vitrum, -trī, *n.,* glass; woad, a paint
used for dyeing blue
vīvō, vīvere, vīxī, vīctum, live
vīvus, -a, -um, alive
vix, *adv.,* with difficulty, barely,
scarcely
vocō, *I,* call for; call; invite
volō, *I,* fly
volō, velle, voluī, ——, wish, be
willing
voluntās, voluntātis, *f.,* will; wish,
desire
voluptās, voluptātis, *f.,* pleasure
vōs, *see* **tū**
vōx, vōcis, *f.,* voice; speech, remark
vulgō, *adv.,* commonly
vulgus, -ī, *n.* (*gender is exceptional*),
the public, the common people;
a crowd
vulnerō, *I,* wound
vulnus, vulneris, *n.,* wound
vultus, -ūs, *m.,* face, expression·
looks, features

X

Xerxēs, Xerxis, *m.,* Xerxes, *King
of Persia 485–465 B.C., defeated
by the Greeks at Salamis*

Z

Zephyrus, -ī, *m.,* west wind

English-Latin Vocabulary

A

a, an. *Latin has no form for the indefinite article,* a *and* an *being implied, according to context, in the noun.*

about, dē, *prep. with abl.*

accord, of one's own accord, ipse, ipsa, ipsum (*gen.*, ipsīus)

advise, moneō, monēre, monuī, monitum

afraid, be afraid, timeō, timēre, timuī, ——

after, *prep.*, post + *acc.*; *conj.* post-quam + *indicative; adv.*, posteā

again, *adv.*, rūrsus

against, contrā, *prep. with acc.*

ago, ab, *with acc. of extent of time or* ante *used adverbially with abl. of degree of difference, e.g.*, multīs ante annīs, **many years ago**

all, omnis, omne; tōtus, -a, -um

allow, sinō, sinere, sīvī, situm; patior, patī, passus sum

ally, socius, socī, *m.*

although, quamquam + *indicative;* cum + *subjunctive*

always, semper

among, inter *with acc.;* in *with abl.*

ancestors, maiōrēs, maiōrum, *m. pl.*

and, -que, *enclitic;* **both . . . and,** et . . . et

angry, īrātus, -a, -um

animal, animal, animālis (*gen. pl.*, animālium), *n.*

announce, nūntiō, *I*

Antony, Antōnius, Antōnī, *m.*

anyone, *after* nē, quis; *after any other negative,* quisquam

appearance, speciēs, speciēī, *f.*

Appian Way, via Appia, *f.*

approach, appropinquō, *I*

approve, probō, *I*

Ariovistus, Ariovistus, -ī, *m.*

arise, orior, orīrī, ortus sum; co-örior, *etc.*

arms (*of war*), arma, armōrum, *n. pl.*

army, exercitus, exercitūs, *m.*

arouse, incitō, excitō, *I*

arrival, adventus, adventūs, *m.*

arrive, perveniō, pervenīre, per-vēnī, perventum

arrogantly, superbē

Asia, Asia, -ae, *f.*

ask, rogō, ōrō, *I;* petō, petere, petīvī *or* petiī, petītum *with* ā, dē *or* ē

as soon as, simul ac (atque); ut prīmum; cum prīmum + *indicative*

assistance, auxilium, auxilī, *n.*

Athens, Athenae, Athenarum, *f. pl.*

attack (*noun*), impetus, impetūs, *m.*

attack (*verb*), oppugnō, *I*

attempt, cōnor, *I*

away, *use* absum *and space or time construction*

B

bad, malus, -a, -um

banquet, epulae, -ārum, *f.*

battle, proelium, -ī, *n.*

be, sum, esse, fuī, futūrus

be able, possum, posse, potuī —— (+ *infinitive*)

be absent, be away from, absum, abesse, āfuī, āfutūrus

beautiful, pulcher, -chra, -chrum

because, quia *followed by indicative;* quod *followed by either indic. or subj. (see sec. 256b and fn.)*

before, ante, *prep. w. acc.*

began, coepī (*see app. 54*)

begin, incipiō, incipere, incēpī, inceptum

be in good health, valeō, valēre, valuī, valitūrus

Belgian, Belga, -ae, *m.*

believe, crēdō, crēdere, crēdidī, crēditum

belong, *use* sum + dative of possessor

belong, sum *and dat. of possessor*

beseech, ōrō, *I;* petō, petere, petīvī *or* petiī, petītum

be sorry, doleō, dolēre, doluī, dolitūrus

be superior to, praestō, praestāre, praestitī, praestitum *or* praestatum *with dative*

be unwilling, nōlō, nōlle, nōluī, ——

be willing, volo, velle, voluī, ——

be without, lack, careō, carēre, caruī, caritūrus

be wrong, errō, *I*

bird, avis (*gen. pl.* avium), *f.*

black, niger, nigra, nigrum; āter, ātra, ātrum

blame, culpō, *I.*

boldness, audācia, -ae, *f.*

book, liber, librī, *m.*

born, be born, nāscor, nāscī, nātus sum

both, ambō, ambae, ambō

bottom of, *use superlative of* infrā *as adj.*

boy, puer, puerī, *m.*

brave, fortis, forte

bravely, fortiter

bread, pānis, pānis, *m.*

break, rumpō, rumpere, rūpī, ruptum

break into, irrumpō in; **break one's word,** fidem violō, violāre

bridge, pōns, pontis (*gen. pl.,* pontium), *m.*

bring, ferō, ferre, tulī, lātum

bring back, referō, referre, rettulī, relātum

broad, lātus, -a, -um

brother, frāter, frātris, *m.*

Brutus, Brūtus, -ī, *m.*

build, aedificō, *I*

buy, emō, emere, ēmī, ēmptum

by, ā, ab, *prep. w. abl.*

C

Caesar, Caesar, Caesaris, *m.*

call, vocō, *I;* appellō, *I*

calm, *noun,* tranquillitās, -tātis, *f.*

camp, castra, castrōrum, *n. pl. with sing. meaning.*

can, be able, possum, posse, potuī, —— (+ *infinitive*)

capture, capiō, capere, cēpī, captum

Capua, Capua,- ae, *f.*

carry, portō, *I;* carry (*a wall or line of fortifications*), dūcō

Carthage, Carthāgō, Carthāginis, *f.*

Carthaginian, Poenus, -ī, *m.*

catch, capiō, capere, cēpī, captum

Catiline, Catilīna, -ae, *m.*

Cato, Catō, Catōnis, *m.*

cautious, cautus, -a, -um

cavalry, equites, equitum, *m. pl.*

centurion, centuriō, centuriōnis, *m.*

charge, impetus, impetūs, *m.*

charioteer, aurīga, -ae, *m.*

cheap, vīlis, -e

chief, prīnceps, prīncipis, *m.*

children, līberī, -ōrum, *m. pl.*

Cicero, Cicerō, Cicerōnis, *m.*

circumstances, under these, quae cum ita sint (essent)

Cisalpine, Cisalpīnus, -a, -um

citizen, cīvis, cīvis (*gen. pl.* cīvium), *c.*

city, oppidum, -ī, *n.*; urbs, urbis, *f.*

city-gate, porta, -ae, *f.*

clan, cīvitās, cīvitātis, *f.*

clear, it is, appāret

clear, manifestus, -a, -um

cloud, nūbes, nūbis (*gen. pl.,* nūbium), *f.*

cohort, cohors, cohortis (*gen. pl.,* cohortium), *f.*

cold, *noun,* frīgus, frīgoris, *n.*; cold, *adj.,* frīgidus, -a, -um

collect, cōgō, cōgere, coēgī, coāctum

come, veniō, venīre, vēnī, ventum

commonwealth, rēs pūblica, reī pūblicae, *f.*

companion, comes, comitis, *m.*

complete, conficiō, conficere, confēcī, confectum

conquer, vincō, vincere, vīcī, victum

consider, habeō, habēre, habuī, habitum

consul, cōnsul, cōnsulis, *m.*

consulship, in the consulship of, cōnsule + *abl. of name of consul*

content, contentus, -a, -um (*with abl.*)

control, regō, regere, rēxī, rēctum

Corinth, Corinthus, -ī, *f.*

cost, *use* stō *with dat. of person and abl. of price*

cottage, casa, -ae, *f.*

country (*as opposed to town*), rūs, rūris, *n.*; **in the country,** rūrī; **country** (*native land*), patria, -ae, *f.*

countryhouse, vīlla, -ae, *f.*

courage, virtūs, virtūtis, *f.*

cover, operiō, operīre, operuī, opertum

credit (**credence**), fidēs, fideī, *f.*; (**praise**), laus, laudis, *f.*

crowd, turba, -ae, *f.*

cruelly, crūdēliter

D

dance, saltō, *I*

danger, perīculum, -ī, *n.*

daring (*noun*), audācia, -ae, *f.*

daring (*adj.*), audāx

dart, tēlum, -ī, *n.*

daughter, fīlia, -ae, *f.*

dawn, daybreak, prīma lūx; **at dawn,** prīmā lūce

day, diēs, diēī, *m. & f.*

daybreak, prīma lūx

dear, cārus, -a, -um

deceive, dēcipiō, dēcipere, dēcēpī, dēceptum

decide, cōnstituō, cōnstituere, cōnstituī, cōnstitūtum

deer, cervus, -ī, *m.*

defeat, vincō, vincere, vīcī, victum

defend, dēfendō, dēfendere, dēfendī, dēfēnsum

delay (*noun*), mora, -ae, *f.*

delay (*verb*), moror, *I*

deprive, prīvō, *I*

deprived of, be deprived of, careō *with abl.*

destroy, dēleō, dēlēre, dēlēvī, dēlētum

devour, dēvorō, *I*

Diana, Diāna, -ae, *f.*

die, morior, morī, mortuus sum

different from, alius, -a, -um (ac, atque)

diligence, dīligentia, -ae, *f.*

discuss, disputō, *I*

disagree, dissentiō, dissentīre, dissēnsī, dissensum, *with* ā
disturb, incitō, *I;* excitō, *I*
ditch, fossa, -ae, *f.*
divide, dīvidō, dīvidere, dīvīsī,
dīvīsum
do, faciō, facere, fēcī, factum
displease, displiceō *and dat.*
doubt, dubitō, *I*
doubtful, dubius, -a, -um
down from, dē, *prep. w. abl.*
draw up (*a line of battle*), īnstruō,
īnstruere, īnstrūxī, īnstructum
drive, agō, agere, ēgī, āctum
drive back, repellō, repellere, reppulī, repulsum
drive out, expellō, expellere, expulī,
expulsum

E

eager, cupidus, -a, -um; eager for,
cupidus + *genitive*
easy, facilis, facile
eat, edo, edere, ēdī, ēsum
eighty-fourth, octōgēsimus (-a,
-um) quārtus (-a, -um)
either . . . or, aut . . . aut; vel
. . . vel
eleventh, ūndecimus, -a, -um
emperor, imperātor, imperātōris, *m.*
empire, imperium, imperī, *n.*
encourage, hortor, *I*
enemy, hostis, hostis (*gen. pl.*,
hostium), *m.*
enjoy, fruor, fruī, fructus sum (*abl.*)
enough, satis (+ *genitive of the
whole*)
enthusiasm, studium, studī, *n.*
envy, invideō, invidēre, invīdī, invīsum (*dat.*)
envoy, lēgātus, -ī, *m.*
everything, omnia, omnium, *n. pl.*

exhausted, cōnfectus, -a, -um; dēfessus, -a, -um
expose, obiciō, obicere, obiēcī, obiectum; expose someone to
something, obiciō + *acc. and dat.*
extend, pateō, patēre, patuī, ——
eye, oculus, -ī, *m.*

F

fail, be wanting, dēsum, dēesse,
dēfuī, dēfutūrus (*w. dat.*)
fall, cadō, cadere, cecidī, cāsum
famous, clārus, -a, -um; praeclārus,
-a, -um
far (*adv.*), longē; far away, procul;
be far away, longē abesse
farmer, agricola, -ae, *m.*
farming, agrīcultūra, -ae, *f. or use
infinitive of* colō *with* agrōs
fast (*adv.*), celeriter
fat, pinguis, pingue
father, pater, patris, *m.*
favor, grātia, grātiae, *f.*
fear, timeō, timēre, timuī, ——;
metuō, metuere, metuī; vereor,
verērī, veritus sum
fever, fēbris, fēbris (*gen. pl.* fe-
brium), *f.*
few, paucī, paucōrum, *m. pl.*
field, ager, agrī, *m.*
fifteen, quīndecim, *indecl.*
fight, pugno, *I*
find, find out, reperiō, reperīre,
repperī, repertum
first, prīmus, -a, -um
first, at first (*adv.*), prīmum
fish, piscis (*gen. pl.*, piscium), *m.*
five, quīnque, *indecl.*
flesh, carō, carnis, *f.*; horse-flesh,
carō equīna
flee, fugiō, fugere, fūgī, fugitūrus
fit, idōneus, -a, -um
flight, fuga, -ae, *f.*

flower, flōs, flōris, *m.*
food, cibus, -ī, *m.*
foolish, stultus, -a, -um
foot, pes, pedis, *m.*
foot-soldier, pedes, peditis, *m.*
for a long time, diū
forces, cōpiae, -ārum, *f. pl.*
foreign, externus, -a, -um
forest, silva, -ae, *f.*
formerly, ōlim, *adv.*
fortify, mūniō, mūnīre, mūnīvī, mūnītum
forum, forum, -ī, *n.*
four, quattuor, *indecl.*
fourth, quārtus, -a, -um
friend, amīcus, -ī, *m.*
friendly, amīcus, -a, -um
frontier, fīnis, fīnis (*gen. pl.*, fīnium)

G

game, lūdus, -ī, *m.*
garden, hortus, -ī, *m.*
gather together (*tr.*), cōgō, cōgere, coēgī, coāctum
Gaul, a, Gallus, -ī, *m.*
Gaul (*the country*), Gallia, -ae, *f.*
general, dux, ducis, *m.*
German, Germānus, -ī, *m.*
get possession of, potior, potīrī, potītus sum (*with abl. or genitive*)
gift, dōnum, -ī, *n.*
girl, puella, -ae, *f.*
give, dō, dare, dedī, datum; give back, reddō, reddere, reddidī, redditum
go, eō, īre, iī, itum
go away, discēdō, discēdere, discessī, discessum; abeō, abīre, abiī, abitum
go off, proficīscor, proficīscī, profectus sum
go on, Use passive of agō.
gold, aurum, -ī, *n.*

good, bonus, -a, -um
grain, frūmentum, -ī, *n.*
great, magnus, -a, -um
Greek, Graecus, -a, -um
greeting, salūs, salūtis, *f.*; send greeting to, salūtem dīcere (*with dative*)
grieve for, doleō, dolēre, doluī, dolitūrus
ground (*places*), loca, -ōrum, *n. pl.;* on the ground that, quod + subjunctive, *see sec. 256b*

H

hand, manus, manūs, *f.*
harbor, portus, -tūs, *m.*
hard, difficult, difficilis, difficile; hard, unyielding, dūrus, -a, -um
harm, noceō, nocēre, nocuī, nocitum (*w. dative*)
has to be, must be, *etc. see sec. 110*
hasten, properō, *I*
have, consider, habeō, habēre, habuī, habitum
he, she, it, is, ea, id
head, caput, capitis, *n.*
health, be in good, valeō
hear, audiō, *I V*
help, auxilium, auxilī, *n.*; help, give help, subveniō *and dat.;* iuvō, iuvāre, iūvī, iūtum
Helvetia, Helvētia, -ae, *f.*
Helvetians, Helvētiī, -ōrum, *m.*
here, hīc
hesitate, dubitō, *I*
high, altus, -a, -um; ēditus, -a, -um
higher, altior, -ius; superior, -ius
highly, at a high price, magnī
himself, sē
Hirtius, Hirtius, Hirtī, *m.*
his, suus, -a, -um *and* eius (*see sec. 166*)

home, domus, domūs, *f.*; **at home,** domī
Horace, Horātius, -ī, *m.*
horn, cornū, -ūs, *n.*
horse, equus, -ī, *m.*; **horse,** *as adj.* **of a horse** *as in* **horseflesh,** equīnus, -a, -um
horseman, eques, equitis, *m.*
hostile, inimīcus, -a, -um
hour, hōra, -ae, *f.*
house, vīlla, -ae, *f.*; domus, domūs, *f.*
however (*adv.*), quamvīs
huge, īngēns, īngentis
hurry, mātūrō, *I;* festīnō, *I*
hurt, noceō, nocēre, nocuī, nocitum (*w. dative*)

I

I, ego, meī
immortal, immortālis, -le
in, in + *abl.;* **in time,** ad diem
incite, excitō, *I*
infantry, peditēs, peditum, *m. pl.*
inferior (*in number*), minor, minus
inform, certiōrem faciō, facere, fēcī, factum; **be informed,** certior fīō, fierī, factus sum
inhabit, incolō, incolere, incoluī, ——
inhabitant, incola, -ae, *c.*
inquire, quaerō, quaerere, quaesīvī, quaesītum
in such a way, ita
intend, I intend, mihi est in animō + *infinitive*
into, in *with acc.*
island, īnsula, -ae, *f.*
Italy, Italia, -ae, *f.*

J

javelin, pīlum, -ī, *n.*
journey, iter, itineris, *n.*

joy, gaudium, gaudī, *n.*
joyfully, *say* "with joy"
Jura, Iūra, -ae, *m.*

K

keep out, prohibeō, prohibēre, prohibuī, prohibitum
key, clāvis (*gen. pl.*, clavium), *f.*
kill, occīdō, occīdere, occīdī, occīsum; interficiō, interficere, interfēcī, interfectum
king, rēx, rēgis, *m.*
know, sciō, *IV*

L

Labienus, Labiēnus, -ī, *m.*
lack, be without, careō, carēre, caruī, caritūrus (*with abl.*)
land, terra, -ae, *f.*
large number, multitūdō, multitūdinis, *f.*
lash, verberō, *I*
Latin, lingua Latīna; **speak Latin,** Latīnē loquī
laugh at, irrīdeō, irrīdēre, irrīsī, irrīsum (*with dative*)
lead, dūcō, dūcere, dūxī, ductum
leading man, prīnceps, prīncipis, *m.*
learn, discō, discere, didicī, ——
leave, relinquō, relinquere, relīquī, relictum
left (*adj.*), sinister, sinistra, sinistrum
left, be left over, supersum, superesse, superfuī, superfutūrus
legion, legiō, legiōnis, *f.*
leisure, ōtium, otī, *n.*
letter, epistula, -ae, *f.*; litterae, -ārum, *f. pl.*
light, lūx, lūcis, *f.*
like, similis, simile *with dative*
like, be fond of, dīligō, dīligere, dīlexī, dīlēctum

line of battle, aciēs, aciēī, *f.*
lion, leō, leōnis, *m.*
little, parvus, -a, -um
live, vīvō, vīvere, vīxī, vīctum;
  live (dwell), habitō, *I*
long, longus, -a, -um
long, a long time, diū
longer, diūtius; **no longer**, nōn iam
long for, dēsīderō, *I;* cupiō, cupere,
  cupīvī, cupitum
look at, spectō, *I*
lose, āmittō, āmittere, āmīsī, amis-
  sum
love, amō, *I*
Lucullus, Lūcullus, -ī, *m.*

M

make war, bellum gerere
man, vir, virī, *m.*
Manlius, Mānlius, Mānlī, *m.*
many, multī, -ae, -a
march (*noun*), iter, itineris, *n.*
marry (wife), dūcō, dūcere, dūxī,
  ductum; **(husband)**, nūbō, nū-
  bere, nūpsī, nuptum (*w. dat.*)
market-place, forum, -ī, *n.*
master, dominus, -ī, *m.*
merchant, mercātor, mercātōris, *m.*
message, nūntius, nūntī, *m.*
messenger, nūntius, nūntī, *m.*
mile, mīlle passūs; **miles**, mīlia
  passuum
molest, vexō, *I*
money, pecūnia, -ae, *f.*
month, mēnsis, mēnsis, *m.* (*gen.
  pl.,* mēnsium)
more, plūs, plūris (*gen. pl.* plūrium)
mother, māter, mātris, *f.*
mountain, mōns, montis (*gen. pl.*
  montium), *m.*
mouse, mūs, mūris, *m.* (*gen. pl.*
  mūrium)

move, commoveō, commovēre,
  commōvī, commōtum
much, multum
Mummius, Mummius, Mummī, *m.*
must, dēbeō *or use gerundive* + *dative of agent* (*if any*)
my, meus, -a, -um

N

need (*verb*), opus est *w. dat. of
  pers. and abl. of thing*
neighbor, vīcīnus, -ī, *m.*; fīnitimus,
  -mī, *m. of adj. used as noun*
neighboring to, fīnitimus, -a, -um
never, numquam
no, *adv.*, minimē
no longer, nōn iam
no one, nēmō (*acc.* nēminem, *gen.*
  nūllīus, *dat.* nūllī, *abl.* nūllō),
  m. & f.
not, nōn
nothing, nihil, *indecl.*
number, numerus, -ī, *m.*

O

oak, quercus, -ūs, *f.*
obey, pāreō, pārēre, pāruī, ——
ocean, ōceanus, -ī, *m.*
Octavian, Octāviānus, -ī, *m.*
officer, dux, ducis, *m.*
often, saepe
old, vetus (*comp.* vetustior *or* nātū
  maior)
old man, senex, senis (*gen. pl.*
  senum), *m.*
on, in *with abl.*
on account of, ob *or* propter *with
  acc.*
on the ground that, quod + *subj.*
orator, ōrātor, ōrātōris, *m.*
other, alius, alia, aliud; **other, the
  other, the remaining**, cēterī, -ae,
  -a; (**the rest, the others**, cēterī,

etc., adj. as noun); **the other**
(**of two**), alter, altera, alterum
ought, dēbeō, dēbēre, dēbuī, dēbitum
our, noster, nostra, nostrum
our men, nostrī, nostrōrum
outrage, iniūria, -ae, *f.*
overcome, superō *I;* vinco, vincere, vīcī, victum

P

Pansa, Pānsa, -ae, *m.*
part, pars, partis (*gen. pl.*, partium),
f.
passion (**anger**), īra, -ae, *f.*
people, populus, -ī, *m.*; **the Roman
people,** populus Rōmānus (*always in this order*)
perceive, sentiō, sentīre, sēnsī, sēnsum
Persian, Persa, -ae, *m.*
persuade, persuādeō, persuādēre,
persuāsī, persuāsum (*dat.*)
Philippi, Philippī, -ōrum, *m. pl.*
philosopher, philosophus, -ī, *m.*
pike, pīlum, -ī, *m.*
pirate, pīrāta, -ae, *m.*
Pisa, Pīsae, Pīsarum, *f. pl.*
pitch, set, pōnō, pōnere, posuī,
positum
place (**put in position**), locō, *I;*
collocō, *I*
place (*noun*), locus, -i, *m.*
plain, campus, -ī, *m.*
play, lūdō, lūdere, lūsī, lūsum
pleasant, pleasing, iūcundus, -a,
-um
pleasure, voluptās, voluptātis, *f.*
pledge, pignus, pignoris, *n.*
poet, poēta, -ae, *m.*
point of, at the, *use future participle*
point out, mōnstrō, *I*
politics, rēs pūblica, *f.*

Pompey, Pompeius, Pompeī, *m.*
praise (*noun*), laus, laudis, *f.*
praise, laudō, *I*
pray, ōrō, *I*
prayer, *say "to pray"*
prefer, mālō, mālle, māluī; **prefer**
(**this to that**), praepōnō, prae-
pōnere, praeposuī, praepositum
prepare, parō, *I*
present, dōnum, -ī, *n.*
prevent, keep from, prohibeō, prohibēre, prohibuī, prohibitum; impediō, *I V*
prey, praeda, -ae, *f.*
prisoner, captīvus, -ī, *m.*
promise, prōmittō, prōmittere,
prōmīsī, prōmissum (*w. dat.*)
promptly, ad diem
provide, parō, *I*
provided that (*conj.*), dummodo
province, prōvincia, -ae, *f.*
pursue, sequor, sequī, secūtus sum
put in charge of, praeficiō, praeficere, praefēcī, praefectum, *with
accusative and dative*
Pyrrhus, Pyrrhus, -ī, *m.*

Q

quickly, celeriter; cito

R

rapidly, celeriter
rate, at a low, parvī
reach, perveniō ad
read, lego, legere, lēgī, lēctum
ready, parātus, -a, -um
receive, accipiō, accipere, accēpī,
acceptum
record, tabula, -ae, *f.*
red, ruber, -bra, -brum
refuse, recūsō, *I*
relying on, frētus, -a, -um (*w. abl.*)
remember, memoriā teneō

remote, be remote from, absum, abesse, āfuī, āfutūrus

resign office, magistrātum dēpōnō

resist, resistō, resistere, restitī, ——, *with dative*

rest, the rest, cēterī, -ōrum, *m.*

rest of, remaining, left over, reliquus, -a, -um

return, redeō, redīre, rediī, reditum

riches, dīvitiae, dīvitiārum, *f. pl.*

right, dexter, dextra, dextrum

river, flūmen, flūminis, *n.*

road, via, -ae, *f.*

rock, saxum -ī, *n.*

Roman, Rōmānus, -a, -um

Rome, Rōma, -ae, *f.*

roof, tēctum, -ī, *n.*

rout, fugō, *I*

rule, rego, regere, rēxī, rēctum; rēgnō, *I*

run, currō, currere, cucurrī, cursum

S

safe, tūtus, -a, -um

sail, nāvigō, *I*

sailor, nauta, -ae, *m.*

same, īdem, eadem, idem; same as, īdem quī, eadem quae, idem quod

save, servō, *I*

say, dīco; say . . . not, nego

school, schola, -ae, *f.*

scout, explōrātor, explōrātōris, *m.*

sea, mare, maris, *n.*

see, videō, vidēre, vīdī, vīsum

seem, videor, vidērī, vīsus sum

seize, occupō, *I;* capiō, capere, cēpī, captum

sell, vēndō, vēndere, vēndidī, vēnditum

senate, senātus, senātūs, *m.*

senators, patrēs cōnscriptī, *m. pl.*

send, mittō, mittere, mīsī, missum

sense, of sense, sensible, prūdens (prūdentis)

set out, proficīscor, proficīscī, profectus sum

severe, gravis, grave

share, pars, *f.* (*gen. pl.* partium)

shield, scūtum, -ī, *n.*

ship, nāvis, nāvis (*gen. pl.* nāvium), *f.*

shop, taberna, tabernae, *f.*

shore, ōra, -ae, *f.*, lītus, litoris, *n.*

short, brevis, breve

show, mōnstrō, *I*

shut, claudō, claudere, clausī, clausum

Sicily, Sicilia, -ae, *f.*

sick, aeger, aegra, aegrum

side (*of a river*), rīpa, -ae, *f.*; (*direction*), pars, partis (*gen. pl.* partium), *f.*

silence, silentium, silentī, *n.*

since (*conj.*), cum

sing, cantō, *I*

six, sex, *indecl.*

sixteen, sēdecim, *indecl.*

size, magnitūdō, magnitūdinis, *f.*

slave, servus, -ī, *m.*

slay, mactō, *I;* occīdō, occīdere, occīdī, occīsum; interficiō; necō, *I*

sleep, somnus, -ī, *m.*

small, parvus, -a, -um

snow, nix, nivis (*gen. pl.* nivium), *f.*

softly (*of voice*), submissē

so great, tantus, -a, -um

soldier, mīles, mīlitis, *m.*

some, nōnnūllī, -ae, -a; there are some who, sunt quī + *subj.;* some . . . others, aliī . . . aliī

son, fīlius, fīlī, *m.*

soon, mox; soon as possible, quam prīmum

sorry, be sorry, doleō, dolēre, doluī, dolitūrus

so that nobody, ut nēmō *in consecutive (result)*; nē quis *in final (purpose) clauses: both with subj.*

soul, anima, animae, *f.*

spare, parcō, parcere, pepercī, parsum *(w. dat.)*

speak, loquor, loquī, locūtus sum; **speak Latin,** Latīnē loquor; **speak with,** loquor cum + abl.

speed, celeritās, celeritātis, *f.*

spring, vēr, vēris, *n.*

stand, stō, stāre, stetī, —

star, stella, -ae, *f.*

start, start out, proficīscor, proficīscī, profectus sum

state, cīvitās, cīvitātis, *f.*

station, put in position, locō, *I;* collocō, *I*

stay, maneō, manēre, mānsī, mānsum

stone, saxum, -ī, *n.*

storm, tempestās, tempestātis, *f.*

street, via, viae, *f.*

strength, vīs, vīs *(gen. pl.* vīrium), *f.*

sturdy, validus, -a, -um

such, tālis, -e

summer, aestās, aestātis, *f.*

sunset, sōlis occāsus

superior, be superior to, praestō, praestāre, praestitī, praestitum *or* praestatum *(w. dat.)*

surround, cingō, cingere, cīnxī, cīnctum

swear, iūrō, *I*

swim, natō, *I*

sword, gladius, gladī, *m.*

Syracuse, Syrācūsae, Syrācūsārum, *f. pl.*

T

tail, cauda, -ae, *f.*

take (receive), accipiō, accipere, accēpī, acceptum

tale, fābula, fābulae, *f.*

talent, talentum, talentī, *n.*

teach, doceō, docēre, docuī, doctum

tear, lacrima, -ae, *f.*

tell, dīcō, dīcere, dīxī, dictum

temple, templum, -ī, *n.*

ten, decem, *indecl.*

Terentia, Terentia, -ae, *f.*

terrify, terreō, terrēre, terruī, territum

than, quam

that, the former, ille, illa, illud

the, *either omit or use* is, ea, id. *Latin has no definite article.*

themselves (*reflexive*), sē, suī

then, deinde, tum

there, ibi

there was, erat

thing, rēs, reī, *f.*

think, putō, *I;* existimō, *I*

third, tertius, -a, -um

thirst, sitis, *f.* (*acc.*, sitim)

this, that, is, ea, id; **this, the latter,** hic, haec, hoc

three, trēs, tria

through, per, *prep. with acc.*

throw, iaciō, iacere, iēcī, iactum

throw forward, prōiciō, prōicere, prōiēcī, prōiectum

time, tempus, temporis, *n.*

tired, fessus, -a, -um; dēfessus, -a, -um

today, hodiē

tomorrow, crās

top of, *use superlative of* suprā *as adj.,* summus

transport, portō, *I*

tree, arbor, arboris, *f.*

tribe, tribus, tribūs, *f.*

tribune, tribūnus, -ī, *m.*

troops, cōpiae, -ārum, *f. pl.*

true, vērus, -a, -um

trust, fīdō, fīdere, fīsus sum; cōnfīdō, *etc.;* **trust something to
somebody,** crēdō, crēdere, crēdidī, crēditum, *w. acc. and dative*

truth, the, *use neuter of adj.* vērus,
-a, -um

try, cōnor, *I*

U

unfriendly to, inimīcus, -a, -um

until (*conj.*), dōnec

unworthy, indignus, -a, -um (*w.
abl.*)

use, ūtor, ūtī, ūsus sum (*w. abl.*)

used to . . . (*in verbs*), *use imperfect tense*

useful, ūtilis, ūtile

useless, inūtilis, inūtile

V

valor, virtūs, virtūtis, *f.*

value, aestimō, *I;* habeō; faciō

very, the very, ipse, ipsa, ipsum

victim, hostia, hostiae, *f.*

villa, vīlla, -ae, *f.*

violence, vīs, vīs (*gen. pl.* vīrium), *f.*

W

wage (war), gerō, gerere, gessī,
gestum

wagon, carrus, -ī, *m.*

wait, exspectō, *I*

walk, ambulō, *I*

wall, mūrus, -ī, *m.*

wander, errō, *I*

war, bellum, ī, *n.*

warlike, bellicōsus, -a, -um

warn, moneō, monēre, monuī, monitum

water, aqua, -ae, *f.*

we, nōs, nostrum (*objective genitive,*
nostrī)

weary, fessus, -a, -um; dēfessus,
-a, -um

weight, pondus, ponderis, *n.*

well, puteus, puteī, *m.*

when (*conj.*), cum; *in indirect questions,* quandō

where, *interr. adv.,* ubi; **where
(whither),** *interr. adv.* quō

whether . . . or, utrum . . . an
(*see secs. 210, 211*)

which (of two), uter, utra, utrum

while (*conj.*), dum; **while + *pres.
participle,** use Latin present participle*

white, albus, -a, -um

who, what, quis, quid

whole, tōtus, -a, -um (*gen.,* tōtīus)

why, *interr. adv.,* cūr

wife, ūxor, ūxōris, *f.*

wine, vīnum, -ī, *n.*

wing (*of an army*), cornū, cornūs,
n.

wisdom, sapientia, -ae, *f.*

wish, volō, velle, voluī, ——

with, cum *with abl.*

withdraw, excēdō, excēdere, excessī,
excessum

within (*of time*), *use abl. without
prep.*

without, sine, *prep. with abl.*

woman, fēmina, -ae, *f.*

wonder, mīror, *I*

wood, forest, silva, -ae, *f.*

word, verbum, -ī, *n.*

work (*noun*), labor, labōris, *m.*

work (*verb*), labōrō, *I*

worth, am, valeō, valēre, valuī,
valitūrus; *or use* dignus *with abl.*

wound (*noun*), vulnus, vulneris, *n.*

wound (*verb*), vulnerō, *I*

wretch, miser, misera

wretched, miser, misera, miserum

wretchedly, miserē

write, scrībō, scrībere, scrīpsī, scrīptum
wrong, be wrong, errō, *I*

Y

year, annus, -ī, *m.*

yesterday, heri
yet, tamen
you *(sing.)*, tū, tuī; **you** *(pl.)*, vōs,
vestrum *(objective gen.,* vestrī)
your, tuus, -a, -um; *of more than one
person,* vester, vestra, vestrum

INDEX

Index

477

A SUBSCRIPTION

(Common in medieval MSS)

Nauta rudis pelagī ut saevīs ēreptus ab undīs
   in portum veniēns pectora laeta tenet;
sīc scrīptor fessus, calamum sub calce labōris
   dēpōnēns, habeat pectora laeta satis.
Ille deō dīcat grātēs prō sospite vītā,
   prōque labōris agat iste suī requiē.[1]

Rescued from pounding of the cruel main
Gladly the mariner sails home again;
So should the writer at his labor's close
Lay down his pen, content with earned repose.
Let each in his peculiar attitude
 Render his Lord a fitting gratitude.

---

[1] Compare the sixteenth century echo of the Latin:

     Sleepe after toyle, port after stormie seas;
  Ease after warre, death after life does greatly please.

                 The Faerie Queene, IX, 40

Supplementary Notes

Page viii, line 24.   The teacher who wishes to complete the book in one
semester can omit lessons 23, 34, 41, 48, 57, and 61–64.

Page 46, sec. 92(b).   From Vergil's time onward, the uncontracted genitive -iī came into favor.

Page 53, Exercise B 8.   nātūrā = by nature, naturally.

Page 57, line 1 from bottom.   *Add at left,* pīrātīs, *to the pirates.*

Page 66, line 16.   *Insert parentheses around* vocat-um īrī *and* vīs-um īrī.

Page 80, Exercise B 3.   *For* over there *read* (over there).

Page 82, line 5.   *For* gender, number, and person *read* gender and number.

Page 114, line 1.   *For* sordidi *read* sordidī.

Page 131, Exercise A 12.   *For* eōrum *read* hostium.

Page 132.   *After* deliver *insert footnote:* habeō, cf. A 14.

Page 134, line 17.   *Add*

    alter . . . alter

    the one . . . the other

    Exercise A 1.   *After* vīgintī *insert* mīlitibus.

    Footnote 3, *add* Illam is the princess Lavinia.

Page 139, Exercise A 11.   *After* vulnus *insert footnote:* Vulnus is here
used figuratively; translate *blow, shock.*

    Footnote 5, *add* This is from Aeneid IX, 37–8.

    Exercise B 4.   *Add* footnote: Use rēs.

Page 144.   *Insert in Vocabulary:* Inscius, -a, -um, ignorant, without
knowledge (of).

Page 145, Exercise B 1.   Distant = longinquus.

    Exercise B 4.   Disease = morbus, -ī, *m.*

Page 148, Footnote 4.   *For* grātiās *read* grātiās.

Page 149.   *Set lines 10–15 within brackets.* This explanation is better
postponed to sec. 189.

Page 150, Footnote 5.   *Add* For this infinitive, see secs. 196–197.

    Exercise B 2.   *After* unwilling, *add footnote:* nōlō, sec. 190.

Page 154, Exercise B 5.   Listen = audiō.

Page 157, Exercise B 7.   See sec. 197.

    Exercise C 8.   Trānscendere = *climb over, across.*

Page 162, sec. 195, line 3.   *After* charge *insert* or punishment.

    Observation: reus, *one who is accused, a defendant.*

Page 163, Exercise A 7.   *For* domī nostrae cf. domī meae in sec. 192d.

    Exercise B 5.   To death; use genitive of caput.

Page 168, Exercise B 6.   *For* alium patriam, *read* alium, patriam.

Page 172, Exercise A 4.   Ipsa, etc., *is sentence 4a.*

Page 181, Exercise A 7.   We expect **vīvatīs,** but Latin uses the singular, as if to say, "May each of you, etc."
Before Ūtāre *insert 7a.*

Page 187, Footnote 5.   *For* **quando** *read* **quandō.**

Page 189, Exercise C 9.   *For* rogant *read* petunt.
Exercise D 8.   **Quā viā = quō modō.**

Page 190, Exercise E 3.   *Commas after* inermibus *and* metū.
Exercise F 2.   *To explain* avāritiae *see sec. 182a.*

Page 191, Exercise G 4.   **Mala rēs =** *slim resources.*

Page 193, sec. **214.**   *Observation.*   These superlatives are found chiefly in the singular, as here, and in neuter plural, cf. Ex. A (5), page 195.   They are often constructed with a *plural* verb.

Page 195, Exercise B 6.   *For* quō *see sec. 159.*

Page 207, Exercise A 9.   *For* existimātus, *read* exīstimātus.

Page 212, Exercise A 7.   **Supplex, supplicis,** *suppliant.*

Page 218, Exercises B 1, 4, 7.   These are examples of a relative clause of result, where **quī = ut is, quae = ut ea,** and so forth.

Page 220, Exercise B 3.   **Cui = ut eī;** *for* ēdīco *read* ēdīcō.
Footnote 2.   *For* past *read* perfect.

Page 221, Exercise D 3.   To explain **ut . . . mitterētur** as the equivalent of an infinitive construction, cf. p. 291, fn. 7.

Page 222, Exercise E 7.   **Tam . . . quam =** *so much . . . as.*

Page 228, Exercise A 10.   *Commas after* eōs *and* suam.

Page 229, Exercise C 4.   *For* while trying *read* while-trying.   *Use present participle.*
Exercise C 5.   **Child = puer;** the-approach-of-the = approaching.
Exercise C 6.   Return = **regredior, -gredī, -gressus;** catch sight of = **cōnspiciō;** as-they-were-advancing = present participle of **prōgredior.**

Page 234, Exercise C 2.   Free = **līber.**

Page 240, Exercise B 3.   *For* repentē *read* repente; **itaque** here = **et ita.**
Exercise C 3.   Chance = **occāsiō.**
Exercise C 4.   Ascertain = find out; send ahead = **praemittō;** commander = **lēgātus;** warship = **nāvis longa.**

Page 244, Exercise C 3.   Use **terriblis + videō** in suitable inflexions.

Page 245.   *For* advexit *in title and first line read* advēxit.   *Translate* Rōmae *as if it were* Rōmam.

Page 249, Exercise A 8.   We would normally expect **aliquis** in the absence of a negative.

Page 255, Exercise A 1.   *For* Illa cum audīsset *read* Nūntium cum audīvisset.

Page 260, Exercise A 9.   The present infinitive here stands for the *imperfect* indicative of direct discourse.
Exercise C 2.   *For* have received *read* received.

Page 266, Exercise C 2.   *For* case, *see sec. 251, last example.*

Page 274, Exercise A 3. Instead of **negās**, we expect **negāveris**, but Cicero chose to be graphic: *if you persist in denying.*

Page 275, Exercise C 3. Be here = **adsum.**

Page 277, sec. **271.** Line 9 from bottom, read: *The Gauls* **started rushing down** *from all sides and* **hurling** *stones and*

Page 278, lines 8 & 9, *beginning with "historical," read: "historical,"* often used for the imperfect indicative (a tense that can have an inceptive force) in narration and description.

Page 280, lines 13 & 14. *After* temperō *add* mihi; *change (oneself) to (myself).*

Page 286, Exercise A 12. Ostendit = *exposed to view.*

Page 287, Footnote 4. Add + **identidem.**

Page 291, Exercise A 10. *After* cito *add* scrībātūr.

Page 292, Exercise D 3. Evening = **vesper, vesperī,** *m.*
 Exercise D 4. Immediately = **statim.**
 Exercise D 5. Use **licet.**

Page 304. In the figure, line 11, **hīs superatīs** should be treated as a unit with the words to the right.

These words should appear as follows:
 Page 334, line 8, Respēxit; line 14, vestīmentīs; line 30, vestēs, perdidī.
 Page 335, line 30, quī.
 Page 337, line 23, nōs.
 Page 339, line 13, quamdiū; line 16, vōs.

Page 342, text, line 5 from bottom, **discurrente** = spreading; line 2 from bottom, **sēcūrus** = confident.

Page 343, line 7, **festīnat** = hurries; line 4 from bottom, **capite mutilātum** = beheaded; line 3 from bottom, **subrīdēns** = smiling.

Page 344, line 7, **praesentent** = bring before; line 10, **festīnanter** = speedily; line 11, **alligātum** = tied to; line 16, **arripit** = snatches; line 19, **ērumpunt** = burst forth, **accurrit** = runs up; line 3 from bottom, **potiōre membrō** = rather important part.

Page 345, line 1, *after* sī *supply* **is;** line 5, **affirmābat** = declared; line 12, **puerulum** = little boy; line 16, **Porrō** = Then; line 6 from bottom, **etiam** = once more, **immō** = but yet.

Page 346, line 3, **īnsūmpsisse** = take up, spend, waste.
 line 16, **infēlīciter** = unhappily.
 line 4 from bottom, **fūrtim** = by stealth.

Page 403. Although conjugated like compounds of **dō** (*give*), **abdō, addō, condō, crēdō, perdō, subdō,** and **indō** (*place on, set over*) are derived from a different **-dō,** a lost simple verb meaning *place* or *put.* The Romans early confused the two verbs.

Page 409, line 596. Letters **IN** in middle of line should appear as if deleted by a diagonal line to indicate an erasure.

Page 417. **Carō** *has gen. pl.* **carnium.**

Page 421. *For* **consūmptum** *read* **cōnsūmptum.**

Page 422.   **Crēdō**: *Insert* put trust in *before* believe.
Page 426.   **Emō**: *After* buy *add* take *or* hold.
Page 432.   *For* **Ianuārius** *read* **Iānuārius.**
       Ign = **īgn** throughout.
Page 434.   *Add* **īnscius, -a, -um,** ignorant, unaware of.
Page 438.   **Maximē**: *Add* most.
Page 442.   *For* **occāsio** *read* **occāsiō.**
Page 453.   *For* **scendō** *read* **scandō.**   *Add* **sanguis; sanguinas,** *m.,* blood.
Page 465.   *Add* **cross, trānseō, -īre, -īi, -itum.**
Page 466.   **Far**: *add* **by far,** longē.
Page 467.   **Frontier**: *add m.*
Page 469.   **Mouse**: *For m. read c.*
Page 470.   *Add* **remain,** maneō, manēre.
Page 471.   **Rule**: *Add* (usually intransitive).
    Sleep: *Add; as verb,* dormiō, IV.